SPSS® Base System
User's Guide

Marija J. Norušis/SPSS Inc.

SPSS Inc.
444 N. Michigan Avenue
Chicago, Illinois 60611
Tel: (312) 329 2400
Fax: (312) 329-3668

For more information about SPSS® software products, please write or call

Marketing Department
SPSS Inc.
444 North Michigan Avenue
Chicago, IL 60611
312/329-2400

SPSS® Base System User's Guide
Copyright © 1990 by SPSS Inc.
All rights reserved.
Printed in the United States of America.
No part of this publication may be reproduced, stored in a retrieval system, or transmitted, in any form or by any means, electronic, mechanical, photocopying, recording, or otherwise, without the prior written permission of the publisher.

4 5 6 7 8 9 0   93

ISBN 0-13-177866-8

Library of Congress Catalog Card Number: 89-062958

Preface

SPSS® is a comprehensive, integrated system for statistical data analysis. It is available on a wide variety of computers and operating systems, including IBM® PC, PS/2®, and compatible computers running OS/2™; Apple Macintosh® computers; workstations, minicomputers, and larger systems under UNIX® and VAX/VMS™; and many other mainframes. All of these versions contain an SPSS Processor that reads and carries out commands in the well-known SPSS language. No matter which version you use, you can issue the same commands and expect the same results.

As of Release 4 (the successor to SPSS-X™ Release 3), most versions of the software now also contain an SPSS Manager that helps you build commands and review output. The Manager includes a menu-based command generator, context-sensitive help, an online glossary, extensive editing capabilities, and other features designed to help you work efficiently with SPSS.

New Features in This Release. In addition to the new SPSS Manager interface available on many systems, Release 4 contains a new procedure for exploring data (EXAMINE), a facility to transpose data files (FLIP), a logistic regression procedure, and a comprehensive matrix manipulation language. (LOGISTIC REGRESSION and MATRIX are part of the Advanced Statistics option on some systems.) For systems where SPSS Graphics is installed, SPSS contains the new GRAPH command that allows you to define a chart and invoke the graphics software from within the SPSS system. In addition, a new option, SPSS Categories™, is available to perform conjoint and correspondence analysis. Finally, the documentation has been fully revised to provide more help for new users and more compact and complete reference material for experienced users.

Manuals for the Base System. Documentation for SPSS Release 4 consists of three parts:

- *SPSS Base System User's Guide* shows how to use SPSS commands to manage and analyze data. It explains many of the statistical concepts involved and includes brief operational instructions for each command.
- *SPSS Reference Guide* documents and gives examples of all of the commands, subcommands, and keywords in the base system and Advanced Statistics option.
- An operations guide tells how to run SPSS on one of the operating systems for which the software is available and explains any differences between that version of SPSS and the system as documented in the user and reference guides. The following operations guides are available: SPSS for OS/2, SPSS for the Macintosh, SPSS for UNIX, SPSS for IBM/CMS™, and SPSS for VAX/VMS.

SPSS Options. The following manuals discuss options available for most versions of SPSS. Advanced Statistics is included with the base system in most versions for larger systems but is a separate option in personal computer versions of the software.

- *SPSS Advanced Statistics User's Guide* contains discussions of advanced statistical analyses such as discriminant analysis, nonlinear and logistic regression analysis, and multivariate analysis of variance. In addition to the statistical discussions, there is a brief discussion of how to run each command.

- *SPSS Trends* documents SPSS's complete time series analysis and forecasting tool. The Trends option includes curve fitting, smoothing, special regression, seasonal adjustment, and Box-Jenkins/ARIMA modeling procedures. The manual contains sample applications and a complete reference to the commands in the Trends option.
- *SPSS Tables* documents the SPSS TABLES procedure, which presents data in presentation quality tables. TABLES can tabulate multiple variables at once and provides great flexibility for displaying totals, percentages, and other statistics. The *SPSS Tables* manual includes a user's guide and a complete reference to TABLES subcommands.
- *SPSS Categories* documents the three conjoint and four correspondence analysis procedures in this new option. The manual includes illustrative applications and a complete reference to the commands.

The SPSS system is constantly undergoing enhancements. For additional information about your system, including any updates since the printing of the most current version of the manual, use the INFO command documented in the reference guide. If you would like to be on our mailing list and you did not buy your system directly from us, write to us at one of the address below. We will send you a copy of our newsletter and let you know about SPSS Inc. activities in your area.

SPSS Inc.
444 North Michigan Ave.
Chicago, IL 60611
Tel: (312) 329-2400
Fax: (312) 329-3668

SPSS Federal Systems
12030 Sunrise Valley Dr.
Suite 300
Reston, VA 22091
Tel: (703) 391-6020
Fax: (703) 391-6002

SPSS Latin America
444 North Michigan Ave.
Chicago, IL 60611
Tel: (312) 329-3556
Fax: (312) 329-3668

SPSS Benelux BV
P.O. Box 115
4200 AC Gorinchem
The Netherlands
Tel: +31.1830.36711
Fax: +31.1830.35839

SPSS UK Ltd.
SPSS House
5 London Street
Chertsey
Surrey KT16 8AP
United Kingdom
Tel: +44.932.566262
Fax: +44.932.567020

SPSS UK Ltd., New Delhi
c/o Ashok Business Centre
Ashok Hotel
50B Chanakyapuri
New Delhi 110 021
India
Tel: +91.11.600121 x1029
Fax: +91.11.6873216

SPSS GmbH Software
Steinsdorfstrasse 19
D-8000 Munich 22
Germany
Tel: +49.89.2283008
Fax: +49.89.2285413

SPSS Scandinavia AB
Gamla Brogatan 36-38
4th Floor
111 20 Stockholm
Sweden
Tel: +46.8.102610
Fax: +46.8.102550

SPSS Asia Pacific Pte. Ltd.
10 Anson Road, #34-07
International Plaza
Singapore 0207
Singapore
Tel: +65.221.2577
Fax: +65.221.9920

SPSS Japan Inc.
AY Bldg.
3-2-2 Kitaaoyama
Minato-ku
Tokyo 107
Japan
Tel: +81.3.5474.0341
Fax: +81.3.5474.2678

SPSS Australasia Pty. Ltd.
121 Walker Street
North Sydney, NSW 2060
Australia
Tel: +61.2.954.5660
Fax: +61.2.954.5616

Contents _____

Chapters

Contents

1 Getting Started: A Few Useful Terms

SPSS is a powerful, comprehensive, and flexible statistical and information analysis system. With SPSS you can perform highly complex data manipulation and analysis with surprisingly simple, straightforward instructions.

SPSS can take data from almost any type of file and use them to generate tabulated reports, plots of distributions and trends, descriptive statistics, and complex statistical analyses. Chapter 2 describes the basic methods for creating data files that can be read by SPSS. Chapter 3 outlines the ways you can transform and manipulate data for analysis, and Chapter 4 demonstrates some of the techniques for transforming and combining different types of data files.

SPSS has many preset values that control settings such as page width and length, upper and lower case for display of labels and messages, and the number of errors allowed before processing ends. Chapter 5 explains how to display these values with the SHOW command and change them with the SET command. Chapter 5 also documents utilities for annotating commands and creating your own commands.

The extensive selection of statistical and reporting procedures available with the SPSS base system is described in Chapters 7 through 27. The statistical chapters are arranged in order of complexity—from procedures for producing simple frequency distributions and descriptive statistics to sophisticated multiple regression models and scaling techniques. The last chapter shows you how to use SPSS to create your own customized output and reports. Each chapter contains an overview of the statistical theory behind the procedure and numerous practical examples, including an explanation of all available subcommands and specifications for the command.

The SPSS "language" consists of descriptive and usually self-explanatory commands. For example, the command to perform regression analysis is RE-GRESSION. SPSS is designed to be easy to learn and use; the syntax rules are kept to a minimum, and the system will even accept many nonambiguous departures from those rules.

Nevertheless, there are *some* rules—and there are also a few terms that you may find useful since they occur frequently in this book and have a specific meaning in SPSS. This chapter describes basic syntax rules and SPSS terms.

1.1
THE SPSS SESSION

Whenever you execute a sequence of SPSS commands, it is called an SPSS *session*. A typical SPSS session consists of three main parts:

- *Data definition* commands provide information about the variables and their location in the data file.
- *Data transformation* commands are used to create new variables, modify existing ones, and select subsets of cases for analyses.
- *Procedure commands* indicate what statistics, reports, or tables are to be produced.

1

Data definition and transformation commands are generally not executed until a command that reads the data is specified. This saves extra passes through the data and reduces processing time. Statistical and reporting procedure commands, such as FREQUENCIES and CROSSTABS, and a number of other commands, such as EXECUTE and SAVE, are commands that read the data.

An SPSS session must begin with at least one data definition command that either defines the data to SPSS or specifies an SPSS system file, which already contains data definition. A session can be a complex series of transformations and statistical procedures, or it can be as simple as the following:

```
GET FILE=ELECTRIC.
FREQUENCIES VARIABLES=DBP58.
```

The GET command is a data definition command, telling SPSS the name of the SPSS system file that contains the data. The FREQUENCIES command is procedure command, instructing SPSS to produce a frequency table for the variable DBP58.

Getting access to SPSS and handling files are very specific to your computer system. Consult the SPSS *Operations Guide* for your system for additional information. You can also use the INFO command to get information about new features and changes to SPSS since publication of this book.

1.2
WAYS TO PROCESS
SPSS COMMANDS

Your SPSS commands can be processed in several different ways, depending on your computer system:

- You can create a file of SPSS commands using a text editor or word processing program. This command file is then submitted for execution through your operating system. This is sometimes called *batch execution,* and the commands within the file are run as a single *job.*
- You can access SPSS and run commands one at time in a prompted (interactive) session.
- In some systems, you can access SPSS and build command files with the help of a command generator. You can run commands within the file during the SPSS session.

For information about the ways your computer system can run SPSS, see the SPSS *Operations Guide* for your system.

1.3
SPSS FILES

Operating SPSS means dealing with files. Depending on the complexity of your session, you may have one or more of the following types of files:

- *Command files* contain SPSS commands. Command files can be created using a text editor or word processor and submitted to SPSS for execution, or on some systems they can be created within an SPSS session. Refer to the SPSS *Operations Guide* for your system for more information.
- *Raw data files* contain your data in almost any form. The raw data can be included within a command file, or they can be in a separate file on disk or tape.
- *SPSS system files* are data files specifically formatted for use by SPSS. An SPSS system file contains both data and the *dictionary* that defines the data. The dictionary contains descriptive information about the data, including variable names and locations, variable and value labels, and formats. SPSS system files speed processing.
- An *active system file* is created whenever you define a raw data file with DATA LIST or MATRIX DATA, or access an SPSS system file or other data file with commands such as GET, IMPORT, and GET TRANSLATE. The active system file will contain any modifications to the data produced by transformation and procedure commands in that session. It exists only for the duration of the SPSS session but can be saved as an SPSS system file or exported as a portable file.

- *Output files* contain data formatted for reading by a computer. Some procedures create output files containing matrix or other materials.
- *Portable files* are system files created by the EXPORT command and formatted for portability to computers other than the one on which they were created.
- *Listing files* contain the tabular output from SPSS procedures and diagnostic information about your session. A listing file is formatted for display on a terminal or printing on a printer.

Information about creating, modifying and accessing files is contained in Chapters 2 and 4. Conventions for naming, printing, deleting, or permanently saving files, and for submitting command files for processing differ considerably from one computer and operating system to another. Use the INFO command, the SPSS *Operations Guide* for your system, and other documentation available for your computer system for information about handling files.

1.4
SPSS SYNTAX

Before learning about individual SPSS commands, you should have some general information about the SPSS language. The rules, or *syntax,* of the SPSS language are easy to learn.

SPSS commands often require more than one line for complete specification. You can indicate command continuation lines in one of two ways, depending on the way your system is processing your SPSS commands.

- Commands entered into an SPSS command file and submitted for execution through your operating system or specified on an INCLUDE command (see Chapter 5) must begin in column 1. Continuation lines are indented at least one column. Anything that appears in the first column is assumed to be the beginning of a new command.
- Commands entered during an SPSS session must end with a command terminator (except the BEGIN DATA command). The default command terminator is a period (.). Anything that appears between the beginning of the command and the command terminator is assumed to be part of the command. Commands can begin in any column, but each command must begin on a new line. This includes commands run during a prompted (interactive) SPSS session.

For more information about the way your system processes commands, see the SPSS *Operations Guide* for your system.

You can add spaces or break lines at almost any point where a single blank is allowed, such as around slashes, parentheses, arithmetic operators, or between variable names. Text included within apostrophes or quotation marks must be contained on a single line.

1.5
Commands and Specifications

All terms in the SPSS language fall into one or more of the following categories:

- *Keyword*: A word already defined by SPSS to identify a command, subcommand, or specification. Most keywords are, or resemble, common English words.
- *Command*: A specific instruction that controls the execution of SPSS.
- *Subcommand*: Additional instructions on SPSS commands. A command can contain more than one subcommand, each with its own specifications.
- *Specifications*: Instructions added to a command or subcommand. Specifications may include subcommands, keywords, numbers, arithmetic operators, variable names, and special delimiters.

These categories are *not* mutually exclusive. Commands are also keywords; subcommands are both keywords and specifications.

Each command begins with a command keyword (which may contain more than one word). The command keyword is followed by at least one blank space and then any specifications required to complete the command, as in

```
LIST VARIABLES=ALL.
```

The command keyword is LIST, and VARIABLES=ALL is a specification.

Many specifications include subcommands. For example, the LIST command above contains a VARIABLES subcommand. Additional subcommands, separated by slashes, can also be specified. For example, the command

```
LIST VARIABLES=ALL /CASES=10.
```

contains a second subcommand, CASES, indicating the number of cases to list. This command could also be written on two lines.

```
LIST VARIABLES=ALL
 /CASES=10.
```

The blank space at the beginning of the second line indicates continuation and the period at the end indicates the end of the LIST procedure.

Most keywords that make up a command can be truncated to the least number of characters needed for identification. Exceptions are the reserved keyword WITH, the END DATA command, and all specifications to the INFO command. For example, the following is identical to the LIST command above:

```
LIST VAR=ALL /CAS=10.
```

1.6
Variable Names

When you define data and create variables with SPSS, you assign *names* to your variables. You use the assigned name to refer to a variable in an SPSS session. Keep in mind the following rules when naming variables:

- The name must begin with a letter. The remaining characters can be any letter, any digit, a period, or the symbols @, #, _, or $.
- The length of the name cannot exceed eight characters.
- Blanks and special characters such as &, !, ?, ', and * cannot occur in a variable name.
- Each variable must have a unique name. Duplication is not allowed.
- The reserved keywords in Table 1.6 cannot be used as variable names since they have special meaning in SPSS.

Table 1.6 SPSS reserved keywords

ALL	AND	BY	EQ	GE	GT	LE
LT	NE	NOT	OR	TO	WITH	

The following are all valid variable names: LOCATION, LOC#5, X.1, and OVER$500.

It is a good idea to assign variable names that help you identify variables. You could give the names X and Y to variables for age and sex, but the names AGE and SEX give you a much better idea of the nature of the variables.

Special *system variables* can be used in data transformation commands. The names of these variables begin with a dollar sign. The available system variables are:

$CASENUM *Case sequence number.* For each case, $CASENUM is the number of cases read up to and including the case.

$SYSMIS *System-missing value.*

$JDATE *Current date in YRMODA format.* For information on YRMODA format, see the *SPSS Reference Guide.*

$DATE *Current date in dd-mmm-yy format.*

$TIME *Current date and time.*

$LENGTH *Current page length.* See the SET command in Chapter 5 for information on controlling page length.

$WIDTH *Current page width.* See the SET command in Chapter 5 for information on controlling page width.

1.7
The TO Keyword

You can both create and refer to a set of variable names by using the keyword TO. When you are assigning new variable names, ITEM1 TO ITEM4 is the equivalent of four names: ITEM1, ITEM2, ITEM3, and ITEM4. When you are referring to a list of variables for a procedure, ITEM TO SCORE can be used to refer to all variables between ITEM and SCORE on the active system file, or, for some procedures, all variables between ITEM and SCORE on the preceding VARIABLES subcommand.

1.8
Annotated Example

```
DATA LIST FILE=WEATHER
 FREE /TEMP1 TEMP2 TEMP3 NEWTEMP HUMIDITY PRESSURE WINDDIR WINDSPD.
COMPUTE AVTEMP=(TEMP1+TEMP2+TEMP3)/3.
REGRESSION VARIABLES=NEWTEMP AVTEMP HUMIDITY TO WINDSPD
 /DEPENDENT=NEWTEMP
 /METHOD=ENTER AVTEMP TO WINDSPD
 /ENTER=AVTEMP TO WINDSPD
 /SAVE=PRED(PREDICT).
SAVE OUTFILE=FORECAST.
```

- The DATA LIST command is a *data definition* command that tells SPSS where to find the data. It also defines and names eight variables. The FILE subcommand indicates that the raw data are contained in a file named WEATHER. The FREE subcommand tells SPSS that the data are in freefield format. Following keyword FREE is the list of variables being defined. For more information about DATA LIST, see Chapter 2.

- The COMPUTE command is a *transformation* command that creates a new variable, AVTEMP, which is the average of three variables defined on DATA LIST. For more information on COMPUTE and other transformation commands, see Chapter 2.

- The REGRESSION command initiates a *procedure.* The VARIABLES subcommand specifies six variables: NEWTEMP, AVTEMP and the four variables from HUMIDITY to WINDSPD on the active system file. The DEPENDENT subcommand specifies NEWTEMP as the dependent variable, and the METHOD subcommand indicates that the five variables from AVTEMP to WINDSPD on the preceding VARIABLES subcommand are the independent variables. The SAVE subcommand saves the predicted values generated by the REGRESSION procedure and assigns the variable name PREDICT to these values. For more information on REGRESSION, see Chapter 19.

- The SAVE command creates a new SPSS system file and names it FORECAST. This system file contains 10 variables: the eight variables defined on the DATA LIST command, plus the two new variables created by the transformation and procedure commands. For more information on the SAVE command, see Chapter 4.

Contents _____

2 Preparing and Defining Data for SPSS Analysis

2.1 PREPARING DATA FOR ANALYSIS

Before information can be analyzed with SPSS, it must be entered into a computer file. This entails two steps:

- Arranging the data into a suitable format.
- Entering the data into the computer.

Sometimes the information to be analyzed is already available on a computer disk or magnetic tape. However, often the data are stored in other forms: in file folders in personnel offices, in patient medical charts, on credit card applications that never leave enough space for the requested information, or some other form that a computer can't read. Sections 2.2 through 2.5 examine the steps necessary to prepare data for analysis.

2.2 Cases, Variables, and Values

Consider Table 2.2, which contains data for five cases from a study designed to identify factors associated with coronary heart disease. In this study, 2,017 male employees of Western Electric with no history of coronary heart disease were followed for 20 years, and the occurrence of heart disease was monitored. Table 2.2 contains only a small portion of the data collected for each man. Each name in the table represents a *case,* or observation, for which *values* are available for a set of *variables.*

Table 2.2 Excerpt from uncoded data for Western Electric study

Name	First event	Age	Diastolic BP	Education	Cholesterol	Cigarettes
John Jones	Nonfatal MI	40	70	B.A.	321	0
Clark Roberts	Nonfatal MI	49	87	11th grade	246	60
Paul Buttons	Sudden death	43	89	High school	262	0
James Smith	Nonfatal MI	50	105	8th grade	275	15
Robert Norris	Sudden death	43	110	Unknown	301	25

Height	Weight	Day of week	Vital10	Family history	Incidence of CHD
68.8	190	None	Alive	Yes	Yes
72.2	204	Thursday	Alive	No	Yes
69.0	162	Saturday	Dead	No	Yes
62.5	152	Wednesday	Alive	Yes	Yes
68.0	148	Monday	Dead	No	Yes

For the first case, employee John Jones, age is a variable with a value of 40. The same variables are recorded for all cases. What differs are the actual values of the variables. Each case has only one value for each variable. "Unknown" and "missing" are acceptable values for a variable, although they require special treatment during analysis.

The case is the basic unit for which values are recorded for variables. In the Western Electric study, the case is an employee. In studies of political opinion or brand preference, the case is usually the individual respondent to a questionnaire. But a case may be a larger unit, such as a school, county, or nation; it may be a time period, such as a year or month, or it may be an event, such as an auto accident.

For any single analysis, all cases must represent the same the basic unit of analysis. If you are studying counties, all cases must be counties, and the values for each variable are values for individual counties. If you are studying states, then all cases must be states, and the values for each variable are the values for individual states.

2.3
Identifying Important Variables

A critical step in any study is the selection of variables to be included. The variables that are relevant to the problem under study must be chosen from a vast array of information available. If important data are excluded from the data file, the results will be of limited use. All potentially relevant variables should be included in the study since it is much easier to exclude unnecessary variables from the analysis than to go back and collect additional information.

2.4
Recording the Data

Once the variables have been selected, you must decide how they will be recorded. Do you need the actual date of birth or simply age in years? It is usually a good idea to record data in as much detail as possible. If you record date of birth, cases can be grouped into age categories later. But if you just record each case as under 50 or over 50, you can never analyze your data using any other age categories.

2.5
Coding the Variables

Once you have all your information, the data must be entered into the computer. One way to simplify data entry is to assign numbers or symbols to represent responses. This is known as *coding* the data. For example, instead of typing "Yes" or "No" as the values for the family history variable, the codes *Y* and *N* can be used. If only numbers are used in a coding scheme, it is called *numeric.* If letters or a combination of numbers, letters, and special characters are used, the code is called *alphanumeric* or *string.* By coding, you substantially decrease the number of symbols that you need to type.

Coding schemes are arbitrary by their very nature. The family history variable could also be coded 0 for no and 1 for yes. All that is necessary is that each possible response have a distinct code.

It is usually helpful to have one variable that uniquely identifies each case. For the Western Electric study, it could be the employee's name—but names are not always unique. The best approach is to assign a unique ID number to each case. This identifier can help you easily locate the data for cases with unusual values or missing information.

Consider the coding scheme in Table 2.5 and the data for the first three cases in Figure 2.5a, coded according to this scheme.

Table 2.5 Coding scheme for employee data form

Variable	Coding scheme
ID	no special code
FIRST CHD EVENT	1=No CHD 2=Sudden death 3=Nonfatal myocardial infarction 4=Fatal myocardial infarction 6=Other CHD
AGE	in years
DIASTOLIC BP	in mm of mercury
EDUCATION	in years
CHOLESTEROL	in milligrams per deciliter
CIGARETTES	number per day
HEIGHT	to nearest 0.1 inch
WEIGHT	in pounds
DAY OF WEEK	1=Sunday 2=Monday 3=Tuesday 4=Wednesday 5=Thursday 6=Friday 7=Saturday 9=Unknown
VITAL10	status at 10 years 0=Alive 1=Dead
FAMILY HISTORY OF CHD	N=No Y=Yes
CHD	0=No 1=Yes

Figure 2.5a Coded data

```
CASEID FIRSTCHD AGE DBP58 EDUYR CHOL58 CGT58  HT58 WT58 DAYOFWK VITAL10 FAMHXCVR CHD
    13        3   40    70    16    321     0  68.8  190       9       0        Y   1
    30        3   49    87    11    246    60  72.2  204       5       0        N   1
    53        2   43    89    12    262     0  69.0  162       7       1        N   1
```

Once the data are coded, a format for arranging the data in a computer file must be determined. Each line of type entered into a computer is called a *record*. Each record is composed of columns in which the numbers or characters are stored. Two decisions that must be made are:

- The number of records needed for each case.
- The column locations for each variable.

Figure 2.5b shows a file containing data for the first three cases in which one record is used for each case. The column locations are also indicated. The ID number is in columns 1–4; first coronary event in column 6; age in columns 17–18; and so forth. This is known as *fixed-column format* (see Section 2.9 for a discussion of fixed versus freefield format).

When there are many variables for each case, more than one record may be necessary. In Figure 2.5c, one case occupies two records. Each record contains the case ID number in columns 1-4 and a record identification number in column 50. It is a good idea to enter the case ID and a record number on all records for each case. You can then easily locate out-of-order or missing records.

Figure 2.5b   One-record file

```
0    0    1    1    2    2    3    3    4    4    5
1    5    0    5    0    5    0    5    0    5    0        Columns
    13 3              40  70 16 321  0 68.8 190 9 0 Y 1
    30 3              49  87 11 246 60 72.2 204 5 0 N 1
    53 2              43  89 12 262  0 69.0 162 7 1 N 1
                     . . .
```

Figure 2.5c   Two-record file

```
0    0    1    1    2    2    3    3    4    4    5
1    5    0    5    0    5    0    5    0    5    0        Column
    13 3 40   70 16 321  0                              1
    13 68.8 190 9 0 Y 1                                 2
                     . . .
```

It is important to allocate a sufficient number of columns for each variable. If only two columns are allocated for the weight variable, only weights less than 100 pounds will fit. Always allocate the maximum number of columns that your data might need. Don't worry if your observed data don't actually require that many columns.

2.6
SPSS DATA DEFINITION

Before you can analyze your data with SPSS, you must first *define* it in SPSS terms. The data definition commands in SPSS answer the following questions:

- Where is the data stored on your computer?
- How many records are there for each case?
- What are the names of the variables, and where are they located in the data file?
- What labels should be attached to variables and values?
- What values are used to represent missing information?

2.7
DATA LIST Command

The most basic component of SPSS data definition is the DATA LIST command. It tells SPSS where the data can be found, indicates how many records there are for each case, defines the variable names, and specifies their column locations.

The DATA LIST command consists of two basic components:

- Subcommands and keywords that indicate where to find the data, the number of records per case, and the basic data format.
- Definition of individual variables and the location of each variable on the case record(s).

Unlike most other SPSS commands, multiple subcommands in DATA LIST are not separated by slashes. A slash in DATA LIST separates the subcommands and keywords from the variable definition section, and each subsequent slash represents the start of a new record. For example, the command

```
DATA LIST FILE=CORONARY RECORDS=2
 /CASEID 1-4 FIRSTCHD 6 AGE 8-9 DBP58 11-13 EDUYR 15-16
  CHOL58 18-20 CGT58 22-23
 /HT58 6-9 WT58 11-13 DAYOFWK 15 VITAL10 17 FAMHXCVR 19 CHD 21.
```

contains two subcommands. The FILE subcommand specifies the name of the file containing the data, and the RECORDS subcommand indicates the number of records per case. Following the two subcommands is a list of variable names and their column locations on two records. (This command reads the data in Figure 2.5c.)

2.8
FILE Subcommand

Use the FILE subcommand to specify the file containing the data described in the DATA LIST command. The specification

```
DATA LIST FILE=CORONARY
```

indicates that the raw data are in a file named CORONARY.

If your data are included in the same file with your data definition commands (*inline* data), you can omit the FILE subcommand. Inline data must be entered between BEGIN DATA and END DATA commands (see Section 2.14).

2.9
FIXED, FREE, and LIST Keywords

Use one of the following keywords on DATA LIST to indicate the format of the data:

FIXED *Fixed-format data.* Each variable is recorded in the same column location on the same record for each case in the data file. FIXED is the default if no format is specified.

FREE *Freefield-format data.* The variables are recorded in the same order for each case, but not necessarily in the same locations. You can enter more than one case on a record. For example, if you define 10 variables, DATA LIST assumes the start of a new case after reading 10 values. Values are separated by blanks or commas.

LIST *Freefield-data with one case on each record.* The variables are recorded in freefield format as described for the keyword FREE, except the variables for each case must be recorded on a separate record, and each case only has one record.

With fixed format, you must specify the exact column locations for each variable, as in:

```
DATA LIST FILE=CORONARY FIXED
 /CASEID 1-4 FIRSTCHD 6 AGE 8-9 . . .
```

With freefield input, you simply provide the variable names, as in:

```
DATA LIST FILE=CORONARY FREE
 /CASEID FIRSTCHD AGE . . .
```

2.10
RECORDS Subcommand

Use the RECORDS subcommand with fixed-format data to specify the number of records per case. The specification

```
DATA LIST FILE=CORONARY RECORDS=2
```

tells SPSS to expect two records per case in file CORONARY.

By default, SPSS assumes one record per case for fixed-format data. You must use the RECORDS subcommand if there is more than one record per case. You should not use the RECORDS subcommand with freefield-format data.

2.11
TABLE and NOTABLE Subcommands

By default for fixed-format data, SPSS displays a table that summarizes your variable definitions immediately following the DATA LIST command. To suppress this table, specify the subcommand NOTABLE, as in:

```
DATA LIST FILE=CORONARY RECORDS=3 NOTABLE
```

The TABLE and NOTABLE subcommands cannot be used with freefield-format data.

2.12
Variable Definition

Use the variable definition portion of the DATA LIST command to assign names to your variables and provide information about the location and format of each variable.

Specifying Variable Names. The names you assign to your variables on the DATA LIST command are used on subsequent SPSS commands to refer to your variables.

Variable names can be up to eight characters long and begin with either an alphabetic letter or one of the following characters: @, #, or $. (For more information about SPSS rules for variable names, see Chapter 1.) The order in which variables are named on the DATA LIST command determines their order in the active system file.

Indicating Column Locations. For fixed-format data, follow the variable name with the column location. If the variable is two or more columns wide, specify the number of the first column, followed by a dash (-), and then the number of the last column, as in:

```
DATA LIST FILE=CORONARY
 /CASEID 1-4 FIRSTCHD 6 AGE 8-9...
```

For fixed-format data, you do not need to define all the variables in the data file—only those you intend to use. SPSS ignores data in columns and on records that you do not mention. Within a record, you do not need to specify variables in the same order in which they appear in the data file. The specification

```
DATA LIST FILE=CORONARY
 /CASEID 1-4 AGE 8-9 FIRSTCHD 6...
```

reads the variables from the correct locations but places AGE before FIRSTCHD on the active system file.

Specifying Multiple Records. The list of variables for each record should be preceded by a slash. You can specify the sequence number for the record immediately after the slash, although it is not required. For example,

```
DATA LIST FILE=CORONARY RECORDS=2
 /1 CASEID 1-4 FIRSTCHD 6 AGE 8-9...
 /2 HT58 6-9 WT58 11-13 DAYOFWK 15...
```

defines two records with sequence numbers 1 and 2.

You can skip over records simply by skipping sequence numbers or by specifying a slash with no subsequent variables for any records you wish to skip.

Specifying Multiple Variables in the Same Location. You can specify multiple variables in the same columns. For example, the specification

```
DATA LIST /MONTH 1-2 DAY 3-4 YEAR 5-6 DATE 1-6
```

specifies three variables MONTH, DAY, and YEAR in separate column locations and then specifies a fourth variable DATE starting in the first column of the field allocated for MONTH and ending in the last column allocated for YEAR. The variable DATE encompasses the values for the other three variables.

Shortcuts. If several variables with the same width and format are recorded in adjacent columns in the data file, you can indicate their column locations with a single specification. For example, the specification

```
DATA LIST /VAR1 1-3 VAR2 4-6 VAR3 7-9
```

could also be expressed as

```
DATA LIST /VAR1 VAR2 VAR3 1-9
```

The DATA LIST command divides the total number of columns equally among the three variables.

You can also use the keyword TO to define consecutive variables. For example, the specification

```
DATA LIST /CASEID 1-4 FIRSTCHD 6 AGE 8-9 DBP58 TO DBP60 11-19
```

defines the variables DBP58, DBP59, and DBP60 in columns 11–13, 14–16, and 17–19, respectively.

2.13
Types of Variables

You can define different types of variables with SPSS. The two most common are numeric and string (alphanumeric). Numeric variables contain only numbers. They can be either decimals (such as 12.345) or integers (such as 1234). A string variable can contain a combination of letters, numbers, and special characters.

There are two types of string variables—short strings and long strings. A string of eight characters or less is considered a short string. Short string variables can be used in some data transformations and procedures in which long strings cannot be used.

Specifying String Variables. By default, SPSS assumes that variables are numeric unless specified otherwise. To identify a string variable on the DATA LIST command, specify (A) after the variable name and column location, as in:

```
DATA LIST FILE=CORONARY /NAME 1-20(A)
```

For freefield-format data, you should also indicate the width of the string variable, as in:

```
DATA LIST FILE=CORONARY FREE /NAME(A20)
```

With freefield format, any preceding variables must also have their formats explicitly specified unless they are separated by an asterisk, as in:

```
DATA LIST FILE=CORONARY FREE
/WT58 HT58 FIRSTCHD * LNAME (A20) FNAME (A20)
```

This command tells SPSS that WT58, HT58, and FIRSTCHD are numeric variables (the default format) and LNAME and FNAME are both string variables with a width of 20 characters.

Indicating Decimal Places. By default, SPSS assumes that decimal points are explicitly coded in the data file. If there are no decimal points, the numeric variables are assumed to be integers. To indicate noninteger values for data that have not been coded with decimal points, you can specify the *implied* number of decimal places in parentheses after the variable name and column location, as in:

```
DATA LIST FILE=CORONARY /HEIGHT 34-36(1)
```

The variable HEIGHT is in columns 34-36. If a value is recorded as 688, it will be assigned a value of 68.8.

Any decimal points explicitly recorded in the data file will override the implied decimal point. Implied decimals on the DATA LIST command can be used only with fixed-format data.

Date Formats. SPSS also recognizes dates in a variety of formats. The two most common are:

DATE   *International date.* This format reads international dates in the form dd/mmm/ yyyy. Dashes, periods, commas, slashes, or blanks can be used as delimiters. Months can be represented in digits, roman numerals, three-character abbreviations, or they can be spelled out fully. If you enter a two-digit year, SPSS assumes a prefix of 19.

For example, 2/12/89, 02-Dec-89, and 2 December 1989 are all acceptable ways to express the date "December 2, 1989."

For DATE format, the width defined on DATA LIST must be at least nine characters. However, dates with fewer characters are correctly evaluated.

ADATE   *American date.* This format reads dates of the general format mm/dd/yyyy. ADATE format follows the same syntax rules as DATE format. For example, 10/28/86, Oct.28.86, and October,28,1986 are all acceptable ways to express the date "October 28, 1986."

For ADATE format, the width defined on DATA LIST must be at least eight characters. However, dates with fewer characters are correctly evaluated.

To define a date variable on the DATA LIST command, specify the date format in parentheses after the variable name and column specifications, as in:

```
DATA LIST /BIRTH 1-8 (ADATE).
```

2.14
BEGIN DATA and END DATA Commands

Sometimes, instead of keeping your data in an external file, you may prefer to enter your data along with your SPSS commands. In such cases, omit the FILE subcommand from the DATA LIST command and separate the inline data from the command lines with the BEGIN DATA and END DATA commands. The BEGIN DATA command follows the DATA LIST command, and the END DATA command follows the last line of data. All procedure commands should come after the END DATA command. Transformation commands can be specified before BEGIN DATA.

For example, the Western Electric data could be included in the same file with DATA LIST and other commands, as in:

```
DATA LIST
/CASEID 1-4 FIRSTCHD 6 AGE 17-18 DBP58 20-22 EDUYR 24-25
CHOL58 27-29 CGT58 31-32 HT58 34-37 WT58 39-41 DAYOFWK 43
VITAL10 45 FAMHXCVR 47 (A) CHD 49.
BEGIN DATA
  13 3            40  70 16 321  0 68.8 190 9 0 Y 1
  30 3            49  87 11 246 60 72.2 204 5 0 N 1
  53 2            43  89 12 262  0 69.0 162 7 1 N 1
                      . . .
END DATA.
FREQUENCIES VARIABLES=DAYOFWK.
```

Note that you do not specify a period ater the BEGIN DATA command.

2.15
MISSING VALUES Command

Sometimes information for a particular variable is not available for a case. For example, an employee in the Western Electric study might not know how many cigarettes he smokes each day, or he might refuse to answer the question. It is often useful to be able to distinguish why information is missing. You can assign values that identify information missing for various reasons, and you can instruct SPSS to flag these values with the MISSING VALUES command. The SPSS statistical procedures and transformation commands recognize this flag, and those cases with missing values are handled specially.

The specification on the MISSING VALUES command consists of a variable name or variable list and the specified missing value or values in parentheses, as in:

```
MISSING VALUES CGT58 (-1, -2) DAYOFWK (9).
```

You can specify missing values for any previously defined numeric or short string variable on the active system file. Variables can be previously defined with DATA LIST or a transformation command (see Chapter 3), or they may be defined in an SPSS system file accessed with the GET or IMPORT commands (see Chapter 4). You can specify missing values for more than one variable on the same MISSING VALUES command.

You can specify up to three individual missing values for each variable. Two of those variables can be the endpoints of a range using the keyword THRU. You can also assign the same missing values to more than one variable by specifying a variable list before the missing value(s). For example, the command

```
MISSING VALUES Q1 TO Q8 (0, 7 THRU 9).
```

defines 0 and all values from 7 through 9 as missing for all variables from Q1 to Q8 on the active system file.

The MISSING VALUES command defines *user-missing* values, which should be distinguished from *system-missing* values (indicated by a period in output). SPSS assigns a system-missing value whenever it encounters a value other than a number for a variable defined as numeric on the DATA LIST command. For example, a blank in a field for a numeric variable is set to system-missing. Leaving a field blank is an alternative to entering special codes for missing values—but you will probably find that assigning user-defined missing values gives you more control in most SPSS procedures.

System-missing values are also assigned when new variables created with transformation commands have undefined values. For example, if a case is missing a value for a variable used to compute the new variable, the system-missing value is assigned to the new variable for that case. The system-missing value is indicated by a period in output.

2.16
Variable and Value Labels

The optional VARIABLE LABELS and VALUE LABELS commands supply information that is used for labeling SPSS display output. Some variables, such as age and weight, can be assigned self-explanatory variable names (e.g. AGE and WEIGHT) and have a wide range of possible values that are inherently meaningful. Such variables do not need additional variable or value labels. But sometimes it is difficult to fully describe a variable with eight characters, and coded values may have no apparent meaning by themselves.

Variable and value labels are enclosed within apostrophes or quotation marks. To include an apostrophe in a label, use quotation marks to enclose the label, as in:

```
VARIABLE LABELS SALARY82 "EMPLOYEE'S ANNUAL SALARY IN 1982".
```

To continue a label from one command line to the next, use the plus sign and enclose both parts of the label in apostrophes or quotation marks. For example, the command

```
VARIABLE LABELS CHD 'INCIDENCE OF CORONARY'
 + ' HEART DISEASE'.
```

produces the label "INCIDENCE OF CORONARY HEART DISEASE". Since a blank space is a valid part of a label, a space must be inserted after CORONARY or before HEART to be included in the label.

2.17
VARIABLE LABELS
Command

Use the VARIABLE LABELS command to assign an extended descriptive label
to variables. Specify the variable name followed by at least one comma or blank
and then the label enclosed in apostrophes or quotation marks, as in:

```
VARIABLE LABELS
  DAYOFWK 'DAY OF DEATH'
  VITAL10 'STATUS AT TEN YEARS'
  FAMHXCVR 'FAMILY HISTORY OF CHD'.
```

This command assigns variable labels to the variables DAYOFWK, VITAL10, and
FAMHXCVR.

You can assign multiple variable labels on the same VARIABLE LABELS
command, but each label applies to only one variable. Variable labels can include
blanks and any other character. Each label can be up to 120 characters long,
although most procedures will print fewer than 120 characters for each label.

The variable must be previously defined on the active system file. Variables
can be defined with DATA LIST or with a transformation command (see Chapter
3), or they may be defined in an SPSS system file accessed with the GET or
IMPORT commands (see Chapter 4).

2.18
VALUE LABELS Command

Use the VALUE LABELS command to provide descriptive labels for values. The
VALUE LABELS command is followed by a variable name, or variable list, and a
list of the values with their associated labels enclosed in apostrophes or quotation
marks, as in:

```
VALUE LABELS
  DAYOFWK 1 'SUNDAY' 2 'MONDAY' 3 'TUESDAY'
  4 'WEDNESDAY' 5 'THURSDAY' 6 'FRIDAY' 7 'SATURDAY'
  /FAMHXCVR 'Y' 'YES' 'N' 'NO'.
```

Value labels can be assigned to any previously defined numeric or short string
variable. For short string variables, such as FAMHXCVR above, the actual value
must be enclosed in apostrophes. Value labels can contain blanks and any
characters. Each value label can be up to 60 characters long, although most
procedures will print fewer than 60 characters for each value.

Value labels for multiple variables can be specified on the same value labels
command. A slash is required to separate labels for one variable or variable list
from the next variable or variable list.

To assign the same labels to the same values of several variables, list all of the
variables followed by the values and associated labels, as in:

```
VALUE LABELS DEPT79 TO DEPT82
  0 'NOT REPORTED' 1 'ADMINISTRATIVE' 2 'PROJECT DIRECTORS'
  3 'CHICAGO OPERATIONS' 4 'ST.  LOUIS OPERATIONS'.
```

2.19
ADDITIONAL DATA
DEFINITION

Once you have defined your data for SPSS analysis, you may want to make some
minor adjustments or refinements without going through the entire data definition
process again. Commands are available to rename variables, add value labels, and
change both print and write formats.

2.20
RENAME VARIABLES
Command

Use the RENAME VARIABLES command to change variable names in the
active system file, while preserving their original order, values, variable labels,
value labels, missing values, and print and write formats.

To rename a variable, specify the old variable name followed by an equals sign and the new variable name, and enclose the entire specification in parentheses, as in:

```
RENAME VARIABLES (MOHIRED=MOSTART) (YRHIRED=YRSTART).
```

Alternatively, for multiple variables you can list all the old variable names before the equals sign and all the new variable names after the equals sign, as in:

```
RENAME VARIABLES (MOHIRED YRHIRED=MOSTART YRSTART).
```

Both variable lists must name or imply the same number of variables. You can use the TO keyword to imply consecutive variables from the active system file to be renamed and to generate new variable names. New variable names generated with the TO keyword are not consecutive on the active system file unless the original variables were consecutive prior to renaming. For example, the command

```
RENAME (INCOME EDUC RACE RELIG=SES1 TO SES4).
```

generates four consecutive new variable *names*—SES1, SES2, SES3, and SES4—but it preserves the original variable *order*, which is not necessarily consecutive since variables can be listed in any order on the RENAME command.

2.21
ADD VALUE LABELS Command

Each time you specify value labels for a variable with the VALUE LABELS command, the new labels completely replace all previously assigned value labels. To add additional value labels for a variable without deleting existing labels, use the ADD VALUE LABELS command. The syntax for ADD VALUE LABELS is the same as VALUE LABELS (see Section 2.18). For example, the command

```
ADD VALUE LABELS
 DAYOFWK 9 'MISSING'
 /FAMHXCHD 'U' 'UNKNOWN'.
```

creates one additional value label for the numeric variable DAYOFWK and one additional value label for the string variable FAMHXCHD.

As with VALUE LABELS, you can add the same labels for several variables by specifying a variable list before the values and labels. For variables that have no previously assigned value labels, the ADD VALUE LABELS command has the same effect as the VALUE LABELS command.

2.22
Print and Write Format Commands

The default print and write formats are determined by several factors:

- For fixed-format data, the default print and write formats are determined by the input field width and implied decimals specified on the DATA LIST command.
- For freefield-format data, the default print and write formats for numeric variables are both F8.2.
- For new numeric variables created with transformation commands (see Chapter 3), the default print and write formats are both F8.2.

A default format of F8.2 specifies a total width of 8 characters, with two decimal places. The decimal point also counts as one character. Numbers greater than 99,999,999 are expressed in scientific notation. For example, the value 235,012,345 appears as 2.4E+08. Values automatically appear with two decimals, provided there is sufficient space in the 8-character width. For example, the number 2,350 appears as 2350.00; the number 235,012 appears as 235012.0; and the number 2,350,123 appears as 2350123.

For fixed-format data, the default print and write formats for decimal places are determined by the number of implied decimals listed in parentheses for the variable on the DATA LIST command. If no implied decimals are specified on DATA LIST, the default print and write formats produce only integers, with no decimals. Explicitly coded decimals are stored in the system file; but they don't appear in the output produced by the default settings.

If a data value exceeds its width specification, SPSS makes an attempt to produce some value nevertheless. It takes out punctuation characters, and then tries scientific notation. If there still is not enough space, it produces asterisks to indicate a value that cannot be printed in the specified width.

SPSS provides a wide variety of formats for numeric variables. Use the PRINT FORMATS, WRITE FORMATS, and FORMATS commands to override the default formats. Table 2.22 shows a few of the more common formats. For a complete list of numeric and string formats, refer to the SPSS *Operations Guide* for your system.

Table 2.22   Common output data formats

Format	Specification	Input	Output
Default*	F8.2*	2350	2350.00
Fw.d	F9.0	2350	2350
COMMAw.d	COMMA9.1	2350	2,350.0
DOLLARw.d	DOLLAR9.2	2350	$2,350.00

*For freefield-format data and transformation commands.

2.23
PRINT FORMATS Command

Use the PRINT FORMATS command to change print formats. Specify the variable name or variable list, followed by the new format specification in parentheses, as in:

```
PRINT FORMATS SALARY79 TO SALARY82 (DOLLAR8).
```

This command specifies dollar print format with 8 positions, including the dollar sign and commas when appropriate.

To specify multiple print formats on the same command, separate the format specifications for each variable or variable list with a slash, as in:

```
PRINT FORMATS SALARY79 TO SALARY82 (DOLLAR8)
 /HOURLY82 (DOLLAR7.2).
```

The formats specified on a PRINT FORMATS command are in effect for the duration of the SPSS session.

2.24
WRITE FORMATS command

The WRITE FORMATS command operates exactly like the PRINT FORMATS command, except that it changes only the write formats of the variables specified. Write formats refer to the format of data sent to computer files to be read by SPSS or other software (see Chapters 4 and 6). They do not affect the format of printed output. There are some additional write formats that are not available as print formats. For a complete list of formats, refer to the SPSS *Operations Guide* for your system.

2.25
FORMATS Command

The FORMATS command operates exactly like the PRINT FORMATS and WRITE FORMATS commands, except that it changes both print and write formats for the variables specified.

2.26
REFORMAT Command

The REFORMAT command converts BMDP files and some earlier versions of SPSS to SPSS Release 4.0 format.

In some earlier versions of SPSS, all variables were printed as integers unless you used a PRINT FORMATS command to specify that the variable was string or to specify the number of decimal places. If you did not use the PRINT FORMATS command when you saved the SPSS system file, the print formats for string and decimal variables were incorrectly indicated as integers.

For a discussion of converting BMDP files, see the *SPSS Reference Guide*.

2.27
COMPLEX DATA DEFINITION

Many data files are not organized into the rectangular, case-ordered structure described at the beginning of this chapter. You may have *matrix files,* which contain summary data in matrix form; *mixed files,* which contain several types of records that define different types of cases; hierarchical or *nested files,* which contain several types of records with defined relationships between the record types; *grouped files,* which contain several records for each case with some records missing or duplicated; or files that contain records with *repeating data.*

Sections 2.28 through 2.39 give a brief overview of many of the SPSS commands available to read and define complex data files. For a complete discussion of these commands, see the *SPSS Reference Guide*.

2.28
MATRIX DATA Command

Some SPSS procedures, such as FACTOR and REGRESSION, allow you to read matrix materials containing summary statistics such as means, correlations, covariances, and factors instead of reading the original cases. This results in a considerable decrease in processing time.

Use the MATRIX DATA command to read raw matrix material and convert the data to an SPSS matrix system file.

The MATRIX DATA command is similar to the DATA LIST command: it defines variable names and their order in the raw data file. It can handle both inline data and data from an external file. The only required subcommand is the VARIABLES subcommand, as in:

```
MATRIX DATA VARIABLES=VAR1 TO VAR5.
```

If the matrix data are in an external file, use the FILE subcommand to specify the file, as in:

```
MATRIX DATA FILE=RAWMTX /VARIABLES=VAR1 TO VAR5.
```

By default, MATRIX DATA assumes the data are the lower triangle of a correlation matrix, including the diagonal. For example, with the commands

```
MATRIX DATA /VARIABLES=ADVERTIS SALES REPS.
BEGIN DATA.
1
0.7763 1
0.8802 0.8818 1
END DATA.
```

each data record represents one line from the lower triangle of the correlation matrix. SPSS will read one value from the first record and assume that it is the correlation between ADVERTIS and itself. It will then read two values from the second record and assume that they are the correlations between ADVERTIS and SALES and between SALES and itself, respectively. In a similar fashion, it will read three correlations from the third record.

If SPSS encounters more values than expected on a record, it will ignore the extraneous values. If it encounters fewer values than expected, it will assume that the coefficients for that line in the correlation matrix are continued on the next record.

MATRIX DATA can also read means, standard deviations, factors, and covariances.

Only statistical procedures that have a MATRIX=IN specification can correctly read matrix system files defined with the MATRIX DATA command. For the FACTOR procedure, the only required specification on MATRIX DATA is the VARIABLES subcommand. For the REGRESSION procedure, the required specifications on MATRIX DATA are the VARIABLES subcommand and the N subcommand, which specifies the number of cases used to compute the correlation coefficients. For both procedures, the matrix system file must contain a matrix of correlation coefficients.

For a complete discussion of all subcommands and specifications for MATRIX DATA and the matrix requirements for procedures other than FACTOR and REGRESSION, see the *SPSS Reference Guide*.

2.29
Complex Files

To define complex files, use the FILE TYPE, RECORD TYPE, DATA LIST, and END FILE TYPE commands. On the FILE TYPE command, specify the type of file, the location of the record type identifier, and optional information for handling duplicate, missing, or invalid record types. Include a RECORD TYPE and a DATA LIST command for each type of record. At the end of the file definition commands, specify the END FILE TYPE command.

2.30
FILE TYPE Command

Use the FILE TYPE command to define the structure of your data file. There are three FILE TYPE keywords:

MIXED   *Each record type defines a case.* Some information may be the same for all record types but recorded in different locations. Other information may be recorded only for specific record types.

GROUPED *Cases are defined by grouping together record types with the same identification number.*

NESTED   *Cases are related to each other in a hierarchical fashion.* Usually, the last record type defined—the lowest level of the hierarchy—defines a case.

For a complete list of FILE TYPE subcommands and keywords, see the *SPSS Reference Guide*.

2.31
RECORD TYPE Command

You must include a RECORD TYPE command after the FILE TYPE command for each type of record that you want to process. The first specification on the RECORD TYPE command is the value of the record type identifier defined on the RECORD subcommand of the FILE TYPE command. For a complete list of RECORD TYPE subcommands and keywords, see the *SPSS Reference Guide*.

2.32
RECORD TYPE with FILE TYPE MIXED

You might want to read the records for chemotherapy treatment in which either Drug A or Drug C was administered. These treatments are coded as 23 and 25 respectively for the record identifier variable, RECID, but the data to be read aren't in the same locations on the two record types. You would specify a separate RECORD TYPE and DATA LIST command for each record type, as in:

```
FILE TYPE MIXED FILE=TREATMNT RECORD=RECID 1-2.
RECORD TYPE 23.
DATA LIST /SEX 5 AGE 6-7 DOSAGE 8-10 RESULT 12.
RECORD TYPE 25.
DATA LIST /SEX 5 AGE 6-7 DOSAGE 10-12 RESULT 15.
END FILE TYPE.
```

2.33
RECORD TYPE with FILE TYPE GROUPED

The FILE TYPE GROUPED command can be used to identify missing records for files with multiple records for each case. For example, the command

```
DATA LIST FILE=CORONARY RECORDS=2
 /RECID 1 CASEID 2-4 FIRSTCHD 6 DAYOFWK 8
 /RECID 1 CASEID 2-4 HT58 6-9 WT58 11-13 AGE 15-16.
```

could be replaced with the commands

```
FILE TYPE GROUPED FILE=CORONARY RECORD=RECID 1 CASE=CASEID 2-4.
RECORD TYPE 1.
DATA LIST /FIRSTCHD 6 DAYOFWK 8.
RECORD TYPE 2.
DATA LIST /HT58 6-9 WT58 11-13 AGE 15-16.
END FILE TYPE.
```

which issue a warning message if a record type is missing for a case.

2.34
Direct Access Files

The SPSS concept of a direct access file is very specific. The file must be one from which individual records can be selected according to their number. The records in a 100-record direct access file, for example, are numbered 1 to 100.

Although the concept of record number applies to almost any file, not all files can be treated by SPSS as direct access files. In fact, some systems contain no direct access capabilities, and others permit only a narrowly defined subset of files to be treated as direct access.

SPSS can read specific records from a direct access file with the KEYED DATA LIST command, and you can also use the POINT command to establish a keyed file location to begin or resume sequential file access. For a complete discussion of these commands, see the *SPSS Reference Guide*.

2.35
INPUT PROGRAM and END INPUT PROGRAM Commands

When a single DATA LIST command does not allow you to define your data, and the complex file definition commands discussed in this chapter are not applicable, you can use one or more DATA LIST commands, transformation commands, and various utility commands described below to build your own input program. The input program must begin with the INPUT PROGRAM command and end with the END INPUT PROGRAM command.

Four utility commands are available for input programs: END CASE, END FILE, REREAD, and REPEATING DATA. For a complete discussion of input programs, see the *SPSS Reference Guide*.

2.36
END CASE Command

Use the END CASE command whenever you change the case structure of your file by building a single case from several cases or by building several cases from a single case. END CASE terminates execution of your SPSS commands and delivers a case to the next procedure (see Section 2.40). For a complete discussion of END CASE, see the *SPSS Reference Guide*.

2.37
END FILE Command

The END FILE command tells SPSS to stop reading data before it actually encounters the end of the file. You can also use END FILE to indicate the end of the file when you are generating data. For a complete discussion of END FILE, see the *SPSS Reference Guide*.

2.38
REREAD Command

The REREAD command allows you to obtain information from a record indicating how to read the remaining portion of the record. For example, a company that manufactures automobile parts might receive orders recorded in different formats for different automobiles, and the variable that describes the type of car indicates how the data should be read. A combination of DATA LIST, DO IF, ELSE IF, and REREAD commands could be used in an input program to read each record, evaluate the information, and then reread each record with a different DATA LIST command (see Section 2.40). For a complete discussion of REREAD, see the *SPSS Reference Guide*.

2.39
REPEATING DATA Command

Use the REPEATING DATA command to read and generate cases from repeating groups of data from the same input record. Each repeating group contains the same information, and a case is built on the active system file for each repeating group. The number of repeating groups can vary for each record. Each input record may include information that is common to all repeating groups that you want to *spread* to each case built on the active file.

For example, each record in a data file might represent a household and contain information about the number of persons living in the household and the number of vehicles. Each record also contains information about each vehicle, such as the make, model, engine size, and so forth. You can use the REPEATING DATA command to create a new file in which each car represents a record or case, with the household information repeated for each new case that was built from the same household record.

The REPEATING DATA command must appear within an input program or in a FILE TYPE—END FILE TYPE structure. For a complete list of REPEATING DATA subcommands and keywords, see the *SPSS Reference Guide*.

2.40
An Input Program Example

As described in Section 2.38, suppose a company that manufactures automobile parts has a data file with different record formats for different types of cars. The REREAD and END CASE commands could be used in the following input program:

```
INPUT PROGRAM.
DATA LIST FILE=CARPARTS /KIND 10-14 (A).
DO IF(KIND EQ 'FORD').
REREAD.
DATA LIST /PARTNO 1-2 PRICE 3-6 QUANTITY 7-9.
END CASE.
ELSE IF (KIND EQ 'CHEVY').
REREAD.
DATA LIST /PARTNO 1-2 PRICE 15-18 QUANTITY 19-21.
END CASE.
END IF.
END INPUT PROGRAM.
```

For a discussion of DO IF and ELSE IF, see Chapter 3.

Contents _____

3 Data Transformation and Selection

In an ideal situation, your raw data are perfectly suitable for the type of analysis you want to perform, and any relationships between variables are either conveniently linear or neatly orthogonal. If this is the case, you can proceed directly from basic data definition to complex statistical analysis. However, you will probably find that this is rarely the case. Preliminary analysis may reveal inconvenient coding schemes or coding errors; complex data transformations may be required to coax out the true relationship between variables; or you may find that only a particular subset of cases is relevant to your analysis.

With SPSS you can perform data transformation ranging from simple tasks, such as collapsing categories for analysis, to creating new variables based on complex equations and conditional statements. You can also select cases for analysis based on an equally complex set of conditions or choose a simple random sample.

This chapter provides an overview of the data transformation and selection commands available with SPSS. For a complete discussion of these commands, see the *SPSS Reference Guide*.

3.1
RECODE COMMAND

The RECODE command tells SPSS to change the values for a variable as the data are being read. The command

```
RECODE X (0=9).
```

instructs SPSS to change all 0's found for variable X to 9's.

The variable or variables to be recoded must already exist on the active SPSS system file. You can specify as many value specifications as needed, enclosing each specification within parentheses, as in:

```
RECODE ITEM1 (0=1) (1=0) (2=-1).
```

You can use multiple input values in a single specification but only one output value following the equals sign, as in:

```
RECODE ITEM2 (8,9=1) (4 THRU 7=2) (1,2=3).
```

The RECODE command is evaluated left to right, and the values for a case are recoded only once per RECODE command. For example, if a case has an input value of 0 for variable ITEM1, the command

```
RECODE ITEM1 (0=1) (1=0) (2=-1).
```

recodes ITEM1 to 1 and SPSS then moves on. The value 1 is *not* recoded back to 0 by the second value specification. Input values not mentioned on the RECODE command are left unchanged.

You can name multiple variables for the same value specifications, as in:

RECODE ITEM1 TO ITEM3 (0=1) (1=0) (2=-1).

In addition, you can specify different values for different variables on the same RECODE command by separating the specifications with a slash, as in:

RECODE AGE (0=9)
/ITEM1 TO ITEM3 (0=1) (1=0) (2=-1).

These rules apply to both numeric and string variables. See Section 3.8 for more information on recoding string variables.

3.2
THRU, LOWEST, and HIGHEST Keywords

To recode ranges of values for numeric variables into a single value, use keyword THRU. Use keyword LO (LOWEST) or HI (HIGHEST) to specify the lowest or highest input value for the variable. For example, to recode all individuals below the United States voting age to 0 and leave all other ages unchanged, specify:

RECODE AGE (LO THRU 17=0).

Keywords LOWEST and HIGHEST do not include the system-missing value. However, user-missing values are included.

3.3
ELSE Keyword

To recode all values not previously mentioned into a single catchall category, use the keyword ELSE. For example, to recode AGE to a dichotomous (two-valued) variable with 0 representing individuals below the voting age and 1 representing potential voters, specify:

RECODE AGE (LO THRU 17=0) (ELSE=1).

ELSE should be the last specification for the variable. Otherwise all subsequent value specifications for that variable are ignored. Keyword ELSE *does* include the system-missing value.

3.4
MISSING and SYSMIS Keywords

To recode a variable that may have missing values, use keyword MISSING or SYSMIS. For example, if −98 and −99 were declared missing for variable AGE, the command

RECODE AGE (MISSING=9).

recodes −98, −99, and any system-missing values (perhaps from input errors) for variable AGE to 9. The command

RECODE AGE (MISSING=SYSMIS).

recodes all missing values to the system-missing value.

You can use keyword MISSING only as an input value. MISSING refers to all missing values including the system-missing value. The output value from a MISSING input specification is not automatically missing; use the MISSING VALUES command to declare the new value missing (see Chapter 2). You can use keyword SYSMIS for either input or output. As an input value, SYSMIS refers to system-missing values. As an output value specification, SYSMIS recodes all values named on the left side of the equals sign to the system-missing value.

3.5
Recoding Continuous Variables

If a numeric variable has noninteger values, some values may not be recoded unless you make certain they are included in a value range. For example, if AGE had noninteger values, the command

```
RECODE AGE (LO THRU 17=0) (18 THRU HI=1).
```

would not recode values between 17 and 18, such as 17.5. You can avoid this problem by using overlapping endpoint values, as in:

```
RECODE AGE (18 THRU HI=1) (LO THRU 18=0).
```

Note that the order of the recode specifications has been reversed. Since a value is recoded only once, any cases with a value of exactly 18 will be recoded to a value of 1.

3.6
INTO Keyword

To recode the values of one variable and store them in another variable, use the keyword INTO, as in:

```
RECODE AGE (18 THRU HI=1) (LO THRU 18=0) INTO VOTER.
```

The recoded AGE values are stored in the *target variable* VOTER, leaving AGE unchanged.

Target variables can be existing or new variables. If you use an existing variable, cases with values not mentioned in the recode specification are not changed. If you recode a variable into a new variable, cases with values not specified for recoding are assigned the system-missing value.

New numeric variables have default print and write formats of F8.2 (see Chapter 2) or the format you specify using the SET command (see Chapter 5).

3.7
COPY Keyword

When you recode a variable into a new variable or use keyword ELSE as a cleanup category, you may want to retain a set of input values. The command

```
RECODE ITEM1 TO ITEM3 (0=1) (1=0) (2=-1) (ELSE=COPY)
   INTO DEFENSE WELFARE HEALTH.
```

creates three new variables. Input values other than 0, 1, or 2 are retained. In other words, if a case has value 9 for variable ITEM1, it will have value 9 for variable DEFENSE, and so forth.

Keyword COPY is an output specification only. Input values to be copied can be a range of values, keywords SYSMIS or MISSING, or keyword ELSE. User-missing values are copied, but their missing-value status is not. The MISSING VALUES command should be used to redeclare missing values for the new variables (see Chapter 2).

3.8
Recoding String Variables

If you are recoding a string variable, enclose each value specification in apostrophes or quotation marks, as in:

```
RECODE STATE ('IO'='IA').
```

The following additional rules apply to recoding string variables:

• The keywords THRU, HIGHEST, LOWEST, MISSING, and SYSMIS cannot be used.

- If a value specification applies to more than one variable, all the named variables must have string values of equal length.
- New string values cannot be longer than the variable length as defined on the DATA LIST or STRING command (see Section 3.23).
- If you specify fewer characters than the defined string variable length, SPSS right-pads the value with blanks to the defined length. For example, if the defined length is A3, and you specify a value of 'NO' on the RECODE command, SPSS reads the value as 'NO '.
- Target variables specified with the INTO keyword must already exist on the active system file. To create a new variable, use the STRING command (see Section 3.23) before the RECODE command to declare new string target variables.

3.9
COMPUTE COMMAND

The COMPUTE command creates new variables through numeric transformations of existing variables. COMPUTE names the variable you want to create (the *target variable*) followed by an *expression* defining the variable. For example, the command

```
COMPUTE TOTSCORE=MIDTERM+FINAL+HOMEWORK.
```

defines the new variable TOTSCORE as the sum of the variables MIDTERM, FINAL, and HOMEWORK.

The target variable can be a variable that already exists or a new variable. If the target variable already exists, its values are replaced with those produced by the specified transformation. If it is a new variable, it is added to the end of the dictionary in your active system file.

The expression on the COMPUTE command can use existing numeric variables, constants, arithmetic operators (such as + and −), and functions such as SQRT (square root) and TRUNC (truncate). For example, the command

```
COMPUTE GRADESCR=.35*MIDTERM+.45*FINAL+.2*HOMEWORK.
```

creates a new variable, GRADESCR, that is the weighted average of the variables MIDTERM, FINAL, and HOMEWORK.

3.10
Arithmetic Operators

The following arithmetic operators are available for transforming numeric variables with COMPUTE:

+   *Addition.*
−   *Subtraction.*
*   *Multiplication.*
/   *Division.*
**   *Exponentiation.*

Arithmetic operators must be explicitly specified. You cannot, for example, write (PROPTAX)(100) instead of (PROPTAX)*100.

You can include blanks in an arithmetic expression to improve readability, as in the command

```
COMPUTE TAXTOTAL = PROPTAX + FICA + STATETAX + FEDTAX.
```

Since fairly complex expressions are possible, it is important to keep in mind the order in which operations are performed. Functions (see Sections 3.11 through 3.13) are evaluated first, then exponentiation, then multiplication and division, and, finally, addition and subtraction. Thus, if you specify

```
COMPUTE NEWRATE=SQRT(RATE1)/SQRT(RATE1)+SQRT(RATE3).
```

the square roots (SQRT) are calculated first, then the division is performed, and then the addition.

You can control the order in which operations are performed by enclosing the operation you want executed first in parentheses. Thus, the command

COMPUTE NEWRATE=SQRT(RATE1)/(SQRT(RATE1)+SQRT(RATE3)).

produces different results than the previous command, since the added parentheses cause the addition to be performed before division. Operations at the same level, as far as order of execution is concerned, are evaluated from left to right. If you are uncertain about the order of execution, you should use parentheses to make the order you want explicit.

3.11
Numeric Functions

Many numeric functions are available with the COMPUTE command. Numeric functions always return numbers (or the system-missing value).

The expression to be transformed by a function is called the *argument*. Most functions have a variable name or variable list as arguments. In numeric functions with two or more arguments, each argument must be separated by a comma. You cannot use blanks alone to separate the variable names, expressions, or constants used as arguments.

For example, to generate the square root of variable X, specify variable X as the argument to the SQRT function, as in SQRT(X). Enclose arguments in parentheses, as in

COMPUTE INCOME=TRUNC(INCOME).

where the TRUNC function returns the integer portion of variable INCOME. Separate multiple arguments with commas, as in

COMPUTE SCALE=MEAN(Q1,Q2,Q3).

where the MEAN function returns the mean of variables Q1, Q2, and Q3.

Sections 3.12 through 3.14 discuss arithmetic, statistical, and other functions for the COMPUTE command. These functions can also be used with the IF, SELECT IF, DO IF, ELSE IF, LOOP IF, and END LOOP IF commands, which are discussed later in this chapter.

3.12
Arithmetic Functions

The following arithmetic functions are available:

ABS(arg)   *Absolute value.* ABS(SCALE) is 4.7 when SCALE equals 4.7 or −4.7.

RND(arg)   *Round the absolute value to an integer and reaffix the sign.* RND(SCALE) is −5 when SCALE equals −4.7.

TRUNC(arg)   *Truncate to an integer.* TRUNC(SCALE) is −4 when SCALE equals −4.7.

MOD(arg,arg)   *Remainder (modulo) of the first argument divided by the second.* MOD(YEAR,100) is 83 when YEAR equals 1983.

SQRT(arg)   *Square root.* SQRT(SIBS) is 1.41 when SIBS equals 2.

EXP(arg)   *Exponential. e is raised to the power of the argument.* EXP(VARA) is 7.39 when VARA equals 2.

LG10(arg)   *Base 10 logarithm.* LG10(VARB) is .48 when VARB equals 3.

LN(arg)   *Natural or Naperian logarithm (base e).* LN(VARC) is 2.30 when VARC equals 10.

ARSIN(arg)   *Arcsine. The result is given in radians (alias ASIN).* ARSIN(ANG) is 1.57 when ANG equals 1.

ARTAN(arg)   *Arctangent. The result is given in radians (alias ATAN).* ARTAN(ANG2) is .79 when ANG2 equals 1.

SIN(arg)   *Sine.* The argument must be specified in radians. SINE(VARC) is .84
                when VARC equals 1.

COS(arg)   *Cosine.* The argument must be specified in radians. COS(VARD) is .54
                when VARD equals 1.

All arithmetic functions except MOD have single arguments; MOD has two. The
arguments to MOD must be separated by a comma. Arguments can be numeric
expressions, as in RND(A**2/B).

3.13
Statistical Functions

Each argument to a statistical function (expression, variable name, or constant)
must be separated by a comma. The available statistical functions are:

SUM(arg list)   *Sum of the values across the argument list.*

MEAN(arg list)   *Mean of the values across the argument list.*

SD(arg list)   *Standard deviation of the values across the argument list.*

VARIANCE(arg list) *Variance of the values across the argument list.*

CFVAR(arg list)   *Coefficient of variation of the values across the argument list. The
                    coefficient of variation is the standard deviation divided by the
                    mean.*

MIN(arg list)   *Minimum value across the argument list.*

MAX(arg list)   *Maximum value across the argument list.*

3.14
Other Functions

Other available functions include:

RANGE(arg,arg list) *Return 1 (true) if the value of the first argument is in the inclusive
                     range(s); otherwise, return 0 (false).* The arguments must be
                     separated by commas. The first argument is usually a variable, and
                     the list usually contains pairs of values. For example, NONWORK
                     =RANGE(AGE,1,17,62,99) returns a value of 1 for ages 1
                     through 17 and ages 62 through 99. The value of NONWORK is 0
                     for any other value of AGE.

ANY(arg, arglist)   *Return 1 (true) if the value of the first argument matches one of the
                     arguments in the list. Otherwise, return 0 (false).* The arguments must
                     be separated by commas. The first argument is usually a variable.
                     For example, PARTIC=ANY(PROJECT, 3, 4, 7, 9) returns a value
                     of 1 if the value of PROJECT is 3, 4, 7, or 9. If PROJECT is any
                     other value, PARTIC has a value of 0.

UNIFORM(arg)   *A uniform pseudo-random number.* The random number is uni-
                     formly distributed with values varying between 0 and the value of
                     the argument. For example, SAMP1=UNIFORM(150) assigns
                     random values between 1 and 150 to the variable SAMP1 for each
                     case in the active system file.

NORMAL(arg)   *A normal pseudo-random number.* The random number is normal-
                     ly distributed, with a mean of approximately 0 and a standard
                     deviation equal to the value of the argument.

VALUE(arg)   *Ignore user-missing values.* User-missing values are treated as valid
                     observations and included in any specified calculations.

MISSING(arg)   *Return 1 (true) if the value of the argument is missing; otherwise
                     return 0 (false).* The argument is a variable name, and the missing
                     values include both user- and system-missing values.

SYSMIS(arg)   *Return 1 (true) if the value of the argument is system-missing;
                     otherwise 0 (false).*

There are also numerous functions that enable you to convert and extract dates and times. For example, you can calculate the number of days between two date variables (see Chapter 2) with the command:

```
COMPUTE DAYDIFF=CTIME.DAYS(VISIT2-VISIT1).
```

SPSS stores all dates as the number of seconds since October 14, 1582. The function CTIME.DAYS converts dates into the number of days. The argument (VISIT2−VISIT1) calculates the difference, in days, between the date variables VISIT2 and VISIT1.

For a complete list of functions, including date and time functions, see the *SPSS Reference Guide*.

3.15
Using Functions in Complex Expressions

You can specify more than one function in an argument as well as combine functions with arithmetic operators. Such arguments will be evaluated in the order described in Section 3.10 or in the order specified by parentheses. For example, if the command

```
COMPUTE PCTTAXES=RND((TAXES/INCOME)*100).
```

is used, TAXES is first divided by INCOME, the result is multiplied by 100, and this result is rounded off to the nearest integer to get the new variable PCTTAXES.

3.16
Missing Values

If a case has missing values for any of the variables used in a COMPUTE arithmetic expression, the case is assigned the system-missing value for the computed variable. For example, if the command

```
COMPUTE AGECUBE=AGE**3.
```

is used, the AGECUBE variable will be system-missing for any case with a missing value for AGE.

A case is also assigned the system-missing value for a computed variable when the specified operation is not defined for that case. For example, if the command

```
COMPUTE PCTTAXES=(TAXES/INCOME)*100.
```

is used, a case with the value 0 for INCOME is assigned the system-missing value for PCTTAXES because division by 0 is not defined. If the result of an expression cannot be represented on the computer (even when valid values are used in the expression itself), the system-missing value is assigned to the new variable.

The assignment of missing values is treated differently for numeric functions. For example, the command

```
COMPUTE MEANSCOR=(SCORE1+SCORE2+SCORE3)/3.
```

will return a missing value for MEANSCOR if a case has a missing value for any one of the variables SCORE1, SCORE2, or SCORE3. However, the command

```
COMPUTE MEANSCOR=MEAN(SCORE1, SCORE2, SCORE3).
```

will return a numeric value unless a case has missing values for all three specified variables.

For a complete discussion of the treatment of missing values with numeric functions, see the *SPSS Reference Guide*.

3.17
Computing String Variables

You can also use the COMPUTE command to compute string variables. With strings, the expression on the right of the equals sign must return a string, and the target variable must already exist on the active system file. To declare a new string variable, use the STRING command (see Section 3.23) before the COMPUTE command, as in:

```
STRING NEWVAR(A2).
COMPUTE NEWVAR='NA'.
```

which declares a new string variable NEWVAR with a length of two characters and assigns a value of NA to NEWVAR for every case.

There are also numerous string functions, including functions for concatenating string values, converting from upper case to lower case (and from lower to upper), and converting strings to numeric values. For a complete list of string functions, see the *SPSS Reference Guide*.

3.18
COUNT COMMAND

The COUNT command is a special data transformation utility used to create a numeric variable that, for each case, counts the occurrences of the same value (or list of values) across a list of numeric or string variables. For example,

```
COUNT  READER=NEWSWEEK,TIME,USNEWS (2).
```

creates a simple index READER that indicates the number of times the value 2 (those who read each magazine) is recorded for the three variables for a case. Thus, the value of reader will be either 0, 1, 2, or 3. You can enter more than one criterion variable list and more than one criterion value enclosed in parentheses, as in

```
COUNT  READER=NEWSWEEK,TIME,USNEWS (2)
 NYTIMES,WPOST,CHIGTRIB,LATIMES (3,4).
```

which adds four more news sources to the previous index. This time, SPSS increases the count for a case by 1 whenever it encounters either value 3 (Sunday only) or 4 (daily plus Sunday) for each newspaper variable.

You can specify a variable more than once in the variable list to increase the count by more than 1 for that variable, thus giving it more weight. You can also use the TO keyword in the variable list and the THRU, LO (LOWEST), and HI (HIGHEST) keywords in the value list. You can also create more than one variable on a COUNT command by separating the specifications with a slash, as in:

```
COUNT LOWCOUNT=Q1 TO Q10 (LO THRU 5)
 /HICOUNT=Q1 TO Q10 (11 THRU HI).
```

3.19
Initialization and Missing Values

The COUNT command ignores the missing-value status of user-missing values. In other words, the COUNT command counts a value even if that value has been previously declared as missing. In the command

```
COUNT LOWCOUNT=Q1 TO Q10 (LO THRU 5).
```

target variable LOWCOUNT is increased for a case with value 0 for variables Q1, Q2, and so forth, even if 0 was declared user-missing for the Q variables.

COUNT will not propagate missing values automatically. In other words, the target variable will never be system-missing. However, you can use the MISSING VALUES command to declare missing values for the target variable.

You can use keyword MISSING to count all missing values (user-defined and system-missing) and keyword SYSMIS to count only system-missing values. Specify these keywords in parentheses, as in:

```
COUNT QMISS=Q1 TO Q10 (MISSING)
 /QSYSMIS= Q1 TO Q10 (SYSMIS).
```

This command creates one variable (QMISS) that counts all missing values for the criterion variables and a second variable (QSYSMISS) that counts only system-missing values.

3.20
WEIGHT COMMAND

The WEIGHT command is used to weight cases differentially for analysis. For example, if you have a sample from a population for which some subgroup has been over- or undersampled, you can apply weights to obtain population estimates. You can also use the WEIGHT command to replicate an example from a table or other aggregated data as shown for the CROSSTABS procedure in Chapter 10.

The variable named after the keyword BY on the WEIGHT command is used to weight cases, as in:

```
WEIGHT BY WTFACTOR.
```

This command tells SPSS to use the value of variable WTFACTOR to weight cases.

Only one variable can be specified on the WEIGHT command, and it must already exist on the active system file. The weight variable must be numeric, and it cannot be a scratch or system variable.

Cases with missing values, negative values, or a value of 0 for the weight variable are not included in statistical procedures.

The weighting variable can be an existing variable or one created through transformation commands. For example, assume your file contains a sample of households in which rural households were oversampled by a factor of 2. To compensate for oversampling, you can weight the rural households by one half, as in:

```
COMPUTE WT=1.
IF (LOCATE EQ 'RURAL') WT=.5.
WEIGHT BY WT.
```

Variable WT is initialized to 1 with the COMPUTE command and then changed to .5 with the IF command (see Section 3.26) for cases where the value of LOCATE equals RURAL. Be sure to initialize the weighting variable to 1 when creating it with IF commands. Otherwise, cases not covered by IF commands will be missing and will have a zero weight.

3.21
Turning Off or Changing Weights

Unless you precede the WEIGHT command with a TEMPORARY command (see Section 3.51), weighting stays in effect. To turn off weighting, simply use a WEIGHT command with the keyword OFF, as in:

```
WEIGHT OFF.
```

To change the weight, use another WEIGHT command specifying a different variable. Weighting is not cumulative. That is, a second WEIGHT command changes the weight; it does not weight the weight. In the following example,

```
GET FILE=CITY.
WEIGHT BY POP81.
DESCRIPTIVES VARIABLES=ALL.
WEIGHT BY POP82.
DESCRIPTIVES VARIABLES=ALL.
```

the first DESCRIPTIVES command computes summary statistics based on cases weighted by POP81, and the second DESCRIPTIVES command computes summary statistics based on cases weighted by POP82.

3.22
NUMERIC COMMAND

Use the NUMERIC command to declare new numeric variables. While you can also create new numeric variables directly with COMPUTE, IF, RECODE, and COUNT, you may need to refer to a numeric variable in the transformation language before it is created. For example, you might want to add a series of variables to your active system file in a fixed order so you can use the TO keyword to refer to variables on procedure commands. The specification

```
NUMERIC SCALE79 IMPACT79 SCALE80 IMPACT80 SCALE81 IMPACT81.
```

declares variables SCALE79 through IMPACT81. Then, regardless of the order in which you determine values for them, the variables remain in that order on the active system file. You can also use the TO keyword to generate consecutive new variable names.

The default format for variables named on a NUMERIC command is F8.2 (or whatever you specify using the SET command), but you can declare formats in parentheses following the variable name or variable list. The specified format applies to all variables that precede it. For example, the command

```
NUMERIC ITEM1(F4.0) ITEM2 ITEM3(F5.2).
```

assigns print and write formats of F4.0 for ITEM1 and F5.2 for ITEM2 and ITEM3.

3.23
STRING COMMAND

A string variable must be declared before it can be used as a target variable in data transformations. If a string variable does not already exist on the active system file, use the STRING command to declare it. The STRING command is followed by the name of the new variable and its simple format in parentheses, as in:

```
STRING SSNUMBER (A11).
```

Multiple string variables can be declared on the same STRING command, and the keyword TO can be used to generate consecutive new variable names. Each format specification applies to the variable or variable list that precedes it. The command

```
STRING ALPHA1 TO ALPHA3(A8)
  BETA1 BETA2(A12).
```

assigns a format of A8 for the new string variables ALPHA1, ALPHA2, and ALPHA3, and a format of A12 for the new string variables BETA1 and BETA2.

The order of the new string variables on the active system file is determined by their order on the STRING command.

3.24
LEAVE COMMAND

Normally, SPSS reinitializes a numeric or string variable each time it reads a new case. Numeric variables are initialized to system-missing for each case, but sometimes it is useful to retain the value from the previous case for certain computations.

To leave a variable at its value for the previous case as each new case is read, specify the variable on a LEAVE command. Numeric variables named on a LEAVE command are initialized to 0 for the first case and string variables are initialized to blanks. For example, to keep a running total of salaries across all cases, specify

```
COMPUTE TSALARY=TSALARY+SALARY82.
LEAVE TSALARY.
FORMAT TSALARY (DOLLAR8)/ SALARY82 (DOLLAR7).
PRINT /SALARY82 TSALARY.
EXECUTE.
```

where SALARY82 is the variable containing the employee's 1982 salary and TSALARY is the new variable containing the cumulative salaries for all previous cases. The results of the PRINT command are shown in Figure 3.24.

Figure 3.24   Accumulating the sum across all variables

```
$10,733    $10,733
 $9,767    $20,500
$11,983    $32,483
$12,888    $45,371
$13,803    $59,174
$24,222    $83,396
$22,111   $105,507
$25,223   $130,730
$27,223   $157,953
$20,100   $178,053
$28,888   $206,941
$21,800   $228,741
$22,338   $251,079
$34,880   $285,959
$28,000   $313,959
$28,888   $342,847
```

You can name more than one variable on a LEAVE command, and you can use the TO keyword to refer to a list of consecutive variables. The variables named on the LEAVE command must already exist and cannot be scratch variables.

3.25
CONDITIONAL TRANSFORMATIONS

You can specify data transformations for selected subsets of cases with conditional transformation commands. The logical expressions used in conditional transformations can include variable names, constants, arithmetic operators, numeric and other functions, logical variables, and relational operators.

3.26
IF Command

The IF command makes COMPUTE-like transformations contingent upon logical conditions found in the data. The IF command is followed by a *logical expression* (see Sections 3.31 through 3.35) followed by an *assignment expression*, which has the same syntax as the COMPUTE command (see Section 3.9). For example, the command

```
IF (X EQ 0) Y=1.
```

assigns a value of 1 to variable Y only for cases with a value of 0 for variable X.

The logical expression is X EQ 0 and the assignment expression is Y=1. The target variable (Y) can be either an existing variable or a new variable. The parentheses enclosing the logical expression are optional.

The assignment expression follows all the rules and possibilities described for the COMPUTE command, but the assignment is executed only if the logical expression is true. The command

```
IF (DEPT82 EQ 2) BONUS=.14*SALARY82.
```

creates the new variable BONUS equal to 0.14 times SALARY82 only for cases with a value of 2 for variable DEPT82.

If a logical expression is false or indeterminate becasue of missing values, the target variable remains unchanged from its original value. If the target variable is a new variable being created by the IF command, it is set to the system-missing value.

3.27
DO IF and END IF Commands

You can perform multiple conditional transformations on the same subset of cases using the DO IF—END IF structure. The DO IF—END IF structure must begin with the DO IF command and end with the END IF command. The DO IF command must be followed by a logical expression. For example, the structure

```
DO IF (X EQ 1).
RECODE Y (1=2) (2=1).
RECODE Z (3=4) (4=3).
END IF.
```

recodes variables Y and Z for cases with a value of 1 for variable X.

The structure can be further defined with the ELSE and ELSE IF commands (see Sections 3.28 and 3.29). You can also nest DO IF—END IF structures as long as each DO IF command has a corresponding END IF command. Conditional data definition can be performed within the DO IF—END IF structure using commands such as DATA LIST, END CASE, END FILE, and REREAD (see Chapter 2).

For a complete discussion of the DO IF—END IF structure, see the *SPSS Reference Guide.*

3.28
ELSE Command

Use the ELSE command to perform transformations when the logical expression on the DO IF command is *not* true, as in:

```
DO IF (X EQ 0).
COMPUTE Y=1.
ELSE.
COMPUTE Y=2.
END IF.
```

In this structure, Y is set to 1 for all cases with a value of 0 for X, and Y is set to 2 for cases with any other valid (nonmissing) value for X. For cases with user-missing or system-missing values for X, Y is set to the system-missing value (see Section 3.30).

You can only use the ELSE command once within the DO IF—END IF structure.

3.29
ELSE IF Command

You can further define subsets within the DO IF—END IF structure by using the ELSE IF command. The ELSE IF command must be followed by a logical expression, as in:

```
DO IF (X EQ 0).
COMPUTE Y=1.
ELSE IF (X LE 9).
COMPUTE (Y=2).
ELSE.
COMPUTE Y=3.
END IF.
```

If X is 0, Y is set to 1; if X is less than or equal to 9, Y is set to 2; and if X is any other valid (nonmissing) value, Y is set to 3. (See Section 3.30 for treatment of missing values.)

You can use multiple ELSE IF commands within a DO IF—END IF structure. If you also include an ELSE command, all ELSE IF commands must precede it.

3.30
Missing Values with DO IF

If SPSS encounters a case with a missing value for the logical expression on the DO IF command, the case is assigned the system-missing value and control passes to the first command after END IF. If a case has a missing value for the logical expression on any subsequent ELSE IF commands, the case is assigned the system-missing value and control also passes to the first command after END IF. In the structure

```
DO IF (X EQ 1).
COMPUTE Y=1.
ELSE IF (Z EQ 1).
COMPUTE Y=2.
ELSE.
COMPUTE Y=3.
END IF.
```

a case with a missing value (user- or system-missing) for variable X will receive the system-missing value for variable Y, regardless of the value of variable Z. A case with a valid value for X other than 1 and a missing value for Z will also receive the system-missing value for Y.

3.31
Logical Expressions

The IF, DO IF, and ELSE IF commands evaluate logical expressions as true, false, or indeterminate. Thus, logical expressions can be any expressions that yield this three-valued logic. The logical expression

```
DO IF (X GE 5).
```

is true if X is 5 or greater, false if X is less than 5, and indeterminate if X is missing.

Logical expressions can be simple logical variables or relations, or they can be complex logical tests involving variables, constants, functions, relational operators, and logical operators.

In addition to the IF, DO IF, and ELSE IF commands, logical expressions can also be used on the LOOP, END LOOP, and SELECT IF commands. For a complete discussion of logical expressions, see the *SPSS Reference Guide*.

3.32
Logical Variables

The simplest logical expression is a logical variable. A logical variable is any variable that has values of 1, 0, or system-missing. For example, the expression

```
DO IF PROMO81.
```

is true if PROMO81 is 1, false if it is 0, and missing if PROMO81 is missing. Any other values will produce a warning message, and SPSS evaluates the expression for that case as 0 and false.

3.33
Relational Operators

A relation is a logical expression that compares two values using a *relational operator*. In the command

```
IF (X EQ 0) Y=1.
```

variable X and 0 are expressions that yield the values to be compared by the EQ relational operator. Relational operators are:

EQ   *Equal to.* Returns true if the expression on the left is exactly equal to the expression on the right.

NE   *Not equal to.* Returns true if the expression on the left does not equal the expression on the right.

LT   *Less than.* Returns true if the expression on the left is less than the expression on the right.

LE   *Less than or equal to.* Returns true if the expression on the left is less than or equal to the expression on the right.

GT   *Greater than.* Returns true if the expression on the left is greater than the expression on the right.

GE   *Greater than or equal to.* Returns true if the expression on the left is greater than or equal to the expression on the right.

You can specify either the relational operators above or their symbolic equivalents: $=$ (EQ), $-=$ or $<>$ (NE), $<$ (LT), $>$ (GT), $<=$ (LE), and $>=$ (GE).

The expressions in a relation can be variables, constants, or more complicated arithmetic expressions, as in:

```
IF (W+Y GT X+Z) NEWX=1.
```

which assigns the value 1 to NEWX if the sum of W and Y is greater than the sum of X and Z. Or you can use one or more of the functions described for the COMPUTE command, as in:

```
IF (MEAN(Q1 TO Q5) LE 5) INDEX=1.
```

which assigns the value 1 to INDEX if the mean of variables Q1 through Q5 is less than or equal to 5.

You must use blanks (not commas) to separate the relational operator from the expressions, but you are free to introduce more blanks and parentheses in order to make the command more readable.

3.34
AND and OR Logical Operators

You can join two or more relations logically using the *logical operators* AND and OR, as in:

```
IF (X EQ 0 AND Z LT 2) Y=2.
```

This command assigns value 2 to variable Y only for cases with X equal to 0 and Z less than 2. The AND logical operator means that both relations must be true. Logical operators combine relations according to the following rules:

AND   *Both relations must be true.*

OR   *Either relation can be true.*

3.35
NOT Logical Operator

The NOT logical operator reverses the true/false outcome of the expression that immediately follows. For example,

```
IF NOT(X EQ 0) Y=3.
```

assigns value 3 to Y for all cases with values other than 0 for variable X.

The NOT operator affects only the expression that immediately follows, unless more than one expression is enclosed in parentheses. The expression

```
DO IF (NOT X EQ 0 AND Z LT 2).
```

is true for cases where X *is not* 0 and Z *is* less than 2. The expression

```
DO IF  NOT(X EQ 0 OR Z EQ 2).
```

is equivalent to

```
DO IF (X NE 0 AND Z NE 2).
```

because the only way the first logical expression can be true is for the parenthetical expression to be false.

The ¬ symbol is a valid substitute for the NOT keyword.

3.36 TRANSFORMATION UTILITIES

SPSS provides various utilties to assist in manipulating data. The basic transformation language should be able to solve most problems you encounter—but you may find that these utility commands make your work substantially easier.

3.37 Scratch Variables

Use scratch variables to create variables that you want to use in data transformations but do not want to analyze or save on the SPSS system file. Scratch variables are initialized to zero for numeric variables and blank for string variables.

To create a scratch variable, use the # as the first character of the numeric or string variable name, as in:

```
COMPUTE #TEMPVAR=VAR1+VAR2.
```

Scratch variables cannot be used in statistical procedures, but they can be useful in transformation utilities, such as the LOOP command (see Section 3.41).

3.38 DO REPEAT Command

If you are doing the same basic transformation on a large set of variables, you can reduce the number of commands by using DO REPEAT—END REPEAT. This utility does not reduce the number of commands SPSS executes, just the number of commands you enter.

The DO REPEAT command should be followed by a user-specified *stand-in variable*, followed by an equals sign and a *replacement list* of variables. The stand-in variable is used in one or more transformation commands within the DO REPEAT—END REPEAT structure. The replacement list is the list of variables that the stand-in variable represents in any transformations specified in the structure. You can also specify values in the replacement list (see Section 3.39).

For example, to initialize a set of five variables to 0 without entering five COMPUTE commands, specify:

```
DO REPEAT R=REGION1 TO REGION5.
COMPUTE R=0.
END REPEAT.
```

The commands between DO REPEAT and END REPEAT are repeated once for each variable in the replacement list. Thus, five COMPUTE commands are generated, one for each REGION variable.

Stand-in variables (R in this example) do not exist outside of the DO REPEAT—END REPEAT utility. You can use any valid variable name you wish—permanent, temporary, scratch, system, and so forth. The stand-in variable has no effect on any variable with the same name. However, you cannot have two stand-in variables with the same name in the same DO REPEAT structure.

In the replacement list you can use the TO keyword to list consecutive existing variables or to create a new set of variables. You can specify multiple stand-in variables on the same DO REPEAT command. Each stand-in variable specification should be separated by a slash, and they must all name or imply the same number of variables, as in:

```
DO REPEAT XTEMP=X1 TO X5.
 /YTEMP=Y1 TO Y5 /ZTEMP=Z1 TO Z5.
COMPUTE ZTEMP=XTEMP+YTEMP.
END REPEAT.
```

You can use the following commands within the DO REPEAT—END REPEAT structure:

• Data transformations COMPUTE, RECODE, IF, COUNT, and SELECT IF.
• Data declarations VECTOR, STRING, NUMERIC, and LEAVE.
• Data definitions DATA LIST and MISSING VALUES (but not VARIABLE LABELS or VALUE LABELS).
• LOOP structure commands LOOP, END LOOP, and BREAK.
• DO IF structure commands DO IF, ELSE IF, ELSE, and END IF.
• Print and write commands PRINT, PRINT EJECT, PRINT SPACE, and WRITE.
• Format commands PRINT FORMATS, WRITE FORMATS, and FORMATS.

3.39
Replacement Value Lists

You can also specify replacement value lists on the DO REPEAT command. A replacement value list can be a list of string or numeric values, or it can be of the form n_1 TO n_2, where n_1 is less than n_2 and both are integers. (Note that the keyword is TO, not THRU.) All stand-in variable lists and replacement value lists must name or imply the same number of items. The commands

```
DO REPEAT R=REGION1 TO REGION5
 /X=1 TO 5.
COMPUTE R=0.
IF (REGION EQ X) R=1.
END REPEAT.
```

create dummy variables REGION1 to REGION5 that equal 0 or 1 for each of five regions, perhaps for use in procedure REGRESSION or REPORT (see Chapters 19 and 27).

3.40
PRINT Subcommand

To see the commands that SPSS generates from the DO REPEAT command, use the PRINT subcommand on the END REPEAT command. Figure 3.40 uses the PRINT subcommand to display the commands generated by the example in Section 3.39. The plus sign marks the generated commands.

Figure 3.40   Display from the PRINT keyword

```
DO REPEAT R=REGION1 TO REGION5
 /X=1 TO 5.
COMPUTE R=0.
IF (REGION EQ X) R=1.
END REPEAT PRINT.
```

```
DO REPEAT R=REGION1 TO REGION5/ X=1 TO 5.
 COMPUTE R=0.
 IF (REGION EQ X) R=1.
 END REPEAT PRINT.

+COMPUTE REGION1=0
+IF (REGION EQ 1) REGION1=1
+COMPUTE REGION2=0
+IF (REGION EQ 2) REGION2=1
+COMPUTE REGION3=0
+IF(REGION EQ 3) REGION3=1
+COMPUTE REGION4=0
+IF(REGION EQ 4) REGION4=1
+COMPUTE REGION5=0
+IF(REGION EQ 5) REGION5=1
```

3.41
Other Transformation Utilities

The following commands may be useful if you require more complex data manipulations:

LOOP—END LOOP   The LOOP—END LOOP structure allows you to repeatedly process a set of commands, until a pre-set limit is reached or a specified condition is true.

VECTOR   The VECTOR command enables you to assign indexed (or subscripted) variable names, as in

```
VECTOR AGES=AGEKID1 TO AGEKID6.
```

in which AGES(1) corresponds to AGEKID1, AGES(2) corresponds to AGEKID2, etc.

MCONVERT   The MCONVERT command converts a covariance matrix to a correlation matrix plus a vector of standard deviations, or a correlation matrix and a vector of standard deviations to a covariance matrix.

For a complete discussion of these commands, including subcommands, keywords, and syntax, see the *SPSS Reference Guide*.

3.42
DATA SELECTION

You can select subgroups of cases for analysis, take a random sample from the data file, and restrict your analysis to a specified number of cases using SPSS data selection commands. You can also split your data file into subgroups and perform separate, simultaneous analyses on each of the subgroups.

3.43
SELECT IF Command

The SELECT IF command selects cases based on logical criteria. The SELECT IF command is followed by a logical expression that can be evaluated as true, false, or missing. For example, the command

```
SELECT IF (SEX EQ 'M').
```

selects cases for which variable SEX has the value M. The syntax of the logical expression for the SELECT IF command is the same as for the IF and DO IF commands (see Sections 3.26 through 3.35). The parentheses around the logical expression are optional. The specification can be as simple as a logical variable (see Section 3.32), as in:

```
SELECT IF (INVAR).
```

This command selects cases for which INVAR is equal to 1.

The expression can also be a complex combination of relational and logical operators, numeric functions, and arithmetic operations, as in:

```
SELECT IF (SEX EQ 'M')
          AND ((MEAN(INC87, INC88, INC89)/FAMSIZE) GT 10000).
```

This command selects males with an average income during a three-year period of over $10,000 per family member. If the logical expression is true the case is selected; if it is false or missing, the case is not selected.

3.44
Missing Values

If the logic of the expression is indeterminate because of missing values, the case is not selected. In a simple relational expression, the logic is indeterminate if the expression on either side of the relational operator is missing. For example,

```
SELECT IF (VSAT GT MSAT).
```

selects only cases for which both VSAT and MSAT are valid and VSAT is greater than MSAT. If either VSAT or MSAT is missing, the logic of the expression is indeterminate and the case is not selected.

If you use a compound expression in which relations are joined by the logical operator OR, as in

```
SELECT IF (VSAT GT 600 OR MSAT GT 600).
```

the case is selected if either relation is true, even if the other is missing.

To select cases with missing values for the variables within the expression, use the missing-value function. For example,

```
SELECT IF MISSING(X).
```

selects all cases missing for variable X. The MISSING function returns 1, which is true, if X is missing. To include cases with values that have been declared user-missing along with other cases, use the VALUE function, as in:

```
SELECT IF VALUE(X) GT 100.
```

This expression is true if X is greater than 100, even if 999 was defined as missing on the MISSING VALUES command (see Chapter 2). The VALUE function does not include the system-missing value, so the above SELECT IF does not select cases for which X is system-missing.

For more information on the MISSING and VALUE functions, see the *SPSS Reference Guide*.

3.45
Multiple SELECT IF Commands

Once specified, a SELECT IF command remains in effect for the remainder of the SPSS session. If you use multiple SELECT IF commands in your session, they must all be true for a case to be selected. For example, the commands

```
SELECT IF (SEX EQ 'M').
SELECT IF (AGE GE 18) AND (AGE LE 65).
```

select all males between the ages of 18 and 65.

If you want to select one subset of cases for one analysis and a different subset of cases for another analysis, you can precede the SELECT IF command with the TEMPORARY command (see Section 3.51).

3.46
SAMPLE Command

The SAMPLE command selects a random sample of cases. To select an approximate percentage of cases, specify a decimal value between 0 and 1, as in:

```
SAMPLE .25.
```

This command samples approximately 25% of the cases in the active system file. When you specify a proportional sample, you usually won't obtain the exact proportion specified. If you know exactly how many cases are in the active file, you can obtain an exact-sized random sample by specifying the number of cases to be sampled from the size of the active file, as in:

```
SAMPLE 60 FROM 200.
```

In this example, the active system file must have exactly 200 cases to obtain a random sample of 60 cases. If the file has fewer than 200 cases, proportionally fewer cases are sampled. If the file has more, the sample is drawn from only the first 200 cases. Note that any SELECT IF commands occurring prior to the SAMPLE command will affect the size of the active system file.

The SAMPLE command uses the internal pseudo-random number generator that depends on a seed value established by SPSS. The first time a random number series is needed, SPSS uses the seed value established by the SEED subcommand of the SET command (see Chapter 5). Since this number defaults to a fixed integer, a SAMPLE command generates the identical sample if the same commands are run in a subsequent session. To generate a different sample each time, use the SET command to reset SEED to a different value for each run.

3.47
Multiple SAMPLE Commands

Once specified, a SAMPLE command remains in effect for the remainder of the SPSS session, unless a TEMPORARY command precedes it (see Section 3.51). Thus, if you use two SAMPLE commands, the second takes a sample of the first, as in:

```
SAMPLE .50.
DESCRIPTIVES   SALARY79 TO SALARY82.
SAMPLE .50.
DESCRIPTIVES   SALARY79 TO SALARY82.
```

In this example, the first DESCRIPTIVES command computes statistics for approximately 50% of the cases, and the second DESCRIPTIVES command computes statistics for approximately 50% of those cases, or 25% of the original cases.

Within a session, you can obtain different random samples of approximately the same size by preceding each SAMPLE command with a TEMPORARY command. The seed value changes each time a random number series is needed within a session.

3.48
N OF CASES Command

You can use the N OF CASES command to select the first *n* cases from a file. For example, if you have a data file containing 1,000 cases but want to use only the first 100 cases to test your SPSS commands, specify:

```
N OF CASES  100.
```

If you specify N OF CASES before the first PROCEDURE command, before BEGIN DATA, or in conjunction with any transformation commands, it remains in effect for the remainder of the session. Subsequent N OF CASES commands should specify a smaller number, or they will be ignored.

If you specify N OF CASES between two procedures (with no intervening transformation commands), it acts like a temporary SELECT IF, as in:

```
DESCRIPTIVES VARIABLES=SALARY79.
N OF CASES 50.
DESCRIPTIVES VARIABLES=SALARY82.
```

3.49
SPLIT FILE Command

You can use the SPLIT FILE command to split the active system file into subgroups that can be analyzed separately by SPSS.

For example, in analyzing attitudes toward abortion, you may want to perform separate analyses for men and women because you suspect the dimensions are very different for each group. Use the SPLIT FILE command to split the active system file into subgroups of men and women.

Since the active system file should be sorted into the appropriate groups before you specify the SPLIT FILE command, you should precede the SPLIT FILE command with the SORT CASES command (see Chapter 4). For both commands, follow the command with the keyword BY and the name of the grouping variable, as in:

```
SORT CASES BY SEX.
SPLIT FILE BY SEX.
```

This command splits the file according to the values for each case for the variable SEX. SPLIT FILE creates a new subgroup each time it reads a case with a different value for SEX than on the previous case. Thus, if SEX is coded 1 for males and 2 for females, SPLIT FILE creates two subgroups for your analyses, assuming that your cases are sorted by SEX.

You can specify or imply up to eight variables on a SPLIT FILE command. You can use both temporary transformations and long string variables. Scratch variables and system variables cannot be used with SPLIT FILE.

For a complete discussion of SPLIT FILE, see the *SPSS Reference Guide*.

3.50
TEMPORARY DATA TRANSFORMATION AND SELECTION

Once specified, most data transformation and selection commands affect all subsequent procedure commands in the SPSS session. You can use the TEMPORARY command to confine the effect of data transformation, data selection, and data definition commands to one procedure, leaving all subsequent procedures unaffected.

Additionally, you can use the CLEAR TRANSFORMATIONS command to discard unwanted transformations in an interactive session.

3.51
TEMPORARY Command

Use the TEMPORARY command before commands that you want to be in effect only for the next procedure. There are no additional specifications on TEMPORARY. For example, the commands

```
TEMPORARY.
RECODE AGE (18 THRU HI=2) (LO THRU 18=1).
FREQUENCIES VARIABLES=AGE.
DESCRIPTIVES VARIABLES=AGE.
```

temporarily recode AGE into two categories for the FREQUENCIES procedure. The subsequent DESCRIPTIVES procedure is not affected by the temporary RECODE and produces descriptive statistics based on the original AGE values.

The following commands can be specified on a temporary basis following the TEMPORARY command:

- Data transformation commands RECODE, COMPUTE, COUNT, WEIGHT, IF, NUMERIC, and STRING.
- Utility commands DO REPEAT, DO IF, LOOP, and VECTOR.
- Data selection commands SELECT IF, SAMPLE, N OF CASES, and SPLIT FILE.
- Data definition commands VARIABLE LABELS, VALUE LABELS, MISSING VALUES, PRINT FORMATS, WRITE FORMATS, and FORMATS.
- Print and write commands PRINT, PRINT EJECT, PRINT SPACE, and WRITE.

Any combination of the above commands can appear between the TEMPORARY command and a procedure command.

Once you specify a TEMPORARY command you cannot refer to previously existing scratch variables, and you cannot use the TEMPORARY command inside a DO IF or LOOP structure.

3.52
CLEAR
TRANSFORMATIONS
Command

In interactive mode, you can use the CLEAR TRANSFORMATIONS command to discard all data transformation and selection commands that have accumulated since the last procedure. Since each command in an interactive session is executed as soon as you finish entering it, CLEAR TRANSFORMATIONS can be helpful if you have made mistakes in selecting or transforming data for analysis.

The command is simply:

```
CLEAR TRANSFORMATIONS.
```

This command only discards commands that have been specified since the last procedure command. Any data transformation or case selection commands prior to the last procedure command will remain in effect.

The CLEAR TRANSFORMATIONS command is intended for use in interactive mode. It has no effect in batch processing, and a warning message will appear if you specify CLEAR TRANSFORMATIONS in a batch SPSS job.

Contents

4 SPSS System Files and File Management

4.1
SPSS SYSTEM FILES

Once you have defined your data file in SPSS, you do not need to repeat the data definition process. You can save the data definition information along with the data in an SPSS *system file*. An SPSS system file is a self-documented file containing data and descriptive information. The descriptive information is called the *dictionary*. It contains variable names and locations, variable and value labels, print and write formats, and missing-value indicators.

You can access an SPSS system file in subsequent SPSS sessions or later in the same session without respecifying any of the data definition commands, such as DATA LIST, VARIABLE LABELS, VALUE LABELS, and MISSING VALUES. You can update the system file, altering the descriptive information or modifying the data, and you can save the updated version in a new system file. You can also combine data from two or more files into a single SPSS system file.

4.2
GET Command

The GET command reads a previously created SPSS system file. The only specification required is the FILE subcommand, which identifies the name of the system file you want to use. Additional subcommands RENAME, DROP, and KEEP allow you to tailor the file, and the MAP subcommand displays the results of these subcommands.

When you access an SPSS system file with the GET command, SPSS creates an *active system file*. This file will contain any modifications to the data produced by transformation and procedure commands issued during that session. The active system file exists only for the duration of the SPSS session, unless you save it with the SAVE or XSAVE command (see Section 4.9).

4.3
FILE Subcommand

The FILE subcommand is required and must be the first specification on the GET command. The FILE subcommand is followed by the name of the SPSS system file. For example, the Western Electric data on coronary heart disease (see Chapter 2) are saved in an SPSS system file named ELECTRIC. The command

```
GET FILE=ELECTRIC.
```

retrieves all the variables and descriptive information from the SPSS system file containing the data for the Western Electric study.

4.4
RENAME Subcommand

You can use the RENAME subcommand to change the names of variables in the active system file. The RENAME subcommand is followed by a variable name or variable list followed by an equals sign and a new variable name or variable list enclosed in parentheses, as in:

```
GET FILE=ELECTRIC
 /RENAME (AGE=AGE58) (FAMHXCVR=HISTORY).
```

This could also be specified as:

```
GET FILE=ELECTRIC
 /RENAME (AGE FAMHXCVR=AGE58 HISTORY).
```

The variable lists on both sides of the equals sign must name or imply the same number of variables. You can use the TO keyword to imply consecutive variables on the active system file and to create consecutive new variable names.

4.5
DROP Subcommand

If the SPSS system file contains variables you don't need, you can use the DROP subcommand to omit them from the active system file. For example, the command

```
GET FILE=ELECTRIC
 /DROP=EDUYR DAYOFWK.
```

does not include the two variables EDUYR and DAYOFWK in the active system file.

You can name variables on the DROP subcommand in any order, and you can use the TO keyword to imply consecutive variables on the SPSS system file.

4.6
KEEP Subcommand

If the SPSS system file contains many variables and you only want to use a few, you can use the KEEP subcommand to select a subset of variables, as in:

```
GET FILE=ELECTRIC
 /KEEP=FIRSTCHD DBP58 CHOL58 VITAL10.
```

You can also use the KEEP subcommand to change the order of variables on the active system file. This can be useful if you want to refer to a variable list in subsequent procedures using the TO keyword. List the variables you want grouped together followed by the keyword ALL, as in:

```
GET FILE=ELECTRIC
 /KEEP=FIRSTCHD DBP58 CHOL58 VITAL10 ALL.
```

This command places the variables FIRSTCHD, DBP58, CHOL58, and VITAL10 together at the beginning of the active system file, followed by the remaining variables in the system file in their original sequence.

4.7
MAP Subcommand

You can use the MAP subcommand to keep track of changes you have made in the active system file with the RENAME, DROP, and KEEP subcommands. Figure 4.7 shows the MAP output display after a RENAME subcommand.

Figure 4.7 Output display of MAP after RENAME

```
GET FILE=ELECTRIC
 /RENAME (AGE FAMHXCVR=AGE58 HISTORY)
 /MAP.
```

Result	Input1	Result	Input1
CASEID	CASEID	HT58	HT58
FIRSTCHD	FIRSTCHD	WT58	WT58
AGE58	AGE	DAYOFWK	DAYOFWK
DBP58	DBP58	VITAL10	VITAL10
EDUYR	EDUYR	HISTORY	FAMHXCVR
CHOL58	CHOL58	CHD	CHD
CGT58	CGT58		

4.8
Multiple Subcommands

You can only use one FILE subcommand on the GET command, and it must be the first subcommand specified. You can use multiple RENAME, DROP, KEEP, and MAP subcommands. Each subcommand refers to the results of the previous subcommand. If you rename variables on one subcommand, they must be referred to by their new names on any subsequent subcommands. If you drop variables on one subcommand, they cannot be specified on subsequent subcommands.

4.9
SAVE and XSAVE Commands

The SAVE and XSAVE commands save the active system file as a permanent SPSS system file. The SAVE command is a procedure and reads the data. The XSAVE command is a transformation command and must be followed by a command that reads the data for the system file to actually be created and saved.

The placement of SAVE or XSAVE relative to other commands determines what is saved on the SPSS system file. Variables created or altered by transformations and procedures prior to the SAVE or XSAVE command are saved in their modified form. Results of temporary transformations are also saved if there are no intervening procedure commands.

The only required specification on the SAVE and XSAVE commands is the OUTFILE subcommand identifying the name of the new SPSS system file. Additional subcommands are RENAME, DROP, KEEP, and MAP. The syntax and operation of these subcommands is the same as for the GET command (see Sections 4.4 through 4.7).

4.10
OUTFILE Subcommand

The OUTFILE subcommand must be the first specification following the SAVE or XSAVE command. The OUTFILE subcommand is followed by the name of the new SPSS system file, as in:

```
SAVE OUTFILE=ELECTRIC.
```

If you use the XSAVE command, it must be followed by a procedure for the new SPSS system file to actually be created and saved. If you don't want to use a statistical procedure, you can follow the XSAVE command with the EXECUTE command (see Chapter 5).

4.11
Saving Multiple System Files

You can use the XSAVE command to selectively send cases to different system files, as in:

```
GET FILE=ELECTRIC.
DO IF (FAMHXCVR EQ 'N').
FILE LABEL 'WESTERN ELECTRIC CHD STUDY: NO CHD FAMILY HISTORY'.
XSAVE OUTFILE=NEWELEC1.
ELSE IF (FAMHXCVR EQ 'Y').
FILE LABEL 'WESTERN ELECTRIC CHD STUDY: FAMILY HISTORY OF CHD'.
XSAVE OUTFILE=NEWELEC2.
END IF.
EXECUTE.
```

These commands create two new SPSS system files. NEWELEC1 contains only cases with no family history of coronary heart disease, and NEWELEC2 contains only cases with a family history of coronary heart disease.

4.12
SAVE and XSAVE Compared

Since SAVE is a procedure, the data are read every time a SAVE command is encountered. Since XSAVE is a transformation, the data are not read until a procedure command is encountered. For large files, reading the data can be time-consuming and costly. In the example above, two XSAVE commands and a single EXECUTE command (or any statistical procedure) read the data only once. Whenever SAVE does not need to be the last command in the SPSS session, you can probably save time by using XSAVE instead.

4.13
FILE LABEL Command

Use the FILE LABEL command to provide a descriptive label for your data file. The FILE LABEL is printed on the first line of each page of output and is included in the SPSS system file dictionary. For example, the commands

```
FILE LABEL 'WESTERN ELECTRIC CORONARY HEART DISEASE DATA'.
SAVE OUTFILE=ELECTRIC.
```

save the SPSS system file ELECTRIC with a file label describing the contents of the file.

A file label can be up to 60 characters long. If it is longer, it will be truncated to 60 characters.

4.14
DOCUMENT Command

Use the DOCUMENT command to save a block of text of any length on your SPSS system file, as in:

```
FILE LABEL 'WESTERN ELECTRIC CORONARY HEART DISEASE DATA'.
DOCUMENT THIS FILE CONTAINS DATA ON THE INCIDENCE OF CORONARY
 HEART DISEASE AMONG WESTERN ELECTRIC EMPLOYEES, INCLUDING
 A TEN-YEAR FOLLOW-UP.
SAVE OUTFILE=ELECTRIC.
```

The block of text specified on the DOCUMENT command is saved on the SPSS system file and is available via the DISPLAY command whenever you need a detailed description of the system file.

4.15
DROP DOCUMENTS Command

When you retrieve an SPSS system file with the GET command, SPSS assumes you want the system file's document text. You can use the DROP DOCUMENTS command to retrieve a system file without document text, as in:

```
GET FILE=ELECTRIC.
DROP DOCUMENTS.
SAVE OUTFILE=NODOCS.
```

In this example, the new system file NODOCS contains all the information from the system file ELECTRIC, except for any document text, which has been dropped.

4.16
DISPLAY Command

The dictionary of an SPSS system file is available at any time via the DISPLAY command for exploring an unfamiliar or forgotten system file or for producing a printed archive document. The DISPLAY command can be used during any SPSS session to display the data definitions in the active system file.

By default, DISPLAY prints an unsorted list of the variables on the active system file. For example, the commands

```
GET FILE=ELECTRIC.
DISPLAY.
```

produce the output shown in Figure 4.16.

Figure 4.16 Display of variable names

```
Currently Defined Variables

CASEID    AGE       EDUYR     CGT58     WT58      VITAL10   FAMHXCVR  CHD
FIRSTCHD  DBP58     CHOL58    HT58      DAYOFWK
```

The following keywords can be specified on the DISPLAY command:

NAMES *Display variable names.* A list of the variables on the active file is displayed. The names are displayed in a compressed format, about eight names across the page, in the order in which they appear on the active system file. This is the default.

DOCUMENTS *Display the text provided by the DOCUMENT command.* No error message is issued if there is no documentary information on the system file.

DICTIONARY *Display complete dictionary information for variables.* Information includes the variable names, labels, sequential position of each variable in the file, print and write formats, missing values, and value labels. Up to 60 characters can be displayed for variable and value labels.

INDEX *Display the variable names and positions.*

VARIABLES *Display the variable names, positions, print and write formats, and missing values.*

LABELS *Display the variable names, positions, and variable labels.*

MACROS *Display a list of the currently defined macros.*

Only one of the above keywords can be specified per DISPLAY command, but you can use as many DISPLAY commands as necessary to obtain the desired information.

In addition, you can use keyword SORTED to display information alphabetically by variable name. SORTED can precede keywords NAMES, DICTIONARY, INDEX, VARIABLES, or LABELS, as in:

```
GET FILE=ELECTRIC.
DISPLAY DOCUMENTS.
DISPLAY SORTED DICTIONARY.
```

The first DISPLAY command displays the document information, and the second displays complete dictionary information for variables sorted alphabetically by variable name.

4.17
VARIABLES Subcommand

To limit DISPLAY information to certain variables, follow any specification other than DOCUMENTS or MACROS with a slash, the VARIABLES subcommand, an optional equals sign, and a list of variables, as in:

```
GET FILE=ELECTRIC.
DISPLAY SORTED DICTIONARY
  /VARIABLES=FIRSTCHD FAMHXCVR VITAL10 DAYOFWK.
```

This specification produces dictionary information only for the variables specified. You can use the TO keyword to imply consecutive variables on the system file.

4.18
FILE TRANSFORMATION COMMANDS

With SPSS, you can transform your active system file in several ways. You can

• Reorder cases in a file with the SORT CASES command.

• Group cases together and create a new file containing one case for each group with the AGGREGATE command.

- Transpose file rows and columns to correctly read spreadsheet-like data with the FLIP command.
- Automatically recode numeric and string variables to consecutive integer variables with the AUTORECODE command.

4.19
SORT CASES Command

Use the SORT CASES command to reorder the sequence of cases on the active system file. The ability to sort cases based on the value of a specified variable is useful in conjunction with commands such as MATCH FILES and ADD FILES (see Sections 4.32 through 4.41), SPLIT FILE (see Chapter 3), and REPORT (see Chapter 27).

The SORT CASES command is followed by the optional keyword BY and the name of the variable to be used to determine the sort order, as in:

```
SORT CASES BY AGE.
```

By default, cases are sorted in ascending order based on the value of the sort variable. In this example, cases with the lowest value for variable AGE will be sorted to the front of the file.

You can specify the default sort order by specifying (A) or (UP) after the variable name, or you can override the default by specifying (D) or (DOWN) for descending order, as in:

```
SORT CASES BY AGE(D).
```

You can also specify multiple sort variables, as in:

```
SORT CASES BY AGE WEIGHT.
```

In this example, cases are sorted by AGE and by WEIGHT within categories of AGE, both in ascending order.

If you specify ascending or descending order with multiple variables, the specification applies to all preceding variables. For example, the command

```
SORT BY AGE WEIGHT(D).
```

sorts cases by AGE and by WEIGHT within categories of AGE, both in descending order. If you want to mix sort orders, you should explicitly specify the sort order after each variable, as in:

```
SORT CASES BY AGE(A) WEIGHT(D).
```

This command sorts cases in ascending order by AGE and in descending order by WEIGHT within categories of AGE.

4.20
AGGREGATE Command

Use the AGGREGATE command to group cases together based on the value of a grouping variable and create a new SPSS system file containing one case for each group. The minimum specifications on the AGGREGATE command are the OUTFILE subcommand, which identifies the name of the new SPSS system file to which the aggregated data are written, the BREAK subcommand, which specifies the grouping variable(s), and the definition of at least one new variable based on an aggregate function.

Sections 4.21 through 4.23 give an overview of the AGGREGATE command. For a complete discussion of AGGREGATE, see the *SPSS Reference Guide*.

4.21
OUTFILE Subcommand

The OUTFILE subcommand must be the first specification after the AGGRE-GATE command. OUTFILE is followed by either a filename or an asterisk. To create and save a new system file, specify a filename after OUTFILE, as in:

```
GET FILE=ELECTRIC.
RECODE FIRSTCHD (1=0) (2 thru 6=1).
AGGREGATE OUTFILE=AGGELEC
 /BREAK=AGE
 /AVWGT=MEAN(WT58) /AVCHOL=MEAN(CHOL58) /AVDBP=MEAN(DBP58)
 /TOTALCHD=SUM(FIRSTCHD).
```

To replace the active system file with the aggregated file, specify an asterisk after OUTFILE, as in:

```
GET FILE=ELECTRIC.
RECODE FIRSTCHD (1=0) (2 thru 6=1).
AGGREGATE OUTFILE=*
 /BREAK=AGE
 /AVWGT=MEAN(WT58) /AVCHOL=MEAN(CHOL58) /AVDBP=MEAN(DBP58)
 /TOTALCHD=SUM(FIRSTCHD).
```

4.22
BREAK Subcommand

The BREAK subcommand follows the OUTFILE subcommand and specifies the grouping variable(s), as in:

```
GET FILE=ELECTRIC.
RECODE FIRSTCHD (1=0) (2 thru 6=1).
AGGREGATE OUTFILE=AGGELEC
 /BREAK=AGE
 /AVWGT=MEAN(WT58) /AVCHOL=MEAN(CHOL58) /AVDBP=MEAN(DBP58)
 /TOTALCHD=SUM(FIRSTCHD).
```

In this example, AGE is the grouping variable, and all cases with the same value for AGE will be grouped together in one case. You can specify multiple BREAK variables. Each unique combination of values defines a group and generates one case in the aggregated file. Optionally you can specify (A) or (UP) for ascending order or (D) or (DOWN) for descending order after each BREAK variable. The default is ascending order.

All BREAK variables are saved on the aggregated system file with their existing names and dictionary information.

4.23
Creating AGGREGATE Variables

New variables on the aggregate file are created by applying aggregate functions to existing variables on the active system file. The specification of each new variable is separated by a slash, as in:

```
GET FILE=ELECTRIC.
RECODE FIRSTCHD (1=0) (2 thru 6=1).
AGGREGATE OUTFILE=AGGELEC
 /BREAK=AGE
 /AVWGT=MEAN(WT58) /AVCHOL=MEAN(CHOL58) /AVDBP=MEAN(DBP58)
 /TOTALCHD=SUM(FIRSTCHD).
```

In this example, four new variables are created and saved on the aggregated system file AGGLEC: AVWGT, the mean weight for each age group; AVCHOL, the mean cholesterol count; AVDBP, the mean diastolic blood pressure; and TOTALCHD, the total number of cases of coronary heart disease in each age group.

You must specify at least one new variable based on an aggregate function.

The following aggregate functions are available:

SUM(varlist)	*Sum across cases.* Dictionary formats are F8.2.
MEAN(varlist)	*Mean across cases.* Dictionary formats are F8.2.
SD(varlist)	*Standard deviation across cases.* Dictionary formats are F8.2.
MAX(varlist)	*Maximum value across cases.* Complete dictionary information is copied from the source variables to the target variables.
MIN(varlist)	*Minimum value across cases.* Complete dictionary information is copied from the source variables to the target variables.
PGT(varlist,value)	*Percentage of cases greater than value.* Dictionary formats are F5.1.
PLT(varlist,value)	*Percentage of cases less than value.* Dictionary formats are F5.1.
PIN(varlist,value1,value2)	*Percentage of cases between value1 and value2 inclusive.* Dictionary formats are F5.1.
POUT(varlist,value1,value2)	*Percentage of cases not between value1 and value2 exclusive.* Dictionary formats are F5.1.
FGT(varlist,value)	*Fraction of cases greater than value.* Dictionary formats are F5.3.
FLT(varlist,value)	*Fraction of cases less than value.* Dictionary formats are F5.3.
FIN(varlist,value1,value2)	*Fraction of cases between value1 and value2 inclusive.* Dictionary formats are F5.3.
FOUT(varlist,value1,value2)	*Fraction of cases not between value1 and value2 exclusive.* Dictionary formats are F5.3.
N(varlist)	*Weighted number of cases in break group.* Dictionary formats are F7.0 for unweighted files and F8.2 for weighted files.
NU(varlist)	*Unweighted number of cases in break group.* Dictionary formats are F7.0.
NMISS(varlist)	*Weighted number of missing cases.* Dictionary formats are F7.0 for unweighted files and F8.2 for weighted files.
NUMISS(varlist)	*Unweighted number of missing cases.* Dictionary formats are F7.0.
FIRST(varlist)	*First nonmissing observed value in break group.* Complete dictionary information is copied from the source variables to the target variables.
LAST(varlist)	*Last nonmissing observed value in break group.* Complete dictionary information is copied from the source variables to the target variables.

4.24
FLIP Command

SPSS assumes a file structure in which the variables are the columns and the cases are the rows. This is the file structure required to correctly read and analyze your data with SPSS. Sometimes, however, data are recorded in just the opposite fashion: the cases are the columns and each variable is a row. You might find this to be the case with spreadsheet data.

Use the FLIP command to get this kind of file into a structure that can be read correctly by SPSS. FLIP switches the columns and rows of your data. For example, if you have two products, each with quarterly sales, and the data are structured like this:

```
           Q1     Q2     Q3     Q4

PROD1      24     36     78     48
PROD2      39     82     31     49
```

The transposed file after FLIP looks like this:

```
        PROD1    PROD2

Q1       24       39
Q2       36       82
Q3       78       31
Q4       48       49
```

The only required specification on the FLIP command is the command keyword FLIP. By default, SPSS transposes all data in the active system file. The optional VARIABLES subcommand names a subset of variables to be transposed. The optional NEWNAMES subcommand specifies a single variable whose values are used to generate new variable names.

Sections 4.25 and 4.26 give a brief overview of these optional subcommands. For a complete discussion of FLIP, see the *SPSS Reference Guide*.

4.25
VARIABLES Subcommand

By default, FLIP transposes all the data in the file. Use the VARIABLES subcommand to name a specific subset of variables (columns) to be transposed. The specified variables become cases (rows) in the new active system file. If you use the VARIABLES subcommand, any variables not named or implied with the TO keyword are not included in the new active system file. For example, the command

```
FLIP VARIABLES=VAR1 TO VAR4.
```

only includes the variables VAR1 through VAR4 as cases on the transposed system file.

4.26
NEWNAMES Subcommand

By default, SPSS assigns new variable names VAR001 to VAR*n* to the transposed data. Use the NEWNAMES subcommand to specify a single variable on the untransposed file whose values will be used as the new variable names. You can only name one variable on the NEWNAMES subcommand, as in:

```
FLIP NEWNAMES=PRODNO.
```

If the variable specified on NEWNAMES is numeric, its values become character strings beginning with the prefix *V*.

4.27
AUTORECODE Command

When category codes are not sequential, the resulting empty cells reduce performance and increase memory requirements for many procedures. For example, if your data only have values of 1, 3, and 14 for a variable, specifying ANOVA with minimum and maximum values of 1 and 14 uses a lot more memory than specifying minimum and maximum values of 1 and 3. For some procedures, such as MANOVA (see the *SPSS Advanced Statistics User's Guide*), consecutive integer values for factor levels are required.

There are also some procedures that cannot use long string variables. For example, the TABLES procedure (see *SPSS Tables*) cannot tabulate long string variables, and you have to create new short string or numeric variables to take the place of long string variables.

Use the AUTORECODE command to recode values of both string and numeric variables to consecutive integers and assign the modified values to new variables. AUTORECODE is similar to RECODE, except that it *automatically* assigns new values. In addition, AUTORECODE automatically uses the original values as value labels.

4.28
VARIABLES and INTO Subcommands

The minimum specifications on the AUTORECODE command are the subcommands VARIABLES, which specifies the variables to be recoded, and INTO, which names the target variables for the new values, as in:

```
AUTORECODE VARIABLES=VAR1 VAR2 VAR4 TO VAR6
 /INTO NEWVAR1 NEWVAR2 NEWVAR4 TO NEWVAR6.
```

You can use the TO keyword to imply consecutive variables on the active system file on the VARIABLES subcommand and to create new variable names on the INTO subcommand. The number of variables named or implied on the VARIABLES subcommand must equal the number of new variables named or implied on the INTO subcommand.

AUTORECODE stores the new values from variables named on the VARIABLES subcommand in target variables listed on the INTO subcommand. The original variables retain their original values. Variable labels are automatically generated for each new variable. If the original value has a label, that label is used for the new value. If the original value doesn't have a label, the original value is used as the label.

4.29
DESCENDING and PRINT Subcommands

By default, AUTORECODE assigns values in ascending order. Use the DESCENDING subcommand to assign values in descending order. Use the PRINT subcommand to display a correspondence table of values for the original and new variables, as in:

```
AUTORECODE VARIABLES=VAR1 VAR2 VAR4 TO VAR6
 /INTO NEWVAR1 NEWVAR2 NEWVAR4 TO NEWVAR6
 /DESCENDING /PRINT.
```

There are no additional specifications on the DESCENDING and PRINT subcommands.

4.30
Missing Values

Missing values are recoded into missing values higher than any nonmissing values, with their order preserved. For example, if the original variable has ten nonmissing values, the value of the first missing value would be recoded to 11, and the value 11 would be a missing value for the new variable.

4.31
COMBINING SYSTEM FILES

With SPSS, you can combine information from two or more files into a single active system file. The MATCH FILES command combines files with the same cases but different variables. The ADD FILES command combines files with the same variables but different cases. The UPDATE command replaces values in a master file with updated values from one or more transaction files.

4.32
MATCH FILES Command

Use the MATCH FILES command to combine files with the same cases but different variables. In the simplest match, you can combine two or more *parallel files*—files with the same cases in the same order but different variables. For parallel files, the only required specification is the FILE subcommand, which identifies the files to be combined.

Nonparallel files have overlapping sets of cases, with some cases appearing in some files but not in others. For nonparallel files, the required specifications on MATCH FILES are the FILE and BY subcommands.

You can also use MATCH FILES with *table lookup files*—files that contain information at one level that can be "spread" across groups of cases on another file. For table lookup files, the required specifications are the FILE, BY, and TABLE subcommands.

Optionally, you can specify the subcommands RENAME, DROP, KEEP, and MAP with all three types of files. The syntax and function of these subcommands is the same as for the GET command (see Sections 4.4 through 4.7).

Sections 4.33 through 4.38 give an overview of the MATCH FILES command. For a complete discussion of MATCH FILES, see the *SPSS Reference Guide*.

4.33
FILE Subcommand

FILE is the only required subcommand for parallel matching files. Parallel files contain the same cases in the same order but different variables. For example, you might have pre-test and post-test data for the same group of subjects in different files. You can combine these files with the MATCH FILES command and the FILE subcommand. Each file should be specified on a separate FILE subcommand, separated by a slash, as in:

```
MATCH FILES FILE=BEFORE /FILE=AFTER.
```

You can combine up to 50 SPSS system files. If cases do not appear in the same order on all files to be combined, you can use the SORT CASES command (see Section 4.19) before MATCH FILES, provided each case has a distinctive value for the sort variable, such as a case ID variable.

The variables in the files to be combined do not have to be similar in number or nature. New cases are built by matching cases and simply appending the variables from each file for that case. For example, if file X contains variables A, B, and C, and file Y contains variables D, E, F and G, the command

```
MATCH FILES FILE=X /FILE=Y.
```

creates a new active system file containing the variables A, B, C, D, E, F, and G for each case.

You can specify the active system file on a FILE subcommand with an asterisk, as in:

```
MATCH FILES FILE=X /FILE=Y /FILE=*.
```

4.34
BY Subcommand

For nonparallel files, there are two required subcommands: FILE, which identifies the files to be combined; and BY, which specifies a key variable or variable list for matching cases.

There are two reasons why files may not have a parallel, one-to-one case structure: cases in one file may be missing in another file, or cases may be duplicated in a file. As long as each case can be identified by a key variable or set of variables, you can still use MATCH FILES to combine the files.

Use the BY subcommand to list the key variable(s) that are used to match cases, as in:

```
MATCH FILES FILE=FIRST /FILE=SECOND /BY ID.
```

All files must be sorted in ascending order on the key variables and the key variables must have the same name on each file. If your files are not already sorted, use the SORT CASES command (see Section 4.19) before MATCH FILES.

4.35
IN Subcommand

With nonparallel matching files, if a case is missing from one of the files, all of the variables from that input file will be set to system-missing for that case on the combined resulting file. Use the optional IN subcommand to create a new variable on the resulting file that indicates whether a case was contained on the associated input file. Each IN subcommand applies to the previously named input file on the FILE subcommand. The only specification on the IN subcommand is the name of the new indicator variable, as in:

```
MATCH FILES FILE=FIRST /IN=INFIRST /FILE=SECOND /IN=INSECOND
/BY ID.
```

The indicator variable named on the IN subcommand has a value of 1 in the combined resulting file for all cases contained in the input file and a value of 0 for any cases not found in the input file.

4.36
TABLE Subcommand

You can also use the MATCH FILES command to transfer information from a table lookup file to another file with a different unit of analysis. For example, you can spread information from a file containing household information to a file containing data on individual household members.

For table lookup files, MATCH FILES has three required subcommands: the TABLE subcommand specifies the name of the table lookup file containing information to be supplied to cases on another file; the FILE subcommand identifies the case file; and the BY subcommand specifies the key variable which is used to look up information on the table file and transfer it to the case file. In the household example, each case on the household file has a variable that identifies the household, and each case on the file containing data on individual household members also has a variable that identifies the household. This variable must have the same name on both the table lookup and case files. The command

```
MATCH FILES TABLE=HOUSE /FILE=PERSONS /BY HOUSEID.
```

creates a combined file containing data for individual household members, with data from the table file HOUSE spread to any cases from the file PERSONS that have the same value for the key variable HOUSEID on both files. Any entries in the table file not matched with entries in the case file are ignored.

4.37
FIRST and LAST
Subcommands

For table lookup files, you will usually have multiple cases with the same value for the key variable. In the household example, for instance, more than one individual will frequently have the same household identifier, and it is sometimes useful to identify either the first or last case in a group sharing a common set of values for key variables.

Use the FIRST subcommand to create a variable that identifies the first case in each group and the LAST subcommand to identify the last case in each group. The FIRST and LAST subcommands refer to the combined file and should be placed after the TABLE, FILE, and BY subcommands, as in:

```
MATCH FILES /TABLE=HOUSE /FILE=PERSONS /BY HOUSEID
/FIRST=OLDEST /LAST=YOUNGEST.
```

The variable OLDEST has the value 1 for the first person in each household, and a value of 0 for all other cases. The variable YOUNGEST has a value of 1 for the last person in each household and a value of 0 for all other cases. Assuming that file PERSONS has been sorted by age, OLDEST will identify the oldest member of each household, and YOUNGEST will identify the youngest.

4.38
RENAME Subcommand

When files are matched, the only variable names that should appear in more than one file are the key variable names used to match cases with the BY subcommand. Other variable names should not appear in more than one file.

Use the optional RENAME subcommand to:

- Change key variable names so they are consistent across all files.
- Change nonunique names for variables not used as keys.

Each RENAME subcommand should follow the FILE subcommand that specifies the file containing the variable(s) to be renamed, as in:

```
MATCH FILES FILE=FIRST /RENAME (GPA=GPA87)
 /FILE=SECOND /RENAME (GPA=GPA88) (IDVAR=CASEID)
 /BY CASEID.
```

In this example, variable GPA from file FIRST is renamed GPA87, and variables GPA and IDVAR from file SECOND are renamed GPA88 and CASEID, respectively.

The syntax for the RENAME subcommand is the same as for the GET command (see Section 4.4).

4.39
ADD FILES Command

Use the ADD FILES command to combine files with the same variables but different cases. For example, you might record the same information for students attending three different schools and maintain the data for each school in a separate file. You can combine these files for analysis with the ADD FILES command.

With ADD FILES, you can either *concatenate* or *interleave* files. Concatenating files simply appends cases from each input file to the combined file. The only required subcommand for concatenating files is the FILE subcommand, which identifies the files to be combined. Interleaving files creates a file sorted by the value of a key variable. Interleaving files requires two subcommands: the FILE subcommand and the BY subcommand, which specifies the key variable(s).

Seven optional subcommands are available with the ADD FILES command: RENAME, DROP, KEEP and MAP have the same syntax and function as for the GET command (see Sections 4.4 through 4.7); IN, FIRST, and LAST have the same syntax and function as for the MATCH FILES subcommand (see Sections 4.35 and 4.37).

Sections 4.40 and 4.41 give a brief overview of ADD FILES. For a complete discussion of the ADD FILES command, see the *SPSS Reference Guide*.

4.40
FILE Subcommand

To concatenate files—to add cases from one file to the end of another—you need to specify only the FILE subcommand, which identifies the input files to be combined in the resulting file. Each input file requires a separate FILE subcommand, separated by a slash, as in:

```
ADD FILES FILE=SCHOOL1 /FILE=SCHOOL2 /FILE=SCHOOL3.
```

You can specify up to 50 SPSS system files on one ADD FILES command. You can specify the active system file with an asterisk, as in:

```
ADD FILES FILE=SCHOOL1 /FILE=SCHOOL2 /FILE=*.
```

4.41
BY Subcommand

To interleave files—to create a file sorted by the value of a key variable or variables—you need to specify two subcommands: FILE, which identifies the files to be combined; and BY, which specifies the key variable(s). For example, to interleave the data from the three school files by grade, specify:

```
ADD FILES FILE=SCHOOL1 /FILE=SCHOOL2 /FILE=SCHOOL3
/BY GRADE.
```

The key variables must have the same names on each input file, and the files must already be sorted in ascending order by the key variables.

If the input files are not sorted, you can either specify a SORT CASES command before ADD FILES (see Section 4.19) for each unsorted input file—or simply omit the BY subcommand, concatenate the unsorted input files, and specify a SORT CASES command after the ADD FILES command to sort the resulting file into the desired order.

The BY subcommand follows all FILE subcommands and any associated RENAME and IN subcommands.

4.42
UPDATE Command

Use the UPDATE command to replace values in a *master file* with values from one or more *transaction files*. Cases in the master and transaction files are matched according to a key variable. For each common variable (a variable that exists on both the master and transaction files), cases in the combined file take on the value of the variable from the transaction file. If more than one transaction file is specified, the value comes from the last transaction file with a nonmissing value for the common variable.

Sections 4.43 and 4.44 provide a brief overview of the UPDATE command. For a complete discussion of UPDATE, see the *SPSS Reference Guide.*

4.43
FILE and BY Subcommands

The UPDATE command has two required subcommands: FILE, which identifies master and transaction files; and BY, which specifies the key variable for matching cases. The first FILE subcommand identifies the master file. All subsequent FILE subcommands identify transaction files. Each SPSS system file must be specified on a separate FILE subcommand, separated by slashes.

For example, if you have a master file containing mailing addresses and a separate file containing only address changes and corrections, you can update the information in the master file with the changes and corrections by specifying:

```
UPDATE FILE=MAILIST /FILE=NEWLIST /BY ID.
```

In this example, MAILIST is the master file, and NEWLIST is the transaction file. Cases are matched based on the value of the key variable ID, specified on the BY subcommand. Cases in both the master and transaction files must be sorted in ascending order by the key variable. If cases are not sorted, specify a SORT CASES command before UPDATE (see Section 4.19).

4.44
Optional Subcommands

There are five optional subcommands for the UPDATE command. RENAME, DROP, KEEP, and MAP have the same syntax and function as for the GET command (see Sections 4.4 through 4.7). The IN subcommand has the same syntax and function as for MATCH FILES (see Section 4.35).

4.45
SPSS FILE INTERFACES

With SPSS, you can read and write *portable files*, as well as read files created with other statistical software.

Portable files are used to transport SPSS files between computers using different conversions of SPSS and to transport files between SPSS and SPSS/PC+ or other software that uses the same portable file format. Use the EXPORT command to write portable files and the IMPORT command to read portable files.

4.46
EXPORT Command

Use the EXPORT command to create a portable file. The EXPORT command is similar to the SAVE command. It can be specified at the same point in the SPSS session, and it saves the current active system file. As with SAVE, the only required specification on the EXPORT command is the OUTFILE subcommand, which names the portable file, as in:

EXPORT OUTFILE=PORTFILE.

Optional subcommands include RENAME, DROP, KEEP, and MAP, which have the same syntax and function as for the GET command (see Sections 4.4 through 4.7), and the TYPE and DIGITS subcommands described below.

4.47
TYPE Subcommand

By default, SPSS creates a portable file suitable for transmission via a communications program (TYPE=COMM) and removes all control characters and replaces them with the character 0. If you want to transport portable files via magnetic tape, specify TAPE on the optional TYPE subcommand, as in:

EXPORT /**TYPE=TAPE** /OUTFILE=PORTFILE.

4.48
DIGITS Subcommand

You can save space on portable files by using the optional DIGITS subcommand to limit the number of decimals used to represent fractional values. The only specification on the DIGITS subcommand is an integer representing the number of digits of precision. For example, the command

EXPORT OUTFILE=PORTFILE /**DIGITS=6**.

will round the number 1.23456789 to 1.234568.

The DIGITS subcommand affects all numbers for which no exact representation is possible with the specified number of digits, so it should be set according to the requirements of the variable that needs the greatest precision.

4.49
IMPORT Command

Use the IMPORT command to read SPSS portable files created with the EXPORT command. The IMPORT command is similar to the GET command. The only required specification is the FILE subcommand which identifies the portable file to be read, as in:

IMPORT FILE=PORTFILE.

Optional subcommands for the IMPORT subcommand are RENAME, DROP, KEEP, and MAP, which have the same syntax and function as for the GET command (see Sections 4.4 through 4.7), and the TYPE subcommand, which has the same syntax and function as for the EXPORT command.

4.50
Interfacing SPSS with Other Statistical Software

With SPSS, you can also read files created with SCSS, SAS, OSIRIS, and BMDP. See the *SPSS Reference Guide* for information on the GET SCSS, GET SAS, GET OSIRIS, and GET BMDP commands.

Contents_____

5 SPSS Session Control

SPSS has a wide variety of commands, giving you a great deal of flexibility and control in both your SPSS session and output display. You can specify your own output titles with the TITLE and SUBTITLE commands. You can use the SET command to override many of the SPSS default settings with your own specifications. You can summarize or document command files with the COMMENT command. You can use the INCLUDE command to incorporate an existing command file into the current session, and you can create your own commands with the macro facility.

5.1
TITLE AND SUBTITLE COMMANDS

SPSS places a heading at the top of each page in a display file. The heading includes the date, a title, and the page number. By default, SPSS assigns a title that indicates the version of the system being used. To specify your own title, use the TITLE command. The title should be enclosed in apostrophes or quotation marks, as in:

```
TITLE 'Western Electric Coronary Heart Disease Study'.
```

If the title includes an apostrophe, enclose the title in quotation marks, as in:

```
TITLE "Western Electric's Coronary Heart Disease Study".
```

Titles can be up to 60 characters long. You can use multiple TITLE commands in an SPSS session. Each TITLE command remains in effect until SPSS encounters a new TITLE command, which then replaces the previous title. For example, the commands

```
FREQUENCIES VARIABLES=DAYOFWK.
TITLE "Descriptive Statistics".
DESCRIPTIVES VARIABLES=AGE HT58 WT58.
TITLE "Crosstabular Analysis".
CROSSTABS TABLES=FIRSTCHD BY AGE.
```

produce a default title for the output pages containing the results of the FREQUENCIES procedure, and separate user-specified titles for the pages containing the results of the DESCRIPTIVES and CROSSTABS procedures.

The SUBTITLE command specifies a subtitle, which prints beneath the title. The subtitle should be enclosed in parentheses or quotation marks, as in:

```
TITLE 'Western Electric Coronary Heart Disease Study'.
SUBTITLE "Crosstabular Analysis".
```

TITLE and SUBTITLE are independent. You can specify SUBTITLE without specifying TITLE, which will change the subtitle and leave the title unaffected.

5.2
COMMENT COMMAND

Use the COMMENT command to insert comments concerning your SPSS commands. Comments can be a useful tool for summarizing the purpose of your commands. The COMMENT command is followed by any message you want, as in:

```
COMMENT   Create uniform distribution for testing computations.
```

You can substitute an asterisk for the command keyword COMMENT, as in:

```
* Create uniform distribution for testing computations.
```

The comment can be continued for as many lines as necessary.

You can place comments at the end of individual command or subcommand lines by separating the comment from the command with a slash, as in:

```
FREQUENCIES VARIABLES=DAYOFWK /* Day of week heart attack occurred.
 /MISSING=INCLUDE /* Include user-defined missing values.
```

5.3
FINISH COMMAND

The FINISH command terminates an SPSS session. The only specification is the command keyword FINISH, as in:

```
FINISH.
```

The FINISH command causes SPSS to stop reading commands and unconditionally ends the session. Placing it within a DO IF structure will not end the session conditionally. Any commands following FINISH are ignored.

5.4
EDIT COMMAND

You can use the EDIT command to check command syntax in a command file that is submitted for execution through your operating system. The EDIT command instructs SPSS to look for syntax errors in the command file without reading or processing the data. This allows you to correct syntax errors before running a potentially time-consuming or costly SPSS session. The EDIT command can appear anywhere in your command file, and the only specification is the command keyword EDIT, as in:

```
EDIT.
```

Although EDIT does not read the data, it does check variable names against the dictionary. Thus, the command file should include a DATA LIST or GET command, which accesses the system file.

You cannot use the EDIT command to check the syntax of commands run from within an SPSS session.

5.5
EXECUTE COMMAND

Some SPSS commands are not executed unless they are followed by a procedure that reads the data. Commands that are not executed immediately include PRINT, WRITE, data transformation commands such as COMPUTE and RECODE, and data selection commands such as SELECT IF.

If your command file doesn't include a data-reading procedure or if you want SPSS to read the data and execute commands before the first data-reading procedure, you can instruct SPSS to do so with the EXECUTE command. The only specification on the EXECUTE command is the command keyword EXE-CUTE. For example, the commands

```
SELECT IF (LNAME EQ 'SMITH').
WRITE OUTFILE=SMITHS /LNAME FNAME.
EXECUTE.
```

select all people with the last name of Smith and writes their last and first names to a file named SMITHS. The EXECUTE command tells SPSS to read the data and execute the preceding SELECT IF and WRITE commands.

5.6
INCLUDE COMMAND

The INCLUDE command enables you to include an SPSS command file in your SPSS session (see Chapter 1). If there is a particular set of commands you use frequently, such as a lengthy set of data transformations, you can put them in a command file and then use the INCLUDE command to incorporate that command file into the command sequence.

The required FILE subcommand indicates the name of the command file to be included in the current session, as in:

```
INCLUDE FILE=TRANSCOM.
```

Commands in an included file must begin in column 1, and continuation lines must be indented at least one column.

You can use multiple INCLUDE commands within a command sequence. You can also create nested INCLUDE commands by specifying additional INCLUDE commands within included files.

5.7
MACRO FACILITY

The macro facility enables you to create your own commands and specifications from existing SPSS commands and specifications. You can use the macro facility to:

• Specify a single macro name which stands for a variable list.
• Execute multiple SPSS commands with a single command.
• Manipulate one or more character strings to produce new character strings.
• Create complex input programs and procedure specifications that can then be executed with simple specifications.

To use the macro facility, you must first define and name the macro. The macro is then invoked every time SPSS encounters the macro name. Sections 5.8 through 5.16 give an overview of the SPSS macro facility. For a complete discussion of the macro facility, including a list of string manipulation functions, see the *SPSS Reference Guide*.

5.8
DEFINE and !ENDDEFINE Commands

Use the DEFINE and !ENDDEFINE commands to define macros. All macro definitions begin with the DEFINE command and end with the !ENDDEFINE command. The general syntax of the macro definition is:

```
DEFINE macro name (macro arguments).
macro body
!ENDDEFINE.
```

The first specification after the DEFINE command is the macro name that will be used to identify and invoke the macro whenever you want to use it. Macro names follow the same syntax rules as variable names (see Chapter 2). In addition, you can begin a macro name with an exclamation point (!) to ensure that the macro name does not conflict with a variable name or command keyword.

The macro name is followed by a set of parentheses that enclose optional macro argument definitions. Although arguments are not required, you must include the parentheses even if your macro has no arguments.

Next, specify the macro body. The macro body can include SPSS commands, variable names, conditional processing statements, string manipulation statements, and macro directives.

After the macro body, indicate the end of the macro definition with the !ENDDEFINE command.

5.9
Macro Call

Once you have defined a macro, you use the macro call to invoke the macro. The macro call simply consists of the macro name and an optional argument list.

The macro name can appear virtually anyplace in an SPSS session, and the macro is invoked whenever SPSS encounters the macro name. If a macro name appears after a command keyword, SPSS assumes that the macro defines additional specifications for the command. If the macro name occurs where SPSS would expect a command, SPSS assumes that the macro defines a command or set of commands to be executed.

5.10
Macros without Arguments

You can define simple macros without arguments. For example, you can use a macro to define a group of variables, as in:

```
DEFINE SESVARS ().
AGE SEX EDUC INCOME.
!ENDDEFINE.
```

In this example, SPSS will substitute the variable names AGE, SEX, EDUC, and INCOME whenever it encounters the macro name SESVARS. So the command

```
FREQUENCIES VARIABLES=SESVARS.
```

is equivalent to

```
FREQUENCIES VARIABLES=AGE SEX EDUC INCOME.
```

You can also use macros without arguments to represent a sequence of commmands. For example, the macro

```
DEFINE SETZERO ().
COMPUTE X=0.
COMPUTE Y=0.
COMPUTE Z=0.
!ENDDEFINE.
```

defines a sequence of COMPUTE commands which set the values of variables X, Y, and Z to 0 whenever SPSS encounters the macro name SETZERO. So the macro call

```
SETZERO.
```

takes the place of the three compute commands.

5.11
Macros with Arguments

Macro arguments let you define more sophisticated and flexible macros. For instance, the macro without arguments in Section 5.10 that executes a series of compute commands is useful only if you want to set exactly three variables to an initial value of 0, and those three variables are always named X, Y, and Z. However, with macro arguments you can create a macro that will generate COMPUTE commands for any number of variables with any valid variable names.

All arguments in a macro are either positional or keyword arguments. A *positional argument* is identified by its position after the macro name. A *keyword argument* is assigned a name in the the macro definition and is identified by name in the macro call.

5.12
Positional Arguments

Positional arguments are declared with the keyword !POSITIONAL, as in:

```
DEFINE SETZERO (!POSITIONAL !CMDEND).
!DO !TEMPVAR !IN(!1).
COMPUTE !TEMPVAR=0.
!DOEND.
!ENDDEFINE.
```

In this example, there is only one positional argument, identified by !1 in the macro body. (See Section 5.16 for a discussion of !DO—!DO END looping constructs.)

The keyword !CMDEND instructs SPSS to assign the positional argument to any arguments found after the macro name on the macro call, up to the start of the next command. For this macro, the macro call

```
SETZERO VAR1 VAR2 VAR3 VAR4.
```

is equivalent to the following four COMPUTE commands:

```
COMPUTE VAR1=0.
COMPUTE VAR2=0.
COMPUTE VAR3=0.
COMPUTE VAR4=0.
```

You could add a second positional argument by specifying:

```
DEFINE SETZERO (!POSITIONAL !CHAREND ('/') /!POSITIONAL !CMDEND).
!DO !TEMPVAR !IN(!1).
COMPUTE !TEMPVAR=0.
!DOEND.
!DO !TEMPVAR !IN(!2).
COMPUTE !TEMPVAR=1.
!DOEND.
!ENDDEFINE.
```

The second conditional argument is identified by !2 in the macro body. The keyword !CHAREND indicates that the first positional argument should be assigned to any arguments on the macro call until a slash (/) is encountered. Any arguments encounted after the slash on the macro call are assigned to the second positional argument. So the macro call

```
SETZERO VAR1 VAR2 VAR3 / VAR4 VAR5 VAR6.
```

is equivalent to the following six COMPUTE commands:

```
COMPUTE VAR1=0.
COMPUTE VAR2=0.
COMPUTE VAR3=0.
COMPUTE VAR4=1.
COMPUTE VAR5=1.
COMPUTE VAR6=1.
```

5.13
Keyword Arguments

Instead of positional arguments, you can specify your own keywords, which can be used to identify arguments in the macro body. The user-specified argument keyword name is followed by an equals sign and a macro keyword, as in:

```
DEFINE SETZERO (SETVAR=!CMDEND).
!DO !TEMPVAR !IN(!SETVAR).
COMPUTE !TEMPVAR=0.
!DOEND.
!ENDDEFINE.
```

In this example, the keyword argument is used like a subcommand on the macro call following the macro name, as in:

```
SETZERO SETVAR=VAR1 VAR2 VAR3.
```

which generates three COMPUTE commands, setting VAR1, VAR2, and VAR3 to 0.

There are no limitations on the number of arguments on the macro definition or macro call. The above macros could be used to generate any number of COMPUTE commands for any valid variable names.

5.14
Macro Argument Keywords

The following keywords are available in macro arguments for both positional and keyword arguments:

!TOKENS(n)   *Assign the next* n *tokens to the argument.* n *can be any positive integer. A* token *is a character or group of characters separated by blanks or SPSS delimiters. For example, DATA LIST is two tokens, and* $1+2$ *is three tokens.*

For example, when the following macro is called

```
DEFINE macname (!POSITIONAL !TOKENS (3)).
     macro body
!ENDDEFINE.
```

as in

```
MACNAME ABC DEFG HI.
```

the three tokens following the macro name MACNAME (ABC, DEFG, and HI) are assigned to the positional argument !1 in the macro body.

!CHAREND('char')   *Assign all tokens up to the specified character to the argument. The character must be a one-character string specified in apostrophes and enclosed in parentheses.* (See example in Section 5.12.)

!ENCLOSE ('char','char')   *Assign all tokens between the indicated characters to the argument. The characters can be any one-character string, each specified in apostrophes. The two strings should be separated by a comma and the entire specification enclosed in parentheses.*

For example, when the following macro is called

```
DEFINE macname (!POSITIONAL !ENCLOSE('(',')')).
     macro body
!ENDDEFINE.
```

as in

```
MACNAME (A B C).
```

the three tokens enclosed in parentheses, A, B, and C, are assigned to the positional argument !1 in the macro body. Note that the starting and ending character can differ.

!CMDEND   *Assign all the remaining text in the macro call to the argument, up to the start of the next command. Since* !CMDEND *reads up to the start of the next command, only the last argument in the argument list can be specified with* !CMDEND. (See example in Section 5.12.)

5.15
Conditional Processing

The !IF construct can be used to specify conditional processing in the macro body. The general format of the !IF construct is:

```
!IF (expression) !THEN statements
                    !ELSE statements.
!IFEND.
```

!IF, !THEN, and !IFEND are required; !ELSE is optional. Valid operators for the expressions include !EQ, !NE, !GT, !GE, !LT, and !LE or =, a=, >, >=, <, and <=. !OR, !NOT, and !AND can also be used.

5.16
Looping Constructs

You can use looping constructs in macros to perform repetitive tasks. The macro facility has two looping constructs, the DO loop and the DO IN loop. The general syntax of the DO loop is:

```
!DO !var = start !TO finish !BY step.
statements.
!BREAK.
!DOEND.
```

!DO, !TO, and !DOEND are required. !BY and !BREAK are optional.

The first specification after !DO must be a variable name that begins with an exclamation point (!). It is used as an index in the loop. Start, finish, and step must be numbers or expressions that evaluate to numbers. The loop begins at the specified start value and continues until the specified finish value, unless it encounters a !BREAK statement. The optional step (!BY) specifies an incremental value. For example, if start is 1, finish is 10, and step is 3, the loop will be executed four times, with the index variable assigned values of 1, 4, 7, and 10.

The statements can be any valid SPSS statements or macro commands. !DOEND specifies the end of the loop. The optional !BREAK specification can be used in conjunction with conditional processing to cause the loop to be exited, as in:

```
!IF (I = 5) !THEN !BREAK   !IFEND
```

For example, in the following macro,

```
DEFINE MACDEF (ARG1 = !TOKENS(1) /ARG2 = !TOKENS(1)).
!DO !I = !ARG1 !TO !ARG2.
FREQUENCIES VARIABLES = !CONCAT(VAR,!I).
!DOEND.
!ENDDEFINE.
MACDEF ARG1 = 1 ARG2 = 3.
```

the variable I is initially assigned the value 1 (ARG1). ARG1 is incremented until it equals 3, at which point the DO loop ends. The loop concatenates VAR and I value 1, VAR and I value 2, and finally VAR and I value 3 on its three iterations. The result of this loop is that FREQUENCIES receives three variables, VAR1, VAR2, and VAR3.

The DO IN loop is a *list processing* loop. The general format is:

```
!DO !var !IN (list).
statements.
!BREAK.
!DOEND.
```

!DO, !IN, and !DOEND are required for a list processing loop. !BREAK is optional.

In a list processing loop, you specify a list after the !IN function, and the variable !var will be set to each member of the list. List processing loops were used in the examples in Sections 5.11 and 5.13, in which the list specification on the !IN function referred to a positional or keyword argument.

5.17
SET AND SHOW COMMANDS

The SET command allows you to control a variety of SPSS settings, overriding the default specifications. The SHOW command displays the current settings, as well as additional information.

The SET command is followed by a subcommand or list of subcommands indicating the settings to be changed. Each subcommand is followed by an equals sign and a user-specified value, as in:

```
SET BLANKS=0 UNDEFINED=NOWARN MXWARNS=200.
```

The SHOW command is followed by a subcommand or list of subcommands for which you want to know the current settings, as in:

```
SHOW BLANKS UNDEFINED NOWARN.
```

If you specify SHOW without any subcommands, all current settings are displayed.

The subcommands listed below are available with both SET and SHOW. For additional SET and SHOW subcommands for the GRAPH procedure (not available in all systems), see the *SPSS Reference Guide*. For additional system-specific subcommands, see the SPSS *Operations Guide* for your system.

BLANKS	*Value to which blanks read in numeric format should be translated.*
BLKSIZE	*Default block length used for scratch data files and SPSS system files.* BLKSIZE can be specified on SHOW only.
BOX	*Characters used to draw boxes.* Both character and hexadecimal representations are given when SHOW is specified.
BUFFNO	*The default number of buffers used for all files managed by the SPSS I/O subsystem.* BUFFNO can be specified on SHOW only.
CASE	*Case for display of labels and error messages.* The specifications are UPPER and UPLOW.
CC	*Custom currency formats.* Five subcommands enable you to customize currency formats for your own applications. These subcommands are CCA, CCB, CCC, CCD, and CCE.
COMPRESSION	*Compression of scratch files.* The specification is either ON or OFF (alias YES or NO).
ENDCMD	*Command terminator.* The specification can be any single character.
FORMAT	*Default print and write formats for numeric variables created by transformations.* The specification can be any F format.
HEADER	*Headings for output.* The specification is either YES or NO (alias ON or OFF).
JOURNAL	*Journal file for commands entered during an SPSS session.* The specification is either ON or OFF (alias YES or NO). This determines whether the journal file keeps a log of commands entered during the SPSS session. In addition to ON or OFF, you can also specify the name of the file.
LENGTH	*Page length for output.* The specification can be any integer in the range 40 through 999,999 inclusive or NONE to suppress page ejects altogether.
MEXPAND	*Macro expansion.* The specification is either ON or OFF (alias YES or NO).
MITERATE	*Maximum loop traversals permitted in macro expansions.* The specification is a positive integer.
MNEST	*Maximum nesting level for macros.* The specification is a positive integer.
MPRINT	*Inclusion of macro expansion command list in the display file.* The specification is either ON and OFF (alias YES or NO).
MXERRS	*Maximum number of errors permitted before session is terminated.* This setting applies only to command files submitted for execution through the operating system.
MXLOOPS	*Maximum executions of a loop on a single case.*
MXWARNS	*Maximum number of warnings and errors permitted, collectively, before session is terminated.* This setting applies only to command files submitted for execution through the operating system.
N	*Unweighted number of cases on the active system file.* N can be specified on SHOW only. Prints UNKNOWN if no active system file has been created yet.

NULLINE	*Null line command terminator for commands entered during a prompted (interactive) session.* The specification is YES or NO (alias ON or OFF).
NUMBERED	*The current status of the switch set by the NUMBERED and UNNUMBERED commands.* NUMBERED can be specified on SHOW only.
PRINTBACK	*Printback of SPSS commands in the display file.* The specification is either YES or NO (alias ON or OFF).
SCOMPRESSION	*Default setting for compression of SPSS system files.* This setting can be overridden by the COMPRESSED or UNCOMPRESSED subcommands on the SAVE or XSAVE commands. SCOMPRESSION can be specified on SHOW only.
SEED	*Seed for the random-number generator.* The specification is a large integer.
SYSMIS	*The system-missing value.* SYSMIS can be specified on SHOW only.
TBFONTS	*Font characters for the TABLES procedure.* Both character and hexadecimal representations are given when TBFONTS is specified on SHOW.
TB1	*Box characters for the TABLES procedure.* Both character and hexadecimal representations are given when TB1 is specified on SHOW.
TB2	*Box overprint characters for the TABLES procedure.* Both character and hexadecimal representations are given when TB2 is specified on SHOW.
UNDEFINED	*Warning message for undefined data.* Specifications are WARN and NOWARN. NOWARN suppresses messages but does not alter the count of warnings toward the MXWARNS total.
WEIGHT	*The name of the variable used to weight cases.* WEIGHT can be specified on SHOW only.
WIDTH	*Maximum page width for the display file.* The specification can be any integer from 80 through 132.
XSORT	*The sort program used to sort data.* The specification is either YES (alias ON) for *use SPSS sort* or NO (alias OFF) for *use another sort program.*
$VARS	*Values of system variables.* Can be specified for SHOW only.
ALL	*Display all settings.* Can be specified for SHOW only.

The default specifications for these settings vary between operating systems. Use the SHOW command to display the default settings for your computer system.

5.18
PRESERVE AND RESTORE COMMANDS

You can use the PRESERVE command to save the current SET specifications and the RESTORE command to change the SET specifications back to the settings saved on the most recent PRESERVE command. The only specifications for these commands are the command keywords PRESERVE and RESTORE.

If you specify PRESERVE before any SET commands, the default settings are saved, and a RESTORE command after any subsequent SET commands will restore the default settings. If you specify RESTORE without a preceding PRESERVE command, SPSS issues a warning and the RESTORE command is ignored.

Contents_____

6 Listing and Writing Cases

It is sometimes necessary or useful to review the actual contents of your data. You may want to see that a DATA LIST command is defining your data as you intend, or you may want to verify results of transformations or examine cases you suspect have coding errors. The LIST and PRINT commands allow you to display the values of variables for each case in your data file.

You may also want to write the values of variables to an output file. For example, you might want to use another program to analyze the data, or you might need to send the data to another computer system. The WRITE command writes values to an output file in a variety of user-specified formats (see Sections 6.17 through 6.19).

6.1
LIST COMMAND

The LIST procedure displays the values of variables for each case in the active system file in a standard format. It can also display a subset of variables or cases.

The minimum specification on the LIST command is the command keyword LIST. By default, LIST displays all variables on the active system file, using the dictionary print format, as shown in Figure 6.1.

Figure 6.1 Default LIST results

```
DATA LIST FILE=HUBDATA RECORDS=3
  /1 MOHIRED YRHIRED 12-15 DEPT82 19
  /2 SALARY79 TO SALARY82 6-25
  /3 NAME 25-48 (A)
LIST.
```

MOHIRED	YRHIRED	DEPT82	SALARY79	SALARY80	SALARY81	SALARY82	NAME
8	69	3	11180	13000	14300	15600	CONNIE E. JANNSEN
3	80	4	0	8190	8840	10050	MARY CHAFEE
2	74	1	13715	14495	16250	18850	HOLLY C. BRADSHAW
10	78	3	6370	7410	0	8872	JACKIE HAMILTON
7	79	2	0	10140	14300	16250	KARIN HEGEL
6	79	1	0	8450	9750	10920	C. M. BROWN
4	80	4	0	13520	16900	18083	VERA D. LOGGINS
9	79	3	0	8060	8866	9840	LUCINDA JACKSON
4	79	3	7605	8255	9750	12328	ANITA PULASKI
1	74	1	14397	15275	16575	19240	REUBEN D. CROSS

Values for each case are always displayed with a blank space between the variables. If a long string variable cannot be listed within the entire page width, it is truncated.

If all the variables fit on a single line, SPSS displays a heading using the variable name. If the variable name is longer than the variable print format width, SPSS centers numeric variables in the column.

When all variables fit on a line, LIST first tries to reserve columns according to the length of the variable name or the print format width, whichever requires more space. If this format is too wide, LIST reduces column widths by displaying variable names vertically.

6.2
VARIABLES Subcommand

By default, all variables are listed. You can limit the listing to specific variables by naming the variables on the VARIABLES subcommand, as in:

```
LIST VARIABLES=MOHIRED YRHIRED DEPT82 NAME.
```

The specified variables must already exist on the active system file. You cannot specify scratch or system variables. You can use the TO keyword to imply consecutive variables on the active system file, as in:

```
LIST VARIABLES=MOHIRED YRHIRED SALARY79 TO SALARY82 NAME.
```

6.3
CASES Subcommand

Use the CASES subcommand to limit the number and pattern of cases listed. Subcommand CASES must be followed by at least one of the following keywords:

FROM n *The case number of the first case to be listed.* The specification CASES FROM 100 starts listing cases at the 100th sequential case. If LIST is preceded by SAMPLE or SELECT IF, it is the 100th case selected. The default is 1, which means the listing begins with the first selected case.

TO n *Upper limit on the cases to be listed.* The specification CASES TO 1000 limits the listing to the 1000th selected case or the end of the file, whichever comes first. The default is to list cases through the end of the file.

BY n *Increment used to choose cases for listing.* The specification CASES BY 5 lists every fifth selected case. The default is 1, which means every case is listed.

You can specify one, two, or all three of these keywords, as in:

```
LIST VARIABLES=MOHIRED YRHIRED DEPT82 SALARY79 TO SALARY82 NAME
/CASES FROM 50 TO 100 BY 5.
```

6.4
FORMAT Subcommand

Use the following keywords on the FORMAT subcommand to control wrapping and numbering of the case listing:

WRAP *Multiple-line format.* If there is not enough room on the line to display the entire variable list, keyword WRAP wraps the listing in multiple lines per case. SPSS then generates a table indicating which variables appear on each line, and the name of the first variable on each line is displayed in the LIST results to identify the line. WRAP is the default.

SINGLE *Single-line format.* If there is not enough room within the line width, SPSS issues an error message and does not execute the listing. Therefore, use SINGLE only if you want one line per case or nothing.

NUMBERED *Number cases.* If you want LIST to number the cases listed, specify keyword NUMBERED (see Figure 6.4).

UNNUMBERED *Do not number cases.* This is the default.

Figure 6.4 List results with numbered format

```
LIST VARIABLES=MOHIRED YRHIRED DEPT82 SALARY79 TO SALARY82 NAME
/CASES FROM 50 TO 100 BY 5
/FORMAT=SINGLE NUMBERED.
```

```
     MOHIRED YRHIRED DEPT82 SALARY79 SALARY80 SALARY81 SALARY82 NAME
        50      2      70      3     11830    12545    13799    18083 FANNIE SMITH
        55     11      72      1      8222     8742     9509    10239 JOHN C. CAMPBELL
        60      6      81      1     10530    12220    13910    13910 CHARLES P. BLACK
        65     11      77      3     10400    11050    12155    15275 PAULINE LATHAN
        70      4      80      4         0     9750    10790    15608 MAUREEN J. WAYNE
        75      2      80      4         0     8190     9750    11240 POLLY E. CHAN
        80     11      73      2      9750    13000    14430    19500 CAROL BEST
        85     10      78      3      9750    11050    12090    15600 JO C. HOAWINSKI
        90      7      78      1      8112     8619     9379    10241 CLIFFORD KOLB
        95      1      76      1     11050    11050    12350    14300 LINDA YOUNG
       100      9      81      3         0     7020        0     8239 PENNY D. STARK

    Number of cases read:  100    Number of cases listed:  11
```

6.5
PRINT COMMAND

The PRINT command is designed to be simple enough for a quick check on reading and transforming data and yet flexible enough for formatting simple reports. As a quick check on data values, the simplest PRINT command consists of the command keyword PRINT, followed by a slash and a variable list, as in Figure 6.5.

Figure 6.5   PRINT results with default settings

```
PRINT /MOHIRED YRHIRED DEPT82 SALARY82 NAME.
EXECUTE.
```

```
8 69 3 15600 CONNIE E. JANNSEN
3 80 4 10050 MARY CHAFEE
2 74 1 18850 HOLLY C. BRADSHAW
7 79 2 16250 KARIN HEGEL
6 79 1 10920 C. M. BROWN
4 80 4 18083 VERA D. LOGGINS
9 79 3  9840 LUCINDA JACKSON
4 79 3 12328 ANITA PULASKI
1 74 1 19240 REUBEN D. CROSS
7 79 1 18460 TANI PATEL
```

By default, PRINT uses the dictionary formats and separates the values for each variable with a blank space. System-missing values are represented by a period.

PRINT is a transformation command. If it is not followed by a procedure command that causes the data to be read, SPSS does nothing. If you want to execute the PRINT command without any subsequent procedures, simply specify the EXECUTE command after PRINT, as shown in Figure 6.5.

Because PRINT is a transformation, it is executed as the data are read, once for each case. If PRINT is followed immediately by a procedure that produces individual case listings, such as REPORT or LIST, the results of PRINT and the procedure will be intermixed. To avoid this, simply place an EXECUTE command between PRINT and the procedure.

6.6
Variable Specifications

Use a slash to separate the variable list from the command keyword PRINT and any subcommands. The variable list can include numeric, string, scratch, temporary, and system variables. You can use the TO keyword to imply consecutive variables on the active system file, as in:

```
PRINT /MOHIRED YRHIRED DEPT82 SALARY79 TO SALARY82 NAME.
```

You can use the keyword ALL to display the values of every variable in the active system file, as in:

```
PRINT /ALL.
```

If you specify more variables than can be displayed in 132 columns, or within the width you specify using the SET command (see Chapter 5), the display will continue on the next line, starting in the second column.

6.7
Formats

You can specify formats for some or all of the *numeric* variables you want to display. (For string variables, the specified format must have a width equal to the dictionary format.) You can use an asterisk (*) to separate lists of variables that use dictionary formats from lists of variables with new formats. The new format should be specified in parentheses after the variable name. For example, the command

```
PRINT /MOHIRED YRHIRED DEPT82 * SALARY82 (DOLLAR8).
```

specifies that the variables in the first list, MOHIRED, YRHIRED and DEPT82, should be displayed using dictionary formats, and the variable in the second list, SALARY82, should be displayed in dollar format, in a space eight characters wide.

If you specify any formats in a variable list, you must specify one for each numeric variable in that list. You can apply one format to multiple variables in a list by preceding the format with an integer indicating the number of variables to which the format applies, as in:

```
PRINT /SALARY79 TO SALARY82 (4DOLLAR8).
```

If you specify formats, the automatic blank between variables is suppressed. To ensure that at least one blank space appears between variables, specify:

```
PRINT /SALARY79 TO SALARY82 (4(DOLLAR8,1X)).
```

For a complete list of PRINT formats, see the *SPSS Reference Guide.*

6.8
Multiple Lines per Case

You can display variables on more than one line for each case. Use a slash to indicate each new line of output. Optionally, you can specify an integer, immediately following the slash, indicating on which line the values are to be displayed.

For example, to display an employee's ID, department, and salary in 1981 on one line, ID, department, and salary in 1982 on the next line, and a blank third line, specify:

```
PRINT /EMPLOYID DEPT81 SALARY81
 /EMPLOYID DEPT82 SALARY82
 /.
```

6.9
Column Locations

You can specify column locations for variables, as in:

```
PRINT /SALARY81 11-20 SALARY82 25-34.
```

If you specify both column location and format, the format should omit the width specification, as in:

```
PRINT /SALARY82 11-20 (DOLLAR).
```

As with formats, you must include column specifications for all variables in the list, unless they are separated by asterisks.

6.10
Strings

You can include strings with your variable specifications on the PRINT command. Strings must be enclosed in apostrophes or quotation marks. For example, in Figure 6.10, strings are used to label the values being displayed and to insert a slash between the month hired (MOHIRED) and the year hired (YRHIRED) to display a composite hiring date. In this example, the F2 format is supplied for variable MOHIRED in order to suppress the blank that would follow it if the dictionary format were used.

Figure 6.10 PRINT display with literal strings

```
PRINT /NAME * "HIRED=" MOHIRED(F2) * "/" YRHIRED *
 "  SALARY82=" SALARY82 (DOLLAR8).
EXECUTE.
```

```
CONNIE E. JANNSEN      HIRED= 8/69   SALARY82= $15,600
MARY CHAFEE            HIRED= 3/80   SALARY82= $10,050
HOLLY C. BRADSHAW      HIRED= 2/74   SALARY82= $18,850
KARIN HEGEL            HIRED= 7/79   SALARY82= $16,250
C. M. BROWN            HIRED= 6/79   SALARY82= $10,920
VERA D. LOGGINS        HIRED= 4/80   SALARY82= $18,083
LUCINDA JACKSON        HIRED= 9/79   SALARY82=  $9,840
ANITA PULASKI          HIRED= 4/79   SALARY82= $12,328
REUBEN D. CROSS        HIRED= 1/74   SALARY82= $19,240
TANI PATEL             HIRED= 7/79   SALARY82= $18,460
```

6.11
Column Headings

You can use strings to create column headings to identify the variables that you are displaying. This can be done using the DO IF—END IF structure (see Chapter 3), as in Figure 6.11.

Figure 6.11 Literal strings as column heads

```
DO IF $CASENUM EQ 1.
PRINT /"    NAME " 1 "DEPT" 25 "HIRED" 30 "   SALARY" 35.
END IF .
PRINT /NAME DEPT82 *
 MOHIRED 30-31 * '/' YRHIRED *
 SALARY82 35-42(DOLLAR).
EXECUTE.
```

```
        NAME            DEPT HIRED  SALARY
    CONNIE E. JANNSEN     3   8/69 $15,600
    MARY CHAFEE           4   3/80 $10,050
    HOLLY C. BRADSHAW     1   2/74 $18,850
    KARIN HEGEL           2   7/79 $16,250
    C. M. BROWN           1   6/79 $10,920
    VERA D. LOGGINS       4   4/80 $18,083
    LUCINDA JACKSON       3   9/79  $9,840
    ANITA PULASKI         3   4/79 $12,328
    REUBEN D. CROSS       1   1/74 $19,240
    TANI PATEL            1   7/79 $18,460
```

Since PRINT is executed once for each case in the data file, you must enclose the PRINT command that specifies column headings within the DO IF—END IF structure. $CASENUM is a system variable with sequential values for each case in the file, starting with a value of 1 for the first case. The DO IF command causes the PRINT command that defines the column heads to be executed only once, as the first case is processed. END IF closes the structure.

The second PRINT command specifies the variables to be displayed. It is executed once for each case in the data file.

6.12
OUTFILE, RECORD, and TABLE Subcommands

Three subcommands are available on the PRINT command. They should appear before the first slash indicating the beginning of the variable list.

OUTFILE Subcommand. OUTFILE specifies the target file for the output. By default, the PRINT command sends the results to the listing file.

RECORDS Subcommand. RECORDS specifies the total number of lines displayed per case. You can either use slashes alone (see Section 6.8) or specify a RECORDS subcommand.

TABLE Subcommand. TABLE requests a format table showing how the variable information is formatted. NOTABLE is the default.

For example, the following command sends output from a PRINT command to a file other than the listing file, specifying the number of lines and requesting a table describing the format of that file:

```
PRINT OUTFILE=PRINTOUT RECORDS=3 TABLE
 /EMPLOYID DEPT82 SALARY82 /NAME.
```

The OUTFILE subcommand names PRINTOUT as the file on which the values specified will be written. The RECORDS subcommand indicates that each case occupies three lines. EMPLOYID, DEPT82, and SALARY82 print on the first line. The second line contains the values of the variable NAME. The third line is blank, creating a blank line between case listings. TABLE requests a summary table describing the PRINT specifications.

The OUTFILE, RECORDS, and TABLE subcommands are optional and can appear in any order before the first slash that indicates the beginning of the variable list. The output from the PRINT command cannot be longer than 132 characters, even if the external file is defined with a longer record length.

6.13
PRINT EJECT
COMMAND

The PRINT EJECT command instructs SPSS to start a new output page. Optionally, you can specify information to be displayed at the beginning of each new page. The syntax for PRINT EJECT is the same as for the PRINT command. As with PRINT, PRINT EJECT is a transformation and is executed as the data are read, once for each case. Therefore, unless you use PRINT EJECT in a conditional processing structure, such as DO IF—END IF, the requested information is displayed on a separate page for each case.

You can use PRINT EJECT to insert titles and column headings by using the DO IF—END IF structure (see Chapter 3). For example, to display the column headings from Figure 6.11 at the top of each output page, you could specify:

```
DO IF MOD($CASENUM,50) EQ 1.
PRINT EJECT /'   NAME ' 1 'DEPT' 25 'HIRED' 30 '  SALARY' 35.
END IF.
PRINT / NAME DEPT82 *
 MOHIRED 30-31 * '/' YRHIRED *
 SALARY82 35-42 (DOLLAR).
EXECUTE.
```

These commands instruct SPSS to start a new page and display the column headings if the remainder of $CASENUM divided by 50 equals 1 (see Chapter 3 for a discussion of the MOD function). The output is essentially the same as that for the Figure 6.11, except that each page has 50 cases (the default page length is 59 lines), and the headings appear at the top of each page.

6.14
PRINT SPACE
COMMAND

The only function of the PRINT SPACE command is to insert blank lines. PRINT SPACE with no specifications produces one blank line on the listing file. The PRINT SPACE command has two optional specifications: the number of blank lines (the default is 1) and the OUTFILE subcommand, which names the target file for the output from the PRINT SPACE command. There are no variable specifications.

For example, to produce a blank line between the the column headings and the data values in Figure 6.11, specify:

```
DO IF $CASENUM EQ 1.
PRINT EJECT /'   NAME ' 1 'DEPT' 25 'HIRED' 30 '  SALARY' 35.
PRINT SPACE.
END IF.
PRINT / NAME DEPT82 *
 MOHIRED 30-31 * '/' YRHIRED *
 SALARY82 35-42 (DOLLAR).
EXECUTE.
```

6.15
OUTFILE Subcommand

Use the OUTFILE subcommand on a PRINT SPACE command to insert blank lines in the output of a PRINT or WRITE command that is directed to a file other than the listing file. The file named on the OUTFILE subcommand of PRINT SPACE should be the same as that specified on the OUTFILE subcommand of the PRINT or WRITE command. (See the example in Section 6.16.)

6.16
Specifying the Number of Blank Lines

You can use a numeric expression with the PRINT SPACE command to specify the number of blank lines. The numeric expression can simply be an integer or it can be a more complex expression.

For example, suppose you have a variable number of input records for each name and address, but you want to print a fixed number of lines for mailing labels. The goal is to know how many lines you have printed for each address and therefore how many blank records to print. Assuming there is already one blank line between each address in the input file and that you want to print eight lines per label, specify:

```
DATA LIST FILE=ADDRESS /RECORD 1-40 (A).
COMPUTE #LINES=#LINES+1.
PRINT OUTFILE=LABELS /RECORD.
DO IF RECORD EQ ' '.
PRINT SPACE OUTFILE=LABELS 8-#LINES.
COMPUTE #LINES=0.
END IF.
EXECUTE.
```

Variable #LINES is the key to this example. #LINES is intialized to 0 as a scratch variable. Then it is incremented for each record printed. When SPSS encounters a blank line (RECORD EQ ' '), PRINT SPACE prints a number of blank lines equal to 8 minus the number already printed, and #LINES is then reset to 0. The first three mailing labels from file LABELS are shown in Figure 6.16.

Figure 6.16 PRINT SPACE with a variable number of lines

```
Dr. Theodore Thomson, Superintendent
Central Offices
Northfield School District 29
Room 101-B
525 Sunset Ridge Road
Northfield, IL  60093


Dr. Susan J. Lewis, Superintendent
Dolton School District 149
15141 Dorchester Avenue
Dolton, IL  60419



Mr. Larry A. Bannes, Superintendent
Kenilworth School District 38
Room 596
542 Abbotsford Road
Kenilworth, IL  60043
```

6.17
WRITE COMMAND

The WRITE command is basically the same as the PRINT command except that it is designed for writing data to be read by other software rather than by people. The WRITE command operates the same as the PRINT command with the following exceptions:

- Blank columns are not inserted automatically between variables.
- There are no carriage-control characters in the output file.
- The system-missing value is by represented by blanks, not by a period.

• You can write records longer than 132 characters.

• The dictionary formats used are the write formats, not the print formats.

As with the PRINT command, WRITE is a transformation. If it is not followed by a procedure that causes the data to be read, SPSS does nothing. To execute the WRITE command without a subsequent procedure command, use the EXECUTE command (see Chapter 5).

6.18
Variable Specifications

The only required specification on the WRITE command is a variable list. Use a slash to separate the variable list from the command keyword WRITE, as in:

```
WRITE /MOHIRED YRHIRED DEPT82 SALARY82 NAME.
EXECUTE.
```

By default, WRITE uses the dictionary formats for all variables. Optionally, you can specify formats for some or all variables. The syntax for specifying formats is the same as for the PRINT command (see Section 6.7). The WRITE command has some additional formats not available with PRINT. For a complete list of WRITE formats, see the *SPSS Reference Guide*.

You can also specify multiple records, column locations, and literal strings. The syntax is the same as for the PRINT command (see Sections 6.8 through 6.10).

If you are writing data, you should consider taking advantage of all of these features of the WRITE command. Within the same machine environment, some data types are more convenient than others. If you are going across machines, you should take into account that some data types cannot be read on another machine.

If long records are less convenient than multiple records per case with shorter record lengths, you can take advantage of the ability to write out a case identifier and to insert a literal as a record identification number. The software at the other end might then be able to check for missing record numbers should something happen to the data in transit.

6.19
OUTFILE, RECORD, and TABLE Subcommands

Three subcommands are available on the WRITE subcommand. They should appear before the slash indicating the beginning of the variable list.

OUTFILE Subcommand. The OUTFILE subcommand specifies the target file for the output from the WRITE command. By default, the WRITE command sends the results to the listing file, which is usually *not* what you want (see Chapter 4).

The RECORDS Subcommand. The RECORDS subcommand specifies the total number of records written for each case. You can use RECORDS instead of using slashes to indicate the number of records.

TABLE Subcommand. TABLE requests a format table on the listing file showing how the variable information is formatted. NOTABLE is the default.

For example, the command

```
WRITE OUTFILE=NEWHUB TABLE
 /EMPLOYID '1' MOHIRED YRHIRED SEX AGE JOBCAT NAME
 /EMPLOYID '2' DEPT79 TO DEPT82 SALARY79 TO SALARY82 *
HOURLY82(F5.2).
EXECUTE.
```

writes the specified variables to the file NEWHUB, and the TABLE subcommand produces the output in Figure 6.19. There are two records for each case, and each record includes both a case identifier variable, EMPLOYID, and a literal string indicating the record number. The dictionary write formats are used for the variables, except for HOURLY82, which has a specified format of F5.2 that overrides the dictionary format.

Figure 6.19 Format table with WRITE command

```
The table for the above 'Write' command is:

Variable    Rec   Start      End       Format

EMPLOYID     1       1         5        F5.0
'1'          1       6         6
MOHIRED      1       7         8        F2.0
YRHIRED      1       9        10        F2.0
SEX          1      11        11        F1.0
AGE          1      12        13        F2.0
JOBCAT       1      14        14        F1.0
NAME         1      15        38        A24
EMPLOYID     2       1         5        F5.0
'2'          2       6         6
DEPT79       2       7         7        F1.0
DEPT80       2       8         8        F1.0
DEPT81       2       9         9        F1.0
DEPT82       2      10        10        F1.0
SALARY79     2      11        15        F5.0
SALARY80     2      16        20        F5.0
SALARY81     2      21        25        F5.0
SALARY82     2      26        30        F5.0
HOURLY82     2      31        35        F5.2
```

Contents_____

7 Data Tabulation: Procedure FREQUENCIES

Few people would dispute the effects of "rainy days and Mondays" on the body and spirit. It has long been known that more suicides occur on Mondays than other days of the week. Recently an excess of cardiac deaths on Mondays has also been noted (Rabkin et al., 1980). In this chapter we will examine the day of the week on which deaths occurred in the Western Electric Study (see Chapter 4) to see if an excess of deaths occurred on Mondays.

7.1
A FREQUENCY TABLE

A first step in analyzing data on day of death might be to count the number of deaths occurring on each day of the week. Figure 7.1a contains this information.

Figure 7.1a   Frequency of death by day of week

```
GET FILE=ELECTRIC.
FREQUENCIES VARIABLES=DAYOFWK.
```

```
DAYOFWK    DAY OF DEATH


                                              Valid    Cum
    Value Label            Value  Frequency  Percent  Percent  Percent
  SUNDAY                      1       19       7.9     17.3     17.3
  MONDAY                      2       11       4.6     10.0     27.3
  TUESDAY                     3       19       7.9     17.3     44.5
  WEDNSDAY                    4       17       7.1     15.5     60.0
  THURSDAY                    5       15       6.3     13.6     73.6
  FRIDAY                      6       13       5.4     11.8     85.5
  SATURDAY                    7       16       6.7     14.5    100.0
  MISSING                     9      130      54.2    Missing

                           Total     240     100.0    100.0

  Valid cases    110    Missing cases    130
```

Each row of the frequency table describes a particular day of the week. The last row represents cases for which the day of death is not known or that have not died. For the table in Figure 7.1a, there are 110 cases for which day of death is known. The first column *(value label)* gives the name of the day, while the second column contains the *value,* which is the symbol given to the computer to represent the day.

The number of people dying on each day is in the third column *(frequency).* Monday is the least-frequent death day with 11 deaths. These 11 deaths are 4.6% (11/240) of all cases. This *percentage* is in the fourth column. However, of the 240 people, 130 had no day of death. The 11 deaths on Monday are 10.0% of the total deaths for which death days are known (11/110). This *valid percentage* is in the fifth column.

The last column of the table contains the *cumulative percentage.* For a particular day, this percentage is the sum of the valid percentages of that day and all other days that precede it in the table. For example, the cumulative percentage for Tuesday is 44.5, which is the sum of the percentage of deaths that occurred on Sunday, Monday, and Tuesday. It is calculated as

$$\frac{19}{110} + \frac{11}{110} + \frac{19}{110} = \frac{49}{110} = 44.5\%$$

Sometimes it is helpful to look at frequencies for a selected subset of cases. Figure 7.1b is a frequency table of day of death for cases who experienced sudden coronary death (FIRSTCHD=2). This is a particularly interesting category since it is thought that sudden death may be related to stressful events such as return to the work environment. In Figure 7.1b there does not appear to be a clustering of deaths on any particular day. Sunday has 22.2% of the deaths, while Thursday has 8.3%. Since the number of sudden deaths in the table is small, the magnitude of the observed fluctuations is not very impressive.

Figure 7.1b Frequency of sudden cardiac death by day of the week

```
GET FILE=ELECTRIC.
SELECT IF (FIRSTCHD EQ 2).
FREQUENCIES VARIABLES=DAYOFWK.
```

```
DAYOFWK    DAY OF DEATH


                                                      Valid      Cum
         Value Label            Value  Frequency  Percent  Percent  Percent
SUNDAY                            1         8      22.2     22.2     22.2
MONDAY                            2         4      11.1     11.1     33.3
TUESDAY                           3         4      11.1     11.1     44.4
WEDNSDAY                          4         7      19.4     19.4     63.9
THURSDAY                          5         3       8.3      8.3     72.2
FRIDAY                            6         6      16.7     16.7     88.9
SATURDAY                          7         4      11.1     11.1    100.0
                                         ----    -----    -----
                        Total             36     100.0    100.0

Valid cases      36     Missing cases      0
```

7.2
Visual Displays

While the numbers in the frequency table can be studied and compared, it is often useful to present results in a visually interpretable form. Figure 7.2a is a pie chart of the data displayed in Figure 7.1a. Each slice represents a day of the week. The size of the slice depends on the frequency of death for that day. Monday is represented by 10.0% of the pie chart since 10.0% of the deaths for which the day is known occurred on Monday.

Figure 7.2a Frequency of death by day of the week
(Pie chart from SPSS Graphics)

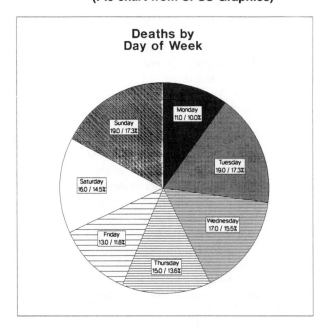

Another way to represent the data is with a bar chart, as shown in Figure 7.2b. There is a bar for each day, and the length of the bar is proportional to the number of deaths observed on that day. At the end of each bar is the number of cases occurring on that day.

Figure 7.2b   Frequency of death by day of the week

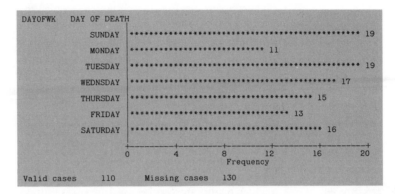

Only values that actually occur in the data are represented in the bar chart from procedure FREQUENCIES. For example, if no deaths took place on Thursday, no space would be left for Thursday and the bar for Wednesday would be followed by the one for Friday. If you chart the number of cars per family, the bar describing 6 cars may be next to the one for 25 cars if no family has 7 to 24 cars. Therefore, you should pay attention to where categories with no cases may occur.

Although the basic information presented by frequency tables, pie charts, and bar charts is the same, the visual displays enliven the data. Differences among the days of the week are apparent at a glance, eliminating the need to pore over columns of numbers.

7.3
What Day?

Although the number of sudden cardiac deaths is small in this study, the data in Figure 7.1b indicate that the number of deaths on Mondays is not particularly large. In fact, Sunday has the most deaths, slightly over 22%. A recent study of over a thousand sudden cardiac deaths in Rochester, Minnesota, also found a slightly increased incidence of death on weekends for men (Beard et al., 1982). The authors speculate that for men, this might mean "the home environment is more stressful than the work environment." But you should be wary of explanations that are not directly supported by data. It is only too easy to find a clever explanation for any statistical finding. (See Chapter 17 for further analysis of these data.)

7.4
Histograms

A frequency table or bar chart of all values for a variable is a convenient way of summarizing a variable that has a relatively small number of distinct values. Variables such as sex, country, and astrological sign are necessarily limited in the number of values they can have. For variables that can take on many different values, such as income to the penny or weight in ounces, a tally of the cases with each observed value may not be very informative. In the worst situation, when all cases have different values, a frequency table is little more than an ordered list of those values.

Variables that have many values can be summarized by grouping the values of the variables into intervals and counting the number of cases with values within each interval. For example, income can be grouped into $5,000 intervals such as 0–4999, 5000–9999, 10000–14999, and so forth, and the number of observations in each group can be tabulated. Such grouping should be done using SPSS during the actual analysis of the data. As indicated in Chapter 2, the values for variables should be entered into the data file in their original, ungrouped form.

A histogram is a convenient way to display the distribution of such grouped values. Consider Figure 7.4, which is a histogram for body weight in pounds of the sample of 240 men from the Western Electric Study. The first column indicates the number of cases with values within the interval, while the second column gives the midpoint, or middle value, for the interval. Each row of asterisks represents the number of cases with values in the interval. For example, the second row of the histogram has 10 asterisks, which represent 10 men who weighed between 130 and 140 pounds in 1958. The number of cases represented by each asterisk depends on the size of the sample and the maximum number of cases falling into an interval. For each histogram, the number of cases represented by an asterisk is printed on the top of the figure. Intervals that have no observations are included in the histogram but no asterisks are printed. This differs from a bar chart, which does not leave space for the empty categories.

A histogram can be used in any situation in which it is reasonable to group adjacent values. Histograms should not be used to display variables in which there is no underlying order to the values. For example, if 100 different religions are arbitrarily assigned codes of 1 to 100, grouping values into intervals is meaningless. Either a bar chart or a histogram in which each interval corresponds to a single value should be used to display such data.

Figure 7.4   A histogram of body weight

```
GET FILE=ELECTRIC.
FREQUENCIES VARIABLES=WT58
 /HISTOGRAM MIN(120) MAX(280) INCREMENT(10).
```

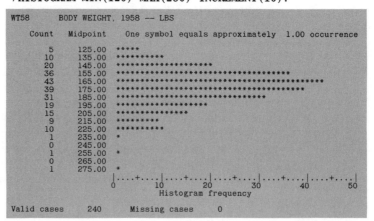

7.5
Screening Data

Frequency tables, bar charts, and histograms can serve purposes other than summarizing data. Unexpected codes in the tables may indicate errors in data entry or coding. Cases with death days coded as 0 or 8 are in error if the numbers 1 through 7 represent the days of the week and 9 stands for unknown. Since errors in the data should be eliminated as soon as possible, it is a good idea to run frequency tables as the first step in analyzing data.

Frequency tables and visual displays can also help you identify cases with values that are unusual but possibly correct. For example, a tally of the number of cars in families may show a family with 25 cars. Although such a value is possible, especially if the survey did not specify cars in working condition, it raises suspicion and should be examined to ensure that it is really correct.

Incorrect data values distort the results of statistical analyses, and correct but unusual values may require special treatment. In either case, early identification is valuable.

7.6 RUNNING PROCEDURE FREQUENCIES

Procedure FREQUENCIES produces frequency tables, histograms, and bar charts for numeric variables and frequency tables and bar charts for string variables. Additionally, you can obtain percentiles and univariate summary statistics. (See Chapter 8 for examples of percentiles and summary statistics produced with FREQUENCIES.) The EXAMINE procedure (see Chapter 9) provides additional facilities for describing and displaying variables.

The only required subcommand on FREQUENCIES is the VARIABLES subcommand, which specifies the variables to be analyzed. Subcommands can be named in any order and are separated from each other by a slash. With the exception of PERCENTILES and NTILES, each subcommand can be used only once per FREQUENCIES command.

7.7 VARIABLES Subcommand

The VARIABLES subcommand names the variables to be analyzed. FREQUENCIES sets up one cell for each unique value encountered in the data. For example, the following command produced the output in Figure 7.1a:

```
FREQUENCIES   VARIABLES=DAYOFWK.
```

The variable and value labels are printed, followed by the value and the number of cases that have the value. The percentage is based on all the observations, and the valid and cumulative percentages are based on those cases that have valid values. The number of valid and missing observations is also provided. FREQUENCIES tabulates any type of variable, including numeric variables with decimal positions and string variables.

You can use the keyword ALL to name all the variables on the active system file or the keyword TO to refer to a set of consecutive variables on the file.

Optionally, you can specify a range of values in parentheses after each variable or variable list. The command

```
FREQUENCIES VARIABLES=DAYOFWK(2,6).
```

only includes cases with values of 2 through 6 in the frequency table for DAYOFWK. If you specify a range, you must do so for every variable listed on the VARIABLES subcommand. The command

```
FREQUENCIES VARIABLES=THING1 THING2 (1,4).
```

uses the value range 1 through 4 for both THING1 and THING2. The command

```
FREQUENCIES VARIABLES=THING1(1,4) THING2.
```

generates an error message and the command is not executed.

7.8 FORMAT Subcommand

The FORMAT subcommand allows you to control the formatting of tables and the order in which values are sorted within the table, suppress tables, produce an index of tables, and write the FREQUENCIES display to another file. FORMAT applies to all variables named on the VARIABLES subcommand.

Specify as many formatting options as desired on the FORMAT subcommand. For example,

```
FREQUENCIES  VARIABLES=POLVIEWS PRESTIGE
 /FORMAT=ONEPAGE DVALUE LIMIT(25).
```

specifies conditional condensed formatting of the tables (keyword ONEPAGE) with values sorted in descending order (keyword DVALUE) and will not display frequency tables for variables with more than 25 categories (keyword LIMIT).

7.9
Table Formats

The following keywords on the FORMAT subcommand control the formatting of tables:

NOLABELS *Supress value labels.* By default, FREQUENCIES displays value labels defined by the VALUE LABELS commands.

DOUBLE *Double-space frequency tables.*

NEWPAGE *Begin each table on a new page.* By default, FREQUENCIES displays as many tables on a page as fit.

CONDENSE *Use condensed format.* This format displays frequency counts in three columns. It does not display value labels and percentages for all cases, and it rounds valid and cumulative percentages to integers.

ONEPAGE *Use conditional condensed format.* Keyword ONEPAGE uses the condensed format for tables that would require more than one page with the default format. All other tables are displayed in default format. If you specify both CONDENSE and ONEPAGE, all tables are displayed in condensed format.

7.10
Order of Values

By default, frequency tables are displayed in ascending order of values. You can override this order with one of three sorting options on the FORMAT subcommand:

AFREQ *Sort categories in ascending order of frequency.*

DFREQ *Sort categories in descending order of frequency.*

DVALUE *Sort categories in descending order of values.*

7.11
Suppressing Tables

You might use FREQUENCIES to obtain univariate statistics not available in other procedures or to display histograms or bar charts, and thus may not be interested in the frequency tables themselves. Or you might want to suppress tables for variables with a large number of values. Two options are available for suppressing tables:

LIMIT(n) *Do not display tables with more categories than the specified value.*

NOTABLE *Suppress all frequency tables.*

If you specify both NOTABLE and LIMIT, NOTABLE overrides LIMIT and no tables are displayed.

7.12
Index of Tables

To obtain both a positional index of frequency tables and an index arranged alphabetically by variable name, use the INDEX keyword on the FORMAT subcommand.

INDEX *Index of tables.*

**7.13
Bar Charts and
Histograms**

You can request bar charts or histograms with the FREQUENCIES command. Use the BARCHART subcommand to produce bar charts (Section 7.2) for all variables named on the VARIABLES subcommand and the HISTOGRAM subcommand to produce histograms (Section 7.4) for all variables. Use the HBAR subcommand to produce bar charts for variables that will fit on one page and histograms for other variables. You can specify only one of these three subcommands on each FREQUENCIES command. If you specify more than one, FREQUENCIES assumes HBAR.

**7.14
BARCHART Subcommand**

No specifications are required on the BARCHART subcommand. In the default bar chart format, all tabulated values are plotted, and the horizontal axis is scaled in frequencies. The scale is determined by the frequency count of the largest single category plotted. For example, the following commands produced Figure 7.2b:

```
FREQUENCIES VARIABLES=DAYOFWK
 /BARCHART.
```

Available formatting options are:

MIN(n) *Lower bound.* Values below the specified minimum are not plotted.

MAX(n) *Upper bound.* Values above the specified maximum are not plotted.

PERCENT(n) *Horizontal axis scaled in percentages.* The *n* specifies the preferred maximum and is not required. If you do not specify an *n* or your *n* is too small, FREQUENCIES chooses 5, 10, 25, 50 or 100, depending on the percentage for the largest category.

FREQ(n) *Horizontal axis scaled in frequencies.* While FREQ is the default scaling method, you can use this keyword to specify a maximum frequency *(n)* for the scale. If you do not specify an *n* or your *n* is too small, FREQUENCIES chooses 10, 20, 50, 100, 200, 500, 1000, 2000, and so forth, depending on the frequency count for the largest category.

You can enter optional specifications in any order, as in

```
FREQUENCIES  VARIABLES=SIBS
 /BARCHART=PERCENT MAX(10).
```

which requests a bar chart for SIBS with values through 10 plotted and the horizontal axis scaled in percentages.

**7.15
HISTOGRAM Subcommand**

No specifications are required on the HISTOGRAM subcommand. In the default histogram format, all tabulated values are included, and the horizontal axis is scaled in frequencies. The scale is determined by the frequency count of the largest category plotted. The number of intervals plotted is 21 (or fewer if the range of values is less than 21).

You can use all of the formatting options available with BARCHART (MIN, MAX, PERCENT, and FREQ) on the HISTOGRAM subcommand. In addition, you can specify the interval width and superimpose a normal curve on the histogram:

INCREMENT(n) *Interval width.* By default, values are collected into 21 intervals for plotting. You can override the default by specifying the actual interval width. For example, if a variable ranges from 1 to 100 and you specify INCREMENT(2), the width of each interval is 2, producing 50 intervals.

NORMAL *Superimpose the normal curve.* The normal curve is based on all valid values for the variable and includes values excluded by MIN and MAX. The default is NONORMAL.

You can enter the optional specifications in any order. For example, the following commands produced Figure 7.4:

```
FREQUENCIES VARIABLES=WT58
/HISTOGRAM MIN(120) MAX(280) INCREMENT(10).
```

7.16
HBAR Subcommand

The HBAR subcommand produces either bar charts or histograms, depending upon the number of values encountered in the data. If a bar chart for a variable fits on a page, HBAR produces a bar chart; otherwise, it produces a histogram. All specifications for HISTOGRAM and BARCHART also work with HBAR.

7.17
Percentiles and Ntiles

You can use either the PERCENTILES or NTILES subcommands to display percentiles for all variables specified on the VARIABLES subcommand. If two or more PERCENTILES and NTILES subcommands are specified, FREQUENCIES displays one table with the values for all requested percentiles.

If a requested percentile cannot be calculated, SPSS displays a period (.) as the value associated with that percentile.

7.18
PERCENTILES Subcommand

Percentiles are the values below which a given percentage of cases fall. Use the PERCENTILES subcommand followed by a list of percentiles between 0 and 100 to display the values for each percentile. For example, to request the values for percentiles 10, 25, 33.3, 66.7, and 75 for variable PRESTIGE, specify:

```
FREQUENCIES VARIABLES=PRESTIGE
/PERCENTILES=10 25 33.3 66.7 75.
```

7.19
NTILES Subcommand

*N*tiles are the values that divide the sample into groups of equal numbers of cases. To display the values for each *n*tile, use the NTILES subcommand followed by an integer value specifying the number of subgroups. For example, to request quartiles for PRESTIGE, specify:

```
FREQUENCIES VARIABLES=PRESTIGE /NTILES=4.
```

SPSS displays one less percentile than the number specified on the NTILES subcommand, since, for example, you only need two values to divide a group into three parts.

7.20
STATISTICS Subcommand

The STATISTICS subcommand specifies univariate statistics for all variables named on the VARIABLES subcommand.

MEAN	*Mean.* The arithmetic average.
SEMEAN	*Standard error of the mean.* A measure of variability of the sample mean.
MEDIAN	*Median.* The median is defined as the value below which half the cases fall. If there is an even number of cases, the median is the average of the (nth/2) and (nth/2+1) cases when the cases are sorted in ascending order. The median is not available if you specify AFREQ or DFREQ on the FORMAT subcommand.
MODE	*Mode.* The most frequently occurring value. If several values are tied for the highest frequency, only the smallest value is displayed.
STDDEV	*Standard deviation.* A measure of how much observations vary from the mean, expressed in the same units as the data.

VARIANCE *Variance.* The same as standard deviation, but expressed in squared units.

SKEWNESS *Skewness.* (See Chapter 8.)

SESKEW *Standard error of the skewness statistic.*

KURTOSIS *Kurtosis.* (See Chapter 8.)

SEKURT *Standard error of the kurtosis statistic.*

RANGE *Range.* The difference between the largest and smallest values.

MINIMUM *Minimum.*

MAXIMUM *Maximum.*

SUM *Sum.*

DEFAULT *Mean, standard deviation, minimum, and maximum.* You can use DE-FAULT jointly with other statistics.

ALL *All available statistics.*

NONE *No statistics.*

You can specify as many keywords as you wish on the STATISTICS subcommand. For example,

```
FREQUENCIES  VARIABLES=PRESTIGE POLVIEWS
 /STATISTICS=MEDIAN DEFAULT.
```

displays the median and the default statistics (the mean, standard deviation, minimum, and maximum). If you use the STATISTICS subcommand with no specifications, the default statistics are displayed.

7.21
MISSING Subcommand

FREQUENCIES recognizes three types of missing values: user-missing, system-missing, and, if you specify a value range for variables on the VARIABLES subcommand, out-of-range values. Both user- and system-missing values are included in frequency tables. They are labeled as missing and are not included in the valid and cumulative percentages. Missing values are not used in the calculation of descriptive statistics, nor do they appear in bar charts and histograms.

To treat user-missing values as valid values, use the MISSING subcommand, which has one specification, INCLUDE. For example,

```
MISSING VALUES  SATFAM TO HAPPY(8,9)
FREQUENCIES  VARIABLES=SATFAM HAPPY (0,9)
 /BARCHART
 /MISSING=INCLUDE.
```

includes values 8 and 9 (which were previously defined as missing with the MISSING VALUES command) in the bar charts.

7.22
Annotated Example

The following commands produce the output in Figure 7.4:

```
GET FILE=ELECTRIC.
FREQUENCIES VARIABLES=WT58
 /FORMAT=NOTABLE
 /HISTOGRAM MIN(120) MAX(280) INCREMENT(10).
```

- The GET command specifies the SPSS file (ELECTRIC) to be read.
- The FREQUENCIES command requests frequencies for the variable WT58.
- The FORMAT subcommand suppresses the frequency table.
- The HISTOGRAM subcommand requests a histogram with a lower boundary value of 120 and an upper boundary value of 280, grouped in interval widths of 10.

Contents_____

8 Descriptive Statistics: Procedure DESCRIPTIVES

Survey data that rely on voluntary information are subject to many sources of error. People deliberately distort the truth, inadvertently fail to recall events correctly, or refuse to participate. Refusals influence survey results by failing to provide information about a particular type of person—one who refuses to answer surveys at all or avoids certain types of questions. For example, if college graduates tend to be unwilling to answer polls, results of surveys will be biased.

One possible way to examine the veracity of responses is to compare them to official records. Systematic differences between the two sources jeopardize the usefulness of the survey. Unfortunately, for many sensitive questions such as illicit drug use, abortion history, or even income, official records are usually unavailable.

Wyner (1980) examined the differences between the true and self-reported numbers of arrests obtained from 79 former heroin addicts enrolled in the Vera Institute of Justice Supported Employment Experiment. As part of their regular quarterly interviews, participants were asked about their arrest histories in New York City. The self-reported value was compared to arrest record data coded from New York City Police Department arrest sheets. The goal of the study was not only to quantify the extent of error but also to identify factors related to inaccurate responses.

8.1
EXAMINING THE DATA

Figure 8.1a shows histograms for the three variables—true number of arrests, reported arrests, and the discrepancy between the two. From a histogram it is possible to see the *shape* of the distribution, that is, how likely the different values are, how much spread or *variability* there is among the values, and where typical values are concentrated. Such characteristics are important because of the direct insight they provide into the data and because many statistical procedures are based on assumptions about the underlying distributions of variables.

Figure 8.1a Reported and true arrests

```
FREQUENCIES VARIABLES=ACTUAL SELF
 /FORMAT=NOTABLE /HISTOGRAM MIN(0) INCREMENT(2).
FREQUENCIES VARIABLES=ERRORS
 /FORMAT=NOTABLE /HISTOGRAM INCREMENT(2).
```

```
ACTUAL    ACTUAL NUMBER OF ARRESTS

   Count  Midpoint   One symbol equals approximately   .40 occurrences

       3     1.00   ********
      15     3.00   *************************************
       9     5.00   ***********************
       8     7.00   *******************
      10     9.00   *************************
       9    11.00   ***********************
       7    13.00   ******************
       6    15.00   ***************
       3    17.00   ********
       3    19.00   ********
       3    21.00   ********
       1    23.00   ***
       0    25.00
       1    27.00   ***
       1    29.00   ***
                    I....+....I....+....I....+....I....+....I....+....I
                    0         4         8        12        16        20
                                 Histogram frequency

Valid cases    79    Missing cases    0
```

- -

```
SELF      SELF-REPORTED ARRESTS

   Count  Midpoint   One symbol equals approximately   .40 occurrences

       7     1.00   ******************
       9     3.00   ************************
      13     5.00   **********************************
      11     7.00   *****************************
      11     9.00   *****************************
       6    11.00   ****************
       2    13.00   *****
       5    15.00   *************
       2    17.00   *****
       1    19.00   ***
      10    21.00   *************************
       1    23.00   ***
       1    25.00   ***
                    I....+....I....+....I....+....I....+....I....+....I
                    0         4         8        12        16        20
                                 Histogram frequency

Valid cases    79    Missing cases    0
```

- -

```
ERRORS    REPORTED ARRESTS MINUS ACTUAL ARRESTS

   Count  Midpoint   One symbol equals approximately   .40 occurrences

       2   -13.00   *****
       0   -11.00
       2    -9.00   *****
       5    -7.00   *************
       6    -5.00   ***************
       7    -3.00   *****************
      16    -1.00   *******************************************
      15     1.00   ***************************************
      12     3.00   ******************************
       7     5.00   ******************
       1     7.00   ***
       2     9.00   *****
       2    11.00   *****
       1    13.00   ***
       1    15.00   ***
                    I....+....I....+....I....+....I....+....I....+....I
                    0         4         8        12        16        20
                                 Histogram frequency

Valid cases    79    Missing cases    0
```

The distributions of the reported and true number of arrests have a somewhat similar shape. Neither distribution has an obvious central value, although the self-reported values have the tallest peak at 4 to 5 arrests, while the actual number of arrests has its peak at 2 to 3 arrests. The distribution of self-reported arrests also has a peak at 20 to 21 arrests. The peaks corresponding to intervals which contain 5, 15, and 20 arrests arouse the suspicion that people may be more likely to report their arrest records as round numbers. Examination of the true number of arrests shows no corresponding peaks at multiples of five.

The distribution of the differences between reported and true number of arrests is not as irregularly shaped as the two distributions from which it is derived. It has two adjacent peaks with midpoint values of −1 and +1. Most cases cluster around the peak values, and cases far from these values are infrequent. Figure 8.1b is a condensed frequency table for the response errors (the adjusted and cumulative percentages are rounded to the nearest integer). Almost 47% of the sample (37 cases) reported their arrest record to within two arrests of the true value. Only 22% (17 cases) misrepresented their records by more than 5 arrests. Underreporting is somewhat more likely than exaggeration, with 39% of the cases overestimating and 48% of the cases underestimating.

Figure 8.1b   Error in reported arrests

FREQUENCIES VARIABLES=ERRORS /FORMAT=CONDENSE.

```
ERRORS     REPORTED ARRESTS MINUS ACTUAL ARRESTS


                         Cum                        Cum                        Cum
        Value   Freq Pct Pct    Value   Freq Pct Pct    Value   Freq Pct Pct
         -14      2   3   3       -2      6   8  35        7      1   1  92
          -9      2   3   5       -1     10  13  48        8      1   1  94
          -8      3   4   9        0     10  13  61        9      1   1  95
          -7      2   3  11        1      5   6  67       10      1   1  96
          -6      1   1  13        2      6   8  75       11      1   1  97
          -5      5   6  19        3      6   8  82       12      1   1  99
          -4      3   4  23        4      4   5  87       15      1   1 100
          -3      4   5  28        5      3   4  91

Valid cases      79      Missing cases     0
```

8.2
Percentile Values

Percentiles are values above and below which certain percentages of the cases fall. For example, 95% of the cases have values less than or equal to the 95th percentile. From the cumulative percentage column in the frequency table in Figure 8.1b, the value for the 95th percentile is 9.

Figure 8.2 contains some commonly used percentiles for the distributions in Figure 8.1a. The three percentiles (25%, 50%, and 75%) divide the observed distributions into approximately four equal parts. The actual and self-reported number of arrests have the same 25th percentile, the value 4. This means that about 75% of the values are greater than or equal to 4, and 25% less than 4.

Figure 8.2   Percentiles for reported and actual arrests and errors

FREQUENCIES VARIABLES=ACTUAL SELF ERRORS
 /FORMAT=NOTABLE /PERCENTILE=25 50 75.

```
ACTUAL     ACTUAL NUMBER OF ARRESTS

Percentile    Value     Percentile    Value     Percentile    Value
   25.00      4.000        50.00      8.000        75.00      13.000

Valid cases      79      Missing cases     0

- - - - - - - - - - - - - - - - - - - - - - - - - - - - - -

SELF      SELF-REPORTED ARRESTS

Percentile    Value     Percentile    Value     Percentile    Value
   25.00      4.000        50.00      7.000        75.00      14.000

Valid cases      79      Missing cases     0

- - - - - - - - - - - - - - - - - - - - - - - - - - - - - -

ERRORS     REPORTED ARRESTS MINUS ACTUAL ARRESTS

Percentile    Value     Percentile    Value     Percentile    Value
   25.00     -3.000        50.00      .000         75.00      3.000

Valid cases      79      Missing cases     0
```

8.3
SUMMARIZING THE DATA

Although frequency tables and bar charts are useful for summarizing and displaying data (see Chapter 7), further condensation and description is often desirable. A variety of summary measures that convey information about the data in single numbers can be computed. The choice of summary measure, or *statistic*, as it is often called, depends upon characteristics of the data as well as of the statistic. One important characteristic of the data that must be considered is the *level of measurement* of each variable being studied.

8.4
Levels of Measurement

Measurement is the assignment of numbers or codes to observations. Levels of measurement are distinguished by ordering and distance properties. A computer does not know what measurement underlies the values it is given. You must determine the level of measurement of your data and apply appropriate statistical techniques.

The traditional classification of levels of measurement into nominal, ordinal, interval, and ratio scales was developed by S. S. Stevens (1946). This remains the basic typology and is the one used throughout this manual. Variations exist, however, and issues concerning the statistical effect of ignoring levels of measurement have been debated (see, for example, Borgatta & Bohrnstedt, 1980).

8.5
Nominal Measurement

The nominal level of measurement is the "lowest" in the typology because no assumptions are made about relations between values. Each value defines a distinct category and serves merely as a label or name (hence, "nominal" level) for the category. For instance, the birthplace of an individual is a nominal variable. For most purposes, there is no inherent ordering among cities or towns. Although cities can be ordered according to size, density, or air pollution, a city thought of as "place of birth" is a concept that is normally not tied to any order. When numeric values are attached to nominal categories, they are merely identifiers. None of the properties of numbers such as relative size, addition, or multiplication, can be applied to these numerically coded categories. Therefore, statistics that assume ordering or meaningful numerical distances between the values do not ordinarily give useful information about nominal variables.

8.6
Ordinal Measurement

When it is possible to rank or order all categories according to some criterion, the ordinal level of measurement is achieved. For instance, classifying employees into clerical, supervisory, and managerial categories is an ordering according to responsibilities or skills. Each category has a position lower or higher than another category. Furthermore, knowing that supervisory is higher than clerical and that managerial is higher than supervisory automatically means that managerial is higher than clerical. However, nothing is known about how much higher; no distance is measured. Ordering is the sole mathematical property applicable to ordinal measurements, and the use of numeric values does not imply that any other property of numbers is applicable.

8.7
Interval Measurement

In addition to order, interval measurements have the property of meaningful distance between values. A thermometer, for example, measures temperature in degrees which are the same size at any point on the scale. The difference between 20°C and 21°C is the same as the difference between 5°C and 6°C. However, an interval scale does not have an inherently determined zero point. In the familiar Celsius and Fahrenheit systems, 0° is determined by an agreed-upon definition, not by the absence of heat. Consequently, interval-level measurement allows us to study differences between items but not their proportionate magnitudes. For example, it is incorrect to say that 80°F is twice as hot as 40°F.

8.8
Ratio Measurement

Ratio measurements have all the ordering and distance properties of an interval scale. In addition, a zero point can be meaningfully designated. In measuring physical distances between objects using feet or meters, a zero distance is naturally defined as the absence of any distance. The existence of a zero point means that ratio comparisons can be made. For example, it is quite meaningful to say that a 6-foot-tall adult is twice as tall as a 3-foot-tall child or that a 500-meter race is five times as long as a 100-meter race.

Because ratio measurements satisfy all the properties of the real number system, any mathematical manipulations appropriate for real numbers can be applied to ratio measures. However, the existence of a zero point is seldom critical for statistical analyses.

8.9
Summary Statistics

Figure 8.9 contains a variety of summary statistics that are useful in describing the distributions of reported arrests, true number of arrests, and the discrepancy. The statistics can be grouped into three categories according to what they quantify: central tendency, dispersion, and shape.

Figure 8.9   Statistics describing arrest data

```
FREQUENCIES VARIABLES=ACTUAL SELF ERRORS
 /FORMAT=NOTABLE /STATISTICS=ALL.
```

```
ACTUAL     ACTUAL NUMBER OF ARRESTS


Mean           9.253    Std err        .703    Median         8.000
Mode           3.000    Std dev       6.248    Variance      39.038
Kurtosis        .597    S E Kurt       .535    Skewness        .908
S E Skew        .271    Range       28.000     Minimum        1.000
Maximum       29.000    Sum         731.000


Valid cases      79     Missing cases     0

- - - - - - - - - - - - - - - - - - - - - - - - - - - - - - -

SELF       SELF-REPORTED ARRESTS


Mean           8.962    Std err        .727    Median         7.000
Mode           5.000    Std dev       6.458    Variance      41.704
Kurtosis       -.485    S E Kurt       .535    Skewness        .750
S E Skew        .271    Range       25.000     Minimum         .000
Maximum       25.000    Sum         708.000


Valid cases      79     Missing cases     0

- - - - - - - - - - - - - - - - - - - - - - - - - - - - - - -

ERRORS     REPORTED ARRESTS MINUS ACTUAL ARRESTS


Mean           -.291    Std err        .587    Median          .000
Mode          -1.000    Std dev       5.216    Variance      27.209
Kurtosis       1.102    S E Kurt       .535    Skewness        .125
S E Skew        .271    Range       29.000     Minimum      -14.000
Maximum       15.000    Sum         -23.000


Valid cases      79     Missing cases     0
```

8.10
Measures of Central Tendency

The mean, median, and mode are frequently used to describe the location of a distribution. The *mode* is the most frequently occurring value (or values). For the true number of arrests, the mode is 3 (see Figure 8.9); for the self-reported values, it is 5. The distribution of the difference between the true and self-reported values is multimodal. That is, it has more than one mode since the values −1 and 0 occur with equal frequency. SPSS, however, displays only one of the modes, as shown in Figure 8.9. The mode can be used for data measured at any level. It is usually not the preferred measure for interval and ordinal data since it ignores much of the available information.

The *median* is the value above and below which one half of the observations fall. For example, if there are 79 observations the median is the 40th largest observation. When there is an even number of observations, no unique center value exists, so the mean of the two middle observations is usually taken as the median value. For the arrest data, the median is 0 for the differences, 8 for the true arrests, and 7 for reported arrests. For ordinal data the median is usually a good measure of central tendency since it uses the ranking information. The median should not be used for nominal data since ranking of the observations is not possible.

The *mean*, also called the arithmetic average, is the sum of the values of all observations divided by the number of observations. Thus

$$\bar{X} = \sum_{i=1}^{N} \frac{X_i}{N} \qquad\qquad \text{Equation 8.10}$$

where N is the number of cases and X_i is the value of the variable for the ith case. Since the mean utilizes the distance between observations, the measurements should be interval or ratio. Mean race, religion, and auto color are meaningless. For dichotomous variables coded as 0 and 1, the mean has a special interpretation: it is the proportion of cases coded 1 in the data.

The three measures of central tendency need not be the same. For example, the mean number of true arrests is 9.25, the median is 8, and the mode is 3 (see Figure 8.9). The arithmetic mean is greatly influenced by outlying observations, while the median is not. Adding a single case with 400 arrests would increase the mean from 9.25 to 14.1, but it would not affect the median. Therefore, if there are values far removed from the rest of the observations, the median may be a better measure of central tendency than the mean.

For symmetric distributions, the observed mean, median, and mode are usually close in value. For example, the mean of the differences between reported and true arrest values is -0.291, the median is 0, and the modes are -1 and 0. All three measures give similar estimates of central tendency in this case.

8.11
Measures of Dispersion

Two distributions can have the same values for measures of central tendency and yet be very dissimilar in other respects. For example, if the true number of arrests for five cases in two methadone clinics is

CLINIC A: 0, 1, 10, 14, 20
CLINIC B: 8, 8, 9, 10, 10

the mean number of arrests (9) is the same in both. However, even a cursory examination of the data indicates that the two clinics are different. In the second clinic, all cases have fairly comparable arrest records while in the first the records are quite disparate. A quick and useful index of dissimilarity, or dispersion, is the *range*. It is the difference between the *maximum* and *minimum* observed values. For Clinic B the range is 2, while for Clinic A it is 20. Since the range is computed only from the minimum and maximum values, it is sensitive to extremes.

Although the range is a useful index of dispersion, especially for ordinal data, it does not take into account the distribution of observations between the maximum and minimum. A commonly used measure of variation that is based on all observations is the *variance*. For a sample, the variance is computed by summing the squared differences from the mean for all observations and then dividing by one less than the number of observations. In mathematical notation this is

$$S^2 = \sum_{i=1}^{N} \frac{(X_i - \bar{X})^2}{N - 1}$$

Equation 8.11

If all observations are identical—that is, if there is no variation—the variance is 0. The more spread out they are, the greater the variance. For the methadone clinic example above, the sample variance for Clinic A is 73, while for Clinic B it is 1.

The square root of the variance is termed the *standard deviation*. The standard deviation is expressed in the same units of measurement as the observations, while the variance is in units squared. This is an appealing property since it is much clearer to think of variability in terms of the number of arrests instead of the number of arrests squared.

8.12
The Normal Distribution

For many variables, most observations are concentrated near the middle of the distribution. As distance from the central concentration increases, the frequency of observation decreases. Such distributions are often described as "bell-shaped." An example is the *normal* distribution (see Figure 8.12a). A broad range of observed phenomena in nature and in society are approximately normally distributed. For example, the distributions of variables such as height, weight, and blood pressure are approximately normal. The normal distribution is by far the most important theoretical distribution in statistics and serves as a reference point for describing the form of many distributions of sample data.

Figure 8.12a A normal curve

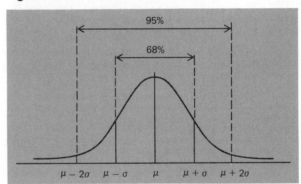

The normal distribution is symmetric: when it is folded in the center, the two sides are identical. Three measures of central tendency—the mean, median, and mode—coincide exactly (see Section 8.10). As shown in Figure 8.12a, 95% of all observations fall within two standard deviations (σ) of the mean (μ), and 68% within one standard deviation. The exact theoretical proportion of cases falling into various regions of the normal curve can be found in tables given in most introductory statistics textbooks.

In SPSS, you can superimpose a normal distribution on a histogram. Consider Figure 8.12b, which contains a histogram of the differences in arrest records. The colons and periods indicate what the distribution of cases would be if the variable had a normal distribution with the same mean and variance. Tests for normality are available in the EXAMINE procedure (see Chapter 9).

Figure 8.12b   Histogram of errors with the normal curve superimposed

```
FREQUENCIES VARIABLES=ERRORS
 /FORMAT=NOTABLE /HISTOGRAM=NORMAL.
```

```
ERRORS    REPORTED ARRESTS MINUS ACTUAL ARRESTS

   Count   Midpoint    One symbol equals approximately   .40 occurrences

      2     -14.5    :****
      0     -13.0    .
      0     -11.5    .
      0     -10.0         .
      5      -8.5    ******:******
      2      -7.0    *****       .
      6      -5.5    *************:*
      3      -4.0    ********
     10      -2.5    *********************.****
     10      -1.0    ********************:**
     15       .5     ********************:****************
      6      2.0     ***************
     10      3.5     ****************:********
      3      5.0     ********        .
      1      6.5     ***
      1      8.0     ***
      2      9.5     ***:*
      1     11.0     *:*
      1     12.5     :**
      0     14.0     .
      1     15.5     ***
                     |....+....|....+....|....+....|....+....|....+....|
                     0        4        8       12       16       20
                                  Histogram frequency

Valid cases     79    Missing cases     0
```

**8.13
Measures of Shape**

A distribution that is not symmetric but has more cases, or more of a "tail," toward one end of the distribution than the other is called *skewed*. If the tail is toward larger values, the distribution is positively skewed or skewed to the right. If the tail is toward smaller values, the distribution is negatively skewed or skewed to the left.

Another characteristic of the form of a distribution is called *kurtosis*, the extent to which, for a given standard deviation, observations cluster around a central point. If cases within a distribution cluster more than those in the normal distribution (that is, the distribution is more peaked), the distribution is called *leptokurtic*. A leptokurtic distribution also tends to have more observations straggling into the extreme tails than does a normal distribution. If cases cluster less than in the normal distribution (that is, it is flatter), the distribution is termed *platykurtic*.

Although examination of a histogram provides some indication of possible skewness and kurtosis, it is often desirable to compute formal indexes that measure these properties. Values for skewness and kurtosis are 0 if the observed distribution is exactly normal. Positive values for skewness indicate a positive skew, while positive values for kurtosis indicate a distribution that is more peaked than normal. For samples from a normal distribution, measures of skewness and kurtosis typically will not be exactly zero but will fluctuate about zero because of sampling variation.

8.14
Standard Scores

It is often desirable to describe the relative position of an observation within a distribution. Knowing that a person achieved a score of 80 in a competitive examination conveys little information about performance. Judgment of performance would depend on whether 80 is the lowest, the median, or the highest score.

One way of describing the location of a case in a distribution is to calculate its *standard score*. This score, sometimes called the Z score, indicates how many standard deviations above or below the mean an observation falls. It is calculated by finding the difference between the value of a particular observation X_i and the mean of the distribution, and then dividing this difference by the standard deviation:

$$Z_i = \frac{X_i - \overline{X}}{S}$$

Equation 8.14

The mean of Z scores is 0, and the standard deviation is 1.

For example, a participant with 5 actual arrests would have a Z score of $(5-9.25)/6.25$, or -0.68. Since the score is negative, the case had fewer arrests than the average for the individuals studied.

Standardization permits comparison of scores from different distributions. For example, an individual with Z scores of -0.68 for actual arrests and 1.01 for the difference between reported and actual arrests had fewer arrests than the average but exaggerated more than the average.

When the distribution of a variable is approximately normal and the mean and variance are known or are estimated from large samples, the Z score of an observation provides more specific information about its location. For example, if actual arrests and response error were normally distributed, 75% of cases would have more arrests than the example individual but only 16% would have exaggerated as much (75% of a standard normal curve lies above a Z score of -0.68, and 16% lies above a score of 1.01).

8.15
Who Lies?

The distribution of the difference between reported and actual arrests indicates that response error exists. Although observing a mean close to zero is comforting, misrepresentation is obvious. What then are the characteristics that influence willingness to be truthful?

Wyner identifies three factors that are related to inaccuracies: the number of arrests before 1960, the number of multiple-charge arrests, and the perceived desirability of being arrested. The first factor is related to a frequently encountered difficulty—the more distant an event in time, the less likely it is to be correctly recalled. The second factor, underreporting of multiple-charge arrests, is probably caused by the general social undesirability of serious arrests. Finally, persons who view arrest records as laudatory are likely to inflate their accomplishments.

8.16
RUNNING
PROCEDURE
DESCRIPTIVES

Procedure DESCRIPTIVES computes univariate summary statistics and standardized variables that are saved on the active system file. Although it computes statistics also available in procedure FREQUENCIES (see Chapter 7), DESCRIPTIVES computes descriptive statistics for continuous variables more efficiently because it does not sort values into a frequencies table.

By default, DESCRIPTIVES calculates the mean, standard deviation, minimum, and maximum. You can request optional statistics and Z-score transformations.

The only required subcommand on DESCRIPTIVES is the VARIABLES subcommand, which specifies the variable list to be analyzed.

8.17
VARIABLES Subcommand

The VARIABLES subcommand names the variable list. You can use keyword TO in the list to refer to consecutive variables in the active system file. The variables must be numeric.

To request the default summary statistics, specify the VARIABLES subcommand and a simple list of variables, as in:

```
DESCRIPTIVES VARIABLES=NTCPRI FOOD RENT.
```

You can also use the keyword ALL to specify all variables in the active system file.

You can specify only one variable list with DESCRIPTIVES, but there is no limit to the number of variables named or implied on one command. Variables named more than once will appear in the output more than once. If there is insufficient space to process all the requested variables, DESCRIPTIVES truncates the variable list.

8.18
Z Scores

The Z-score variable transformation standardizes variables with different observed scales to the same scale. DESCRIPTIVES generates new variables, each with a mean of 0 and a standard deviation of 1, and stores them on the active system file. Z scores can be created by using the SAVE subcommand (Section 8.19) or by naming Z-score variable names on the VARIABLES subcommand (Section 8.20).

8.19
SAVE Subcommand

Use the SAVE subcommand to obtain one Z-score variable for each variable specified on the DESCRIPTIVES variable list. The SAVE subcommand calculates standardized variables and stores them on the active system file. The command

```
DESCRIPTIVES VARIABLES=ALL
 /SAVE.
```

produces new Z-score variables for all the variables on the active system file.

DESCRIPTIVES automatically supplies variable names and labels for the new variables. The new variable name is created by prefixing the letter Z to the first seven characters of the variable name. For example, ZFOOD is the Z-score variable for FOOD. When DESCRIPTIVES creates new Z-score variables, it displays a table containing the original variable name, the new variable name and its label, and the number of cases for which the Z score is computed.

If DESCRIPTIVES cannot use the default naming convention because it would produce duplicate names, it uses an alternative naming convention: first

ZSC001 through ZSC099, then STDZ01 through STDZ09, then ZZZZ01 through ZZZZ09, then ZQZQ01 through ZQZQ09.

DESCRIPTIVES automatically supplies variable labels for the new variables by prefixing *ZSCORE:* to the first 31 characters of the original variable's label. If it uses a name like ZSC001, it prefixes *ZSCORE(varname)* to the first 31 characters of the original variable's label. If the original variable has no label, it uses *ZSCORE(varname)* for the label.

8.20
Creating Z Scores on the VARIABLES Subcommand

If you want *Z* scores for a subset of the variables listed on DESCRIPTIVES, specify the name of the new variable in parentheses following the original variable on the VARIABLES subcommand, and *do not use the SAVE subcommand.* For example,

```
DESCRIPTIVES VARIABLES=NTCSAL NTCPUR (PURCHZ) NTCPRI (PRICEZ).
```

creates *Z*-score variables for NTCPUR and NTCPRI.

If you specify new names on the VARIABLES subcommand *and* use the SAVE subcommand, DESCRIPTIVES creates one new variable for each variable on the VARIABLES subcommand, using the default names for variables that are not explicitly assigned names. For example,

```
DESCRIPTIVES VARIABLES=NTCSAL NTCPUR (PURCHZ) NTCPRI (PRICEZ)
/SAVE.
```

creates PURCHZ and PRICEZ and assigns a default name to the *Z*-score variable for NTCSAL. When you specify the name of the new variable, you can use any acceptable eight-character variable name, including any default variable name, that is not already part of the active system file.

8.21
STATISTICS Subcommand

By default, DESCRIPTIVES displays the mean, standard deviation, minimum, and maximum values. If you use the STATISTICS subcommand and any of its keywords, you can specify alternative statistics. When you specify statistics, DESCRIPTIVES displays *only* those statistics you request.

You can use the keyword ALL to obtain all statistics. When requesting the default statistics plus additional statistics, you can specify DEFAULT to obtain the default statistics without having to name MEAN, STDDEV, MIN, and MAX.

The following keywords can be specified on the STATISTICS subcommand:

MEAN	*Mean.*
SEMEAN	*Standard error of the mean.*
STDDEV	*Standard deviation.*
VARIANCE	*Variance.*
KURTOSIS	*Kurtosis.* Also displays standard error.
SKEWNESS	*Skewness.* Also displays standard error.
RANGE	*Range.*
MIN	*Minimum.*
MAX	*Maximum.*
SUM	*Sum.*
DEFAULT	*Mean, standard deviation, minimum, and maximum.* These are the default statistics if you omit the STATISTICS subcommand.
ALL	*All the statistics available on DESCRIPTIVES.*

8.22
MISSING Subcommand

By default, DESCRIPTIVES deletes cases with missing values on a variable-by-variable basis. A case missing on a variable will not be included in the summary statistics for that variable, but the case *will* be included for variables where it is not missing.

The MISSING subcommand controls missing values, and three keywords are available:

VARIABLE *Exclude missing values on a variable-by-variable basis.* A case is excluded from the computation of statistics for a variable if it has a missing value for that variable. This is the default if you omit the MISSING subcommand.

LISTWISE *Exclude missing values listwise.* Cases missing on any variable named on the VARIABLES subcommand are excluded from the computation of summary statistics for all variables.

INCLUDE *Include user-defined missing values.*

The VARIABLE and LISTWISE keywords cannot be specified together. However, each can be specified with INCLUDE. For example, to include user-missing values in an analysis that excludes missing values listwise, specify

```
DESCRIPTIVES VARIABLES=ALL
  /MISSING=INCLUDE LISTWISE.
```

When you use the keyword VARIABLE or the default missing-value treatment, DESCRIPTIVES reports the number of valid cases for each variable. It always displays the number of cases that would be available if listwise deletion of missing values had been selected.

8.23
FORMAT Subcommand

The FORMAT subcommand controls the formatting options available in DESCRIPTIVES. The following keywords can be specified on it:

LABELS *Display variable labels.* This is the default if you omit the FORMAT subcommand.

NOLABELS *Suppress variable labels.*

INDEX *Display reference indexes.* INDEX displays a positional and an alphabetic reference index following the statistical display. The index shows the page location in the output of the statistics for each variable. The variables are listed by their position in the active file and alphabetically.

NOINDEX *Suppress reference indexes.* This is the default if you omit the FORMAT subcommand.

LINE *Display statistics in line format.* LINE displays statistics on the same line as the variable name. It is the default if you omit the FORMAT subcommand.

SERIAL *Display statistics in serial format.* SERIAL displays statistics below the variable name, permitting greater field widths and more decimal digits for very large or very small numbers. DESCRIPTIVES automatically forces this format if the number of statistics requested does not fit in the column format.

8.24
SORT Subcommand

By default, DESCRIPTIVES lists variables in the order in which they appear on the VARIABLES subcommand. You can use the SORT subcommand to list variables in ascending or descending alphabetical order or by numerical value of any of the statistics available with DESCRIPTIVES.

The following keywords can be specified on the SORT subcommand:

MEAN *Sort by mean.* This is the default.

SEMEAN *Sort by standard error of the mean.*

STDDEV *Sort by standard deviation.*

VARIANCE	*Sort by variance.*
KURTOSIS	*Sort by kurtosis.*
SKEWNESS	*Sort by skewness.*
RANGE	*Sort by range.*
MIN	*Sort by minimum observed value.*
MAX	*Sort by maximum observed value.*
SUM	*Sort by sum.*
NAME	*Sort by variable name.*
(A)	*Sort in ascending order.* This is the default.
(D)	*Sort in descending order.*

If you specify SORT without any of the optional keywords, variables are listed by mean in ascending order.

The SORT subcommand sorts variables by the value of any of the statistics available with DESCRIPTIVES, but only those statistics specified on the STATISTICS subcommand are displayed. If you specify SORT without STATIS-TICS, the default statistics are displayed. The command

```
DESCRIPTIVES VARIABLES=A B C
  /STATISTICS=DEFAULT RANGE
  /SORT=RANGE (D).
```

sorts variables A, B, and C by range in descending order and displays the mean, standard deviation, minimum and maximum values, number of cases, value labels, and the range.

8.25
Annotated Example

Figures 8.25a and 8.25b show the statistics for original variables and new Z-score variables produced by the following DESCRIPTIVES commands:

```
DESCRIPTIVES VARIABLES=ACTUAL SELF ERRORS
  /SAVE.
DESCRIPTIVES VARIABLES=ZACTUAL, ZSELF, ZERRORS
  /STATISTICS=DEFAULT RANGE /FORMAT=NOLABELS.
```

- The first DESCRIPTIVES command produces the default statistics for all three variables.
- The SAVE subcommand saves three new Z-score variables and assigns them the names ZACTUAL, ZSELF, and ZERRORS.
- The second DESCRIPTIVES command requests statistics for the three new Z-score variables.
- The STATISTICS subcommand produces the default statistics plus the range.
- The FORMAT subcommand suppresses the value labels for the new Z-score variables.

Figure 8.25a   Default statistics available with DESCRIPTIVES

```
Number of valid observations (listwise) =        79.00

                                             Valid
Variable     Mean    Std Dev   Minimum   Maximum    N   Label

ACTUAL       9.25     6.25        1        29       79   ACTUAL NUMBER OF ARRESTS
SELF         8.96     6.46        0        25       79   SELF-REPORTED ARRESTS
ERRORS       -.29     5.22     -14.00      15       79   REPORTED ARRESTS MINUS ACTUAL ARRESTS
```

Figure 8.25b   Statistics for new Z-score variables

```
                                                         Valid
Variable     Mean    Std Dev   Range    Minimum   Maximum    N

ZACTUAL       .00      1.00     4.48    -1.32093   3.16050    79
ZSELF         .00      1.00     3.87    -1.38777   2.48349    79
ZERRORS       .00      1.00     5.56    -2.62812   2.93146    79
```

Contents_____

9 Looking First: Procedure EXAMINE

The first step of data analysis should always be a detailed examination of the data. It doesn't matter whether the problem you're solving is simple or complex, whether you're planning to do a t-test or a multivariate repeated measures analysis of variance. First you should take a careful look at the data. In this chapter, we'll consider some methods for exploring data using the SPSS EXAMINE procedure.

9.1 REASONS FOR EXAMINING DATA

There are several important reasons for examining your data carefully before you begin your analysis. Let's start with the simplest.

9.2 Identifying Mistakes

Data must make a hazardous journey before they find final rest in a computer file. First a measurement is made or a response elicited, sometimes with a faulty instrument or by a sleepy experimenter. The result is then recorded, often barely legibly, in a lab notebook, medical chart, or personnel record. Often this information is not actually coded and entered onto a data form until much later. From this form the numbers must yet find their way into their designated slot in the computer file. Then they must be properly introduced to a computer program. Their correct location and missing values must be specified.

Errors can be introduced at any step. Some errors are easy to spot. For example, forgetting to declare a value as missing, using an invalid code, or entering the value 701 for age will be apparent from a frequency table. Other errors, like entering an age of 54 instead of 45, may be difficult, if not impossible, to spot. Unless your first step is to carefully check your data for mistakes, errors may contaminate all of your analyses.

9.3 Exploring the Data

After the commotion of data acquisition, entry, and checking, it's time to actually look at the data—not to search frantically for statistical significance, but to examine the data carefully using simple exploratory techniques. Why bother, you might ask? Why not just begin your analysis?

Data analysis has often been compared to detective work. Before the actual trial of a hypothesis there is much evidence to be gathered and sifted. Based on the clues, the hypothesis itself may be altered, or the methods for testing it may have to be changed. For example, if a display of the distribution of data values reveals a "gap," that is, a range where no values occur, we must ask why. If there are some values far removed from the others, we must also ask why. If the pattern of numbers is strange, for example if all values are even, we must determine why. If we see unexpected variability in the data, we must look for possible explanations. Perhaps there are additional variables that might explain some of the variability.

9.4
Preparing for Hypothesis Testing

Looking at the distribution of the values is also important for evaluating the appropriateness of the statistical techniques we are planning to use for hypothesis testing or model building. Perhaps the data must be transformed so that the distribution is approximately normal, or so that the variances in the groups are similar. Or perhaps a nonparametric technique is needed.

9.5
WAYS OF DISPLAYING DATA

Now that we've established why it's important to look at data, we'll consider some of the techniques that are available for exploring data. To illustrate the methods, we'll use the Western Electric data (see Chapter 4) and the bank salary data (see Chapter 11).

9.6
The Histogram

The histogram is a commonly used display. The range of observed values is subdivided into equal intervals and then the number of cases in each interval is obtained. Each row of symbols in a histogram represents the number of cases with values within the interval.

Figure 9.6 is a histogram of diastolic blood pressure for a sample of 239 men from the Western Electric study. The first column, labeled **Frequency,** is the number of cases with values in the intervals. The second column, **Bin Center,** is the midpoint of each of the bins. For example, the midpoint of the first bin is 65. The text underneath the histogram shows that the length of each bin is 10. Thus, the first interval contains cases with diastolic blood pressures in the 60's. Cases with diastolic blood pressures in the 70's go into the next interval. The last bin center is labeled 125 and includes cases with values in the 120's.

Figure 9.6   Histogram of diastolic blood pressure

```
GET FILE=ELECTRIC.
EXAMINE VARIABLES=DBP58 /PLOT=HISTOGRAM.

    Frequency    Bin Center

        7.00           65    ***
       45.00           75    ***********************
       89.00           85    ********************************************
       58.00           95    *****************************
       24.00          105    ************
       10.00          115    *****
        2.00          125    *
        4.00      Extremes    **

    Bin width :      10
    Each star:         2 case(s)
```

The last row of this histogram is for cases whose values are much larger than the rest. These are labeled **Extremes.** The reason the histogram is not extended to accommodate these cases is to avoid having too many intervals, or intervals that are very wide. For example, if there is a person with a diastolic blood pressure of 200, the histogram would have a lot of empty bins between the bin centers of 125 and 205. Of course, we could have fewer bins and make them wider but this would obscure potentially interesting information. That's why the histogram contains special bins for very large and very small values.

9.7
The Stem-and-Leaf Plot

A display closely related to the histogram is the stem-and-leaf plot. The stem-and-leaf plot provides more information about the actual values than does a histogram. Consider Figure 9.7a, which is a stem-and-leaf plot of the diastolic blood pressures. As in a histogram, the length of each row corresponds to the number of cases that fall into a particular interval. However, instead of representing all cases with the same symbol, say a star, the stem-and-leaf plot represents each case with a symbol that corresponds to the actual observed value. This is done by dividing observed values into two components—the leading digit or digits, called the stem, and a trailing digit, called the leaf. For example, the value 75 has a stem of 7 and a leaf of 5. In the plot, each row represents a stem and each case is represented by its leaf value.

Figure 9.7a   Stem-and-leaf plot of diastolic blood pressure

EXAMINE VARIABLES=DBP58 /**PLOT=STEMLEAF**.

```
 Frequency      Stem &  Leaf

        .00       6  *
       7.00       6  .  5558889
      13.00       7  *  0000111223344
      32.00       7  .  55555555667777777777788888889999
      44.00       8  *  00000000000000000000001111122222333333334444
      45.00       8  .  555555555566666666777777777777788888999999999
      31.00       9  *  0000000001111111122222222333334
      27.00       9  .  556666677777788888888899999
      13.00      10  *  00001222333333
      11.00      10  .  55555577899
       5.00      11  *  00003
       5.00      11  .  55789
       2.00      12  *  01
       4.00  Extremes     (125), (133), (160)

 Stem width:    10
 Each leaf:       1 case(s)
```

In this example, each stem is subdivided into two rows. The first row of each pair has cases with leaves of 0 through 4, while the second row has cases with leaves of 5 through 9. Consider the two rows that correspond to the stem of 11. From the first of these rows, we can see that there are four cases with diastolic blood pressures of 110, and one case with a pressure of 113. Similarly there are two cases with values of 115, and one each with values of 117, 118, and 119.

The last row of the stem-and-leaf plot is for cases with values removed from the rest. In this row the actual values are displayed in parentheses. From the frequency column we see that there are four extreme cases. Their values are 125, 133, and 160. Only distinct values are listed.

To identify cases with extreme values, you can display a table containing identifying information for cases with the largest and smallest values. Figure 9.7b shows the five cases with the largest and smallest values for diastolic blood pressure. When the data file contains names or other information that can be used to identify cases, this can be listed. Otherwise, the sequence of the case in the data file is reported.

Figure 9.7b   Extreme cases

EXAMINE VARIABLES=DBP58 /**STATISTICS=EXTREME**.

			Extreme Values			
5	Highest	Case #		5	Lowest	Case #
	160	CASE120			65	CASE73
	133	CASE56			65	CASE157
	125	CASE163			65	CASE156
	125	CASE42			68	CASE34
	121	CASE26			68	CASE175

9.8
Other Stems   In Figure 9.7a each stem was subdivided into two parts—one for leaves of 0 thru 4, the other for leaves of 5 thru 9. When there are few stems, it is sometimes useful to subdivide each stem even further. Consider Figure 9.8, which is a stem-and-leaf plot of cholesterol levels for the men in the Western Electric study. In this figure stems are divided into five parts—each is used to represent two leaf values. The first, designated by an asterisk, is for leaves of 0 and 1; the next, designated by **t**, is for leaves of 2's and 3's the **f** is for leaves of 4's and 5's; **s** for 6's and 7's; and a period for 8's and 9's.

This stem-and-leaf plot differs from the previous in yet another way. Since cholesterol values have a wide range, in this example from 106 to 515, using the first two digits for the stem would result in an unnecessarily detailed plot. To avoid this, we will use only the hundreds digit as the stem instead of the first two digits. The line after the stem-and-leaf plot tells us that the stems are in hundreds. The leaf is then the tens digit. The last digit is ignored. Thus from this stem-and-leaf plot it is not possible to determine the exact cholesterol level for a case. Instead, each case is classified only by its first two digits.

Figure 9.8   Stem-and-leaf plot of cholesterol levels

EXAMINE VARIABLES=CHOL58 /PLOT=STEMLEAF.

```
Frequency     Stem &  Leaf

     1.00  Extremes    (106)
     2.00        1  f  55
     6.00        1  s  677777
    12.00        1  .  888889999999
    23.00        2  *  00000000000001111111111
    36.00        2  t  222222222222222223333333333333333333
    35.00        2  f  44444444444444444445555555555555555
    42.00        2  s  666666666666666666666677777777777777777777
    28.00        2  .  8888888888888889999999999999
    18.00        3  *  000000011111111111
    17.00        3  t  22222222222233333
     9.00        3  f  444445555
     6.00        3  s  666777
     1.00        3  .  8
     3.00  Extremes    (393), (425), (515)

Stem width:    100
Each leaf:       1 case(s)
```

9.9
The Boxplot   Both the histogram and the stem-and-leaf plot provide useful information about the distribution of observed values. We can see how tightly cases cluster together. We can see if there is a single peak or several peaks. We can determine if there are extreme values.

A display that further summarizes information about the distribution of the values is the boxplot. Instead of plotting the actual values, a boxplot displays summary statistics for the distribution. It plots the median, the 25th percentile, the 75th percentile, and values that are far removed from the rest.

Figure 9.9a shows an annotated sketch of a boxplot. The lower boundary of the box is the 25th percentile, and the upper boundary is the 75th percentile. (These percentiles are sometimes called Tukey's hinges and are calculated a little differently from ordinary percentiles.) The asterisk in the box represents the median. Fifty percent of the cases have values within the box. The length of the box corresponds to the interquartile range, which is the difference between the 75th and 25th percentiles.

The boxplot includes two categories of cases with outlying values. Cases with values more than 3 box-lengths from the upper or lower edge of the box are called *extreme values*. On the boxplot these are designated with the letter E. Cases with values between 1.5 and 3 box-lengths from the edge of the box are called *outliers* and are designated with the letter O. The largest and smallest observed values

Figure 9.9a Annotated sketch of a boxplot

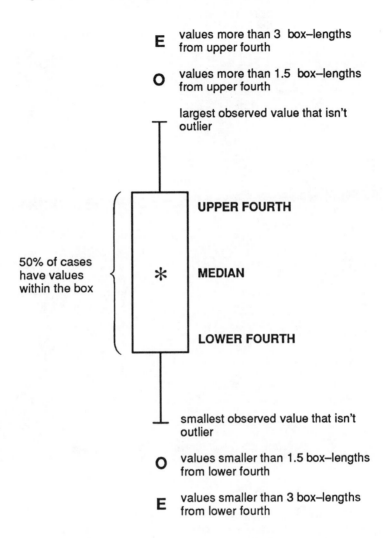

E   values more than 3 box–lengths from upper fourth

O   values more than 1.5 box–lengths from upper fourth

largest observed value that isn't outlier

UPPER FOURTH

50% of cases have values within the box

✳   MEDIAN

LOWER FOURTH

smallest observed value that isn't outlier

O   values smaller than 1.5 box–lengths from lower fourth

E   values smaller than 3 box–lengths from lower fourth

that aren't outliers are also shown. Lines are drawn from the ends of the box to these values. (These lines are sometimes called whiskers and the plot is called a box-and-whiskers plot.)

What can you tell about your data from a boxplot? From the median you can determine the central tendency, or location. From the length of the box you can see the spread, or variability, of your observations. If the median is not in the center of the box you know that the observed values are skewed. If the median is closer to the bottom of the box than the top, the data are positively skewed. There is a tail with large values. If the median is closer to the top of the box than the bottom, the opposite is true. The distribution is negatively skewed. The length of the tail is shown by the whiskers and the outlying and extreme points.

Boxplots are particularly useful for comparing the distribution of values in several groups. For example, suppose you want to compare the distribution of beginning salaries for people employed in several different positions at a bank. Figure 9.9b contains boxplots of the bank salary data. From this plot you can see that the first two job categories have similar distributions for salary, although the first has several extreme values. The third job category has little variability. All 27 people in this category earn similar amounts of money. The last two groups have much higher median salaries than the other groups, and larger spread as well.

Figure 9.9b   Boxplots for bank salary data

```
GET FILE=BANK.
SELECT IF (JOBCAT LE 5).
EXAMINE VARIABLES=SALBEG BY JOBCAT /PLOT=BOXPLOT.
```

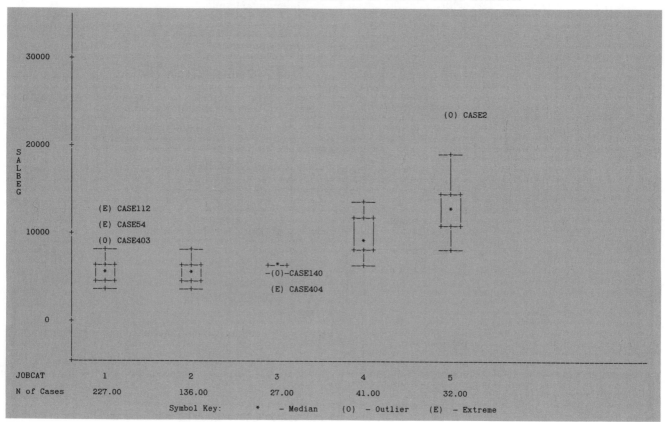

9.10
EVALUATING
ASSUMPTIONS

Many statistical procedures, such as analysis of variance, require that all groups come from normal populations with the same variance. Therefore, before using them, we often wish to test the hypothesis that all the group variances are equal or that the samples are from normal populations. If it appears that the assumptions are violated, we may want to determine appropriate transformations.

9.11
The Levene Test

There is a wide variety of tests available for evaluating the assumption that all groups come from populations with equal variances. Many of these tests, however, are heavily dependent on the data being samples from normal populations. Analysis of variance procedures, on the other hand, are reasonably robust to departures from normality. The Levene test is a homogeneity of variance test that is less dependent on the assumption of normality than most tests and thus is particularly useful with analysis of variance. It is obtained by computing for each case the absolute difference from its cell mean and then performing a one-way analysis of variance on these differences.

From Figure 9.11 you can see that, for the salary data, the null hypothesis that all group variances are equal is rejected. We should consider transforming the data if we plan to use a statistical procedure which requires equality of variance. Next we'll consider how to select a transformation.

Figure 9.11 The Levene test

Test of homogeneity of variance		df1	df2	Significance
Levene Statistic	28.9200	4	458	.0000

9.12
Spread-and-Level Plots

Often there is a relationship between the average value, or level, of a variable, and the variability or spread associated with it. For example, we can see in Figure 9.9b that as salaries increase, so does the variability.

One way of studying the relationship between spread and level is to plot the values of spread and level for each group. If there is no relationship, the points should cluster around a horizontal line. If this is not the case, we can use the observed relationship between the two variables to choose an appropriate transformation.

9.13
Determining the Transformation

A power transformation is frequently used to stabilize variances. All a power transformation does is raise each data value to a specified power. For example, a power transformation of 2 squares all of the data values. A transformation of 1/2 indicates that the square root of all the values be taken. If the power is 0, the log of the numbers is used.

To determine an appropriate power for transforming the data we can plot, for each group, the log of the median against the log of the interquartile range. Figure 9.13 shows such a plot for the salary data shown in Figure 9.9b. You see that there is a fairly strong linear relationship between spread and level. From the slope of the line, we can estimate the power value that will eliminate or lessen this relationship. The power is obtained by subtracting the slope from 1. That is,

$$\text{Power} = 1 - \text{slope}$$

Equation 9.13

Figure 9.13 Spread-and-level plot of bank data

EXAMINE VARIABLES=SALBEG BY JOBCAT **/PLOT=SPREADLEVEL**.

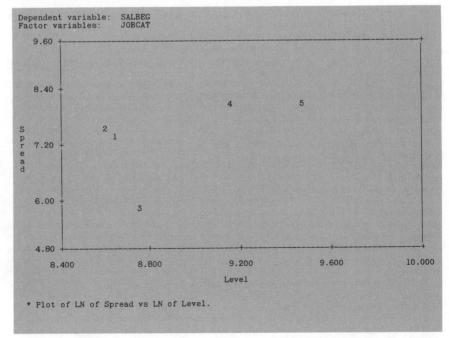

Although this formula can result in all sorts of powers, for simplicity and interpretability we usually choose the closest powers that are multiples of 1/2. Table 9.13 shows the most commonly used transformations.

Table 9.13 Commonly used transformations

Power	Transformation
3	Cube
2	Square
1	No change
1/2	Square root
0	Logarithm
−1/2	Reciprocal of the square root
−1	Reciprocal

As shown in Figure 9.13, the slope of the least-squares line for the bank data is 1.475, so the power for the transformation is −.475. Rounding to the nearest multiple of a half, we will use the reciprocal of the square root.

After applying the power transformation, it is wise to obtain a spread-and-level plot for the transformed data. From this plot you can judge the success of the transformation.

9.14
Tests of Normality

Since the normal distribution is very important to statistical inference, we often want to examine the assumption that our data come from a normal distribution. One way to do this is with a normal probability plot. In a normal probability plot each observed value is paired with its expected value from the normal distribution. (The expected value from the normal distribution is based on the number of cases in the sample and the rank order of the case in the sample.) If the sample is from a normal distribution, we expect that the points will fall, more or less, on a straight line.

Figure 9.14a is a normal probability plot of a sample of 200 points from a normal distribution. Note how the points cluster about a straight line. You can also plot the actual deviations of the points from a straight line. This is called a detrended normal plot and is shown in Figure 9.14b. If the sample is from a normal population, the points should cluster around a horizontal line through 0 and there should be no pattern. A striking pattern suggests departure from normality.

Figure 9.14a Normal probability plot   **Figure 9.14b Detrended normal plot**

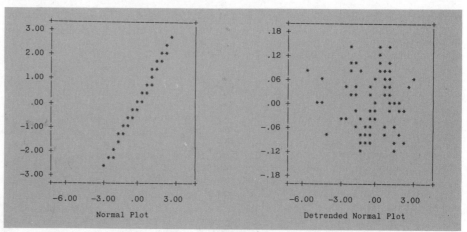

Figure 9.14c shows a normal probability plot and a detrended plot for data from a uniform distribution. The points do not cluster around a straight line, and the deviations from a straight line are not randomly distributed about 0.

Figure 9.14c Normal plots for a uniform distribution

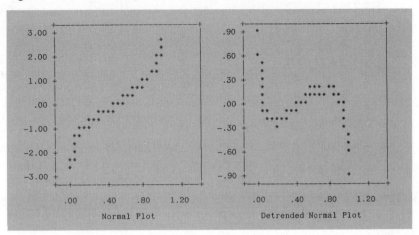

Although normal probability plots provide a visual basis for checking normality, it is often desirable to compute a statistical test of the hypothesis that the data are from a normal distribution. Two commonly used tests are the Shapiro-Wilks and the Lilliefors. The Lilliefors test is based on a modification of the Kolmogorov-Smirnov test for the situation when means and variances are not known but must be estimated from the data. The Shapiro-Wilks test has been found to have good power in many situations when compared to other tests of normality (Conover, 1980).

Figure 9.14d contains normal probability plots and tests of normality for the diastolic blood pressure data. From the small observed significance levels you see that the hypothesis of normality can be rejected. However, it is important to remember that whenever the sample size is large almost any goodness-of-fit test will result in rejection of the null hypothesis. It is almost impossible to find data that are *exactly* normally distributed. For most statistical tests, it is sufficient that the data are approximately normally distributed. Thus, for large data sets you should look not only at the observed significance level but also at the actual departure from normality.

Figure 9.14d Normal plots for diastolic blood pressure

```
SET WIDTH=90.
EXAMINE VARIABLES=DBP58 /PLOT=NPPLOT.
```

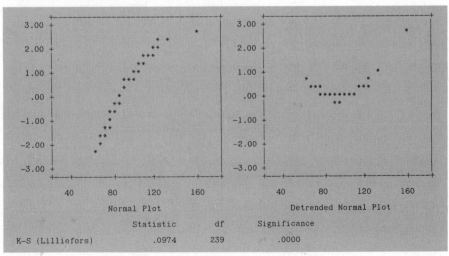

9.15
ESTIMATING LOCATION WITH ROBUST ESTIMATORS

We often use the arithmetic mean to estimate central tendency, or location. We know, however, that the mean is heavily influenced by outliers. One very large or very small value can change the mean dramatically. The median, on the other hand, is insensitive to outliers. Addition or removal of extreme values has little effect on the median. The median is called a *resistant* measure, since its value depends on the "main body" of the data and not on outliers. The advantage of resistant measures are easy to see. Their values are not unduly influenced by a few observations. They don't change much if small amounts of data are added or removed.

Although the median is an intuitive, simple measure of location, there are better estimators of location if we are willing to make some assumptions about the population from which our data originate. Estimators that depend on simple, fairly nonrestrictive assumptions about the underlying distribution and are not sensitive to these assumptions are called *robust* estimators. We will now consider some robust estimators of central tendency that depend only on the assumption that the data are from a symmetric population.

9.16
The Trimmed Mean

A simple robust estimator of location can be obtained by "trimming" the data to exclude values that are far removed from the others. For example, a 20% trimmed mean disregards the smallest 20% and the largest 20% of all observations. The estimate is based only on the 60% of data values that are in the middle. What's the advantage of the trimmed mean? Like the median, it results in an estimate that is not influenced by extreme values. However, unlike the median it is not based solely on a single value, or two values, that are in the middle. It is based on a much larger number of "middle" values. (The median can be considered a 50% trimmed mean, since half of the values above and below the median are ignored!) In general a trimmed mean makes better use of the data than does the median.

9.17
M-Estimators

When calculating a trimmed mean we subdivide our cases into two groups—those which are included and those which are excluded from the computation of the mean. We can consider the trimmed mean as a weighted mean in which cases have weights of 0 or 1, depending on whether they are included or excluded from the computations. (A weighted mean is calculated by assigning to each case a weight and then using the formula $\overline{X} = \Sigma w_i x_i / \Sigma w_i$.) In the trimmed mean we treat observations that are far from most of the others pretty harshly. We exclude them altogether. A more lenient alternative is to include them but give them smaller weights than cases that are closer to the center. An estimator that does this is the M-estimator. (The M stands for generalized *maximum-likelihood estimator*.)

Since there are many different schemes that can be used to assign weights to cases, there are many different M-estimators. (The usual mean can be viewed as an M-estimator with all cases having a weight of 1.) All commonly used M-estimators assign weights so that they decrease as distance from the center of the distribution increases. Figures 9.17a through 9.17d show the weights used by four common M-estimators.

Consider Figure 9.17a, which is for Huber's M-estimators. The value on the horizontal axis is a standardized distance from the estimate of location. It is computed using the following formula:

$$u_i = \frac{|\text{value for } i\text{th case} - \text{estimate of location}|}{\text{estimate of spread}}$$

Equation 9.17

Common M-estimators

Figure 9.17a   Huber's (c=1.339)

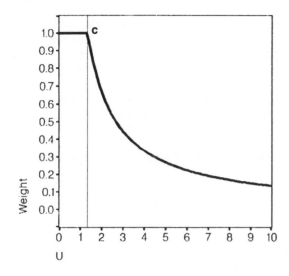

Figure 9.17b   Tukey's biweight (c=4.685)

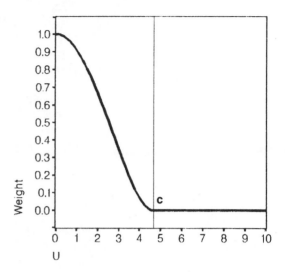

Figure 9.17c   Hampel's (a=1.7, b=3.4, c=8.5)

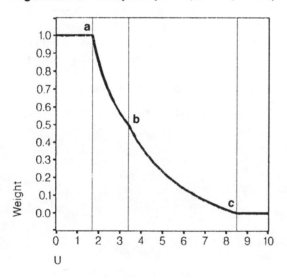

Figure 9.17d   Andrew's (c=1.339π)

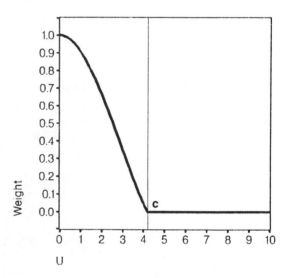

The estimate of spread used is the median of the absolute deviations from the sample median, commonly known as MAD. It is calculated by first finding the median for the sample and then for each case computing the absolute value of the deviation from the median. The MAD is then the median of these absolute values. Since the weights for cases depend on the value of the estimate of central location, M-estimators must be computed iteratively.

From Figure 9.17a, you can see that cases have weights of 1 up to a certain critical point, labeled **c**. After the critical point, the weights decrease as *u*, standardized distance from the location estimate, increases. The SPSS default values for these critical points are given in parentheses in Figures 9.17a through 9.17d.

The four M-estimators in Figures 9.17a through 9.17d differ from each other in the way they assign weights. The Tukey biweight does not have a point at which weights shift abruptly from 1. Instead weights gradually decline to 0. Cases with values greater than *c* standardized units from the estimate are assigned weights of 0.

Hampel's three-part redescending M-estimator (Figure 9.17c) has a more complicated weighting scheme than the Huber or Tukey biweight. It uses four schemes for assigning weights. Cases with values less than *a* receive a weight of 1, cases with values between *a* and *b* receive a weight of a/u, while cases between *b* and *c* receive a weight of

$$\frac{a}{u} \cdot \frac{c-u}{c-b}$$

Cases with values greater than *c* receive a weight of 0. With Andrew's M-estimator (Figure 9.17d), there is no abrupt change in the assignment of weights. A smooth function replaces the separate pieces.

Figure 9.17e contains basic descriptive statistics and values for the M-estimators for the diastolic blood pressure data. As expected, the estimates of location differ for the various methods. The mean produces the largest estimate, 88.79. That's because we have a positively skewed distribution and the mean is heavily influenced by the large values. Of the M-estimators, the Huber and Hampel estimates have the largest values. They too are influenced by the large data values. The remaining two M-estimates are fairly close in value.

Figure 9.17e   M-estimates for blood pressure variable

```
EXAMINE VARIABLES=DBP58 /STATISTICS=DESCRIPTIVES /MESTIMATORS.
```

```
      DBP58        AVERAGE DIAST BLOOD PRESS

   Valid cases:       239.0   Missing cases:        1.0   Percent missing:      .4


   Mean      88.7908  Std Err      .8441  Min       65.0000  Skewness    1.2557
   Median    87.0000  Variance  170.3006  Max      160.0000  S E Skew     .1575
   5% Trim   88.0065  Std Dev    13.0499  Range     95.0000  Kurtosis    3.5958
                                          IQR       17.0000  S E Kurt     .3137

                                   M-Estimators

   Huber  (1.339)                  87.1219   Tukey  (4.685)         86.4269
   Hampel (1.700,3.400,8.500)      87.1404   Andrew (1.340 * pi)    86.4105
```

In summary, M-estimators are good alternatives to the usual mean and median. The Huber is a good estimator when the distribution is close to normal but is not recommended if there are extreme values. For further discussion of robust estimators see Hogg and Tanis (1988) and Hoaglin et al. (1983).

9.18 SUMMARY

Examination of the data is the most essential step of good data analysis. This chapter has shown a variety of descriptive statistics and displays that is useful as a preliminary step in data analysis. All of these statistics and displays are available in the SPSS EXAMINE procedure. With EXAMINE, you can screen your data, visually examine the distributions of values for various groups, and test for normality and homogeneity of variance.

9.19
RUNNING PROCEDURE EXAMINE

The EXAMINE procedure provides a variety of descriptive plots and statistics, including stem-and-leaf plots, boxplots, normal probability plots, and spread-and-level plots. Also available are the Levene test for homogeneity of variance, the Shapiro-Wilks and Lilliefors tests for normality, and several robust maximum-likelihood estimators of location. Cases can be subdivided into groups and statistics obtained for each group.

9.20
VARIABLES Subcommand

The only required specification is the VARIABLES subcommand and a list of variables for which descriptive statistics are to be calculated. For example, to obtain descriptive statistics for the variables SALBEG and EDUC, specify

EXAMINE VARIABLES=SALBEG EDUC.

The VARIABLES subcommand can be specified only once.

9.21
Specifying Cells

To subdivide cases into cells based on their values for grouping (factor) variables, specify the factor variables after keyword BY. String variables can be used as factors, but only the first eight characters are used.

For example, to obtain summary statistics for SALBEG and EDUC when cases are subdivided into employment categories (JOBCAT), specify

EXAMINE VARIABLES=SALBEG EDUC BY JOBCAT.

If several variables are listed after keyword BY, separate analyses are obtained for each factor variable. For example, the command

EXAMINE VARIABLES=SALBEG EDUC BY JOBCAT SEX.

will produce summary statistics for salary and education for categories of JOBCAT and for categories of SEX. To obtain summary statistics for cells based on the combination of values of JOBCAT and SEX, use the keyword BY to separate the factor names. The command

EXAMINE VARIABLES=SALBEG EDUC BY JOBCAT BY SEX.

will produce descriptive statistics for cells formed by the combination of values of sex and job category. That is, there will be cells for males and females within each job category. If there are five job categories, you will obtain 11 analyses: one for all cases combined, and one for each of the ten cells formed by the combinations of JOBCAT and SEX. Note that you will not obtain analyses for each individual job category and for each sex. To obtain this additional output, specify

EXAMINE VARIABLES=SALBEG EDUC BY SEX JOBCAT JOBCAT BY SEX.

Note that specifying many cells will generate a large amount of output. Be sure to request only the analyses that you need.

9.22
ID Subcommand

Individual cases can be identified in the output according to their values for a selected variable specified on the ID subcommand. For example, to identify cases by their values for EMPLNO, specify:

EXAMINE VARIABLES=SALBEG BY JOBCAT /ID=EMPLNO.

If the ID subcommand is not specified, the SPSS system variable $CASENUM is used.

9.23
STATISTICS Subcommand

Use the STATISTICS subcommand to control the output of basic descriptive statistics. The following keywords can be specified:

DESCRIPTIVE   *Basic descriptive statistics only.* This includes the mean, median, 5% trimmed mean, standard error, variance, standard deviation, minimum, maximum, range, interquartile range and skewness and kurtosis, and their standard errors. Interquartile range computations are based on the method specified with the PERCENTILES subcommand.

EXTREMES (n)   *The cases with the* n *largest and* n *smallest values.* If *n* is omitted, the cases with the five largest and five smallest values are displayed. Cases are identified by their values for the variable specified on the ID subcommand. If the ID subcommand is not used, cases are identified by their values for the SPSS system variable $CASENUM.

ALL   *Basic descriptive statistics and extreme values.* All statistics available with DESCRIPTIVE and EXTREMES are displayed. The default *n* of 5 is used for EXTREMES.

NONE   *Neither basic descriptive statistics nor extreme values.*

9.24
MESTIMATORS Subcommand

Use the MESTIMATORS subcommand to obtain robust maximum-likelihood estimators of location. If the MESTIMATORS subcommand is specified without keywords, all four M-estimators are calculated. Individual estimators and constants at which the weighting scheme changes can be selected with the following keywords:

HUBER(c)   *Huber's M-estimator with constant* c. By default, $c=1.339$.

ANDREWS(c)   *Andrews' wave estimator with constant* c. The constant is multiplied by pi. By default, $c=1.34$.

HAMPEL(a,b,c)   *Hampel's redescending M-estimator with constants* a, b, *and* c. By default, $a=1.7$, $b=3.4$, and $c=8.5$.

TUKEY(c)   *Tukey's biweight estimator with constant* c. By default, $c=4.685$.

ALL   *All four M-estimators.* This is the default when MESTIMATORS is specified without a keyword.

NONE   *No M-estimators.* This is the default if MESTIMATORS is omitted.

For example, to calculate all four M-estimators for the variable DBP58, specify:

EXAMINE VARIABLES=DBP58 /MESTIMATORS.

To obtain only the Andrew's estimator with a constant of 2 pi, specify:

EXAMINE VARIABLES=DBP58 /MESTIMATORS ANDREWS(2).

9.25
FREQUENCIES Subcommand

Use the FREQUENCIES subcommand to obtain frequency tables. You can specify starting values and increment sizes. For example, to obtain a frequency table for DBP58 using increments of 5 and starting at 70, specify

EXAMINE VARIABLES=DBP58 /FREQUENCIES FROM (70) BY (5).

If you do not specify a starting value or increment, EXAMINE will select a value based on the data. If you specify an increment of 0, a frequency table for each distinct value is produced.

9.26
PERCENTILES Subcommand

Use the PERCENTILES subcommand to obtain percentiles. You can also select the method of estimation. For example, to calculate the 25th, 50th, and 75th percentiles using the default method of estimation, specify

```
EXAMINE VARIABLES=DBP58 /PERCENTILES(25,50,75).
```

If you specify the PERCENTILES subcommand without percentile values in parentheses, the default percentiles are 5, 10, 25, 50, 75, 90, and 95.

The following methods are available for calculating the percentiles, where W is the sum of weights for all nonmissing cases, p is the percentile divided by 100, i is the rank of the case when cases are sorted in ascending order, and X_i is the value for the ith case.

HAVERAGE *Weighted average at* $X_{(W+1)p}$. The percentile value is the weighted average of X_i and X_{i+1} using the formula $(1\text{-}f)X_i + fX_{i+1}$, where $(W+1)p$ is decomposed into an integer part i and fractional part f. This is the default if PERCENTILES is specified without a keyword.

WAVERAGE *Weighted average at* X_{Wp}. The percentile value is the weighted average of X_i and X_{i+1} using the formula $(1\text{-}f)X_i + fX_{i+1}$, where i is the integer part of Wp.

ROUND *Observation closest to* Wp. The percentile value is X_i, where i is the integer part of $(Wp + 0.5)$.

EMPIRICAL *Empirical distribution function.* The percentile value is X_i when the fractional Wp is equal to 0 and i is the integer part. The percentile value is X_{i+1} when the fractional part of Wp is greater than 0.

AEMPIRICAL *Empirical distribution with averaging.* The percentile value is $(X_i + X_{i+1})/2$ when the fractional part of Wp equals 0. The percentile value is X_{i+1} when the fractional part of Wp is greater than 0.

NONE *No percentile output.* This is the default if PERCENTILES is omitted.

The keyword for the method to be used for calculating the percentiles follows the list of percentile values, as in:

```
EXAMINE  VARIABLES=DBP58 /PERCENTILES(25 50 75)=WAVERAGE.
```

To obtain default percentiles for a specified method, specify the method keyword in parentheses after the PERCENTILES subcommand, as in:

```
EXAMINE VARIABLES=DBP58 /PERCENTILES=EMPIRICAL.
```

9.27
PLOT Subcommand

EXAMINE produces boxplots, stem-and-leaf plots, histograms, normal probability plots, and spread-and-level plots. If the PLOT subcommand is specified without any keywords or if the subcommand is omitted, stem-and-leaf plots and boxplots are produced. If any plots are specified on PLOT, only the requested plots are displayed.

The following keywords can be used with the PLOT subcommand:

BOXPLOT *Boxplot.* The boundaries of the box are Tukey's hinges. The median is identified by an asterisk. The length of the box is the interquartile range (IQR) based on Tukey's hinges. Values more than 3 IQR's from the end of the box are labeled as extreme (E). Values more than 1.5 IQR's from the end of the box but less than 3 IQR's are labeled as outliers (O). This is produced by default.

STEMLEAF *Stem-and-leaf plot.* Plot in which each observed value is divided into two components—the leading digits (stem) and trailing digits (leaf). This is produced by default.

HISTOGRAM *Histogram.*

SPREADLEVEL(p) *Spread-and-level plot.* If the keyword appears alone, for each cell, the natural log of the interquartile range is plotted against the log of the median. If the power for transforming the data (p) is supplied, the power transformation is performed and the IQR and median of the transformed data are plotted. If p=0 is specified, a natural log transformation of the data is done. The slope of the regression line and Levene's test for homogeneity of variance are also displayed. Levene's test is based on the original data if no transformation is specified and on the transformed data if a transformation is done.

NPPLOT   *Normal probability and detrended probability plots.* The Shapiro-Wilks statistic and the Kolmogorov-Smirnov statistic with a Lilliefors significance level for testing normality are calculated. The Shapiro-Wilks statistic is not calculated when the sample size exceeds 50.

ALL   *All available plots.*

NONE   *No plots.*

For example, to request stem-and-leaf plots and normal probability plots, specify:

```
EXAMINE VARIABLES=DBP58 /PLOT=STEMLEAF NPPLOT.
```

To determine an appropriate transformation of the data based on a plot of the logs of the interquartile ranges against the logs of the medians, specify:

```
EXAMINE VARIABLES=SALBEG BY JOBCAT /PLOT=SPREADLEVEL.
```

To obtain a plot of interquartile ranges against medians when the data values are squared, specify:

```
EXAMINE VARIABLES=SALBEG BY JOBCAT /PLOT=SPREADLEVEL(2).
```

To obtain a plot of the interquartile ranges against the medians after the data have been log transformed, specify:

```
EXAMINE VARIABLES=SALBEG BY JOBCAT /PLOT=SPREADLEVEL(0).
```

The following commands produced Figures 9.9b, 9.11, and 9.13:

```
SELECT IF (JOBCAT LE 5).
EXAMINE VARIABLES=SALBEG BY JOBCAT
 /PLOT=BOXPLOT SPREADLEVEL.
```

9.28
COMPARE Subcommand

Use the COMPARE subcommand to control how boxplots are displayed. Two methods are available. For each variable you can display the boxplots for all cells side by side, or you can display all of the boxplots for a cell together. (You will only have several boxplots for a single cell if you specify more than one dependent variable.)

The method you use depends on the comparisons of interest. If you display the boxplots for all cells together you can see how the distribution of a particular variable differs for the cells. For example, suppose you have variables SAL1, SAL2, SAL3, and SAL4, containing yearly salaries for the first four years of employment. If you specify

```
EXAMINE VARIABLES=SAL1 SAL2 SAL3 SAL4 BY JOBCAT BY SEX
 /COMPARE GROUPS.
```

you could easily compare each of the yearly salaries for the JOBCAT/SEX groups, since the distribution of SAL1 would be shown for all groups, followed by the distribution of SAL2 for all groups, and so forth. However, if you specify

```
EXAMINE VARIABLES=SAL1 SAL2 SAL3 SAL4 BY JOBCAT BY SEX
 /COMPARE VARIABLES.
```

for each group the boxplots for the four salaries will be displayed together. This allows you to examine salary changes over time for each group.

9.29
SCALE Subcommand

By default, the histogram and stem-and-leaf scale are based on the values of the cases in a particular plot. You can, however, use the same scale for all plots for each dependent variable by specifying the SCALE subcommand. The following keywords are available:

PLOTWISE *Scales are based on the values of cases in each plot.* This is the default.
UNIFORM *All plots for each dependent variable use the same scale.*

For example, if you specify

```
EXAMINE VARIABLES=SAL1 BY JOCBCAT /SCALE=UNIFORM.
```

the same scale is used for all stem-and-leaf plots. If histograms are requested they will also be on the same scale.

9.30
MISSING Subcommand

By default, cases with either system- or user-missing values for any variable specified on the VARIABLES subcommand are excluded from the analysis. You can specify other missing-value treatments using the MISSING subcommand. The following keywords are available:

LISTWISE *Cases with any missing values are deleted.* This is the default.
PAIRWISE *Cases with nonmissing values for a cell are included in the analysis of that cell.* The case may have missing values for variables used in other cells.
REPORT *Missing values for factor variables are treated as a separate category.* All output is produced for this additional category. Frequency tables include categories for missing values.
INCLUDE *Cases with user-missing values are included.* Only cases with system-missing values are excluded from the analysis. This keyword can be used together with LISTWISE, PAIRWISE, or REPORT.

For example, the command

```
EXAMINE VARIABLES=SALBEG EDUC BY JOBCAT /MISSING PAIRWISE.
```

excludes cases from the analysis of SALBEG only if they have missing values for SALBEG or JOBCAT. It doesn't matter whether the value of EDUC is missing or not. Only cases with missing values for EDUC or JOBCAT will be excluded from the analysis of EDUC.

9.31
Annotated Example

```
GET FILE=ELECTRIC.
SET WIDTH=90.
EXAMINE VARIABLES=DBP58
 /PLOT=STEMLEAF NPPLOT
 /STATISTICS=ALL
 /MESTIMATORS.
```

- The GET command specifies the SPSS system file (ELECTRIC) to be read.
- The SET command sets the page width to 90 characters (allowing enough space for the plots in Figure 9.14d to be displayed side-by-side) in the output.
- The EXAMINE command and VARIABLES subcommand name the variable to be examined.
- The PLOT subcommand produces the stem-and-leaf plot in Figure 9.7a and the side-by-side normal probability and detrended normal plots in Figure 9.14d.
- The STATISTICS subcommand displays the default five lowest and five highest extreme values in Figure 9.7b and the descriptive statistics in Figure 9.17e.
- The MESTIMATORS subcommand produces the four default M-estimators in Figure 9.17e.

Contents _____

10 Crosstabulation and Measures of Association Procedure CROSSTABS

Newspapers headline murders in subway stations, robberies on crowded main streets, suicides cheered by onlookers. All are indications of the social irresponsibility and apathy said to characterize city residents. Since overcrowding, decreased sense of community, and other urban problems are usually blamed, you might ask whether small town residents are more responsible and less apathetic than their urban counterparts.

Hansson and Slade (1977) used the "lost letter technique" to test the hypothesis that altruism is higher in small towns than in cities, unless the person needing assistance is a social deviant. In this technique, stamped and addressed letters are "lost," and the rate at which they are returned is examined. A total of 216 letters were lost in Hansson and Slade's experiment. Half were dropped within the city limits of Tulsa, Oklahoma, the others in 51 small towns within a 50-mile radius of Tulsa. The letters were addressed to three fictitious people at a post-office box in Tulsa: M. J. Davis; Dandee Davis, c/o Pink Panther Lounge; and M. J. Davis, c/o Friends of the Communist Party. The first person is considered a normal "control," the second a person whose occupation is questionable, and the third a subversive or political deviant.

10.1 CROSSTABULATION

To see whether the return rate is similar for the three addresses, the letters found and mailed and those not mailed must be tallied separately for each address. Figure 10.1 is a *crosstabulation* of address type and response. The number of cases (letters) for each combination of values of the two variables is displayed in a *cell* in the table, together with various percentages. These cell entries provide information about relationships between the variables.

Figure 10.1 Crosstabulation of status of letter by address

```
CROSSTABS TABLES=RETURNED BY ADDRESS
  /CELLS.
```

RETURNED FOUND AND MAILED by ADDRESS ADDRESS ON LETTER				
	ADDRESS			Page 1 of 1
Count Row Pct Col Pct Tot Pct	CONTROL 1	DANDEE 2	COMMUNIS T 3	Row Total
RETURNED				
1 YES	35 45.5 48.6 16.2	32 41.6 44.4 14.8	10 13.0 13.9 4.6	77 35.6
2 NO	37 26.6 51.4 17.1	40 28.8 55.6 18.5	62 44.6 86.1 28.7	139 64.4
Column Total	72 33.3	72 33.3	72 33.3	216 100.0

Number of Missing Observations: 0

In Figure 10.1, the address is called the *column* variable since each address is displayed in a column of the table. Similarly, the status of the letter, whether it was returned or not, is called the *row* variable. With three categories of the column variable and two of the row, there are six cells in the table.

10.2
Cell Contents and Marginals

The first entry in the table is the number of cases, or *frequency*, in that cell. It is labeled as **Count** in the key displayed in the upper-left corner of the table. For example, 35 letters addressed to the control were returned, and 62 letters addressed to the Communist were not returned. The second entry in the table is the *row percentage* (**Row Pct**). It is the percentage of all cases in a row that fall into a particular cell. Of the 77 letters returned, 45.5% were addressed to the control, 41.6% to Dandee, and 13.0% to the Communist.

The *column percentage* (**Col Pct**), the third item in each cell, is the percentage of all cases in a column that occur in a cell. For example, 48.6% of the letters addressed to the control were returned and 51.4% were not. The return rate for Dandee is similar (44.4%), while that for the Communist is markedly lower (13.9%).

The last entry in the table is the *table percentage* (**Tot Pct**). The number of cases in the cell is expressed as a percentage of the total number of cases in the table. For example, the 35 letters returned to the control represent 16.2% of the 216 letters in the experiment.

The numbers to the right and below the table are known as *marginals*. They are the counts and percentages for the row and column variables taken separately. In Figure 10.1, the row marginals show that 77 (35.6%) of the letters were returned, while 139 (64.4%) were not.

10.3
Choosing Percentages

Row, column, and table percentages convey different types of information, so it is important to choose carefully among them.

In this example, the row percentage indicates the distribution of address types for returned and "lost" letters. It conveys no direct information about the return rate. For example, if twice as many letters were addressed to the control, an identical return rate for all letters would give row percentages of 50%, 25%, and 25%. However, this does not indicate that the return rate is higher for the control. In addition, if each category had the same number of returned letters, the row percentages would have been 33.3%, 33.3%, and 33.3%, regardless of whether one or all letters were returned.

The column percentage is the percentage of letters returned and not returned for each address. By looking at column percentages across rows, you can compare return rates for the address types. Interpretation of this comparison would not be affected if unequal numbers of letters had been addressed to each category.

Since it is always possible to interchange the rows and columns of any table, general rules about when to use row and column percentages cannot be given. The percentages to use depend on the nature of the two variables. If one of the two variables is under experimental control, it is termed an *independent variable*. This variable is hypothesized to affect the response, or *dependent variable*. If variables can be classified as dependent and independent, the following guideline may be helpful: If the independent variable is the row variable, select row percentages; if the independent variable is the column variable, select column percentages. In this example the dependent variable is the status of the letter, whether it was mailed or not. The type of address is the independent variable. Since the independent variable is the column variable in Figure 10.1, column percentages should be used for comparisons of return rates.

10.4
Adding a Control Variable

Since Figure 10.1 combines results from both the city and the towns, differences between the locations are obscured. Two separate tables, one for the city and one for the towns, are required. Figure 10.4 shows crosstabulations of response and address for each of the locations. SPSS produces a separate table for each value of the location (control) variable.

Figure 10.4 Crosstabulations of status of letter by address controlled for location

```
CROSSTABS TABLES=RETURNED BY ADDRESS BY LOCATION
  /CELLS=COUNT COLUMN /STATISTICS=CHISQ.
```

```
RETURNED  FOUND AND MAILED  by  ADDRESS  ADDRESS ON LETTER
Controlling for..
LOCATION  LOCATION LOST  Value = 1  CITY

                 ADDRESS                      Page 1 of 1
         Count
         Col Pct |CONTROL  DANDEE   COMMUNIS
                 |                       T      Row
                 |    1  |    2  |    3  | Total
RETURNED    -----+-------+-------+-------+
            1    |   16  |   14  |    9  |   39
  YES            | 44.4  | 38.9  | 25.0  | 36.1
            -----+-------+-------+-------+
            2    |   20  |   22  |   27  |   69
  NO             | 55.6  | 61.1  | 75.0  | 63.9
            -----+-------+-------+-------+
         Column      36      36      36     108
          Total    33.3    33.3    33.3   100.0

     Chi-Square                Value          DF         Significance
  ------------------------------------------------------------------
  Pearson                    3.13043           2            .20904
  Likelihood Ratio           3.21256           2            .20063
  Mantel-Haenszel            2.92252           1            .08735

  Minimum Expected Frequency -   13.000



RETURNED  FOUND AND MAILED  by  ADDRESS  ADDRESS ON LETTER
Controlling for..
LOCATION  LOCATION LOST  Value = 2  TOWN

                 ADDRESS                      Page 1 of 1
         Count
         Col Pct |CONTROL  DANDEE   COMMUNIS
                 |                       T      Row
                 |    1  |    2  |    3  | Total
RETURNED    -----+-------+-------+-------+
            1    |   19  |   18  |    1  |   38
  YES            | 52.8  | 50.0  |  2.8  | 35.2
            -----+-------+-------+-------+
            2    |   17  |   18  |   35  |   70
  NO             | 47.2  | 50.0  | 97.2  | 64.8
            -----+-------+-------+-------+
         Column      36      36      36     108
          Total    33.3    33.3    33.3   100.0

     Chi-Square                Value          DF         Significance
  ------------------------------------------------------------------
  Pearson                   24.92932           2            .00000
  Likelihood Ratio          31.25342           2            .00000
  Mantel-Haenszel           19.54962           1            .00001

  Minimum Expected Frequency -   12.667


Number of Missing Observations:  0
```

These tables show interesting differences between cities and towns. Although the overall return rates are close, 36.1% for the city and 35.2% for the towns, there are striking differences between the addresses. Only 2.8% of the Communist letters were returned in towns, while 25.0% of them were returned in Tulsa. (At least two of the Communist letters were forwarded by small-town residents to the FBI for punitive action!) The return rates for both the control (52.8%) and Dandee (50.0%) are higher in towns.

The results support the hypothesis that, in small towns, suspected social deviance influences the response more than in big cities, although it is surprising that Dandee and the Pink Panther Lounge were deemed worthy of as much assistance as they received. If the Communist letter is excluded, inhabitants of small towns are somewhat more helpful than city residents, returning 51% of the other letters, in comparison to the city's 42%.

10.5 GRAPHICAL REPRESENTATION OF CROSSTABULATIONS

As with frequency tables, visual representation of a crosstabulation often simplifies the search for associations. Figure 10.5 is a bar chart of letters returned from the crosstabulations shown in Figure 10.4. In a bar chart, the length of each bar represents the frequencies or percentages for each category of a variable. In Figure 10.5, the percentages plotted are the column percentages shown in Figure 10.4 for the returned letters only. This chart clearly shows that the return rates for the control and Dandee are high compared to the return rate for the Communist. Also, it demonstrates more vividly than the crosstabulation that the town residents' return rates for the control and Dandee are higher than city residents' return rates but that the reverse is true for the Communist.

Figure 10.5   Status of letter by address by location (bar chart from SPSS Graphics)

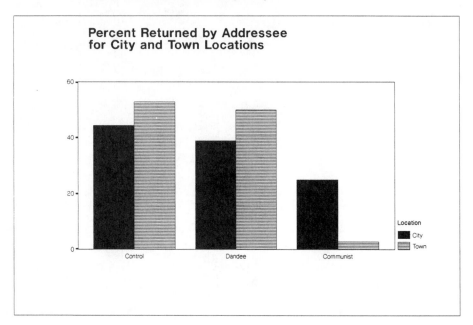

10.6 USING CROSSTABULATION FOR DATA SCREENING

Errors and unusual values in data entry that cannot be spotted with FREQUEN-CIES can sometimes be identified using crosstabulation. For example, a case coded as a male with a history of three pregnancies would not be identified as suspicious in FREQUENCIES tables of sex and number of pregnancies. When considered separately, the code for male is acceptable for variable sex and the value 3 is acceptable for number of pregnancies. Jointly, however, the combination is unexpected.

Whenever possible, crosstabulations of related variables should be obtained so that anomalies can be identified and corrected before further statistical analysis of the data.

10.7
CROSSTABULATION STATISTICS

Although examination of the various row and column percentages in a crosstabulation is a useful first step in studying the relationship between two variables, row and column percentages do not allow for quantification or testing of that relationship. For these purposes, it is useful to consider various indexes that measure the extent of association as well as statistical tests of the hypothesis that there is no association.

10.8
The Chi-Square Test of Independence

The hypothesis that two variables of a crosstabulation are *independent* of each other is often of interest to researchers. Two variables are by definition independent if the probability that a case falls into a given cell is simply the product of the marginal probabilities of the two categories defining the cell.

For example, in Figure 10.1 if returns of the letter and address type are independent, the probability of a letter being returned to a Communist is the product of the probability of a letter being returned and the probability of a letter being addressed to a Communist. From the table, 35.6% of the letters were returned and 33.3% of the letters were addressed to a friend of the Communist party. Thus, if address type and status of the letter are independent, the probability of a letter being returned to the Communist is estimated to be

P(return) P(Communist)$=0.356 \times 0.333 = 0.119$

The *expected* number of cases in that cell is 25.7, which is 11.9% of the 216 cases in the sample. From the table, the *observed* number of letters returned to the Communist is 10 (4.6%), nearly 16 fewer than expected if the two variables are independent.

To construct a statistical test of the independence hypothesis, you repeat the above calculations for each cell in the table. The probability under independence of an observation falling into cell (ij) is estimated by

$$P(\text{row} = i \text{ and column} = j) = \left(\frac{\text{count in row } i}{N}\right) \left(\frac{\text{count in column } j}{N}\right) \quad \textbf{Equation 10.8a}$$

To obtain the expected number of observations in cell (ij), the probability is multiplied by the total sample size.

$$E_{ij} = N\left(\frac{\text{count in row } i}{N}\right) \left(\frac{\text{count in column } j}{N}\right)$$
$$= \frac{(\text{count in row } i) (\text{count in column } j)}{N} \quad \textbf{Equation 10.8b}$$

Figure 10.8 contains the observed and expected frequencies and the *residuals*, which are the observed minus the expected frequencies for the data in Figure 10.1.

Figure 10.8 Observed, expected, and residual values

```
CROSSTABS TABLES=RETURNED BY ADDRESS
 /CELLS=COUNT EXPECTED RESID
 /STATISTICS=CHISQ.
```

```
RETURNED   FOUND AND MAILED   by   ADDRESS   ADDRESS ON LETTER

                  ADDRESS                          Page 1 of 1
          Count
          Exp Val  CONTROL  DANDEE  COMMUNIS
          Residual                  T            Row
                      1  |     2  |     3  |    Total
RETURNED        -------+--------+--------+--------+
             1  |   35 |    32 |    10 |     77
 YES            | 25.7 |  25.7 |  25.7 |  35.6%
                |  9.3 |   6.3 | -15.7 |
                +--------+--------+--------+
             2  |   37 |    40 |    62 |    139
 NO             | 46.3 |  46.3 |  46.3 |  64.4%
                | -9.3 |  -6.3 |  15.7 |
                +--------+--------+--------+
        Column      72 |    72 |    72 |    216
        Total    33.3%   33.3%   33.3%  100.0%

     Chi-Square                    Value             DF           Significance
   _____

   Pearson                       22.56265             2               .00001
   Likelihood Ratio              24.68680             2               .00000
   Mantel-Haenszel               18.83234             1               .00001

   Minimum Expected Frequency -   25.667


   Number of Missing Observations:  0
```

A statistic often used to test the hypothesis that the row and column variables are independent is the *Pearson chi-square*. It is calculated by summing over all cells the squared residuals divided by the expected frequencies.

$$\chi^2 = \sum_i \sum_j \frac{(O_{ij} - E_{ij})^2}{E_{ij}}$$

Equation 10.8c

The calculated chi-square is compared to the critical points of the theoretical chi-square distribution to produce an estimate of how likely (or unlikely) this calculated value is if the two variables are in fact independent. Since the value of the chi-square depends on the number of rows and columns in the table being examined, you must know the *degrees of freedom* for the table. The degrees of freedom can be viewed as the number of cells of a table that can be arbitrarily filled when the row and column totals (marginals) are fixed. For an $r \times c$ table, the degrees of freedom are $(r - 1) \times (c - 1)$, since once $(r-1)$ rows and $(c-1)$ columns are filled, frequencies in the remaining row and column cells must be chosen so that marginal totals are maintained.

In this example, there are two degrees of freedom (1×2), and the Pearson chi-square value is 22.56 (see Figure 10.8). If type of address and return rate are independent, the probability that a random sample would result in a chi-square value of at least that magnitude is less than 0.00001. This probability is also known as the *observed significance level* of the test. If the probability is small enough (usually less than 0.05 or 0.01), the hypothesis that the two variables are independent is rejected.

Since the observed significance level in Figure 10.1 is very small (based on the combined city and town data), the hypothesis that address type and return rate are independent is rejected. When the chi-square test is calculated for the city and town data separately (Figure 10.4), different results are obtained. The observed significance level of the city data is 0.209, so the independence hypothesis is not rejected. For the towns, the observed significance level is less than 0.000005, and the hypothesis that address and return rate are independent is rejected. These results support the theory that city and town residents respond differently.

An alternative to the commonly used Pearson chi-square is the likelihood ratio chi-square (see Figure 10.8). This test is based on maximum likelihood theory and is often used in the analysis of categorical data. For large samples, the Pearson and likelihood ratio chi-square statistics give very similar results. (The test labeled **Mantel-Haenszel** is discussed in section 10.15.)

The chi-square test is a test of independence; it provides little information about the strength or form of the association between two variables. The magnitude of the observed chi-square depends not only on the goodness of fit of the independence model but also on the sample size. If the sample size for a particular table increases n-fold, so does the chi-square value. Thus, large chi-square values can arise in applications where residuals are small relative to expected frequencies but where the sample size is large.

Certain conditions must be met for the chi-square distribution to be a good approximation of the distribution of the statistic in the equation given above. The data must be random samples from multinomial distributions and the expected values must not be too small. While it has been recommended that all expected frequencies be at least 5, recent studies indicate that this is probably too stringent and can be relaxed (Everitt, 1977). CROSSTABS displays the number of cells with expected frequencies less than 5 and the minimum expected cell value.

To improve the approximation for a 2×2 table, *Yates' correction for continuity* is sometimes applied. Yates' correction for continuity involves subtracting 0.5 from positive differences between observed and expected frequencies (the residuals) and adding 0.5 to negative differences before squaring. For a discussion of some of the controversy regarding the merits of this correction, see Conover (1974) and Mantel (1974).

An alternative test for the 2×2 table is based on the hypergeometric distribution. Exact probabilities of obtaining the observed results if the two variables are independent and the marginals fixed are calculated. This is called *Fisher's exact test*. It is most useful when the total sample size and the expected values are small. SPSS calculates Fisher's exact test if any expected cell value in a 2×2 table is less than 5.

10.9
Measures of Association

In many research situations, the strength and nature of the dependence of variables is of central concern. Indexes that attempt to quantify the relationship between variables in a cross-classification are called *measures of association*. No single measure adequately summarizes all possible types of association. Measures vary in their interpretation and in the way they define perfect and intermediate association. These measures also differ in the way they are affected by various factors such as marginals. For example, many measures are "margin sensitive" in that they are influenced by the marginal distributions of the rows and columns. Such measures reflect information about the marginals along with information about association.

A particular measure may have a low value for a given table, not because the two variables are not related but because they are not related in the way to which the measure is sensitive. No single measure is best for all situations. The type of data, the hypothesis of interest, as well as the properties of the various measures must all be considered when selecting an index of association for a given table. It is not, however, reasonable to compute a large number of measures and then to report the most impressive as if it were the only one examined.

The measures of association available in CROSSTABS are computed only from bivariate tables. For example, if three dichotomous variables are specified in the table, two sets of measures are computed, one for each subtable produced by the values of the controlling variable. In general, if relationships among more than two variables are to be studied, examination of bivariate tables is only a first step. For an extensive discussion of various more sophisticated multivariate procedures for the analysis of qualitative data, see Feinberg (1977), Everitt (1977), and Haberman (1978).

10.10
Nominal Measures

Consider measures that assume only that both variables in the table are nominally measured. As such, these measures can only provide some indication of the strength of association between variables; they cannot indicate direction or anything about the nature of the relationship. The measures provided are of two types: those based on the chi-square statistic and those that follow the logic of proportional reduction in error, denoted PRE.

10.11
Chi-Square-Based Measures

As explained above, the chi-square statistic itself is not a good measure of the degree of association between two variables. But its widespread use in tests of independence has encouraged the use of measures of association based upon it. Each of these measures based on the chi-square attempts to modify the chi-square statistic to minimize the influence of sample size and degrees of freedom as well as to restrict the range of values of the measure to those between 0 and 1. Without such adjustments, comparison of chi-square values from tables with varying dimensions and sample sizes is meaningless.

The *phi-coefficient* modifies the Pearson chi-square by dividing it by the sample size and taking the square root of the result:

$$\phi = \sqrt{\frac{\chi^2}{N}}$$

Equation 10.11a

For tables in which one dimension is greater than 2, phi may not lie between 0 and 1 since the chi-square value can be greater than the sample size. To obtain a measure that must lie between 0 and 1, Pearson suggested the use of

$$C = \sqrt{\frac{\chi^2}{\chi^2 + N}}$$

Equation 10.11b

which is called the *coefficient of contingency*. Although the value of this measure is always between 0 and 1, it cannot generally attain the upper limit of 1. The maximum value possible depends upon the number of rows and columns. For example, in a 4×4 table, the maximum value of C is 0.87.

Cramér introduced the following variant:

$$V = \sqrt{\frac{\chi^2}{N(k-1)}}$$

Equation 10.11c

where k is the smaller of the number of rows and columns. This statistic, known as *Cramér's V*, can attain the maximum of 1 for tables of any dimension. If one of the table dimensions is 2, V and phi are identical.

Figure 10.11 shows the values of the chi-square based measures for the letter data. The test of the null hypothesis that a measure is 0 is based on the Pearson chi-square probability.

Figure 10.11 Chi-square-based measures

```
CROSSTABS TABLES=RETURNED BY ADDRESS
  /STATISTICS=PHI CC.
```

```
RETURNED  FOUND AND MAILED  by  ADDRESS  ADDRESS ON LETTER

                     ADDRESS                    Page 1 of 1
             Count  |
                    |CONTROL  DANDEE  COMMUNIS
                    |                      T     Row
                    |    1   |    2   |    3   | Total
RETURNED     -------+--------+--------+--------+
             1   |    35  |    32  |    10  |    77
  YES            |        |        |        |   35.6
             ----+--------+--------+--------+
             2   |    37  |    40  |    62  |   139
  NO             |        |        |        |   64.4
             ----+--------+--------+--------+
           Column     72       72       72      216
            Total    33.3     33.3     33.3    100.0


                                                       Approximate
       Statistic            Value     ASE1   T-value   Significance
    _____       _____   _____   _____   _____

Phi                        .32320                        .00001 *1
Cramer's V                 .32320                        .00001 *1
Contingency Coefficient    .30753                        .00001 *1

*1 Pearson chi-square probability

Number of Missing Observations:  0
```

The chi-square-based measures are hard to interpret. Although when properly standardized they can be used to compare strength of association in several tables, the "strength of association" being compared is not easily related to an intuitive concept of association.

10.12
Proportional Reduction in Error

Common alternatives to chi-square-based measurements are those based on the idea of *proportional reduction in error* (PRE), introduced by Goodman and Kruskal (1954). With PRE measures, the meaning of association is clearer. These measures are all essentially ratios of a measure of error in predicting the values of one variable based on knowledge of that variable alone and the same measure of error applied to predictions based on knowledge of an additional variable.

For example, Figure 10.12 is a crosstabulation of depth of hypnosis and success in treatment of migraine headaches by suggestion (Cedercreutz, 1978). The best guess of the results of treatment when no other information is available is the outcome category with the largest proportion of observations (the modal category). In Figure 10.12, "no change" is the largest outcome category, with 45% of the subjects. The estimate of the probability of incorrect classification is 1 minus the probability of the modal category:

$$P(1) = 1 - 0.45 = 0.55$$

Equation 10.12a

Figure 10.12   Depth of hypnosis and success of treatment

```
CROSSTABS TABLES=HYPNOSIS BY MIGRAINE
 /CELLS=COUNT COLUMN TOTAL
 /STATISTICS=LAMBDA.
```

```
HYPNOSIS  DEPTH OF HYPNOSIS  by  MIGRAINE  OUTCOME

                      MIGRAINE                    Page 1 of 1
              Count
              Col Pct  CURED   BETTER   NO
              Tot Pct                   CHANGE    Row
                        1.00    2.00     3.00|   Total
HYPNOSIS      -------+-------+-------+-------+
              1.00  |   13  |    5  |       |     18
DEEP                |  56.5 |  15.6 |       |   18.0
                    |  13.0 |   5.0 |       |
              -------+-------+-------+-------+
              2.00  |   10  |   26  |   17  |     53
MEDIUM              |  43.5 |  81.3 |  37.8 |   53.0
                    |  10.0 |  26.0 |  17.0 |
              -------+-------+-------+-------+
              3.00  |       |    1  |   28  |     29
LIGHT               |       |   3.1 |  62.2 |   29.0
                    |       |   1.0 |  28.0 |
              -------+-------+-------+-------+
              Column     23      32      45       100
               Total    23.0    32.0    45.0    100.0


                                                              Approximate
      Statistic                  Value     ASE1    T-value    Significance
      _____


Lambda :
    symmetric                   .35294    .11335   2.75267
    with HYPNOSIS dependent     .29787    .14702   1.72276
    with MIGRAINE dependent     .40000    .10539   3.07580
Goodman & Kruskal Tau :
    with HYPNOSIS dependent     .29435    .06304              .00000 *2
    with MIGRAINE dependent     .34508    .04863              .00000 *2

*2 Based on chi-square approximation

Number of Missing Observations:  0
```

Information about the depth of hypnosis can be used to improve the classification rule. For each hypnosis category, the outcome category that occurs most frequently for that hypnosis level is predicted. Thus, no change is predicted for participants achieving a light level of hypnosis, better for those achieving a medium level, and cured for those achieving a deep level. The probability of error when depth of hypnosis is used to predict outcome is the sum of the probabilities of all the cells that are not row modes:

$$P(2)=0.05+0.10+0.17+0.01=0.33 \qquad \text{Equation 10.12b}$$

Goodman and Kruskal's *lambda*, with outcome as the predicted (dependent) variable, is calculated as

$$\lambda_{\text{outcome}} = \frac{P(1) - P(2)}{P(1)} = \frac{0.55 - 0.33}{0.55} = 0.40 \qquad \text{Equation 10.12c}$$

Thus, a 40% reduction in error is obtained when depth of hypnosis is used to predict outcome.

Lambda always ranges between 0 and 1. A value of 0 means the independent variable is of no help in predicting the dependent variable. A value of 1 means that the independent variable perfectly specifies the categories of the dependent variable (perfection can occur only when each row has at most one nonzero cell). When the two variables are independent, lambda is 0; but a lambda of 0 need not imply statistical independence. As with all measures of association, lambda is constructed to measure association in a very specific way. In particular, lambda reflects the reduction in error when values of one variable are used to predict values of the other. If this particular type of association is absent, lambda is 0. Other measures of association may find association of a different kind even when lambda is 0. A measure of association sensitive to every imaginable type of association does not exist.

For a particular table, two different lambdas can be computed, one using the row variable as the predictor and the other using the column variable. The two do not usually have identical values, so care should be taken to specify which is the dependent variable, that is, the variable whose prediction is of primary interest. In some applications, dependent and independent variables are not clearly distinguished. Then, a symmetric version of lambda, which predicts the row variable and column variable with equal frequency, can be computed. When the lambda statistic is requested, SPSS displays the symmetric lambda as well as the two asymmetric lambdas.

10.13
Goodman and Kruskal's Tau

When lambda is computed, the same prediction is made for all cases in a particular row or column. Another approach is to consider what happens if the prediction is randomly made in the same proportion as the marginal totals. For example, if you're trying to predict migraine outcome without any information about the depth of the hypnosis, you can use the marginal distributions in Figure 10.12 instead of the modal category to guess cured for 23% of the cases, better for 32% of the cases, and no change for 45% of the cases.

Using these marginals, you would expect to correctly classify 23% of the 23 cases in the cured category, 32% of the 32 cases in the better category, and 45% of the 45 cases in the no change category. This results in the correct classification of 35.78 out of 100 cases. When additional information about the depth of hypnosis is incorporated into the prediction rule, the prediction is based on the probability of the different outcomes for each depth of hypnosis. For example, for those who experienced deep hypnosis, you would predict cure 72% of the time (13/18) and better 28% of the time (5/18). Similarly, for those with light hypnosis, you would predict better 3% of the time and no change 97% of the time. This results in correct classification for about 58 of the cases.

Kruskal and Goodman's tau is computed by comparing the probability of error in the two situations. In this example, when predicting only from the column marginal totals, the probability of error is 0.64. When predicting from row information the probability of error is 0.42. Thus:

$$\text{tau (migraine|hypnosis)} = (0.64 - 0.42)/0.64 = 0.34 \qquad \textbf{Equation 10.13}$$

By incorporating information about the depth of hypnosis we have reduced our error of prediction by about 34%.

A test of the null hypothesis that tau is 0 can be based on the value of $(N\text{-}1)(c - 1)$ tau (col|row), which has a chi-square distribution with $(c - 1) \times (r - 1)$ degrees of freedom. In this example, the observed significance level for tau is very small, and you can reject the null hypothesis that tau is 0. The asymptotic standard error for the statistic is shown in the column labeled **ASE1**. The asymptotic standard error can be used to construct confidence intervals.

10.14
Measuring Agreement

Measures of agreement allow you to compare the ratings of two observers for the same group of objects. For example, consider the data reported in Bishop et al. (1975), shown in Figure 10.14.

Figure 10.14   Student teachers rated by supervisors

```
CROSSTABS TABLES=SUPRVSR1 BY SUPRVSR2
  /CELLS=COUNT TOTAL
  /STATISTICS=KAPPA.
```

```
SUPRVSR1   Supervisor 1  by  SUPRVSR2   Supervisor 2

                    SUPRVSR2                      Page 1 of 1
           Count
           Tot Pct  Authorit Democrat Permissi
                    arian    ic       ve          Row
                        1.00     2.00     3.00 | Total
SUPRVSR1   ------+--------+--------+--------+
              1.00 |   17   |    4   |    8   |   29
         Authoritarian |  23.6 |   5.6  |  11.1 |  40.3
                  +--------+--------+--------+
              2.00 |    5   |   12   |        |   17
         Democratic |   6.9 |  16.7  |        |  23.6
                  +--------+--------+--------+
              3.00 |   10   |    3   |   13   |   26
         Permissive |  13.9 |   4.2  |  18.1 |  36.1
                  +--------+--------+--------+
           Column      32       19       21       72
           Total      44.4     26.4     29.2    100.0


                                                              Approximate
        Statistic                   Value      ASE1    T-value  Significance
  _____              _____      ____    _____  _____


  Kappa                            .36227     .09144   4.32902


Number of Missing Observations:  0
```

Two supervisors rated the classroom style of 72 teachers. You are interested in measuring the agreement between the two raters. The simplest measure that comes to mind is just the proportion of cases for which the raters agree. In this case it is 58.3%. The disadvantage of this measure is that no correction is made for the amount of agreement expected by chance. That is, you would expect the supervisors to agree sometimes even if they were assigning ratings by tossing dice.

To correct for chance agreement you can compute the proportion of cases that you would expect to be in agreement if the ratings are independent. For example, Supervisor 1 rated 40.3% of the teachers as authoritarian, while Supervisor 2 rated 44.4% of the teachers as authoritarian. If their rankings are independent, you would expect that 17.9% ($40.3\% \times 44.4\%$) of the teachers would be rated as authoritarian by both. Similarly, 6.2% would be rated as democratic ($23.6\% \times 26.4\%$) and 10.5% ($36.1\% \times 29.2\%$) as permissive. Thus, 34.6% of all the teachers would be classified the same merely by chance.

The difference between the observed proportion of cases in which the raters agree and that expected by chance is 0.237 ($0.583 - 0.346$). *Cohen's kappa* (1960) normalizes this difference by dividing it by the maximum difference possible for the marginal totals. In this example, the largest possible "non-chance" agreement is $1 - 0.346$ (the chance level). Therefore:

$$\text{kappa} = 0.237/(1 - 0.346) = 0.362 \qquad \text{Equation 10.14}$$

The test of the null hypothesis that kappa is 0 can be based on the t statistic shown in Figure 10.14. (See Benedetti & Brown, 1978, for further discussion of standard errors for measures of association as well as discussion of the degrees of freedom for the t statistic.) The t value is the ratio of the value of kappa to its asymptotic standard error when the null hypothesis is true. (This asymptotic error is not the one shown on the output. The asymptotic standard error on the output, ASE1, does not assume that the true value is 0.)

Since the kappa statistic measures agreement between two raters, the two variables that contain the ratings must have the same range of values. If this is not true, CROSSTABS will not compute kappa.

10.15
Ordinal Measures

Although relationships among ordinal variables can be examined using nominal measures, other measures reflect the additional information available from ranking. Consideration of the kind of relationships that may exist between two ordered variables leads to the notion of direction of relationship and to the concept of *correlation*. Variables are positively correlated if cases with low values for one variable also tend to have low values for the other and cases with high values on one also tend to be high on the other. Negatively correlated variables show the opposite relationship: the higher the first variable, the lower the second tends to be.

The Spearman correlation coefficient is a commonly used measure of correlation between two ordinal variables. For all of the cases, the values of each of the variables are ranked from smallest to largest and the Pearson correlation coefficient is computed on the ranks. The Mantel-Haenszel chi-square is another measure of linear association between the row and column variables in a crosstabulation. It is computed by multiplying the Pearson correlation coefficient by the number of cases minus 1. The resulting statistic has one degree of freedom (Mantel & Haenszel, 1959). (Although the Mantel-Haenszel statistic is displayed whenever chi-square is requested, it should not be used for nominal data.)

10.16
Ordinal Measures Based On Pairs

For a table of two ordered variables, several measures of association based on a comparison of the values of both variables for all possible *pairs* of cases or observations are available. Cases are first compared to determine if they are *concordant, discordant,* or *tied.* A pair of cases is *concordant* if the values of both variables for one case are higher (or both are lower) than the corresponding values for the other case. The pair is *discordant* if the value of one variable for a case is larger than the corresponding value for the other case, and the direction is reversed for the second variable. When the two cases have identical values on one or on both variables, they are *tied.*

Thus, for any given pair of cases with measurements on variables X and Y, the pair may be concordant or discordant, or tied in one of three ways: they may be tied on X but not on Y, they may be tied on Y but not on X, or they may be tied on both variables. When data are arranged in crosstabulated form, the number of concordant, discordant, and tied pairs can be easily calculated since all possible pairs can be conveniently determined.

If the preponderance of pairs is concordant, the association is said to be positive: as ranks of variable X increase (or decrease), so do ranks of variable Y. If the majority of pairs is discordant, the association is negative: as ranks of one variable increase, those of the other tend to decrease. If concordant and discordant pairs are equally likely, no association is said to exist.

The ordinal measures presented here all have the same numerator: the number of concordant pairs (P) minus the number of discordant pairs (Q) calculated for all distinct pairs of observations. They differ primarily in the way in which $P-Q$ is normalized. The simplest measure involves subtracting Q from P and dividing by the total number of pairs. If there are no pairs with ties, this measure (Kendall's tau-a) is in the range from -1 to $+1$. If there are ties, the range of possible values is narrower; the actual range depends on the number of ties. Since all observations within the same row are tied, so also are those in the same column, and the resulting tau-a measures are difficult to interpret.

A measure that attempts to normalize $P-Q$ by considering ties on each variable in a pair separately but not ties on both variables in a pair is tau-b:

$$\tau_b = \frac{P - Q}{\sqrt{(P + Q + T_X)(P + Q + T_Y)}}$$

Equation 10.16a

where T_X is the number of pairs tied on X but not on Y, and T_Y is the number of pairs tied on Y but not on X. If no marginal frequency is 0, tau-b can attain $+1$ or -1 only for a square table.

A measure that can attain, or nearly attain, $+1$ or -1 for any $r \times c$ table is tau-c

$$\tau_c = \frac{2m(P - Q)}{N^2(m - 1)}$$

Equation 10.16b

where m is the smaller of the number of rows and columns. The coefficients tau-b and tau-c do not differ much in value if each margin contains approximately equal frequencies.

Goodman and Kruskal's *gamma* is closely related to the tau statistics and is calculated as

$$G = \frac{P - Q}{P + Q}$$

Equation 10.16c

Gamma can be thought of as the probability that a random pair of observations is concordant minus the probability that the pair is discordant, assuming the absence of ties. The absolute value of gamma is the proportional reduction in error between guessing concordant and discordant ranking of each pair depending on which occurs more often and guessing ranking according to the outcome of the toss of a fair coin. Gamma is 1 if all observations are concentrated in the upper-left to lower-right diagonal of the table. In the case of independence, gamma is 0. However, the converse (that a gamma of 0 necessarily implies independence) need not be true except in the 2×2 table.

In the computation of gamma, no distinction is made between the independent and dependent variable; the variables are treated symmetrically. Somers (1962) proposed an asymmetric extension of gamma that differs only in the inclusion of the number of pairs not tied on the independent variable (X) in the denominator. Somers' d is

$$d_Y = \frac{P - Q}{P + Q + T_Y}$$

Equation 10.16d

The coefficient d_Y indicates the proportionate excess of concordant pairs over discordant pairs among pairs not tied on the independent variable. The symmetric variant of Somers' *d* uses for the denominator the average value of the denominators of the two asymmetric coefficients.

These ordinal measures for the migraine data are shown in Figure 10.16. All of the measures indicate that there is a fairly strong linear association between the two variables.

Figure 10.16 Ordinal measures

```
CROSSTABS TABLES=HYPNOSIS BY MIGRAINE
 /FORMAT=NOTABLE
 /STATISTICS=CORR BTAU CTAU GAMMA D.
```

```
HYPNOSIS  DEPTH OF HYPNOSIS  by  MIGRAINE  OUTCOME

Number of valid observations = 100


                                                          Approximate
        Statistic                Value     ASE1   T-value Significance
    _____             _____     ____   _____ _____


    Kendall's Tau-b             .67901    .04445  11.96486
    Kendall's Tau-c             .63360    .05296  11.96486
    Gamma                       .94034    .02720  11.96486
    Somers' D :
        symmetric               .67866    .04443  11.96485
        with HYPNOSIS dependent .65774    .05440  11.96485
        with MIGRAINE dependent .70096    .03996  11.96486


    Pearson's R                 .71739    .04484  10.19392    .00000
    Spearman Correlation        .72442    .04317  10.40311    .00000


Number of Missing Observations:  0
```

10.17
Measures Involving Interval Data

If the two variables in the table are measured on an interval scale, various coefficients that make use of this additional information can be calculated. A useful symmetric coefficient that measures the strength of the *linear* relationship is the Pearson correlation coefficient, or *r*. It can take on values from -1 to $+1$, indicating negative or positive linear correlation.

The *eta* coefficient is appropriate for data in which the dependent variable is measured on an interval scale and the independent variable on a nominal or ordinal scale. When squared, eta can be interpreted as the proportion of the total variability in the dependent variable that can be accounted for by knowing the values of the independent variable. The measure is asymmetric and does not assume a linear relationship between the variables.

10.18
Estimating Risk in Cohort Studies

Often you want to identify variables that are related to the occurrence of a particular event. For example, you may want to determine if smoking is related to heart disease. A commonly used index that measures the strength of the association between presence of a factor and occurence of an event is the *relative risk ratio*. It is estimated as the ratio of two incidence rates, for example, the incidence rate of heart disease in those who smoke and the incidence rate of heart disease in those who do not smoke.

For example, suppose you observe for five years 1000 smokers without a history of heart disease and 1000 non-smokers without a history of heart disease, and you determine how many of each group develop heart disease during this time period. (Studies in which a group of disease-free people are studied to see who develops the disease are called *cohort* or *prospective* studies.) Figure 10.18 contains hypothetical results from such a cohort study.

Figure 10.18 Hypothetical cohorts

```
CROSSTABS TABLES=SMOKING BY HDISEASE
/STATISTICS=RISK.
```

```
SMOKING  Smoking  by  HDISEASE  Heart Disease

                    HDISEASE        Page 1 of 1
            Count
                    Yes      No
                                        Row
                      1.00|    2.00| Total
SMOKING     --------+--------+--------+
            1.00 |   100  |   900  |  1000
   Yes      |        |        |    50.0
            +--------+--------+
            2.00 |    50  |   950  |  1000
    No      |        |        |    50.0
            +--------+--------+
          Column     150     1850    2000
          Total      7.5     92.5   100.0




     Statistic               Value        95% Confidence Bounds

Relative Risk Estimate (SMOKING 1.0 / SMOKING 2.0) :
   case control                2.11111     1.48544      3.00032
   cohort (HDISEASE 1.0 Risk)  2.00000     1.44078      2.77628
   cohort (HDISEASE 2.0 Risk)   .94737      .92390       .97143

Number of Missing Observations:  0
```

The five-year incidence rate for smokers is 100/1000, while the incidence rate for nonsmokers is 50/1000. The relative risk ratio is 2 (100/1000 divided by 50/1000). This indicates that, in the sample, smokers are twice as likely to develop heart disease as nonsmokers.

The estimated relative risk and its 95% confidence interval are in the row labeled **cohort (HDISEASE 1.0 Risk)** in Figure 10.18. In CROSSTABS, the ratio is always computed by taking the incidence in the first row and dividing it by the incidence in the second row. Since either column can represent the event, separate estimates are displayed for each column. The 95% confidence intervals do not include the value of 1, so you can reject the null hypothesis that the two incidence rates are the same.

10.19
Estimating Risk in Case-Control Studies

In the cohort study described above, we took a group of disease-free people (the cohort) and watched what happened to them. Another type of study that is commonly used is called a retrospective, or *case-control* study. In this type of study, we take a group of people with the disease of interest (the cases) and a comparable group of people without the disease (the controls) and see how they differ. For example, we could take 100 people with documented coronary heart disease and 100 controls without heart disease and establish how many in each group smoked. The hypothetical results are shown in Figure 10.19.

Figure 10.19 Hypothetical Smoking Control

```
CROSSTABS TABLES=GROUP BY SMOKING
  /CELLS=COUNT ROW
  /STATISTICS=RISK.
```

```
GROUP   by   SMOKING

                            SMOKING      Page 1 of 1
                    Count
                    Row Pct  Yes        No
                                                       Row
                             1.00|     2.00|   Total
      GROUP         --------+--------+--------+
                    1.00       30        70        100
        Cases                30.0      70.0       50.0
                           --------+--------+--------+
                    2.00       10        90        100
        Controls             10.0      90.0       50.0
                           --------+--------+--------+
                    Column     40       160        200
                    Total     20.0      80.0      100.0


        Statistic                    Value          95% Confidence Bounds
      ---------------------          -------        ---------------------
      Relative Risk Estimate (GROUP 1.0 / GROUP 2.0) :
        case control                3.85714         1.76660      8.42156
        cohort (SMOKING 1.0 Risk)   3.00000         1.55083      5.80334
        cohort (SMOKING 2.0 Risk)    .77778          .67348       .89823

      Number of Missing Observations:  0
```

From a case-control study we cannot estimate incidence rates. Thus we cannot compute the relative risk ratio. Instead we estimate relative risk using what is called an *odds ratio*. We compute the odds that a "case" smokes and divide it by the odds that a control smokes.

For example, from Figure 10.19, the odds that a case smokes are 30/70. The odds that a control smokes is 10/90. The odds ratio is then 30/70 divided by 10/90, or 3.85. The odds ratio and its confidence interval are in the row labeled **case control** in Figure 10.19. The CROSSTABS procedure expects the cases to be in the first row and the controls in the second. Similarly, the event of interest of interest must be in the first column. For further discussion of measures of risk, see Kleinbaum et al. (1982).

10.20
RUNNING PROCEDURE CROSSTABS

Procedure CROSSTABS produces two-way to *n*-way crosstabulations and related statistical measures for variables with numeric or string values. In addition to cell counts, you can obtain cell percentages and expected values. You can alter the handling of missing values, reorder rows, request an index of tables, and write cell frequencies to a file.

10.21
TABLES Subcommand

The only required subcommand for CROSSTABS is the TABLES subcommand. The minimum specification for the TABLES subcommand is a list of one or more variables followed by the keyword BY and a second list of one or more variables, as in:

```
CROSSTABS TABLES=RETURNED BY ADDRESS.
```

The first variable list specifies the *row variables*, and the variable list following the first BY keyword specifies the *column variables*.

Optionally, you can specify *control variables* with additional BY keywords and variable lists, as in:

```
CROSSTABS TABLES=RETURNED BY ADDRESS BY LOCATION.
```

A separate subtable is generated for each value of the control variable(s). In this example, the control variable LOCATION has two values, producing two subtables (as in Figure 10.4).

You can specify more than one variable in each dimension. Use the TO keyword to imply consecutive variables on the active system file, as in:

```
CROSSTABS  TABLES=CONFINAN TO CONARMY BY SEX TO REGION.
```

This command will produce CROSSTABS tables for all the variables between and including CONFINAN and CONARMY by all the variables between and including SEX and REGION.

You can specify multiple TABLES subcommands. Each subcommand should be separated by a slash.

10.22
VARIABLES Subcommand

To run CROSSTABS in *integer mode*, use the VARIABLES subcommand. Integer mode builds tables more quickly than general mode but requires more space if the table has many empty cells. You must specify an integer value range enclosed in parentheses for each variable, as in:

```
CROSSTABS VARIABLES=RETURNED(1,2) ADDRESS(1,3)
 /TABLES=RETURNED BY ADDRESS.
```

Since only values within the specified range will be included, you can use the VARIABLES subcommand to select subsets of cases for analysis. If multiple variables have the same range, you need to specify the range only once, as in:

```
CROSSTABS VARIABLES=ADDRESS(1,3) RETURNED LOCATION(1,2)
 /TABLES=RETURNED BY ADDRESS BY LOCATION.
```

which specifies the same range for variables RETURNED and LOCATION.

If used, the VARIABLES subcommand must be the first subcommand specified, and it must include all variables specified on subsequent TABLES subcommands. The TO keyword on subsequent TABLES subcommands refers to the order of variables on the VARIABLES subcommand, not the order of variables on the active system file.

10.23
CELLS Subcommand

By default, CROSSTABS displays only the number of cases in each cell. Use the CELLS subcommand to display row, column, or total percentages, expected values, residuals. These items are calculated separately for each bivariate table or subtable.

You can specify the CELLS subcommand by itself, or with one or more keywords. If you specify the CELLS subcommand by itself, CROSSTABS displays cell counts plus row, column, and total percentages for each cell. If you specify keywords, CROSSTABS displays only the cell information you request.

The following keywords can be specified on the CELLS subcommand:

COUNT   *Cell counts.* This is the default if you omit the CELLS subcommand.

ROW   *Row percentages.* Row percentages are the number of cases in each cell in a row expressed as a percentage of all cases in that row.

COLUMN *Column percentages.* Column percentages are the number of cases in each cell in a column expressed as a percentage of all cases in that column.

TOTAL   *Two-way table total percentages.* This is the number of cases in each cell of a subtable expressed as a percentage of all cases in that subtable.

EXPECTED *Expected frequencies.* Expected frequencies are the number of cases expected in each cell if the two variables in the subtable were statistically independent.

RESID *Residuals.* The residual is the value of the observed cell count minus the expected value.

SRESID *Standardized residuals.* (Haberman, 1978).

ASRESID *Adjusted standardized residuals.* (Haberman, 1978).

ALL *All cell information.* This includes cell counts, row, column, and total percentages, expected values, residuals, standardized residuals, and adjusted standardized residuals.

NONE *No cell information.* Use NONE to write tables to a file without displaying any tables. This has the same effect as specifying FORMAT=NOTABLES (see Section 10.26).

For example, the command

```
CROSSTABS TABLES=RETURNED BY ADDRESS
 /CELLS.
```

produces Figure 10.1, and the command

```
CROSSTABS TABLES=RETURNED BY ADDRESS
 /CELLS=COUNT EXPECTED RESID.
 /STATISTICS=CHISQ.
```

produces Figure 10.8.

10.24
STATISTICS Subcommand

CROSSTABS can calculate a number of summary statistics for each subtable. Unless you specify otherwise, it calculates statistical measures of association for the cases with valid values included in the subtable. If you include user-missing values with the MISSING subcommand, cases with user-missing values are included in the tables as well as in the calculation of statistics.

The STATISTICS subcommand requests summary statistics. You can specify the STATISTICS subcommand by itself, or with one or more keywords. If you specify STATISTICS by itself, CROSSTABS calculates CHISQ. If you include a keyword or keywords on the STATISTICS subcommand, CROSSTABS calculates all the statistics you request.

Asymptotic standard errors (ASE1) that are not based on the assumption that the true value is 0 are also calculated. The t statistics displayed are the ratio of the measure to an asymptotic standard error which assumes the true coefficient is 0.

The following keywords can be specified on the STATISTICS subcommand:

CHISQ *Chi-square.* The output includes the Pearson chi-square, likelihood-ratio chi-square, and Mantel-Haenszel linear association chi-square. For 2×2 tables, Fisher's exact test is computed when a table that does not result from missing rows or columns in a larger table has a cell with an expected frequency less than 5; Yates' corrected chi-square is computed for all other 2 × 2 tables. This is the default if STATISTICS is specified without keywords.

PHI *Phi and Cramer's V.*

CC *Contingency coefficient.*

LAMBDA *Lambda, symmetric and asymmetric, and Goodman and Kruskal's tau.*

UC *Uncertainty coefficient, symmetric and asymmetric.*

BTAU *Kendall's tau-b.*

CTAU *Kendall's tau-c.*

GAMMA *Gamma.* Partial and zero-order gammas for 3-way to 8-way tables are available in integer mode only (see Section 10.22). Zero-order gammas are displayed for 2-way tables and conditional gammas are displayed for 3-way to 10-way tables in general mode and 3-way to 8-way tables in integer mode.

D	*Somers' d, symmetric and asymmetric.*
ETA	*Eta.* Available for numeric data only.
CORR	*Pearson's* r, *and Spearman's correlation coefficient.* Available for numeric data only.
KAPPA	*Kappa coefficient.* Kappa can only be computed for square tables in which the row and column values are identical. If there is a missing row or column, use integer mode to specify the square table since a missing column or row in general mode would keep the table from being square (see Section 10.22). (Kraemer, 1982.)
RISK	*Relative risk.* Relative risk can be calculated only for 2 × 2 tables. (Kleinbaum et al., 1982).
ALL	*All available statistics.*
NONE	*No summary statistics.* This is the default if STATISTICS is omitted.

For example, the command

```
CROSSTABS TABLES=RETURNED BY ADDRESS
 /STATISTICS=PHI CC.
```

produces Figure 10.11.

10.25
MISSING Subcommand

By default, CROSSTABS deletes cases with missing values on a table-by-table basis. A case missing on any of the variables specified for a table is not used either in the table or in the calculation of the statistics. Missing values are handled separately for each TABLES subcommand. The number of missing cases is displayed at the end of the table, following the last subtable and after any requested statistics.

The MISSING subcommand controls missing values. The following keywords can be specified on the MISSING subcommand:

TABLE	*Delete cases with missing values on a table-by-table basis.* This is the default if you omit the MISSING subcommand.
INCLUDE	*Include cases with user-missing values.*
REPORT	*Report missing values in the tables.* This option includes missing values in tables but not in the calculation of percentages or statistics. The letter **M** is used to indicate that cases within a cell are missing. REPORT is available only in integer mode (see Section 10.22).

10.26
FORMAT Subcommand

Use the FORMAT subcommand to modify the default formats. The following keywords can be specified:

LABELS	*Display both variable and value labels for each table.* This is the default. The values for the row variables are displayed in order from lowest to highest. CROSSTABS uses only the first 16 characters of the value labels. Value labels for the columns are displayed on two lines with eight characters per line.
NOLABELS	*Suppress variable and value labels.*
NOVALLABS	*Suppress value labels but display variable labels.*
AVALUE	*Display row variables ordered from lowest to highest.* This is the default.
DVALUE	*Display row variables ordered from highest to lowest.*
NOINDEX	*Suppress a table index.* This is the default.
INDEX	*Display an index of tables.* The index lists all tables produced by the CROSSTABS command and the page number where each table begins. The index follows the last page of tables produced by the tables list.

TABLES	*Display the crosstabulation tables.* This is the default.
NOTABLES	*Suppress table display.* If you use the STATISTICS subcommand (see Section 10.24) and specify NOTABLES, only the statistics are displayed. If you do not use the STATISTICS subcommand and specify NOTA-BLES, the CROSSTABS command produces no output.
BOX	*Use box drawing characters around every cell.* This is the default.
NOBOX	*Suppress the box drawing characters around each cell.* The banner and stub are still separated from the table by by box drawing characters.

10.27
WRITE Subcommand

The WRITE subcommand writes cell frequencies to a procedure output file (specified on the PROCEDURE OUTPUT command), for subsequent use by SPSS or some other program. The output file contains one record per cell.

NONE	*Do not write the cell counts to the file.* This is the default if you omit the WRITE subcommand.
CELLS	*Write the cell count for nonempty cells to a file.*
ALL	*Write the cell count for all cells to a file.* This is only available in integer mode. (See the VARIABLES subcommand, Section 10.22.)

For more information about the WRITE subcommand, see the *SPSS Reference Guide.*

10.28
Entering Crosstabulated Data

You can use the CROSSTABS procedure to calculate statistics for a pre-existing crosstabulation without entering the individual case data. Each cell of the table is considered a case. The variables for each case are the cell count and the values of the row, column, and control variables.

Define this file as you would any other file. Then use the WEIGHT command (see Chapter 2) to count each "case" as many times as the value of the cell count variable. For example, Figure 10.18 was produced from a table, rather than raw data, using the following commands:

```
DATA LIST FREE /SMOKING HDISEASE COUNT.
BEGIN DATA.
1 1 100
1 2 900
2 1 50
2 2 950
END DATA.
VARIABLE LABELS
  SMOKING 'Smoking'
  HDISEASE 'Heart Disease'.
VALUE LABELS SMOKING HDISEASE 1 'Yes' 2 'No'.
WEIGHT BY COUNT.
CROSSTABS TABLES=SMOKING by HDISEASE
 /STATISTICS=RISK.
```

- The DATA LIST command names three variables: SMOKING is the row variable; HDISEASE is the column variable, and COUNT is the cell count.

- The optional VARIABLE LABELS and VALUE LABELS commands identify the variables and values in the tables.

- The WEIGHT command weights each case by the cell count.

- The CROSSTABS command re-creates the table, and the STATISTICS subcommand provides summary statistics not provided with the original table.

Contents

11 Describing Subpopulation Differences: Procedure MEANS

The 1964 Civil Rights Act prohibits discrimination in the workplace based on sex or race. Employers who violate the act by unfair hiring or advancement practices can be prosecuted. Numerous lawsuits have been filed on behalf of women, blacks, and other groups offered equal protection under the law.

The courts have ruled that statistics can be used as *prima facie* evidence of discrimination, and many lawsuits depend heavily on complex statistical analyses, which attempt to demonstrate that similarly qualified individuals are not treated equally. Identifying and measuring all variables that legitimately influence promotion and hiring is difficult, if not impossible, especially for nonroutine jobs. Years of schooling and prior work experience can be quantified, but what about the more intangible attributes such as enthusiasm and creativity? How are they to be objectively measured so as not to become convenient smoke screens for concealing discrimination?

11.1 SEARCHING FOR DISCRIMINATION

In this chapter, employee records for 474 individuals hired between 1969 and 1971 by a bank engaged in Equal Employment Opportunity (EEO) litigation are analyzed. Two types of unfair employment practices are of particular interest: shunting (placing some employees in lower job categories than others with similar qualifications) and salary and promotion inequities.

Although extensive and intricate statistical analyses are usually involved in studies of this kind (see, for example, Roberts, 1980), the discussion here is necessarily limited. The SPSS MEANS procedure is used to calculate average salaries for groups of employees based on race and sex. Additional grouping variables are introduced to help "explain" some of the observed variability in salary.

11.2
Who Does What?

Figure 11.2 is a crosstabulation of job category at the time of hiring with sex and race characteristics. The first three job classifications contain 64% of white males (adding column percents), 94% of both nonwhite males and white females, and 100% of nonwhite females. Among white males, 17% are in the college trainee program, compared to 4% of white females.

Figure 11.2 Crosstabulation of job category by sex-race

```
COMPUTE    SEXRACE=1.
IF (MINORITY EQ 1 AND SEX EQ 0) SEXRACE=2.
IF (MINORITY EQ 0 AND SEX EQ 1) SEXRACE=3.
IF (MINORITY EQ 1 AND SEX EQ 1) SEXRACE=4.
CROSSTABS TABLES=JOBCAT BY SEXRACE /CELLS=COUNT, COLUMN, TOTAL.
```

JOBCAT EMPLOYMENT CATEGORY by SEXRACE SEX & RACE CLASSIFICATION

Count Col Pct Tot Pct	WHITE MALES 1	MINORITY MALES 2	WHITE FEMALES 3	MINORITY FEMALES 4	Row Total
JOBCAT					
1 CLERICAL	75 38.7 15.8	35 54.7 7.4	85 48.3 17.9	32 80.0 6.8	227 47.9
2 OFFICE TRAINEE	35 18.0 7.4	12 18.8 2.5	81 46.0 17.1	8 20.0 1.7	136 28.7
3 SECURITY OFFICER	14 7.2 3.0	13 20.3 2.7			27 5.7
4 COLLEGE TRAINEE	33 17.0 7.0	1 1.6 .2	7 4.0 1.5		41 8.6
5 EXEMPT EMPLOYEE	28 14.4 5.9	2 3.1 .4	2 1.1 .4		32 6.8
6 MBA TRAINEE	3 1.5 .6	1 1.6 .2	1 .6 .2		5 1.1
7 TECHNICAL	6 3.1 1.3				6 1.3
Column Total	194 40.9	64 13.5	176 37.1	40 8.4	474 100.0

Number of Missing Observations: 0

Although these observations are interesting, they do not imply discriminatory placement into beginning job categories because the qualifications of the various groups are not necessarily similar. If women and nonwhites are more qualified than white males in the same beginning job categories, discrimination may be suspected.

11.3
Level of Education

One easily measured employment qualification is years of education. Figure 11.3a shows the average years of education for the entire sample (labeled **For Entire Population**) and then for each of the two sexes (labeled **SEX** and **MALES** or **FEMALES**) and then for each of the two race categories within each sex category (labeled **MINORITY** and **WHITE** or **NONWHITE**).

Figure 11.3a Education broken down by race within sex

```
MEANS  TABLES=EDLEVEL BY SEX BY MINORITY.
```

```
                    - - Description of Subpopulations - -

Summaries of     EDLEVEL      EDUCATIONAL LEVEL
By levels of     SEX          SEX OF EMPLOYEE
                 MINORITY     MINORITY CLASSIFICATION


Variable       Value  Label                    Mean     Std Dev   Cases

For Entire Population                          13.4916   2.8848    474

SEX               0   MALES                    14.4302   2.9793    258
  MINORITY        0   WHITE                    14.9227   2.8484    194
  MINORITY        1   NONWHITE                 12.9375   2.8888     64

SEX               1   FEMALES                  12.3704   2.3192    216
  MINORITY        0   WHITE                    12.3409   2.4066    176
  MINORITY        1   NONWHITE                 12.5000   1.9081     40

  Total Cases = 474
```

The entire sample has an average of 13.49 years of education. Males have more years of education than females—an average of 14.43 years compared to 12.37. White males have the highest level of education, almost 15 years, which is 2 years more than nonwhite males and approximately 2.5 years more than either group of females.

Figure 11.3b Education by sex-race and job category

```
MEANS VARIABLES=EDLEVEL (LO,HI) SEXRACE(1,4) JOBCAT(1,7)
 /CROSSBREAK=EDLEVEL BY JOBCAT BY SEXRACE.
```

```
                         - - Cross-Breakdown - -

Summaries of      EDLEVEL      EDUCATIONAL LEVEL
By levels of      JOBCAT       EMPLOYMENT CATEGORY
                  SEXRACE      SEX & RACE CLASSIFICATION
```

	Mean Count Std Dev	SEXRACE WHITE MALES 1	MINORITY MALES 2	WHITE FEMALES 3	MINORITY FEMALES 4	Row Total
JOBCAT						
CLERICAL	1	13.87 75 2.30	13.77 35 2.31	11.46 85 2.43	12.63 32 2.12	12.78 227 2.56
OFFICE TRAINEE	2	13.89 35 1.41	12.58 12 2.61	12.81 81 1.93	12.00 8 .00	13.02 136 1.89
SECURITY OFFICER	3	10.29 14 2.05	10.08 13 2.47			10.19 27 2.22
COLLEGE TRAINEE	4	17.21 33 1.34	17.00 1 .	16.00 7 .00		17.00 41 1.28
EXEMPT EMPLOYEE	5	17.61 28 1.77	14.00 2 2.83	16.00 2 .00		17.28 32 1.97
MBA TRAINEE	6	18.33 3 1.15	19.00 1 .	16.00 1 .		18.00 5 1.41
TECHNICAL	7	18.17 6 1.47				18.17 6 1.47
Column Total		14.92 194 2.85	12.94 64 2.89	12.34 176 2.41	12.50 40 1.91	13.49 474 2.88

In Figure 11.3b, the cases are further subdivided by their combined sex-race characteristics and by their initial job category. For each cell in the table, the average years of education, the standard deviation, and number of cases are displayed. White males have the highest average years of education in all job categories except MBA trainees, where the single nonwhite male MBA trainee has nineteen years of education. From this table, it does not appear that females and nonwhites are overeducated when compared to white males in similar job categories. However, it is important to note that group means provide information about a particular class of employees. While discrimination may not exist for a class as a whole, some individuals within that class may be victims (or beneficiaries) of discrimination.

11.4
Beginning Salaries

The average beginning salary for the 474 persons hired between 1969 and 1971 is $6,806. The distribution by the four sex-race categories is shown in Figure 11.4a.

Figure 11.4a   Beginning salary by sex-race

MEANS TABLES=SALBEG BY SEXRACE.

```
            - - Description of Subpopulations - -

Summaries of       SALBEG       BEGINNING SALARY
By levels of       SEXRACE      SEX & RACE CLASSIFICATION


Variable      Value  Label                    Mean      Std Dev   Cases

For Entire Population                       6806.4346  3148.2553   474

SEXRACE          1   WHITE   MALES           8637.5258  3871.1017   194
SEXRACE          2   MINORITY MALES          6553.5000  2228.1436    64
SEXRACE          3   WHITE   FEMALES         5340.4886  1225.9605   176
SEXRACE          4   MINORITY FEMALES        4780.5000   771.4188    40

   Total Cases = 474
```

White males have the highest beginning salaries—an average of $8,638—followed by nonwhite males. Since males are in higher job categories than females, this difference is not surprising.

Figure 11.4b   Beginning salary by sex-race and job category

MEANS VARIABLES=SALBEG(LO,HI) SEXRACE(1,4) JOBCAT(1,7)
  /CROSSBREAK=SALBEG BY JOBCAT BY SEXRACE /CELLS=MEAN.

```
                        - - Cross-Breakdown - -

Summaries of       SALBEG       BEGINNING SALARY
By levels of       JOBCAT       EMPLOYMENT CATEGORY
                   SEXRACE      SEX & RACE CLASSIFICATION
```

	Mean	SEXRACE				
		WHITE MALES 1	MINORITY MALES 2	WHITE FEMALES 3	MINORITY FEMALES 4	Row Total
JOBCAT						
CLERICAL	1	6553.44	6230.74	5147.32	4828.13	5733.95
OFFICE TRAINEE	2	6262.29	5610.00	5208.89	4590.00	5478.97
SECURITY OFFICER	3	6102.86	5953.85			6031.11
COLLEGE TRAINEE	4	10467.64	11496.00	7326.86		9956.49
EXEMPT EMPLOYEE	5	13255.29	15570.00	10998.00		13258.88
MBA TRAINEE	6	14332.00	13992.00	7200.00		12837.60
TECHNICAL	7	19996.00				19996.00
Column Total		8637.53	6553.50	5340.49	4780.50	6806.43

Figure 11.4b shows beginning salaries subdivided by race, sex, and job category. For most of the job categories, white males have higher beginning salaries than the other groups. There is a $1,400 salary difference between white males and white females in the clerical jobs and a $1,000 difference in the general office trainee classification. In the college trainee program, white males averaged over $3,000 more than white females. However, Figure 11.3b shows that white females in the college trainee program had only an undergraduate degree, while white males had an average of 17.2 years of schooling.

11.5
Introducing More Variables

The differences in mean beginning salaries between males and females are somewhat suspect. It is, however, unwise to conclude that salary discrimination exists since several important variables, such as years of prior experience, have not been considered. It is necessary to control (or to adjust statistically) for other relevant variables. Crossclassifying cases by the variables of interest and comparing salaries across the subgroups is one way of achieving control. However, as the number of variables increases, the number of cases in each cell rapidly diminishes, making statistically meaningful comparisons difficult. To circumvent these problems, regression methods, which achieve control by specifying certain statistical relations that may describe what is happening, are used. Regression methods are described in Chapter 19.

11.6
RUNNING PROCEDURE MEANS

MEANS calculates means and variances for a dependent variable within subgroups defined by control variables. For most applications, you can specify your variables on the TABLES subcommand. If your control variables are discrete, integer values and you want the special crosstabulation-like format, you can use the VARIABLES and CROSSBREAK subcommands.

11.7
TABLES Subcommand

Use the TABLES subcommand followed by one or more dependent variables, the keyword BY, and one or more control variables. For example,

MEANS **TABLES=SALBEG BY SEXRACE.**

describes SALBEG within categories of SEXRACE, as in Figure 11.4a. Additional BY keywords and control variables can subdivide the the sample into further subgroups. For example,

MEANS TABLES=EDLEVEL BY SEX BY MINORITY.

calculates statistics for EDLEVEL for each category of SEX and for each category of MINORITY within categories of SEX, producing the output in Figure 11.3a. A maximum of six dimensions can be specified on a TABLES subcommand: one dependent variable followed by up to five BY keywords and control variables.

The first variable is always the dependent variable. The control variables appear in the table in the order in which they are specified. MEANS displays subpopulation statistics for each category of the first control variable. However, for subsequent variables, it displays statistics only for each category of the variable within a category of the preceding control variable.

You can specify more than one dependent variable and more than one control variable in each dimension. Use the keyword TO to name a set of adjacent variables in the active system file, as in:

MEANS TABLES=RAISE79 TO RAISE81 BY DEPT TO AGE.

This command will produce summary tables for each variable from RAISE79 to RAISE81 within categories of each variable from DEPT to AGE. The variables to the right of the last BY change most quickly. Within lists separated with a BY, variables rotate from left to right. For example,

```
MEANS  TABLES=VAR1 TO VAR3 BY VAR4 VAR5 BY VAR6 TO VAR8.
```

produces 18 tables. The first table is VAR1 by VAR4 by VAR6, the second is VAR1 by VAR4 by VAR7, and the third is VAR1 by VAR4 by VAR8. The combinations of VAR1 and VAR5 follow the combinations of VAR1 and VAR4. The last table produced is VAR3 by VAR5 by VAR8.

To specify multiple tables lists, use multiple TABLES subcommands or a slash to separate tables lists on one TABLES subcommand. For example,

```
MEANS  TABLES=RAISE82 BY GRADE/SALARY BY DEPT.
```

specifies two tables: RAISE82 by GRADE, and SALARY by DEPT.

11.8
VARIABLES Subcommand

Use the VARIABLES subcommand to define a list of variables and their value ranges for subsequent TABLES and CROSSBREAK subcommands. Specify the lowest and highest values in parentheses after each variable. For control variables, these must be integer values.

You do not have to specify an explicit range for dependent variables because they are usually continuous and are not assumed to be integers. However, you must provide bounds. You can use the keyword LOWEST (LO) and HIGHEST (HI) for dependent, or criterion, variables. You can also use explicit bounds to eliminate outliers from the calculation of summary statistics. For example, (0,HI) excludes negative values. You cannot use LOWEST, LO, HIGHEST, HI with control variables. For variables with the same range, the lowest and highest values only have to be specified once.

The final variable or set of variables must be followed by a slash and either the TABLES or CROSSBREAK subcommand. The variables may appear in any order. However, the order in which you place them on the VARIABLES subcommand affects their implied order on the TABLES and CROSSBREAK subcommands.

For example,

```
MEANS VARIABLES=DEPT80 DEPT81 DEPT82 (1,3) GRADE81S (1,4)
 SALARY82 (LO,HI)
 /TABLES=SALARY82 BY DEPT80 TO DEPT82 BY GRADE81S.
```

defines 1 as the lowest value and 3 as the highest value for DEPT80, DEPT81, and DEPT82. The TABLES subcommand will produce the following tables:

- SALARY82 by DEPT80 and by GRADE81S within categories of DEPT80.
- SALARY82 by DEPT81 and by GRADE81S within categories of DEPT81.
- SALARY82 by DEPT82 and by GRADE81S within categories of DEPT82.

11.9
CROSSBREAK Subcommand

To display tables in a crosstabular format when the values of all control variables are integers, use the VARIABLES and CROSSBREAK subcommands. Tables displayed in crossbreak format resemble CROSSTABS tables, but their contents are considerably different. The cells contain means, counts, and standard deviations for the dependent variable.

The VARIABLES subcommand specifies the variables to be used and the minimum and maximum values for building tables, and the CROSSBREAK subcommand specifies the tables. CROSSBREAK has exactly the same specification field as the TABLES subcommand.

The CROSSBREAK format is especially suited to breakdowns with two control variables. The first control variable defines the rows and the second control variable defines the columns. For example, Figure 11.3b was produced with the following commands:

```
MEANS VARIABLES=EDLEVEL(LO,HI) SEXRACE(1,4) JOBCAT(1,7)
 /CROSSBREAK=EDLEVEL BY JOBCAT BY SEXRACE.
```

The CROSSBREAK subcommand displays separate subtables for each combination of values when you specify three or more dimensions (two or more BY keywords).

11.10
CELLS Subcommand

By default, MEANS displays the means, standard deviations, and cell counts in each cell. Use the CELLS subcommand to modify cell information.

If you specify the CELLS subcommand with no keywords, MEANS displays all cell information (keyword ALL below). If you specify a keyword or keywords, MEANS displays only the information you request.

The following keywords can be specified on the CELLS subcommand:

DEFAULT   *Means, standard deviations, and cell counts in each cell.* This is the default if you omit the CELL subcommand.

MEAN   *Cell means.*

STDDEV   *Cell standard deviations.*

COUNT   *Cell frequencies.*

SUM   *Cell sums.*

VARIANCE   *Variances.*

ALL   *Means, counts, standard deviations, sums, and variances in each cell.* This is the default if you specify the CELLS subcommand with no keyword(s).

The following commands produced Figure 11.4b:

```
MEANS  VARIABLES=SALBEG(LO,HI) SEXRACE(1,4) JOBCAT(1,7)
 /CROSSBREAK=SALBEG BY JOBCAT BY SEXRACE
 /CELLS=MEAN.
```

11.11
STATISTICS Subcommand

MEANS automatically computes means, standard deviations, and counts for subpopulations. Optionally, you can obtain a one-way analysis of variance for each table as well as a test of linearity. The STATISTICS subcommand computes these additional statistics. Statistics you request on the STATISTICS subcommand are computed *in addition to* the default statistics or those you request on the CELLS subcommand.

If you specify the STATISTICS subcommand with no keyword, MEANS computes an analysis of variance for each table (keyword ANOVA below). If you specify a keyword, MEANS computes the additional statistics you request.

The following keywords can be specified on the STATISTICS subcommand:

ANOVA   *Analysis of variance.* Displays a standard analysis of variance table and calculates *ETA* and *ETA²*. This is the default if you specify the STATISTICS subcommand with no keyword.

LINEARITY   *Test of linearity.* Calculates the sums of squares, degrees of freedom, and mean square associated with linear and nonlinear components, as well as the *F* ratio, Pearson's *r*, and *r²*. ANOVA *must* be requested to obtain LINEARITY. LINEARITY is ignored if the control variable is a short string.

ALL   *Both ANOVA and LINEARITY.*

NONE   *No additional statistics.* This is the default if you omit the STATISTICS subcommand.

If you specify a two-way or higher-order breakdown, the second and subsequent dimensions are ignored in the analysis of variance table. To obtain a two-way and higher analysis of variance, use procedure ANOVA (see Chapter 16).

11.12
MISSING Subcommand

By default, MEANS deletes cases with missing values on a tablewide basis. A case missing on any of the variables specified for a table is not used. Every case contained in a table will have a complete set of nonmissing values for all variables in that table. When you separate tables requests with a slash, missing values are handled separately for each list.

The MISSING subcommand controls missing values, and the following keywords can be specified on it:

TABLE *Delete cases with missing values on a tablewide basis.* This is the default if you omit the MISSING subcommand.

INCLUDE *Include user-defined missing values.* User-defined missing values are treated as nonmissing.

DEPENDENT *Exclude cases with missing values for the dependent variable only.* A case is included if it has a valid value for the dependent variable, although it may have missing values for the control variables. Categories of the control variables defined as missing are not included in the tables.

11.13
FORMAT Subcommand

By default, MEANS displays variable and value labels and the names and values of control variables. All tables are in report format.

The FORMAT subcommand controls table formats. The following keywords can be specified:

LABELS *Display both variable and value labels for each table.* This is the default if you omit the FORMAT subcommand.

NOLABELS *Suppress variable and value labels.*

NOCATLABS *Suppress value (category) labels.*

NAMES *Display the names of control variables.* This is the default if you omit the FORMAT subcommand.

NONAMES *Suppress names of control variables.*

VALUES *Display the values of control variables.* This is the default if you omit the FORMAT subcommand.

NOVALUES *Suppress values of control variables.* This is useful when there are category labels.

TABLE *Display each table in report format.* This is the default if you omit the FORMAT subcommand.

TREE *Display each table in tree format.*

11.14
Annotated Example

The following SPSS command file produced Figures 11.3a and 11.4b:

```
GET FILE=BANK.
COMPUTE SEXRACE=1.
IF (MINORITY EQ 1 AND SEX EQ 0) SEXRACE=2.
IF (MINORITY EQ 0 AND SEX EQ 1) SEXRACE=3.
IF (MINORITY EQ 1 AND SEX EQ 1) SEXRACE=4.
PRINT FORMATS SEXRACE(F1.0).
MEANS  TABLES=EDLEVEL BY SEX BY MINORITY.
VALUE LABELS  SEXRACE 1 'WHITE   MALES' 2 'MINORITYMALES'
 3 'WHITE  FEMALES' 4 'MINORITYFEMALES'.
MEANS  VARIABLES=SALBEG(LO,HI) SEXRACE(1,4) JOBCAT(1,7)
 /CROSSBREAK=SALBEG BY JOBCAT BY SEXRACE
 /CELLS=MEAN.
```

• The COMPUTE command and the three IF commands create a single four-category variable that combines the sex and race variables already on the file. The COMPUTE command sets the new variable SEXRACE to 1, which will be the white-male category. The IF commands change the value to 2 for nonwhite males, 3 for white females, and 4 for nonwhite females. Refer to Chapter 4 for an additional discussion of the COMPUTE and IF commands.

- The first MEANS command summarizes education for race within each sex category (see Figure 11.3a).

- A set of VALUE LABELS is assigned to the new variable SEXRACE for the second MEANS command. These labels are specially formatted to display well in the CROSSBREAK tables in Figures 11.3b and 11.4b, as described for CROSSTABS in Chapter 10.

- The second MEANS command requests crosstabular format (see Figure 11.4b). The keywords LO and HI specify the minimum and maximum values for variable SALBEG.

- The CELLS subcommand requests only means in each cell.

Contents_____

12 Testing Hypotheses about Differences in Means: Procedure T-TEST

Would you buy a disposable raincoat, vegetables in pop-top cans, or investment counseling via closed-circuit television? These products and 17 others were described in questionnaires administered to 100 married couples (Davis & Ragsdale, 1983). Respondents were asked to rate on a scale of 1 (definitely want to buy) to 7 (definitely do not want to buy) their likelihood of buying the product. Of the 100 couples, 50 received questionnaires with pictures of the products and 50 received questionnaires without pictures. In this chapter we will examine whether pictures affect consumer preferences and whether husbands' and wives' responses differ.

12.1 TESTING HYPOTHESES

The first part of the table in Figure 12.1 contains basic descriptive statistics for the buying scores of couples receiving questionnaires with and without pictures. A couple's buying score is simply the sum of all ratings assigned to products by the husband and wife individually. Low scores indicate buyers while high scores indicate reluctance to buy. The 50 couples who received questionnaires without pictures (Group 1) had a mean score of 168 while the 48 couples who received forms with pictures had an average score of 159. (Two couples did not complete the questionnaire and are not included in the analysis.) The standard deviations show that scores for the second group were somewhat more variable than those for the first.

Figure 12.1 Family buying scores by questionnaire type

```
T-TEST GROUPS=VISUAL(0,1) /VARIABLES=FAMSCORE.
```

```
- - - - - - - - - - - - - - - - - - - - - - - - - - T - T E S T - - - - - - - - - - - - - - - - - - - - - - - - - - - - -

GROUP 1 - VISUAL  EQ  0:  NO PICTURES
GROUP 2 - VISUAL  EQ  1:  PICTURES
                                                      * Pooled Variance estimate * Separate Variance Estimate
                                                    *                           *
Variable          Number              Standard   Standard *   F    2-tail *    t   Degrees of 2-tail *    t   Degrees of 2-tail
                 of Cases     Mean    Deviation    Error  * Value  Prob.  *  Value   Freedom   Prob. *  Value   Freedom   Prob.

FAMSCORE  FAMILY BUYING SCORE                       *                  *                           *
         GROUP 1    50     168.0000    21.787     3.081  *                  *                           *
                                                    * 1.60   .106  * 1.78    96     .078 * 1.77   89.43    .080
         GROUP 2    48     159.0833    27.564     3.979  *                  *                           *
```

If you are willing to restrict the conclusions to the 98 couples included in the study, it is safe to say that couples who received forms with pictures indicated a greater willingness to purchase the products than couples who received forms without pictures. However, this statement is not very satisfying. What is needed is some type of statement about the effect of the two questionnaire types for all couples—or at least some larger group of couples—not just those actually studied.

12.2
Samples and Populations

The totality of all cases about which conclusions are desired is called the *population*, while the observations actually included in the study are the *sample*. The couples in this experiment can be considered a sample from the population of couples in the United States.

The field of statistics helps us draw inferences about populations based on observations obtained from *random samples,* or samples in which the characteristics and relationships of interest are independent of the probabilities of being included in the sample. The necessity of a good research design cannot be overemphasized. Unless precautions are taken to ensure that the sample is from the population of interest and that the cases are chosen and observed without bias, the results obtained from statistical analyses may be misleading. For example, if a sample contains only affluent suburban couples, conclusions about all couples may be unwarranted.

If measurements are obtained from an entire population, the population can be characterized by the various measures of central tendency, dispersion, and shape described in Chapter 8. The results describe the population exactly. If, however, you obtain information from a random sample—the usual case—the results serve as *estimates* of the unknown population values. Special notation is used to identify population values, termed *parameters*, and to distinguish them from sample values, termed *statistics*. The mean of a population is denoted by μ, and the variance by σ^2. The symbols $\bar{X}$ and S^2 are reserved for the mean and variance of samples.

12.3
Sampling Distributions

The observations actually included in a study are just one of many random samples that could have been selected from a population. For example, if the population consists of married couples in the United States, the number of different samples that could be chosen for inclusion in a study is mind-boggling. The estimated value of a population parameter depends on the particular sample chosen. Different samples usually produce different estimates.

Figure 12.3 is a histogram of 400 means. Each mean is calculated from a random sample of 25 observations from a population which has a normal distribution with a mean value of 0 and a standard deviation of 1. The estimated means are not all the same. Instead, they have a distribution. Most sample means are fairly close to 0, the population mean. The mean of the 400 means is 0.010 and the standard deviation of these means is 0.205. In fact, the distribution of the means appears approximately normal.

Although Figure 12.3 gives some idea of the appearance of the distribution of sample means of size 25 from a standard normal population, it is only an approximation since all possible samples of size 25 have not been taken. If the number of samples taken is increased to 1000, an even better picture of the distribution could be obtained. As the number of samples of a fixed size increases, the observed (or empirical) distribution of the means approaches the underlying or theoretical distribution.

The theoretical distribution of all possible values of a statistic obtained from a population is called the *sampling distribution* of the statistic. The mean of the sampling distribution is called the *expected value* of the statistic. The standard deviation is termed the *standard error*. The sampling distributions of most commonly used statistics calculated from random samples are tabulated and readily accessible. Knowing the sampling distribution of a statistic is very important for hypothesis testing, since from it you can calculate the probability of obtaining an observed sample value if a particular hypothesis is true. For example, from Figure 12.3, it appears quite unlikely that a sample mean based on a sample of size 25 from a standard normal distribution would be greater than 0.5 if the population mean were 0.

Figure 12.3   Means of 400 samples of size 25 from a normal distribution

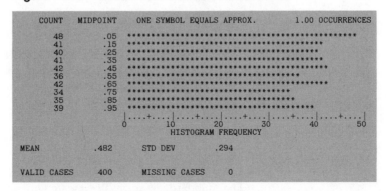

```
     COUNT    MIDPOINT    ONE SYMBOL EQUALS APPROX.              1.50 OCCURRENCES

         0      -.800
         0      -.725
         1      -.650    *
         2      -.575    :
         4      -.500    *.*
         5      -.425    ***.
        13      -.350    *******.*
        23      -.275    **************:
        31      -.200    ********************* .
        41      -.125    *****************************       .
        53      -.050    ************************************** .
        72       .025    ******************************************:********
        46       .100    *******************************        .
        47       .175    *******************************:***
        28       .250    ******************.
        18       .325    **********:
         9       .400    *****:
         5       .475    **:
         2       .550    :
         0       .625
         0       .700
                         |....+....|....+....|....+....|....+....|....+....|
                         0        15        30        45        60        75
                                           HISTOGRAM FREQUENCY

     MEAN          .010      STD DEV        .205

     VALID CASES   400       MISSING CASES      0
```

12.4
Sampling Distribution of the Mean

Since hypotheses about population means are often of interest, the sampling distribution of the mean is particularly important. If samples are taken from a normal population, the sampling distribution of the sample mean is also normal. As expected, the observed distribution of the 400 means in Figure 12.3 is approximately normal. The theoretical distribution of the sample mean, based on all possible samples of size 25, is exactly normal.

Even when samples are taken from a nonnormal population, the distribution of the sample means will be approximately normal for sufficiently large samples. This is one reason for the importance of the normal distribution in statistical inference. Consider Figure 12.4a, which shows a sample from a uniform distribution. In a uniform distribution all values of a variable are equally likely, and hence the proportion of cases in each bin of the histogram is roughly the same.

Figure 12.4a   Values from a uniform distribution

```
     COUNT    MIDPOINT    ONE SYMBOL EQUALS APPROX.              1.00 OCCURRENCES

        48       .05    ****************************************************
        41       .15    *****************************************
        40       .25    ****************************************
        41       .35    *****************************************
        42       .45    ******************************************
        36       .55    ************************************
        42       .65    ******************************************
        34       .75    **********************************
        35       .85    ***********************************
        39       .95    ***************************************
                        |....+....|....+....|....+....|....+....|....+....|
                        0        10        20        30        40        50
                                          HISTOGRAM FREQUENCY

     MEAN          .482      STD DEV        .294

     VALID CASES   400       MISSING CASES      0
```

Figure 12.4b is a histogram of 400 means calculated from samples of size 25 from a uniform distribution. Note that the observed distribution is approximately normal even though the distribution from which the samples were taken is markedly nonnormal.

Figure 12.4b   Distribution of 400 means calculated from samples of size 25 from a uniform distribution

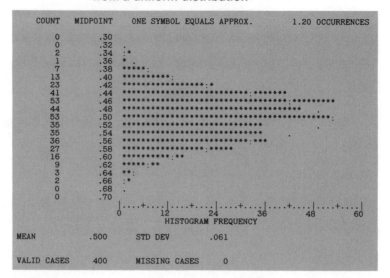

Both the size of a sample and the shape of the distribution from which samples are taken affect the shape of the sampling distribution of the mean. If samples are small and come from distributions that are far from normal, the distribution of the means will not be even approximately normal. As the size of the sample increases, the sampling distribution of the mean will approach normality.

The mean of the theoretical sampling distribution of the means of samples of size n is μ, the population mean. The standard error, which is another name for the standard deviation of the sampling distribution of the mean, is

$$\sigma_{\bar{X}} = \frac{\sigma}{\sqrt{N}}$$ **Equation 12.4a**

where σ is the standard deviation of the population, and N is the sample size.

The standard deviation of the observed sampling distribution of means in Figure 12.3 is 0.205. This is close to the value of the standard error for the theoretical distribution which, from the previous formula, is 1/5, or 0.20.

Usually the value of the standard error is unknown and is estimated from a single sample using

$$S_{\bar{x}} = \frac{S}{\sqrt{N}}$$ **Equation 12.4b**

where S is the *sample* standard deviation. The estimated standard error is displayed in the FREQUENCIES procedure and is also part of the output shown in Figure 12.1. For example, for Group 1 the estimated standard error of the mean is

$$\frac{21.787}{\sqrt{50}} = 3.081$$ **Equation 12.4c**

This value is displayed in the column labeled **Standard Error** in Figure 12.1.

The standard error of the mean depends on both the sample standard deviation and the sample size. As the size of a sample increases, the standard error decreases. This is intuitively clear, since the more data are gathered, the more confident you can be that the sample mean is not too far from the population mean. Also, as the standard deviation of the observations decreases, the standard error decreases as well. Small standard deviations occur when observations are fairly homogeneous. In this case, means based on different samples should also not vary much.

12.5
THE TWO-SAMPLE
T-TEST

Consider again whether there is evidence that the type of form administered influences couples' buying decisions. The question is not whether the two sample means are equal, but whether the two population means are equal.

To test the hypothesis that, in the population, buying scores for the two questionnaire types are the same, the following statistic can be calculated:

$$t = \frac{\overline{X}_1 - \overline{X}_2}{\sqrt{S_1^2/N_1 + S_2^2/N_2}}$$

Equation 12.5a

$\overline{X}_1$ is the sample mean of Group 1, S_1^2 is the variance, and N_1 is the sample size.

Based on the sampling distribution of the above statistic, you can calculate the probability that a difference at least as large as the one observed would occur if the two population means (μ_1 and μ_2) are equal. This probability is called the *observed significance level*. If the observed significance level is small enough, usually less than 0.05, or 0.01, the hypothesis that the population means are equal is rejected.

The t value and its associated probability are given in Figure 12.1 in the section labeled **Separate Variance Estimate**. The t value is

$$t = \frac{168.0 - 159.08}{\sqrt{\frac{21.787^2}{50} + \frac{27.564^2}{48}}} = 1.77$$

Equation 12.5b

If $\mu_1 = \mu_2$, the probability of observing a difference at least as large as the one in the sample is estimated to be about 0.08. Since this probability is greater than 0.05, the hypothesis that mean buying scores in the population are equal for the two types of forms is not rejected. The entry under **Degrees of Freedom** in Figure 12.1 is a function of the sample size in the two groups and is used together with the t value in establishing the observed significance level.

Another statistic based on the t distribution can be used to test the equality of means hypothesis. This statistic, known as the *pooled-variance t-test*, is based on the assumption that the population variances in the two groups are equal and is obtained using a pooled estimate of that common variance. The test statistic is identical to the equation for t given previously except that the individual group variances are replaced by a pooled estimate S_p^2. That is,

$$t = \frac{\overline{X}_1 - \overline{X}_2}{\sqrt{S_p^2/N_1 + S_p^2/N_2}}$$

Equation 12.5c

where S_p^2, the pooled variance, is a weighted average of the individual variances and is calculated as

$$S_p^2 = \frac{(N_1 - 1)S_1^2 + (N_2 - 1)S_2^2}{N_1 + N_2 - 2}$$

Equation 12.5d

From the output in Figure 12.1, the pooled t-test value for the study is 1.78. The degrees of freedom for the pooled t-test are 96, the sum of the sample sizes in both groups minus 2. If the pooled-variance t-test is used when the population variances are not equal, the probability level associated with the statistic may be in error. The amount of error depends on the inequality of the sample sizes and of the variances. However, using the separate-variance t value when the population variances are equal will usually result in an observed significance level somewhat larger than it should be. For large samples, the discrepancy between the two methods is small. In general, it is a good idea to use the separate-variance t-test whenever you suspect that the variances are unequal.

The statistic used to test the hypothesis that the two population variances are equal is the F value, which is the ratio of the larger sample variance to the smaller. In Figure 12.1, this value is ($27.6^2/21.8^2 = 1.6$). If the observed significance level for the F test is small, the hypothesis that the population variances are equal is rejected, and the separate-variance t-test for means should be used. In this example, the significance level for the F test is large, and thus the pooled-variance t-test is appropriate. The F test for the equality of two variances depends heavily on the data being from normal populations, while the t-test does not. Thus, the F test is not a very good test for the hypothesis.

12.6
Significance Levels

The commonsense interpretation of a small observed significance level is straight-forward: it appears unlikely that the two population means are equal. Of course, there is a possibility that the means are equal and the observed difference is due to chance. The *observed significance level* is the probability that a difference at least as large as the one observed would have arisen if the means were really equal.

When the observed significance level is too large to reject the equality hypothesis, the two population means may indeed be equal, or the means may be unequal but the difference cannot be detected. Failure to detect can be due to a true difference that is very small. For example, if a new cancer drug prolongs survival time by only one day when compared to the standard treatment, it is unlikely that such a difference will be detected, especially if survival times vary substantially and the additional day represents a small increment.

There are other reasons why true differences may not be found. If the sample sizes in the two groups are small or the variability large, even substantial differences may not be detected. Significant t values are obtained when the numerator of the t statistic is large when compared to the denominator. The numerator is the difference between the sample means, and the denominator depends on the standard deviations and sample sizes of the two groups. For a given standard deviation, the larger the sample size, the smaller the denominator. Thus, a difference of a given magnitude may be significant if obtained with a sample size of 100, but not significant with a sample size of 25.

12.7
One-Tailed vs. Two-Tailed Tests

A two-tailed test is used to detect a difference in means between two populations regardless of the direction of the difference. For example, in the study of buying scores presented in this chapter, we are interested in whether buying scores without pictures are larger *or* smaller than buying scores with pictures. In applications where you are interested in detecting a difference in one direction—such as whether a new drug is better than the current treatment—a so-called one-tailed test can be performed. The procedure is the same as for the two-tailed test, but the resulting probability value is divided by 2, adjusting for the fact that the equality hypothesis is rejected only when the difference between the two means is sufficiently large and in the direction of interest. In a two-tailed test, the equality hypothesis is rejected for large positive or negative values of the statistic.

12.8
What's the Difference?

It appears that the questionnaire type has no significant effect on couples' willingness to purchase products. Overall buying scores for the two conditions are similar. Pictures of the products do not appear to enhance their perceived desirability. In fact, the pictures actually appear to make several products somewhat less desirable. However, since the purpose of the questionnaires is to ascertain buying intent, including a picture of the actual product may help gauge true product response. Although the concept of disposable raincoats may be attractive, if they make the owner look like a walking trash bag their appeal may diminish considerably.

12.9
USING PROCEDURE CROSSTABS TO TEST HYPOTHESES

The T-TEST procedure is used to test hypotheses about the equality of two means for variables measured on an interval or ratio scale. Procedure CROSSTABS and the Pearson chi-square statistic can be used to test hypotheses about a dichotomous variable, such as purchase of a particular product.

Figure 12.9 is a crosstabulation showing the number of husbands who would definitely want to buy (value 1) vegetables in pop-top cans when shown a picture and when not shown a picture of the product. The vegetables in pop-top cans were chosen by 6.0% of the husbands who were tempted with pictures and 16.0% of the husbands who were not shown pictures. The chi-square statistic provides a test of the hypothesis that the proportion of husbands selecting the vegetables in pop-top cans is the same for the picture and no-picture forms.

Figure 12.9   Preference of husbands for vegetables in pop-top cans

```
CROSSTABS TABLES=H2S BY VISUAL
  /CELLS=COUNT COLUMN /STATISTICS=CHISQ.
```

```
H2S  POP-TOP CANS HUSB SELF  by  VISUAL  PICTURE ACCOMPANIED QUESTION

                    VISUAL
          Count
          Col Pct |NO PICTU PICTURES
                  |RES               Row
                  |      0 |      1 | Total
H2S       --------+--------+--------+
              1   |      8 |      3 |    11
    DEFINITELY    |   16.0 |    6.0 |  11.0
          --------+--------+--------+
              2   |     42 |     47 |    89
    VERY LIKELY   |   84.0 |   94.0 |  89.0
          --------+--------+--------+
          Column        50       50      100
          Total       50.0     50.0    100.0

      Chi-Square                  Value          DF         Significance

   Pearson                       2.55362          1            .11004
   Continuity Correction         1.63432          1            .20111
   Likelihood Ratio              2.63925          1            .10425
   Mantel-Haenszel               2.52809          1            .11184

   Minimum Expected Frequency -    5.500

   Number of Missing Observations:  0
```

The probability of 0.11 associated with the Pearson chi-square in Figure 12.9 is the probability that a difference at least as large as the one observed would occur in the sample if in the population there were no difference in the selection of the product between the two formats. Since the probability is large, the hypothesis of no difference between the two formats is not rejected.

12.10
INDEPENDENT VS.
PAIRED SAMPLES

Several factors contribute to the observed differences in response between two groups. Part of the observed difference in scores between the picture and no-picture formats may be attributable to form type. Another component is due to differences between individuals. Not all couples have the same buying desires, so even if the type of form does not affect buying, differences between the two groups will probably be observed due to differences between the couples within the two groups.

One method of minimizing the influence of individual variation is to choose the two groups so that the couples within them are comparable on characteristics that can influence buying behavior, such as income, education, family size, and so forth.

It is sometimes possible to obtain pairs of subjects, such as twins, and assign one member of each pair to each of the two treatments. Another frequently used experimental design is to expose the same individual to both types of conditions. (In this design, care must be taken to ensure that the sequential administration of treatments does not influence response by providing practice, decreasing attention span, or affecting the second treatment in other ways.) In both designs, subject-to-subject variability has substantially less effect. These designs are called *paired-samples designs*, since for each subject there is a corresponding pair in the other group. In the second design, a person is paired with himself or herself. In an *independent-samples design*, there is no pairing of cases; all observations are independent.

12.11
Analysis of Paired Data

Although the interpretation of the significance of results from paired experiments is the same as those from the two independent samples discussed previously, the actual computations are different. For each pair of cases, the difference in the responses is calculated. The statistic used to test the hypothesis that the mean difference in the population is 0 is

$$t = \frac{\overline{D}}{S_D/\sqrt{N}}$$

Equation 12.11

where $\overline{D}$ is the observed difference between the two means and S_D is the standard deviation of the differences of the paired observations. The sampling distribution of t, if the differences are normally distributed with a mean of 0, is Student's t with $N-1$ degrees of freedom, where N is the number of pairs. If the pairing is effective, the standard error of the difference will be smaller than the standard error obtained if two independent samples with N subjects each were chosen. However, if the variables chosen for pairing do not affect the responses under study, pairing may result in a test that is less powerful since true differences can be detected less frequently.

For example, to test the hypothesis that there is no difference between husbands' and wives' buying scores, a paired t-test should be calculated. A paired test is appropriate since husbands and wives constitute matched observations. Hopefully, including both members of a couple controls for some nuisance effects like socioeconomic status, age, and so forth. The observed differences are more likely to be attributable to differences in sex.

Figure 12.11 contains output from the paired t-test. The entry under number of cases is the number of pairs of observations. The mean difference is the difference between the mean scores for males and females. The t value is the mean difference divided by the standard error of the difference (0.55/1.73=0.32). The two-tailed probability for this test is 0.75, so there is insufficient evidence to reject the null hypothesis that married males and females have similar mean buying scores.

Figure 12.11 Husbands' versus wives' buying scores

T-TEST PAIRS=HSSCALE, WSSCALE.

Variable	Number of Cases	Mean	Standard Deviation	Standard Error	*(Difference) Mean	Standard Deviation	Standard Error	* 2-tail Corr. Prob.	t Value	Degrees of Freedom	2-tail Prob.
HSSCALE	HUSBAND SELF SCALE	82.0918	14.352	1.450							
	98				.5510	17.095	1.727	.367 .000	.32	97	.750
		81.5408	15.942	1.610							
WSSCALE	WIFE SELF SCALE										

The correlation coefficient between husbands' and wives' scores is 0.367. A positive correlation indicates that pairing has been effective in decreasing the variability of the mean difference. The larger the correlation coefficient, the greater the benefit of pairing.

12.12
HYPOTHESIS TESTING: A REVIEW

The purpose of hypothesis testing is to help draw conclusions about population parameters based on results observed in a random sample. The procedure remains virtually the same for tests of most hypotheses.

- A hypothesis of no difference (called a *null hypothesis*) and its alternative are formulated.
- A test statistic is chosen to evaluate the null hypothesis.
- For the sample, the test statistic is calculated.
- The probability, if the null hypothesis is true, of obtaining a test value at least as extreme as the one observed is determined.
- If the observed significance level is judged small enough, the null hypothesis is rejected.

12.13
The Importance of Assumptions

In order to perform a statistical test of any hypothesis, it is necessary to make certain assumptions about the data. The particular assumptions depend on the statistical test being used. Some procedures require stricter assumptions than others. For *parametric tests*, some knowledge about the distribution from which samples are selected is required.

The assumptions are necessary to define the sampling distribution of the test statistic. Unless the distribution is defined, correct significance levels cannot be calculated. For the pooled t-test, the assumption is that the observations are random samples from normal distributions with the same variance.

For many procedures, not all assumptions are equally important. Moderate violation of some assumptions may not always be serious. Therefore, it is important to know for each procedure not only what assumptions are needed but also how severely their violation may influence results. For example the *F* test for equality of variances is quite sensitive to departures from normality, while the t-test for equality of means is less so.

The responsibility for detecting violations of assumptions rests with the researcher. Unfortunately, unlike the experimenter in chemistry, no explosions or disintegrating terminals threaten the investigator who does not comply with good statistical practice. However, from a research viewpoint, the consequences can be just as severe.

Wherever possible, tests of assumptions—often called diagnostic checks of the model—should be incorporated as part of the hypothesis-testing procedures. Throughout SPSS, attempts have been made to provide facilities for examining assumptions. For example, in the EXAMINE procedure there are several tests for normality. Discussions of other such diagnostics are included with the individual procedures.

12.14
RUNNING
PROCEDURE T-TEST

Procedure T-TEST computes the Student's *t* statistic for testing the significance of a difference in means for independent or paired samples. For independent samples, procedure T-TEST provides both separate- and pooled-variance estimates.

12.15
Independent Samples

An independent-samples test divides the cases into two groups and compares the group means on a single variable (Section 12.5). This test requires the GROUPS and VARIABLES subcommands.

12.16
GROUPS Subcommand

The GROUPS subcommand names the variable and the criterion for dividing the cases into two groups. You can name only one variable. You can use any of three different methods to define the two groups. In the first method, a single value in parentheses groups all cases with a value equal to or greater than the specified value into one group and the remaining cases with nonmissing values into the other group. For example, the command

```
T-TEST GROUPS=WORLD(2) /VARIABLES=NTCPUR.
```

groups together all cases with the value of WORLD greater than or equal to 2. The remaining cases go into the other group.

Alternatively, if you specify two values in parentheses, one group includes cases with the first value on the grouping variable, and the other includes cases with the second value. For example, the following command produced Figure 12.1:

```
T-TEST   GROUPS=VISUAL(0,1) /VARIABLES=FAMSCORE.
```

In this example, any cases with values other than 0 and 1 for variable VISUAL would not be used. You can also use the RECODE command (see Chapter 3) to collapse or combine categories of the variable named on the GROUPS subcommand.

If the grouping variable has only two values, coded 1 and 2, you do not have to specify a value list. For example, the command

```
T-TEST   GROUPS=SEX /VARIABLES=GRADES.
```

groups all cases having the value 1 for SEX into one group and cases having the value 2 for SEX into the other group. All other cases are not used.

12.17
VARIABLES Subcommand

The VARIABLES subcommand names the variables being analyzed. You can use only numeric variables. The command

```
T-TEST   GROUPS=WORLD(1,3) /VARIABLES=NTCPRI NTCSAL NTCPUR.
```

compares the means of the two groups defined by WORLD for the variables NTCPRI, NTCSAL, and NTCPUR, while

```
T-TEST   GROUPS=WORLD(1,3) /VARIABLES=NTCPRI TO MCLOTHES.
```

compares the means of the groups defined by WORLD for all variables on the active system file between and including NTCPRI and MCLOTHES.

12.18
PAIRS Subcommand

To compute tests for paired samples (Section 12.10) you need two variables that represent values for the two members of the pair for each case, such as pre- and post-test scores for students in a class. Figure 12.11, comparing husbands' and wives' buying scores, was produced with the following command:

```
T-TEST  PAIRS=HSSCALE, WSSCALE.
```

You can name only numeric variables. If you specify a list of variables, each variable is compared with every other variable. For example, the command

```
T-TEST PAIRS=TEACHER CONSTRUC MANAGER.
```

compares TEACHER with CONSTRUC, TEACHER with MANAGER, and CONSTRUC with MANAGER.

You can use the keyword WITH to request a test comparing every variable to the left of the keyword with every variable to the right of the keyword. For example,

```
T-TEST  PAIRS=TEACHER MANAGER WITH CONSTRUC ENGINEER.
```

compares TEACHER with CONSTRUC, TEACHER with ENGINEER, MANAGER with CONSTRUC, and MANAGER with ENGINEER. TEACHER is not compared with MANAGER, and CONSTRUC is not compared with ENGINEER.

You can use the slash to separate lists of variables, as in

```
T-TEST  PAIRS=WCLOTHES MCLOTHES/NTCPRI WITH NTCPUR NTCSAL.
```

which specifies two lists.

You can also use the keyword (PAIRED) to specify multiple paired-sample analyses. Each variable before the keyword WITH is paired with a variable after the WITH keyword, as in:

```
T-TEST  PAIRS=TEACHER MANAGER WITH CONSTRUC ENGINEER (PAIRED).
```

TEACHER is paired with CONSTRUC and MANAGER is paired with ENGINEER. You must name or imply the same number of variables on each side of the keyword WITH. If the number of variables is not equal, SPSS will generate as many t-tests as it can and will then issue a warning indicating that the number of variables is not equal.

12.19
Independent and Paired Designs

You can request both independent- and paired-samples tests on a single T-TEST command, but you must specify the independent-samples test first. Thus, the GROUPS subcommand is first, followed by the VARIABLES subcommand, and finally the PAIRS subcommand, as in the following example:

```
T-TEST GROUPS=VISUAL(0,1) /VARIABLES=FAMSCORE
 /PAIRS=HSSCALE WSSCALE.
```

12.20
One-Tailed Significance Levels

By default, the probability is based on the two-tailed test. This is appropriate when differences in either direction are of interest. When theoretical considerations predict that the difference will be in a given direction (such as the Group 1 mean will be higher than the Group 2 mean), a one-tailed test is appropriate. To calculate the one-tailed probability, divide the two-tailed probability by 2.

12.21
MISSING Subcommand

By default, T-TEST deletes cases with missing values on an analysis-by-analysis basis. For independent-samples tests, cases missing on either the grouping variable or the analysis variable are excluded from the analysis of that variable. For paired-samples tests, a case missing on either of the variables in a given pair is excluded from the analysis of that pair. The following keyword options are available using the MISSING subcommand:

ANALYSIS   *Delete cases with missing values on an analysis-by-analysis basis.* This is the default if you omit the MISSING subcommand.

LISTWISE   *Exclude missing values listwise.* A case missing for any variable specified on either the GROUPS or the VARIABLES subcommand is excluded from any independent sample analysis. A case missing for any variable specified on the PAIRS subcommand is excluded from any paired sample analysis.

INCLUDE   *Include user-missing values.* Cases with user-missing values are included in the analysis. By default, cases with user-missing values are excluded.

The ANALYSIS and LISTWISE keywords are mutually exclusive; however, each can be specified with INCLUDE.

12.22
FORMAT Subcommand

By default, T-TEST displays variable labels. You can suppress variable labels by specifying NOLABELS on the FORMAT subcommand:

LABELS   *Display variable labels.* This is the default if you omit the FORMAT subcommand.

NOLABELS   *Suppress variable labels.*

Contents

13 Plotting Data: Procedure PLOT

Today the quest for the Fountain of Youth has been replaced by the Search for Slimness. It's almost acceptable to grow old, as long as one remains trim and fit. Programs for weight loss are assuming ever-increasing attention, and behavioral psychologists are studying the effectiveness of many different weight-loss strategies. Black and Sherba (1983) studied the effects of two different types of behavior programs on weight loss. One group of subjects was taught behavioral weight-loss techniques, while the second was taught weight-loss techniques and problem-solving behavior. Their data set is examined in this chapter.

13.1 DESCRIBING WEIGHT LOSS

As discussed in Chapter 9, a stem-and-leaf plot is a convenient method for displaying the distribution of a variable that can have many values. Figure 13.1a shows the percentage of excess weight actually lost during the treatment for each of the twelve cases in the study. From this figure we can see that about one-third of the participants lost 20% or more of the required weight during treatment. To see if weight loss is maintained, consider Figure 13.1b, which shows the percentage of weight loss one year after treatment. It appears that subjects did not gain back the weight but maintained weight loss.

Figure 13.1a Stem-and-leaf plot of weight loss during treatment

```
EXAMINE VARIABLES=TREATRED
 /PLOT=STEMLEAF /SCALE=UNIFORM.

    Frequency     Stem &  Leaf

        4.00      -2  .   1445
        5.00      -1  .   23449
        2.00      -0  .   05
        1.00       0  .   0

 Stem width:      10.00
 Each leaf:          1 case(s)
```

Figure 13.1b Stem-and-leaf plot of weight loss after one year

```
EXAMINE VARIABLES=TWELVRED
 /PLOT=STEMLEAF /SCALE=UNIFORM.

    Frequency     Stem &  Leaf

        3.00      -4  .   057
        1.00      -3  .   9
        1.00      -2  .   0
        3.00      -1  .   279
        2.00      -0  .   27
        2.00       0  .   15

 Stem width:      10.00
 Each leaf:          1 case(s)
```

Although the stem-and-leaf plots provide information about the weight loss during treatment and weight loss after twelve months, they reveal nothing about the relationship between the two variables since they each describe single variables. To determine whether lost weight during treatment is maintained or replaced at twelve months, the two variables must be studied together.

Figure 13.1c is a scatterplot of the percentage of weight loss during treatment and at one year for the twelve cases. Each symbol 1 on the plot represents one case, showing the values for that case on two variables: loss during treatment and loss at one year. For example, the circled point represents a case with a treatment loss of 25% and a twelve month value of −18%.

Figure 13.1c Scatterplot for weight loss during treatment and after one year

PLOT PLOT=TREATRED WITH TWELVRED.

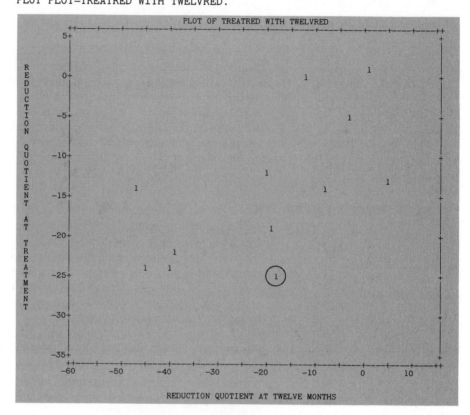

Since plots generated for terminals and printers have a limited number of positions in which to display points, it may not be possible to distinguish cases with similar values for the two variables. When two or more cases with similar values fall on the same point on the scatterplot, a number is displayed indicating how many cases overlap at that point. The scale of the plot depends on the minimum and maximum values for the two variables plotted. If the values for a few cases are far removed from the others, the majority of cases may appear bunched together in order to permit the outlying cases to appear on the same plot.

Figure 13.1d contains the symbols used to represent multiple cases at each point. For example, the symbol **D** is used when there are 13 coincident points.

Figure 13.1d Scatterplot symbols for multiple cases

```
Frequencies and symbols used (not applicable for control or overlay plots)
         1 - 1      11 - B      21 - L      31 - V
         2 - 2      12 - C      22 - M      32 - W
         3 - 3      13 - D      23 - N      33 - X
         4 - 4      14 - E      24 - O      34 - Y
         5 - 5      15 - F      25 - P      35 - Z
         6 - 6      16 - G      26 - Q      36 - *
         7 - 7      17 - H      27 - R
         8 - 8      18 - I      28 - S
         9 - 9      19 - J      29 - T
        10 - A      20 - K      30 - U
```

13.2
Controlled Scatterplots

Often it is informative to identify each point on a scatterplot by its value on a third variable. For example, cases may be designated as males or females, or as originating from the West, Midwest, or East. Figure 13.2 is the same plot as Figure 13.1c except each case is identified as being a participant in the behavior program (value 1) or the problem-solving program (value 2). A dollar sign is displayed if cases from different groups coincide.

Figure 13.2   Scatterplot identifying the two programs

PLOT PLOT=TREATRED WITH TWELVRED BY TREATMNT.

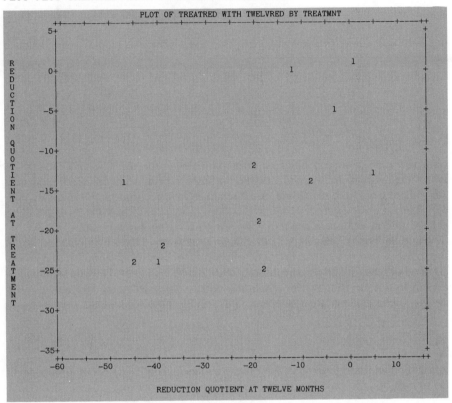

By examining Figure 13.2 you can see if the weight-loss-maintenance relationships are similar for the two groups.

13.3
Plotting Multiple Variables

Weight-loss maintenance may be associated with many variables, including age. Figure 13.3a is a plot of age with weight loss during treatment while Figure 13.3b is a plot of weight loss at twelve months with age. There appears to be a somewhat negative relationship between age and weight loss. Older people appear to have lost a greater percentage of weight than younger ones.

Figure 13.3a   Scatterplot of age with weight loss during treatment

PLOT PLOT=TREATRED WITH AGE.

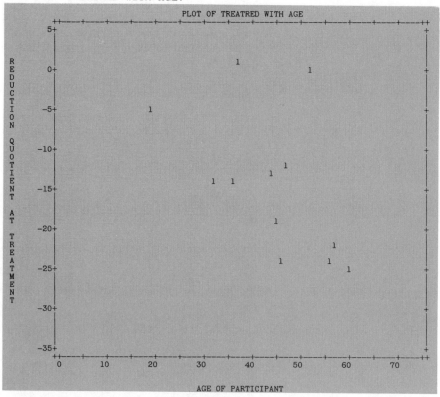

Figure 13.3b   Scatterplot of age with weight loss at twelve months

PLOT PLOT=TWELVRED WITH AGE.

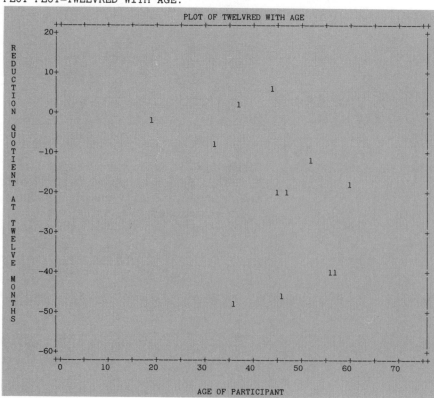

Figures 13.3a and 13.3b can be combined into a single plot, as shown in Figure 13.3c. Each case appears twice on Figure 13.3c, once with treatment weight loss (denoted as **1**) and once with twelve-month loss (denoted as **2**).

Figure 13.3c   Overlay plot of weight loss during treatment and at twelve months

```
PLOT FORMAT=OVERLAY
  /PLOT=TREATRED TWELVRED WITH AGE.
```

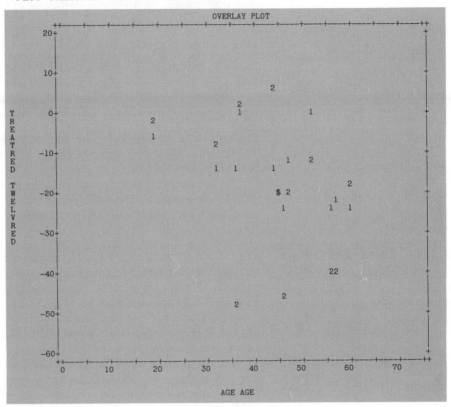

13.4
RUNNING
PROCEDURE PLOT

You can use the PLOT procedure to obtain bivariate scatterplots or regression plots (with or without control variables), contour plots, overlay plots, and some regression statistics. (For complete regression analysis, use procedure REGRESSION, described in Chapter 19.) Formatting options enable you to control axis size and scale, the plotting symbols used, and the frequency they represent. You can also label the plot and axes, request reference lines, and plot standardized variables.

The only required subcommand on PLOT is the PLOT subcommand. There are two types of optional subcommands: global subcommands (HSIZE, VSIZE, CUTPOINT, SYMBOLS, and MISSING) and local subcommands (FORMAT, TITLE, HORIZONTAL, and VERTICAL).

You can specify each of the global subcommands only once, and each must be prior to the first occurrence of the PLOT subcommand. You can use the PLOT subcommand and accompanying local subcommands more than once within a PLOT command. However, local subcommands apply only to the *immediately following* PLOT subcommand. A PLOT subcommand must be the last subcommand you specify.

13.5
PLOT Subcommand

Use the PLOT subcommand to specify the variables to be plotted. Variables to be plotted on the vertical (Y) axis are specified first, followed by the WITH keyword, followed by the variables to be plotted on the horizontal (X) axis.

By default, PLOT produces bivariate scatterplots. For example, the following command produces the output in Figure 13.1c:

```
PLOT PLOT=TREATRED WITH TWELVRED.
```

You can produce multiple plots with one PLOT subcommand. For example, the command

```
PLOT PLOT=IQ GRE WITH GPA SAT.
```

produces four plots: IQ with GPA, IQ with SAT, GRE with GPA, and GRE with SAT.

You can also use semicolons to separate multiple plot lists. For example,

```
PLOT PLOT=BONUS WITH TENURE SALNOW; SALNOW WITH SALBEG.
```

requests three scatterplots. The first request produces plots of BONUS with TENURE and BONUS with SALNOW. The second request produces the plot of SALNOW with SALBEG.

In the output, an information table precedes the plots you request on a PLOT subcommand. This table shows the number of cases used, the size of the plot, and a list of symbols and frequencies.

13.6
Control and Contour Variables

Use the BY keyword on the PLOT subcommand to specify a control variable or a contour variable (see Section 13.2) for a set of plots. You can specify only one such variable on any plot list. To produce a contour plot you must also use a FORMAT subcommand (see Section 13.9).

PLOT uses the first character of the control variable's value label as the plot symbol. If no value labels are supplied, PLOT uses the first character of the actual value. For the numeric value 28, the symbol would be 2; for the string value MALE, the symbol would be M. (PLOT does not check uniqueness of symbols, but you can use the VALUE LABELS command to create appropriate value labels that prevent ambiguity.) When cases with different values for the control value fall in the same position on the plot, they are represented by a single $.

The following command produced Figure 13.2:

```
PLOT PLOT=TREATRED WITH TWELVRED BY TREATMNT.
```

13.7
TITLE Subcommand

You can provide a title for a plot by enclosing the title in apostrophes on the TITLE subcommand. The default plot title uses either the names of the variables for a bivariate plot or the type of plot requested on the FORMAT subcommand (see Section 13.9). The command

```
PLOT TITLE='Plot of Beginning Salary on Current Salary'
 /PLOT=SALNOW WITH SALBEG.
```

requests a title that overrides the default.

A title can contain up to 60 characters. A title longer than the horizontal width specified on the HSIZE subcommand (see Section 13.10) will be truncated.

13.8
VERTICAL and
HORIZONTAL
Subcommands

Use the HORIZONTAL and VERTICAL subcommands to control axis labels, minimum and maximum values plotted, standardization of axes, reference lines, and uniform scales across plots.

Adjusting minimum and maximum values is especially useful when you want to focus on a subset of a larger plot. The minimum and maximum value specifications function like a TEMPORARY SELECT IF transformation (see Chapter 4). PLOT excludes values outside the specified range from the immediately following PLOT subcommand. The axes are scaled to include the specified values, but PLOT may extend the scales slightly beyond the specified minimum and maximum to ensure that integers or simple decimals are on the axes.

The VERTICAL and HORIZONTAL subcommands have the same keyword specifications:

'label'	*Axis label.* You can specify a label of up to 40 characters. The default is the variable label for the variable on the axis. If there is no variable label, PLOT uses the variable name. If you specify a label longer or wider than the plot frame size (see Section 13.10), the label will be truncated.
MIN(min)	*Minimum value plotted for that axis.* The default is the minimum observed value. With the MIN option, only data values greater than or equal to *min* are plotted. The axis scale includes this value.
MAX(max)	*Maximum value plotted for that axis.* The default is the maximum observed value. With the MAX option, only data values less than or equal to *max* are plotted. The axis scale includes this value.
UNIFORM	*Uniform values on axis.* This option specifies that all plots will have scales with the same values on the vertical or horizontal axis. Uniform scales also result if you specify both MIN and MAX. If you specify UNIFORM but not MIN and MAX, PLOT determines the minimum and maximum across all variables for the axis.
REFERENCE(value list)	*Reference lines for axis.* The value list specifies values at which to draw reference lines perpendicular to the axis.
STANDARDIZE	*Standardize variables on axis.* With this option, PLOT standardizes variables to have a mean of 0 and a standard deviation of 1. This option is useful if you want to overlay plots of variables that otherwise would have different scales.

The command

```
PLOT TITLE='Annual Salary by Age, XYZ Corporation  1983'
 /VERTICAL='Annual salary before taxes' MIN (500) MAX (75000)
 REFERENCE(25000,50000)
 /HORIZONTAL='Age of employee' MIN (18) MAX (65)
 REFERENCE (33,48)
 /PLOT=INCOME WITH AGE.
```

produces a bivariate scatterplot with labeled axes that include values of INCOME between 500 and 75,000 and values of AGE between 18 and 65. The keyword REFERENCE requests reference lines at 25,000 and 50,000 on the vertical axis and at 33 and 48 on the horizontal axis.

**13.9
FORMAT Subcommand**

Use the FORMAT subcommand to specify the type of plot you want to produce. Four types of plots are available: scatterplots, regression plots, contour plots, and overlay plots. If FORMAT is not used, or is specified without keywords, scatterplots are displayed. To specify plot type, use the following keywords:

DEFAULT   *Bivariate scatterplot.* When there are no control variables each symbol represents the case count at that plot position. When a control variable is specified, each symbol represents the first character of the value label of the control variable.

REGRESSION   *Scatterplot plus regression statistics.* The vertical-axis variable is regressed on the horizontal-axis variable, and the regression line intercepts on each axis are indicated with the letter R. In a control plot, regression statistics are pooled over all categories.

CONTOUR(n)   *Contour plot with* n *levels.* Contour plots use a continuous variable as the control variable. The control variable is specified after BY on the PLOT subcommand. The contour variable is recoded into *n* intervals of equal width. Up to 35 contour levels can be specified. If *n* is omitted, the default is 10 levels.

OVERLAY   *Overlay plots.* All plots specified on the next PLOT subcommand are displayed in one plot frame. A unique plotting symbol is used for each overlaid plot. An additional symbol indicates multiple plot points at the same position. Control plots cannot be overlaid.

Specify the FORMAT subcommand before the PLOT subcommand to which it refers. One FORMAT subcommand can be specified before each PLOT subcommand.

For example, the command

```
PLOT FORMAT=OVERLAY
/PLOT=TREATRED TWELVRED WITH AGE.
```

produces the overlay plot in Figure 13.3c.

Overlay plots are useful when several variables represent the same type of measurement or when the same variable is measured at different times (see Figure 13.11). Contour plots evaluate the effects of a continuous variable as a control variable. If you use symbols (see Section 13.12) with degrees of density, you can produce visual representation of the density of the control variable (see Figure 13.16).

**13.10
HSIZE and VSIZE
Subcommands**

Use the HSIZE and VSIZE subcommands to specify dimensions for your plots. The HSIZE and VSIZE subcommands must precede all PLOT subcommands and can be specified only once. All plots requested on one PLOT command are drawn to the same specified size.

The default size of your plot depends on current page size. With a typical computer page, the default width is 80 positions and the default length is 40 lines. You can override the defaults by using the VSIZE and HSIZE subcommands. The VSIZE subcommand specifies the vertical frame size (length) of the plot, and the HSIZE subcommand specifies the horizontal frame size (width). For example,

```
PLOT VSIZE=30/HSIZE=70
/PLOT=Y WITH X.
```

requests a length of 30 print lines and a width of 70 print positions. The specified size does *not* include print lines for the plot frames or for auxiliary information such as titles, axis scale numbers, regression statistics, or the symbol table.

**13.11
HSIZE and VSIZE with
HORIZONTAL and VERTICAL**

If you specify both MIN and MAX values on the HORIZONTAL or VERTICAL subcommands, your axes may contain some fractional values, even if your data contain only integer values. You can control the axis values displayed and the interval between values by specifying HSIZE and VSIZE in conjunction with MIN and MAX values on the HORIZONTAL and VERTICAL subcommands.

For the horizontal axis, use the formula

$$\frac{\text{MAX} - \text{MIN}}{\text{interval}} \times 10 = \text{HSIZE}$$

For the vertical axis, use the formula

$$\frac{\text{MAX} - \text{MIN}}{\text{interval}} \times 5 = \text{VSIZE}$$

For example, to display the years from 1880 to 2000 in 20 year increments on the horizontal axis, you would calculate the HSIZE as

$$\frac{2000 - 1880}{20} \times 10 = 60$$

and you would specify

```
/HSIZE=60
/HORIZONTAL MIN(1880) MAX(2000)
```

The results are shown in Figure 13.11.

If the result of (MAX − MIN)/interval is not an integer, some of your axis values will be fractional. You can compensate by adjusting either your MIN, MAX, or interval values.

Figure 13.11   Overlay plot of marriage and divorce rates

```
PLOT SYMBOLS='MD'
 /FORMAT=OVERLAY
 /TITLE='MARRIAGE AND DIVORCE RATES  1900-1981'
 /VSIZE=20 /HSIZE=60
 /VERTICAL='RATES PER 1000 POPULATION' MIN(0) MAX(20)
 /HORIZONTAL='YEAR' REFERENCE (1918,1945) MIN(1880) MAX(2000)
 /PLOT=MARRATE DIVRATE WITH YEAR.
```

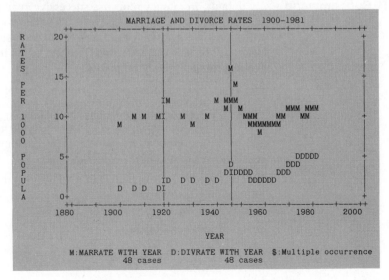

13.12
Controlling Plot Symbols

Two subcommands, CUTPOINT and SYMBOLS, control the frequencies that plotted symbols represent and the characters for the symbols in plots.

Use the CUTPOINT subcommand to adjust the frequencies represented by each plot symbol in bivariate plots (simple scatterplots and regression plots). Use the SYMBOLS subcommand to specify which characters represent a given frequency value in bivariate scatter and regression plots, overlay, and contour plots. Both CUTPOINT and SYMBOLS must precede the first PLOT subcommand and can be specified only once on a PLOT command. All requested plots use the same cutpoint values and symbols.

13.13
SYMBOLS Subcommand

Use the SYMBOLS subcommand to specify the plotting symbols. The SYMBOLS subcommand applies to bivariate, overlay, and contour plots. It does not apply to control plots. You can use only one SYMBOLS subcommand on a PLOT command. The available keywords are:

ALPHANUMERIC
Alphanumeric plotting symbols. PLOT uses the characters 1–9, A–Z, and * as plot symbols. Thus, * represents 36 or more cases at a print position. This is the default symbol set.

NUMERIC
Numeric plotting symbols. PLOT uses the characters 1–9 and * as plot symbols. Thus, * represents 10 or more cases at a print position.

'symbols'[,'ovprnt']
List of plot symbols. You can provide your own list of symbols enclosed in apostrophes. You can also specify a second list of overprinting symbols, separated from the first list by a comma or space and enclosed in apostrophes or quotation marks. A blank space can be used as an overprint "symbol" if you only want to overprint some symbols (see Figure 13.16). The overprinting symbols can be either hexadecimal representations (preceded by an X) or keyboard characters.

X'hexsym'[,'ovprnt']
List of hexadecimal plot symbols. Indicate hexadecimal symbols by specifying X before the hexadecimal representation list enclosed in apostrophes. Optionally, you can specify a second list of overprinting symbols separated from the first list by a comma or space. The overprinting symbols can be either hexadecimal representations or keyboard characters.

13.14
CUTPOINT Subcommand

By default, frequency plots use successive symbols in print positions corresponding to 1, 2, 3... cases, respectively. To define your own set of frequency values for the successive symbols, use the CUTPOINT subcommand. You can specify the desired interval width on the EVERY keyword, or you can use a value list in parentheses to specify cutpoints:

EVERY(n)
Frequency intervals of width n. The default is an interval size of 1, meaning that each individual frequency up to 35 has a different symbol. The last default frequency interval includes all frequencies greater than 35. If you specify SYMBOLS as well as EVERY, the last symbol specified will represent all frequencies greater than those for the next-to-last symbol.

(value list)
Cutpoints at the values specified.

You can specify only one CUTPOINT subcommand on a PLOT command, and it applies only to bivariate plots, not to control, overlay, or contour plots. If you specify

```
PLOT   CUTPOINT=EVERY(4)
 /PLOT = Y WITH X.
```

1 will represent 1 to 4 cases at a print position, 2 will represent 5 to 8 cases, and so forth. If you specify

```
PLOT  CUTPOINT=(4, 10, 25)
 /PLOT = Y WITH X.
```

1 will represent 1 to 4 cases at a print position, 2 will represent 5 to 10 cases, 3 will represent 11 to 25 cases, and 4 will represent 26 or more cases.

13.15
MISSING Subcommand

Use the MISSING subcommand to change or make explicit the treatment of cases with missing values. You can use only one MISSING subcommand on a PLOT command. Three specifications are available:

PLOTWISE *Exclude cases with missing values plotwise.* For each plot within a single frame, cases that have missing values on any variable for that plot are excluded. This is the default.

LISTWISE *Exclude cases with missing values listwise.* Cases with missing values on any variable named on any PLOT subcommand are excluded from all plots specified on the PLOT command.

INCLUDE *Include user-defined missing values as valid.*

If you specify

```
PLOT MISSING = LISTWISE
 /FORMAT=REGRESSION
 /PLOT = Y WITH A; Z WITH B.
```

PLOT excludes cases with missing values on any of the variables Y, A, Z, and B.

For overlay plots, plotwise deletion applies to each subplot requested. With the command

```
PLOT FORMAT=OVERLAY
 /PLOT = INCOME82 TAXES82 WITH YEAR82.
```

cases with missing values on INCOME82 or YEAR82 will be deleted from that subplot only, and cases with missing values on TAXES82 or YEAR82 will be deleted from the other subplot. The complete overlay plot may have a different number of cases for each subplot that is overlaid. The number of cases plotted in each subplot is stated below the plot frame.

13.16
Annotated Example

The following commands produce the output in Figure 13.16:

```
PLOT FORMAT=CONTOUR (10)
 /HSIZE=100 /VSIZE=60
 /SYMBOLS='.-=*+OXOXM','        -OW'
 /TITLE='SOLUBILITY OF AMMONIA IN WATER'
 /HORIZONTAL='ATMOSPHERIC PRESSURE'
 /VERTICAL='TEMPERATURE'
 /PLOT=TEMP WITH PRESSURE BY CONCENT.
```

- The FORMAT subcommand requests a contour plot with the control variable divided into 10 equal width intervals, corresponding to 10 plotting symbols.
- The HSIZE and VSIZE subcommands specify a plot width of 100 characters and a length of 60 lines.
- The SYMBOLS subcommand specifies the plotting symbols and overprint symbols to be used.
- The TITLE subcommand names a title to override the default title.

• The HORIZONTAL and VERTICAL subcommands indicate labels for the X and Y axes.

• The PLOT subcommand requests a plot of TEMP on the vertical (Y) axis with PRESSURE on the horizontal (X) axis. The keyword BY specifies CONCENT as the control, or contour, variable.

Figure 13.16   A contour plot

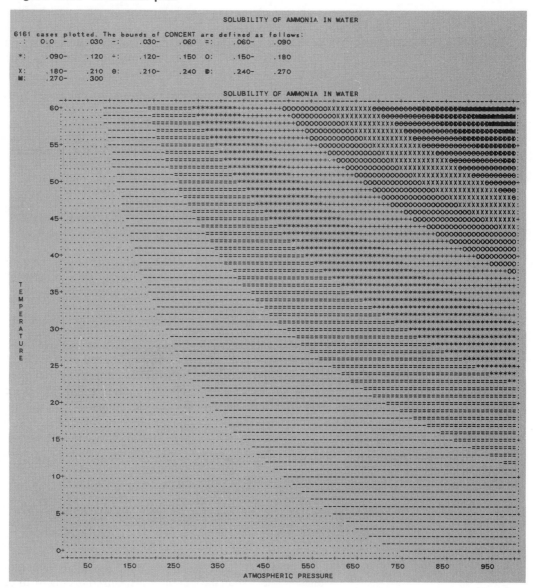

Contents

14 Measuring Linear Association: Procedure CORRELATIONS

Youthful lemonade-stand entrepreneurs as well as balding executives of billion-dollar corporations share a common concern—increasing sales. Hand-lettered signs affixed to neighborhood trees, television campaigns, siblings and friends canvassing local playgrounds, and international sales forces are known to be effective tactics. However, the impact of various intertwined factors on sales can be difficult to isolate, and much effort in the business world is expended on determining exactly what makes a product sell.

Churchill (1979) describes a study undertaken by the manufacturer of Click ball-point pens on the effectiveness of the firm's marketing efforts. A random sample of forty sales territories is selected, and sales, amount of advertising, and number of sales representatives are recorded. This chapter looks at the relationship between sales and these variables.

14.1 EXAMINING RELATIONSHIPS

Figure 14.1a is a scatterplot of the amount of sales and the number of television spots in each of forty territories. A scatterplot can reveal various types of associations between two variables. Figure 14.1b contains some commonly encountered patterns. In the first panel there appears to be no discernible relationship between the two variables. The variables are related exponentially in the second panel. That is, Y increases very rapidly for increasing values of X. In the third panel, the relationship between the two variables is U-shaped. Small and large values of the X variable are associated with large values of the Y variable.

From Figure 14.1a there appears to be a positive association between sales and advertising. That is, as the amount of advertising increases, so does the number of sales. The relationship between sales and advertising may also be termed *linear,* since the observed points cluster more or less around a straight line.

Figure 14.1a   Scatterplot showing a linear relationship

PLOT PLOT=SALES WITH ADVERTIS.

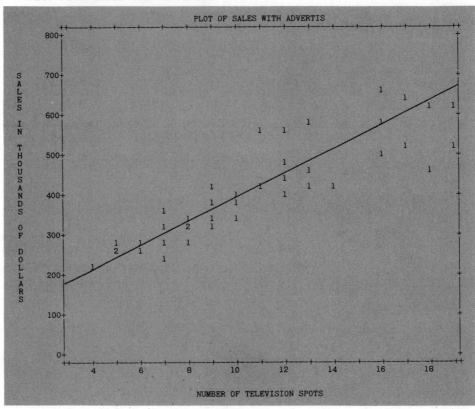

Figure 14.1b   Some common relationships

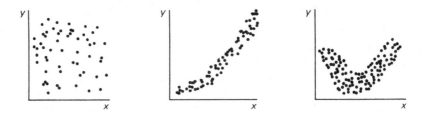

14.2
THE CORRELATION COEFFICIENT

Although a scatterplot is an essential first step in studying the association between two variables, it is often useful to quantify the strength of the association by calculating a summary index. One commonly used measure is the Pearson correlation coefficient, denoted by r. It is defined as

$$r = \frac{\sum_{i=1}^{N} (X_i - \overline{X})(Y_i - \overline{Y})}{(N-1)S_X S_Y}$$

Equation 14.2

where N is the number of cases and S_x and S_y are the standard deviations of the two variables. The absolute value of r indicates the strength of the linear relationship. The largest possible absolute value is 1, which occurs when all points fall exactly on the line. When the line has a positive slope, the value of r is positive, and when the slope of the line is negative, the value of r is negative (see Figure 14.2a).

Figure 14.2a   Scatterplots with correlation coefficients of +1 and −1

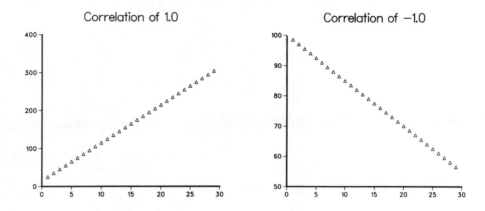

A value of 0 indicates no *linear* relationship. Two variables can have a strong association but a small correlation coefficient if the relationship is not linear. Figure 14.2b shows two plots with correlation coefficients of 0.

Figure 14.2b   Scatterplots with correlation coefficients of 0

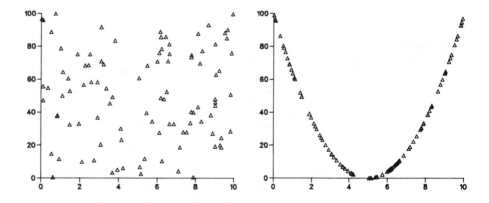

It is important to examine correlation coefficients together with scatterplots since the same coefficient can result from very different underlying relationships. The variables plotted in Figure 14.2c have a correlation coefficient greater than 0.8, as do the variables plotted in Figure 14.1a. But note how different the relationships are between the two sets of variables. In Figure 14.2c there is a strong positive linear association only for part of the graph. The relationship between the two variables is basically nonlinear. The scatterplot in Figure 14.1a is very different. The points cluster more or less around a line. Thus, the correlation coefficient should be used only to summarize the strength of linear association.

Figure 14.2c Scatterplot of percentage no facial hair with year

`PLOT PLOT=CLEAN WITH YEAR.`

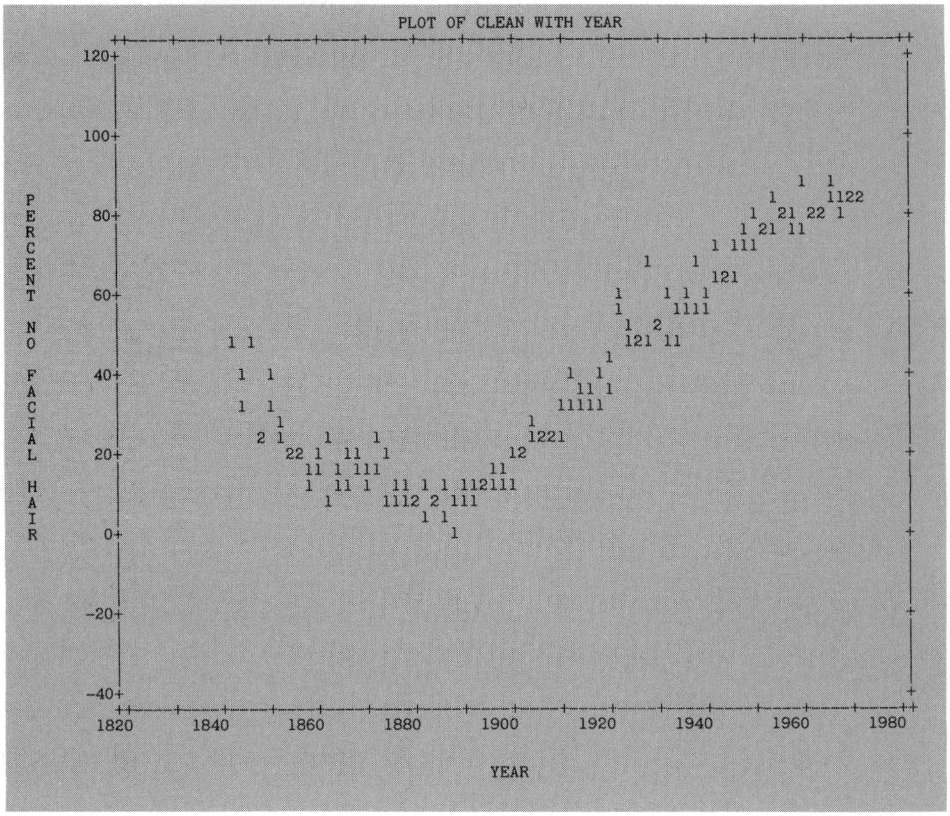

14.3
Some Properties of the Correlation Coefficient

A common mistake in interpreting the correlation coefficient is to assume that correlation implies causation. No such conclusion is automatic. While sales are highly correlated with advertising, they are also highly correlated with other variables, such as the number of sales representatives in a territory. Advertising alone does not necessarily result in increased sales. For example, territories with high sales may simply have more money to spend on TV spots, regardless of whether the spots are effective.

The correlation coefficient is a symmetric measure since interchanging the two variables X and Y in the formula does not change the results. The correlation coefficient is not expressed in any units of measure, and it is not affected by linear transformations such as adding or subtracting constants or multiplying or dividing all values of a variable by a constant.

14.4
Calculating Correlation Coefficients

Figure 14.4 is a table of correlation coefficients for the number of television spots, number of sales representatives, and amount of sales. The entry in each cell is the correlation coefficient. For example, the correlation coefficient between advertising and sales is 0.8802. This value indicates that there is a fairly strong linear association between the two variables, as shown in Figure 14.1a. The table is symmetric since the correlation between X and Y is the same as the correlation between Y and X. The values on the diagonal are all 1 since a variable is perfectly related to itself.

Figure 14.4 Correlation coefficients

CORRELATIONS VARIABLES=ADVERTIS REPS SALES.

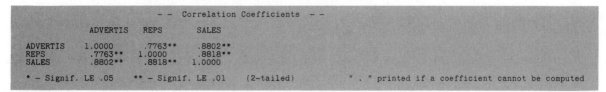

```
                    - - Correlation Coefficients - -

                  ADVERTIS   REPS      SALES

       ADVERTIS   1.0000    .7763**   .8802**
       REPS        .7763**  1.0000    .8818**
       SALES       .8802**   .8818**  1.0000

       * - Signif. LE .05    ** - Signif. LE .01    (2-tailed)        " . " printed if a coefficient cannot be computed
```

14.5
Hypothesis Tests about the Correlation Coefficient

Although the correlation coefficient is sometimes used only as a summary index to describe the observed strength of the association, in some situations description and summary are but a first step. The primary goal may be to test hypotheses about the unknown population correlation coefficient—denoted as ρ—based on its estimate, the sample correlation coefficient r. In order to test such hypotheses, certain assumptions must be made about the underlying joint distribution of the two variables. A common assumption is that independent random samples are taken from a distribution in which the two variables together are distributed normally. If this condition is satisfied, the test that the population coefficient is 0 can be based on the statistic

$$t = r\sqrt{\frac{N - 2}{1 - r^2}}$$

Equation 14.5

which, if $\rho=0$, has a Student's t distribution with $N-2$ degrees of freedom. Either one- or two-tailed tests can be calculated. If nothing is known in advance, a two-tailed test is appropriate. That is, the hypothesis that the coefficient is zero is rejected for both extreme positive and extreme negative values of t. If the direction of the association can be specified in advance, the hypothesis is rejected only for t values that are of sufficient magnitude and in the direction specified.

In SPSS, coefficients with two-tailed observed significance levels less than 0.05 are designated with a single asterisk. Those with two-tailed significance levels less than 0.01 are designated with two asterisks. From Figure 14.4, the probability that a correlation coefficient of at least 0.88 is obtained when there is no linear association in the population between sales and advertising is less than 0.01. Care should be exercised when examining the significance levels for large tables. Even if there is no association between the variables, if many coefficients are computed some would be expected to be statistically significant by chance alone.

Special procedures must be employed to test more general hypotheses of the form $\rho=\rho_0$, where ρ_0 is a constant. If the assumptions of bivariate normality appear unreasonable, a variety of *nonparametric* measures, which make limited assumptions about the underlying distributions of the variables, can be calculated. See Chapter 17 for further discussion.

14.6
Correlation Matrices and Missing Data

For a variety of reasons, data files frequently contain incomplete observations. Respondents in surveys scrawl illegible responses or refuse to answer certain questions. Laboratory animals die before experiments are completed. Patients fail to keep scheduled clinic appointments.

Analysis of data with missing values is troublesome. Before even considering possible strategies, you should determine whether there is evidence that the missing-value pattern is not random. That is, are there reasons to believe that missing values for a variable are related to the values of that variable or other variables? For example, people with low incomes may be less willing to report their financial status than more affluent people. This may be even more pronounced for people who are poor but highly educated.

One simple method of exploring such possibilities is to subdivide the data into two groups—those observations with missing data for a variable and those with complete data—and examine the distributions of the other variables in the file across these two groups. The SPSS procedures CROSSTABS and T-TEST are particularly useful for this. For a discussion of more sophisticated methods for detecting nonrandomness, see Frane (1976).

If it appears that the data are not missing randomly, use great caution in attempting to analyze the data. It may be that no satisfactory analysis is possible, especially if there are only a few cases.

If you are satisfied that the missing data are random, several strategies are available. First, if the same few variables are missing for most cases, exclude those variables from the analysis. Since this luxury is not usually available, you can alternatively keep all variables but eliminate the cases with missing values on any of them. This is termed *listwise* missing-value treatment since a case is eliminated if it has a missing value on any variable in the list.

If many cases have missing data for some variables, listwise missing-value treatment could eliminate too many cases and leave you with a very small sample. One common technique is to calculate the correlation coefficient between a pair of variables based on all cases with complete information for the two variables regardless of whether the cases have missing data on any other variable. For example, if a case has values only for variables 1, 3, and 5, it is used only in computations involving variable pairs 1 and 3, 1 and 5, and 3 and 5. This is *pairwise* missing-value treatment.

14.7
Choosing Pairwise Missing-Value Treatment

Several problems can arise with pairwise matrices, one of which is inconsistency. There are some relationships between coefficients that are clearly impossible but may seem to occur when different cases are used to estimate different coefficients. For example, if age and weight and age and height have a high positive correlation, it is impossible in the same sample for height and weight to have a high negative correlation. However, if the same cases are not used to estimate all three coefficients, such an anomaly can occur.

There is no single sample size that can be associated with a pairwise matrix since each coefficient can be based on a different number of cases. Significance levels obtained from analyses based on pairwise matrices must be viewed with caution since little is known about hypothesis testing in such situations.

It should be emphasized that missing-value problems should not be treated lightly. You should base your decision on careful examination of the data and not leave the choices up to system defaults.

14.8
RUNNING PROCEDURE CORRELATIONS

Procedure CORRELATIONS produces Pearson product-moment correlations with significance levels and, optionally, univariate statistics, covariances, and cross-product deviations. The only required subcommand on CORRELATIONS is the VARIABLES subcommand, which specifies the variable list to be analyzed. Optional subcommands can be entered in any order after the variable list.

14.9
VARIABLES Subcommand

CORRELATIONS displays either a square (symmetric) or rectangular (asymmetric) matrix, depending on how you specify the variable list. Both forms of the specification allow you to use the keyword TO to refer to consecutive variables on the active system file.

If you provide a simple list of variables, CORRELATIONS displays the correlations of each variable with every other variable in the list in a symmetric, square matrix. The correlation of a variable with itself is always 1.0000 and can be found on the diagonal of the matrix. Each pair of variables appears twice in the matrix (e.g., FOOD with RENT and RENT with FOOD) with identical coefficients, and the upper and lower triangles of the matrix are mirror images.

The square correlation matrix in Figure 14.4 was produced with the following command:

```
CORRELATIONS VARIABLES=ADVERTIS REPS SALES.
```

If you specify two variable lists separated by the keyword WITH, SPSS produces an asymmetic matrix of variables in the first list correlated with variables in the second list. For example,

```
CORRELATIONS VARIABLES=MECHANIC BUS WITH PUBTRANS.
```

produces two correlations, MECHANIC with PUBTRANS and BUS with PUBTRANS, while

```
CORRELATIONS VARIABLES=FOOD RENT WITH COOK TEACHER MANAGER.
```

produces six correlations. The variables listed before the keyword WITH define the rows of the matrix and those listed after the keyword WITH define the columns. Unless a variable is in both lists, there are no redundant coefficients in the matrix.

You can request more than one matrix on a CORRELATIONS command. Use a slash (/) to separate the specifications for each of the requested matrices. For example,

```
CORRELATIONS VARIABLES=FOOD RENT WITH COOK TEACHER MANAGER
 /FOOD TO MANAGER /PUBTRANS WITH MECHANIC.
```

produces three separate correlation matrices. The first matrix contains six nonredundant coefficients, the second matrix is a square matrix of all the variables from FOOD to MANAGER, and the third matrix consists of one coefficient for PUBTRANS and MECHANIC.

If all cases have a missing value for a given pair of variables or if they all have the same value for a variable, the coefficient cannot be computed. A period is displayed if a coefficient cannot be calculated.

14.10
PRINT Subcommand

By default, CORRELATIONS calculates two-tailed significance levels. A single asterisk appears next to the coefficient if it is significant at the 0.05 level; two asterisks indicate significance at the 0.01 level.

The PRINT subcommand allows you to switch to a one-tailed test and/or display both the number of cases and the significance level. The following keywords can be specified on the PRINT subcommand:

TWOTAIL   *Use two-tailed test of significance.* This test is appropriate when the direction of the relationship cannot be determined in advance, as is often the case in exploratory data analysis. This is the default.

ONETAIL   *Use one-tailed test of significance.* This test is appropriate when the direction of the relationship between a pair of variables can be specified in advance of the analysis.

NOSIG   *Suppress the display of the number of cases and significance level.* This is the default.

SIG   *Display the number of cases and significance level.*

14.11
STATISTICS Subcommand

The STATISTICS subcommand provides the following keywords for obtaining additional statistics:

DESCRIPTIVES *Mean, standard deviation, and number of nonmissing cases for each variable.* Missing values are handled on a variable-by-variable basis regardless of the missing-value option in effect for the correlations.

XPROD *Cross-product deviations and covariance for each pair of variables.*

ALL *All additional statistics available in CORRELATIONS.* Includes the mean, standard deviation, and number of nonmissing cases for each variable. Also includes the cross-product deviations and covariance for each pair of variables.

For example, the following command produces the statistics shown in Figure 14.11:

```
CORRELATIONS VARIABLES=ADVERTIS REP SALES
 /STATISTICS=DESCRIPTIVES.
```

Figure 14.11   Univariate statistics

VARIABLE	CASES	MEAN	STD DEV
ADVERTIS	40	10.9000	4.3074
REPS	40	5.0000	1.6486
SALES	40	411.2875	123.8540

14.12
MISSING Subcommand

By default, CORRELATIONS deletes cases with missing values for one or both of the pair of variables for a correlation coefficient. Since each coefficient is based on all cases that have valid codes on that particular pair of variables, the maximum information available is used in every calculation. This can result in a set of coefficients based on a varying number of cases.

The MISSING subcommand controls missing values. The following keywords can be specified on the MISSING subcommand:

PAIRWISE *Exclude missing values pairwise.* Cases missing for one or both of a pair of variables for a correlation coefficient are excluded from the analysis. This is the default.

LISTWISE *Exclude missing values listwise.* Cases missing on any variable named in a list are excluded from all analyses.

INCLUDE *Include user-missing values.* User-missing values are included in the analysis.

The PAIRWISE and LISTWISE keywords are mutually exclusive; however, each can be specified with INCLUDE.

14.13
FORMAT Subcommand

By default, CORRELATIONS includes redundant coefficients in the correlation and uses matrix format. The FORMAT subcommand has two keywords that control matrix format:

MATRIX *Use matrix format with redundant coefficients.* This is the default.

SERIAL *Use in serial string format with nonredundant coefficients.*

If you specify FORMAT=SERIAL, the number of cases and significance levels will also be displayed, overriding the PRINT=NOSIG default.

14.14
MATRIX Subcommand

Use the MATRIX subcommand to write matrix materials to an SPSS system file. The matrix materials include the mean, standard deviation, number of cases used to compute each coefficient, and Pearson correlation coefficient for each variable.

The OUT keyword on MATRIX specifies the file to which the matrix is written. Specify the matrix file in parentheses. There are two options:

(file) *Write the correlation matrix to an SPSS system file.* Specify the filename in the parentheses. CORRELATIONS creates a system file containing the matrix materials. The system file is stored on disk and can be retrieved at any time.

(*) *Replace the active system file with the correlation matrix system file.* The matrix materials replace the active system file. The correlation matrix is *not* stored on disk unless the active system file is saved.

14.15
Annotated Example

The following commands produced Figure 14.15:

```
CORRELATION VARIABLES=ADVERTIS REPS SALES
 /MISSING=LISTWISE
 /PRINT=ONETAIL SIG
 /MATRIX=OUT(CORRFILE).
```

- The VARIABLES subcommand specifies that correlation coefficients should be computed for all possible pairs of the variables ADVERTIS, REPS, and SALES.
- The MISSING subcommand indicates that if a case has a missing value for any of the three specified variables, the case should be excluded from the computation of all correlation coefficients.
- The PRINT subcommand computes significance levels based on a one-tailed test and displays the significance levels and the number of cases used in the calculation of each coefficient.
- The MATRIX subcommand creates a matrix system file called CORRFILE, which contains the matrix of correlation coefficients.

Figure 14.15 Correlation coefficients with significance levels

```
                        - - Correlation Coefficients  - -

                ADVERTIS    REPS        SALES

ADVERTIS        1.0000      .7763       .8802
                (   40)     (   40)     (   40)
                P= .        P= .000     P= .000

REPS             .7763     1.0000       .8818
                (   40)     (   40)     (   40)
                P= .000     P= .        P= .000

SALES            .8802      .8818      1.0000
                (   40)     (   40)     (   40)
                P= .000     P= .000     P= .

(Coefficient / (Cases) / 1-tailed Sig)          " . " is printed if a coefficient cannot be computed
```

Contents

15 One-Way Analysis of Variance: Procedure ONEWAY

Rotund Italians washing down carbohydrate-laden feasts with jugs of chianti, somber Jews ritualistically sipping Sabbath wine, melancholy Irish submerging grief and frustration in a bottle—all are common ethnic stereotypes. Is there any evidence to support these notions? In *Ethnic Drinking Subcultures,* Greeley et al. (1980) examine drinking habits in a sample of five ethnic populations within four major American cities.

A total of 1,107 families completed questionnaires detailing their drinking behavior and ancestral origins. Irish, Italian, Jewish, Swedish, and English families were included. Greeley investigates possible differences in drinking habits and a variety of cultural and psychological explanations for them. In this chapter, only differences in total alcohol consumption are considered.

15.1 DESCRIPTIVE STATISTICS AND CONFIDENCE INTERVALS

Figure 15.2 contains basic descriptive statistics for total yearly alcohol consumption in pints for the adult males in the study. The Italians and Irish are the biggest consumers, drinking an average of 24 pints a year. The Jewish males drink the least, an average of slightly more than 9 pints a year.

The sample mean for a group provides the single best guess for the unknown population value μ_i. It is unlikely that the value of the sample mean is exactly equal to the population parameter. Instead, it is probably not too different. Based on the sample mean, it is possible to calculate a range of values that, with a designated likelihood, include the population value. Such a range is called a *confidence interval*. For example, as shown in Figure 15.2, the 95% confidence interval for μ_{Irish} is the range 19.61 to 28.89 pints. This means that if repeated samples are selected from a population under the same conditions and 95% confidence intervals are calculated, 95% of the intervals will contain the unknown parameter μ_{Irish}. Since the parameter value is unknown, it is not possible to determine whether a particular interval contains it.

15.2 ANALYSIS OF VARIANCE

Looking at the sample means in Figure 15.2, you might wonder whether the observed differences can be reasonably attributed to chance or whether there is reason to suspect true differences between the five groups. One of the statistical procedures commonly used to test the hypothesis that several population means are equal is *analysis of variance,* or ANOVA.

Figure 15.2 Total yearly alcohol consumption for adult males (in pints)

ONEWAY AMOUNT BY ETHNIC(1,5)   /STATISTICS=DESCRIPTIVES.

GROUP	COUNT	MEAN	STANDARD DEVIATION	STANDARD ERROR	MINIMUM	MAXIMUM	95 PCT CONF INT FOR MEAN		
IRISH	119	24.2500	25.5620	2.3433	0.0	145.0	19.6097	TO	28.8903
ITALIAN	84	24.3120	24.1880	2.6391	0.0	128.0	19.0629	TO	29.5611
JEWISH	41	9.2500	21.6250	3.3773	0.0	87.0	2.4243	TO	16.0757
SWEDISH	74	16.5630	26.7500	3.1096	0.0	112.0	10.3655	TO	22.7605
ENGLISH	90	21.8750	21.5630	2.2729	0.0	117.0	17.3587	TO	26.3913
TOTAL	408	20.8373	24.6519	1.2204	0.0	145.0	18.4381	TO	23.2365

Certain assumptions are required for correct application of the ANOVA test. Independent samples from normally distributed populations with the same variance must be selected. In subsequent discussion, it is assumed that the populations sampled constitute the entire set of populations about which conclusions are desired. For example, the five ethnic groups are considered to be the only ones of interest. They are not viewed as a sample from all possible ethnic groups. This is called a *fixed-effects model*.

15.3
Partitioning Variation

In analysis of variance, the observed variability in the sample is subdivided into two components—variability of the observations within a group about the group mean and variability of the group means. If the amount of alcohol consumed doesn't vary much for individuals within the same ethnic group—for example, all the Swedes seem to drink about the same—but the group means differ substantially, there is evidence to suspect that the population means are not all equal.

The *within-groups sum of squares* is a measure of the variability within groups. It is calculated as

$$\text{SSW} = \sum_{i=1}^{k} (N_i - 1)S_i^2$$

Equation 15.3a

where S_i^2 is the variance of group i about its mean, and N_i is the number of cases in group i. For the data shown in Figure 15.2, the within-groups sum of squares is

$$\text{SSW} = 25.56^2(118) + 24.19^2(83) + 21.63^2(40) + 26.75^2(73)$$
$$+ 21.56^2(89) = 237,986.20$$

Equation 15.3b

Variability of the group means is measured by the *between-groups sum of squares*, which is

$$\text{SSB} = \sum_{i=1}^{k} N_i (\overline{X}_i - \overline{X})^2$$

Equation 15.3c

The mean of the ith group is denoted $\overline{X}_i$, and the mean of the entire sample is $\overline{X}$. For the drinking study, the between-groups sum of squares is

$$\text{SSB} = (24.25-20.84)^2(119) + (24.31-20.84)^2(84)$$
$$+ (9.25-20.84)^2(41) + (16.56-20.84)^2(74)$$
$$+ (21.88-20.84)^2(90) = 9,353.89$$

Equation 15.3d

The sums of squares, and other related statistics, are usually displayed in an analysis of variance table, as shown in Figure 15.3.

Figure 15.3 Analysis of variance table

ONEWAY AMOUNT BY ETHNIC(1,5).

```
- - - - - - - - - - - - - - - - - - - - - O N E W A Y - - - - - - - - - - - - - - - - - - - - - - - -
   VARIABLE   AMOUNT    AMOUNT OF ALCOHOL CONSUMED IN PINTS
BY VARIABLE   ETHNIC    ETHNIC BACKGROUND

                                  ANALYSIS OF VARIANCE

                SOURCE      D.F.    SUM OF SQUARES   MEAN SQUARES    F RATIO    F PROB.

       BETWEEN GROUPS         4         9353.8877      2338.4717      3.960     0.0036

       WITHIN GROUPS        403       237986.2031       590.5364

       TOTAL               407       247340.0625
```

The mean squares in Figure 15.3 are obtained by dividing the sums of squares by their degrees of freedom. The between-groups degrees of freedom are $k-1$, where k is the number of groups. The within-groups degrees of freedom are $N-k$, where N is the number of cases in the entire sample.

15.4
Testing the Hypothesis

To test the hypothesis that the five ethnic groups under study consume the same average amount of alcohol—that is, that

$$\mu_{Irish} = \mu_{Italian} = \mu_{Jewish} = \mu_{Swedish} = \mu_{English}$$

the following statistic is calculated (see Figure 15.3):

$$F = \frac{\text{BETWEEN GROUPS MEAN SQUARE}}{\text{WITHIN GROUPS MEAN SQUARE}} = \frac{2338.47}{590.54} = 3.96 \qquad \textbf{Equation 15.4}$$

When the assumptions described in Section 15.2 are met, the observed significance level is obtained by comparing the calculated F to values of the F distribution with $k-1$ and $N-k$ degrees of freedom. The observed significance level is the probability of obtaining an F statistic at least as large as the one calculated when all population means are equal. If this probability is small enough, the hypothesis that all population means are equal is rejected. In this example, the observed significance level is approximately 0.0036 (Figure 15.3). Thus, it appears unlikely that men in the five ethnic populations consume the same mean amount of alcohol.

15.5
MULTIPLE
COMPARISON
PROCEDURES

A significant F statistic indicates only that the population means are probably unequal. It does not pinpoint where the differences are. A variety of special techniques, termed *multiple comparison* procedures, are available for determining which population means are different from each other.

You may question the need for special techniques—why not just calculate the t-test described in Chapter 12 for all possible pairs of means? The problem is that when many comparisons are made, some will appear to be significant even when all population means are equal. With five groups, for example, there are ten possible comparisons between pairs of means. When all population means are equal, the probability that at least one of the ten observed significance levels will be less than 0.05 is about 0.29 (Snedecor & Cochran, 1967).

Multiple comparison procedures protect against calling too many differences significant. These procedures set up more stringent criteria for declaring differences significant than does the usual t-test. That is, the difference between two sample means must be larger to be identified as a true difference.

15.6
The Scheffé Test

Many multiple comparison procedures are available, and they all provide protection in slightly different ways (for further discussion, see Winer, 1971, or Neter & Wasserman, 1985). Figure 15.6a is output from the Scheffé multiple comparison procedure for the ethnic drinking data. The Scheffé method is conservative for pairwise comparisons of means. It requires larger differences between means for significance than most of the other methods.

Figure 15.6a   The Scheffé multiple comparison procedure

```
ONEWAY AMOUNT BY ETHNIC(1,5)
 /RANGES=SCHEFFE /FORMAT=LABELS.
```

```
        VARIABLE  AMOUNT     AMOUNT OF ALCOHOL CONSUMED IN PINTS
        BY VARIABLE  ETHNIC    ETHNIC BACKGROUND


MULTIPLE RANGE TEST


SCHEFFE PROCEDURE
RANGES FOR THE 0.050 LEVEL -

         4.38  4.38  4.38  4.38


THE RANGES ABOVE ARE TABLE RANGES.  THE VALUE ACTUALLY COMPARED WITH MEAN(J)-MEAN(I) IS..
     17.1834 * RANGE * SQRT(1/N(I) + 1/N(J))


 (*) DENOTES PAIRS OF GROUPS SIGNIFICANTLY DIFFERENT AT THE 0.050 LEVEL


                        J S E I I
                        E W N R T
                        W E G I A
                        I D L S L
                        S I I H I
                        H S S H A
                        H H   N
    MEAN      GROUP

    9.2500   JEWISH
   16.5630   SWEDISH
   21.8750   ENGLISH
   24.2500   IRISH     *
   24.3120   ITALIAN   *
```

The means are ordered and displayed from smallest to largest, as shown in Figure 15.6a. Pairs of means that are significantly different at the 0.05 level in this case are indicated with an asterisk in the lower half of the matrix at the bottom of the output. In this example, the asterisks under the vertical column labeled **JEWISH** mean that Jews are significantly different from the Irish and the Italians. No other pair is found to be significantly different. If no pairs are significantly different, a message is displayed and the matrix is suppressed.

The formula above the matrix indicates how large an observed difference must be to attain significance using the particular multiple comparison procedure. The table ranges are the values for the range variable in the formula.

If the sample sizes in all groups are equal, or an average sample size is used in the computations, a somewhat modified table is also displayed (Figure 15.6b). Instead of indicating which groups are significantly different, means that are not different are grouped. Subset 1 shows that Jews, Swedes, and English are not different. Subset 2 groups Swedes, English, Irish, and Italians. Jews do not appear in the same subset as Irish and Italians since they are significantly different from these two.

Figure 15.6b   Homogeneous subsets

```
         VARIABLE   AMOUNT       AMOUNT OF ALCOHOL CONSUMED IN PINTS
      BY VARIABLE   ETHNIC       ETHNIC BACKGROUND


MULTIPLE RANGE TEST


SUBSET  1

GROUP       JEWISH          SWEDISH          ENGLISH
MEAN        9.2500          16.5630          21.8750
- - - - - - - - - - - - - - - - - - - - - - - - - -

SUBSET  2

GROUP       SWEDISH         ENGLISH          IRISH            ITALIAN
MEAN        16.5630         21.8750          24.2500          24.3120
```

15.7
EXPLANATIONS

Both cultural and psychological explanations for differences in drinking habits among ethnic groups have been suggested (Greeley et al., 1980). In Jewish culture, the religious symbolism associated with drinking, as well as strong cultural norms against drunkenness, seem to discourage alcohol consumption. For the Irish, alcohol is a vehicle for promotion of fun and pleasure, as well as a potent tranquilizer for dissipating grief and tension. Such high expectations of alcohol make it a convenient escape and foster dependency. Italians have accepted drinking as a natural part of daily life. Alcohol is treated almost as a food and not singled out for its special pleasures.

15.8
Tests for Equality of Variance

As previously discussed, one of the assumptions needed for applying analysis of variance properly is that of equality of variances. That is, all of the populations from which random samples are taken must not only be normal but must also have the same variance σ^2. Several procedures are available for testing this assumption of *homogeneity of variance*. Unfortunately, many of them are not very useful since they are influenced by characteristics of the data other than the variance. The Levene test, available in the EXAMINE procedure (see Chapter 9), is the best test to use for testing if all variances are equal.

Figure 15.8   Tests for homogeneity of variance

```
ONEWAY AMOUNT BY ETHNIC(1,5)
 /STATISTICS=HOMOGENEITY.
```

```
TESTS FOR HOMOGENEITY OF VARIANCES

    COCHRANS C = MAX. VARIANCE/SUM(VARIANCES) = 0.2479, P = 0.248 (APPROX.)
    BARTLETT-BOX F =                             1.349, P = 0.249
    MAXIMUM VARIANCE / MINIMUM VARIANCE =        1.539
```

Figure 15.8 contains the three tests for homogeneity of variance available in the ONEWAY procedure. If the significance levels are not small, there is no reason to worry. Also, even if the variances appear different but the sample sizes in all groups are similar, there is no cause for alarm since the ANOVA test is not particularly sensitive to violations of equality of variance under such conditions. However, if the sample sizes are quite dissimilar and the variances are unequal, you should consider transforming the data or using a statistical procedure that requires less stringent assumptions (Chapter 17).

15.9
RUNNING
PROCEDURE
ONEWAY

Procedure ONEWAY produces a one-way analysis of variance for an interval-level variable by one independent variable. You can test for trends across categories, specify contrasts, and use a variety of range tests. Procedure ONEWAY requires a dependent variable list and the independent variable with its range of integer values. All ONEWAY subcommands are optional and may be entered in any order, provided they appear after the variable list.

15.10
Specifying the Design

A ONEWAY analysis list contains a dependent variable list and one independent (grouping) variable with its minimum and maximum values. Use only one analysis list per ONEWAY command. Dependent variables must be numeric. The independent variable follows the keyword BY and must include a value range specifying the highest and lowest values to be used in the analysis. These values are separated by a comma and are enclosed in parentheses. For example, the following command produced Figure 15.3:

```
ONEWAY AMOUNT BY ETHNIC(1,5).
```

While you can specify any number of categories for the independent variable, contrasts and multiple comparison tests are not available for more than 50 groups. ONEWAY deletes empty groups for the analysis of variance and range tests. The independent variable must have integer values. Noninteger values encountered in the independent variable are truncated.

15.11
RANGES Subcommand

The RANGES subcommand specifies any of seven different tests appropriate for multiple comparisons between means (see Section 15.5). Each RANGES subcommand specifies one test. For example,

```
ONEWAY AMOUNT BY ETHNIC(1,5)
 /RANGES=SCHEFFE
 /RANGES=SNK.
```

produces the Scheffé range test in Figure 15.6a and one additional range test. RANGES subcommands cannot be separated by CONTRAST or POLYNOMIAL subcommands. The available tests are:

LSD (alpha)   *Least-significant difference.* Any alpha between 0 and 1 can be specified. The default is 0.05. This is equivalent to doing multiple t-tests between all pairs of groups. No "multiple comparisons" protection is provided.

DUNCAN (alpha)   *Duncan's multiple range test.* Only 0.01, 0.05, and 0.10 are available as the alpha value. The default alpha is 0.05. DUNCAN uses 0.01 if the alpha specified is less than 0.05; 0.05 if the alpha specified is greater than or equal to 0.05 but less than 0.10; and 0.10 if the alpha specified is greater than or equal to 0.10.

SNK   *Student-Newman-Keuls.* Only 0.05 is available as the alpha value.

TUKEYB   *Tukey's alternate procedure.* Only 0.05 is available as the alpha value.

TUKEY   *Honestly significant difference.* Only 0.05 is available as the alpha value.

LSDMOD (alpha)   *Modified LSD.* Any alpha between 0 and 1 can be specified. The default alpha is 0.05. This is the Bonferroni test.

SCHEFFE (alpha)   *Scheffé's test.* Any alpha between 0 and 1 can be specified. The default alpha is 0.05.

Range tests always produce multiple comparisons between all groups. Nonempty group means are sorted in ascending order. Asterisks in the matrix indicate significantly different group means. In addition to this output, homogeneous subsets are calculated for balanced designs and for all designs that use either the Duncan (DUNCAN) or the Student-Newman-Keuls (SNK) procedure to calculate multiple range tests.

15.12
User-Specified Ranges

You can specify any other type of range by coding specific range values. You can specify up to $k - 1$ range values in ascending order, where k is the number of groups and where the range value times the standard error of the combined subset is the critical value. If fewer than $k - 1$ values are specified, the last value specified is used for the remaining ones. You can also specify n repetitions of the same value with the form $n * r$. To use a single critical value for all subsets, specify one range value, as in:

```
ONEWAY  WELL BY EDUC6(1,4)
   /RANGES=5.53.
```

15.13
HARMONIC Subcommand

The HARMONIC subcommand determines the sample size estimate to be used when the sample sizes are not equal in all groups. Either the sample sizes in the two groups being compared are used, or an average sample size of all groups is used.

The default keyword for HARMONIC is NONE, which uses the harmonic mean of the sizes of just the two groups being compared. To use the harmonic mean of *all* group sizes, specify keyword ALL. If ALL is used, ONEWAY calculates homogeneous subsets for SCHEFFE, TUKEY, TUKEYB, and LSDMOD tests on unbalanced designs. Specify only one keyword on the HARMONIC subcommand.

NONE *Harmonic mean of the sizes of the two groups being compared.* This is the default. You can also use keyword PAIR as an alias for NONE.

ALL *Harmonic mean of group sizes as sample sizes for range tests.* If the harmonic mean is used for unbalanced designs, ONEWAY determines homogeneous subsets for all range tests.

15.14
STATISTICS Subcommand

By default ONEWAY calculates the analysis of variance table. It also calculates any statistics specified by the CONTRAST and RANGES subcommands.

Use the STATISTICS subcommand to request additional statistics. The default keyword for STATISTICS is NONE, for no additional statistics. You can specify any one or all of the following statistics:

NONE *No optional statistics.* This is the default if you specify STATISTICS without keywords.

DESCRIPTIVES *Group descriptive statistics.* Displays the number of cases, mean, standard deviation, standard error, minimum, maximum, and 95% confidence interval for each dependent variable for each group.

EFFECTS *Fixed- and random-effects statistics.* Displays the standard deviation, standard error, and 95% confidence interval for the fixed-effects model, and the standard error, 95% confidence interval, and estimate of between-component variance for the random-effects model.

> **HOMOGENEITY** *Homogeneity-of-variance tests.* Displays Cochran's *C*, the Bartlett-Box *F*, and Hartley's *F* max.
>
> **ALL** *All statistics available for ONEWAY.*

The following commands produce the output in Figures 15.2 and 15.8:

```
ONEWAY AMOUNT BY ETHNIC(1,5)
 /STATISTICS=DESCRIPTIVES HOMOGENEITY.
```

15.15
MISSING Subcommand

Use the MISSING subcommand to control the treatment of cases with missing values. The following keywords are available:

> **ANALYSIS** *Exclude missing values on a pair-by-pair basis.* A case missing on either the dependent variable or grouping variable for a given analysis is not used for that analysis. Also, a case outside the range specified for the grouping variable is not used. This is the default.
>
> **LISTWISE** *Exclude missing values listwise.* Cases missing on any variable named are excluded from all analyses.
>
> **EXCLUDE** *Exclude cases with user-missing values.* This is the default.
>
> **INCLUDE** *Include cases with user-missing values.* User-defined missing values are included in the analysis.

Keywords ANALYSIS and LISTWISE are mutually exclusive. Each can be used with either INCLUDE or EXCLUDE. The defaults are ANALYSIS and EXCLUDE.

15.16
FORMAT Subcommand

By default, ONEWAY identifies groups as GRP1, GRP2, GRP3, etc. Use the FORMAT subcommand to identify the groups by their value labels. The FORMAT subcommand has only two keywords, NOLABELS and LABELS. NOLABELS is the default.

> **NOLABELS** *Suppress value labels.* This is the default.
>
> **LABELS** *Use the first eight characters from value labels for group labels.* The value labels are those defined for the independent variable.

The following commands produced Figure 15.6a:

```
ONEWAY AMOUNT BY ETHNIC
 /RANGES=SCHEFFE  /FORMAT=LABELS.
```

15.17
MATRIX Subcommand

ONEWAY writes means, standard deviations, and frequencies to a matrix system file that can be used by subsequent ONEWAY procedures. In addition, it can read a matrix containing means, frequencies, pooled variance, and degrees of freedom for the pooled variance.

The OUT keyword on MATRIX specifies the file to which the matrix is written. The IN keyword specifies the file from which the matrix is read. In both cases, specify the matrix file in parentheses, with one of the following options:

> **(file)** *Write the correlation matrix to, or read it from, the SPSS system file specified in the parentheses.*
>
> **(*)** *Replace the active system file with the correlation matrix, or read the matrix from the system active file.*

In addition to OUT and IN, ONEWAY allows the keyword NONE to explicitly indicate that the data are not matrix materials.

15.18
POLYNOMIAL Subcommand

The POLYNOMIAL subcommand partitions the between-groups sum of squares into linear, quadratic, cubic, or higher-order trend components. The value specified in the POLYNOMIAL subcommand indicates the highest-degree polynomial to be used. This value must be a positive integer less than or equal to 5 and less than the number of groups. Use only one POLYNOMIAL subcommand per ONEWAY command.

Specify this subcommand after the analysis specification, as in:

```
ONEWAY  WELL BY EDUC6 (1,4)
  /POLYNOMIAL = 2.
```

When you use the POLYNOMIAL subcommand with balanced designs, ONEWAY computes the sum of squares for each order polynomial from weighted polynomial contrasts, using the group code as the metric. These contrasts are orthogonal; hence the sum of squares for each order polynomial is statistically independent. If the design is unbalanced and there is equal spacing between groups, ONEWAY also computes sums of squares using the unweighted polynomial contrasts. These contrasts are not orthogonal. The deviation sums of squares are always calculated from the weighted sums of squares (Speed, 1976).

15.19
CONTRAST Subcommand

The CONTRAST subcommand specifies a priori contrasts to be tested by the t statistic. The specification for the CONTRAST subcommand is a vector of coefficients, with each coefficient corresponding to a category of the grouping variable. For example, the command

```
ONEWAY  WELL BY EDUC6(1,6)
  /CONTRAST = -1 -1 -1 -1 2 2.
```

contrasts the combination of the first four groups with the combination of the last two groups.

You can also specify fractional weights, as in:

```
/CONTRAST = -1 0 0 0 .5 .5
```

This subcommand contrasts Group 1 and the combination of Groups 5 and 6.

For most applications, the coefficients should sum to 0. Those sets that do not sum to 0 are used, but a warning message is displayed. In addition, you can use the repeat notation $n * c$ to specify the same coefficient for a consecutive set of means. For example,

```
/CONTRAST = 1 4*0 -1
```

specifies a contrast coefficient of 1 for Group 1, 0 for Groups 2 through 5, and −1 for Group 6. You must specify a contrast for every group implied by the range specification in the analysis list, even if a group is empty. However, you do not have to specify trailing zeros. For example,

```
/CONTRAST = -1 0 0 1 0 0
```

```
/CONTRAST = -1 2*0 1 2*0
```

```
/CONTRAST = -1 2*0 1
```

all specify the same set of contrast coefficients for a six-group analysis.

You can specify only one set of contrast coefficients per CONTRAST subcommand and no more than 50 coefficients per set. Output for each contrast list includes the value of the contrast, the standard error of the contrast, the t statistic, the degrees of freedom for t, and the two-tailed probability of t. Both pooled- and separate-variance estimates are displayed.

15.20
Annotated Example   The SPSS commands that produce the output in this chapter are:

```
TITLE 'DRINKING STUDY'.
DATA LIST /1 ETHNIC 1 AMOUNT 2-6 (2).
BEGIN DATA.
[data records]
END DATA.
VARIABLE LABELS
 AMOUNT 'AMOUNT OF ALCOHOL CONSUMED IN PINTS'
 /ETHNIC 'ETHNIC BACKGROUND'.
VALUE LABELS
  ETHNIC  1 'IRISH' 2 'ITALIAN' 3 'JEWISH' 4 'SWEDISH' 5 'ENGLISH'.
ONEWAY AMOUNT BY ETHNIC(1,5)
 /RANGES=SCHEFFE
 /FORMAT=LABELS
 /STATISTICS=DESCRIPTIVES HOMOGENEITY.
```

- The TITLE command puts the text, DRINKING STUDY, at the top of each page of output.

- The DATA LIST, VARIABLE LABELS, and VALUE LABELS commands define the variables used in this analysis. To define the variable AMOUNT with two decimal places, specify the number 2 enclosed in parentheses following the column specification, as shown in the DATA LIST command.

- The ONEWAY command requests a one-way analysis of variance of variable AMOUNT for five ethnic groups (variable ETHNIC). The RANGES subcommand requests Scheffé tests for comparing group means.

- The FORMAT subcommand instructs SPSS to use the first eight characters of the value labels to label output.

- The STATISTICS subcommand requests the group means, standard deviations, standard errors, minimum, maximum, 95% confidence intervals, and homogeneity-of-variance statistics.

Contents_____

16 Analysis of Variance: Procedure ANOVA

Despite constitutional guarantees, any mirror will testify that all citizens are not created equal. The consequences of this inequity are pervasive. Physically attractive persons are perceived as more desirable social partners, more persuasive communicators, and generally more likeable and competent. Even cute children and attractive burglars are disciplined more leniently than their homely counterparts (Sigall & Ostrove, 1975).

Much research on physical attractiveness focuses on its impact on heterosexual relationships and evaluations. Its effect on same-sex evaluations has received less attention. Anderson and Nida (1978) examined the influence of attractiveness on the evaluation of writings by college students. In the study, 144 male and 144 female students were asked to appraise essays purportedly written by college freshmen. A slide of the "author" was projected during the rating as part of supplemental information. Half of the slides were of authors of the same sex as the rater; the other half were of authors of the opposite sex. The slides had previously been determined to be of high, medium, and low attractiveness. Each participant evaluated one essay for creativity, ideas, and style. The three scales were combined to form a composite measure of performance.

16.1 DESCRIPTIVE STATISTICS

Figure 16.1 contains average composite scores for the essays, subdivided by the three categories of physical attractiveness and the two categories of sex similarity. The table is similar to the summary table shown for the one-way analysis of variance in Chapter 15. The difference here is that there are two independent (or grouping) variables, attractiveness and sex similarity. The first mean displayed (25.11) is for the entire sample. The number of cases (288) is shown in parentheses. Then for each of the independent variables, mean scores are displayed for each of the categories. The attractiveness categories are ordered from low (coded 1) to high (coded 3). Evaluations in which the rater and author are of the same sex are coded as 1, while opposite-sex evaluations are coded as 2. Finally, a table of means is displayed for cases classified by both grouping variables. Attractiveness is the row variable, and sex is the column variable. Each mean is based on the responses of 48 subjects.

Figure 16.1 Table of group means

```
ANOVA  VARIABLES=SCORE BY ATTRACT(1,3) SEX(1,2)
 /STATISTICS=MEAN.
```

```
                      * * *  C E L L   M E A N S  * * *

                    SCORE     COMPOSITE SCORE
                 BY ATTRACT   ATTRACTIVENESS LEVEL
                    SEX       SEX SIMILARITY


TOTAL POPULATION

      25.11
   (   288)


ATTRACT
       1           2           3

      22.98       25.78       26.59
   (    96)   (     96)   (     96)


SEX
       1           2

      25.52       24.71
   (   144)   (    144)



          SEX
                   1           2
ATTRACT
       1          22.79       23.17
               (     48)   (     48)

       2          28.63       22.92
               (     48)   (     48)

       3          25.13       28.04
               (     48)   (     48)
```

The overall average score is 25.11. Highly attractive individuals received the highest average score (26.59), while those rated low in physical appeal had the lowest score (22.98). There doesn't appear to be much difference between the average scores assigned to same (25.52) and opposite-sex (24.71) individuals. Highly attractive persons received an average rating of 25.13 when evaluated by individuals of the same sex and 28.04 when evaluated by students of the opposite sex.

16.2 ANALYSIS OF VARIANCE

Three hypotheses are of interest in the study: Does attractiveness relate to the composite scores? Does sex similarity relate to the scores? And is there an interaction between the effects of attractiveness and sex? The statistical technique used to evaluate these hypotheses is an extension of the one-way analysis of variance outlined in Chapter 15. The same assumptions as before are needed for correct application: the observations should be independently selected from normal populations with equal variances. Again, discussion here is limited to the situation in which both grouping variables are considered fixed. That is, they constitute the populations of interest.

The total observed variation in the scores is subdivided into four components: the sums of squares due to attractiveness, sex, their interaction, and the residual. This can be expressed as

TOTAL SS = ATTRACTIVENESS SS + SEX SS
     + INTERACTION SS + RESIDUAL SS
          Equation 16.2

Figure 16.2 is the analysis of variance table for this study. The first column lists the sources of variation. The sums of squares attributable to each of the components are given in the second column. The sums of squares for each independent variable alone are sometimes termed the "main effect" sums of squares. The "explained" sum of squares is the total sum of squares for the main effect and interaction terms in the model.

The degrees of freedom for sex and attractiveness, listed in the third column, are one fewer than the number of categories. For example, since there are three levels of attractiveness, there are two degrees of freedom. Similarly, sex has one degree of freedom. Two degrees of freedom are associated with the interaction term (the product of the degrees of freedom of each of the individual variables). The degrees of freedom for the residual are $N-1-k$, where k equals the degrees of freedom for the explained sum of squares.

Figure 16.2   Analysis of variance table

```
ANOVA VARIABLES=SCORE BY ATTRACT(1,3) SEX(1,2).
```

```
                    * * * A N A L Y S I S   O F   V A R I A N C E * * *

                 SCORE      COMPOSITE SCORE
          by     ATTRACT    ATTRACTIVENESS LEVEL
                 SEX        SEX SIMILARITY

                                 Sum of                Mean              Sig
   Source of Variation           Squares      DF       Square      F     of F

   Main Effects                  733.700       3       244.567    3.276  .022
      ATTRACT                    686.850       2       343.425    4.600  .011
      SEX                         46.850       1        46.850    0.628  .429

   2-Way Interactions            942.350       2       471.175    6.311  .002
      ATTRACT  SEX               942.350       2       471.175    6.311  .002

   Explained                    1676.050       5       335.210    4.490  .000

   Residual                    21053.140     282        74.656

   Total                       22729.190     287        79.196
```

The mean squares shown in Figure 16.2 are obtained by dividing each sum of squares by its degrees of freedom. Hypothesis tests are based on the ratios of the mean squares of each source of variation to the mean square for the residual. When the assumptions are met and the true means are in fact equal, the distribution of the ratio is an F with the degrees of freedom for the numerator and denominator terms.

16.3
Testing for Interaction

The F value associated with the attractiveness and sex interaction is 6.311. The observed significance level is approximately 0.002. Therefore, it appears that there is an interaction between the two variables. What does this mean?

**Figure 16.3a   Cell means
(Plot from SPSS Graphics)**

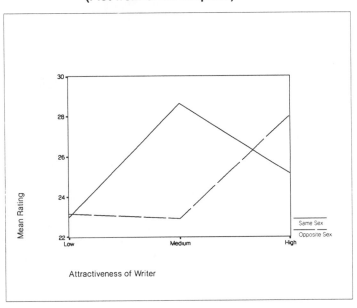

Consider Figure 16.3a, which is a plot of the cell means in Figure 16.1. Notice how the mean scores relate not only to the attractiveness of the individual and to the sex of the rater, but also to the particular combination of the values of the variables. Opposite-sex raters assign the highest scores to highly attractive individuals. Same-sex raters assign the highest scores to individuals of medium attractiveness. Thus, the ratings for each level of attractiveness depend on the sex variable. If there were no interaction between the two variables, a plot like that shown in Figure 16.3b might result, where the difference between the two types of raters is the same for the three levels of attractiveness.

Figure 16.3b   Cell means with no interaction
(Plot from SPSS Graphics)

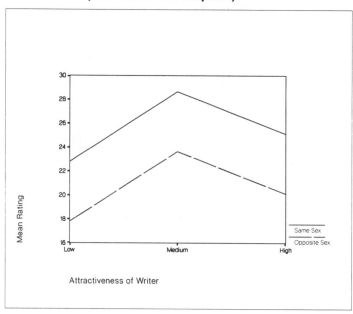

16.4
Tests for Sex and Attractiveness

Once the presence of interaction has been established, it is not particularly useful to continue hypothesis testing since the two variables *jointly* affect the dependent variable. If there is no significant interaction, the grouping variables can be tested individually. The F value associated with attractiveness would provide a test of the hypothesis that attractiveness does not affect the rating. Similarly, the F value associated with sex would test the hypothesis that sex has no main effect on evaluation.

Note that the small F value associated with sex does not indicate that response is unaffected by sex, since sex *is* included in the significant interaction term. Instead, it shows that when response is averaged over attractiveness levels, the two sex category means are not significantly different.

16.5
EXPLANATIONS

Several explanations are consistent with the results of this study. Since most people consider themselves moderately attractive, the highest degree of identification should be with same-sex individuals of moderate attractiveness. The higher empathy may result in the higher scores. An alternative theory is that moderately attractive individuals are generally perceived as more desirable same-sex friends: they have more favorable personality profiles and don't encourage unfavorable comparisons. Their writing scores may benefit from their perceived popularity.

Although we don't want friends who outshine us, handsome (and beautiful) dates provide a favorable reflection and enhance our status. Physical beauty is advantageous for heterosexual relationships, but not same-sex friendships. This prejudice may affect all evaluations of highly attractive members of the opposite sex. Regardless of the explanation, certain practical conclusions are apparent. Students, choose your instructors carefully! Authors, think twice before including your photo on the book jacket!

16.6 EXTENSIONS

Analysis of variance techniques can be used with any number of grouping variables. For example, the data in Table 16.1 originated from a more complicated experiment than described here. There were four factors—essay quality, physical attractiveness, sex of writer, and sex of subject. The original data were analyzed with a 3 × 3 × 2 × 2 ANOVA table. (The numbers indicate how many categories each grouping variable has.) The conclusions from our simplified analysis are the same as those from the more elaborate analysis.

Each of the cells in our experiment had the same number of subjects. This greatly simplifies the analysis and its interpretation. When unequal sample sizes occur in the cells, the total sum of squares cannot be partitioned into nice components that sum to the total. A variety of techniques are available for calculating sums of squares in such "nonorthogonal" designs. The methods differ in the way they adjust the sums of squares to account for other effects in the model. Each method results in different sums of squares and tests different hypotheses. However, when all cell frequencies are equal, the methods yield the same results. For discussion of various procedures for analyzing designs with unequal cell frequencies, see Kleinbaum and Kupper (1978) and Overall and Klett (1972).

16.7 RUNNING PROCEDURE ANOVA

Analysis of variance tests the hypothesis that the group means of the dependent variable are equal. The dependent variable must be interval level, and one or more categorical variables define the groups. These categorical variables are termed *factors.* The ANOVA procedure also allows you to include continuous explanatory variables, termed *covariates.* When there are five or fewer factors, the default model is *full factorial,* meaning that all interaction terms are included. If there are more than five factors, only interaction terms up to order five are included.

The only required subcommand on ANOVA is the VARIABLES subcommand, which specifies the variable list to be analyzed.

16.8 VARIABLES Subcommand

The VARIABLES subcommand specifies the name of at least one dependent variable, the keyword BY, and one to ten independent variables followed by their minimum and maximum values separated by a comma and enclosed in parentheses. To produce the analysis of variance table in Figure 16.2, specify:

```
ANOVA VARIABLES=SCORE BY ATTRACT(1,3) SEX (1,2).
```

By default, the model effects are the ATTRACT and SEX main effects and the ATTRACT by SEX interaction.

16.9 Specifying Covariates

The *covariate list* follows the keyword WITH. You do not specify a value range for the covariates. For example, the command

```
ANOVA VARIABLES=PRESTIGE BY REGION(1,9) SEX(1,2) WITH EDUC.
```

names EDUC as the covariate.

16.10
COVARIATES
Subcommand

By default, ANOVA assesses the covariates before it assesses the factor main effects. Use the COVARIATES subcommand to specify a different order for assessing blocks of covariates and factor main effects. The following keywords can be specified on the COVARIATES subcommand:

FIRST *Process covariates before main effects for factors.* This is the default if you omit the COVARIATES subcommand.

WITH *Process covariates concurrently with main effects for factors.*

AFTER *Process covariates after main effects for factors.*

Note that the order of entry is irrelevant when METHOD=UNIQUE (see Section 16.12).

16.11
MAXORDERS
Subcommand

By default, ANOVA examines all the interaction effects up to and including the fifth order. Use the MAXORDERS subcommand to suppress the effects of various orders of interaction. The following keywords can be specified on the MAXORDERS subcommand:

ALL *Examine all the interaction effects up to and including the fifth order.* This is the default if you omit the MAXORDERS subcommand.

n *Examine all the interaction effects up to and including the n-order effect.* For example, if you specify MAXORDERS=3, ANOVA examines all the interaction effects up to and including the third order. All higher-order interaction sums of squares are pooled into the error term.

NONE *Delete all interaction terms from the model.* All interaction sums of squares are pooled into the error sum of squares. Only main effects and covariate effects appear in the ANOVA table.

For example, to suppress all interaction effects, specify

```
ANOVA VARIABLES=PRESTIGE BY REGION(1,9) SEX, RACE(1,2)
 /MAXORDERS=NONE.
```

16.12
METHOD Subcommand

By default, ANOVA uses what is termed the *classic experimental approach* for decomposing sums of squares. Optionally, you can request the *regression approach* or the *hierarchical approach* on the METHOD subcommand. The following keywords can be specified on METHOD:

EXPERIMENTAL *Classic experimental approach.* This is the default if you omit the METHOD subcommand.

UNIQUE *Regression approach.* UNIQUE overrides any specifications on the COVARIATES subcommand. All effects are assessed simultaneously for their partial contribution, so order is irrelevant. The MCA and MEAN specifications on the STATISTICS subcommand are not available with the regression approach.

HIERARCHICAL *Hierarchical approach.*

If you select the default classic-experimental approach and the default treatment of covariates (before the main effects), effects are assessed in the following order: covariates, main effects, two-way interactions, three-way interactions, four-way interactions, and five-way interactions. This means that covariates are not adjusted for any other terms in the model except for other covariates, main effects are adjusted only for covariates and other main effects, and interactions are adjusted for all interactions of the same and lower order as well as for all main effects and covariates.

The effects within each type are adjusted for all other effects of that type and also for the effects of all prior types. For example, all two-way interactions are adjusted for other two-way interactions and, as described above, for all main effects and covariates.

In the regression approach all effects are assessed simultaneously. That is, each effect is adjusted for all other effects in the model. The COVARIATE subcommand has no effect if METHOD=UNIQUE.

The hierarchical approach differs from the experimental approach only in the treatment of covariates and main effects. In the hierarchical approach, covariates and main effects are adjusted only for effects that precede them on the VARIABLES subcommand. (By default, covariates are considered to precede all other effects on VARIABLES, even though they are actually specified after the main effects.) For example, if the command is

```
ANOVA VARIABLES=DEP BY F1 F2 F3 (1,4) WITH COV1 COV2 COV3
   /METHOD=HIERARCHICAL.
```

COV1 is not adjusted for any other terms, COV2 is adjusted only for COV1, and COV3 is adjusted for both COV1 and COV2. Similarly, F1 is adjusted only for the covariates, F2 is adjusted for the covariates and F1, and F3 is adjusted for F1, F2, and all of the covariates. Note that interactions are not processed hierarchically; they are adjusted for all covariates, factors and other interactions of the same and lower orders, just as in the default classical experimental approach.

The COVARIATES subcommand allows you to change the order in which covariates are entered into the model. For example, if you select the default experimental approach but request COVARIATES=AFTER, main effects are entered first and adjusted only for other main effects, covariates are entered after the main effects and adjusted for other covariates and main effects. If, instead, you select the default experimental approach with COVARIATES=WITH, covariates are entered together with the main effects. This means that all covariates and main effects are adjusted for each other.

16.13
STATISTICS Subcommand

By default, ANOVA calculates only the statistics needed for analysis of variance. Optionally, you can request a means and counts table, unstandardized regression coefficients, and multiple classification analysis on the STATISTICS subcommand.

You can specify the STATISTICS subcommand by itself or with one or more keywords. If you specify the STATISTICS subcommand with no keywords, ANOVA calculates MEAN and REG, if there are covariates. If you include a keyword or keywords on the STATISTICS subcommand, ANOVA calculates only the additional statistics you request.

The following keywords can be specified on the STATISTICS subcommand:

MEAN *Means and counts table.* MEAN requests means and counts for each dependent variable for groups defined by each factor and each combination of factors up to the fifth level. This statistic is not available with METHOD=UNIQUE.

REG *Unstandardized regression coefficients for the covariates.* The coefficients are computed at the point where the covariates are entered into the equation. Thus, their values depend on the type of design you have specified.

MCA *Multiple classification analysis.* The MCA table is not available with METHOD=UNIQUE. In the MCA table, effects are expressed as deviations from the grand mean. The table includes a listing of unadjusted category effects for each factor, category effects adjusted for other factors, category effects adjusted for all factors and covariates, and eta and beta values.

ALL   *Means and counts table, unstandardized regression coefficients, and multiple classification analysis.*

NONE   *No additional statistics.* This is the default if you omit the STATISTICS subcommand.

For example, the following commands produce Figure 16.1:

```
ANOVA VARIABLES=SCORE BY ATTRACT(1,3) SEX(1,2)
 /STATISTICS=MEAN.
```

16.14
MISSING Subcommand

By default, a case that is missing for any variable named in the analysis list is deleted for all analyses specified by that list. Use the MISSING subcommand to ignore missing-data indicators and to include all cases in the computations. Two keywords can be specified on the MISSING subcommand:

EXCLUDE   *Exclude cases with missing data.* This is the default if you omit the MISSING subcommand.

INCLUDE   *Include cases with user-missing data.*

16.15
FORMAT Subcommand

By default, ANOVA displays variable or value labels if they have been defined. Use the FORMAT subcommand to suppress variable and value labels. Two keywords can be specified on the FORMAT subcommand:

LABELS   *Display variable and value labels.* This is the default if you omit the FORMAT subcommand.

NOLABELS   *Suppress variable and value labels.*

16.16
Annotated Example

The SPSS commands used to produce the results in Figures 16.1 and 16.2 are:

```
TITLE 'ANALYSIS OF VARIANCE'.
DATA LIST  /1 ATTRACT 1-2 SEX 3 SCORE 4-5.
BEGIN DATA.
data records
END DATA.
RECODE  ATTRACT (1=1) (5=2) (10=3).
VARIABLE LABELS
 ATTRACT 'ATTRACTIVENESS LEVEL'
 SEX 'SEX SIMILARITY'
 SCORE 'COMPOSITE SCORE'.
VALUE LABELS
  ATTRACT  1 'LOW' 2 'MEDIUM' 3 'HIGH'
 /SEX  1 'SAME' 2 'OPPOSITE'.
ANOVA   VARIABLES=SCORE BY ATTRACT (1,3) SEX (1,2)
 /STATISTICS=MEAN.
FINISH.
```

Thess commands assume that the variable ATTRACT is originally coded 1=low, 5=medium, and 10=high.

- The TITLE command displays the title ANALYSIS OF VARIANCE at the top of each page of output.

- The DATA LIST command defines the variables.

- The RECODE command changes the values of ATTRACT to consecutive values of 1, 2, and 3 so that the ANOVA procedure will be more efficient. The recode specification (1=1), although unnecessary, is included to give a complete description of the values of ATTRACT. All values not mentioned on the RECODE command remain unchanged. See Chapter 2 for a discussion of the RECODE command.

- The VARIABLE LABELS and VALUE LABELS commands assign variable and value labels.
- The ANOVA command requests an analysis of variance of variable SCORE by SEX and three categories of attractiveness (variable ATTRACT).
- The STATISTICS command requests the means and counts table.

Contents _____

17 Distribution-Free or Nonparametric Tests: Procedures NONPAR CORR and NPAR TESTS

Coffee and carrots have recently joined saccharin, tobacco, Laetrile, and interferon on the ever-expanding list of rumored causes of and cures for cancer. This list is necessarily tentative and complicated. The two major sources of evidence—experiments on animals and examination of the histories of afflicted persons—are fraught with problems. It is difficult to predict, based on large doses of suspect substances given to small animals, the consequences of small amounts consumed by humans over a long time span.

In studies of people, lifestyle components are difficult to isolate, and it is challenging—if not impossible—to unravel the contribution of a single factor. For example, what is the role of caffeine based on a sample of overweight, sedentary, coffee- and alcohol-drinking, cigarette-smoking, urban dwellers?

Nutrition is also thought to be an important component in cancer development and progression. For example, the per capita consumption of dietary fats is positively correlated with the incidence of mammary and colon cancer in humans (Wynder, 1976). In a recent study, King et al. (1979) examined the relationship between diet and tumor development in rats. Three groups of animals of the same age, species, and physical condition were injected with tumor cells. The rats were divided into three groups and fed diets of either low, saturated, or unsaturated fat.

One hypothesis of interest is whether the length of time until a tumor develops in rats fed saturated diets differs from the length of time in rats fed unsaturated diets. If it is tenable to assume that tumor-free time is normally distributed, the two-sample t-test described in Chapter 12 can be used to test the hypothesis that the population means are equal. However, if the distribution of times does not appear to be normal, and especially if the sample sizes are small, statistical procedures that do not require assumptions about the shapes of the underlying distributions should be considered.

17.1 THE MANN-WHITNEY TEST

The *Mann-Whitney test*, also known as the Wilcoxon test, does not require assumptions about the shape of the underlying distributions. It tests the hypothesis that two independent samples come from populations having the same distribution. The form of the distribution need not be specified. The test does not require that the variable be measured on an interval scale; an ordinal scale is sufficient.

17.2
Ranking the Data

To compute the test, the observations from both samples are first combined and ranked from smallest to largest. Consider Table 17.2, which shows a sample of the King data reported by Lee (1980). Case 4 has the shortest elapsed time to development of a tumor, 68 days. It is assigned a rank of 1. The next shortest time is for Case 3, so it is assigned a rank of 2. Cases 5 and 6 both exhibited tumors on the same day. They are both assigned a rank of 3.5, the average of the ranks (3 and 4) for which they are tied. Case 2, the next largest, is given a rank of 5, and Case 1 is given a rank of 6.

Table 17.2   Ranking the data

Saturated			**Unsaturated**		
Case	Time	Rank	Case	Time	Rank
1	199	6	4	68	1
2	126	5	5	112	3.5
3	81	2	6	112	3.5

17.3
Calculating the Test

The statistic for testing the hypothesis that the two distributions are equal is the sum of the ranks for each of the two groups. If the groups have the same distribution, their sample distributions of ranks should be similar. If one of the groups has more than its share of small or large ranks, there is reason to suspect that the two underlying distributions are different.

Figure 17.3 shows the output from the Mann-Whitney test for the complete King data. For each group, the mean rank and number of cases is given. (The mean rank is the sum of the ranks divided by the number of cases.) Note that the saturated-diet group has only 29 cases since one rat died of causes unrelated to the experiment. The entry displayed under W is the sum of the ranks for the group with the smaller number of observations. If both groups have the same number of observations, W is the rank sum for the group named first in the NPAR TESTS command (see Section 17.33). For this example, W is 963, the sum of the ranks for the saturated-diet group.

Figure 17.3   Mann-Whitney output

```
NPAR TESTS M-W=TUMOR BY DIET(0,1).
```

```
- - - - - Mann-Whitney U - Wilcoxon Rank Sum W Test

      TUMOR
   by DIET


     Mean Rank      Cases

        26.90          30   DIET = 0   UNSATURATED
        33.21          29   DIET = 1   SATURATED
                      ---
                       59   Total

                                      Corrected for ties
          U                W            Z       2-Tailed P
        342.0            963.0       -1.4112        .1582
```

The number identified on the output as U is the number of times a value in the unsaturated-diet group precedes a value in the saturated-diet group. To understand what this means, consider the data in Table 17.2 again. All three cases in the unsaturated-diet group have smaller ranks than the first case in the saturated-diet group, so they all precede Case 1 in the rankings. Similarly, all three cases in the unsaturated-diet group precede Case 2. Only one unsaturated-diet case (Case 4) is smaller in value than Case 3. Thus, the number of times the value for an unsaturated-diet case precedes the value for a saturated-diet case is

3+3+1=7. The number of times the value of a saturated-diet case precedes the value of an unsaturated-diet case is 2, since Case 3 has a smaller rank than both Cases 5 and 6. The smaller of these two numbers is displayed on the output as U. If the two distributions are equal, values from one group should not consistently precede values in the other.

The significance levels associated with U and W are the same. They can be obtained by transforming the score to a standard normal deviate (Z). If the total sample size is less than 30, an exact probability level based on the distribution of the score is also displayed. From Figure 17.3, the observed significance level for this example is 0.158. Since the significance level is large, the hypothesis that tumor-free time has the same distribution for the two diet groups is not rejected.

17.4
Which Diet?

You should not conclude from these findings that it doesn't matter—as far as tumors are concerned—what kind of fat you (or rats) eat. King et al. found that rats fed the unsaturated diet had a total of 96 tumors at the end of the experiment, while rats fed the saturated diet had only 55 tumors. They also found that large tumors were more common in the unsaturated-diet group than in the saturated-diet group. Thus, unsaturated fats may be more hazardous than saturated fats.

17.5
Assumptions

The Mann-Whitney test requires only that the observations be a random sample and that values can be ordered. These assumptions, especially randomness, are not to be made lightly, but they are less restrictive than those for the two-sample t-test for means. The t-test further requires that the observations be selected from normally distributed populations with equal variances. (An approximate test for the case of unequal variances is presented in Chapter 12).

Since the Mann-Whitney test can always be calculated instead of the t-test, what determines which should be used? If the assumptions needed for the t-test are met, the t-test is more powerful than the Mann-Whitney test. That is, the t-test will detect true differences between the two populations more often than will the Mann-Whitney test since the t-test uses more information from the data. Substitution of ranks for the actual values loses potentially useful information. On the other hand, using the t-test when its assumptions are substantially violated may result in an erroneous observed significance level.

In general, if the assumptions of the t-test appear reasonable, it should be used. When the data are ordinal—or interval but from a markedly nonnormal distribution—the Mann-Whitney test is the procedure of choice.

17.6
NONPARAMETRIC
TESTS

Many statistical procedures, like the Mann-Whitney test, require limited distributional assumptions about the data. Collectively these procedures are termed *distribution-free* or *nonparametric tests*. Like the Mann-Whitney test, distribution-free tests are generally less powerful than their parametric counterparts. They are most useful in situations where parametric procedures are not appropriate: when the data are nominal or ordinal, or when interval data are from markedly nonnormal distributions. Significance levels for certain nonparametric tests can be determined regardless of the shape of the population distribution since they are based on ranks.

In the following sections, various nonparametric tests will be used to reanalyze some of the data described in previous chapters. Since the data were chosen to illustrate the parametric procedures, they satisfy assumptions that are more restrictive than those for nonparametric procedures. However, they provide an opportunity for learning new procedures with familiar data and for comparing results from different types of analyses.

17.7
The Sign Test

In Chapter 12, the paired t-test for means is used to test the hypothesis that the mean buying scores for husbands and wives are equal. Remember that the assumption that the differences are normally distributed is required for this test.

The *sign test* is a nonparametric procedure used with two related samples to test the hypothesis that the distributions of two variables are the same. This test makes no assumptions about the shape of these distributions.

To compute the sign test, the difference between the buying scores of husbands and wives is calculated for each case. Next, the numbers of positive and negative differences are obtained. If the distributions of the two variables are the same, the numbers of positive and negative differences should be similar.

Figure 17.7 Sign test output

NPAR TESTS SIGN=HSSCALE WITH WSSCALE.

```
- - - - - Sign Test

       HSSCALE    HUSBAND SELF SCALE
with WSSCALE    WIFE SELF SCALE


        Cases

          56    - Diffs (WSSCALE LT HSSCALE)          Z =      1.6416
          39    + Diffs (WSSCALE GT HSSCALE)
           3      Ties                         2-Tailed P =       .1007
         ----
          98      Total
```

The output in Figure 17.7 shows that the number of negative differences is 56, while the number of positive differences is 39. The total number of cases is 98, including 3 with 0 differences. The observed significance level is 0.1007. Since this value is large, the hypothesis that the distributions are the same is not rejected.

17.8
The Wilcoxon
Signed-Ranks Test

The sign test uses only the direction of the differences between the pairs and ignores the magnitude. A discrepancy of 15 between husbands' and wives' buying scores is treated in the same way as a discrepancy of 1. The *Wilcoxon signed-ranks test* incorporates information about the magnitude of the differences and is therefore more powerful than the sign test.

To compute the Wilcoxon signed-ranks test, the differences are ranked ignoring the signs. In the case of ties, average ranks are assigned. The sums of the ranks for positive and negative differences are then calculated.

Figure 17.8 Wilcoxon signed-ranks test output

NPAR TESTS WILCOXON=HSSCALE WITH WSSCALE.

```
- - - - - Wilcoxon Matched-Pairs Signed-Ranks Test

       HSSCALE    HUSBAND SELF SCALE
with WSSCALE    WIFE SELF SCALE


     Mean Rank    Cases

        45.25         56    - Ranks (WSSCALE LT HSSCALE)
        51.95         39    + Ranks (WSSCALE GT HSSCALE)
                       3      Ties (WSSCALE EQ HSSCALE)
                     ----
                      98      Total

      Z =    -.9428              2-Tailed P =   .3458
```

From Figure 17.8, the average rank of the 56 negative differences is 45.25. The average positive rank is 51.95. There are 3 cases with the same value for both variables. This is the entry under TIES in Figure 17.8. The observed significance level associated with the test is large (0.3458), and again the hypothesis of no difference is not rejected.

17.9
The Kruskal-Wallis Test

The experiment described in the first sections of this chapter investigates the effects of three diets on tumor development. The Mann-Whitney test was calculated to examine possible differences between saturated and unsaturated diets. To test for differences between all three diets, an extension of the Mann-Whitney test can be used. This test is known as the *Kruskal-Wallis one-way analysis of variance*.

The procedure for computing the Kruskal-Wallis test is similar to that used in the Mann-Whitney test. All cases from the groups are combined and ranked. Average ranks are assigned in the case of ties. For each group, the ranks are summed, and the Kruskal-Wallis *H* statistic is computed from these sums. The *H* statistic has approximately a chi-square distribution under the hypothesis that the three groups have the same distribution.

Figure 17.9   Kruskal-Wallis one-way analysis of variance output

```
NPAR TESTS K-W=TUMOR BY DIET(0,2).
```

```
- - - - - Kruskal-Wallis 1-Way Anova

      TUMOR
   by DIET


    Mean Rank      Cases

       34.12          30     DIET = 0     UNSATURATED
       43.50          29     DIET = 1     SATURATED
       56.24          29     DIET = 2     LOW-FAT

                      ---

                       88    Total

                                                      Corrected for ties
        Cases      Chi-Square  Significance    Chi-Square  Significance
          88        11.1257       .0038          11.2608      .0036
```

The output in Figure 17.9 shows that the third group, the low-fat-diet group, has the largest average rank. The value of the Kruskal-Wallis statistic is 11.1257. When the statistic is adjusted for the presence of ties, the value changes to 11.2608. The small observed significance level suggests that the time until development of a tumor is not the same for all three groups.

17.10
The One-Sample Chi-Square Test

In Chapter 7, frequencies of deaths for the days of the week are examined. The FREQUENCIES output suggests that the days of the week are equally hazardous in regard to death. To test this conclusion, the *one-sample chi-square test* can be used. This nonparametric test requires only that the data be a random sample.

To calculate the one-sample chi-square statistic, the data are first classified into mutually exclusive categories of interest—days of the week in this example—and then expected frequencies for these categories are computed. Expected frequencies are the frequencies that would be expected if a given hypothesis is true. For the death data, the hypothesis to be tested is that the probability of death is the same for each day of the week. The day of death is known for 110 subjects. The hypothesis implies that the expected frequency of deaths for each weekday is 110 divided by 7, or 15.71. Once the expected frequencies are obtained, the chi-square statistic is computed as

$$\chi^2 = \sum_{i=1}^{k} (O_i - E_i)^2 / E_i \qquad \text{\textbf{Equation 17.10}}$$

where O_i is the observed frequency for the ith category, E_i is the expected frequency for the ith category, and k is the number of categories.

Figure 17.10   One-sample chi-square output

NPAR TESTS CHISQUARE=DAYOFWK.

```
- - - - - Chi-Square Test
   DAYOFWK    DAY OF DEATH

                                    Cases
                         Category  Observed   Expected   Residual
              SUNDAY         1         19       15.71       3.29
              MONDAY         2         11       15.71      -4.71
              TUESDAY        3         19       15.71       3.29
              WEDNSDAY       4         17       15.71       1.29
              THURSDAY       5         15       15.71       -.71
              FRIDAY         6         13       15.71      -2.71
              SATURDAY       7         16       15.71        .29
                                     ----
                           Total      110

              Chi-Square            D.F.           Significance
                3.400                 6                 .757
```

If the hypothesis is true, the chi-square statistic has approximately a chi-square distribution with $k-1$ degrees of freedom. This statistic will be large if the observed and expected frequencies are substantially different. Figure 17.10 is the output from the one-sample chi-square test for the death data. The codes associated with the days of the week are listed in the column labeled **Category.** The observed frequencies are in the next column, labeled **Cases Observed.** The observed significance level is 0.757, so it appears that the day of the week does not affect the chance of death.

17.11
The Rank Correlation Coefficient

The Pearson product-moment correlation discussed in Chapter 14 is appropriate only for data that attain at least an interval level of measurement, such as the sales and advertising data used as examples in that chapter. Normality is also assumed when testing hypotheses about this correlation coefficient. For ordinal data or interval data that do not satisfy the normality assumption, another measure of the linear relationship between two variables, *Spearman's rank correlation coefficient,* is available.

The rank correlation coefficient is the Pearson correlation coefficient based on the ranks of the data if there are no ties (adjustments are made if some of the data are tied). If the original data for each variable have no ties, the data for each variable are first ranked and then the Pearson correlation coefficient between the ranks for the two variables is computed. Like the Pearson correlation coefficient, the rank correlation ranges between -1 and $+1$, where -1 and $+1$ indicate a perfect linear relationship between the ranks of the two variables. The interpretation is therefore the same except that the relationship between *ranks* and not values is examined.

Figure 17.11   The rank correlation coefficient

NONPAR CORR VARIABLES=ADVERTIS REPS SALES.

```
- - - - - - - - - - - - - SPEARMAN  CORRELATION  COEFFICIENTS - - - - - - - - - - - - -


REPS          .7733
          N(   40)
          SIG .000


SALES         .9182        .8636
          N(   40)     N(   40)
          SIG .000      SIG .000


          ADVERTIS       REPS

" . " IS PRINTED IF A COEFFICIENT CANNOT BE COMPUTED.
```

Figure 17.11 shows the matrix of rank correlation coefficients for the sales and advertising data. As expected, these coefficients are similar in sign and magnitude to the Pearson coefficients obtained in Chapter 14.

17.12
RUNNING PROCEDURE NONPAR CORR

NONPAR CORR computes two rank-order correlation coefficients, Spearman's rho and Kendall's tau-*b*, with their significance levels. You can obtain either or both coefficients.

The only required subcommand on NONPAR CORR is the VARIABLES subcommand, which specifies the list of variables to be analyzed. VARIABLES must be specified first. You can specify the optional subcommands in any order, separated by slashes.

17.13
VARIABLES Subcommand

The VARIABLES subcommand names the variable list. You can use the keyword TO in the list to refer to consecutive variables in the active system file. The variables must be numeric.

Depending on how you specify the variable list, NONPAR CORR displays either a lower-triangular or a rectangular matrix. If you provide a simple list of variables, NONPAR CORR displays the correlations of each variable with every other variable in the list in a lower-triangular matrix. For example, the triangular matrix in Figure 17.11 was produced with the following command:

```
NONPAR CORR VARIABLES=ADVERTIS REPS SALES.
```

The correlation of a variable with itself (the diagonal) and redundant coefficients are not displayed.

To obtain the rectangular matrix, specify two variable lists separated by the keyword WITH. NONPAR CORR then displays a rectangular matrix of variables in the first list correlated with variables in the second list. For example,

```
NONPAR CORR VARIABLES=PRESTIGE SPPRES PAPRES16
  WITH DEGREE PADEG MADE.
```

produces nine correlations. The variables listed before keyword WITH define the rows of the matrix, and those listed after keyword WITH define the columns. Unless a variable is in both lists, there are no identity coefficients in the matrix.

You can request more than one matrix on a NONPAR CORR command. Use a slash to separate the specifications for each of the requested matrices. For example,

```
NONPAR CORR VARIABLES=SPPRES PAPRES16 PRESTIGE
 /SATCITY WITH SATHOBBY SATFAM.
```

produces two correlation matrices. The first matrix contains three coefficients in triangular form. The second matrix is rectangular and contains two coefficients.

If all cases have a missing value for a given pair of variables, or if they all have the same value for a variable, the coefficient cannot be computed and NONPAR CORR displays a period for the coefficient.

17.14
PRINT Subcommand

By default, NONPAR CORR displays Spearman correlation coefficients. Below each coefficient it displays the number of cases and the significance level. The significance level is based on a one-tailed test.

Use the PRINT subcommand to request the Kendall correlation coefficient or both Spearman and Kendall coefficients. Both coefficients are based on ranks.

You can also use PRINT to switch to a two-tailed test and to suppress the display of the number of cases and significance level.

The following keywords are available on PRINT:

SPEARMAN   *Spearman's rho.* Only Spearman coefficients are displayed. This is the default.

KENDALL   *Kendall's tau-b.* Only Kendall coefficients are displayed.

BOTH   *Kendall and Spearman coefficients.* Both coefficients are displayed.

SIG   *Display the number of cases and significance level.* This is the default.

NOSIG   *Suppress the display of the number of cases and significance level.*

ONETAIL   *One-tailed test of significance.* This is the default.

TWOTAIL   *Two-tailed test of significance.*

If you specify both FORMAT=SERIAL (Section 17.17) and PRINT=NOSIG, only FORMAT=SERIAL will be in effect.

17.15
SAMPLE Subcommand

NONPAR CORR must store cases in memory to build matrices. You may not have sufficient computer resources to store all the cases to produce the coefficients requested. The SAMPLE subcommand allows you to select a random sample of cases when there is not enough space to store all the cases. To request a random sample, simply specify the subcommand, as in:

```
NONPAR CORR VARIABLES=PRESTIGE SPPRES PAPRES16
 DEGREE PADEG MADEG
  /SAMPLE.
```

The SAMPLE subcommand has no additional specifications.

17.16
MISSING Subcommand

By default, NONPAR CORR deletes a case from the computation of a coefficient if it is missing on one or both of the pair of variables. Because each coefficient is based on all cases that have valid codes on that particular pair of variables, the maximum information available is used in every calculation. This can result in a set of coeffients based on a varying number of cases.

Use the MISSING subcommand to specify alternative missing-value treatments. The following keywords are available:

PAIRWISE   *Exclude missing values pairwise.* Cases missing on one or both variables in a pair for a specific correlation coefficient are excluded from the computation of that coefficient. This is the default.

LISTWISE   *Exclude missing values listwise.* Cases missing on any variable named in a list are excluded from all analyses. Each variable list on a command is evaluated separately. If you specify multiple variable lists, a case missing for one list might be used in another list. This option decreases the amount of memory required and significantly decreases computational time.

INCLUDE   *Include user-missing values.* Cases with user-missing values are included in the analysis.

Only one of these keywords can be specified on MISSING.

17.17
FORMAT Subcommand

The FORMAT subcommand controls the format of the correlation matrix. The following keywords are available:

MATRIX   *Print correlations in matrix format.* This is the default.

SERIAL   *Print correlations in serial string format.*

17.18
RUNNING PROCEDURE NPAR TESTS

Procedure NPAR TESTS is a collection of nonparametric tests that make minimal assumptions about the underlying distributions of data. In addition to the nonparametric tests available in NPAR TESTS, the k-sample chi-square and Fisher's exact test are available in procedure CROSSTABS (see Chapter 10).

Each NPAR TESTS subcommand names a specific test, followed by a variable list. You can use the keyword TO to reference consecutive variables in the active system file. The form of the variable list differs with the data organization required for the test. You can request any or all of the available tests, separated by slashes, on one NPAR TESTS command. Some tests require additional parameters, and the CHISQUARE test has an optional subcommand.

17.19
One-Sample Tests

In a one-sample test, variables being tested are not subdivided into groups (see Section 17.10). Specify the name of the test and one or more variables. The test is repeated for each variable specified.

17.20
CHISQUARE Subcommand

Subcommand CHISQUARE tabulates a variable into categories and computes a chi-square statistic based on the differences between observed and expected frequencies. By default, the CHISQUARE test assumes equal expected frequencies. The following command produced Figure 17.10:

NPAR TESTS **CHISQUARE=DAYOFWK**.

Optionally, you can specify a range after a variable or variable list. If you do not specify a range, each distinct value encountered is defined as a category. If you do specify a range, integer-valued categories are established for each value within the inclusive range. Noninteger values are truncated, and cases with values outside the bounds are excluded. For example,

NPAR TESTS CHISQUARE=RANK(**1,4**).

uses only the integer values 1 through 4 for the chi-square test of the variable RANK.

EXPECTED Subcommand. To specify expected frequencies, percentages, or proportions for the chi-square test, use the EXPECTED subcommand and a value list. You must specify a value greater than 0 for each observed category of the data. The values listed after the EXPECTED subcommand are summed. Each value is then divided by this sum to calculate the proportion of cases expected in the corresponding category. For example,

NPAR TESTS CHISQUARE=RANK(1,4) /**EXPECTED = 3 4 5 4**.

specifies expected proportions of 3/16, 4/16, 5/16, and 4/16 for categories 1, 2, 3, and 4, respectively. You can specify the same expected proportion for two or more consecutive categories with an asterisk (*), as in:

NPAR TESTS CHISQUARE=A(1,5) /EXPECTED=12, **3*16**, 18.

This command tests the observed frequencies for variable A against the hypothetical proportions of 12/78 for category 1; 16/78 each for categories 2, 3, and 4; and 18/78 for category 5.

The EXPECTED subcommand applies to all variables named on the preceding CHISQUARE subcommand. If you want to specify different expected proportions for each variable, use multiple combinations of the CHISQUARE and EXPECTED subcommands. If you want to test the same variable against different proportions, you can also use multiple combinations.

17.21
K-S Subcommand (One-Sample Test)

Subcommand K-S compares the observed cumulative distribution function for a variable with a specified distribution, which may be uniform, normal, or Poisson. The Kolmogorov-Smirnov Z is computed from the largest difference (in absolute value) between the observed and theoretical distribution functions. Each of these distributions has optional parameters:

(UNIFORM,lo,hi)   *Uniform distribution.* The optional parameters are user-specified minimum and maximum values (in that order). If you do not specify them, K-S uses the observed minimum and maximum values.

(NORMAL,m,sd)   *Normal distribution.* The optional parameters are user-specified mean and standard deviation (in that order). If you do not specify them, K-S uses the observed mean and standard deviation.

(POISSON,m)   *Poisson distribution.* The one optional parameter is a user-specified mean. If you do not specify it, K-S uses the observed mean. A word of caution about testing against a Poisson distribution: if the mean of the test distribution is large, evaluating the probabilities is a very time-consuming process. If a mean of 100,000 or larger is used, K-S uses a normal approximation to the Poisson distribution.

For example, the command

```
NPAR TESTS  K-S(UNIFORM)=A.
```

compares the distribution for variable A with a uniform distribution which has the same range as variable A, while the command

```
NPAR TESTS  K-S(NORMAL,0,1)=B.
```

compares the distribution for variable B with a normal distribution that has a mean of 0 and standard deviation of 1.

K-S assumes that the test distribution is entirely specified in advance. When parameters of the test distribution are estimated from the sample, the distribution of the test statistic changes. NPAR TESTS does not provide any correction for this. Tests for normality are also available with the EXAMINE procedure.

The K-S subcommand can also be used for tests of two independent samples (see Section 17.34).

17.22
RUNS Subcommand

Subcommand RUNS performs the runs test to test whether the two values of a dichotomous variable occur randomly. A run is defined as a sequence of one of the values which is preceded and followed by the other data value (or the end of the series). For example, the following sequence

| 1 1 | 0 0 0 | 1 | 0 0 0 0 | 1 | 0 | 1 |

contains seven runs (vertical bars are used to separate the runs).

You must specify a cutpoint (enclosed in parentheses) to dichotomize the variable. Use either the observed mean, median, or mode, or a specified value, as the cutpoint. One category comes from cases with values below the cutpoint and the other category comes from cases with values equal to or greater than the cutpoint. To specify the cutpoint, use either the keywords MEAN, MEDIAN, MODE, or a value. Even if the variable is already dichotomized, you still must specify a cutting point. For example, if the variable has values 0 and 1, you can use 1 as the cutting point. The command

```
NPAR TESTS RUNS(MEDIAN)=RANK.
```

uses the median as the cutpoint, assigning cases with values below the median to one category, and cases with values equal to or above the median to the other category.

17.23
BINOMIAL Subcommand

Subcommand BINOMIAL compares the observed frequency in each category of a dichotomous variable with expected frequencies from the binomial distribution. BINOMIAL tabulates a variable into two categories based on the way you specify a cutpoint. The command

```
NPAR TESTS BINOMIAL=RANK(2).
```

specifies the value 2 as the cutting point for the variable RANK. Cases with values less than or equal to 2 for RANK are assigned to one group, and cases with values greater than 2 are assigned to the other group. If you specify *two* values in parentheses following the variable list, all cases with the first value will be in the first category, and all cases with the second value will be in the second category. If you specify two values and the variable is not a dichotomy, only cases with the two values specified are included in the analysis.

By default, the null hypothesis is that the data are from a binomial distribution with a probability of 0.5 for both values. You can change the probabilities by specifying a probability for the first value in parentheses after the subcommand BINOMIAL. For example, the command

```
NPAR TESTS BINOMIAL(.25)=RANK(2).
```

tests the null hypothesis that the data are from a binomial distribution with a probability of 0.25 for the first value and a probability of 0.75 for the second value.

17.24
Tests for Two Related Samples

Tests for two related samples compare pairs of variables (see Section 17.7). Specify the name of the test and two or more variables to be tested. If you specify a simple variable list, a test is performed for each variable paired with every other variable on the list. To obtain tests for specific pairs of variables, use two variable lists separated by keyword WITH. Each variable in the first list is tested with each variable in the second list. For example,

```
NPAR TESTS  SIGN=A WITH B C.
```

produces sign tests for A with B and A with C. No test is performed for B with C.

The keyword (PAIRED) used in conjunction with the keyword WITH provides additional control over which variables are paired together. When you specify (PAIRED), the first variable in the first list is paired with the first variable in the second list, the second variable in the first list is paired with the second variable in the second list, and so on. You must name or imply the same number of variables in both lists. For example,

```
NPAR TESTS  MCNEMAR=A B WITH C D (PAIRED).
```

pairs A with C and B with D. You must specify (PAIRED) after the second variable list. You cannot use (PAIRED) if keyword WITH is not specified.

17.25
MCNEMAR Subcommand

McNemar's test looks at the cases with different values for two related variables. The hypothesis that both combinations of different values are equally likely is tested.

Subcommand MCNEMAR produces a 2×2 table for each pair of dichotomous variables. Pairs of variables being tested must be coded with the same two values. A chi-square statistic is computed for cases with different values for the two variables. If fewer than 25 cases have different values for the two variables, the binomial distribution is used to compute the significance level. The command

```
NPAR TESTS MCNEMAR=A B C D.
```

produces tests for A with B, A with C, A with D, B with C, B with D, and C with D.

17.26
SIGN Subcommand

The sign test analyzes the signs of the differences between two paired values. Subcommand SIGN counts the positive and negative differences between each pair of variables and ignores 0 differences. Under the null hypothesis for large sample sizes, the test statistic Z is approximately normally distributed with mean 0 and variance 1. The binomial distribution is used to compute an exact significance level if 25 or fewer differences are observed. The following command produced Figure 17.7:

```
NPAR TESTS SIGN=HSSCALE WITH WSSCALE.
```

17.27
WILCOXON Subcommand

Subcommand WILCOXON computes differences between pairs of variables, ranks the absolute differences, sums ranks for the positive and negative differences, and computes the test statistic Z from the positive and negative rank sums. Under the null hypothesis, Z is approximately normally distributed with mean 0 and variance 1 for large sample sizes. The following command produced Figure 17.8:

```
NPAR TESTS WILCOXON=HSSCALE WITH WSSCALE.
```

17.28
Tests for *k* Related Samples

Tests for k related samples compare sets of variables. Specify the name of the test and two or more variables to be tested. The k variables in the list produce one test for k related samples. The COCHRAN, FRIEDMAN, and KENDALL tests are available for k related samples.

17.29
COCHRAN Subcommand

Cochran's test is used to test the null hypothesis that the proportion of cases in a particular category is the same for several related variables.

Subcommand COCHRAN produces a $k \times 2$ contingency table (variable vs. category) for dichotomous variables and computes the proportions for each variable. If your data are not dichotomous, recode them (see Chapter 3). Cochran's Q statistic has approximately a chi-square distribution. The command

```
NPAR TESTS COCHRAN=A B C.
```

produces a 3×2 with three rows for the variables A, B, and C, and two columns for the dichotomous values.

17.30
FRIEDMAN Subcommand

The Friedman test is used to test the hypothesis that k-related variables are from the same distribution. Subcommand FRIEDMAN ranks k variables from 1 to k for each case, calculates the mean rank for each variable over all the cases, and then calculates a test statistic with approximately a chi-square distribution. The command

```
NPAR TESTS FRIEDMAN=A B C D.
```

tests whether the four variables are from the same distribution.

17.31
KENDALL Subcommand

Subcommand KENDALL ranks k variables from 1 to k for each case, calculates the mean rank for each variable over all the cases, and then calculates Kendall's W and a corresponding chi-square statistic, correcting for ties. W ranges between 0 and 1, with 0 signifying no agreement and 1 signifying complete agreement. The command

```
NPAR TESTS KENDALL=A B C.
```

produces mean ranks for the three variables listed.

This test assumes that each case is a judge or rater. If you want to perform this test with variables as judges and cases as entities, you must first transpose your data matrix (see Chapter 4).

17.32
Tests for Two Independent Samples

Tests for two independent samples compare two groups of cases on one variable (see Section 17.1). Specify the name of the test and one or more variables to be tested. Each variable in the list produces one test. The variable following the keyword BY splits the file into two groups or samples, based on two values specified in parentheses after the grouping variable. All cases with the first value are in the first group, and all cases with the second value are in the second group. If the grouping variable is not a dichotomy, only cases with the two specified values are included in the analysis.

17.33
M-W Subcommand

Subcommand M-W (Mann-Whitney) ranks all the cases in order of increasing size and computes the test statistic U, the number of times a score from Group 1 precedes a score from Group 2. If the samples are from the same population, the distribution of scores from the two groups in the ranked list should be random; an extreme value of U indicates a nonrandom pattern. For samples with fewer than 30 cases, the exact significance level for U is computed using the algorithm of Dineen and Blakesly (1973). For larger samples, U is transformed into a normally distributed Z statistic. The following command produces Figure 17.3:

```
NPAR TESTS M-W=TUMOR BY DIET(0,1).
```

17.34
K-S Subcommand (Two-Sample Test)

Subcommand K-S computes the observed cumulative distributions for both groups and the maximum positive, negative, and absolute differences. The Kolmogorov-Smirnov Z is then computed along with the two-tailed probability level based on the Smirnov (1948) formula. The one-tailed test can be used to determine whether the values of one group are generally larger than the values of the other group. For example, the command

```
NPAR TESTS K-S = PCTERR BY GRADE (7,11)
```

analyzes PCTERR by GRADE.

17.35
W-W Subcommand

Subcommand W-W combines observations from both groups and ranks them from lowest to highest. If the samples are from the same population, the two groups should be randomly scattered throughout the ranking. A runs test is performed using group membership as the criterion. If there are ties involving observations from both groups, both the minimum and maximum number of runs possible are calculated. If the total sample size is 30 cases or fewer, the exact one-tailed significance level is calculated. Otherwise, the normal approximation is used. For example, the command

```
NPAR TESTS  W-W = SCORE BY SEX (1,2)
```

tests SCORE by SEX.

17.36
MOSES Subcommand

Subcommand MOSES arranges the scores from the groups in a single ascending sequence. The span of the control group is computed as the number of cases in the sequence containing the lowest and highest control score. The exact significance level can be computed for the span. Chance outliers can easily distort the range of the span. To minimize this problem, you can specify that a certain number of outliers be trimmed from each end of the span. No adjustments are made for tied observations.

The number of outliers to be trimmed is specified in parentheses after the MOSES subcommand. If you do not specify the percentage, MOSES automatically trims 5% of the cases from each end. The control group is defined by the first grouping value specified. For example,

```
NPAR TESTS MOSES (10) = SCORE BY SECTION (1,2)
```

trims 10 cases from each end. The control group is defined as the group with value 1 for SECTION.

17.37
Tests for *k* Independent Samples

Tests for *k* independent samples compare *k* groups of cases on one variable. Specify the name of the test and one or more variables to be tested. Each variable in the list produces one test. The variable following the keyword BY splits the file into *k* groups. You must specify a minimum and maximum value (enclosed in parentheses) for the grouping variable. If the first value specified is *greater* than the second value, only cases with those two values are included in the analysis.

17.38
MEDIAN Subcommand (*k*-Sample Test)

Subcommand MEDIAN produces a $2 \times k$ contingency table with counts of the number of cases with values greater than the median and less than or equal to the median for the *k* groups. A chi-square statistic for the table is computed. The command

```
NPAR TESTS MEDIAN=TUMOR BY DIET(0,2).
```

produces a 2×3 table, with categories for values 0, 1, and 2 for the grouping variable DIET. The command

```
NPAR TESTS MEDIAN=TUMOR BY DIET(2,0).
```

produces a 2×2 table and a two-sample test for cases with values of 0 and 2 on the grouping variable DIET.

By default, the observed median is used as the test median, but you can specify any value. For example, the command

```
NPAR TESTS MEDIAN(100)=TUMOR BY DIET(0,2).
```

divides cases into three groups based on the value of DIET and compares the proportion of cases in each group with values less than or equal to 100 and with values greater than 100.

17.39
K-W Subcommand

Subcommand K-W ranks all cases from the *k* groups in a single series, computes the rank sum for each group, and computes the Kruskal-Wallis *H* statistic, which has approximately a chi-square distribution. The following command produced Figure 17.9:

```
NPAR TESTS K-W=TUMOR BY DIET(0,2).
```

17.40
STATISTICS Subcommand

In addition to the statistics provided for each test, you can also obtain two types of summary statistics for variables named on each of the subcommands. Use the STATISTICS subcommand to request the following statistics for NPAR TESTS:

DESCRIPTIVES *Univariate statistics.* Displays the mean, maximum, minimum, standard deviation, and number of nonmissing cases for each variable named on the combined subcommands.

QUARTILES *Quartiles and number of cases.* Displays values corresponding to the 25th, 50th, and 75th percentiles for each variable named on the combined subcommands.

ALL *All statistics available on NPAR TESTS.*

17.41
MISSING Subcommand

By default, NPAR TESTS deletes cases with missing values on a test-by-test basis. For subcommands where you can specify several tests, it evaluates each test separately for missing values. For example,

```
NPAR TESTS  MEDIAN=A B BY GROUP (1,5).
```

specifies two tests, A by GROUP and B by GROUP. A case missing for GROUP is excluded from both tests, but a case missing for A is not excluded from the test for B if it is not missing for B.

Use the MISSING subcommand to specify alternative missing-value treatments. The following keywords can be specified:

ANALYSIS *Exclude missing values on a test-by-test basis.* This is the default.

LISTWISE *Exclude missing values listwise.* Cases missing on any variable named on any subcommand are excluded from all analyses.

INCLUDE *Include user-missing values.* User-missing values are treated as if they were not missing.

The ANALYSIS and LISTWISE keywords are mutually exclusive; however, each can be specified with INCLUDE.

17.42
SAMPLE Subcommand

NPAR TESTS must store cases in memory. You may not have sufficient computer resources to store all the cases to produce the tests requested. The SAMPLE subcommand allows you to select a random sample of cases when there is not enough space to store all the cases. The SAMPLE subcommand has no additional specifications.

Because sampling would invalidate a runs test, this option is ignored when you use the RUNS subcommand.

Contents

18 Establishing Order: Procedure RANK

Ranks are sometimes the most natural way to collect data. Market researchers ask us to rank products from least favorite to most favorite; sportscasters give us their lists of the top twenty basketball or football teams. Ranks are also useful for interpreting measurements when we have reason to suspect that the underlying scale is not really interval. Registrars often convert grade point averages to class ranks, perhaps suspecting that grades aren't really measured on a consistent interval scale.

Similarly, when you have reason to suspect that your data are not measured on a good interval scale or do not have the kind of distribution required for many statistical techniques, you might choose to analyze them using a nonparametric procedure which requires very limited assumptions about the underlying distribution. Many nonparametric procedures replace data values with ranks.

18.1
COMPUTING RANKS

The basic idea of rank assignment is straightforward. You order the data values and then assign sequential integers, from 1 to the number of cases, to the ordered values. If the data values are sorted from smallest to largest—that is, the data are in ascending order—the smallest value receives the rank of 1. If the data are sorted in descending order, from largest to smallest, the largest value receives a rank of 1.

Difficulties with the assignment of ranks occur when there are tied values. For example, if the data values are 10, 10, 11, and 20, several different schemes can be used to assign ranks to the tied values of 10. The most frequently used method assigns the average of the ranks for which they are tied. If you are assigning ranks based on ascending data values, the two cases with values of 10 are tied for ranks of 1 and 2, so each is assigned a rank of 1.5, $((1+2)/2)$. If you had three values of 10, each of them would receive a rank of $(1+2+3)/3$, or 2.

The SPSS RANK procedure offers several other possibilities for the treatment of ties. For example, in Figure 18.1, class ranks are assigned in descending order (so that the highest grade point average receives rank 1). Students that have the same grade point average are assigned the smallest rank. For example, the two students tied for second both receive rank 2.

Figure 18.1 Class ranks using descending order and low scores for ties

```
DATA LIST / NAME 1-24 (A) GPA 26-28 (2).
BEGIN DATA.
MARK ANDERSON           325
ANDREW BROWN            400
YVONNE HIRSCHFIELD      275
HAROLD THOMPSON         400
SALLY WILSON            425
END DATA.
RANK VARIABLES=GPA (D) /TIES=LOW.
SORT CASES BY RGPA.
LIST.
```

NAME	GPA	RGPA
SALLY WILSON	4.25	1.000
ANDREW BROWN	4.00	2.000
HAROLD THOMPSON	4.00	2.000
MARK ANDERSON	3.25	4.000
YVONNE HIRSCHFIELD	2.75	5.000

18.2
ORDERING THE DATA
INTO CATEGORIES

Based on the ranks assigned to cases you can classify them into several distinct groups. For example, you can subdivide the cases into quartiles—that is, classify the cases into four groups of approximately equal size based on the values of their ranks. You can subdivide the cases into as many groups as you like using the RANK procedure.

Figure 18.2 shows average weights of the men in the Western Electric study (see Chapter 4) when they are grouped into quartiles based on their diastolic blood pressure. (Quartiles are determined by the RANK procedure and saved in the variable NDBP58, which is then used as the BY variable in the MEANS procedure. See Chapter 11 for a discussion of MEANS.) You can see that the average weights increase across the quartiles. The four groups are not exactly of the same size since there are many tied values for diastolic blood pressure (see the stem-and-leaf plots in Chapter 9). All tied values are assigned to the same quartile group.

Figure 18.2   Mean weight of subjects within quartiles

```
GET FILE=ELECTRIC.
RANK VARIABLES=DBP58 /NTILES(4).
VALUE LABELS NDBP58 1 "FIRST QUARTILE OF DBP58" 2 "SECOND QUARTILE"
 3 "THIRD QUARTILE" 4 "FOURTH QUARTILE".
MEANS TABLES=WT58 BY NDBP58.
```

```
               - - Description of Subpopulations - -

Summaries of      WT58        BODY WEIGHT, 1958 -- LBS
By levels of      NDBP58      NTILES of DBP58


Variable        Value  Label                    Mean     Std Dev   Cases

For Entire Population                          173.4812   24.7644     239

NDBP58              1  FIRST QUARTILE OF DB    167.0962   22.2994      52
NDBP58              2  SECOND QUARTILE         171.8525   24.0720      61
NDBP58              3  THIRD QUARTILE          176.4697   25.9847      66
NDBP58              4  FOURTH QUARTILE         177.3833   25.4313      60

   Total Cases = 240
Missing Cases = 1 or     .4 Pct
```

18.3
PROGRAMMING
STATISTICAL TESTS
BASED ON RANKS

The SPSS NPAR TESTS procedure (see Chapter 17) contains most of the commonly used nonparametric tests. However, you may want to use a test that is not available in NPAR TESTS. Using the RANK procedure and some other simple SPSS commands, you should be able to implement most nonparametric tests.

18.4
Conover's Test for
Equality of Variance

Conover (1980) describes a nonparametric test for the hypothesis that two samples come from populations with equal variance. He describes a food packaging company that wants to compare two methods for packaging cereal. Table 18.4 contains data for the two methods, conveniently designated as "present" and "new."

Table 18.4   Conover cereal packaging data

	Amount in box	
	Present	New
	10.8	10.8
	11.1	10.5
	10.4	11.0
	10.1	10.9
	11.3	10.8
		10.7
		10.8
Mean	10.74	10.79

The test statistic for evaluating the null hypothesis of equal variances is

$$T = \frac{T_1 - n\,\overline{R^2}}{\sqrt{\dfrac{nm}{N(N-1)}\,\Sigma R_i^4 - \dfrac{nm}{(N-1)}\,(\overline{R^2})^2}}$$

Equation 18.4a

where T_1 is the sum of squared ranks for the smaller group, and n and m are the group sizes. In this test the ranks are based not on the original data but on the absolute value of the deviation from the group mean.

To calculate the test statistic you enter the data as two variables, one containing the measurements of amounts of cereal in the box and the other indicating the group for each measurement. A preliminary run of the MEANS procedure provides the means for each group. You can then proceed, as in Figure 18.4, to compute the absolute values of the differences from the group means, rank them, and then square the ranks and raise them to the fourth power. Descriptive statistics from the MEANS procedure for the new variables then give us the needed information to compute the test statistic.

Figure 18.4   Calculating numbers for equality of variance test

```
IF (GROUP EQ 1) ABSDIF=ABS(AMOUNT-10.74).
IF (GROUP EQ 2) ABSDIF=ABS(AMOUNT-10.79).
RANK VARIABLES=ABSDIF /RANK INTO R.
COMPUTE R2=R**2.
COMPUTE R4=R**4.
VARIABLE LABELS R2 'SQUARED RANKS' R4 'RANKS TO THE FOURTH POWER'.
MEANS TABLES=R2 R4 BY GROUP / CELLS=MEAN SUM COUNT.
```

```
                 - - Description of Subpopulations - -

Summaries of      R2        SQUARED RANKS
By levels of      GROUP


Variable      Value Label                  Sum       Mean      Cases

For Entire Population                     648.00    54.0000     12

GROUP          1.00                       462.00    92.4000      5
GROUP          2.00                       186.00    26.5714      7

  Total Cases = 12


                 - - Description of Subpopulations - -

Summaries of      R4        RANKS TO THE FOURTH POWER
By levels of      GROUP


Variable      Value Label                  Sum       Mean      Cases

For Entire Population                   60660.00   5055.0000    12

GROUP          1.00                     52194.00  10438.8000     5
GROUP          2.00                      8466.00   1209.4286     7

  Total Cases = 12
```

From the numbers in Figure 18.4 we calculate

$$T = \frac{462 - 5\,(54)}{\sqrt{\dfrac{5 \times 7}{12 \times 11} \times 60{,}660 - \dfrac{5 \times 7}{11} \times (54)^2}} = 2.3273$$

Equation 18.4b

The observed significance level is obtained from tables available in Conover (1980). In this case the observed significance level is less than 0.05, so you reject the null hypothesis that both methods have equal variability.

18.5
Spearman Correlation Coefficient

The Spearman rank correlation coefficient is available with the SPSS procedure NONPAR CORR (see Chapter 17), but it can also be calculated with the RANK procedure. This is a nonparametric correlation coefficient based on ranks. In fact, it is just the usual Pearson correlation coefficient applied to ranks. For example, to calculate the Spearman correlation coefficient between diastolic blood pressure and weight in the Western Electric study, you could use the RANK procedure to rank the two variables and then calculate a correlation coefficient on the ranks (Figure 18.5).

Figure 18.5 Calculating the Spearman correlation coefficient

```
GET FILE=ELECTRIC.
RANK VARIABLES=DBP58 WT58.
CORRELATION VARIABLES=RDBP58 RWT58 /PRINT=SIG ONETAIL.
```

```
              RDBP58     RWT58

RDBP58        1.0000      .1474
             (  239)    (  239)
             P= .        P= .011

RWT58          .1474    1.0000
             (  239)    (  240)
             P= .011     P= .

(COEFFICIENT / (CASES) / 1-TAILED SIG)              " . " IS PRINTED IF A COEFFICIENT CANNOT BE COMPUTED
```

18.6
Normal Scores in Statistical Tests

When analyzing ranks you ignore the actual distance between observations. For example, if you have the values 1, 3, 9, and 10, or the values 1, 2, 70, and 100, you assign them the same ranks. The distance between the observations doesn't matter; only their order matters.

There is a class of statistical tests which attempts to replace the ranks with other numbers that more closely resemble the observations from a particular distribution. For example, if you have five observations, you can replace the ranks 1 to 5 with quantiles from a particular distribution, usually the standard normal. That is, you find the five numbers that divide the area of a normal distribution into six equal parts and then analyze them. In this case you would analyze the scores -0.9674, -0.4307, 0, 0.4307, and 0.9674. If you analyze the normal scores instead of the ranks, the resulting statistical tests will have, under certain conditions, somewhat better statistical properties, even if the population from which the sample is obtained is not normal.

18.7
The van der Waerden Test for Several Independent Samples

To see how normal scores can be used to test the null hypothesis that all population distributions are identical, consider the van der Waerden test for several independent samples. The test statistic is

$$T = \frac{\sum n_i \bar{A}_i^2}{S^2}$$

Equation 18.7

where n_i is the number of cases in group i, $\bar{A}_i$ is the average normal score in group i, and S^2 is the variance of all of the normal scores. To compute this statistic, you must compute the average score in each group, square these averages, multiply them by the sample size in each group, and then sum them across all groups. Finally, you divide this sum by the variance of the scores.

Conover (1980) presents data for comparing four methods of growing corn. Figure 18.7a contains the SPSS commands to calculate the van der Waerden test for the hypothesis that the four populations from which the samples were taken are in fact identical. Figure 18.7b, the output from the LIST procedure, shows the data, the ranks, and the normal scores for all four methods. Figure 18.7c contains the relevant portions of the output from the two DESCRIPTIVES commands. The first gives the variance for all the cases; the second gives the sum of the squared means multiplied by the sample sizes. Dividing that sum by the variance yields the

test statistic

21.31 / .846 = 25.19

The significance level is based on the chi-squared distribution with degrees of freedom equal to one less than the number of groups. The observed significance level is less than 0.001, so the null hypothesis is rejected.

Figure 18.7a   SPSS commands for van der Waerden Test

```
DATA LIST FREE/ GROUP YIELD.
BEGIN DATA.
1 83 1 91 1 94 1 89 1 89 1 96 1 91 1 92 1 90
2 91 2 90 2 81 2 83 2 84 2 83 2 88 2 91 2 89 2 84
3 101 3 100 3 91 3 93 3 96 3 95 3 94
4 78 4 82 4 81 4 77 4 79 4 81 4 80 4 81
END DATA.
FORMATS YIELD GROUP(F3.0).
RANK VARIABLES=YIELD /RANK /NORMAL INTO VWSCORE /FRACTION VW.
LIST.
DESCRIPTIVES VARIABLES=VWSCORE /STATISTICS=VARIANCE.
AGGREGATE OUTFILE=* /BREAK=GROUP
 /MEAN=MEAN(VWSCORE) /COUNT=N(VWSCORE).
COMPUTE PRODUCT=MEAN**2 * COUNT.
DESCRIPTIVES VARIABLES=PRODUCT /STATISTICS=SUM.
```

Figure 18.7b   Data, ranks, and normal scores for Conover data

GROUP	YIELD	RYIELD	VWSCORE
1	83	11.000	-.4837
1	91	23.000	.4047
1	94	28.500	.8938
1	89	17.000	-.0358
1	89	17.000	-.0358
1	96	31.500	1.2816
1	91	23.000	.4047
1	92	26.000	.6522
1	90	19.500	.1437
2	91	23.000	.4047
2	90	19.500	.1437
2	81	6.500	-.8938
2	83	11.000	-.4837
2	84	13.500	-.2905
2	83	11.000	-.4837
2	88	15.000	-.1800
2	91	23.000	.4047
2	89	17.000	-.0358
2	84	13.500	-.2905
3	101	34.000	1.9022
3	100	33.000	1.5792
3	91	23.000	.4047
3	93	27.000	.7436
3	96	31.500	1.2816
3	95	30.000	1.0676
3	94	28.500	.8938
4	78	2.000	-1.579
4	82	9.000	-.6522
4	81	6.500	-.8938
4	77	1.000	-1.902
4	79	3.000	-1.368
4	81	6.500	-.8938
4	80	4.000	-1.204
4	81	6.500	-.8938

Figure 18.7c   Output from DESCRIPTIVES

Variable	Variance	Valid N	Label
VWSCORE	.85	34	NORMAL of YIELD using VW

Variable	Sum	Valid N	Label
PRODUCT	21.31	4	

18.8
Graphical Tests of Normality

Normal scores can also be used to examine the hypothesis that data come from a normal distribution. You can use RANK to generate normal scores for each of the cases based on their ranks and then plot the observed values against the normal scores. If the underlying distribution is normal, the points should cluster around a straight line.

Figure 18.8 is a plot of the observed diastolic blood pressures for the Western Electric men against the normal scores. (In this case, instead of using the normal scores proposed by van der Waerden, we use a modification suggested by Blom (1958) that results in scores which are somewhat closer to the exact expected values for the order statistics.) From this plot we see that the observed distribution differs somewhat from normal. Similar normal probability plots can also be obtained with the EXAMINE procedure (see Chapter 9).

Figure 18.8   Normal probability plot

```
GET FILE=ELECTRIC.
RANK VARIABLES=DBP58 /NORMAL INTO NORMAL.
PLOT PLOT=NORMAL WITH DBP58.
```

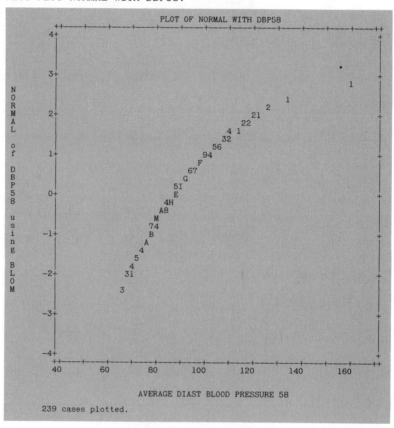

239 cases plotted.

18.9
Scores for an Exponential Distribution

If you have reason to believe that your data are a sample from an exponential distribution, instead of computing normal scores you can compute scores based on the exponential distribution. These scores are sometimes called Savage scores. (The length of time between consecutive events, when the events occur randomly in time, follows an exponential distribution.) To see whether a sample of data might originate from an exponential distribution, you can plot Savage scores against the observed values. Again, if the data are from an exponential distribution, the points should cluster around a straight line. Figure 18.9 is a plot of data values that appear to come from an exponential distribution.

Figure 18.9 Savage scores (problem 5 from Conover, 1980, p. 367)

```
DATA LIST FREE/DISTANCE.
BEGIN DATA.
0.3 6.1 4.3 3.3 1.9 4.8 .3 1.2 .8 10.3 1.2 .1 10 1.6 27.6
12 14.2 19.7 15.5
END DATA.
RANK VARIABLES=DISTANCE /SAVAGE INTO SAVDIST.
PLOT PLOT=SAVDIST WITH DISTANCE.
```

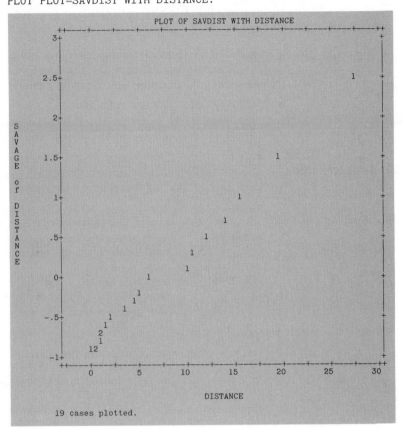

18.10
RUNNING
PROCEDURE RANK

The RANK procedure produces new variables containing ranks, normal and Savage scores, and related statistics for numeric variables. It can also be used to classify cases into groups based on percentile values. You can rank variables in ascending or descending order, choose the method(s) used for computing ranks, and name the new rank variables. Ranks, scores, and group memberships are saved as variables on the active system file. The procedure does not require that the file be sorted.

18.11
VARIABLES Subcommand

The VARIABLES subcommand specifies the variables to be ranked. By default, the RANK command ranks data in ascending order and creates a new variable name by adding the first letter of the RANK function subcommand (see Section 18.13) to the first seven characters of the original variable name. For example, the command

```
RANK VARIABLES=INCOME.
```

creates a new variable, RINCOME, which contains ranks based on ascending values of INCOME.

Optionally, you can specify the direction for ranking. Specify the keyword (A) for ascending or (D) for descending after the variable name or variable list. (Ascending order means that the rank of 1 goes to the case with the smallest value and the rank of *n,* where *n* is the number of cases, goes to the case with the largest value.) (A) is the default. The command

```
RANK VARIABLES=INCOME JOBCAT (D).
```

assigns ranks for both variables based on descending values. The command

```
RANK VARIABLES=INCOME(A) JOBCAT(D).
```

ranks INCOME in ascending order and JOBCAT in descending order.

You can organize rankings into subgroups with the keyword BY followed by the name of a grouping variable. The command

```
RANK VARIABLES=INCOME BY JOBCAT.
```

ranks INCOME within categories of JOBCAT.

18.12
Function Subcommands

The optional rank function subcommands specify methods for computing rank. Each of the following function subcommands can be specified once:

RANK	*Simple rank.* Rank can be either ascending or descending (see Section 18.11). This is the default.
RFRACTION	*Fractional ranks.* Each rank is divided by the number of cases with valid values, or by the sum of weights if the WEIGHT command is used.
PERCENT	*Fractional rank as a percent.* Each rank is divided by the number of cases with valid values and multiplied by 100.
N	*Sum of case weight.* The value of the variable is a constant for all cases in the same group.
NTILES(k)	*Percentile groups.* Cases are divided into k approximately equal groups based on the values of the variable. Cases are assigned to groups from 1 to $k,$ where the lowest values are in the first group and the largest values are in the kth group. Cases are assigned to groups using the formula $\text{group}_i = \text{TRUNCATE}(1 + (R_i \times k / (W+1)))$, where TRUNCATE signifies the integer part of the result, R_i is the rank of case $i,$ k is the number of groups, and W is the sum of case weights.
PROPORTION	*Proportion estimates.* This is the estimate of the cumulative proportion (area) of the distribution corresponding to a particular rank. Several different methods are available for estimating the cumulative proportion with subcommand FRACTION (see Section 18.15).
NORMAL	*Normal scores computed from the ranks.* The new variable contains the Z score from the standard normal which corresponds to the estimated cumulative proportion. For example, if the estimated cumulative proportion for an observation is 0.50, its normal score is 0. Several different methods are available for estimating the cumulative proportion with subcommand FRACTION (see Section 18.15).
SAVAGE	*Savage scores.* Scores based on an exponential distribution.

18.13
INTO Keyword

By default, new variable names are created by adding the first letter of the function name to the first seven characters of the variable name. For example, for variable INCOME, the name RINCOME is used for the ranks (function RANK) and the name NINCOME for the normal scores (function NORMAL).

You can specify your own variable names with the keyword INTO. For example, in Figure 18.7a the command

```
RANK VARIABLES=YIELD /RANK /NORMAL INTO VWSCORE
```

creates two new variables from the variable YIELD. The default name RYIELD is assigned to the new variable created by the RANK function, and the name VWSCORE is assigned to the new variable created by the NORMAL function.

If a new variable name is not unique, it is named XXXnnn, where XXX is the first three letters of the function name and nnn is a sequence number. If this still results in a non-unique name, the variable is named RNKXXnn, where XX is the first two letters of the function, and nn is a sequence number.

RANK assigns descriptive variable labels that include both the name of the original variable and the function used to create the new variable. For example, the new variable RYIELD has the variable label RANK OF YIELD.

18.14
TIES Subcommand

By default, cases with the same values for a variable are assigned the average of the ranks for the tied values. For example, consider a data set of six cases with the values 10, 15, 15, 15, 16, and 20. If you are assigning ranks in ascending order of the values, the case with the value of 10 is assigned a rank of 1. The next three cases, all with values of 15, are tied for the ranks of 2, 3, and 4. By default each is assigned the rank $(2+3+4)/3$, which is 3. The last two cases are assigned ranks of 5 and 6.

Options for the treatment of ties are selected with the TIES subcommand. The following keywords are available.

MEAN   *Average rank assigned to tied values.* This is the default.
LOW   *Lowest rank assigned to tied values.*
HIGH   *Highest rank assigned to tied values.*
CONDENSE   *Only distinct values of the variable are ranked.* That is, ranks are assigned from 1 to *D*, where *D* is the number of distinct values. Cases with the same values receive the same ranks.

Table 18.14 shows the ranks assigned to the data described above using each method.

Table 18.14 Options for handling ties in ranks

Case	Value	MEAN	LOW	HIGH	CONDENSE
1	10	1	1	1	1
2	15	3	2	4	2
3	15	3	2	4	2
4	15	3	2	4	2
5	16	5	5	5	3
6	20	6	6	6	4

The ranks in Figure 18.1 were generated with the following command:

```
RANK VARIABLES=GPA(D) /TIES=LOW.
```

18.15
FRACTION Subcommand

FRACTION specifies the way to compute a proportion estimate P for the NORMAL and PROPORTION rank functions. This optional subcommand can be used only with the rank function subcommands NORMAL or PROPORTION.

Only one of the following methods can be specified for each RANK procedure:

BLOM *Blom's transformation, defined by the formula* $(r − 3/8) / (w + 1/4)$. *w is the number of observations and r is the rank, ranging from 1 to w.* (See Blom, 1958.) This is the default.

RANKIT *Uses the formula* $(r − 1/2) / w$. *w is the number of observations and r is the rank, ranging from 1 to w.* (See Chambers et al., 1983.)

TUKEY *Tukey's transformation, defined by the formula* $(r − 1/3) / (w + 1/3)$. *w is the sum of case weights and r is the rank, ranging from 1 to w.* (See Tukey, 1962.)

VW *Van der Waerden's transformation, defined by the formula* $r / (w + 1)$. *w is the sum of case weights and r is the rank, ranging from 1 to w.* (See Lehmann, 1975.)

The following command created the variable VWSCORE in Figure 18.7b:

```
RANK VARIABLES=YIELD /RANK /NORMAL INTO VWSCORE
 /FRACTION=VW.
```

The new variable VWSCORE contains normal scores computed with Van der Waerden's transformation. For the RANK function subcommand, the FRACTION subcommand is ignored, and the new variable RYIELD contains simple ranks.

18.16
PRINT Subcommand

PRINT determines whether the summary tables are displayed with the output. The specifications on PRINT are

YES *Display the summary table.* YES is the default.
NO *Do not display the summary table.*

18.17
MISSING Subcommand

MISSING controls the treatment of cases with user-missing values. The default is EXCLUDE.

INCLUDE *Include cases with user-missing values.*
EXCLUDE *Exclude cases with user- or system-missing values.*

The command

```
RANK VARIABLES=INCOME /MISSING=INCLUDE.
```

treats user-missing values as valid values. System-missing values are assigned system-missing values for any variable created by the RANK procedure.

Contents _____

19 Multiple Linear Regression Analysis: Procedure REGRESSION

The 1964 Civil Rights Act prohibits discrimination in the workplace based on sex or race. Employers who violate the act, by unfair hiring or advancement, are liable to prosecution. Numerous lawsuits have been filed on behalf of women, blacks, and other groups on these grounds.

The courts have ruled that statistics can be used as *prima facie* evidence of discrimination. Many lawsuits depend heavily on complex statistical analyses, which attempt to demonstrate that similarly qualified individuals are not treated equally (Roberts, 1980). In this chapter, employee records for 474 individuals hired between 1969 and 1971 by a bank engaged in Equal Employment Opportunity litigation are analyzed. A mathematical model is developed that relates beginning salary and salary progression to various employee characteristics such as seniority, education, and previous work experience. One objective is to determine whether sex and race are important predictors of salary.

The technique used to build the model is linear regression analysis, one of the most versatile data analysis procedures. Regression can be used to summarize data as well as to study relations among variables.

19.1
LINEAR REGRESSION

Before examining a model that relates beginning salary to several other variables, consider the relationship between beginning salary and current (as of March 1977) salary. For employees hired during a similar time period, beginning salary should serve as a reasonably good predictor of salary at a later date. Although superstars and underachievers might progress differently from the group as a whole, salary progression should be similar for the others. The scatterplot of beginning salary and current salary produced by the PLOT procedure and shown in Figure 19.1 supports this hypothesis.

Figure 19.1 Scatterplot of beginning and current salaries

```
PLOT VERTICAL=MIN(0) /HORIZONTAL=MIN(0) /VSIZE=30 /HSIZE=90
     /CUTPOINTS=EVERY(3) /SYMBOLS='.+*#@'
     /PLOT=SALNOW WITH SALBEG.
```

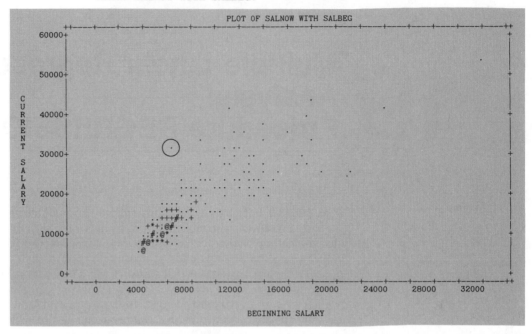

A scatterplot may suggest what type of mathematical functions would be appropriate for summarizing the data. A variety of functions are useful in fitting models to data. Parabolas, hyperbolas, polynomials, trigonometric functions, and many more are potential candidates. For the scatterplot in Figure 19.1, current salaries tend to increase linearly with increases in beginning salary. If the plot indicates that a straight line is not a good summary measure of the relationship, you should consider other possibilities, including attempts to transform the data to achieve linearity (see Section 19.27).

19.2
Outliers

A plot may also indicate the presence of points suspiciously different from the others. Examine such observations, termed *outliers*, carefully to see if they result from errors in gathering, coding, or entering data. The circled point in Figure 19.1 appears to be an outlier. Though neither the value of beginning salary ($6,300) nor the value of current salary ($32,000) is unique, jointly they are unusual.

The treatment of outliers can be difficult. If the point is really incorrect, due to coding or entry problems, you should correct it and rerun the analysis. If there is no apparent explanation for the outlier, consider interactions with other variables as a possible explanation. For example, the outlier may represent an employee who was hired as a low-paid clerical worker while pursuing an MBA degree. After graduation, a rapid rise in position was possible, making education the variable that explains the unusual salary characteristics of the employee.

19.3
Choosing a Regression Line

Since current salary tends to increase linearly with beginning salary, a straight line can be used to summarize the relationship. The equation for the line is

$$\text{predicted current salary} = B_0 + B_1(\text{beginning salary})$$ **Equation 19.3a**

The *slope* (B_1) is the dollar change in the fitted current salary for a dollar change in the beginning salary. The *intercept* (B_0) is the theoretical estimate of current salary if there were a beginning salary of 0.

However, the observed data points do not all fall on a straight line but cluster about it. Many lines can be drawn through the data points; the problem is to select among them. The method of *least squares* results in a line that minimizes the sum of squared vertical distances from the observed data points to the line. Any other line has a larger sum. Figure 19.3a shows the least-squares line superimposed on the salary scatterplot. Several vertical distances from points to the line are also shown.

Figure 19.3a   Regression line for beginning and current salaries

```
PLOT FORMAT=REGRESSION
    /VERTICAL=MIN(0) /HORIZONTAL=MIN(0) /VSIZE=30 /HSIZE=90
    /CUTPOINTS=EVERY(3) /SYMBOLS='.+*#@'
    /PLOT=SALNOW WITH SALBEG.
```

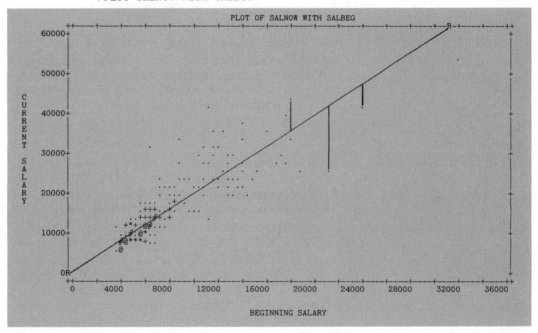

You can use the SPSS REGRESSION procedure to calculate the least-squares line. For the data in Figure 19.1, that line is

predicted current salary = 771.28 + 1.91(beginning salary)   **Equation 19.3b**

The slope and intercept values are shown in the column labeled **B** in the output shown in Figure 19.3b.

Figure 19.3b   Statistics for variables in the equation

```
REGRESSION
  /DEPENDENT=SALNOW
  /METHOD=ENTER SALBEG.
```

```
------------------- Variables in the Equation -------------------

Variable              B         SE B      Beta          T   Sig T

SALBEG          1.909450     .047410    .880117    40.276   .0000
(Constant)    771.282303   355.471941               2.170   .0305
```

19.4
The Standardized Regression Coefficient

The *standardized regression coefficient*, labeled **Beta** in Figure 19.3b, is defined as

$$BETA = B_1 \frac{S_X}{S_Y}$$ **Equation 19.4**

Multiplying the regression coefficient (B_1) by the ratio of the standard deviation of the independent variable (S_X) to the standard deviation of the dependent variable (S_Y) results in a dimensionless coefficient. In fact, the beta coefficient is the slope of the least-squares line when both X and Y are expressed as Z scores. The beta coefficient is further discussed in Section 19.38.

19.5
From Samples to Populations

Generally, more is sought in regression analysis than a description of observed data. You usually want to draw inferences about the relationship of the variables in the population from which the sample was taken. How are beginning and current salaries related for all employees, not just those included in the sample? To draw inferences about population values based on sample results, the following assumptions are needed:

Normality and Equality of Variance. For any fixed value of the independent variable X, the distribution of the dependent variable Y is normal, with mean $\mu_{Y/X}$ (the mean of Y for a given X) and a constant variance of σ^2 (see Figure 19.5). This assumption specifies that not all employees with the same beginning salary have the same current salary. Instead, there is a normal distribution of current salaries for each beginning salary. Though the distributions have different means, they have the same variance σ^2.

Figure 19.5 Regression assumptions

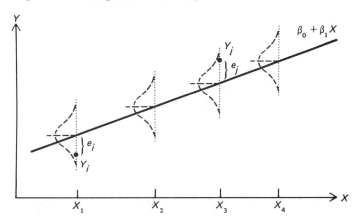

Independence. The Y's are statistically independent of each other. That is, observations are in no way influenced by other observations. For example, observations are *not* independent if they are based on repeated measurements from the same experimental unit. If three observations are taken from each of four families, the twelve observations are not independent.

Linearity. The mean values $\mu_{Y/X}$ all lie on a straight line, which is the population regression line. This line is drawn in Figure 19.5. An alternative way of stating this assumption is that the linear model is correct.

When there is a single independent variable, the model can be summarized by

$$Y_i = \beta_0 + \beta_1 X_i + e_i$$ **Equation 19.5**

The population parameters (values) for the slope and intercept are denoted by β_1 and β_0. The term e_i, often called an error or disturbance, is the difference between the observed value of Y_i and the subpopulation mean at the point X_i. The e_i are assumed to be normally distributed, independent, random variables with a mean of 0 and variance of σ^2 (see Figure 19.5).

**19.6
Estimating Population
Parameters**

Since β_0 and β_1 are unknown population parameters, they must be estimated from the sample. The least-squares coefficients B_0 and B_1, discussed in Section 19.3, are used to estimate the population parameters.

However, the slope and intercept estimated from a single sample typically differ from the population values and vary from sample to sample. To use these estimates for inference about the population values, the sampling distributions of the two statistics are needed. When the assumptions of linear regression are met, the sampling distributions of B_0 and B_1 are normal with means of β_0 and β_1.

The standard error of B_0 is

$$\sigma_{B_0} = \sigma \sqrt{\frac{1}{N} + \frac{\bar{X}^2}{(N-1)S_X^2}}$$ **Equation 19.6a**

where $S_X{}^2$ is the sample variance of the independent variable. The standard error of B_1 is

$$\sigma_{B_1} = \frac{\sigma}{\sqrt{(N-1)S_X{}^2}}$$
Equation 19.6b

Since the population variance of the errors, σ^2, is not known, it must also be estimated. The usual estimate of σ^2 is

$$S^2 = \frac{\sum_{i=1}^{N}(Y_i - B_0 - B_1 X_i)^2}{N-2}$$
Equation 19.6c

The positive square root of σ^2 is termed the *standard error of the estimate,* or the standard deviation of the residuals. (The reason for this name is discussed in Section 19.15.) The estimated standard errors of the slope and intercept are displayed in the third column (labeled **SE B**) in Figure 19.3b.

19.7
Testing Hypotheses

A frequently tested hypothesis is that there is no linear relationship between X and Y—that the slope of the population regression line is 0. The statistic used to test this hypothesis is

$$t = \frac{B_1}{S_{B_1}}$$
Equation 19.7a

The distribution of the statistic, when the assumptions are met and the hypothesis of no linear relationship is true, is Student's t distribution with $N-2$ degrees of freedom. The statistic for testing the hypothesis that the intercept is 0 is

$$t = \frac{B_0}{S_{B_0}}$$
Equation 19.7b

Its distribution is also Student's t with $N-2$ degrees of freedom.

These t statistics and their two-tailed observed significance levels are displayed in the last two columns of Figure 19.3b. The small observed significance level (less than 0.00005) associated with the slope for the salary data supports the hypothesis that beginning and current salary are linearly related.

19.8
Confidence Intervals

A statistic calculated from a sample provides a point estimate of the unknown parameter. A point estimate can be thought of as the single best guess for the population value. While the estimated value from the sample is typically different from the value of the unknown population parameter, the hope is that it isn't too far away. Based on the sample estimate, it is possible to calculate a range of values that, with a designated likelihood, includes the population value. Such a range is called a *confidence interval.* For example, as shown in Figure 19.8, the 95% confidence interval for β_1, the population slope, is 1.816 to 2.003.

Figure 19.8   Confidence intervals

```
REGRESSION
  /STATISTICS=CI
  /DEPENDENT=SALNOW
  /METHOD=ENTER SALBEG.
```

Variable	95% Confdnce Intrvl B	
SALBEG	1.816290	2.002610
(Constant)	72.779206	1469.785399

Ninety-five percent confidence means that, if repeated samples are drawn from a population under the same conditions and 95% confidence intervals are calculated, 95% of the intervals will contain the unknown parameter β_1. Since the parameter value is unknown, it is not possible to determine whether or not a particular interval contains it.

19.9
Goodness of Fit

An important part of any statistical procedure that builds models from data is establishing how well the model actually fits. This topic encompasses the detection of possible violations of the required assumptions in the data being analyzed. Sections 19.10 through 19.16 are limited to the question of how close to the fitted line the observed points fall. Subsequent sections discuss other assumptions and tests for their violation.

19.10
The R^2 Coefficient

A commonly used measure of the goodness of fit of a linear model is R^2, sometimes called the *coefficient of determination.* It can be thought of in a variety of ways. Besides being the square of the correlation coefficient between variables X and Y, it is the square of the correlation coefficient between Y, the observed value of the dependent variable, and $\widehat{Y}$, the predicted value of Y from the fitted line. If for each employee you compute (based on the coefficients in the output in Figure 19.3b) the predicted salary

predicted current salary $= 771.28 + 1.91$(beginning salary)   **Equation 19.10a**

and then calculate the square of the Pearson correlation coefficient between predicted current salary and observed current salary, R^2 is obtained. If all the observations fall on the regression line, R^2 is 1. If there is no linear relationship between the dependent and independent variables, R^2 is 0.

Note that R^2 is a measure of the goodness of fit of a particular model and that an R^2 of 0 does not necessarily mean that there is no association between the variables. Instead, it indicates that there is no *linear relationship.*

In the output in Figure 19.10, R^2 is labeled **R Square.** Its square root is called **Multiple R.** The sample R^2 tends to be an optimistic estimate of how well the model fits the population. The model usually does not fit the population as well as it fits the sample from which it is derived. The statistic *adjusted R^2* attempts to correct R^2 to more closely reflect the goodness of fit of the model in the population.

Adjusted R^2 is given by

$$R_a{}^2 = R^2 - \frac{p(1 - R^2)}{N - p - 1}$$ **Equation 19.10b**

where p is the number of independent variables in the equation (1 in the salary example).

Figure 19.10   Summary statistics for the equation

```
REGRESSION
   /DEPENDENT=SALNOW
   /METHOD=ENTER SALBEG.
```

```
   Multiple R              .88012
   R Square                .77461
   Adjusted R Square       .77413
   Standard Error     3246.14226
```

19.11
Analysis of Variance

To test the hypothesis of no linear relationship between X and Y, several equivalent statistics can be computed. When there is a single independent variable, the hypothesis that the population R^2 is 0 is identical to the hypothesis that the population slope is 0. The test for $R^2_{pop}=0$ is usually obtained from the *analysis of variance* (ANOVA) table (see Figure 19.11a).

Figure 19.11a   Analysis of variance table

```
REGRESSION
   /DEPENDENT=SALNOW
   /METHOD=ENTER SALBEG.
```

```
   Analysis of Variance
                       DF      Sum of Squares      Mean Square
   Regression           1   17092967800.01931  17092967800.0193
   Residual           472    4973671469.79484    10537439.55465

   F =    1622.11776      Signif F =   .0000
```

The total observed variability in the dependent variable is subdivided into two components—that which is attributable to the regression (labeled **Regression**) and that which is not (labeled **Residual**). Consider Figure 19.11b. For a particular point, the distance from Y_i to $\overline{Y}$ (the mean of the Y's) can be subdivided into two parts:

$$Y_i - \overline{Y} = (Y_i - \hat{Y}_i) + (\hat{Y}_i - \overline{Y})$$ **Equation 19.11a**

Figure 19.11b   Components of variability

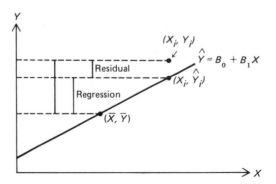

The distance from Y_i, the observed value, to $\hat{Y}_i$, the value predicted by the regression line, or $Y_i - \hat{Y}_i$, is 0 if the regression line passes through the point. It is called the *residual from the regression.* The second component $(\hat{Y}_i - \bar{Y})$ is the distance from the regression line to the mean of the Y's. This distance is "explained" by the regression in that it represents the improvement in the estimate of the dependent variable achieved by the regression. Without the regression, the mean of the dependent variable $(\bar{Y})$ is used as the estimate. It can be shown that

$$\sum_{i=1}^{N}(Y_i - \bar{Y})^2 = \sum_{i=1}^{N}(Y_i - \hat{Y}_i)^2 + \sum_{i=1}^{N}(\hat{Y}_i - \bar{Y})^2 \qquad \textbf{Equation 19.11b}$$

The first quantity following the equals sign is called the *residual sum of squares* and the second quantity is the *regression sum of squares.* The sum of these is called the *total sum of squares.*

The analysis of variance table displays these two sums of squares under the heading **Sum of Squares** (Figure 19.11a). The **Mean Square** for each entry is the sum of squares divided by the degrees of freedom (**DF**). If the regression assumptions are met, the ratio of the mean square regression to the mean square residual is distributed as an F statistic with p and $N-p-1$ degrees of freedom. F serves to test how well the regression model fits the data. If the probability associated with the F statistic is small, the hypothesis that $R^2_{pop}=0$ is rejected. For this example, the F statistic is

$$F = \frac{\text{MEAN SQUARE REGRESSION}}{\text{MEAN SQUARE RESIDUAL}} = 1622 \qquad \textbf{Equation 19.11c}$$

The observed significance level (SIGNIF F) is less than 0.00005.

The square root of the F value (1622) is 40.28, which is the value of the t statistic for the slope in Figure 19.3b. The square of a t value with k degrees of freedom is an F value with 1 and k degrees of freedom. Therefore, either t or F values can be computed to test that $\beta_i = 0$.

Another useful summary statistic is the standard error of the estimate, S, which can also be calculated as the square root of the residual mean square (Section 19.15).

**19.12
Another Interpretation of R^2**

Partitioning the sum of squares of the dependent variable allows another interpretation of R^2. It is the proportion of the variation in the dependent variable "explained" by the model.

$$R^2 = 1 - \frac{\text{RESIDUAL SUM OF SQUARES}}{\text{TOTAL SUM OF SQUARES}} = 0.775 \qquad \textbf{Equation 19.12a}$$

Similarly, adjusted R^2 is

$$R^2_a = 1 - \frac{\text{RESIDUAL SUM OF SQUARES}/(N-p-1)}{\text{TOTAL SUM OF SQUARES}/(N-1)} \qquad \textbf{Equation 19.12b}$$

where p is the number of independent variables in the equation (1 in the salary example).

19.13
Predicted Values and Their Standard Errors

By comparing the observed values of the dependent variable to the values predicted by the regression equation, you can learn a good deal about how well a model and the various assumptions fit the data (see the discussion of residuals beginning with Section 19.17). Predicted values are also of interest when the results are used to predict new data. You may wish to predict the mean Y for all cases with a given value of X, denoted X_0, or to predict the value of Y for a single case. For example, you can predict either the mean salary for all employees with a beginning salary of \$10,000 or the salary for a particular employee with a beginning salary of \$10,000. In both situations, the predicted value

$$\hat{Y}_0 = B_0 + B_1 X_0 = 771 + 1.91 \times 10,000 = 19,871$$

Equation 19.13

is the same. What differs is the standard error.

19.14
Predicting Mean Response

The estimated standard error for the predicted mean Y at X_0 is

$$S_{\hat{Y}} = S \sqrt{\frac{1}{N} + \frac{(X_0 - \overline{X})^2}{(N-1)S_X{}^2}}$$

Equation 19.14a

The equation for the standard error shows that the smallest value occurs when X_0 is equal to $\overline{X}$, the mean of X. The larger the distance from the mean, the greater the standard error. Thus, the mean of Y for a given X is better estimated for central values of the observed X's than for outlying values. Figure 19.14a is a plot from the PLOT procedure of the standard errors of predicted mean salaries for different values of beginning salary.

Figure 19.14a   Standard errors for predicted mean responses

```
REGRESSION
  /DEPENDENT=SALNOW
  /METHOD=ENTER SALBEG
  /SAVE=SEPRED(SE).
PLOT VERTICAL=MIN(0) /VSIZE=25
  /CUTPOINTS=EVERY(20) /SYMBOLS='*'
  /PLOT=SE WITH SALBEG.
```

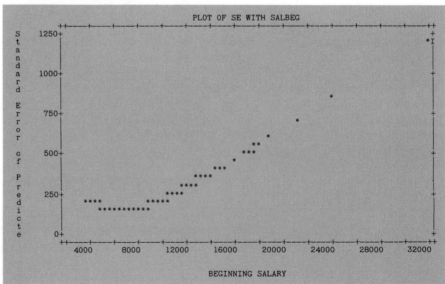

Prediction intervals for the mean predicted salary are calculated in the standard way. The 95% confidence interval at X_0 is

$$\hat{Y} \pm t_{\left(1-\frac{\alpha}{2}, N-2\right)} S_{\hat{Y}}$$

Equation 19.14b

Figure 19.14b shows a typical 95% confidence band for predicted mean responses. It is narrowest at the mean of X and increases as the distance from the mean $(X_0 - \overline{X})$ increases.

Figure 19.14b   95% confidence band for mean prediction

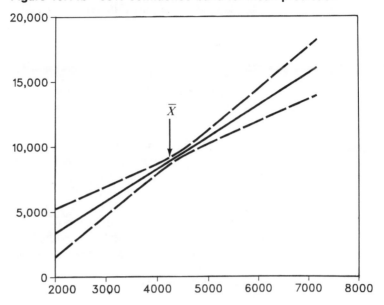

19.15
Predicting a New Value

Although the predicted value for a single new observation at X_0 is the same as the predicted value for the mean at X_0, the standard error is not. The two sources of error when predicting an individual observation are illustrated in Figure 19.15. They are

1 The individual value may differ from the population mean of Y for X_0.

2 The estimate of the population mean at X_0 may differ from the population mean.

Figure 19.15   Sources of error in predicting individual observations

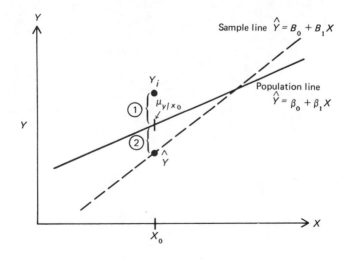

When estimating the mean response, only the second error component is considered. The variance of the individual prediction is the variance of the mean prediction plus the variance of Y_i for a given X. This can be written as

$$S^2_{ind\hat{Y}} = S^2_{\hat{Y}} + S^2 = S^2\left(1 + \frac{1}{N} + \frac{(X_0 - \overline{X})^2}{(N-1)S_X^2}\right) \qquad \textbf{Equation 19.15a}$$

Prediction intervals for the new observation are obtained by substituting $S_{ind\hat{Y}}$ for S_Y in the equation for the confidence intervals for the mean given in Section 19.14. If the sample size is large, the terms $1/N$ and

$$\frac{(X_0 - \overline{X})^2}{(N-1)S_X^2} \qquad \textbf{Equation 19.15b}$$

are negligible. In that case, the standard error is simply S, which explains the name *standard error of the estimate* for S (see Section 19.6).

19.16
Reading the Casewise Plot

Figure 19.16 shows the output from the beginning and end of a plot of the salary data. The sequence number of the case and an optional labeling variable (SEXRACE) are listed first, followed by the plot of standardized residuals, the observed (SALNOW), predicted (PRED), and residual (RESID) values, and, finally, the standard error of the mean prediction (SEPRED). In the REGRESSION procedure you can generate predicted values and confidence intervals for the mean responses (MCIN) and for individual responses (ICIN), and you can display these values for all cases or for a subset of cases along with a casewise plot.

Figure 19.16   Casewise plot with predicted values and standard errors

```
REGRESSION
  /DEPENDENT=SALNOW
  /METHOD=ENTER SALBEG
  /RESIDUALS=ID(SEXRACE)
  /CASEWISE=ALL DEPENDENT PRED RESID SEPRED.
```

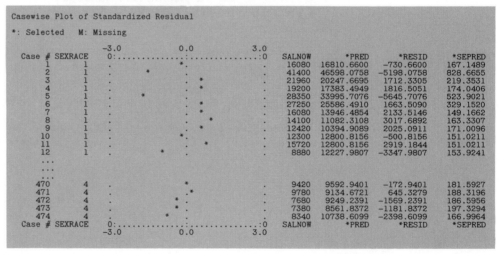

19.17
Searching for Violations of Assumptions

You usually don't know in advance whether a model such as linear regression is appropriate. Therefore, it is necessary to conduct a search focused on residuals to look for evidence that the necessary assumptions are violated.

19.18
Residuals

In model building, a *residual* is what is left after the model is fit. It is the difference between an observed value and the value predicted by the model.

$$E_i = Y_i - B_0 - B_1 X_i = Y_i - \hat{Y}_i \qquad\qquad \textbf{Equation 19.18}$$

In regression analysis, the true errors e_i are assumed to be independent normal values with a mean of 0 and a constant variance of σ^2. If the model is appropriate for the data, the observed residuals E_i, which are estimates of the true errors e_i, should have similar characteristics.

If the intercept term is included in the equation, the mean of the residuals is always 0, so it provides no information about the true mean of the errors. Since the sum of the residuals is constrained to be 0, they are *not* strictly independent. However, if the number of residuals is large when compared to the number of independent variables, the dependency among the residuals can be ignored for practical purposes.

The relative magnitudes of residuals are easier to judge when they are divided by estimates of their standard deviations. The resulting standardized residuals are expressed in standard deviation units above or below the mean. For example, the fact that a particular residual is -5198.1 provides little information. If you know that its standardized form is -3.1, you know not only that the observed value is less than the predicted value but also that the residual is larger than most in absolute value.

Residuals are sometimes adjusted in one of two ways. The *standardized residual* for case i is the residual divided by the sample standard deviation of the residuals. Standardized residuals have a mean of 0 and a standard deviation of 1. The *Studentized residual* is the residual divided by an estimate of its standard deviation that varies from point to point, depending on the distance of X_i from the mean of X. Usually standardized and Studentized residuals are close in value, but not always. The Studentized residual reflects more precisely differences in the true error variances from point to point.

19.19
Linearity

For the bivariate situation, a scatterplot is a good means for judging how well a straight line fits the data. Another convenient method is to plot the residuals against the predicted values. If the assumptions of linearity and homogeneity of variance are met, there should be no relationship between the predicted and residual values. You should be suspicious of any observable pattern.

For example, fitting a least-squares line to the data in the two left-hand plots in Figure 19.19a yields the residual plots shown on the right. The two residual plots show patterns since straight lines do not fit the data well. Systematic patterns between the predicted values and the residuals suggest possible violations of the linearity assumption. If the assumption was met, the residuals would be randomly distributed in a band about the horizontal straight line through 0, as shown in Figure 19.19b.

Figure 19.19a   Standardized residuals scatterplots

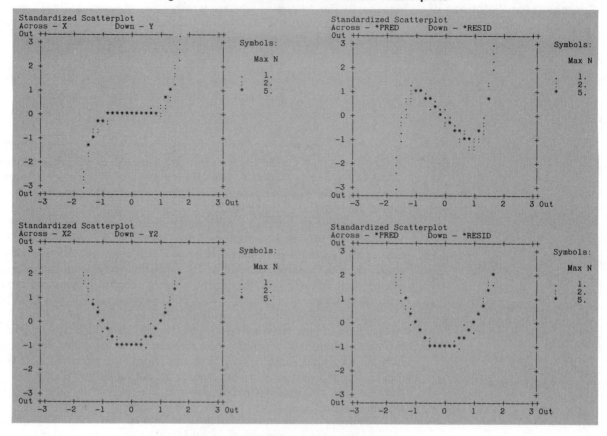

Figure 19.19b   Randomly distributed residuals

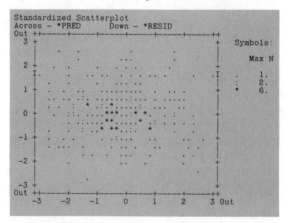

    Residuals can also be plotted against individual independent variables. Again, if the assumptions are met, you should see a horizontal band of residuals. Consider plotting the residuals against independent variables not in the equation as well. If the residuals are not randomly distributed, you may want to include the variable in the equation for a multiple regression model (see Sections 19.32 through 19.55).

19.20
Equality of Variance

You can also use the previously described plots to check for violations of the equality of variance assumption. If the spread of the residuals increases or decreases with values of the independent variables or with predicted values, you should question the assumption of constant variance of Y for all values of X.

Figure 19.20 is a plot of the Studentized residuals against the predicted values for the salary data. The spread of the residuals increases with the magnitude of the predicted values, suggesting that the variability of current salaries increases with salary level. Thus, the equality of variance assumption appears to be violated.

Figure 19.20   Unequal variance

```
REGRESSION
  /DEPENDENT=SALNOW
  /METHOD=ENTER SALBEG
  /SCATTERPLOT=(*SRESID,*PRED).
```

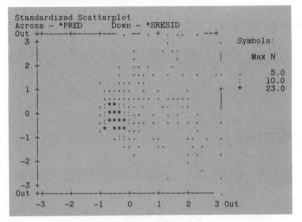

19.21
Independence of Error

Whenever the data are collected and recorded sequentially, you should plot residuals against the sequence variable. Even if time is not considered a variable in the model, it could influence the residuals. For example, suppose you are studying survival time after surgery as a function of complexity of surgery, amount of blood transfused, dosage of medication, and so forth. In addition to these variables, it is also possible that the surgeon's skill increased with each operation and that a patient's survival time is influenced by the number of prior patients treated. The plot of residuals corresponding to the order in which patients received surgery shows a shorter survival time for earlier patients than for later patients (see Figure 19.21). If sequence and the residual are independent, you should not see a discernable pattern.

Figure 19.21   Casewise serial plot

```
Casewise Plot of Studentized Residual
                   -3.0      0.0      3.0     LIFE     *PRED    *RESID   *SRESID
Case #    TIME    0:.........:.........:0
     1    78012        .  *     .        .   15.0000   19.5624  -4.5624  -2.2598
     2    78055        .  *     .        .   13.5000   17.8974  -4.3974  -2.1856
     3    78122        .   *    .        .    9.9000   13.8390  -3.9390  -1.9871
     4    78134        .    *   .        .   15.5000   18.5218  -3.0218  -1.4997
     5    78233        .    *   .        .   35.0000   38.2933  -3.2933  -1.7466
     6    78298        .     * .         .   14.7000   16.6487  -1.9487   -.9720
     7    78344        .      *.         .   34.8000   36.0040  -1.2040   -.6258
     8    79002        .       *.        .   20.8000   20.8111   -.0111   -.0055
     9    79008        .       . *       .   15.9000   14.8796   1.0204    .5123
    10    79039        .       . *       .   22.0000   21.6436    .3564    .1762
    11    79101        .       .   *     .   13.7000   11.7578   1.9422    .9910
    12    79129        .       .   *     .   14.2000   11.4456   2.7544   1.4082
    13    79178        .       .    *    .   33.2000   30.3847   2.8153   1.4144
    14    79188        .       .    *    .   26.2000   22.4761   3.7239   1.8401
    15    79189        .       .     *   .   37.4000   33.2984   4.1016   2.0920
    ...
```

The *Durbin-Watson* statistic, a test for sequential correlation of adjacent error terms, is defined as

$$D = \frac{\sum_{t=2}^{N} (E_t - E_{t-1})^2}{\sum_{t=1}^{N} E_t^2}$$

Equation 19.21

The differences between successive residuals tend to be small when error terms are positively correlated and large when error terms are negatively correlated. Thus, small values of D indicate positive correlation and large values of D indicate negative correlation. Consult tables of the D statistic for bounds upon which significance tests can be based (Neter & Wasserman, 1985).

19.22
Normality

The distribution of residuals may not appear to be normal for reasons other than actual nonnormality: misspecification of the model, nonconstant variance, a small number of residuals actually available for analysis, etc. Therefore, you should pursue several lines of investigation. One of the simplest is to construct a histogram of the residuals such as the one shown in Figure 19.22a for the salary data.

Figure 19.22a   Histogram of Studentized residuals

```
REGRESSION
  /DEPENDENT=SALNOW
  /METHOD=ENTER SALBEG
  /RESIDUALS=HISTOGRAM(SRESID) SIZE(SMALL).
```

```
Histogram - Studentized Residual

  N   Exp N        (* = 2 Cases,     . : = Normal Curve)
  7     .37   Out  ****
  2     .73  3.00  *
  4    1.85  2.67  :*
  2    4.23  2.33  *.
  6    8.65  2.00  ***.
 12   15.85  1.67  ******  .
  7   26.01  1.33  ****        .
 18   38.23  1.00  *********        .
 35   50.34   .67  ******************  .
 63   59.38   .33  *******************************:.**
 87   62.74   .00  *********************************. **************
114   59.38  -.33  *********************************:.******************************
 64   50.34  -.67  *************************:.*******
 32   38.23 -1.00  ****************    .
  9   26.01 -1.33  *****         .
  6   15.85 -1.67  ***      .
  1    8.65 -2.00  *  .
  1    4.23 -2.33  *.
  2    1.85 -2.67  :
  0     .73 -3.00  :
  2     .37   Out  *
```

The REGRESSION histogram contains a tally of the observed number of residuals (labeled **N**) in each interval and the number expected in a normal distribution with the same mean and variance as the residuals (**Exp N**). The first and last intervals (**Out**) contain residuals more than 3.16 standard deviations from the mean. Such residuals deserve examination. A histogram of expected N's is superimposed on that of the observed N's. Expected frequencies are indicated by a period. When observed and expected frequencies overlap, a colon is displayed. However, it is unreasonable to expect the observed residuals to be exactly normal—some deviation is expected because of sampling variation. Even if the errors are normally distributed in the population, sample residuals are only approximately normal.

In the histogram in Figure 19.22a, the distribution does not seem normal since there is an exaggerated clustering of residuals toward the center and a straggling tail toward large positive values. Thus, the normality assumption may be violated.

Another way to compare the observed distribution of residuals to that expected under the assumption of normality is to plot the two cumulative distributions against each other for a series of points. If the two distributions are identical, a straight line results. By observing how points scatter about the expected straight line, you can compare the two distributions.

Figure 19.22b is a cumulative probability plot of the salary residuals. Initially, the observed residuals are below the straight line, since there is a smaller number of large negative residuals than expected. Once the greatest concentration of residuals is reached, the observed points are above the line, since the observed cumulative proportion exceeds the expected. Tests for normality are available in the EXAMINE procedure (see Chapter 9).

Figure 19.22b   A normal probability (P-P) plot

```
REGRESSION
  /DEPENDENT=SALNOW
  /METHOD=ENTER SALBEG
  /RESIDUALS=HISTOGRAM(SRESID) NORMPROB.
```

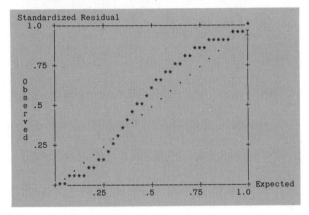

19.23
Locating Outliers

You can spot outliers readily on residual plots since they are cases with very large positive or negative residuals. In the histogram, cases with values greater than $+3.16$ or less than -3.16 appear in the interval labeled **Out**. In the scatterplots, they appear on the borders of the plot, again labeled **Out**. Since you usually want more information about outliers, you can use the casewise plotting facility to display identification numbers and a variety of other statistics for cases having residuals beyond a specified cutoff point.

Figure 19.23 lists information for the nine cases with Studentized residuals greater than 3 in absolute value. Only two of these nine employees have current salaries less than those predicted by the model (Cases 67 and 122), while the others have larger salaries. The second column contains identifier information that indicates that all outliers are white males (SEXRACE=1). They all have large salaries, an average of $33,294, while the average for the sample is only $13,767. Thus, there is some evidence that the model may not fit well for the highly paid cases.

Figure 19.23   Casewise plot of residuals outliers

```
REGRESSION
  /DEPENDENT=SALNOW
  /METHOD=ENTER SALBEG
  /CASEWISE=PLOT(SRESID)
  /RESIDUALS=ID(SEXRACE).
```

```
Casewise Plot of Studentized Residual

Outliers = 3.      *: Selected    M: Missing

                -6.    -3.  3.    6.
   Case #  SEXRACE   0:.......:  :.......:0    SALNOW     *PRED      *RESID
      24       1     .        ..*         .    28000   17383.4949   10616.5051
      60       1     .         ..       *.     32000   12800.8156   19199.1844
      67       1     .      * ..         .     26400   37043.1894  -10643.1894
     114       1     .         ..*        .    38800   27511.2163   11288.7837
     122       1     .     *   ..         .    26700   40869.7266  -14169.7266
     123       1     .         ..*        .    36250   24639.4039   11610.5961
     129       1     .         ..      *  .    33500   17383.4949   16116.5051
     149       1     .         ..        *     41500   21782.8671   19717.1329
     177       1     .         ..    *   .     36500   23295.1513   13204.8487

       9 Outliers found.
```

In Section 19.2, an employee was identified as an outlier because the combination of values for beginning and current salaries was atypical. This case, which is Case 60, shows up in Figure 19.23 since it has a large value for the Studentized residual. Another unusual employee (Case 56) has a beginning salary of $31,992. Since the average beginning salary for the entire sample is only $6,806 and the standard deviation is 3148, the case is eight standard deviations above the mean. But since the Studentized residual is not large, this case does not appear in Figure 19.23.

However, cases that have unusual values for the independent variables can have a substantial impact on the results of analysis and should be identified. One measure of the distance of cases from average values of the independent variables is *Mahalanobis' distance*. In the case of a regression equation with a single independent variable, it is the square of the standardized value of X:

$$D_i = \left(\frac{X_i - \overline{X}}{S_X}\right)^2$$

Equation 19.24

Thus, for Case 56, the Mahalanobis' distance shown in Figure 19.24 is 64 (8^2). When there is more than one independent variable—where Mahalanobis' distance is most valuable—the computations are more complex.

Figure 19.24   Mahalanobis' distances

```
REGRESSION
  /DEPENDENT=SALNOW
  /METHOD=ENTER SALBEG
  /RESIDUALS=OUTLIERS(MAHAL)  ID(SEXRACE).
```

```
Outliers - Mahalanobis' Distance

   Case #  SEXRACE      *MAHAL

      56       1      63.99758
       2       1      29.82579
     122       1      20.32559
      67       1      14.99121
     132       1      12.64145
      55       1      12.64145
     415       2      11.84140
       5       1      11.32255
     172       1      10.49188
      23       1      10.46720
```

**19.25
Influential Cases:
Deleted Residuals and
Cook's Distance**

Certain observations in a set of data can have a large influence on estimates of the parameters. Figure 19.25a shows such a point. The regression line obtained for the data is quite different if the point is omitted. However, the residual for the circled point is not particularly large when the case (Case 8) is included in the computations and does not therefore arouse suspicion (see the plot in Figure 19.25b).

Figure 19.25a   Influential observation

```
REGRESSION
    /STATISTICS=DEFAULTS CI
    /DEPENDENT=Y /METHOD=ENTER X
    /SCATTERPLOT=(Y,X).
```

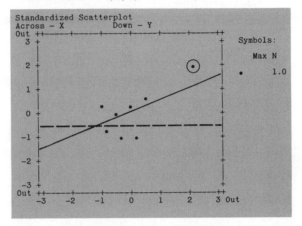

One way to identify an influential case is to compare the residuals for a case when the suspected case is included in the equation and when it is not. The *adjusted predicted value* (ADJPRED) for case *i* when it is not included in the computation of the regression line is

$$\hat{Y}_i^{(i)} = B_0^{(i)} + B_1^{(i)} X_i$$

Equation 19.25a

where the superscript *i* indicates that the *i*th case is excluded. The change in the predicted value when the *i*th case is deleted (DFFIT) is

$$\hat{Y}_i - \hat{Y}_i^{(i)}$$

Equation 19.25b

The residual calculated for a case when it is not included is called the *deleted residual* (DRESID), computed as

$$Y_i - \hat{Y}_i^{(i)}$$

Equation 19.25c

The deleted residual can be divided by its standard error to produce the *Studentized deleted residual* (SDRESID).

Although the difference between the deleted and ordinary residual for a case is useful as an index of the influence of that case, this measure does not reflect changes in residuals of other observations when the ith case is deleted. *Cook's distance* does consider changes in all residuals when case i is omitted (Cook, 1977). It is defined as

$$C_i = \frac{\sum_{j=1}^{N} (\hat{Y}_j^{(i)} - \hat{Y}_j)^2}{(p+1)S^2}$$

Equation 19.25d

The casewise plot for the data in Figure 19.25a is shown in Figure 19.25b. The line for Case 8 describes the circled point. It has neither a very large Studentized residual nor a very large Studentized deleted residual. However, the deleted residual is 5.86 ($Y-ADJPRED=12-6.14$), which is somewhat larger than the ordinary residual (1.24). The large Mahalanobis' distance identifies the case as having an X value far from the mean, while the large Cook's D identifies the case as an influential point.

Figure 19.25b   Casewise plot to study influential observation

```
REGRESSION
  /STATISTICS=DEFAULTS CI
  /DEPENDENT=Y /METHOD=ENTER X
  /CASEWISE=ALL DEPENDENT RESID SRESID DSRESID ADJPRED MAHAL COOK.
```

```
Casewise Plot of Standardized Residual

*: Selected   M: Missing

            -3.0        0.0        3.0
  Case #   0:..............:..............:0   Y    *RESID   *SRESID  *SDRESID  *ADJPRED   *MAHAL   *COOK D
       1   .              .        *      . :0    7   2.9394    1.4819   1.6990    2.9096   1.0947    .4300
       2   .           *  .               .      4   -.5758    -.2780   -.2554    4.7349    .6401    .0107
       3   .              . *             .      6    .9091     .4262    .3951    4.9062    .3068    .0184
       4   .        *     .               .      3  -2.6061   -1.2000  -1.2566    6.0252    .0947    .1158
       5   .              . *             .      7    .8788     .4016    .3717    5.9950    .0038    .0116
       6   .      *       .               .      3  -3.6364   -1.6661  -2.0747    7.1791    .0341    .2071
       7   .              .*              .      8    .8485     .3937    .3641    7.0000    .1856    .0138
       8   .              . *             . :    12   1.2425    1.1529   1.1929    6.1426   4.6402   2.4687
  Case #   0:..............:..............:0   Y    *RESID   *SRESID  *SDRESID  *ADJPRED   *MAHAL   *COOK D
            -3.0        0.0        3.0
```

The regression coefficients with and without Case 8 are shown in Figures 19.25c and 19.25d. Both $B_0^{(8)}$ and $B_1^{(8)}$ are far removed from B_0 and B_1, since Case 8 is an influential point.

Figure 19.25c   Regression results from all cases

```
REGRESSION
  /STATISTICS=DEFAULTS CI
  /DEPENDENT=Y /METHOD=ENTER X.
```

			———— Variables in the Equation ————				
Variable	B	SE B	95% Confdnce Intrvl B		Beta	T	Sig T
X	.515145	.217717	-.017587	1.047876	.694761	2.366	.0558
(Constant)	3.545466	1.410980	.092944	6.997987		2.513	.0457

Figure 19.25d   Regression coefficients without Case 8

```
REGRESSION
 /SELECT=CASEID NE 8
 /STATISTICS=DEFAULTS CI
 /DEPENDENT=Y /METHOD=ENTER X.
```

────────── Variables in the Equation ──────────							
Variable	B	SE B	95% Confdnce Intrvl B		Beta	T	Sig T
X	.071407	.427380	-1.027191	1.170004	.074513	.167	.8739
(Constant)	5.142941	1.911317	.229823	10.056060		2.691	.0433

You can examine the change in the regression coefficients when a case is deleted from the analysis by looking at the intercept and X values for DFBETA on the casewise plot. For Case 8 in Figure 19.25e, you see that the change in the intercept is -1.5975 and the change in slope (**X**) is 0.4437.

Figure 19.25e   Diagnostic statistics for influential observations

```
REGRESSION
 /DEPENDENT=Y /METHOD=ENTER X
 /CASEWISE=ALL DEPENDENT DFBETA.
```

```
Casewise Plot of Standardized Residual

*: Selected  M: Missing

         -3.0        0.0        3.0
  Case #  0:.................:.................:0   Y   *DFBETA_____
          ·              ·              ·               Intercept          X
     1    ·              ·    *         ·        7       1.3015       -.1505
     2    ·              *·             ·        4       -.2004        .0207
     3    ·              ·  *           ·        6        .2486       -.0213
     4    ·         *     ·             ·        3       -.5500        .0327
     5    ·              · *            ·        7        .1370       -.0022
     6    ·       *      ·             ·        3       -.3799       -.0271
     7    ·              · *            ·        8        .0455        .0152
     8    ·              ·  *           ·       12      -1.5975        .4437
  Case #  0:.................:.................:0   Y   *DFBETA_____
         -3.0        0.0        3.0
```

19.26
When Assumptions Appear To Be Violated

When evidence of violation of assumptions appears, you can pursue one of two strategies. You can either formulate an alternative model, such as weighted least squares, or you can transform the variables so that the current model will be more adequate. For example, taking logs, square roots, or reciprocals can stabilize the variance, achieve normality, or linearize a relationship.

19.27
Coaxing a Nonlinear Relationship to Linearity

To try to achieve linearity, you can transform either the dependent or independent variables, or both. If you alter the scale of independent variables, linearity can be achieved without any effect on the distribution of the dependent variable. Thus, if the dependent variable is normally distributed with constant variance for each value of X, it remains so.

When you transform the dependent variable, its distribution is changed. This new distribution must then satisfy the assumptions of the analysis. For example, if logs of the values of the dependent variable are taken, log Y—not the original Y—must be normally distributed with constant variance.

The choice of transformations depends on several considerations. If the form of the true model governing the relationship is known, it should dictate the choice. For instance, if it is known that $\hat{Y}=AC^X$ is an adequate model, taking logs of both sides of the equation results in

$$\log \hat{Y}_i = \underset{[B_0]}{(\log A)} + \underset{[B_1]}{(\log C)} X_i$$

Equation 19.27

Thus log Y is linearly related to X.

Figure 19.27   A transformed relationship

```
REGRESSION
  /DEPENDENT=Y /ENTER=X
  /SCATTERPLOT=(Y,X)
  /DEPENDENT=LOGY /ENTER=X
  /SCATTERPLOT=(LOGY,X).
```

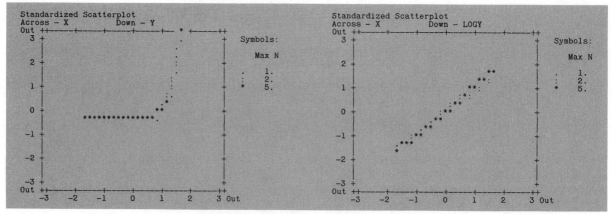

If the true model is not known, you should choose the transformation by examining the plotted data. Frequently, a relationship appears nearly linear for part of the data but is curved for the rest. The first plot in Figure 19.27 is an example. Taking the log of the dependent variable results in the second plot—an improved linear fit.

Other transformations that may diminish curvature are the square root of Y and $-1/Y$. The choice depends, to a certain extent, on the severity of the problem.

19.28
Coping with Skewness

When the distribution of residuals is positively skewed, the log transformation of the dependent variable is often helpful. For negatively skewed distributions, the square transformation is common. It should be noted that the F tests used in regression hypothesis testing are usually quite insensitive to moderate departures from normality.

19.29
Stabilizing the Variance

If the variance of the residuals is not constant, you can try a variety of remedial measures:

- When the variance is proportional to the mean of Y for a given X, use the square root of Y if all Y_i are positive.
- When the standard deviation is proportional to the mean, try the logarithmic transformation.
- When the standard deviation is proportional to the square of the mean, use the reciprocal of Y.
- When Y is a proportion or rate, the arc sine transformation may stabilize the variance.

19.30
Transforming the Salary Data

The assumptions of constant variance and normality appear to be violated with the salary data (see Figures 19.20 and 19.22a). A regression equation using logs of beginning and current salary was developed to obtain a better fit to the assumptions. Figure 19.30a is a scatterplot of Studentized residuals against predicted values when logs of both variables are used in the regression equation.

Figure 19.30a   Scatterplot of transformed salary data

```
COMPUTE LOGBEG=LG10(SALBEG).
COMPUTE LOGNOW=LG10(SALNOW).
REGRESSION
  /DEPENDENT=LOGNOW
  /METHOD=ENTER LOGBEG
  /SCATTERPLOT=(*SRESID,*PRED).
```

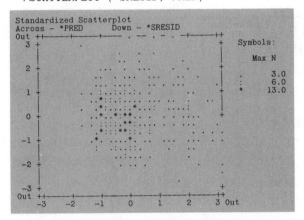

Compare Figures 19.20 and 19.30a and note the improvement in the behavior of the residuals. The spread no longer increases with increasing salary level. Also compare Figures 19.22a and 19.30b and note that the distribution in Figure 19.30b is nearly normal.

Figure 19.30b   Histogram of transformed salary data

```
COMPUTE LOGBEG=LG10(SALBEG).
COMPUTE LOGNOW=LG10(SALNOW).
REGRESSION
  /DEPENDENT=LOGNOW
  /METHOD=ENTER LOGBEG
  /RESIDUALS=HISTOGRAM(SRESID) SIZE(SMALL).
```

```
Histogram - Studentized Residual

  N Exp N        (* = 1 Cases,    . : = Normal Curve)
  3   .37   Out ***
  1   .73  3.00 :
  3  1.85  2.67 *:*
  4  4.23  2.33 ***:
 10  8.65  2.00 ********:*
 14 15.85  1.67 **************
 21 26.01  1.33 *********************
 31 38.23  1.00 *******************************     .
 48 50.34   .67 ************************************************    .
 55 59.38   .33 *******************************************************        .
 63 62.74   .00 ****************************************************************:*****
 64 59.38  -.33 ****************************************************************:*****
 62 50.34  -.67 *************************************************:************
 44 38.23 -1.00 ********************************************:******
 28 26.01 -1.33 ****************************:**
 14 15.85 -1.67 **************.
  7  8.65 -2.00 *******.
  1  4.23 -2.33 *  .
  1  1.85 -2.67 *.
  0   .73 -3.00 .
  0   .37   Out
```

For the transformed data, the multiple R increases slightly to 0.8864, and the outlier plot contains only four cases (compare with Figures 19.10 and 19.23). Thus, the transformation appears to have resulted in a better model.

19.31
A Final Comment on Assumptions

Rarely are assumptions not violated one way or another in regression analysis and other statistical procedures. However, this is not a justification for ignoring the assumptions. Cranking out regressions with little thought to possible departures from the necessary assumptions can lead to problems in interpreting and applying results. Significance levels, confidence intervals, and other results are sensitive to certain types of violations and cannot be interpreted in the usual fashion if serious departures exist.

By carefully examining residuals and, if need be, using transformations or other methods of analysis, you are in a much better position to pursue analyses that solve the problems you are investigating. Even if everything isn't perfect, you can at least knowledgeably gauge the possible extent of difficulties.

19.32
MULTIPLE REGRESSION MODELS

Beginning salary seems to be a good predictor of current salary, given the evidence shown above. Nearly 80% ($R^2 = 0.77$ from Figure 19.10) of the observed variability in current salaries can be explained by beginning salary levels. But how do variables such as education level, years of experience, race, and sex affect the salary level at which one enters the company?

19.33
Predictors of Beginning Salary

Multiple linear regression extends bivariate regression by incorporating multiple independent variables. The model can be expressed as:

$$Y_i = \beta_0 + \beta_1 X_{1i} + \beta_2 X_{2i} + \ldots + \beta_p X_{pi} + e_i \qquad \text{Equation 19.33}$$

The notation X_{pi} indicates the value of the pth independent variable for case i. Again, the β terms are unknown parameters and the e_i terms are independent random variables that are normally distributed with mean 0 and constant variance σ^2. The model assumes that there is a normal distribution of the dependent variable for every combination of the values of the independent variables in the model. For example, if child's height is the dependent variable and age and maternal height are the independent variables, it is assumed that for every combination of age and maternal height there is a normal distribution of children's heights and, though the means of these distributions may differ, all have the same variance.

19.34
The Correlation Matrix

One of the first steps in calculating an equation with several independent variables is to calculate a correlation matrix for all variables, as shown in Figure 19.34. The variables are the log of beginning salary, years of education, sex, years of work experience, race, and age in years. Variables sex and race are represented by *indicator variables,* that is, variables coded as 0 or 1. SEX is coded 1 for female and 0 for male, and MINORITY is coded 1 for nonwhite and 0 for white.

Figure 19.34 The correlation matrix

```
COMPUTE LOGBEG=LG10(SALBEG).
REGRESSION
  /DESCRIPTIVES=CORR
  /VARIABLES=LOGBEG,EDLEVEL,SEX,WORK,MINORITY,AGE
  /DEPENDENT=LOGBEG
  /METHOD=ENTER EDLEVEL TO AGE.
```

	LOGBEG	EDLEVEL	SEX	WORK	MINORITY	AGE
LOGBEG	1.000	.686	-.548	.040	-.173	-.048
EDLEVEL	.686	1.000	-.356	-.252	-.133	-.281
SEX	-.548	-.356	1.000	-.165	-.076	.052
WORK	.040	-.252	-.165	1.000	.145	.804
MINORITY	-.173	-.133	-.076	.145	1.000	.111
AGE	-.048	-.281	.052	.804	.111	1.000

The matrix shows the correlations between the dependent variable (LOGBEG) and each independent variable, as well as the correlations between the independent variables. Particularly note any large intercorrelations between the independent variables, since such correlations can substantially affect the results of multiple regression analysis.

19.35
Correlation Matrices and Missing Data

For a variety of reasons, data files frequently contain incomplete observations. Respondents in surveys scrawl illegible responses or refuse to answer certain questions. Laboratory animals die before experiments are completed. Patients fail to keep scheduled clinic appointments. Thus, before computing the correlation matrix, you must usually decide what to do with cases that have missing values for some of the variables.

Before even considering possible strategies, you should determine whether there is evidence that the missing-value pattern is not random. That is, are there reasons to believe that missing values for a variable are related to the values of that variable or other variables? For example, people with low incomes may be less willing to report their financial status than more affluent people. This may be even more pronounced for people who are poor but highly educated.

One simple method of exploring such possibilities is to subdivide the data into two groups—those observations with missing data on a variable and those with complete data—and examine the distributions of the other variables in the file across these two groups. The SPSS procedures CROSSTABS and T-TEST are particularly useful for this. For a discussion of more sophisticated methods for detecting nonrandomness, see Frane (1976).

If it appears that the data are not missing randomly, use great caution in attempting to analyze the data. It may be that no satisfactory analysis is possible, especially if there are only a few cases.

If you are satisfied that the missing data are random, several strategies are available. First, if the same few variables are missing for most cases, consider excluding those variables from the analysis. Since this luxury is not usually available, you can alternatively keep all variables but eliminate the cases with missing values on any of them. This is termed *listwise* missing-value treatment since a case is eliminated if it has a missing value on any variable in the list.

If many cases have missing data for some variables, listwise missing-value treatment may eliminate too many cases and leave you with a very small sample. One common technique is to calculate the correlation coefficient between a pair of variables based on all cases with complete information for the two variables, regardless of whether the cases have missing data on any other variable. For example, if a case has values only for variables 1, 3, and 5, it is used only in computations involving variable pairs 1 and 3, 1 and 5, and 3 and 5. This is *pairwise* missing-value treatment.

Several problems can arise with pairwise matrices, one of which is inconsistency. There are some relationships between coefficients that are impossible but may occur when different cases are used to estimate different coefficients. For example, if age and weight and age and height have a high positive correlation, it is impossible in the same sample for height and weight to have a high negative correlation. However, if the same cases are not used to estimate all three coefficients, such an anomaly can occur.

Another problem with pairwise matrices is that no single sample size can be obtained since each coefficient may be based on a different number of cases. In addition, significance levels obtained from analyses based on pairwise matrices must be viewed with caution, since little is known about hypothesis testing in such situations.

Missing-value problems should not be treated lightly. You should always select a missing-value treatment based on careful examination of the data and not leave the choices up to system defaults. In this example, complete information is available for all cases, so missing values are not a problem.

19.36
Partial Regression
Coefficients

The summary output when all independent variables are included in the multiple regression equation is shown in Figure 19.36a. The *F* test associated with the analysis of variance table is a test of the null hypothesis that

$$\beta_1 = \beta_2 = \beta_3 = \beta_4 = \beta_5 = 0$$ **Equation 19.36a**

In other words, it is a test of whether there is a linear relationship between the dependent variable and the entire set of independent variables.

Figure 19.36a   Statistics for the equation and analysis of variance table

```
COMPUTE LOGBEG=LG10(SALBEG).
REGRESSION VARIABLES=LOGBEG EDLEVEL SEX WORK MINORITY AGE
   /DEPENDENT=LOGBEG
   /METHOD=ENTER EDLEVEL TO AGE.
```

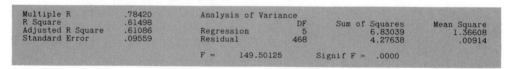

Multiple R	.78420	Analysis of Variance			
R Square	.61498		DF	Sum of Squares	Mean Square
Adjusted R Square	.61086	Regression	5	6.83039	1.36608
Standard Error	.09559	Residual	468	4.27638	.00914
		F = 149.50125	Signif F =	.0000	

The statistics for the independent variables in Figure 19.36b are parallel to those obtained in regression with a single independent variable (see Figure 19.3b). In multiple regression, the coefficients labeled **B** are called *partial regression coefficients* since the coefficient for a particular variable is adjusted for other independent variables in the equation. The equation that relates the predicted log of beginning salary to the independent variables is

$$\text{LOGBEG} = 3.3853 + 0.00102(\text{AGE}) \\ - 0.10358(\text{SEX}) - 0.05237(\text{MINORITY}) \\ + 0.03144(\text{EDLEVEL}) + 0.00161(\text{WORK})$$

Equation 19.36b

Figure 19.36b Statistics for variables in the equation

```
COMPUTE LOGBEG=LG10(SALBEG).
REGRESSION VARIABLES=LOGBEG EDLEVEL SEX WORK MINORITY AGE
   /DEPENDENT=LOGBEG
   /METHOD=ENTER EDLEVEL TO AGE.
```

```
------------------ Variables in the Equation ------------------

Variable            B         SE B        Beta         T    Sig T

AGE              .001015   6.6132E-04    .078106     1.535   .1254
SEX             -.103576     .010318    -.336987   -10.038   .0000
MINORITY        -.052366     .010837    -.141573    -4.832   .0000
EDLEVEL          .031443     .001748     .591951    17.988   .0000
WORK             .001608   9.2407E-04    .091428     1.740   .0826
(Constant)      3.385300     .033233               101.866   .0000
```

19.37
Determining Important Variables

In multiple regression, you sometimes want to assign relative importance to each independent variable. For example, you might want to know whether education is more important in predicting beginning salary than previous work experience. There are two possible answers, depending on which of the following questions is asked:

- How important are education and work experience when each one is used alone to predict beginning salary?
- How important are education and work experience when they are used to predict beginning salary along with other independent variables in the regression equation?

The first question is answered by looking at the correlation coefficients between salary and the independent variables. The larger the absolute value of the correlation coefficient, the stronger the linear association. Figure 19.34 shows that education correlates more highly with the log of salary than does previous work experience (0.686 and 0.040, respectively). Thus, you would assign more importance to education as a predictor of salary.

The answer to the second question is considerably more complicated. When the independent variables are correlated among themselves, the unique contribution of each is difficult to assess. Any statement about an independent variable is contingent upon the other variables in the equation. For example, the regression coefficient (B) for work experience is 0.0007 when it is the sole independent variable in the equation, compared to 0.00161 when the other four independent variables are also in the equation. The second coefficient is more than twice the size of the first.

19.38
Beta Coefficients

It is also inappropriate to interpret the B's as indicators of the relative importance of variables. The actual magnitude of the coefficients depends on the units in which the variables are measured. Only if all independent variables are measured in the same units—years, for example—are their coefficients directly comparable. When variables differ substantially in units of measurement, the sheer magnitude of their coefficients does not reveal anything about relative importance.

One way to make regression coefficients somewhat more comparable is to calculate *beta* weights, which are the coefficients of the independent variables when all variables are expressed in standardized (Z-score) form (see Figure 19.36b). The beta coefficients can be calculated directly from the regression coefficients using

$$BETA_k = B_k\left(\frac{S_k}{S_Y}\right)$$

Equation 19.38

where S_k is the standard deviation of the kth independent variable.

However, the values of the beta coefficients, like the B's, are contingent on the other independent variables in the equation. They are also affected by the correlations of the independent variables and do not in any absolute sense reflect the importance of the various independent variables.

19.39
Part and Partial Coefficients

Another way of assessing the relative importance of independent variables is to consider the increase in R^2 when a variable is entered into an equation that already contains the other independent variables. This increase is

$$R^2_{change} = R^2 - R^2_{(i)}$$

Equation 19.39a

where $R^2_{(i)}$ is the square of the multiple correlation coefficient when all independent variables except the ith are in the equation. A large change in R^2 indicates that a variable provides unique information about the dependent variable that is not available from the other independent variables in the equation. The signed square root of the increase is called the *part correlation coefficient.* It is the correlation between Y and X_i when the linear effects of the other independent variables have been removed from X_i. If all independent variables are uncorrelated, the change in R^2 when a variable is entered into the equation is simply the square of the correlation coefficient between that variable and the dependent variable.

The output in Figure 19.39 shows that the addition of years of education to an equation that contains the other four independent variables results in a change in R^2 of 0.266 (0.51593^2). The square of the part coefficient tells only how much R^2 increases when a variable is added to the regression equation. It does not indicate what proportion of the unexplained variation this increase constitutes. If most of the variation had been explained by the other variables, a small part correlation is all that is possible for the remaining variable. It may therefore be difficult to compare part coefficients.

Figure 19.39 Zero-order, part, and partial correlation coefficients

```
COMPUTE LOGBEG=LG10(SALBEG).
REGRESSION VARIABLES=LOGBEG,EDLEVEL,SEX,WORK,MINORITY,AGE
  /STATISTICS=R CHA ZPP F
  /DEPENDENT=LOGBEG
  /METHOD=ENTER AGE /ENTER SEX /ENTER MINORITY /ENTER WORK /ENTER
  EDLEVEL.
```

```
Variable(s) Entered on Step Number  5..     EDLEVEL    EDUCATIONAL LEVEL


Multiple R               .78420
R Square                 .61498           R Square Change      .26619
Adjusted R Square        .61086           F Change          323.55404
Standard Error           .09559           Signif F Change      .0000

F =       149.50125        Signif F =   .0000




------------- Variables in the Equation ---------------

Variable      Correl Part Cor  Partial          F   Sig F
AGE          -.047795  .044040  .070796      2.357   .1254
SEX          -.548020 -.287918 -.420903    100.761   .0000
MINORITY     -.172836 -.138596 -.217989     23.349   .0000
WORK          .039940  .049897  .080154      3.026   .0826
EDLEVEL       .685719  .515935  .639342    323.554   .0000
(Constant)                               10376.613   .0000
```

A coefficient that measures the proportional reduction in variation is

$$Pr_i^2 = \frac{R^2 - R_{(i)}^2}{1 - R_{(i)}^2}$$

Equation 19.39b

The numerator is the square of the part coefficient; the denominator is the proportion of unexplained variation when all but the ith variable are in the equation. The signed square root of Pr_i^2 is the *partial correlation coefficient*. It can be interpreted as the correlation between the ith independent variable and the dependent variable when the linear effects of the other independent variables have been removed from both X_i and Y. Since the denominator of Pr_i^2 is always less than or equal to 1, the part correlation coefficient is never larger in absolute value than the partial correlation coefficient.

Plots of the residuals of Y and X_i, when the linear effects of the other independent variables have been removed, are a useful diagnostic aid. They are discussed in Section 19.49.

19.40
Building a Model

Our selection of the five variables to predict beginning salary has been arbitrary to some extent. It is unlikely that all relevant variables have been identified and measured. Instead, some relevant variables have no doubt been excluded, while others that were included may not be very important determinants of salary level. This is not unusual; you must try to build a model from available data, as voluminous or scanty as the data may be. Before considering several formal procedures for model building, we will examine some of the consequences of adding and deleting variables from regression equations. The REGRESSION statistics for variables not in the equation are also described.

19.41
Adding and Deleting
Variables

The first step in Figure 19.41 shows the equation and summary statistics when years of education is the sole independent variable and log of beginning salary is the dependent variable. Consider the second step in the same figure, when another variable, sex, is added. The value displayed as **R Square Change** in the second step is the change in R^2 when sex is added. R^2 for education alone is 0.47021, so R^2_{change} is 0.57598−0.47021, or 0.10577.

Figure 19.41   Adding a variable to the equation

```
COMPUTE LOGBEG=LG10(SALBEG).
REGRESSION VARIABLES=LOGBEG,EDLEVEL,SEX
   /STATISTICS=DEFAULTS CHA
   /DEPENDENT=LOGBEG
   /METHOD=ENTER EDLEVEL /ENTER SEX.
```

```
Beginning Block Number  1.  Method:  Enter     EDLEVEL


Variable(s) Entered on Step Number  1..   EDLEVEL    EDUCATIONAL LEVEL

Multiple R          .68572                                        Analysis of Variance
R Square            .47021        R Square Change    .47021                            DF     Sum of Squares      Mean Square
Adjusted R Square   .46909        F Change        418.92011       Regression            1            5.22252          5.22252
Standard Error      .11165        Signif F Change    .0000        Residual            472            5.88425           .01247

                                                                  F =    418.92011      Signif F =  .0000


----------------- Variables in the Equation ------------------           -------------- Variables not in the Equation --------------

Variable            B        SE B       Beta        T    Sig T       Variable    Beta In  Partial  Min Toler      T  Sig T

EDLEVEL          .036424   .001780    .685719   20.468  .0000       SEX        -.348017 -.446811    .873274  -10.839  .0000
(Constant)      3.310013   .024551             134.821  .0000


End Block Number   1   All requested variables entered.

Beginning Block Number  2.  Method:  Enter     SEX

Variable(s) Entered on Step Number  2..   SEX       SEX OF EMPLOYEE

Multiple R          .75893                                        Analysis of Variance
R Square            .57598        R Square Change    .10577                            DF     Sum of Squares      Mean Square
Adjusted R Square   .57418        F Change        117.48552       Regression            2            6.39725          3.19863
Standard Error      .09999        Signif F Change    .0000        Residual            471            4.70951           .01000

                                                                  F =    319.89574      Signif F =  .0000


----------------- Variables in the Equation ------------------

Variable            B        SE B       Beta        T    Sig T

EDLEVEL          .029843   .001705    .561830   17.498  .0000
SEX             -.106966   .009869   -.348017  -10.839  .0000
(Constant)      3.447542   .025386             135.806  .0000


End Block Number   2   All requested variables entered.
```

The null hypothesis that the true population value for the change in R^2 is 0 can be tested using

$$F_{change} = \frac{R^2_{change}(N - p - 1)}{q(1 - R^2)} = \frac{(0.1058)\,(474\text{-}2\text{-}1)}{1(1\text{-}0.5760)} = 117.48 \qquad \textbf{Equation 19.41}$$

where N is the number of cases in the equation, p is the total number of independent variables in the equation, and q is the number of variables entered at this step. Sometimes, this is referred to as a *partial F test*. Under the hypothesis that the true change is 0, the significance of the value labeled **F Change** can be obtained from the F distribution with q and $N-p-1$ degrees of freedom.

The hypothesis that the real change in R^2 is 0 can also be formulated in terms of the β parameters. When only the ith variable is added in a step, the hypothesis that the change in R^2 is 0 is equivalent to the hypothesis that β_i is 0. The F value displayed for the change in R^2 is the square of the t value displayed for the test of the coefficient, as shown in Figure 19.41. For example, the t value for sex from Figure 19.41 is -10.839. This value squared is 117.48, the value displayed for **F Change.**

When q independent variables are entered in a single step, the test that R^2 is 0 is equivalent to the simultaneous test that the coefficients of all q variables are 0. For example, if sex and age were added in the same step to the regression equation that contains education, the F test for R^2 change would be the same as the F test which tests the hypothesis that $\beta_{sex} = \beta_{age} = 0$.

Entering sex into the equation with education has effects in addition to changing R^2. For example, note the decrease in magnitude of the regression coefficient for education from Step 1 to Step 2 (from 0.03642 to 0.02984) in Figure 19.41. This is attributable to the correlation between sex and level of education.

When highly intercorrelated independent variables are included in a regression equation, results may appear anomalous. The overall regression may be significant while none of the individual coefficients are significant. The signs of the regression coefficients may be counterintuitive. High correlations between independent variables inflate the variances of the estimates, making individual coefficients quite unreliable without adding much to the overall fit of the model. The problem of linear relationships between independent variables is discussed further in Section 19.51.

19.42
Statistics for Variables Not in the Equation

When you have independent variables that have not been entered into the equation, you can examine what would happen if they were entered at the next step. Statistics describing these variables are shown in Figure 19.42. The column labeled **Beta In** is the standardized regression coefficient that would result if the variable were entered into the equation at the next step. The F test and level of significance are for the hypothesis that the coefficient is 0. (Remember that the partial F test and the t test for the hypothesis that a coefficient is 0 are equivalent.) The partial correlation coefficient with the dependent variable adjusts for the variables already in the equation.

Figure 19.42 Coefficients for variables not in the equation

```
COMPUTE LOGBEG=LG10(SALBEG).
REGRESSION WIDTH=80
  /VARIABLES=LOGBEG,EDLEVEL,SEX,WORK,MINORITY,AGE
  /STATISTICS=OUTS F
  /DEPENDENT=LOGBEG
  /METHOD=FORWARD.
```

Variable	Beta In	Partial	Min Toler	F	Sig F
WORK	.144245	.205668	.773818	20.759	.0000
MINORITY	-.129022	-.194642	.847583	18.507	.0000
AGE	.139419	.205193	.804253	20.659	.0000

From statistics calculated for variables not in the equation, you can decide what variable should be entered next. This process is detailed in Section 19.45.

19.43
The "Optimal" Number of
Independent Variables

Having seen what happens when sex is added to the equation containing education (Figure 19.41), consider now what happens when the remaining three independent variables are entered one at a time in no particular order. Summary output is shown in Figure 19.43. Step 5 shows the statistics for the equation with all independent variables entered. Step 3 describes the model with education, sex, and work experience as the independent variables.

Figure 19.43   All independent variables in the equation

```
COMPUTE LOGBEG=LG10(SALBEG).
REGRESSION VARIABLES=LOGBEG,EDLEVEL,SEX,WORK,AGE,MINORITY
    /STATISTICS=HISTORY F
    /DEPENDENT=LOGBEG
    /METHOD=ENTER EDLEVEL /ENTER SEX /ENTER WORK /ENTER AGE
    /ENTER MINORITY.
```

				Summary table									
Step	MultR	Rsq	AdjRsq	F(Eqn)	SigF	RsqCh	FCh	SigCh		Variable	BetaIn	Correl	
1	.6857	.4702	.4691	418.920	.000	.4702	418.920	.000 In:	EDLEVEL	.6857	.6857	EDUCATIONAL LEVEL
2	.7589	.5760	.5742	319.896	.000	.1058	117.486	.000 In:	SEX	-.3480	-.5480	SEX OF EMPLOYEE
3	.7707	.5939	.5913	229.130	.000	.0179	20.759	.000 In:	WORK	.1442	.0399	WORK EXPERIENCE
4	.7719	.5958	.5923	172.805	.000	.0019	2.149	.143 In:	AGE	.0763	-.0478	AGE OF EMPLOYEE
5	.7842	.6150	.6109	149.501	.000	.0192	23.349	.000 In:	MINORITY	-.1416	-.1728	MINORITY CLASSIFICATION

Examination of Figure 19.43 shows that R^2 never decreases as independent variables are added. This is always true in regression analysis. However, this does not necessarily mean that the equation with more variables better fits the population. As the number of parameters estimated from the sample increases, so does the goodness of fit to the sample as measured by R^2. For example, if a sample contains six cases, a regression equation with six parameters fits the sample exactly, even though there may be no true statistical relationship at all between the dependent variable and the independent variables.

As indicated in Section 19.10, the sample R^2 in general tends to overestimate the population value of R^2. Adjusted R^2 attempts to correct the optimistic bias of the sample R^2. Adjusted R^2 does not necessarily increase as additional variables are added to an equation and is the preferred measure of goodness of fit because it is not subject to the inflationary bias of unadjusted R^2. This statistic is shown in the column labeled **AdjRsq** in the output.

Although adding independent variables increases R^2, it does not necessarily decrease the standard error of the estimate. Each time a variable is added to the equation, a degree of freedom is lost from the residual sum of squares and one is gained for the regression sum of squares. The standard error may increase when the decrease in the residual sum of squares is very slight and not sufficient to make up for the loss of a degree of freedom for the residual sum of squares. The F value for the test of the overall regression decreases when the regression sum of squares does not increase as fast as the degrees of freedom for the regression.

Including a large number of independent variables in a regression model is never a good strategy, unless there are strong, previous reasons to suggest that they all should be included. The observed increase in R^2 does not necessarily reflect a better fit of the model in the population. Including irrelevant variables increases the standard errors of all estimates without improving prediction. A model with many variables is often difficult to interpret.

On the other hand, it is important not to exclude potentially relevant independent variables. The following sections describe various procedures for selecting variables to be included in a regression model. The goal is to build a concise model that makes good prediction possible.

19.44
Additional Statistics for Comparing Models

In addition to R^2 and adjusted R^2, many other criteria have been suggested for comparing models and selecting among them (Judge et al., 1985). One of the most commonly used alternatives to R^2 is called Mallow's C_p, which measures the standardized total mean squared error of prediction for the observed data. It is defined as

$$C_p = \frac{SSE}{\hat{\sigma}^2} + 2p - N$$ **Equation 19.44a**

where $\hat{\sigma}^2$ is an estimate of σ^2 usually obtained from the full set of variables, SSE is the error sum of squares from a model with p coefficients, including the constant, and N is the sample size.

The first part of Mallow's C_p is called the "variance" component, the second the bias component. Subsets of variables that produce values close to p are considered good. Graphical methods for evaluation of models based on C_p are discussed in Daniel and Wood (1980) and Draper and Smith(1981).

Amemiya's prediction criteria PC, is akin to adjusted R^2 with a higher penalty for adding variables. It is defined as

$$PC = \frac{N+p}{N-p}(1-R^2)$$ **Equation 19.44b**

Aikake's information criterion is based on an information measure of model selection. It is computed as

$$AIC = N\,ln\left(\frac{SSE}{N}\right) + 2p$$ **Equation 19.44c**

The Schwarz Bayesian criterion is

$$SBC = N\,ln\left(\frac{SSE}{N}\right) + p\,ln(N)$$ **Equation 19.44d**

Detailed discussions of these criteria can be found in Judge et al. (1985).

19.45
Procedures for Selecting Variables

You can construct a variety of regression models from the same set of variables. For instance, you can build seven different equations from three independent variables: three with only one independent variable, three with two independent variables, and one with all three. As the number of variables increases, so does the number of potential models (ten independent variables yield 1,023 models).

Although there are procedures for computing all possible regression equations, several other methods do not require as much computation and are more frequently used. Among these procedures are forward selection, backward elimination, and stepwise regression. None of these variable selection procedures is "best" in any absolute sense; they merely identify subsets of variables that, for the sample, are good predictors of the dependent variable.

19.46
Forward Selection

In *forward selection*, the first variable considered for entry into the equation is the one with the largest positive or negative correlation with the dependent variable. The F test for the hypothesis that the coefficient of the entered variable is 0 is then calculated. To determine whether this variable (and each succeeding variable) is entered, the F value is compared to an established criterion. You can specify one of two criteria in SPSS. One criterion is the minimum value of the F statistic that a variable must achieve in order to enter, called *F-to-enter* (keyword FIN), with a default value of 3.84. The other criterion you can specify is the probability associated with the F statistic, called *probability of F-to-enter* (keyword PIN), with a default of 0.05. In this case, a variable enters into the equation only if the probability associated with the F test is less than or equal to the default 0.05 or the value you specify. By default, the probability of F-to-enter is the criterion used.

These two criteria are not necessarily equivalent. As variables are added to the equation, the degrees of freedom associated with the residual sum of squares decrease while the regression degrees of freedom increase. Thus, a fixed F value has different significance levels depending on the number of variables currently in the equation. For large samples, the differences are negligible.

The actual significance level associated with the F-to-enter statistic is not the one usually obtained from the F distribution, since many variables are being examined and the largest F value is selected. Unfortunately, the true significance level is difficult to compute since it depends not only on the number of cases and variables but also on the correlations between independent variables.

If the first variable selected for entry meets the criterion for inclusion, forward selection continues. Otherwise, the procedure terminates with no variables in the equation. Once one variable is entered, the statistics for variables not in the equation are used to select the next one. The partial correlations between the dependent variable and each of the independent variables not in the equation, adjusted for the independent variables in the equation, are examined. The variable with the largest partial correlation is the next candidate. Choosing the variable with the largest partial correlation in absolute value is equivalent to selecting the variable with the largest F value.

If the criterion is met, the variable is entered into the equation and the procedure is repeated. The procedure stops when there are no other variables that meet the entry criterion.

To include a specific number of independent variables in the equation, you can specify the number of steps and REGRESSION will select only the first n variables that meet entry requirements. Another criterion that is always checked before a variable is entered is the tolerance, which is discussed in Section 19.51.

Figure 19.46a shows output generated from a forward-selection procedure using the salary data. The default entry criterion is PIN=0.05. In the first step, education (variable EDLEVEL) is entered since it has the highest correlation with beginning salary. The significance level associated with education is less than 0.0005, so it certainly meets the criterion for entry.

Figure 19.46a   Summary statistics for forward selection

```
COMPUTE LOGBEG=LG10(SALBEG).
REGRESSION VARIABLES=LOGBEG,EDLEVEL,SEX,WORK,MINORITY,AGE
    /STATISTICS=HISTORY F
    /DEPENDENT=LOGBEG
    /METHOD=FORWARD.
```

Step	MultR	Rsq	AdjRsq	F(Eqn)	SigF	RsqCh	FCh	SigCh		Variable	BetaIn	Correl
1	.6857	.4702	.4691	418.920	.000	.4702	418.920	.000	In:	EDLEVEL	.6857	.6857
2	.7589	.5760	.5742	319.896	.000	.1058	117.486	.000	In:	SEX	-.3480	-.5480
3	.7707	.5939	.5913	229.130	.000	.0179	20.759	.000	In:	WORK	.1442	.0399
4	.7830	.6130	.6097	185.750	.000	.0191	23.176	.000	In:	MINORITY	-.1412	-.1728

To see how the next variable, SEX, was selected, look at the statistics shown in Figure 19.46b for variables not in the equation when only EDLEVEL is in the equation. The variable with the largest partial correlation is SEX. If entered at the next step, it would have an F value of approximately 117 for the test that its coefficient is 0. Since the probability associated with the F is less than 0.05, variable SEX is entered in the second step.

Figure 19.46b   Status of the variables at the first step

```
COMPUTE LOGBEG=LG10(SALBEG).
REGRESSION WIDTH=80
    /VARIABLES=LOGBEG,EDLEVEL,SEX,WORK,MINORITY,AGE
    /STATISTICS=F
    /DEPENDENT=LOGBEG
    /METHOD=FORWARD.
```

```
------------------ Variables in the Equation ------------------

Variable              B         SE B       Beta         F    Sig F

EDLEVEL          .036424     .001780    .685719    418.920   .0000
(Constant)      3.310013     .024551              18176.773   .0000


-------------- Variables not in the Equation --------------

Variable     Beta In  Partial  Min Toler        F   Sig F

SEX         -.348017 -.446811    .873274   117.486   .0000
WORK         .227473  .302405    .936316    47.408   .0000
MINORITY    -.083181 -.113267    .982341     6.121   .0137
AGE          .157180  .207256    .921128    21.140   .0000
```

Once variable SEX enters at Step 2, the statistics for variables not in the equation must be examined (see Figure 19.42). The variable with the largest absolute value for the partial correlation coefficient is now years of work experience. Its F value is 20.759 with a probability less than 0.05, so variable WORK is entered in the next step. The same process takes place with variable MINORITY and it is entered, leaving AGE as the only variable out of the equation. However, as shown in Figure 19.46c, the significance level associated with the AGE coefficient F value is 0.1254, which is too large for entry. Thus, forward selection yields the summary table for the four steps shown in Figure 19.46a.

Figure 19.46c The last step

```
COMPUTE LOGBEG=LG10(SALBEG).
REGRESSION WIDTH=80
  /VARIABLES=LOGBEG,EDLEVEL,SEX,WORK,MINORITY,AGE
  /STATISTICS=F
  /DEPENDENT=LOGBEG
  /METHOD=FORWARD.
```

```
------------- Variables not in the Equation -------------

Variable      Beta In  Partial  Min Toler        F  Sig F

AGE           .078106  .070796  .297843      2.357  .1254
```

19.47
Backward Elimination

While forward selection starts with no independent variables in the equation and sequentially enters them, *backward elimination* starts with all variables in the equation and sequentially removes them. Instead of entry criteria, removal criteria are specified.

Two removal criteria are available in SPSS. The first is the minimum F value (FOUT) that a variable must have in order to remain in the equation. Variables with F values less than this *F-to-remove* are eligible for removal. The second criterion available is the maximum probability of *F*-to-remove (keyword POUT) a variable can have. The default FOUT value is 2.71 and the default POUT value is 0.10. The default criterion is POUT.

Figure 19.47a Backward elimination at the first step

```
COMPUTE LOGBEG=LG10(SALBEG).
REGRESSION VARIABLES=LOGBEG,EDLEVEL,SEX,WORK,MINORITY,AGE
  /STATISTICS=COEFF ZPP F
  /DEPENDENT=LOGBEG
  /METHOD=BACKWARD.
```

```
--------------------------------- Variables in the Equation ---------------------------------

Variable            B         SE B         Beta   Correl Part Cor  Partial            F    Sig F

AGE           .001015  6.6132E-04      .078106 -.047795   .044040   .070796        2.357   .1254
SEX          -.103576     .010318     -.336987 -.548020  -.287918  -.420903      100.761   .0000
MINORITY     -.052366     .010837     -.141573 -.172836  -.138596  -.217989       23.349   .0000
EDLEVEL       .031443     .001748      .591951  .685719   .515935   .639342      323.554   .0000
WORK          .001608  9.2407E-04      .091428  .039940   .049897   .080154        3.026   .0826
(Constant)   3.385300     .033233                                               10376.613   .0000
```

Look at the salary example again, this time constructing the model with backward elimination. The output in Figure 19.47a is from the first step, in which all variables are entered into the equation. The variable with the smallest partial correlation coefficient, AGE, is examined first. Since the probability of its F

(0.1254) is greater than the default POUT criterion value of 0.10, variable AGE is removed.

Figure 19.47b Backward elimination at the last step

```
COMPUTE LOGBEG=LG10(SALBEG).
REGRESSION VARIABLES=LOGBEG,EDLEVEL,SEX,WORK,MINORITY,AGE
    /STATISTICS=COEFF ZPP F
    /DEPENDENT=LOGBEG
    /METHOD=BACKWARD.
```

Variable	B	SE B	Beta	Correl	Part Cor	Partial	F	Sig F	Variable	F	Sig F
SEX	-.099042	.009901	-.322234	-.548020	-.287333	-.419331	100.063	.0000	AGE	2.357	.1254
MINORITY	-.052245	.010853	-.141248	-.172836	-.138282	-.216998	23.176	.0000			
EDLEVEL	.031433	.001751	.591755	.685719	.515768	.638270	322.412	.0000			
WORK	.002753	5.4582E-04	.156592	.039940	.144891	.226848	25.444	.0000			
(Constant)	3.411953	.028380					14454.046	.0000			

(Variables in the Equation — left block; not in — right block)

The equation is then recalculated without AGE, producing the statistics shown in Figure 19.47b. The variable with the smallest partial correlation is MINORITY. However, its significance is less than the 0.10 criterion, so backward elimination stops. The equation resulting from backward elimination is the same as the one from forward selection. This is not always the case, however. Forward- and backward-selection procedures can give different results, even with comparable entry and removal criteria.

19.48
Stepwise Selection

Stepwise selection of independent variables is really a combination of backward and forward procedures and is probably the most commonly used method. The first variable is selected in the same manner as in forward selection. If the variable fails to meet entry requirements (either FIN or PIN), the procedure terminates with no independent variables in the equation. If it passes the criterion, the second variable is selected based on the highest partial correlation. If it passes entry criteria, it also enters the equation.

After the first variable is entered, stepwise selection differs from forward selection: the first variable is examined to see whether it should be removed according to the removal criterion (FOUT or POUT) as in backward elimination. In the next step, variables not in the equation are examined for entry. After each step, variables already in the equation are examined for removal. Variables are removed until none remain that meet the removal criterion. To prevent the same variable from being repeatedly entered and removed, PIN must be less than POUT (or FIN greater than FOUT). Variable selection terminates when no more variables meet entry and removal criteria.

In the salary example, stepwise selection with the default criteria results in the same equation produced by both forward selection and backward elimination (see Figure 19.48).

Figure 19.48 Stepwise output

```
COMPUTE LOGBEG=LG10(SALBEG).
REGRESSION VARIABLES=LOGBEG EDLEVEL SEX WORK MINORITY AGE
    /STATISTICS=R COEFF OUTS F
    /DEPENDENT=LOGBEG
    /METHOD=STEPWISE.
```

```
Listwise Deletion of Missing Data

Equation Number 1    Dependent Variable..  LOGBEG

Beginning Block Number  1.  Method: Stepwise

Variable(s) Entered on Step Number  1..    EDLEVEL    EDUCATIONAL LEVEL


Multiple R           .68572
R Square             .47021
Adjusted R Square    .46909
Standard Error       .11165

F =      418.92011      Signif F =  .0000
```

Variable	B	SE B	Beta	F	Sig F
EDLEVEL	.036424	.001780	.685719	418.920	.0000
(Constant)	3.310013	.024551		18176.773	.0000

Variable	Beta In	Partial	Min Toler	F	Sig F
SEX	-.348017	-.446811	.873274	117.486	.0000
WORK	.227473	.302405	.936316	47.408	.0000
MINORITY	-.083181	-.113267	.982341	6.121	.0137

```
Equation Number 1    Dependent Variable..  LOGBEG

Variable(s) Entered on Step Number  2..    SEX        SEX OF EMPLOYEE


Multiple R           .75893
R Square             .57598
Adjusted R Square    .57418
Standard Error       .09999

F =      319.89574      Signif F =  .0000
```

Variable	B	SE B	Beta	F	Sig F
EDLEVEL	.029843	.001705	.561830	306.191	.0000
SEX	-.106966	.009869	-.348017	117.486	.0000
(Constant)	3.447542	.025386		18443.284	.0000

Variable	Beta In	Partial	Min Toler	F	Sig F
WORK	.144245	.205668	.773818	20.759	.0000
MINORITY	-.129022	-.194642	.847583	18.507	.0000
AGE	.139419	.205193	.804253	20.659	.0000

```
Variable(s) Entered on Step Number  3..    WORK       WORK EXPERIENCE


Multiple R           .77066
R Square             .59391
Adjusted R Square    .59132
Standard Error       .09796

F =      229.13001      Signif F =  .0000
```

Variable	B	SE B	Beta	F	Sig F
EDLEVEL	.032572	.001775	.613209	336.771	.0000
SEX	-.094035	.010076	-.305945	87.099	.0000
WORK	.002536	5.5664E-04	.144245	20.759	.0000
(Constant)	3.384569	.028452		14150.645	.0000

Variable	Beta In	Partial	Min Toler	F	Sig F
MINORITY	-.141248	-.216998	.759669	23.176	.0000
AGE	.076331	.067540	.298392	2.149	.1433

```
Equation Number 1    Dependent Variable..  LOGBEG

Variable(s) Entered on Step Number  4..    MINORITY   MINORITY CLASSIFICATION


Multiple R           .78297
R Square             .61304
Adjusted R Square    .60974
Standard Error       .09573

F =      185.74958      Signif F =  .0000
```

Variable	B	SE B	Beta	F	Sig F
EDLEVEL	.031433	.001751	.591755	322.412	.0000
SEX	-.099042	.009901	-.322234	100.063	.0000
WORK	.002753	5.4582E-04	.156592	25.444	.0000
MINORITY	-.052245	.010853	-.141248	23.176	.0000
(Constant)	3.411953	.028380		14454.046	.0000

Variable	Beta In	Partial	Min Toler	F	Sig F
AGE	.078106	.070796	.297843	2.357	.1254

```
End Block Number  1   PIN =      .050 Limits reached.
```

The three procedures do not always result in the same equation, though you should be encouraged when they do. The model selected by any method should be carefully studied for violations of the assumptions. It is often a good idea to develop several acceptable models and then choose among them based on interpretability, ease of variable acquisition, parsimony, and so forth.

19.49
Checking for Violation of Assumptions

The procedures discussed in Sections 19.17 through 19.22 for checking for violations of assumptions in bivariate regression apply in the multivariate case as well. Residuals should be plotted against predicted values as well as against each independent variable. The distribution of residuals should be examined for normality.

Several additional residual plots may be useful for multivariate models. One of these is the partial regression plot. For the jth independent variable, it is obtained by calculating the residuals for the dependent variable when it is predicted from all the independent variables excluding the jth and by calculating the residuals for the jth independent variable when it is predicted from all of the other independent variables. This removes the linear effect of the other independent variables from both variables. For each case, these two residuals are plotted against each other.

A partial regression plot for educational level for the regression equation that contains work experience, minority, sex, and educational level as the independent variables is shown in Figure 19.49a. (Summary statistics for the regression equation with all independent variables are displayed in the last step of Figure 19.48.)

Figure 19.49a Partial regression plot from PLOT

```
COMPUTE LOGBEG=LG10(SALBEG).
REGRESSION VARIABLES=LOGBEG SEX MINORITY EDLEVEL WORK
   /DEPENDENT=LOGBEG
   /METHOD=ENTER MINORITY SEX WORK
   /SAVE=RESID(RES1)
   /DEPENDENT=EDLEVEL
   /METHOD=ENTER MINORITY SEX WORK
   /SAVE=RESID(RES2).
PLOT FORMAT=REGRESSION /VSIZE=30 /HSIZE=70
 /PLOT=RES1 WITH RES2.
```

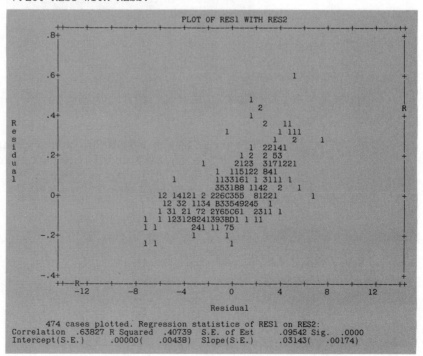

Several characteristics of the partial regression plot make it a particularly valuable diagnostic tool. The slope of the regression line for the two residual variables (0.03143) is equal to the coefficient for the EDLEVEL variable in the multiple regression equation after the last step (Step 4 in Figure 19.48). Thus, by examining the bivariate plot, you can conveniently identify points that are influential in the determination of the particular regression coefficient (see Sections 19.23 through 19.25). The correlation coefficient between the two residuals, 0.638, is the partial correlation coefficient discussed in Section 19.39. The residuals from the least-squares line in Figure 19.49a are equal to the residuals from the final multiple regression equation, which includes all the independent variables.

The partial regression plot also helps you assess inadequacies of the selected model and violations of the underlying assumptions. For example, the partial regression plot of educational level does not appear to be linear, suggesting that an additional term, such as years of education squared, might also be included in the model. This violation is much easier to spot using the partial regression plot than the plot of the independent variable against the residual from the equation with all independent variables. Figures 19.49b and 19.49c show the residual scatterplot and partial regression plot produced by the REGRESSION procedure. Note that the nonlinearity is much more apparent in the partial regression plot.

Figure 19.49b   Residual scatterplot from REGRESSION

```
COMPUTE LOGBEG=LG10(SALBEG).
REGRESSION VARIABLES=LOGBEG SEX MINORITY EDLEVEL WORK
  /DEPENDENT=LOGBEG
  /METHOD=STEPWISE
  /SCATTERPLOT=(*RESID,EDLEVEL).
```

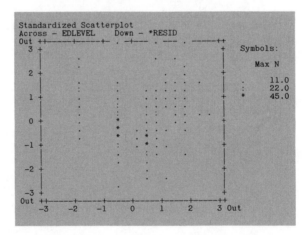

Figure 19.49d contains the summary statistics when the number of years of education squared is included in the multiple regression equation. The multiple R^2 increases from 0.61 (Step 4 in Figure 19.48) to 0.71, a significant improvement.

Figure 19.49c   Partial regression plot from REGRESSION

```
COMPUTE LOGBEG=LG10(SALBEG).
REGRESSION VARIABLES=LOGBEG SEX MINORITY EDLEVEL WORK
   /DEPENDENT=LOGBEG
   /METHOD=STEPWISE
   /PARTIALPLOT=EDLEVEL.
```

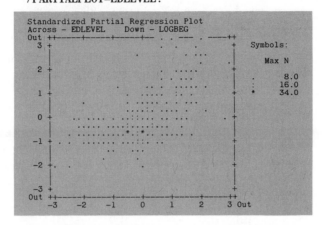

Figure 19.49d   The regression equation with education squared

```
COMPUTE LOGBEG=LG10(SALBEG).
COMPUTE ED2=EDLEVEL*EDLEVEL.
REGRESSION VARIABLES=LOGBEG SEX MINORITY EDLEVEL ED2 WORK
   /DEPENDENT=LOGBEG
   /METHOD=ENTER.
```

Variable(s) Entered on Step Number	1..	WORK	WORK EXPERIENCE
	2..	MINORITY	MINORITY CLASSIFICATION
	3..	SEX	SEX OF EMPLOYEE
	4..	EDLEVEL	EDUCATIONAL LEVEL
	5..	ED2	

		Analysis of Variance			
Multiple R	.84302				
R Square	.71068		DF	Sum of Squares	Mean Square
Adjusted R Square	.70759	Regression	5	7.89331	1.57866
Standard Error	.08286	Residual	468	3.21345	.00687
		F =	229.91286	Signif F =	.0000

19.50
Looking for Influential Points

As discussed in Sections 19.23 through 19.25 when building a regression model it is important to identify cases that are influential, or that have a disproportionately large effect on the estimated model. We can look for cases that change the values of the regression coefficients and of predicted values, cases that increase the variances of the coefficients, and cases that are poorly fitted by the model.

Among the important influence measures is the leverage (LEVER) of a case. The predicted values of the dependent variable can be expressed as

$$\hat{Y} = H\,Y$$

Equation 19.50a

The diagonal elements of the H matrix (commonly called the hat matrix) are called leverages. The leverage for a case describes the impact of the observed value of the dependent variable on the prediction of the fitted value. Leverages are important in their own right and as fundamental building blocks for other diagnostic measures. For example, the Mahalanobis' distance for a point is obtained by multiplying the leverage value by $N-1$.

The REGRESSION procedure computes centered leverages (LEVER). They range from 0 to $(N-1)/N$, where N is the number of observations. The mean value for the centered leverage is p/N, where p is the number of independent variables in the equation. A leverage of 0 identifies a point with no influence on the fit, while a point with a leverage of $(N-1)/N$ indicates that a degree of freedom has been devoted to fitting the data point. Ideally, you would like each observation to exert a roughly equal influence. That is, you want all of the leverages to be near p/N. It is a good idea to examine points with leverage values that exceed $(2p)/N$.

To see the effect of a case on the estimation of the regression coefficients, you can look at the change in each of the regression coefficients when the case is removed from the analysis. REGRESSION can display or save the actual change in each of the coefficients, including the intercept (DFBETA) and the standardized change (SDBETA).

Figure 19.50a is a plot of SDBETA for the MINORITY variable against a case ID number. Note that, as expected, most of the points cluster in a horizontal band around 0. However, there are a few points far removed from the rest. Belsley et al. (1980) recommend examining SDBETA values that are larger than

$$\frac{2}{\sqrt{N}}$$

Equation 19.50b

Figure 19.50a   Plot of SDBETA values for variable MINORITY

```
COMPUTE LOGBEG=LG10(SALBEG).
COMPUTE ED2=EDLEVEL*EDLEVEL.
REGRESSION VARIABLES=LOGBEG SEX MINORITY EDLEVEL ED2 WORK
 /DEPENDENT=LOGBEG /METHOD=ENTER
 /SAVE SDBETA.
PLOT PLOT=SDB2_1 WITH ID.
```

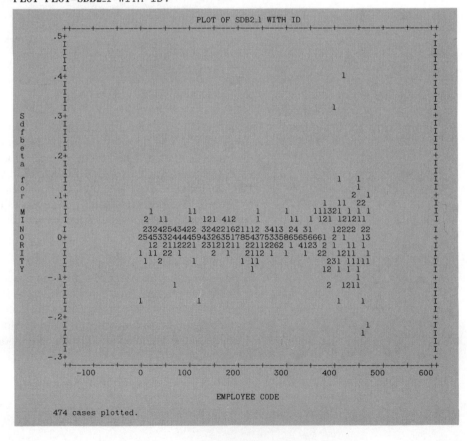

474 cases plotted.

In addition to looking at the change in the regression coefficients when a case is deleted from an analysis, we can look at the change in the predicted value (DFFIT) or at the standardized change (SDFFIT). Cases with large values far removed from the rest should be examined. As a rule of thumb, you may want to look at standardized values larger than

$$2\sqrt{p/N}$$

Equation 19.50c

Another type of influential observation is one that influences the variance of the estimated regression coefficients. A measure of the impact of an observation on the variance-covariance matrix of the parameter estimates is called the covariance ratio (COVRATIO). It is computed as the ratio of the determinant of the variance-covariance matrix computed without the case to the determinant of the variance-covariance matrix computed with all cases. If this ratio is close to 1, the case leaves the variance-covariance matrix relatively unchanged. Belsley et al. (1980) recommend examining points for which the absolute value of the ratio minus 1 is greater than $3p/N$.

Figure 19.50b is a plot of COVRATIO for the salary example. Note the circled point which has a COVRATIO substantially smaller than the rest.

Figure 19.50b   Plot of the covariance ratio (COVRATIO)

```
COMPUTE LOGBEG=LG10(SALBEG).
COMPUTE ED2=EDLEVEL*EDLEVEL.
REGRESSION VARIABLES=LOGBEG SEX MINORITY EDLEVEL ED2 WORK
 /DEPENDENT=LOGBEG /METHOD=ENTER
 /SAVE COVRATIO.
PLOT PLOT=COV_1 WITH ID.
```

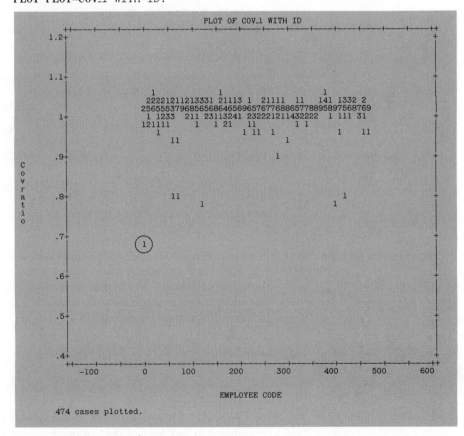

19.51
Measures of Collinearity

Collinearity refers to the situation in which there is a high multiple correlation when one of the independent variables is regressed on the others (i.e., when there is a high correlation between independent variables). The problem with collinear variables is that they provide very similar information, and it is difficult to separate out the effects of the individual variables. Diagnostics are available which allow you to detect the presence of collinear data and to assess the extent to which the collinearity has degraded the estimated parameters.

The tolerance of a variable is a commonly used measure of collinearity. The tolerance (TOL) of variable i is defined as $1-R_i^2$, where R_i is the multiple correlation coefficient when the ith independent variable is predicted from the other independent variables. If the tolerance of a variable is small, it is almost a linear combination of the other independent variables.

The variance inflation factor (VIF) is closely related to the tolerance. In fact, it is defined as the reciprocal of the tolerance. That is, for the ith variable

$$\text{VIF}_i = \frac{1}{(1-R_i^2)}$$

Equation 19.51

This quantity is called the variance inflation factor since the term is involved in the calculation of the variance of the ith regression coefficient. As the variance inflation factor increases, so does the variance of the regression coefficient.

Figure 19.51 shows the tolerances and VIFs for the variables in the final model. Note the low tolerances and high VIFs for EDLEVEL and ED2 (the square of EDLEVEL). This is to be expected since there is a relationship between these two variables.

Figure 19.51 Measures of collinearity: tolerance and VIF

```
COMPUTE LOGBEG=LG10(SALBEG).
COMPUTE ED2=EDLEVEL*EDLEVEL.
REGRESSION VARIABLES=LOGBEG SEX MINORITY EDLEVEL ED2 WORK
 /STATISTICS=COEF TOL
 /DEPENDENT=LOGBEG /METHOD=ENTER.
```

Variable	B	SE B	Beta	Tolerance	VIF	T	Sig T
WORK	.001794	4.7859E-04	.102038	.834367	1.199	3.749	.0002
MINORITY	-.038225	.009460	-.103342	.945107	1.058	-4.041	.0001
SEX	-.082503	.008671	-.268426	.776799	1.287	-9.515	.0000
EDLEVEL	-.089624	.009751	-1.687260	.018345	54.511	-9.191	.0000
ED2	.004562	3.6303E-04	2.312237	.018263	54.756	12.567	.0000
(Constant)	4.173910	.065417				63.804	.0000

Two useful tools for examining the collinearity of a data matrix are the eigenvalues of the scaled, uncentered cross-products matrix and the decomposition of regression variance corresponding to the eigenvalues.

19.52
Eigenvalues and Condition Indexes

We can compare the eigenvalues of the scaled, uncentered cross-products matrix to see if some are much larger than others. If this is the case, the data matrix is said to be "ill-conditioned." If a matrix is ill-conditioned, small changes in the values of the independent or dependent variables may lead to large changes in the solution. The condition index is defined as

$$cond\ index_i = \sqrt{\frac{EIGENVALUE_{max}}{EIGENVALUE_i}}$$

Equation 19.52

There are as many near dependencies among the variables as there are large condition indexes.

Figure 19.52 shows the eigenvalues and condition indexes for the salary example. You can see that the last two eigenvalues are much smaller than the rest. Their condition indexes are 10.29 and 88.22.

Figure 19.52 Measures of collinearity: eigenvalues and condition indexes

```
COMPUTE LOGBEG=LG10(SALBEG).
COMPUTE ED2=EDLEVEL*EDLEVEL.
REGRESSION VARIABLES=LOGBEG SEX MINORITY EDLEVEL ED2 WORK
 /STATISTICS=COLLIN
 /DEPENDENT=LOGBEG /METHOD=ENTER.
```

Collinearity Diagnostics

Number	Eigenval	Cond Index	Constant	SEX	MINORITY	EDLEVEL	ED2	WORK
				Variance Proportions				
1	4.08812	1.000	.00019	.01223	.01375	.00004	.00013	.01466
2	.79928	2.262	.00005	.08212	.65350	.00002	.00009	.04351
3	.59282	2.626	.00001	.37219	.22139	.00003	.00022	.17437
4	.48061	2.917	.00005	.14964	.05421	.00012	.00091	.51370
5	.03864	10.286	.05223	.37811	.04876	.00004	.02337	.20721
6	.00053	88.221	.94746	.00571	.00839	.99975	.97527	.04655

19.53
Variance Proportions

The variances of each of the regression coefficients, including the constant, can be decomposed into a sum of components associated with each of the eigenvalues. If a high proportion of the variance of two or more coefficients is associated with the same eigenvalue, there is evidence for a near dependency.

Consider Figure 19.52 again. Each of the columns after the condition index tells you the proportion of the variance of each of the coefficients associated with each of the eigenvalues. Consider the column for the SEX coefficient. You see that 1.22% of the variance of the coefficient is attributable to the first eigenvalue, 8.2% to the second, and similarly 0.57% to the sixth (the proportions in each column sum to 1).

In this table you're looking for variables with high proportions for the same eigenvalue. For example, looking at the last eigenvalue, you see that it accounts for 95% of the variance of the constant, almost 100% of the variance of EDLEVEL, and 98% of the variance of ED2. This tells you that these three variables are highly dependent. Since the other independent variables have small variance proportions for the sixth eigenvalue, it does not appear that the observed dependencies are affecting their coefficients. (See Belsley et al., 1980, for an extensive discussion of these diagnostics.)

19.54
Interpreting the Equation

The multiple regression equation estimated above suggests several findings. Education appears to be the best predictor of beginning salary, at least among the variables included in this study (Figure 19.47a). The sex of the employee also appears to be important. Women are paid less than men since the sign of the regression coefficient is negative (men are coded 0 and women are coded 1). Years of prior work experience and race are also related to salary, but when education and sex are included in the equation, the effect of experience and race is less striking.

Do these results indicate that there is sex discrimination at the bank? Not necessarily. It is well recognized that all education is not equally profitable. Master's degrees in business administration and political science are treated quite differently in the marketplace. Thus, a possible explanation of the observed results is that women enter areas that are just not very well paid. Although this may suggest inequities in societal evaluation of skills, it does not necessarily imply discrimination at the bank. Further, many other potential job-related skills or qualifications are not included in the model. Also, some of the existing variables, such as age, may make nonlinear as well as linear contributions to the fit. Such contributions can often be approximated by including new variables that are simple functions of the existing one. For example, the age values squared may improve the fit.

19.55
Statistics for Unselected Cases

As previously noted, a model usually fits the sample from which it is derived better than it fits the population. A sometimes useful strategy for obtaining an estimate of how well the model fits the population is to split the sample randomly into two parts. One part is then used to estimate the model, while the remaining cases are reserved for testing the goodness of fit.

It is also sometimes interesting to split the data on some characteristics of the sample. For example, you can develop the salary equation for males alone and then apply it to females to see how well it fits. For example, Figure 19.55 shows histograms of residuals for males (denoted as selected cases) and females (unselected cases). Note that the females' salaries are too large when predicted from the male equation since most of the residuals are negative. The multiple R for the females is 0.45596, which is smaller than the 0.73882 for males (stepwise selection was used).

Figure 19.55   Histograms for males (selected) and females (unselected)

```
COMPUTE LOGBEG=LG10(SALBEG).
COMPUTE ED2=EDLEVEL*EDLEVEL.
REGRESSION WIDTH=90
  /SELECT SEX EQ 0
  /VARIABLES=LOGBEG,EDLEVEL,ED2,SEX,WORK,MINORITY,AGE
  /DEPENDENT=LOGBEG
  /METHOD=STEPWISE
  /RESIDUALS=HISTOGRAM.
```

```
Histogram - Standardized Residual
- Selected Cases
 N  Exp N        (* = 1 Cases.    . : = Normal Curve)
 6   .20    Out ******
 0   .40   3.00 .
 0  1.01   2.67 .
 1  2.30   2.33 *.
 1  4.71   2.00 * .
 6  8.63   1.67 ****** .
 7 14.16   1.33 *******    .
14 20.81   1.00 ************** .
24 27.40    .67 ************************* .
36 32.32    .33 *********************************:****
39 34.15    .00 *************************************:*****
48 32.32   -.33 **********************************:*****************
41 27.40   -.67 ***************************:***************
17 20.81  -1.00 ***************** .
12 14.16  -1.33 ************ .
 3  8.63  -1.67 *** .
 0  4.71  -2.00    .
 2  2.30  -2.33 *:
 1  1.01  -2.67 :
 0   .40  -3.00
 0   .20    Out


Histogram - Standardized Residual
- Unselected Cases
 N  Exp N        (X = 1 Cases.    . : = Normal Curve)
 0   .17    Out
 0   .33   3.00
 0   .84   2.67 .
 0  1.93   2.33 .
 0  3.94   2.00  .
 1  7.22   1.67 X
 2 11.85   1.33 XX      .
 2 17.42   1.00 XX          .
 3 22.94    .67 XXX            .
 5 27.06    .33 XXXXX             .
23 28.59    .00 XXXXXXXXXXXXXXXXXXXXXXX .
23 27.06   -.33 XXXXXXXXXXXXXXXXXXXXXXX
36 22.94   -.67 XXXXXXXXXXXXXXXXXXXXXX:XXXXXXXXXXXXX
49 17.42  -1.00 XXXXXXXXXXXXXXX:XXXXXXXXXXXXXXXXXXXXXXXXXXXXXXXX
20 11.85  -1.33 XXXXXXXXXXX:XXXXXXXX
14  7.22  -1.67 XXXXXX:XXXXXXX
15  3.94  -2.00 XXX:XXXXXXXXXX
15  1.93  -2.33 X:XXXXXXXXXXXX
 4   .84  -2.67 :XXX
 0   .33  -3.00
 4   .17    Out XXXX
```

19.56
RUNNING
PROCEDURE
REGRESSION

The REGRESSION procedure provides five equation-building methods: forward selection, backward elimination, stepwise selection, forced entry, and forced removal. The subcommands for residual analysis help detect influential data points, outliers, and violations of the regression model assumptions.

19.57
Building the Equation

To build a simple regression model, you must specify two required subcommands: a DEPENDENT subcommand that indicates the dependent variable and a METHOD subcommand that names the method to be used. For example, to build the simple bivariate model of beginning salary and current salary discussed earlier in the chapter, specify

```
REGRESSION DEPENDENT=SALNOW
   /METHOD=ENTER SALBEG.
```

The beginning (SALBEG) and current (SALNOW) salaries are named, with the latter specified as the dependent variable. The ENTER keyword enters beginning salary into the equation. The output produced by this command is shown in Figures 19.3b, 19.10, and 19.11a.

19.58
VARIABLES Subcommand

The optional VARIABLES subcommand lists all variables to be used in the regression analysis. The order of variables on the VARIABLES subcommand determines the order of variables in the correlation matrix. The keyword TO can be used on the VARIABLES subcommand to imply consecutive variables on the active system file. On subsequent DEPENDENT and METHOD subcommands, the keyword TO refers to the order of variables on the VARIABLES subcommand.

The VARIABLES subcommand is followed by a variable list or either one of the following keywords:

ALL *Include all user-defined variables in the active system file.*

(COLLECT) *Include all variables named on the DEPENDENT and METHOD subcommands.* This is the default if the VARIABLES subcommand is not included.

If you do not include a VARIABLES subcommand or you specify the keyword (COLLECT), the METHOD subcommand(s) must include a variable list. If used, the VARIABLES subcommand must precede the first DEPENDENT and METHOD subcommands, as in:

```
REGRESSION VARIABLES=SALBEG SALNOW LOGBEG
   EDLEVEL SEX WORK MINORITY AGE
   /DEPENDENT=LOGBEG
   /METHOD=ENTER EDLEVEL TO AGE.
```

19.59
DEPENDENT Subcommand

The DEPENDENT subcommand indicates the dependent variable for the regression analysis. The DEPENDENT subcommand is followed by a variable name or variable list. If you specify more than one variable on the DEPENDENT subcommand, SPSS produces a separate equation for each dependent variable specified.

You can specify more than one analysis with multiple DEPENDENT and METHOD subcommands. For example, to run both a bivariate and multivariate analysis in the same REGRESSION procedure, specify

```
REGRESSION VARIABLES=SALBEG SALNOW LOGBEG
 EDLEVEL SEX WORK MINORITY AGE
  /DEPENDENT=SALNOW
  /METHOD=ENTER SALBEG
  /DEPENDENT=LOGBEG
  /METHOD=ENTER EDLEVEL TO AGE.
```

The first DEPENDENT subcommand defines a single equation with SALNOW as the dependent variable, and the METHOD subcommand enters SALBEG into the equation. The second DEPENDENT subcommand defines another equation, with LOGBEG as the dependent variable. The associated METHOD subcommand enters variables EDLEVEL to AGE into the equation. The TO convention for naming consecutive variables used in the second METHOD subcommand refers to the order in which the variables are named on the VARIABLES subcommand, not their order on the active system file. See Figures 19.36a and 19.36b for the output from the second equation.

    If you specify more than one variable on the DEPENDENT subcommand, SPSS produces a separate equation for each dependent variable specified.

19.60
METHOD Subcommand

At least one METHOD subcommand must immediately follow each DEPENDENT subcommand, specifying the method to be used in developing the regression equation. The available methods are:

FORWARD (varlist)   *Forward variable selection.* The variables named are entered one at a time based on entry criteria (Section 19.46).

BACKWARD (varlist)   *Backward variable elimination.* All variables named are entered and then removed one at a time based on removal criteria (Section 19.47).

STEPWISE (varlist)   *Stepwise variable entry and removal.* The variables named are examined at each step for entry or removal (Section 19.48).

ENTER (varlist)   *Forced entry.* All variables named are entered in a single step.

REMOVE (varlist)   *Forced removal.* The variables named are removed in a single step. REMOVE must have an accompanying variable list.

TEST (varlist)   *Test indicated subsets of independent variables.* TEST offers an easy way to test a variety of models using R^2 change and its test of significance as the criterion for the "best" model. TEST must have an accompanying variable list.

A variable list is required with the REMOVE and TEST keywords and is optional for the other METHOD keywords, provided you include a VARIABLES subcommand. The default variable list for methods FORWARD, BACKWARD, STEPWISE, and ENTER includes all variables named on the VARIABLES subcommand that are not named on the preceding DEPENDENT subcommand. For example, to request the backward-elimination method discussed in Section 19.47, specify:

```
REGRESSION VARIABLES=LOGBEG EDLEVEL SEX WORK MINORITY AGE
 /DEPENDENT=LOGBEG
  /METHOD=BACKWARD.
```

The keyword METHOD is optional and may be omitted. For example, the command

```
REGRESSION VARIABLES=LOGBEG EDLEVEL SEX WORK MINORITY AGE
 /DEPENDENT=LOGBEG
  /BACKWARD.
```

produces the same results as the previous example.

You can specify multiple METHOD subcommands. For example, you might want to force one variable into the equation first and then enter the remaining variables in a forward-selection fashion, as in:

```
REGRESSION VARIABLES=LOGBEG EDLEVEL SEX WORK MINORITY AGE
   /DEPENDENT=LOGBEG
   /METHOD=ENTER EDLEVEL
   /METHOD=FORWARD SEX TO AGE.
```

19.61
STATISTICS Subcommand

By default, REGRESSION displays the four sets of statistics described for keywords R, ANOVA, COEFF, and OUTS below. These statistics are shown in Figures 19.3b, 19.10, and 19.11a for the bivariate equation, and in Figures 19.36a and 19.36b for the multivariate equation. You can specify exactly which statistics you want displayed by any of the following keywords on the STATISTICS subcommand.

DEFAULTS *R, ANOVA, COEFF, and OUTS.* These statistics are displayed when the STATISTICS subcommand is omitted or if no keywords are specified on the subcommand. If you specify statistics keywords on a STATISTICS subcommand, the default statistics will not appear unless you specify them explicitly, either individually or with the DEFAULTS keyword.

ALL *All statistics except F, LINE, and END.*

R *Multiple R. Displays multiple R, R^2, adjusted R^2, and the standard error. (See Figure 19.10.)*

ANOVA *Analysis of variance table.* Displays degrees of freedom, sums of squares, mean squares, F value for multiple R, and the observed significance level of F. (See Figure 19.11a.)

CHA *Change in R^2 between steps, F value for change in R^2, and significance of F.* (See Figure 19.41.)

BCOV *Variance-covariance matrix of regression coefficients.* Displays a matrix with covariances below the diagonal, correlations above the diagonal, and variances on the diagonal.

XTX *Swept correlation matrix.*

COLLIN *Collinearity diagnostics.* Includes the variance inflation factor (VIF), the eigenvalues of the scaled and uncentered cross-products matrix, condition indices, and variance-decomposition proportions (Belsley et al., 1980).

SELECTION *Aids to selecting set of regressors.* Includes Akaike information criterion (AIK), Amemiya's prediction criterion (PC), Mallow's conditional mean squared error of prediction criterion (Cp), and Schwarz Bayesian criterion (SBC) (Judge et al., 1980).

COEFF *Statistics for variables in the equation.* Displays regression coefficient B, standard error of B, standardized coefficient beta, t value for B, and two-tailed significance level of t. (See Figure 19.47a.)

OUTS *Statistics for variables not in the equation that have been named on the VARIABLES subcommand.* Statistics are beta if the variable were entered, t value for beta, significance level of t, partial correlation with the dependent variable controlling for variables in the equation, and minimum tolerance. (See Figure 19.42.)

ZPP *Zero-order, part, and partial correlation.* (See Figure 19.39.)

CI *Confidence intervals.* Displays the 95% confidence interval for the unstandardized regression coefficient. (See Figure 19.8.)

SES *Approximate standard error of the standardized regression coefficients.* (See Meyer and Younger, 1976.)

TOL	*Tolerance.* Displays tolerance and VIF for variables in the equation and, for variables not in the equation, the tolerance a variable would have if it were the only variable entered next. (See Figure 19.51.)
F	F *value for* B *and significance of* F. Displayed instead of *t* for COEFF and OUTS. (See, for example, Figures 19.46b, 19.46c, 19.47a, and 19.47b.)
LINE	*Summary line for each step in step methods.* Displays a single summary line for each step in BACKWARD, FORWARD, or STEPWISE methods and the default or requested statistics at the end of each method block (BACKWARD, FORWARD, STEPWISE, ENTER, REMOVE, or TEST).
HISTORY	*Step history.* Displays a summary report with a summary line for each method (ENTER, REMOVE, or TEST, if the equation changes) or step if the method entails steps (FORWARD, BACKWARD, or STEPWISE). If history is the only statistic requested, COEFF is displayed for the final equation. (See Figures 19.43 and 19.46a.)
END	*One summary line per step or method block.* Displays a summary line per step for BACKWARD, FORWARD, or STEPWISE, and one summary line per block for ENTER, REMOVE, or TEST, if the equation changes.

The STATISTICS subcommand must appear before the DEPENDENT subcommand that initiates the equation and remains in effect until overridden by another STATISTICS subcommand. For example, to produce the output in Figure 19.8, specify

```
REGRESSION VARIABLES=SALBEG SALNOW
  /STATISTICS=CI
  /DEPENDENT=SALNOW
  /METHOD=ENTER SALBEG.
```

19.62
CRITERIA Subcommand

You can control the statistical criteria by which REGRESSION chooses variables for entry into or removal from an equation with the CRITERIA subcommand. Place the CRITERIA subcommand after the VARIABLES subcommand and before the DEPENDENT subcommand. A CRITERIA subcommand affects any subsequent DEPENDENT and METHOD subcommands and remains in effect until overridden with another CRITERIA subcommand.

The CRITERIA keywords are

DEFAULTS	*PIN(0.05), POUT(0.10), and TOLERANCE(0.0001).* These are the defaults if no CRITERIA subcommand is specified. If criteria have been changed, DEFAULTS restores the default values.
PIN(value)	*Probability of* F-to-enter. The default value is 0.05.
POUT(value)	*Probability of* F-to-remove. The default value is 0.10.
FIN(value)	F-to-enter. The default value is 3.84. FIN overrides the default PIN criteria. If both FIN and PIN are specified on the same CRITERIA subcommand, only the last one specified will be in effect.
FOUT(value)	F-to-remove. The default value is 2.71. FOUT overrides the default POUT criteria. If both FOUT and POUT are specified on the same CRITERIA subcommand, only the last one specified will be in effect.
TOLERANCE(value)	*Tolerance.* The default value is 0.0001. All variables must pass both tolerance and minimum tolerance tests before entering the equation. The minimum tolerance is the smallest tolerance for that variable or any other variable in the equation if the variable is entered.

MAXSTEPS(n)	*Maximum number of steps.* For the STEPWISE method, the default is twice the number of independent variables. For the FORWARD and BACKWARD methods, the default maximum is the number of variables meeting the PIN and POUT or FIN and FOUT criteria. The MAXSTEPS value applies to the total model. The default value for the total model is the sum of the maximum number of steps over each method in the model.
CIN (value)	*Reset the value of the percent for confidence intervals.* The default is 95%. This sets the percent interval used in the computation of the temporary variables MCIN and ICIN.

For example, to change stepwise entry and removal criteria to FIN and FOUT and use their default values of 3.84 and 2.71, respectively, specify

```
REGRESSION VARIABLES=LOGBEG EDLEVEL SEX WORK MINORITY AGE
  /CRITERIA=FIN,FOUT
  /DEPENDENT=LOGBEG
  /METHOD=STEPWISE.
```

19.63
ORIGIN Subcommand

The regression model contains a constant term. You can use the ORIGIN subcommand to suppress this term and obtain regression through the origin. The NOORIGIN subcommand, which is the default, requests that equations include a constant term.

Place the ORIGIN or NOORIGIN subcommand between the VARIABLES subcommand and the DEPENDENT subcommand for the equation. For example,

```
REGRESSION VARIABLES=SALBEG SALNOW,EDLEVEL
  /DEPENDENT=SALNOW
  /METHOD=ENTER SALBEG
  /ORIGIN
  /DEPENDENT=SALBEG
  /METHOD=ENTER EDLEVEL.
```

requests two equations, the first with a constant term (the default) and the second with regression through the origin.

There are no specifications for the ORIGIN and NOORIGIN subcommands. Once specified, the ORIGIN subcommand remains in effect until NOORIGIN is requested.

19.64
SELECT Subcommand

Use the SELECT subcommand to select a subset of cases for computing the regression equation. Only selected cases contribute to the correlation coefficients and to the regression equation. Residuals and predicted values are calculated and reported separately for both selected and unselected cases. The SELECT subcommand can precede or immediately follow the VARIABLES subcommand and is in effect for the entire REGRESSION procedure. The form of the SELECT subcommand is:

/SELECT= varname relation value

The *relation* can be EQ, NE, LT, LE, GT, or GE.

For example, to generate separate residuals histograms for males and females based on the equation developed for males alone (SEX=0), as shown in Figure 19.55, specify:

```
REGRESSION SELECT SEX EQ 0
  /VARIABLES=LOGBEG EDLEVEL SEX WORK MINORITY AGE
  /DEPENDENT=LOGBEG
  /METHOD=STEPWISE
  /RESIDUALS=HISTOGRAM.
```

19.65
MISSING Subcommand

Use the MISSING subcommand to specify the treatment of cases with missing values. If the MISSING subcommand is omitted, a case with user- or system-missing values for any variable named on the VARIABLES subcommand is excluded from the computation of the correlation matrix on which all analyses are based. The MISSING subcommand can precede or immediately follow the VARIABLES subcommand and is in effect for the entire REGRESSION procedure.

The available keywords are:

LISTWISE
Delete cases with missing values listwise. Only cases with valid values for all variables listed on the VARIABLES subcommand are included in analyses. If INCLUDE is also specified, only cases with system-missing values are deleted listwise. LISTWISE is the default.

PAIRWISE
Delete cases with missing values pairwise. Cases with complete data on the pair of variables being correlated are used to compute the correlation coefficient. If INCLUDE is also specified, only cases with system-missing values are deleted pairwise.

MEANSUBSTITUTION
Replace missing values with the variable mean. All cases are used for computations, with the mean of a variable substituted for missing observations. If INCLUDE is also specified, user-missing values are included in the computation of the means and only system-missing values are substituted.

INCLUDE
Include all cases with user-missing values. Only cases with system-missing values are excluded.

If you specify any combination of LISTWISE, PAIRWISE, and MEANSUBSTITUTION on the same MISSING subcommand, only the last one specified will be in effect. If INCLUDE is also specified, it will also be in effect.

19.66
DESCRIPTIVES Subcommand

You can request a variety of descriptive statistics with the DESCRIPTIVES subcommand. These statistics are displayed for all variables specified on the VARIABLES subcommand, regardless of which variables you specify for computations. Descriptive statistics are based on all valid cases for each variable if you have specified PAIRWISE or MEANSUB on the MISSING subcommand. Otherwise, only cases that are included in the computation of the correlation matrix are used. If you specify the DESCRIPTIVES subcommand without any keywords, the statistics listed for keyword DEFAULTS are displayed. If you name any statistics on DESCRIPTIVES, only those explicitly requested are displayed.

The following descriptive statistics are available:

DEFAULTS
MEAN, STDDEV, and CORR. This is the default if DESCRIPTIVES is specified without any keywords.

MEAN
Variable means.

STDDEV
Variable standard deviations.

VARIANCE
Variable variances.

CORR
Correlation matrix.

SIG
One-tailed significance levels for the correlation coefficients.

BADCORR
Correlation matrix only if some coefficients cannot be computed.

COV
Covariance matrix.

XPROD
Cross-product deviations from the mean.

N
Number of cases used to compute the correlation coefficients.

ALL
All descriptive statistics.

For example, to produce the correlation matrix shown in Figure 19.34, specify:

```
REGRESSION DESCRIPTIVES=CORR
  /VARIABLES=LOGBEG EDLEVEL SEX WORK MINORITY AGE
  /DEPENDENT=LOGBEG
  /METHOD=ENTER EDLEVEL TO AGE.
```

19.67
Analyzing Residuals

Once you have built an equation, REGRESSION can calculate 21 temporary variables containing several types of residuals, predicted values, and related measures. You can use these variables to detect outliers and influential data points and to examine the regression assumptions described in Sections 19.17 through 19.22.

The following temporary variables are available for the analysis of residuals:

PRED	*Unstandardized predicted values.*
RESID	*Unstandardized residuals.*
DRESID	*Deleted residuals.*
ADJPRED	*Adjusted predicted values.*
ZPRED	*Standardized predicted values.*
ZRESID	*Standardized residuals.*
SRESID	*Studentized residuals.*
SDRESID	*Studentized deleted residuals.* (See Hoaglin & Welsch, 1978.)
SEPRED	*Standard errors of the predicted values.*
MAHAL	*Mahalanobis' distances.*
COOK	*Cook's distances.* (See Cook, 1977.)
LEVER	*Centered leverage values.* (See Velleman & Welsch, 1981.)
DFBETA	*DFBETA.* The change in the regression coefficient that results from the deletion of the *i*th case. A DFBETA value is computed for each case for each regression coefficient generated in a model.
SDBETA	*Standardized DFBETA.* An SDBETA value is computed for each case for each regression coefficient generated in a model. (See Belsley et al., 1980.)
DFFIT	*DFFIT.* DFFIT is the change in the predicted value when the *i*th case is deleted. (See Belsley et al., 1980.)
SDFIT	*Standardized DFFIT.* (See Belsley et al., 1980.)
COVRATIO	*COVRATIO.* Ratio of the determinant of the covariance matrix with the *i*th case deleted to the determinant of the covariance matrix with all cases included. (See Belsley et al., 1980.)
MCIN	*Lower and upper bounds for the prediction interval of the mean predicted response.* A lower bound LMCIN and an upper bound UMCIN are generated. The default confidence interval is 95%. The interval may be reset with the CIN subcommand. (See Dillon & Goldstein, 1984.)
ICIN	*Lower and upper bounds for the prediction interval for a single observation.* (See Dillon & Goldstein, 1978.) A lowerbound LICIN and an upperbound UICIN are generated. The default confidence interval is 95%. The interval may be reset with the CIN subcommand.

Residuals analysis is specified with four subcommands: RESIDUALS, CASE-WISE, PARTIALPLOT, and SCATTERPLOT. You can specify these subcommands in any order, but you cannot specify more than one of each per equation, and they must immediately follow the last METHOD subcommand that completes an equation. The residuals subcommands affect only the equation they follow. Requesting any residuals analysis always produces descriptive statistics on at least four of the temporary variables (PRED, ZPRED, RESID, and ZRESID).

All variables are standardized before plotting. If an unstandardized version of a variable is requested, the standardized version is plotted.

19.68
RESIDUALS Subcommand

Use the RESIDUALS subcommand to obtain the statistics and plots listed below. Specifying the RESIDUALS subcommand without any specifications produces the display described for keyword DEFAULTS. If any keywords are specified on RESIDUALS, *only* the displays for those keywords are produced.

DEFAULT
HISTOGRAM(ZRESID), NORMPROB(ZRESID), and OUTLIERS(ZRESID) plots, SIZE(LARGE), and DURBIN. These are produced if RESIDUALS is specified without any specifications.

HISTOGRAM(tempvars)
Histogram of temporary variables named. The default temporary variable is ZRESID. Other variables that can be plotted are PRED, RESID, ZPRED, DRESID, ADJPRED, SRESID, and SDRESID. (See Figure 19.22a.) PRED and RESID are standardized in the output.

NORMPROB(tempvars)
Normal probability $(P - P)$ *plot.* The default variable is ZRESID. Other variables that can be plotted are PRED, RESID, ZPRED, DRESID, ADJPRED, SRESID, and SDRESID. (See Figure 19.22b.) PRED and RESID are standardized in the output.

SIZE(plotsize)
Plot sizes. The default is LARGE if the display width is at least 120 and the page length is at least 55.

OUTLIERS(tempvars)
The ten most extreme values for the temporary variables named. The default temporary variable is ZRESID. Other variables can be RESID, DRESID, SRESID, SDRESID, MAHAL, and COOK. (See Figure 19.24.)

DURBIN
Durbin-Watson test statistic. (See Section 19.21.)

ID(varname)
Identification labels for casewise and outlier plots. Cases are labeled with values of the variable named after the ID keyword. By default, the plots are labeled with the sequential case number. ID also labels the CASEWISE list of cases. (See Figures 19.23 and 19.24.)

POOLED
Pooled plots and statistics when the SELECT subcommand is in effect. All cases in the active system file are used. The default is separate reporting of residuals statistics and plots for selected and unselected cases.

For example, to produce the output shown in Figures 19.22a, 19.22b, and 19.24, specify:

```
REGRESSION VARIABLES=SALBEG SALNOW
  /DEPENDENT=SALNOW
  /METHOD=ENTER SALBEG
  /RESIDUALS=HISTOGRAM(SRESID)  NORMPROB
   OUTLIERS(MAHAL)  ID(SEXRACE)  SIZE(SMALL).
```

19.69
CASEWISE Subcommand

You can display a casewise plot of one of the temporary variables accompanied by a listing of the values of the dependent and the temporary variables. The plot can be requested for all cases or limited to outliers. Specifying the CASEWISE subcommand without keywords produces the output listed for DEFAULTS.

The following can be specified on the CASEWISE subcommand:

DEFAULTS
OUTLIERS(3), PLOT(ZRESID), DEPENDENT, PRED, and RESID. This is the default if CASEWISE is specified without any keywords.

OUTLIERS(value)
Limit plot to cases with a standardized absolute value of the plotted variable greater than the specified value. The default value is 3. (See Figure 19.23.)

ALL
Include all cases in the casewise plot. The plot includes all cases, including outliers. The keyword OUTLIERS is ignored when ALL is specified.

PLOT(tempvar)   *Plot the values of the temporary variable named.* The default variable is ZRESID. The other variables that can be plotted are RESID, DRESID, SRESID, and SDRESID. (See Figure 19.23.)

varlist   *List values of the DEPENDENT and temporary variables named.* Any temporary variable can be listed. The defaults are DEPENDENT (the dependent variable), PRED, and RESID. (See Figures 19.16 and 19.23.)

For example, to produce the casewise plot shown in Figure 19.16, specify:

```
REGRESSION VARIABLES=SALBEG SALNOW
   /DEPENDENT=SALNOW
   /METHOD=ENTER SALBEG
   /RESIDUALS=ID(SEXRACE)
   /CASEWISE=ALL DEPENDENT PRED RESID SEPRED.
```

To plot outliers whose absolute values are equal to or greater than 3 based on ZRESID, you need only specify the CASEWISE subcommand. To base the plot on Studentized residuals and label it with an ID variable, as shown in Figure 19.23, specify:

```
REGRESSION VARIABLES=SALBEG SALNOW
   /DEPENDENT=SALNOW
   /METHOD=ENTER SALBEG
   /RESIDUALS=ID(SEXRACE)
   /CASEWISE=PLOT(SRESID).
```

If you request more variables than will fit on the page width set either with the SET WIDTH command or the WIDTH subcommand in REGRESSION, your output will be truncated (see Section 19.75).

**19.70
SCATTERPLOT Subcommand**

Use the SCATTERPLOT subcommand to generate scatterplots for the variables in the equation. You must name at least one pair of variables on the SCATTERPLOT subcommand, and you must precede temporary variable names with an asterisk. You can also specify the SIZE keyword to control the size of the plots. All scatterplots are standardized.

The specifications for SCATTERPLOT are:

(varname,varname)   *The pair of variables to be plotted.* Available variables are PRED, RESID, ZPRED, ZRESID, DRESID, ADJPRED, SRESID, SDRESID, and any variable named on the VARIABLES subcommand. Temporary variables should be preceded by an asterisk on this subcommand.

SIZE(plotsize)   *Plot sizes.* The plot size can be SMALL or LARGE. The default is SMALL.

The first variable named inside the parentheses is plotted on the vertical (Y) axis, and the second is plotted on the horizontal (X) axis. For example, to generate the scatterplot shown in Figure 19.20, specify:

```
REGRESSION VARIABLES=SALBEG SALNOW
   /DEPENDENT=SALNOW
   /METHOD=ENTER SALBEG
   /SCATTERPLOT=(*SRESID,*PRED).
```

To produce a scatterplot for SRESID and PRED based on the logarithmic transformation of both the dependent and independent variables, as shown in Figure 19.30a, use the SCATTERPLOT subcommand above along with the following transformation commands:

```
COMPUTE LOGBEG=LG10(SALBEG).
COMPUTE LOGNOW=LG10(SALNOW).
REGRESSION VARIABLES=LOGBEG,LOGNOW
   /DEPENDENT=LOGNOW
   /METHOD=ENTER LOGBEG
   /SCATTERPLOT=(*SRESID,*PRED).
```

To produce more than one scatterplot, simply add pairs of variable names in parentheses, as in

```
/SCATTERPLOT=(*SRESID,*PRED) (SALBEG,*PRED)
```

19.71
PARTIALPLOT Subcommand

Use the PARTIALPLOT subcommand to generate partial residual plots. Partial residual plots are scatterplots of the residuals of the dependent variable and an independent variable when both variables are regressed on the rest of the independent variables.

If no variable list is given on the PARTIALPLOT subcommand, a partial residual plot is produced for every independent variable in the equation. Plots are displayed in descending order of the standard errors of the regression coefficients. All plots are standardized.

The specifications on the PARTIALPLOT subcommand are:

varlist *Independent variables for partial residual plot.* At least two independent variables must be in the equation (determined by the METHOD subcommand) for a partial residual plot to be produced. You can specify the keyword ALL to obtain the default plots for every independent variable in the equation.

SIZE(plotsize) *Plot sizes.* The plot size can be specified as SMALL or LARGE. The default plot size is SMALL.

For example, the following commands produced Figure 19.49a:

```
COMPUTE LOGBEG=LG10(SALBEG).
REGRESSION VARIABLES=LOGBEG SEX MINORITY EDLEVEL WORK
 /DEPENDENT=LOGBEG /METHOD=STEPWISE
 /PARTIALPLOT=EDLEVEL.
```

19.72
SAVE Subcommand

Use the SAVE subcommand to save any or all of the 12 temporary variables described in Section 19.67. The format is the name of the temporary variable followed by an optional new variable name in parentheses, as in:

```
GET FILE=BANK.
REGRESSION VARIABLES=SALBEG, SALNOW
 /DEPENDENT=SALNOW
 /METHOD=ENTER SALBEG
 /SAVE=SEPRED(SE).
PLOT CUTPOINTS=EVERY(20) /SYMBOLS='*'
 /PLOT=SE WITH SALBEG.
```

This example saves the standard errors of the predicted values with variable name SE. Then the PLOT procedure is used to plot the standard errors against the values of the independent variable SALBEG. Figure 19.14a shows the plot.

If you don't specify a new variable name, SPSS generates a new variable name by default.

If you specify DFBETA or SDBETA, the number of new variables saved is equal to the total number of variables in the equation, including the constant. For example, the command

```
REGRESSION DEPENDENT=SALBEG
 /METHOD=ENTER AGE SEX
 /SAVE=DFBETA(DFBVAR).
```

will create and save three new variables with the names DFBVAR0, DFBVAR1, and DFBVAR2.

You can use the keyword FITS to automatically save the temporary variables DFFIT, SDFIT, DFBETA, SDBETA, and COVRATIO, as in:

```
/SAVE=FITS.
```

If you specify FITS, you cannot specify new variable names. SPSS automatically generates new variable names.

19.73
REGWGT Subcommand

The REGWGT subcommand specifies a variable for estimating weighted least-squares models. The only specification on REGWGT is the name of the single variable containing the weights, as in

```
REGRESSION VARIABLES=IQ TO ACHIEVE /REGWGT=WGT1
    /DEPENDENT=VARY /METHOD=ENTER /SAVE=PRED(P) RESID(R).
```

REGWGT remains in effect for all analyses specified on the REGRESSION command. If you specify more than one REGWGT subcommand, only the last one specified will be in effect.

19.74
MATRIX Subcommand

Procedure REGRESSION can read and write matrix materials, which can be processed more quickly than cases. When MATRIX is used, it must be the first subcommand specified. Use the following keywords to specify matrix input and output:

OUT *Write matrix materials.* After OUT, specify in parentheses either a name for the matrix file or an asterisk to replace the active system file with the matrix. The matrix file contains the correlation coefficients as well as the mean, standard deviation, and number of cases used to compute each coefficient.

IN *Read matrix materials.* After IN, specify in parentheses either the name of the matrix file to read or an asterisk to read the matrix materials from the active system file.

For example, the command

```
REGRESSION MATRIX IN(CORMTRX)
    /VARIABLES=SALBEG SALNOW
    /DEPENDENT=SALNOW
    /METHOD=ENTER SALBEG.
```

uses the matrix data file REGMTRX to produce the regression equation.

If you are reading a matrix from the active system file with the specification

```
REGRESSION MATRIX IN (*)
```

you cannot use the RESIDUALS, CASEWISE, SCATTERPLOT, PARTIALPLOT, or SAVE subcommands. See the *SPSS Reference Guide* for complete instructions on using matrix materials.

19.75
WIDTH Subcommand

You can use the WIDTH subcommand to control the width of the display produced by the REGRESSION procedure. The default is the width specified on the SET command. The WIDTH subcommand in REGRESSION overrides the width specified on SET.

You can use the WIDTH subcommand to change the appearance of your output. For example, in Figure 19.41 statistics for variables in the equation and variables not in the equation are displayed side by side. In Figure 19.46b, the command

```
REGRESSION WIDTH=80
    /VARIABLES=LOGBEG EDLEVEL SEX WORK MINORITY AGE
    /STATISTICS=F /DEPENDENT=LOGBEG /METHOD=FORWARD.
```

displays the statistics for variables not in the equation below the statistics for variables in the equation.

A smaller page width limits the number of statistics that can be displayed in a summary line and may also cause casewise output to be truncated (see Section 19.69). Specifying a smaller page width may also reduce the size of scatterplots and normal-probability plots in the residuals output.

Contents _____

20 Partial Correlation Analysis: Procedure PARTIAL CORR

Whenever you examine the relationship between two variables, you must be concerned with the effects of other variables on the relationship of interest. For example, if you are studying the relationship between education and income, you must worry about controlling for the effects of age and work experience. It may be that a small observed relationship between education and income is due to younger people being more highly educated but less experienced in the work force. If you control for job experience and age, the relationship between education and income may appear stronger.

The partial correlation coefficient, a technique closely related to multiple linear regression, provides us with a single measure of linear association between two variables, while adjusting for the effects of one or more additional variables. Properly used, partial correlation is a useful technique for uncovering spurious relationships, identifying intervening variables, and detecting hidden relationships.

20.1 COMPUTING A PARTIAL CORRELATION COEFFICIENT

Consider the steps involved in computing a partial correlation coefficient between salary and education, controlling for age. First, two regression equations must be estimated. The first equation predicts salary from age, and the second predicts education from age. For each of the regression equations we compute the residuals for each case. The partial correlation coefficient between salary and education, controlling for age, is simply the usual Pearson correlation coefficient between the two sets of residuals.

In our example, the first regression equation removes the linear effects of age from salary. The residuals represent salary after the adjustment for age. The second regression equation removes the linear effects of age from education. The residuals represent education after the adjustment for age. The partial correlation coefficient estimates the linear association between the two variables, after the effects of age are removed.

Since we used linear regression analysis to control for the age variable, we had to make the assumption that the relationships of interest are linear. If there is reason to suspect that the variables are related in a nonlinear way, the partial correlation coefficient is not an appropriate statistical technique to use.

20.2 The Order of the Coefficient

In the previous example, we controlled for the effect of only one variable, age. However, partial correlation analysis is not limited to a single control variable. The same procedure can be applied to several control variables.

The number of control variables determines the order of the partial correlation coefficient. If there is one control variable, the partial correlation coefficient is a first-order partial. If there are five control variables, it is a fifth-order partial. Sometimes the ordinary correlation coefficient is called a zero-order correlation since there are no control variables.

(In fact it is not necessary to keep computing regression equations since partial correlation coefficients of a particular order can be computed recursively from coefficients of a lower order.)

20.3
Tests of Statistical Significance

The assumption of multivariate normality is required to test the null hypothesis that the population partial coefficient is 0. The test statistic is

$$t = r \sqrt{\frac{N - \theta - 2}{1 - r^2}}$$

Equation 20.3

where θ is the order of the coefficient and r is the partial correlation coefficient. The degrees of freedom for t are $N-\theta-2$.

20.4
DETECTING SPURIOUS RELATIONSHIPS

Partial correlation analysis can be used to detect spurious correlations between two variables. A spurious correlation is one in which the correlation between two variables results solely from the fact that one of the variables is correlated with a third variable that is the true predictor.

Consider the following example described by Kendall and Stuart (1973). Figure 20.4a is the correlation matrix between four variables measured in 16 large cities: crime rate, percentage of foreign-born males, number of children under 5 per 1000 women between 15 and 44, and percentage of church membership.

Figure 20.4a   Zero-order correlation matrix

```
PARTIAL CORR VARIABLES=CRIME CHURCH BY PCTFRNM UNDER5 (1)
    /STATISTICS=CORR.
```

```
- - - - - - - - - - - - - -  P A R T I A L   C O R R E L A T I O N   C O E F F I C I E N T S  - - - - - - - - - - - - - -
   ZERO ORDER PARTIALS

                CRIME      CHURCH     PCTFRNM    UNDER5

   CRIME        1.0000     -.1400     -.3400     -.3100
               (    0)    (   14)    (   14)    (   14)
                P= .       P= .303    P= .099    P= .121

   CHURCH       -.1400     1.0000      .3300      .8500
               (   14)    (    0)    (   14)    (   14)
                P= .303    P= .       P= .106    P= .000

   PCTFRNM      -.3400      .3300     1.0000      .4400
               (   14)    (   14)    (    0)    (   14)
                P= .099    P= .106    P= .       P= .044

   UNDER5       -.3100      .8500      .4400     1.0000
               (   14)    (   14)    (   14)    (    0)
                P= .121    P= .000    P= .044    P= .

    (COEFFICIENT / (D.F.) / SIGNIFICANCE)      (" . " IS PRINTED IF A COEFFICIENT CANNOT BE COMPUTED)
```

You can see that the correlation coefficient between crime rate (CRIME) and church membership (CHURCH) is negative (-.14). The simplest conclusion is that church membership is a deterrent to crime. Although such a conclusion is no doubt comforting to theologians, let's examine the observed relationship further.

From Figure 20.4a you see that the crime rate is negatively correlated with the percentage of foreign-born males (PCTFRNM) and with the number of children per women (UNDER5). Both of these variables are positively correlated with church membership. That is, both foreigners and women with many children tend to be church members.

Let's see what happens to the relationship between crime and church membership when we control for the linear effects of being foreign born and having many children. Figure 20.4b shows the partial correlation coefficient between crime and church membership when the percentage of foreign-born males is held constant. Note that the correlation coefficient, -0.03, is now close to 0.

Figure 20.4b First-order partials, controlling for percentage of foreign born males

```
PARTIAL CORR VARIABLES=CRIME CHURCH BY PCTFRNM (1).
```

```
- - - - - - - - - - - -  P A R T I A L   C O R R E L A T I O N   C O E F F I C I E N T S  - - - - - - - - - - - - -
CONTROLLING FOR..    PCTFRNM


              CRIME      CHURCH
CRIME        1.0000      -.0313
            (     0)    (    13)
            P= .        P= .456

CHURCH       -.0313      1.0000
            (    13)    (     0)
            P= .456     P= .

(COEFFICIENT / (D.F.) / SIGNIFICANCE)      (" . " IS PRINTED IF A COEFFICIENT CANNOT BE COMPUTED)
```

Figure 20.4c First-order partials, controlling for number of children

```
PARTIAL CORR VARIABLES=CRIME CHURCH BY UNDER5 (1).
```

```
- - - - - - - - - - - -  P A R T I A L   C O R R E L A T I O N   C O E F F I C I E N T S  - - - - - - - - - - - - -
CONTROLLING FOR..    UNDER5

              CRIME      CHURCH
CRIME        1.0000       .2466
            (     0)    (    13)
            P= .        P= .188

CHURCH        .2466      1.0000
            (    13)    (     0)
            P= .188     P= .

(COEFFICIENT / (D.F.) / SIGNIFICANCE)      (" . " IS PRINTED IF A COEFFICIENT CANNOT BE COMPUTED)
```

Similarly, Figure 20.4c is the partial correlation coefficient between crime and church membership when the number of young children per woman is held constant. The partial correlation coefficient is now positive, 0.25. The second-order partial correlation coefficient controlling for both foreign-born males and number of children is shown in Figure 20.4d. Again, the relationship between church membership and crime is positive, 0.23.

Figure 20.4d   Second-order partial correlations

```
PARTIAL CORR VARIABLES=CRIME CHURCH BY PCTFRNM UNDER5 (2).
```

```
- - - - - - - - - - - - PARTIAL CORRELATION COEFFICIENTS - - - - - - - - - - - - -
CONTROLLING FOR..    PCTFRNM    UNDER5

                  CRIME     CHURCH
    CRIME        1.0000      .2321
                (    0)    (   12)
                 P= .       P= .212

    CHURCH        .2321     1.0000
                (   12)    (    0)
                 P= .212    P= .

   (COEFFICIENT / (D.F.) / SIGNIFICANCE)       (" . " IS PRINTED IF A COEFFICIENT CANNOT BE COMPUTED)
```

From examination of the partial coefficients it appears that the original negative relationship between church membership and crime may be due to the presence of law-abiding foreigners with large families. In 1935, when the study was done, foreigners were less likely to commit crimes and more likely to be church members. These relationships cause the overall coefficient between the two variables to be negative. However, when these two variables are controlled for, the relationship between church membership and crime changes drastically.

20.5 DETECTING HIDDEN RELATIONSHIPS

Theory or intuition sometimes suggests that there should be a relationship between two variables even though the data indicate no correlation. In this situation it is possible that one or more additional variables are suppressing the expected relationship. For example, it may be that A is not correlated with B because A is negatively related to C which is positively related to B.

For example, assume that a marketing research company wants to examine the relationship between the need for transmission rebuilding kits and the intent to purchase such a kit. Initial examination of the data finds almost no correlation (0.01) between the need for such a kit and the intent to buy. However, the data show a *negative* relationship (−0.5) between income and the need to buy, and a *positive* relationship (0.6) between income and intent to buy. If we control for the effect of income using a partial correlation coefficient, the first-order partial between need and intent, controlling for income, is 0.45. Thus, income hid the relationship between need and intent to buy.

20.6 INTERPRETING THE RESULTS OF PARTIAL CORRELATION ANALYSIS

Proper interpretation of partial correlation analysis requires knowledge about the way the variables may be related. You must know, for example, the nature of the relationship between need for a transmission and family income; that is, does income influence need, or need influence income? If you assume that need for a transmission influences family income, then need is specified as the control variable. One way of codifying the requisite assumptions in using partials in multivariate analysis is known as "path analysis" (see Wright, 1960, and Duncan, 1966).

20.7
RUNNING PROCEDURE PARTIAL CORR

Procedure PARTIAL CORR produces partial correlation coefficients that describe the relationship between two variables while adjusting for the effects of one or more additional variables. PARTIAL CORR first calculates a matrix of Pearson product-moment (zero-order) correlations and bases the partial correlations on this matrix. Alternatively, it can read the zero-order correlation matrix as input. Other procedures that produce zero-order correlation matrices that can be read by PARTIAL CORR include CORRELATIONS (Chapter 14), REGRESSION (Chapter 19), FACTOR (Chapter 21), and DISCRIMINANT (see the *SPSS Advanced Statistics User's Guide*). For more information on matrices, see the *SPSS Reference Guide*.

20.8
VARIABLES Subcommand

The VARIABLES subcommand is the only required subcommand for the PARTIAL CORR procedure. There are three required specifications on the VARIABLES subcommand:

- A *correlation list* of one or more pairs of variables for which partial correlations are computed. This list does *not* include the control variables.
- A *control list* of one or more variables that will be used as controls for the variables in the correlation list. Use the keyword BY to separate the control list from the correlation list.
- One or more *order values*, enclosed in parentheses, indicating the order of partials desired from the correlation and control list. The value(s) specified in parentheses should not exceed the number of variables on the control list.

For example, the command

```
PARTIAL CORR VARIABLES=CRIME CHURCH BY PCTFRNM (1).
```

produces a first-order partial correlation between CRIME and CHURCH, controlling for the effects of PCTFRNM. This command produces Figure 20.4b.

You can use the TO keyword on the correlation or control list to imply consecutive variables on the active system file.

20.9
Correlation List

The correlation list specifies pairs of variables to be correlated while controlling for the variable(s) in the control list. If you provide a simple list of variables, PARTIAL CORR computes the partial correlation of each variable with every other variable in the list, producing a square, symmetric matrix. Since the partial correlation coefficient is a symmetrical measure, the upper and lower triangles of the matrix are mirror images of each other.

You can request specific variable pairs by using the keyword WITH. Each variable specified before the keyword WITH is correlated with each variable specified after the keyword, and there are no redundant coefficients. The first variable list defines the rows of the matrix and the second list defines the columns. For example,

```
PARTIAL CORR VARIABLES=VAR1 VAR2 VAR3 WITH VAR4 VAR5 BY VAR6(1).
```

produces a 3 × 2 rectangular partial correlation matrix with no redundant coefficients.

20.10
Control List and Order Values

The control list names the variables to be used as controls for each pair of variables specified on the correlation list. You can specify up to 100 control variables. The control list is followed by the order values, enclosed in parentheses, that specify the orders of partials to be computed. You can specify up to 5 order values. The order values must be integers between 1 and the number of control variables.

The correlation between a pair of variables is referred to as a zero-order correlation; controlling for one variable produces a first-order partial correlation; controlling for two variables produces a second-order partial; and so on. The number of control variables determines the orders that can be requested, while the order value or values indicate the partial correlation matrix or matrices to be produced.

One partial will be produced for every unique combination of control variables that add up to the order value. For example, the command

```
PARTIAL CORR VARIABLES=CRIME CHURCH BY PCTFRNM UNDER5 (1).
```

produces two first-order correlation matrices: the partial correlation between CRIME and CHURCH, controlling for PCTFRNM, and the partial correlation between CRIME and CHURCH, controlling for UNDER5. The command

```
PARTIAL CORR VARIABLES=CRIME CHURCH BY PCTFRNM UNDER5 (2).
```

produces one second-order partial correlation between CRIME and CHURCH, controlling for both PCTFRNM and UNDER5. This command produces Figure 20.4d. The command

```
PARTIAL CORR VARIABLES=CRIME CHURCH BY PCTFRNM UNDER5 (1 2).
```

produces three partial correlation matrices: two first-order partials and one second-order partial.

20.11
Specifying Multiple Analyses

You can specify up to 25 partial correlation analyses on one PARTIAL CORR command using multiple VARIABLES subcommands, separated by slashes, as in:

```
PARTIAL CORR VARIABLES=CRIME CHURCH BY PCTFRNM UNDER5 (1 2)
/VARIABLES=CRIME PCTMALE BY PCTFRNM CHURCH UNDER5 (3).
```

You can name or imply up to 400 variables.

20.12
SIGNIFICANCE Subcommand

The optional SIGNIFICANCE subcommand determines whether the significance level is based on a one-tailed or two-tailed test. The available keywords are:

ONETAIL *One-tailed test of significance.* This is the default if you omit the SIGNIFICANCE subcommand.

TWOTAIL *Two-tailed test of significance.*

20.13
STATISTICS Subcommand

By default, PARTIAL CORR displays the matrix of partial correlation coefficients, degrees of freedom, and significance levels. You can obtain additional statistics with the STATISTICS subcommand.

The available keywords are:

CORR   *Zero-order correlations with degrees of freedom and significance level.*

DESCRIPTIVES *Mean, standard deviation, and number of nonmissing cases.* Descriptive statistics are not available with matrix input.

BADCORR   *Zero-order correlation coefficients if and only if any of the zero-order correlations cannot be computed.* Coefficients that cannot be computed are printed as a period (.).

ALL   *All additional statistics available with PARTIAL CORR.*

NONE   *No additional statistics.* This is the default if you omit the STATISTICS subcommand.

If you specify both CORR and BADCORR, CORR will be in effect, and the zero-order correlation matrix will be displayed. For example, the command

```
PARTIAL CORR VARIABLES=CRIME CHURCH BY PCTFRNM UNDER5 (1)
 /STATISTICS=CORR.
```

produces the zero-order correlation matrix in Figure 20.4a.

20.14
MISSING Subcommand

By default, cases are excluded from the analysis on a listwise basis. If a case has a missing value for any of the specified variables, it is not used in the computation of any of the partial correlation coefficients. If you specify multiple analysis lists with multiple VARIABLES subcommands, missing values are handled separately for each analysis list.

Use the keyword ANALYSIS on the MISSING subcommand to exclude cases with missing values on a pair-by-pair basis when the zero-order correlation matrix is computed. A case missing on one or both of a pair of variables is not used. Pairwise deletion has the advantage of using as much of the data as possible. However, there are two problems in using pairwise deletion. First, the number of cases differs across coefficients; second, the coefficients represent different populations since they are based on different cases (with some overlap). When pairwise deletion is in effect, the degrees of freedom for a particular partial coefficient are based on the smallest number of cases used in the calculation of any of the zero-order correlations.

You can specify one of the following two keywords:

LISTWISE *Exclude missing values listwise.* Cases missing on any of the variables listed, including the set of control variables, are not used in the calculation of zero-order correlation coefficients. This is the default.

ANALYSIS *Exclude cases with missing values on a pair-by-pair basis.* Cases missing on one or both of a pair of variables are not used in the calculation of zero-order correlation coefficients.

Additionally, you can also specify one of the following two keywords:

EXCLUDE *Exclude cases with user-missing values.* Cases with user-missing values are excluded from the analysis. This is the default.

INCLUDE *Include cases with user-missing values.* Cases with user-missing values are included in the analysis.

By default, SPSS assumes MISSING=LISTWISE EXCLUDE.

20.15
FORMAT Subcommand

By default, the partial correlation matrix produced by PARTIAL CORR requires four lines per coefficient, one line for each of the following: the partial correlation coefficient, the degrees of freedom, the significance level, and a blank line between coefficients. Use the FORMAT subcommand to change the matrix to a condensed format or to display coefficients in serial form instead of matrix form.

Specify one of the following keywords after the FORMAT subcommand:

MATRIX *Display the coefficients, degrees of freedom, and significance level in matrix format.* This is the default.

CONDENSED *Suppress the display of the degrees of freedom and significance level.* A single asterisk after the coefficient indicates significance at the 0.01 level, and two asterisks indicate significance at the 0.001 level.

SERIAL *Display only the nonredundant coefficients in serial string format.* Degrees of freedom and significance levels are also displayed.

20.16
MATRIX Subcommand

Procedure PARTIAL CORR can read and write matrix materials, which can be processed more quickly than individual cases. Use the following keywords to specify matrix input and output:

OUT *Write matrix materials.* After the keyword OUT, specify in parentheses either a name for the matrix system file or an asterisk (*) to replace the active system file. The matrix file contains the correlation coefficients, as well as the mean, standard deviation, and number of cases used to compute each coefficient.

IN *Read matrix materials.* After IN, specify in parentheses either the name of the matrix system file to read or an asterisk (*) to read matrix materials from the active system file.

For example, the command

```
PARTIAL CORR MATRIX=IN(CORMTRX)
 /VARIABLES=CRIME CHURCH BY PCTFRNM UNDER5 (1 2).
```

uses the matrix system file CORMTRX to produce the partial correlation analysis.

The matrix system file used for the analysis must contain at least a correlation matrix and the number of cases used to compute the coefficients. For more information about matrix data files, see Chapter 2 or the *SPSS Reference Guide*.

Contents

21 Factor Analysis: Procedure FACTOR

What are creativity, love, and altruism? Unlike variables such as weight, blood pressure, and temperature, they cannot be measured on a scale, sphygmomanometer, or thermometer, in units of pounds, millimeters of mercury, or degrees Fahrenheit. Instead they can be thought of as unifying constructs or labels that characterize responses to related groups of variables. For example, answers of "strongly agree" to items such as he (or she) sends me flowers, listens to my problems, reads my manuscripts, laughs at my jokes, and gazes deeply into my soul, may lead you to conclude that the love "factor" is present. Thus, love is not a single measurable entity but a construct which is derived from measurement of other, directly observable variables. Identification of such underlying dimensions or factors greatly simplifies the description and understanding of complex phenomena, such as social interaction. For example, postulating the existence of something called "love" explains the observed correlations between the responses to numerous and varied situations.

Factor analysis is a statistical technique used to identify a relatively small number of factors that can be used to represent relationships among sets of many interrelated variables. For example, variables such as scores on a battery of aptitude tests may be expressed as a linear combination of factors that represent verbal skills, mathematical aptitude, and perceptual speed. Variables such as consumer ratings of products in a survey can be expressed as a function of factors such as product quality and utility. Factor analysis helps identify these underlying, not directly observable, constructs.

A huge number of variables can be used to describe a community—degree of industrialization, commercial activity, population, mobility, average family income, extent of home ownership, birth rate, and so forth. However, descriptions of what is meant by the term "community" might be greatly simplified if it were possible to identify underlying dimensions, or factors, of communities. This was attempted by Jonassen and Peres (1960), who examined 82 community variables from 88 counties in Ohio. This chapter uses a subset of their variables (shown in Table 21.0) to illustrate the basics of factor analysis.

Table 21.0 Community variables

POPSTABL	population stability
NEWSCIRC	weekly per capita local newspaper circulation
FEMEMPLD	percentage of females 14 years or older in labor force
FARMERS	percentage of farmers and farm managers in labor force
RETAILNG	per capita dollar retail sales
COMMERCL	total per capita commercial activity in dollars
INDUSTZN	industrialization index
HEALTH	health index
CHLDNEGL	total per capita expenditures on county aid to dependent children
COMMEFFC	index of the extent to which a community fosters a high standard of living
DWELGNEW	percentage of dwelling units built recently
MIGRNPOP	index measuring the extent of in- and out-migration
UNEMPLOY	unemployment index
MENTALIL	extent of mental illness

21.1
THE FACTOR
ANALYSIS MODEL

The basic assumption of factor analysis is that underlying dimensions, or factors, can be used to explain complex phenomena. Observed correlations between variables result from their sharing these factors. For example, correlations between test scores might be attributable to such shared factors as general intelligence, abstract reasoning skill, and reading comprehension. The correlations between the community variables might be due to factors like amount of urbanization, the socioeconomic level or welfare of the community, and the population stability. The goal of factor analysis is to identify the not-directly-observable factors based on a set of observable variables.

The mathematical model for factor analysis appears somewhat similar to a multiple regression equation. Each variable is expressed as a linear combination of factors which are not actually observed. For example, the industrialization index might be expressed as

$$\text{INDUSTZN} = a(\text{URBANISM}) + b(\text{WELFARE}) + c(\text{INFLUX}) \qquad \textbf{Equation 21.1a}$$
$$+ \ U_{\text{INDUSTZN}}$$

This equation differs from the usual multiple regression equation in that URBANISM, WELFARE, and INFLUX are not single independent variables. Instead, they are labels for groups of variables that characterize these concepts. These groups of variables constitute the factors. Usually, the factors useful for characterizing a set of variables are not known in advance but are determined by factor analysis.

URBANISM, WELFARE, and INFLUX are called *common factors,* since all variables are expressed as functions of them. The *U* in Equation 21.1a is called a *unique factor,* since it represents that part of the industrialization index that cannot be explained by the common factors. It is unique to the industrialization index variable.

In general, the model for the ith standardized variable is written as

$$X_i = A_{i1}F_1 + A_{i2}F_2 + \ldots + A_{ik}F_k + U_i \qquad \textbf{Equation 21.1b}$$

where the F's are the common factors, the U is the unique factor, and the A's are the constants used to combine the k factors. The unique factors are assumed to be uncorrelated with each other and with the common factors.

The factors are inferred from the observed variables and can be estimated as linear combinations of them. For example, the estimated urbanism factor is expressed as

URBANISM = C$_1$ POPSTABL + C$_2$ NEWSCIRC **Equation 21.1c**

    + . . . + C$_{14}$ MENTALIL

While it is possible that all of the variables contribute to the urbanism factor, we hope that a only subset of variables characterizes urbanism, as indicated by their large coefficients. The general expression for the estimate of the jth factor F_j is

$$F_j = \sum_{i=1}^{p} W_{ji}X_i = W_{j1}X_1 + W_{j2}X_2 + \ldots + W_{jp}X_p \qquad \textbf{Equation 21.1d}$$

The W_i's are known as factor score coefficients, and p is the number of variables.

21.2
Ingredients of a Good Factor Analysis Solution

Before examining the mechanics of a factor analysis solution, let's consider the characteristics of a successful factor analysis. One goal is to represent relationships among sets of variables parsimoniously. That is, we would like to explain the observed correlations using as few factors as possible. If many factors are needed, little simplification or summarization occurs. We would also like the factors to be meaningful. A good factor solution is both simple and interpretable. When factors can be interpreted, new insights are possible. For example, if liquor preferences can be explained by such factors as sweetness and regional tastes (Stoetzel, 1960), marketing strategies can reflect this.

21.3
STEPS IN A FACTOR ANALYSIS

Factor analysis usually proceeds in four steps.

- First, the correlation matrix for all variables is computed, as in Figure 21.4a. Variables that do not appear to be related to other variables can be identified from the matrix and associated statistics. The appropriateness of the factor model can also be evaluated. At this step you should also decide what to do with cases that have missing values for some of the variables.

- In the second step, factor extraction—the number of factors necessary to represent the data and the method of calculating them—must be determined. At this step, you also ascertain how well the chosen model fits the data.

- The third step, rotation, focuses on transforming the factors to make them more interpretable.

- At the fourth step, scores for each factor can be computed for each case. These scores can then be used in a variety of other analyses.

21.4
Examining the Correlation Matrix

The correlation matrix for the 14 community variables is shown in Figure 21.4a. Since one of the goals of factor analysis is to obtain "factors" that help explain these correlations, the variables must be related to each other for the factor model to be appropriate. If the correlations between variables are small, it is unlikely that they share common factors. Figure 21.4a shows that almost half the coefficients are greater than 0.3 in absolute value. All variables, except the extent of mental illness, have large correlations with at least one of the other variables in the set.

Figure 21.4a   Correlation matrix of 14 community variables

```
FACTOR VARIABLES=
 POPSTABL NEWSCIRC FEMEMPLD FARMERS RETAILNG COMMERCL INDUSTZN
 HEALTH CHLDNEGL COMMEFFC DWELGNEW MIGRNPOP UNEMPLOY MENTALIL
 /PRINT=CORRELATION KMO AIC.
```

CORRELATION MATRIX:

	POPSTABL	NEWSCIRC	FEMEMPLD	FARMERS	RETAILNG	COMMERCL	INDUSTZN	HEALTH	CHLDNEGL	COMMEFFC	DWELGNEW	MIGRNPOP
POPSTABL	1.00000											
NEWSCIRC	-.17500	1.00000										
FEMEMPLD	-.27600	.61600	1.00000									
FARMERS	.36900	-.62500	-.63700	1.00000								
RETAILNG	-.12700	.62400	.73600	-.51900	1.00000							
COMMERCL	-.06900	.65200	.58900	-.30600	.72700	1.00000						
INDUSTZN	-.10600	.71200	.74200	-.54500	.78500	.91100	1.00000					
HEALTH	-.14900	-.03000	.24100	-.06800	.10000	.12300	.12900	1.00000				
CHLDNEGL	-.03900	-.17100	-.58900	.25700	-.55700	-.35700	-.42400	-.40700	1.00000			
COMMEFFC	-.00500	.10000	.47100	-.21300	.45200	.28700	.35700	.73200	-.66000	1.00000		
DWELGNEW	-.67000	.18800	.41300	-.57900	.16500	.03000	.20300	.29000	-.13800	.31100	1.00000	
MIGRNPOP	-.47600	-.08600	.06400	-.19800	.00700	-.06800	-.02400	.08300	.14800	.06700	.50500	1.00000
UNEMPLOY	.13700	-.37300	-.68900	.45000	-.65000	-.42400	-.52800	-.34800	.73300	-.60100	-.26600	.18100
MENTALIL	.23700	.04600	-.23700	.12100	-.19000	-.05500	-.09500	-.27900	.24700	-.32400	-.26600	-.30700

	UNEMPLOY	MENTALIL
UNEMPLOY	1.00000	
MENTALIL	.21700	1.00000

Bartlett's test of sphericity can be used to test the hypothesis that the correlation matrix is an identity matrix. That is, all diagonal terms are 1 and all off-diagonal terms are 0. The test requires that the data be a sample from a multivariate normal population. From Figure 21.4b, the value of the test statistic for sphericity (based on a chi-square transformation of the determinant of the correlation matrix) is large and the associated significance level is small, so it appears unlikely that the population correlation matrix is an identity. If the hypothesis that the population correlation matrix is an identity cannot be rejected because the observed significance level is large, you should reconsider the use of the factor model.

Figure 21.4b   Test statistic for sphericity

```
FACTOR VARIABLES=POPSTABL TO MENTALIL
 /PRINT=CORRELATION KMO AIC.
```

```
KAISER-MEYER-OLKIN MEASURE OF SAMPLING ADEQUACY =   .76968

BARTLETT TEST OF SPHERICITY = 946.15313, SIGNIFICANCE =    .00000
```

Another indicator of the strength of the relationship among variables is the partial correlation coefficient. If variables share common factors, the partial correlation coefficients between pairs of variables should be small when the linear effects of the other variables are eliminated. The partial correlations are then estimates of the correlations between the unique factors and should be close to 0 when the factor analysis assumptions are met. (Recall that the unique factors are assumed to be uncorrelated with each other.)

The negative of the partial correlation coefficient is called the anti-image correlation. The matrix of anti-image correlations is shown in Figure 21.4c. If the proportion of large coefficients is high, you should reconsider the use of the factor model.

Figure 21.4c   Anti-image correlation matrix

```
FACTOR VARIABLES=POPSTABL TO MENTALIL
      /PRINT=CORRELATION  KMO  AIC.
```

```
ANTI-IMAGE CORRELATION MATRIX:


           POPSTABL  NEWSCIRC  FEMEMPLD   FARMERS  RETAILNG  COMMERCL  INDUSTZN    HEALTH  CHLDNEGL  COMMEFFC  DWELGNEW  MIGRNPOP

POPSTABL    .58174
NEWSCIRC    .01578    .82801
FEMEMPLD    .10076   -.24223    .90896
FARMERS     .03198    .43797   -.00260    .73927
RETAILNG    .14998   -.14295   -.12037    .16426    .86110
COMMERCL    .20138   -.27622    .20714   -.49344   -.19535    .68094
INDUSTZN   -.23815    .08231   -.32790    .41648   -.04602   -.85499    .75581
HEALTH      .26114   -.02839   -.02332    .05845    .38421   -.16150    .08627    .59124
CHLDNEGL    .10875   -.24685    .27281   -.03446    .13062    .07043   -.07979    .02899    .87023
COMMEFFC   -.39878    .05772    .03017   -.16386   -.33700    .09427   -.06742   -.70853    .19554    .68836
DWELGNEW    .55010    .04505   -.09493    .33479    .26678    .13831   -.13726    .07480   -.04008   -.30434    .70473
MIGRNPOP    .20693    .22883   -.06689    .11784   -.15886   -.07421    .06501    .07460   -.10809   -.14292   -.24074    .61759
UNEMPLOY   -.17774   -.05946    .18631   -.12699    .19591   -.01262   -.02503   -.02904   -.33523    .19240    .02181   -.38208
MENTALIL   -.08437   -.10058    .07770    .03053    .07842   -.02921   -.00056    .06821   -.04163    .04728   -.02505    .20487


           UNEMPLOY  MENTALIL

UNEMPLOY    .87230
MENTALIL   -.02708    .88390


MEASURES OF SAMPLING ADEQUACY (MSA) ARE PRINTED ON THE DIAGONAL.
```

The Kaiser-Meyer-Olkin measure of sampling adequacy is an index for comparing the magnitudes of the observed correlation coefficients to the magnitudes of the partial correlation coefficients. It is computed as

$$\text{KMO} = \frac{\sum_{i \neq j} \sum r_{ij}^2}{\sum_{i \neq j} \sum r_{ij}^2 + \sum_{i \neq j} \sum a_{ij}^2}$$

Equation 21.4a

where r_{ij} is the simple correlation coefficient between variables i and j, and a_{ij} is the partial correlation coefficient between variables i and j. If the sum of the squared partial correlation coefficients between all pairs of variables is small when compared to the sum of the squared correlation coefficients, the KMO measure is close to 1. Small values for the KMO measure indicate that a factor analysis of the variables may not be a good idea, since correlations between pairs of variables cannot be explained by the other variables. Kaiser (1974) characterizes measures in the 0.90's as marvelous, in the 0.80's as meritorious, in the 0.70's as middling, in the 0.60's as mediocre, in the 0.50's as miserable, and below 0.5 as unacceptable. The value of the overall KMO statistic for this example is shown in Figure 21.4b. Since it is close to 0.8, we can comfortably proceed with the factor analysis.

A measure of sampling adequacy can be computed for each individual variable in a similar manner. Instead of including all pairs of variables in the summations, only coefficients involving that variable are included. For the *i*th variable, the measure of sampling adequacy is

$$MSA_i = \frac{\sum_{j \neq i} r_{ij}^2}{\sum_{j \neq i} r_{ij}^2 + \sum_{j \neq i} a_{ij}^2}$$

Equation 21.4b

These measures of sampling adequacy are displayed on the diagonals of Figure 21.4c. Again, reasonably large values are needed for a good factor analysis. Thus, you might consider eliminating variables with small values for the measure of sampling adequacy.

The squared multiple correlation coefficient between a variable and all other variables is another indication of the strength of the linear association among the variables. These values are shown in the column labeled **COMMUNALITY** in Figure 21.9a. The extent of mental illness variable has a small multiple R^2, suggesting that it should be eliminated from the set of variables being analyzed. It will be kept in the analysis for illustrative purposes.

21.5 Factor Extraction

The goal of the factor extraction step is to determine the factors. In this example, we will obtain estimates of the initial factors from principal components analysis. Other methods for factor extraction are described in Section 21.10. In principal components analysis, linear combinations of the observed variables are formed. The first principal component is the combination that accounts for the largest amount of variance in the sample. The second principal component accounts for the next largest amount of variance and is uncorrelated with the first. Successive components explain progressively smaller portions of the total sample variance, and all are uncorrelated with each other.

It is possible to compute as many principal components as there are variables. If all principal components are used, each variable can be exactly represented by them, but nothing has been gained since there are as many factors (principal components) as variables. When all factors are included in the solution, all of the variance of each variable is accounted for, and there is no need for a unique factor in the model. The proportion of variance accounted for by the common factors, or the *communality* of a variable, is 1 for all the variables, as shown in Figure 21.5a. In general, principal components analysis is a separate technique from factor analysis. That is, it can be used whenever uncorrelated linear combinations of the observed variables are desired. All it does is transform a set of correlated variables to a set of uncorrelated variables (principal components).

To help us decide how many factors we need to represent the data, it is helpful to examine the percentage of total variance explained by each. The total variance is the sum of the variance of each variable. For simplicity, all variables and factors are expressed in standardized form, with a mean of 0 and a standard deviation of 1. Since there are 14 variables and each is standardized to have a variance of 1, the total variance is 14 in this example.

Figure 21.5a contains the initial statistics for each factor. The total variance explained by each factor is listed in the column labeled **EIGENVALUE.** The next column contains the percentage of the total variance attributable to each factor. For example, the linear combination formed by Factor 2 has a variance of 2.35, which is 16.8% of the total variance of 14. The last column, the cumulative percentage, indicates the percentage of variance attributable to that factor and those that precede it in the table. Note that the factors are arranged in descending order of variance explained. Note also that although variable names and factors are displayed on the same line, there is no correspondence between the lines in the two halves of the table. The first two columns provide information about the individual variables, while the last four columns describe the factors.

Figure 21.5a   Initial statistics

FACTOR VARIABLES=POPSTABL TO MENTALIL.

```
EXTRACTION  1  FOR ANALYSIS  1, PRINCIPAL-COMPONENTS ANALYSIS (PC)


INITIAL STATISTICS:


VARIABLE      COMMUNALITY  *  FACTOR   EIGENVALUE   PCT OF VAR   CUM PCT
                           *
POPSTABL       1.00000     *    1       5.70658       40.8        40.8
NEWSCIRC       1.00000     *    2       2.35543       16.8        57.6
FEMEMPLD       1.00000     *    3       2.00926       14.4        71.9
FARMERS        1.00000     *    4        .89745        6.4        78.3
RETAILNG       1.00000     *    5        .75847        5.4        83.8
COMMERCL       1.00000     *    6        .53520        3.8        87.6
INDUSTZN       1.00000     *    7        .50886        3.6        91.2
HEALTH         1.00000     *    8        .27607        2.0        93.2
CHLDNEGL       1.00000     *    9        .24511        1.8        94.9
COMMEFFC       1.00000     *   10        .20505        1.5        96.4
DWELGNEW       1.00000     *   11        .19123        1.4        97.8
MIGRNPOP       1.00000     *   12        .16982        1.2        99.0
UNEMPLOY       1.00000     *   13        .10202         .7        99.7
MENTALIL       1.00000     *   14        .03946         .3       100.0
```

Figure 21.5a shows that almost 72% of the total variance is attributable to the first three factors. The remaining eleven factors together account for only 28.1% of the variance. Thus, a model with three factors may be adequate to represent the data.

Several procedures have been proposed for determining the number of factors to use in a model. One criterion suggests that only factors that account for variances greater than 1 (the eigenvalue is greater than 1) should be included. Factors with a variance less than 1 are no better than a single variable, since each variable has a variance of 1. Although this is the default criterion in FACTOR, it is not always a good solution (see Tucker, Koopman, & Linn, 1969).

Figure 21.5b is a plot of the total variance associated with each factor. Typically, the plot shows a distinct break between the steep slope of the large factors and the gradual trailing off of the rest of the factors. This gradual trailing off is called the *scree* (Cattell, 1966) because it resembles the rubble that forms at the foot of a mountain. Experimental evidence indicates that the scree begins at the kth factor, where k is the true number of factors. From the scree plot, it again appears that a three-factor model should be sufficient for the community example.

Figure 21.5b   Scree plot

```
FACTOR VARIABLES=POPSTABL TO MENTALIL
 /PLOT=EIGEN.
```

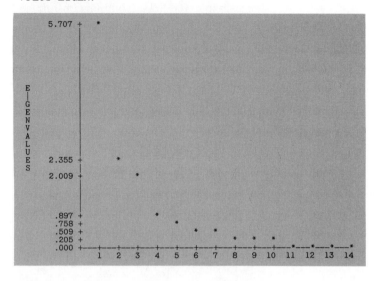

21.6
The Three Factors

Figure 21.6 contains the coefficients that relate the variables to the three factors. The figure shows that the industrialization index can be expressed as

$$\text{INDUSTZN} = 0.844F_1 + 0.300F_2 + 0.238F_3 \qquad \qquad \textbf{Equation 21.6a}$$

Similarly, the health index is

$$\text{HEALTH} = 0.383F_1 - 0.327F_2 - 0.635F_3 \qquad \qquad \textbf{Equation 21.6b}$$

Figure 21.6   Factor matrix

```
FACTOR VARIABLES=POPSTABL TO MENTALIL.
```

```
FACTOR MATRIX:

                 FACTOR 1      FACTOR 2      FACTOR 3

   POPSTABL      -.30247        .68597        -.36451
   NEWSCIRC       .67238        .28096         .49779
   FEMEMPLD       .89461        .01131         .08063
   FARMERS       -.68659        .20002        -.40450
   RETAILNG       .85141        .24264         .09351
   COMMERCL       .72503        .39394         .19896
   INDUSTZN       .84436        .29956         .23775
   HEALTH         .38347       -.32718        -.63474
   CHLDNEGL      -.67430       -.12139         .52896
   COMMEFFC       .63205       -.15540        -.64221
   DWELGNEW       .45886       -.73940         .18706
   MIGRNPOP       .07894       -.74371         .24335
   UNEMPLOY      -.78714       -.09777         .30110
   MENTALIL      -.30025        .45463         .27134
```

Each row of Figure 21.6 contains the coefficients used to express a standardized variable in terms of the factors. These coefficients are called *factor loadings*, since they indicate how much weight is assigned to each factor. Factors with large coefficients (in absolute value) for a variable are closely related to the variable. For example, Factor 1 is the factor with the largest loading for the INDUSTZN variable. The matrix of factor loadings is called the *factor pattern* matrix.

When the estimated factors are uncorrelated with each other (orthogonal), the factor loadings are also the correlations between the factors and the variables. Thus, the correlation between the health index and Factor 1 is 0.383. Similarly, there is a slightly smaller correlation (-0.327) between the health index and Factor 2. The matrix of correlations between variables and factors is called the *factor structure* matrix. When the factors are orthogonal, the factor structure matrix and the factor pattern matrix are equivalent. As shown in Figure 21.6, such a matrix is labeled the factor matrix in SPSS output.

21.7
More on the Factor Matrix

There is yet another interpretation of the factor matrix in Figure 21.6. Whether the factors are orthogonal or not, the factor loadings are the standardized regression coefficients in the multiple regression equation with the original variable as the dependent variable and the factors as the independent variables. If the factors are uncorrelated, the values of the coefficients are not dependent on each other. They represent the unique contribution of each factor, and are the correlations between the factors and the variable.

To judge how well the three-factor model describes the original variables, we can compute the proportion of the variance of each variable explained by the three-factor model. Since the factors are uncorrelated, the total proportion of variance explained is just the sum of the variance proportions explained by each factor.

Consider, for example, the health index. Factor 1 accounts for 14.7% of the variance for this variable. This is obtained by squaring the correlation coefficient for Factor 1 and HEALTH (0.383). Similarly, Factor 3 explains 40.3% (-0.635^2) of the variance. The total percentage of variance in the health index accounted for by this three-factor model is therefore 65.7% (14.7 + 10.7 + 40.3). The proportion of variance explained by the common factors is called the *communality* of the variable.

The communalities for the variables are shown in Figure 21.7, together with the percentage of variance accounted for by each of the retained factors. This table is labeled **FINAL STATISTICS,** since it shows the communalities and factor statistics after the desired number of factors has been extracted. When factors are estimated using the method of principal components, the factor statistics are the same in the tables labeled as initial and final. However, the communalities are different since all of the variances of the variables are not explained when only a subset of factors is retained.

Figure 21.7 Communality of variables

FACTOR VARIABLES=POPSTABL TO MENTALIL.

```
FINAL STATISTICS:

VARIABLE      COMMUNALITY  *  FACTOR   EIGENVALUE   PCT OF VAR   CUM PCT
                           *
POPSTABL         .69491    *    1       5.70658        40.8        40.8
NEWSCIRC         .77882    *    2       2.35543        16.8        57.6
FEMEMPLD         .80696    *    3       2.00926        14.4        71.9
FARMERS          .67503    *
RETAILNG         .79253    *
COMMERCL         .72044    *
INDUSTZN         .85921    *
HEALTH           .65699    *
CHLDNEGL         .74921    *
COMMEFFC         .83607    *
DWELGNEW         .79226    *
MIGRNPOP         .61855    *
UNEMPLOY         .71981    *
MENTALIL         .37047    *
```

Communalities can range from 0 to 1, with 0 indicating that the common factors explain none of the variance, and 1 indicating that all the variance is explained by the common factors. The variance that is not explained by the common factors is attributed to the unique factor and is called the *uniqueness* of the variable.

21.8
The Reproduced Correlation Matrix

One of the basic assumptions of factor analysis is that the observed correlation between variables is due to the sharing of common factors. Therefore, the estimated correlations between the factors and the variables can be used to estimate the correlations between the variables. In general, if factors are orthogonal, the estimated correlation coefficient for variables i and j is

$$r_{ij} = \sum_{f=1}^{k} r_{fi} r_{fj} = r_{1i} r_{1j} + r_{2i} r_{2j} + \ldots r_{ki} r_{kj}$$ **Equation 21.8a**

where k is the number of common factors, and r_{fi} is the correlation between the fth factor and the ith variable.

From Figure 21.6 and Equation 21.8a, the estimated correlation coefficient for HEALTH and COMMEFFC, based on the three-factor model, is

$$r_{8,10} = (0.38)(0.63) + (-0.33)(-0.16) + (-0.63)(-0.64) = 0.70.$$ **Equation 21.8b**

Figure 21.4a shows that the observed correlation coefficient between HEALTH and COMMEFFC is 0.73, so the diffeence between the observed correlation coefficient and that estimated from the model is about –0.03. This difference is called a residual.

The estimated correlation coefficients and the residuals are shown in Figure 21.8. The residuals are listed above the diagonal and the estimated correlation coefficients are below the diagonal. The values with asterisks (on the diagonal) are estimates of the communalities discussed in Section 21.7.

Figure 21.8 Estimated correlations and residuals

```
FACTOR VARIABLES=POPSTABL TO MENTALIL
      /PRINT=REPR.
```

```
REPRODUCED CORRELATION MATRIX:

                POPSTABL    NEWSCIRC    FEMEMPLD     FARMERS    RETAILNG    COMMERCL    INDUSTZN      HEALTH    CHLDNEGL

POPSTABL         .69491*      .01709      .01623     -.12332     -.00183     -.04741      .03056     -.03994      .03312
NEWSCIRC        -.19209      .77882*     -.02883     -.01820     -.06320     -.04521     -.05824      .12005      .05318
FEMEMPLD        -.29223      .64483      .80696*      .00758     -.03597     -.08012     -.03593     -.04718     -.02704
FARMERS          .49232     -.60680     -.64458      .67503*      .05486      .19348      .07098      .00398      .03227
RETAILNG        -.12517      .68720      .77197     -.57386      .79253*     -.00449      .13350      .10014     -.00290
COMMERCL        -.02159      .69721      .66912     -.49948      .73149      .72044*      .13350      .10014      .07447
INDUSTZN        -.13656      .77024      .77793     -.61598      .81382      .77750      .85921*      .65699*      .14761
HEALTH          -.10906     -.15005      .28818     -.07198      .18775      .02286      .07487      .65699*      .74921*
CHLDNEGL        -.07212     -.22418     -.56196      .22473     -.55410     -.43147     -.47996     -.55461      .74921*
COMMEFFC        -.06368      .06163      .51190     -.20527      .44037      .26927      .33444      .70086     -.74703
DWELGNEW        -.71418      .19390      .41722     -.53861      .22876      .07863      .21042      .29914     -.12070
MIGRNPOP        -.62274     -.03474      .08183     -.30139     -.09049     -.18732     -.09828      .11913      .16577
UNEMPLOY         .06126     -.40684     -.68101      .39909     -.66575     -.54931     -.62233     -.46098      .70191
MENTALIL         .30378      .06093     -.24158      .18733     -.11995      .01539     -.05282     -.43612      .29080


                COMMEFFC    DWELGNEW    MIGRNPOP    UNEMPLOY    MENTALIL

POPSTABL         .05868      .04418      .14674      .07574     -.06678
NEWSCIRC         .03837     -.00590     -.05126      .03384     -.01493
FEMEMPLD        -.04090     -.00422     -.01783     -.00799      .00458
FARMERS         -.00773     -.04039      .10339      .05091     -.06633
RETAILNG         .01163     -.06376      .09749      .01575     -.07005
COMMERCL         .01773     -.04863      .11932      .12531     -.07039
INDUSTZN         .02256     -.00742      .07428      .09433     -.04218
HEALTH           .03114     -.00914     -.03613      .11298      .15712
CHLDNEGL         .08703     -.01730     -.01777      .03109     -.04380
COMMEFFC         .83607*      .02621      .05782      .07469      .11068
DWELGNEW         .28479      .79226*     -.12664     -.03343      .15717
MIGRNPOP         .00918      .63164      .61855*      .09715     -.01121
UNEMPLOY        -.67569     -.23257      .08385      .71981*     -.05659
MENTALIL        -.43468     -.42317     -.29579      .27359      .37047*

THERE ARE   42 (46.0%) RESIDUALS (ABOVE DIAGONAL) THAT ARE > 0.05
```

Below the matrix is a message indicating how many residuals are greater than 0.05 in absolute value. In the community example, less than half (46%) are greater than 0.05 in absolute value. The magnitudes of the residuals indicate how well the fitted model reproduces the observed correlations. If the residuals are large, the model does not fit the data well and should probably be reconsidered.

21.9
Some Additional Considerations

If a method other than principal components analysis is used to extract the initial factors, there are differences in parts of the factor output. Consider, for example, Figure 21.9a, which contains the initial statistics obtained when the maximum-likelihood algorithm is used.

Figure 21.9a Maximum-likelihood extractions

```
FACTOR VARIABLES=POPSTABL TO MENTALIL
      /EXTRACTION=ML.
```

```
INITIAL STATISTICS:

VARIABLE    COMMUNALITY  *  FACTOR    EIGENVALUE   PCT OF VAR   CUM PCT
                         *
POPSTABL       .62385    *     1        5.70658       40.8        40.8
NEWSCIRC       .71096    *     2        2.35543       16.8        57.6
FEMEMPLD       .77447    *     3        2.00926       14.4        71.9
FARMERS        .74519    *     4         .89745        6.4        78.3
RETAILNG       .79259    *     5         .75847        5.4        83.8
COMMERCL       .90987    *     6         .53520        3.8        87.6
INDUSTZN       .92914    *     7         .50886        3.6        91.2
HEALTH         .66536    *     8         .27607        2.0        93.2
CHLDNEGL       .67987    *     9         .24511        1.8        94.9
COMMEFFC       .79852    *    10         .20505        1.5        96.4
DWELGNEW       .72576    *    11         .19123        1.4        97.8
MIGRNPOP       .50560    *    12         .16982        1.2        99.0
UNEMPLOY       .72549    *    13         .10202         .7        99.7
MENTALIL       .23825    *    14         .03946         .3       100.0
```

Regardless of the algorithm used, by default the number of factors to be retained is determined by the principal components solution because it is easily obtainable. Thus most of the output in Figure 21.9a is identical to that displayed in Figure 21.5a. The only exception is the column of communalities. In the principal components solution, all initial communalities are listed as 1's. In all other solutions, the initial estimate of the communality of a variable is the multiple R^2 from the regression equation that predicts that variable from all other variables. These initial communalities are used in the estimation algorithm.

When a method other than principal components analysis is used to estimate the final factor matrix, the percentage of variance explained by each final factor is usually different. Figure 21.9b contains the final statistics from a maximum-likelihood solution. The final three factors extracted explain only 63% of the total variance, as compared to 72% for the first three principal components. The first factor accounts for 35.5% of the total variance, as compared to 40.8% for the first principal component.

Figure 21.9b Maximum-likelihood final statistics

```
FACTOR VARIABLES=POPSTABL TO MENTALIL
  /EXTRACTION=ML.
```

```
FINAL STATISTICS:

VARIABLE     COMMUNALITY  *  FACTOR   EIGENVALUE   PCT OF VAR   CUM PCT
                          *
POPSTABL       .52806     *    1       4.96465        35.5        35.5
NEWSCIRC       .57439     *    2       2.17833        15.6        51.0
FEMEMPLD       .75057     *    3       1.67661        12.0        63.0
FARMERS        .56808     *
RETAILNG       .72089     *
COMMERCL       .87128     *
INDUSTZN       .96817     *
HEALTH         .33383     *
CHLDNEGL       .78341     *
COMMEFFC       .62762     *
DWELGNEW       .87445     *
MIGRNPOP       .35074     *
UNEMPLOY       .70833     *
MENTALIL       .15977     *
```

The proportion of the total variance explained by each factor can be calculated from the factor matrix. The proportion of the total variance explained by Factor 1 is calculated by summing the proportions of variance of each variable attributable to Factor 1. Figure 21.9c, the factor matrix for the maximum-likelihood solution, shows that Factor 1 accounts for -0.16^2 of the POPSTABL variance, 0.72^2 of the NEWSCIRC variance, 0.81^2 of the FEMEMPLD variance, and so on for the other variables. The total variance attributable to Factor 1 is therefore

Total variance   **Equation 21.9**
for Factor 1 $= (-0.16)^2 + 0.72^2 + 0.81^2 + (-0.59)^2$
$\qquad\qquad + 0.83^2 + 0.89^2 + 0.97^2 + 0.20^2 + (-0.52)^2 + 0.44^2 + 0.27^2$
$\qquad\qquad + (-0.00)^2 + (-0.62)^2 + (-0.15)^2 = 4.96$

This is the eigenvalue displayed for Factor 1 in Figure 21.9b.

Figure 21.9c Maximum-likelihood factor matrix

```
FACTOR VARIABLES=POPSTABL TO MENTALIL
  /EXTRACTION=ML.

FACTOR MATRIX:

                FACTOR  1     FACTOR  2     FACTOR  3

POPSTABL        -.16474       -.62235       -.33705
NEWSCIRC         .71934       -.04703        .23394
FEMEMPLD         .80703        .27934       -.14573
FARMERS         -.58607       -.43787       -.18130
RETAILNG         .83267        .00538       -.16588
COMMERCL         .88945       -.27142        .08063
INDUSTZN         .97436       -.10452        .08869
HEALTH           .19912        .35743       -.40795
CHLDNEGL        -.51856       -.17816        .69481
COMMEFFC         .44351        .33795       -.56277
DWELGNEW         .27494        .86373        .22983
MIGRNPOP        -.00353        .49141        .33052
UNEMPLOY        -.62354       -.25283        .50558
MENTALIL        -.14756       -.33056        .16948
```

**21.10
Methods for Factor
Extraction**

Several different methods can be used to obtain estimates of the common factors. These methods differ in the criterion used to define "good fit." Principal axis factoring proceeds much as principal components analysis, except that the diagonals of the correlation matrix are replaced by estimates of the communalities. At the first step, squared multiple correlation coefficients can be used as initial estimates of the communalities. Based on these, the requisite number of factors is extracted. The communalities are reestimated from the factor loadings, and factors are again extracted with the new communality estimates replacing the old. This continues until negligible change occurs in the communality estimates.

The method of unweighted least squares produces, for a fixed number of factors, a factor pattern matrix that minimizes the sum of the squared differences between the observed and reproduced correlation matrices (ignoring the diagonals). The generalized least-squares method minimizes the same criterion; however, correlations are weighted inversely by the uniqueness of the variables. That is, correlations involving variables with high uniqueness are given less weight than correlations involving variables with low uniqueness.

The maximum-likelihood method produces parameter estimates that are the most likely to have produced the observed correlation matrix if the sample is from a multivariate normal distribution. Again, the correlations are weighted by the inverse of the uniqueness of the variables, and an iterative algorithm is employed.

The alpha method considers the variables in a particular analysis to be a sample from the universe of potential variables. It maximizes the alpha reliability of the factors. This differs from the previously described methods, which consider the cases to be a sample from some population and the variables to be fixed. With alpha factor extraction, the eigenvalues can no longer be obtained as the sum of the squared factor loadings and the communalities for each variable are not the sum of the squared loadings on the individual factors. See Harman (1967) and Kim and Mueller (1978) for discussions of the different factor estimation algorithms.

21.11
Goodness of Fit of the Factor Model

When factors are extracted using generalized least squares or maximum-likelihood estimation and it is assumed that the sample is from a multivariate normal population, it is possible to obtain goodness-of-fit tests for the adequacy of a k-factor model. For large sample sizes, the goodness-of-fit statistic tends to be distributed as a chi-squared variate. In most applications, the number of common factors is not known, and the number of factors is increased until a reasonably good fit is obtained—that is, until the observed significance level is no longer small. The statistics obtained in this fashion are not independent and the true significance level is not the same as the observed significance level at each step.

The value of the chi-squared goodness-of-fit statistic is directly proportional to the sample size. The degrees of freedom are a function of only the number of common factors and the number of variables. (For the chi-squared statistic to have positive degrees of freedom, the number of common factors cannot exceed the largest integer satisfying

$$m < 0.5(2p + 1 - \sqrt{8p + 1})$$

Equation 21.11

where m is the number of common factors to be extracted and p is the number of variables). For large sample sizes, the goodness-of-fit test may cause rather small discrepancies in fit to be deemed statistically significant, resulting in a larger number of factors being extracted than is really necessary.

Table 21.11 contains the goodness-of-fit statistics for maximum-likelihood extraction for different numbers of common factors. Using this criterion, six common factors are needed to adequately represent the community data.

Table 21.11 Goodness-of-fit statistics

Number of factors	Chi-square statistic	Iterations required	Significance
3	184.8846	13	0.0000
4	94.1803	8	0.0000
5	61.0836	11	0.0010
6	27.3431	15	0.1985

21.12
Summary of the Extraction Phase

In the factor extraction phase, the number of common factors needed to adequately describe the data is determined. This decision is based on eigenvalues and percentage of the total variance accounted for by different numbers of factors. A plot of the eigenvalues (the scree plot) is also helpful in determining the number of factors.

21.13
The Rotation Phase

Although the factor matrix obtained in the extraction phase indicates the relationship between the factors and the individual variables, it is usually difficult to identify meaningful factors based on this matrix. Often the variables and factors do not appear correlated in any interpretable pattern. Most factors are correlated with many variables. Since one of the goals of factor analysis is to identify factors that are substantively meaningful (in the sense that they summarize sets of closely related variables) the *rotation* phase of factor analysis attempts to transform the initial matrix into one that is easier to interpret.

Consider Figure 21.13a, which is a factor matrix for four hypothetical variables. From the factor loadings, it is difficult to interpret any of the factors, since the variables and factors are intertwined. That is, all factor loadings are quite high, and both factors explain all of the variables.

Figure 21.13a Hypothetical factor matrix

```
FACTOR MATRIX:

                  FACTOR  1        FACTOR  2

    V1              .50000           .50000
    V2              .50000          -.40000
    V3              .70000           .70000
    V4             -.60000           .60000
```

Figure 21.13b Rotated hypothetical factor matrix

```
ROTATED FACTOR MATRIX:

                  FACTOR  1        FACTOR  2

    V1              .70684          -.01938
    V2              .05324          -.63809
    V3              .98958          -.02713
    V4              .02325           .84821
```

In the factor matrix in Figure 21.13b, variables V1 and V3 are highly related to Factor 1, while V2 and V4 load highly on Factor 2. By looking at what variables V2 and V4 have in common (such as a measurement of job satisfaction, or a characterization of an anxious personality), we may be able to identify Factor 2. Similar steps can be taken to identify Factor 1. The goal of rotation is to transform complicated matrices like that in Figure 21.13a into simpler ones like that in Figure 21.13b.

Consider Figure 21.13c, which is a plot of variables V1 to V4 using the factor loadings in Figure 21.13a as the coordinates, and Figure 21.13d, which is the corresponding plot for Figure 21.13b. Note that Figure 21.13c would look exactly like Figure 21.13d if the dotted lines were rotated to be the reference axes. When the axes are maintained at right angles, the rotation is called orthogonal. If the axes are not maintained at right angles, the rotation is called oblique. Oblique rotation is discussed in Section 21.16.

Figure 21.13c   Prior to rotation

```
FACTOR VARIABLES=V1 V2 V3 V4
 /ROTATION=NOROTATE
 /PLOT=ROTATION(1,2).
```

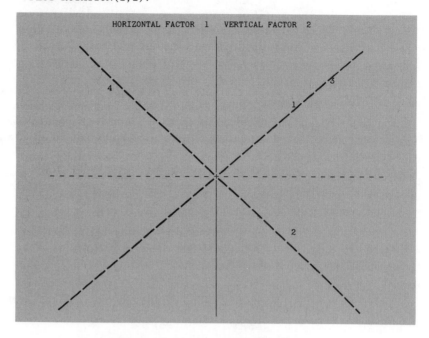

The purpose of rotation is to achieve a simple structure. This means that we would like each factor to have nonzero loadings for only some of the variables. This helps us interpret the factors. We would also like each variable to have nonzero loadings for only a few factors, preferably one. This permits the factors to be differentiated from each other. If several factors have high loadings on the same variables, it is difficult to ascertain how the factors differ.

Rotation does not affect the goodness of fit of a factor solution. That is, although the factor matrix changes, the communalities and the percentage of total variance explained do not change. The percentage of variance accounted for by each of the factors does, however, change. Rotation redistributes the explained variance for the individual factors. Different rotation methods may actually result in the identification of somewhat different factors.

A variety of algorithms are used for orthogonal rotation to a simple structure. The most commonly used method is the *varimax* method, which attempts to minimize the number of variables that have high loadings on a factor. This should enhance the interpretability of the factors.

Figure 21.13d Orthogonal rotation

```
FACTOR VARIABLES=V1 V2 V3 V4
  /ROTATION=VARIMAX
   /PLOT=ROTATION(1,2).
```

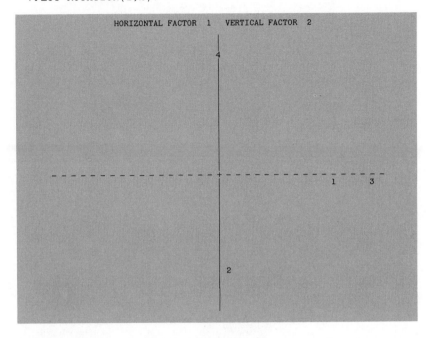

The *quartimax* method emphasizes simple interpretation of variables, since the solution minimizes the number of factors needed to explain a variable. A quartimax rotation often results in a general factor with high-to-moderate loadings on most variables. This is one of the main shortcomings of the quartimax method.

The *equamax* method is a combination of the varimax method, which simplifies the factors, and the quartimax method, which simplifies variables.

Consider Figure 21.13e, which shows the factor matrices for the community data before rotation and again after a varimax (and quartimax and equamax) orthogonal rotation procedure.

The unrotated factor matrix is difficult to interpret. Many variables have moderate-size correlations with several factors. After rotation, the number of large and small factor loadings increases. Variables are more highly correlated with single factors. Interpretation of the factors also appears possible. For

Figure 21.13e Factor matrices for community data

```
FACTOR VARIABLES=POPSTABL TO MENTALIL
 /EXTRACTION=PC
 /ROTATION=VARIMAX
 /ROTATION=QUARTIMAX
 /ROTATION=EQUAMAX.
```

FACTOR MATRIX (unrotated):

	FACTOR 1	FACTOR 2	FACTOR 3
POPSTABL	-.30247	.68597	-.36451
NEWSCIRC	.67238	.28096	.49779
FEMEMPLD	.89461	.01131	.08063
FARMERS	-.68659	.20002	-.40450
RETAILNG	.85141	.24264	.09351
COMMERCL	.72503	.39394	.19896
INDUSTZN	.84436	.29956	.23775
HEALTH	.38347	-.32718	-.63474
CHLDNEGL	-.67430	-.12139	.52896
COMMEFFC	.63205	-.15540	-.64221
DWELGNEW	.45886	-.73940	.18706
MIGRNPOP	.07894	-.74371	.24335
UNEMPLOY	-.78714	-.09777	.30110
MENTALIL	-.30025	.45463	.27134

ROTATED FACTOR MATRIX (varimax):

	FACTOR 1	FACTOR 2	FACTOR 3
POPSTABL	-.13553	.00916	-.82247
NEWSCIRC	.86634	-.14256	.08920
FEMEMPLD	.78248	.37620	.23055
FARMERS	-.65736	-.04537	-.49077
RETAILNG	.83993	.29454	.01705
COMMERCL	.83432	.11068	-.11000
INDUSTZN	.91325	.15773	.01730
HEALTH	-.05806	.79424	.15101
CHLDNEGL	-.39791	-.75492	.14486
COMMEFFC	.21186	.88794	.05241
DWELGNEW	.17484	.22931	.84208
MIGRNPOP	-.12119	-.00660	.77706
UNEMPLOY	-.57378	-.62483	.01311
MENTALIL	.03133	-.47460	-.37979

ROTATED FACTOR MATRIX (quartimax):

	FACTOR 1	FACTOR 2	FACTOR 3
POPSTABL	-.14884	.00769	-.82018
NEWSCIRC	.85549	-.20254	.07706
FEMEMPLD	.81105	.32272	.21214
FARMERS	-.66736	-.00515	-.47920
RETAILNG	.85885	.23432	-.00105
COMMERCL	.83802	.04963	-.12529
INDUSTZN	.92229	.09267	.00000
HEALTH	.00097	.79832	.14028
CHLDNEGL	-.44778	-.72272	.16242
COMMEFFC	.27508	.87127	.03590
DWELGNEW	.20527	.22763	.83565
MIGRNPOP	-.10781	.01249	.77896
UNEMPLOY	-.61627	-.58226	.03168
MENTALIL	-.00897	-.48069	-.37326

ROTATED FACTOR MATRIX (equamax):

	FACTOR 1	FACTOR 2	FACTOR 3
POPSTABL	-.12961	.01218	-.82338
NEWSCIRC	.86917	-.12003	.09470
FEMEMPLD	.77037	.39514	.23949
FARMERS	-.65223	-.05898	-.49613
RETAILNG	.83157	.31678	.02580
COMMERCL	.83185	.13387	-.10273
INDUSTZN	.90854	.18199	.02554
HEALTH	-.08047	.79116	.15682
CHLDNEGL	-.37857	-.76645	.13585
COMMEFFC	.18756	.89284	.06103
DWELGNEW	.16236	.22710	.84518
MIGRNPOP	-.12675	-.01613	.77603
UNEMPLOY	-.55688	-.64006	.00379
MENTALIL	.04688	-.47050	-.38327

example, the first factor shows string positive correlation with newspaper circulation, percentage of females in the labor force, sales, commercial activity, and the industrialization index. It also shows a strong negative correlation with the number of farmers. Thus Factor 1 might be interpreted as measuring something like "urbanism." The second factor is positively correlated with health and a high standard of living and negatively correlated with aid to dependent children, unemployment, and mental illness. This factor describes the affluence or welfare of a community. The last factor is associated with the instability or influx of a community. Thus, communities may be fairly well characterized by three factors—urbanism, welfare, and influx.

21.14
Factor Loading Plots

A convenient means of examining the success of an orthogonal rotation is to plot the variables using the factor loadings as coordinates. In Figure 21.14a, the variables are plotted using Factors 1 and 2 after varimax rotation of the two factors. The plotted numbers represent the number of the variable; e.g., 7 represents the seventh variable (INDUSTZN). The coordinates correspond to the factor loadings in Figure 21.13e for the varimax-rotated solution. The coordinates are also listed under each plot (these have been omitted in Figure 21.14b). In Figure 21.14b, the variables are plotted using Factors 1 and 2 before rotation.

Figure 21.14a   Varimax-rotated solution

```
FACTOR VARIABLES=POPSTABL TO MENTALIL
 /WIDTH=80
 /ROTATION=VARIMAX
 /PLOT=ROTATION(1,2).
```

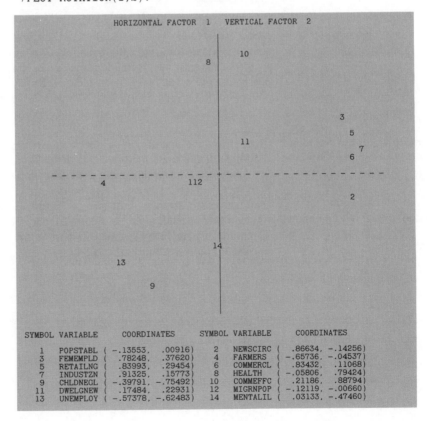

Figure 21.14b   Unrotated solution

```
FACTOR VARIABLES=POPSTABL TO MENTALIL
 /WIDTH=80
 /ROTATION=NOROTATE
 /PLOT=ROTATION(1,2).
```

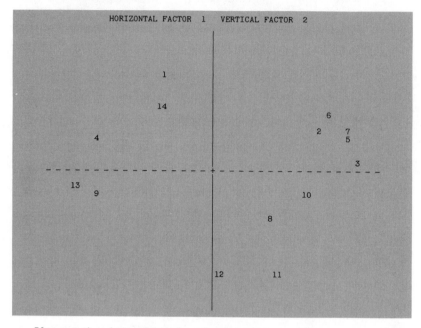

If a rotation has achieved a simple structure, clusters of variables should occur near the ends of the axes and at their intersection. Variables at the end of an axis are those that have high loadings on only that factor. Variables near the origin of the plot have small loadings on both factors. Variables that are not near the axes are explained by both factors. If a simple structure has been achieved, there should be few, if any, variables with large loadings on more than one factor.

21.15
Interpreting the Factors

To identify the factors, it is necessary to group the variables that have large loadings for the same factors. Plots of the loadings, as discussed in Section 21.14, are one way of determining the clusters of variables. Another convenient strategy is to sort the factor pattern matrix so that variables with high loadings on the same factor appear together, as shown in Figure 21.15a. Small factor loadings can be omitted from such a table. In Figure 21.15b, no loadings less than 0.5 in absolute value are displayed. Note that the mental illness variable, as expected, does not correlate highly with any of the factors.

Figure 21.15a Sorted loadings

```
FACTOR VARIABLES=POPSTABL TO MENTALIL
 /FORMAT=SORT
 /ROTATION=VARIMAX.
```

```
ROTATED FACTOR MATRIX:

                 FACTOR  1      FACTOR  2      FACTOR  3

INDUSTZN          .91325         .15773         .01730
NEWSCIRC          .86634        -.14256         .08920
RETAILNG          .83993         .29454         .01705
COMMERCL          .83432         .11068        -.11000
FEMEMPLD          .78248         .37620         .23055
FARMERS          -.65736        -.04537        -.49077
COMMEFFC          .21186         .88794         .05241
HEALTH           -.05806         .79424         .15101
CHLDNEGL         -.39791        -.75492         .14486
UNEMPLOY         -.57378        -.62483         .01311
MENTALIL          .03133        -.47460        -.37979
DWELGNEW          .17484         .22931         .84208
POPSTABL         -.13553         .00916        -.82247
MIGRNPOP         -.12119        -.00660         .77706
```

Figure 21.15b Sorted and blanked loadings

```
FACTOR VARIABLES=POPSTABL TO MENTALIL
 /FORMAT=SORT BLANK(.5)
 /ROTATION=VARIMAX.
```

```
ROTATED FACTOR MATRIX:

                 FACTOR  1      FACTOR  2      FACTOR  3

INDUSTZN          .91325
NEWSCIRC          .86634
RETAILNG          .83993
COMMERCL          .83432
FEMEMPLD          .78248
FARMERS          -.65736

COMMEFFC                         .88794
HEALTH                           .79424
CHLDNEGL                        -.75492
UNEMPLOY         -.57378        -.62483
MENTALIL

DWELGNEW                                        .84208
POPSTABL                                       -.82247
MIGRNPOP                                        .77706
```

21.16
Oblique Rotation

Orthogonal rotation results in factors that are uncorrelated. Although this is an appealing property, sometimes allowing for correlations among factors simplifies the factor pattern matrix. Consider Figure 21.16a, which is a plot of the factor loadings for six variables. Note that if the axes went through the points (the solid line), a simpler factor pattern matrix would result than with an orthogonal rotation (the dotted lines). Factor pattern matrices for both rotations are shown in Figure 21.16b.

Figure 21.16a   Plot of factor loadings

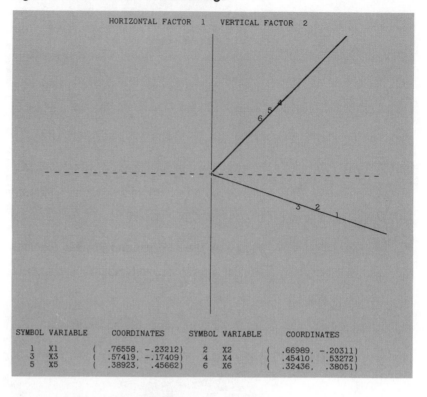

SYMBOL	VARIABLE	COORDINATES	SYMBOL	VARIABLE	COORDINATES
1	X1	(.76558, −.23212)	2	X2	(.66989, −.20311)
3	X3	(.57419, −.17409)	4	X4	(.45410, .53272)
5	X5	(.38923, .45662)	6	X6	(.32436, .38051)

Figure 21.16b   Rotated varimax and oblique factor loadings

ROTATED FACTOR MATRIX varimax:

	FACTOR 1	FACTOR 2
X1	.78313	.16345
X2	.68523	.14302
X3	.58734	.12259
X4	.14302	.68523
X5	.12259	.58734
X6	.10215	.48945

PATTERN MATRIX oblique:

	FACTOR 1	FACTOR 2
X1	.80000	.00000
X2	.70000	.00000
X3	.60000	.00000
X4	.00000	.70000
X5	.00000	.60000
X6	.00000	.50000

There are several reasons why oblique rotation has come into favor. It is unlikely that influences in nature are uncorrelated. And even if they are uncorrelated in the population, they need not be so in the sample. Thus, oblique rotations have often been found to yield substantively meaningful factors.

**21.17
Factor Pattern and Structure
Matrices**

Oblique rotation preserves the communalities of the variables, as does orthogonal rotation. When oblique rotation is used, however, the factor loadings and factor variable correlations are no longer identical. The factor loadings are still partial regression coefficients, but since the factors are correlated, they are no longer equal to the simple factor variable correlations. (Remember that the regression coefficients depend on the interrelationships of the independent variables when these are correlated.) Therefore, separate factor loading and factor structure matrices are displayed as part of the output.

21.18
Algorithm for Oblique Rotation

The method for oblique rotation available in FACTOR is called OBLIMIN. A parameter called δ (delta) controls the extent of obliqueness. When δ is 0, the factors are most oblique. For negative values of δ, the factors become less oblique as δ becomes more negative. Harman (1967) recommends that δ be either 0 or negative.

The factor loadings for the communities data after an oblique rotation are shown in the factor pattern matrix in Figure 21.18a. The loadings are no longer constrained to a range from -1 to $+1$. The correlations between the factors and variables are shown in Figure 21.18b, the factor structure matrix.

Figure 21.18a Factor pattern matrix

```
FACTOR VARIABLES=POPSTABL TO MENTALIL
 /FORMAT=SORT
 /ROTATION=OBLIMIN.
```

```
PATTERN MATRIX:

               FACTOR  1      FACTOR  2      FACTOR  3

  INDUSTZN       .91577         .02882        -.04731
  NEWSCIRC       .90594        -.06987         .26053
  COMMERCL       .84325         .15024        -.01504
  RETAILNG       .82253         .03760        -.19782
  FEMEMPLD       .74906        -.17274        -.27862
  FARMERS       -.65969         .46636        -.06041

  POPSTABL      -.12570         .82380        -.06787
  DWELGNEW       .13426        -.82258        -.17248
  MIGRNPOP      -.13720        -.78724         .03070

  COMMEFFC       .09940         .02770        -.88775
  HEALTH        -.16689        -.08909        -.81993
  CHLDNEGL      -.31128        -.22218         .73693
  UNEMPLOY      -.50651        -.08531         .57387
  MENTALIL       .10140         .34462         .47495
```

Figure 21.18b Factor structure matrix

```
STRUCTURE MATRIX:

               FACTOR  1      FACTOR  2      FACTOR  3

  INDUSTZN       .92553        -.04717        -.27457
  RETAILNG       .86963        -.05222        -.40031
  NEWSCIRC       .84545        -.10235         .02205
  COMMERCL       .83566         .08423        -.20712
  FEMEMPLD       .83252        -.26822        -.49178
  FARMERS       -.67979         .50798         .17096

  DWELGNEW       .24017        -.85671        -.32064
  POPSTABL      -.17101         .82390         .07829
  MIGRNPOP      -.08527        -.77258        -.04400

  COMMEFFC       .32149        -.10314        -.90901
  HEALTH         .04692        -.19032        -.79016
  CHLDNEGL      -.48053        -.09623         .78468
  UNEMPLOY      -.64496         .03280         .68993
  MENTALIL      -.04466         .40290         .49721
```

The correlation matrix for the factors is in Figure 21.18c. Note that there are small correlations between all three factors. In the case of an orthogonal rotation, the factor correlation matrix is an identity matrix: that is, there are 1's on the diagonal and 0's elsewhere.

Figure 21.18c   Factor correlation matrix

```
FACTOR CORRELATION MATRIX:

                  FACTOR  1      FACTOR  2      FACTOR  3
FACTOR   1        1.00000
FACTOR   2        -.07580        1.00000
FACTOR   3        -.25253         .13890        1.00000
```

The oblique rotation resulted in the same grouping of variables as did the orthogonal rotation. The interpretation of the factors does not change based on it.

21.19
Factor Scores

Since one of the goals of factor analysis is to reduce a large number of variables to a smaller number of factors, it is often desirable to estimate factor scores for each case. The factor scores can be used in subsequent analyses to represent the values of the factors. Plots of factor scores for pairs of factors are useful for detecting unusual observations.

Recall from Section 21.1 that a factor can be estimated as a linear combination of the original variables. That is, for case k, the score for the jth factor is estimated as

$$\hat{F}_{jk} = \sum_{i=1}^{p} W_{ji} X_{ik}$$

Equation 21.19a

where X_{ik} is the standardized value of the ith variable for case k and W_{ji} is the factor score coefficient for the jth factor and the ith variable. Except for principal components analysis, exact factor scores cannot be obtained. Estimates are obtained instead.

There are several methods for estimating factor score coefficients. Each has different properties and results in different scores (see Tucker, 1971; Harman, 1967). The three methods available in SPSS FACTOR (Anderson-Rubin, regression, and Bartlett) all result in scores with a mean of 0. The Anderson-Rubin method always produces uncorrelated scores with a standard deviation of 1, even when the original factors are estimated to be correlated. The regression factor scores (the default) have a variance equal to the squared multiple correlation between the estimated factor scores and the true factor values. (These are shown on the diagonal in Figure 21.19b.) Regression method factor scores can be correlated even when factors are assumed to be orthogonal. If principal components extraction is used, all three methods result in the same factor scores, which are no longer estimated but are exact.

Figure 21.19a contains the factor score coefficients used to calculate regression method factor scores for the community data. The correlation matrix for the estimated scores is shown in Figure 21.19b.

Figure 21.19a Factor coefficient matrix

```
FACTOR VARIABLES=POPSTABL TO MENTALIL
 /PRINT=FSCORES
 /EXTRACTION=ML /ROTATION=VARIMAX.
```

```
FACTOR SCORE COEFFICIENT MATRIX:

                FACTOR  1      FACTOR  2      FACTOR  3

POPSTABL         -.00150         .03191        -.15843
NEWSCIRC          .05487        -.06095         .03524
FEMEMPLD          .01729         .14014         .05328
FARMERS          -.01797         .00113        -.11462
RETAILNG          .03728         .09460        -.03577
COMMERCL          .20579        -.11667        -.10723
INDUSTZN          .77285        -.27024         .00882
HEALTH           -.02786         .09971        -.00161
CHLDNEGL          .08404        -.44657         .16521
COMMEFFC         -.05030         .23211        -.03623
DWELGNEW         -.05117         .07034         .68792
MIGRNPOP          .00029        -.03198         .09778
UNEMPLOY          .03856        -.26435         .05378
MENTALIL          .01264        -.04224        -.01691
```

Figure 21.19b Covariance matrix for estimated regression factor scores

```
FACTOR VARIABLES=POPSTABL TO MENTALIL
 /PRINT=FSCORES
 /EXTRACTION=ML /ROTATION=VARIMAX.
```

```
COVARIANCE MATRIX FOR ESTIMATED REGRESSION FACTOR SCORES:

                FACTOR  1      FACTOR  2      FACTOR  3

FACTOR  1        .96763
FACTOR  2        .03294         .87641
FACTOR  3        .00042         .02544         .89452
```

To see how factor scores are calculated, consider Table 21.19, which contains standardized values for the original 14 variables for 5 counties, and factor score values for the three factors. For each factor, the factor scores are obtained by multiplying the standardized values by the corresponding factor score coefficients. Thus, for Adams county the value for Factor 1 is -1.328.

$$-.00150 \times -.36 + .05487 \times -.93 + .01729 \times -1.06 + \cdots + .01264 \times -.76 = -1.328$$

Equation 21.19b

Table 21.19 Standardized values and factor scores

County

Variable	Adams	Butler	Crawford	Cuyahoga	Hamilton
POPSTABL	−0.36	−1.49	2.44	−0.13	−0.30
NEWSCIRC	−0.93	0.39	−0.26	2.04	1.17
FEMEMPLD	−1.06	0.41	0.24	1.30	1.03
FARMERS	2.20	−0.67	0.01	−0.93	−0.90
RETAILNG	−1.41	0.49	0.58	1.15	1.07
COMMERCL	−0.89	−0.30	−0.07	1.58	2.02
INDUSTZN	−1.14	−0.11	0.03	1.53	1.85
HEALTH	−0.25	−0.56	−1.32	−0.36	−1.17
CHLDNEGL	−1.26	0.79	−0.61	0.63	0.99
COMMEFFC	−0.20	0.78	−0.87	−0.78	−1.66
DWELGNEW	−0.52	0.52	−1.09	−0.01	−0.22
MIGRNPOP	−0.98	0.16	−0.60	0.63	1.13
UNEMPLOY	−0.75	−0.36	−0.44	1.56	0.76
MENTALIL	−0.76	−0.77	−0.46	−0.14	0.61

Factor			Scores		
Factor 1	−1.328	−0.089	0.083	1.862	2.233
Factor 2	0.897	0.027	0.197	−1.362	−1.79
Factor 3	−0.830	0.831	−1.290	0.342	0.226

21.20 RUNNING PROCEDURE FACTOR

A variety of extraction and rotation techniques are available in the SPSS FACTOR procedure. The extraction methods available include principal components analysis (Section 21.5) and the maximum-likelihood factor method (Section 21.9). The factor rotation methods are varimax, equamax, quartimax, and oblimin.

You can also request scree plots and factor loading plots to help in selecting and interpreting factors. FACTOR will accept a correlation matrix or a factor loading matrix as input, as well as actual data values.

21.21 Global and Analysis Block Subcommands

There are two basic types of FACTOR subcommands: global and analysis block. Global subcommands are specified once and are in effect for the entire FACTOR procedure. Analysis block subcommands apply only to the ANALYSIS subcommand that precedes them.

The global subcommands are VARIABLES, MISSING, WIDTH, and MATRIX. The VARIABLES subcommand identifies the variables from the active system file available for analysis by FACTOR. The MISSING subcommand provides several alternative missing-value treatments. WIDTH controls the width of the display. The MATRIX subcommand enables you to perform factor analyis from a matrix of correlations or factors.

An analysis block begins with an ANALYSIS subcommand, which names a subset of variables from the list specified on the VARIABLES subcommand. If you omit the ANALYSIS subcommand, all variables named on the VARIABLES subcommand are used. The analysis block subcommands are ANALYSIS, EXTRACTION, ROTATION, DIAGONAL, PLOT, PRINT, and SAVE.

The EXTRACTION subcommand initiates the extraction phase. (A principal components analysis is performed if there is no EXTRACTION subcommand.) The ROTATION subcommand, which specifies the rotation method to use, initiates the rotation phase. The default varimax rotation is obtained if you omit both EXTRACTION and ROTATION. No rotation occurs if EXTRACTION is specified without ROTATION.

The CRITERIA and FORMAT subcommands may be specified for each analysis block, but once specified they remain in effect for subsequent analysis blocks unless explicitly overridden.

21.22
Subcommand Order

The global subcommands VARIABLES and MISSING must be the first specifications. If the MATRIX subcommand is used, it must appear before the analysis block. WIDTH can appear anywhere.

The placement of CRITERIA is important, since it affects any extractions and rotations that follow, until a new CRITERIA subcommand is specified. More than one CRITERIA subcommand may be specified within an analysis block.

21.23
VARIABLES Subcommand

The VARIABLES subcommand lists the variables to analyze. If you do not specify a subsequent EXTRACTION or ROTATION subcommand, the default principal components analysis with varimax rotation is produced. For example, the command

```
FACTOR VARIABLES= POPSTABL NEWSCIRC FEMEMPLD FARMERS RETAILNG
  COMMERCL INDUSTZN  HEALTH CHLDNEGL COMMEFFC DWELGNEW MIGRNPOP
  UNEMPLOY MENTALIL.
```

produces a principal components analysis with varimax rotation for the specified variables. If the variables exist in that order on the active system file, the command

```
FACTOR VARIABLES=POPSTABL TO MENTALIL.
```

produces the same results. The output is shown in Figures 21.5a, 21.6, and 21.7.

VARIABLES is the only required subcommand and must be placed before all other subcommands except MISSING, WIDTH, and MATRIX. Only variables named on the VARIABLES subcommand can be referred to in subsequent subcommands. You can specify only one VARIABLES subcommand on a FACTOR command.

21.24
MISSING Subcommand

FACTOR results are based on the correlation matrix for the variables listed on the VARIABLES subcommand. Use the MISSING subcommand to specify the missing-value treatment for this matrix. If you omit the MISSING subcommand, or include it with no specifications, missing values are deleted listwise.

LISTWISE *Delete missing values listwise.* Only cases with valid values on all variables on the VARIABLES subcommand are used. This is the default.

PAIRWISE *Delete missing values pairwise.* Cases with complete data on each pair of variables correlated are used.

MEANSUB *Replace missing values with the variable mean.* This includes both user-missing and system-missing values.

INCLUDE *Include missing values.* Cases with user-missing values are treated as valid observations. System-missing values are excluded from analysis.

For example, the command

```
FACTOR VARIABLES=IQ GPA TESTSCOR STRESS SAT PSYCHTST
 /MISSING=PAIRWISE.
```

requests a default analysis that uses pairwise missing-value treatment in calculating the correlation matrix.

You can specify only one MISSING subcommand per FACTOR command. The MISSING subcommand must be placed before all other subcommands except VARIABLES and WIDTH. MISSING is ignored with matrix input.

21.25
WIDTH Subcommand

The WIDTH subcommand controls the display width for factor output. For example, the subcommand

```
/WIDTH=80
```

requests output that is 80 characters wide. The value on WIDTH must be an integer. This value overrides the one specified on the SET command. You can specify only one WIDTH subcommand per FACTOR command. The WIDTH subcommand can be placed anywhere.

21.26
ANALYSIS
Subcommand

The ANALYSIS subcommand allows you to perform analyses on subsets of variables named on the VARIABLES subcommand. For example, the command

```
FACTOR VARIABLES=POPSTABL TO MENTALIL
 /ANALYSIS=FEMEMPLD FARMERS INDUSTZN HEALTH CHILDNEGL DWELGNEW
 /ANALYSIS=POPSTABL NEWSCIRC FEMEMPLD COMMERCL UNEMPLOY MENTALIL.
```

requests two default principal components analyses. The first uses variables FEMEMPLD, FARMERS, INDUSTZN, HEALTH, CHLDNEGL, and DWELGNEW, and the second uses variables POPSTABL, NEWSCIRC, FEMEMPLD, COMMERCL, UNEMPLOY, and MENTALIL.

If you do not include the ANALYSIS subcommand, FACTOR uses all of the variables listed on the VARIABLES subcommand for the analysis and produces the following message:

```
>NOTE    11284
>Since the ANALYSIS subcommand is not used, all variables on the VARIABLES
>subcommand will be used for the first analysis.
```

The TO keyword in a variable list on the ANALYSIS subcommand refers to the order of variables on the VARIABLES subcommand, not to their order in the file. Otherwise, the usual SPSS conventions for variable lists are followed. You can use the keyword ALL to refer to all of the variables listed on the VARIABLES subcommand.

If you follow the VARIABLES subcommand with another analysis block subcommand prior to the ANALYSIS subcommand, you implicitly initiate an analysis block. For example, the command

```
FACTOR VARIABLES=POPSTABL TO MENTALIL
 /PRINT=DEFAULT CORRELATION
 /ANALYSIS=FEMEMPLD FARMERS INDUSTZN HEALTH CHILDNEGL DWELGNEW
 /ANALYSIS=POPSTABL NEWSCIRC FEMEMPLD COMMERCL UNEMPLOY MENTALIL.
```

requests three analyses. The first uses all variables and displays the correlation matrix along with the defaults, and the second and third use different subsets of the variable list and display only the defaults.

21.27 EXTRACTION Subcommand

To specify the extraction method, use the EXTRACTION subcommand with one of the following keywords:

PC *Principal components analysis.* This is the default.
PAF *Principal axis factoring.*
ML *Maximum likelihood.*
ALPHA *Alpha factoring.*
IMAGE *Image factoring.*
ULS *Unweighted least squares.*
GLS *Generalized least squares.*

You can specify more than one EXTRACTION subcommand. For example, the command

```
FACTOR VARIABLES=IQ GPA TESTSCOR STRESS SAT PSYCHTST
/EXTRACTION=ML
/EXTRACTION=PC.
```

produces output based on two extraction methods—maximum likelihood and principal components. You can specify multiple EXTRACTION subcommands in each analysis block to produce output for different extraction methods.

If you use the EXTRACTION subcommand without a subsequent ROTATION subcommand, the factor pattern matrix is not rotated (see Section 21.30).

21.28 DIAGONAL Subcommand

Use the DIAGONAL subcommand to specify initial diagonal values in conjunction with principal axis factoring (EXTRACTION=PAF). You can specify any one of the following:

value list *Diagonal values.* User-supplied diagonal values are used only for principal axis factoring.
DEFAULT *1's on the diagonal for principal components or initial communality estimates on the diagonal for factor methods.*

You must supply the same number of diagonal values as there are variables in the analysis. For example, the command

```
FACTOR VARIABLES=IQ GPA TESTSCOR SAT EDYEARS
/DIAGONAL=.55 .45 .35 .40 .50
/EXTRACTION=PAF.
```

assigns five diagonal values for the specified principal axis factoring. You can use the prefix *n* and an asterisk to indicate replicated values. For example, 5*0.80 is the same as specifying 0.80 five times.

21.29 CRITERIA Subcommand

Use CRITERIA to control criteria for extractions and rotations that follow the subcommand. The following keywords are available:

FACTORS(nf) *Number of factors extracted.* The default is the number of eigenvalues greater than MINEIGEN (see MINEIGEN).
MINEIGEN(eg) *Minimum eigenvalue used to control the number of factors.* The default value is 1.
ITERATE(ni) *Number of iterations for the factor solution.* The default value is 25.
ECONVERGE(e1) *Convergence criterion for extraction.* The default value is 0.001.
RCONVERGE(e2) *Convergence criterion for rotation.* The default value is 0.0001.

KAISER	*Kaiser normalization in rotation.* This is the default.
NOKAISER	*No Kaiser normalization.*
DELTA(d)	*Value of delta for direct oblimin rotation.* The default value is 0.
DEFAULT	*Use default values for all criteria.*

More than one CRITERIA subcommand may be specified within an analysis block. Each CRITERIA subcommand affects the subsequent extractions and rotations. Once specified, criteria stay in effect for subsequent analysis blocks unless explicitly overridden by new CRITERIA subcommands. For example, the command

```
FACTOR VARIABLES=IQ GPA TESTSCOR STRESS SAT PSYCHTST
 /CRITERIA=FACTORS(2)
 /EXTRACTION=ML
 /ANALYSIS=ALL
 /EXTRACTION=ULS
 /CRITERIA=DEFAULT
 /EXTRACTION=ML.
```

produces three factor analyses for the same set of variables. The first analysis limits the number of factors extracted to 2, using the maximum-likelihood extraction method. The second analysis also limits the number of factors to 2 but uses the unweighted least squares extraction method. The third analysis extracts all factors whose eigenvalue is greater than 1, using the maximum-likelihood extraction method.

21.30
Rotating Factors

Four rotation methods are available in FACTOR: varimax, equamax, quartimax, and oblimin (see Section 21.13). When both the EXTRACTION and ROTATION subcommands are omitted, the factors are rotated using the varimax method. However, if EXTRACTION is specified but ROTATION is not, the factors are not rotated. To specify a rotation method other than these defaults, use the ROTATION subcommand.

VARIMAX	*Varimax rotation.* This is the default if both EXTRACTION and ROTATION are omitted.
EQUAMAX	*Equamax rotation.*
QUARTIMAX	*Quartimax rotation.*
OBLIMIN	*Direct oblimin rotation.* OBLIMIN uses a default delta value of 0. Use the CRITERIA subcommand to change this default (see Section 21.29).
NOROTATE	*No rotation.* This is the default if EXTRACTION is specified but ROTATION is not.

To obtain a factor loading plot based on unrotated factors, use the PLOT subcommand (see Section 21.33) and specify NOROTATE in the ROTATION subcommand. For example, the following command produced Figure 21.14b:

```
FACTOR VARIABLES=POPSTABL TO MENTALIL
 /WIDTH=80
 /ROTATION=NOROTATE
 /PLOT=ROTATION(1,2).
```

You can specify more than one rotation for a given extraction by using multiple ROTATION subcommands. See Section 21.29 for information on controlling rotation criteria.

21.31
PRINT Subcommand

By default, the statistics listed below under INITIAL, EXTRACTION, and ROTATION are displayed. Use the PRINT subcommand to request additional statistics. If you specify PRINT, only those statistics explicitly named are displayed. You can use only one PRINT subcommand for each analysis block.

UNIVARIATE	*Numbers of valid observations, means, and standard deviations for the variables named on the ANALYSIS subcommand.*
INITIAL	*Initial communalities, eigenvalues, and percentage of variance explained. (See Sections 21.5 and 21.7.)*
CORRELATION	*Correlation matrix for the variables named on the ANALYSIS subcommand.*
SIG	*Significance levels of correlations.* These are one-tailed probablities.
DET	*The determinant of the correlation matrix.*
INV	*The inverse of the correlation matrix.*
AIC	*The anti-image covariance and correlation matrices.*
KMO	*The Kaiser-Meyer-Olkin measure of sampling adequacy and Bartlett's test of spericity. (See Section 21.4.)*
EXTRACTION	*Communalities, eigenvalues, and unrotated factor loadings. (See Sections 21.5 through 21.10.)*
REPR	*Reproduced correlations and their residuals. (See Section 21.8.)*
ROTATION	*Rotated factor pattern and structure matrices, factor transformation matrix, and factor correlation matrix. (See Section 21.13.)*
FSCORE	*The factor score coefficient matrix.* By default, this is based on a regression solution.
DEFAULT	*INITIAL, EXTRACTION, AND ROTATION statistics.* If you use the EXTRACTION subcommand without a subsequent ROTATION subcommand, only the statistics specified by INITIAL and EXTRACTION are displayed by default.
ALL	*All available statistics.*

For example,

```
FACTOR VARIABLES=POPSTABL TO MENTALIL
 /PRINT=REPR.
```

produces the output in Figure 21.8.

21.32
FORMAT
Subcommand

Use the FORMAT subcommand to reformat the display of the factor loading and structure matrices to help you interpret the factors (see Section 21.15). You can use only one FORMAT subcommand per analysis block. The following keywords may be specified on FORMAT:

SORT	*Order the factor loadings by magnitude.*
BLANK(n)	*Suppress coefficients lower in absolute value than* n.
DEFAULT	*Turn off blanking and sorting.*

For example, the command

```
FACTOR VARIABLES=POPSTABL TO MENTALIL
 /FORMAT=SORT BLANK(.5).
```

produces the output in Figure 21.15b.

The FORMAT subcommand should only be specified once within each analysis block. Once specified, the FORMAT subcommand remains in effect for subsequent analysis blocks, unless it is explicitly overridden with a new FORMAT subcommand.

21.33
PLOT Subcommand

To obtain a scree plot (Section 21.5) or a factor loading plot (Section 21.14), use the PLOT subcommand with the following keywords:

EIGEN   *Scree plot.* Plots the eigenvalues in descending order.

ROTATION(n1 n2)   *Factor loading plot.* The specifications *n*1 and *n*2 refer to the factor numbers used as the axes. Several pairs of factors in parentheses can be specified on one ROTATION specification. A plot is displayed for each pair of factors enclosed in parentheses.

You can specify only one PLOT subcommand per analysis block. Plots are based on rotated factors. To get an unrotated factor plot, you must explicitly specify NOROTATE on the ROTATION subcommand (see Section 21.30).

The plots in Figures 21.5b and 21.14a as well as two additional factor plots can be produced by specifying

```
FACTOR VARIABLES=POPSTABL TO MENTALIL
 /PLOT=EIGEN ROTATION(1 2)(1 3)(2 3).
```

21.34
SAVE Subcommand

Use the SAVE subcommand to compute and save factor scores on the active system file. (Factor scores cannot be produced from matrix input.) The specifications on the SAVE subcommand include the method for calculating factor scores, how many factor scores to calculate, and a *rootname* to be used in naming the factor scores. Rotated factor scores are saved unless you specify NOROTATE on the ROTATION subcommand.

REG   *The regression method.* This is the default.

BART   *The Bartlett method.*

AR   *The Anderson-Rubin method.*

Next, specify within parentheses the number of desired factor scores and a rootname up to seven characters long to be used in naming the scores. The maximum number of scores equals the order of the factor solution. You can use keyword ALL to calculate factor scores for all extracted factors.

FACTOR uses the rootname to name the factor scores sequentially, as in root1, root2, root3, etc. If you are calculating factor scores for a many-factor solution, make sure that the rootname is short enough to accommodate the number of the highest-order factor score variable. When FACTOR saves the variables on the active system file, it automatically supplies a variable label indicating the method used to calculate it, its positional order, and the analysis number.

For example, the following FACTOR command saves factor scores for a study of abortion items:

```
FACTOR VARIABLES=ABDEFECT TO ABSINGLE
 /MISSING=MEANSUB
 /CRITERIA=FACTORS(2)
 /EXTRACTION=ULS
 /ROTATION=VARIMAX
 /SAVE AR (ALL FSULS).
```

FACTOR calculates two factor scores named FSULS1 and FSULS2 using the Anderson-Rubin method and saves them on the active system file.

You can use multiple SAVE subcommands for an extraction. For example,

```
FACTOR VARIABLES=ABDEFECT TO ABSINGLE
 /MISSING=MEANSUB
 /EXTRACTION=ULS
 /ROTATION=VARIMAX
 /SAVE AR (ALL FSULS)
 /SAVE BART (ALL BFAC).
```

saves two sets of factor scores. The first set is computed using the Anderson-Rubin method and the second is computed using the Bartlett method.

21.35
MATRIX Subcommand

The MATRIX subcommand allows FACTOR to read matrix materials written by procedures that generate correlation coefficient matrices and write matrix materials in the form of either a correlation matrix or a factor-loading matrix. This subcommand should appear before any analysis blocks.

The MATRIX subcommand has two keywords, IN and OUT, which specify whether the matrix is to be read or written, along with the matrix type and filename in parentheses. If you use both of the keywords IN and OUT, you can specify them in either order.

With MATRIX=IN, the VARIABLES subcommand should not be used. By default, all variables used to create the matrix are included. For correlation matrix input, you can use subsets of variables by specifying ANALYSIS subcommands. For factor matrix input, any ANALYSIS subcommands must specify all the variables used to create the matrix. Analysis of subsets of variables is not available with factor matrix input.

The keywords IN and OUT each have the same four options:

(COR=file) *Read the correlation matrix from an SPSS system file or write it to a system file.* The name of the file follows the equal sign.

(COR=*) *Read the correlation matrix from the active system file or write it to the active system file.* With keyword OUT, the matrix materials replace the active file.

(FAC=file) *Read the factor-loading matrix from an SPSS system file or write it to a system file.* The name of the file follows the equals sign.

(FAC=*) *Read the factor-loading matrix from the active system file or write it to the active file.* With keyword OUT, the matrix materials replace the active system file.

FACTOR writes only COR values for correlation matrix materials and FACTOR values for factor-loading matrix materials. It neither reads nor writes additional statistics with its matrix materials. (When FACTOR reads matrix materials, it skips vectors that represent mean, standard deviation, and N values.)

In the example below, FACTOR reads a factor-loading matrix from a file called FACLOAD:

FACTOR MATRIX=IN (FAC=facload)

In the example below, FACTOR writes a correlation matrix, which replaces the active system file:

FACTOR MATRIX=OUT (COR=*)

21.36
Annotated Example
All of the factor analyses for the community data in this chapter (with the exception of the factor scores in Table 21.19) can be generated from the correlation matrix in Figure 21.4a, using matrix data and the MATRIX subcommand. For example, the output in Figures 21.4a, 21.4b, 21.4c, 21.5a, 21.5b, 21.6, 21.7, 21.8, and 21.14a could be produced with the following commands:

```
MATRIX DATA VARIABLES=POPSTABL NEWSCIRC FEMEMPLD FARMERS RETAILNG
 COMMERCL INDUSTZN HEALTH CHLDNEGL COMMEFFC DWELGNEW MIGRNPOP
 UNEMPLOY MENTALIL
 /CONTENTS=CORR /N=88.
BEGIN DATA.
1.
-.175 1.
-.276 .616 1.
 .369 -.625 -.637 1.
etc.
END DATA.
FACTOR MATRIX=IN (COR=*)
 /PRINT=DEFAULT CORRELATION KMO AIC REPR
 /PLOT=EIGEN ROTATION(1,2).
```

- The MATRIX DATA command defines the variable names. The CONTENTS subcommand identifies the data as correlation coefficients. The N subcommand indicates the original number of cases used to generate the correlation matrix (in this case, 88 counties).

- The FACTOR command and MATRIX subcommand produce factor analyses based on the correlation matrix in the active system file. By default the analysis includes all variables in a principle component analysis, using varimax rotation.

- The PRINT subcommand displays the correlation matrix (Figure 21.4a), the Kaiser-Meyer-Olkin measure (Figure 21.4b), the anti-image correlation matrix (Figure 21.4c), and the reproduced correlation matrix (Figure 21.8). It also displays the default INITIAL and EXTRACTION statistics (Figures 21.5a, 21.6, and 21.7).

- The PLOT subcommand produces the scree plot of eigenvalues in Figure 21.15b and the varimax-rotated plot of the first two factors in Figure 21.14a.

Contents

22 Cluster Analysis: Procedure CLUSTER

Despite the old adage that opposites attract, it appears instead that likes cluster together. Birds of a feather, yuppies, and many other animate and inanimate objects that share similar characteristics are found together. By studying such clusters, you can determine the characteristics the objects share, as well as those in which they differ. In statistics, the search for relatively homogeneous groups of objects is called *cluster analysis.*

In biology, cluster analysis is used to classify animals and plants. This is called numerical taxonomy. In medicine, cluster analysis is used to identify diseases and their stages. For example, by examining patients who are diagnosed as depressed, you might find that there are several distinct subgroups of patients with different types of depression. In marketing, cluster analysis is used to identify persons with similar buying habits. By examining their characteristics, you may be able to target future marketing strategies more efficiently. See Romesburg (1984) for more examples of the use of cluster analysis.

Although both cluster analysis and discriminant analysis classify objects or cases into categories, discriminant analysis requires you to know group membership for the cases used to derive the classification rule. For example, if you are interested in distinguishing among several disease groups, cases with known diagnoses must be available. Then, based on cases whose group membership is known, discriminant analysis derives a rule for allocating undiagnosed patients. In cluster analysis, group membership for all cases is unknown. In fact, even the number of groups is often unknown. The goal of cluster analysis is to identify homogeneous groups or clusters.

In this chapter the fundamentals of cluster analysis are illustrated using a subset of data presented in a Consumer Reports (1983) survey of beer. Each of 20 beers is characterized in terms of cost per 12 ounces, alcohol content, sodium content, and the number of calories per 12-ounce serving. From these variables is it possible to identify several distinct subgroups of beer.

22.1
BASIC STEPS

As in other statistical procedures, a number of decisions must be made before you embark on the actual analysis. Which variables will serve as the basis for cluster formation? How will the distance between cases be measured? What criteria will be used for combining cases into clusters?

Selecting the variables to include in an analysis is always crucial. If important variables are excluded, poor or misleading findings may result. For example, in a regression analysis of salary, if variables such as education and experience are not included, the results may be questionable. In cluster analysis, the initial choice of variables determines the characteristics that can be used to identify subgroups. If you are interested in clustering schools within a city and do not include variables like the number of students or the number of teachers, size is automatically excluded as a criterion for establishing clusters. By excluding all measures of taste or quality from the beer data, only physical characteristics and price will determine which beers are deemed similar.

22.2
How Alike are the Cases?

The concepts of distance and similarity are basic to many statistical techniques. Distance is a measure of how far apart two objects are, and similarity measures closeness. Distance measures are small and similarity measures are large for cases that are similar. In cluster analysis, these concepts are especially important, since cases are grouped on the basis of their "nearness." There are many different definitions of distance and similarity. Selection of a distance measure should be based both on the properties of the measure and on the algorithm for cluster formation. See Section 22.11 for further discussion of distance measures.

To see how a simple distance measure is computed, consider Table 22.2a, which shows the values of calories and cost for two of the beers. There is a 13-calorie and 5-cent difference between the two beers. This information can be combined into a single index or distance measure in many different ways. A commonly used index is the *squared Euclidean distance,* which is the sum of the squared differences over all of the variables. In this example, the squared Euclidean distance is $13^2 + 5^2$, or 194.

Table 22.2a   Values of calories and cost for two beers

	Calories	Cost
Budweiser	144	43
Lowenbrau	157	48

The squared Euclidean distance has the disadvantage that it depends on the units of measurement for the variables. For example, if the cost were given as pennies per ounce instead of per twelve ounces, the distance measure would change. Another disadvantage is that when variables are measured on different scales, as in this example, variables that are measured in larger numbers will contribute more to the distance than variables that are recorded in smaller numbers. For example, the 13-calorie difference contributes much more to the distance score than does the 5-cent difference in cost.

One means of circumventing this problem is to express all variables in standardized form. That is, all variables have a mean of 0 and a standard deviation of 1. This is not always the best strategy, however, since the variability of a particular measure can provide useful information (see Sneath & Sokal, 1973).

Table 22.2b shows the Z scores for calories and cost for Budweiser and Lowenbrau based on the means and standard deviations for all twenty beers. The squared Euclidean distance based on the standardized variables is $(0.38-0.81)^2 + (-0.46-(-0.11))^2$, or 0.307. The differences in calories and cost are now weighted equally.

Table 22.2b Z scores for the calories and cost variables

	Calories	Cost
Budweiser	0.38	-0.46
Lowenbrau	0.81	-0.11

22.3
Forming Clusters

Just as there are many methods for calculating distances between objects, there are many methods for combining objects into clusters. A commonly used method for forming clusters is hierarchical cluster analysis, using one of two methods: agglomerative, or divisive. In *agglomerative* hierarchical clustering, clusters are formed by grouping cases into bigger and bigger clusters until all cases are members of a single cluster. *Divisive* hierarchical clustering starts out with all cases grouped into a single cluster and splits clusters until there are as many clusters as there are cases. For a discussion of nonhierarchical clustering methods, see Everitt (1980).

22.4
Agglomerative Clustering

Before discussing the rules for forming clusters, consider what happens during the steps of agglomerative hierarchical cluster analysis. At the first step all cases are considered separate clusters: there are as many clusters as there are cases. At the second step, two of the cases are combined into a single cluster. At the third step, either a third case is added to the cluster already containing two cases, or two additional cases are merged into a new cluster. At every step, either individual cases are added to clusters or already existing clusters are combined. Once a cluster is formed, it cannot be split; it can only be combined with other clusters. Thus, hierarchical clustering methods do not allow cases to separate from clusters to which they have been allocated. For example, if two beers are deemed members of the same cluster at the first step, they will always be members of the same cluster, although they may be combined with additional cases at a later step.

22.5
Criteria for Combining Clusters

There are many criteria for deciding which cases or clusters should be combined at each step. All of these criteria are based on a matrix of either distances or similarities between pairs of cases. One of the simplest methods is *single linkage*, sometimes called "nearest neighbor." The first two cases combined are those that have the smallest distance (or largest similarity) between them. The distance between the new cluster and individual cases is then computed as the minimum distance between an individual case and a case in the cluster. The distances between cases that have not been joined do not change. At every step, the distance between two clusters is the distance between their two closest points.

Another commonly used method is called *complete linkage*, or the "furthest neighbor" technique. In this method, the distance between two clusters is calculated as the distance between their two furthest points. Other methods for combining clusters are described in Section 22.11.

22.6
PERFORMING A CLUSTER ANALYSIS

Before considering other distance measures and methods of combining clusters, consider Figure 22.6a, which shows the original and standardized values for calories, sodium, alcohol, and cost for the 20 beers, and Figure 22.6b, which displays the squared Euclidean distance coefficients for all possible pairs of the 20 beers, based on the standardized values.

Figure 22.6a   Original and standardized values for the 20 beers from procedure LIST

```
DESCRIPTIVES CALORIES SODIUM ALCOHOL COST
  /SAVE.
LIST VARIABLES=ID BEER CALORIES SODIUM ALCOHOL COST ZCALORIE TO
  ZCOST.
```

```
ID BEER                      CALORIES SODIUM ALCOHOL COST ZCALORIE ZSODIUM ZALCOHOL ZCOST

 1 BUDWEISER                    144     15     4.7    .43    .38      .01     .34    -.46
 2 SCHLITZ                      151     19     4.9    .43    .61      .62     .61    -.46
 3 LOWENBRAU                    157     15     4.9    .48    .81      .01     .61    -.11
 4 KRONENBOURG                  170      7     5.2    .73   1.24    -1.2    1.00    1.62
 5 HEINEKEN                     152     11     5.0    .77    .65     -.60     .74    1.90
 6 OLD MILWAUKEE                145     23     4.6    .28    .42     1.22     .21   -1.5
 7 AUGSBERGER                   175     24     5.5    .40   1.41     1.38    1.40    -.67
 8 STROHS BOHEMIAN STYLE        149     27     4.7    .42    .55     1.83     .34    -.53
 9 MILLER LITE                   99     10     4.3    .43   -1.1     -.75    -.18    -.46
10 BUDWEISER LIGHT              113      8     3.7    .44    -.64    -1.1    -.97    -.39
11 COORS                        140     18     4.6    .44    .25      .46     .21    -.39
12 COORS LIGHT                  102     15     4.1    .46   -1.0      .01    -.45    -.25
13 MICHELOB LIGHT               135     11     4.2    .50    .09     -.60    -.32     .02
14 BECKS                        150     19     4.7    .76    .58      .62     .34    1.83
15 KIRIN                        149      6     5.0    .79    .55    -1.4     .74    2.04
16 PABST EXTRA LIGHT             68     15     2.3    .38   -2.1      .01    -2.8    -.81
17 HAMMS                        136     19     4.4    .43    .12      .62    -.05    -.46
18 HEILEMANS OLD STYLE          144     24     4.9    .43    .38     1.38    -.46    -.46
19 OLYMPIA GOLD LIGHT            72      6     2.9    .46   -2.0    -1.4    -2.0     -.25
20 SCHLITZ LIGHT                 97      7     4.2    .47   -1.2    -1.2    -.32    -.18

Number of cases read:  20    Number of cases listed:  20
```

Figure 22.6b   The squared Euclidean distance coefficient matrix

```
CLUSTER ZCALORIE ZSODIUM ZALCOHOL ZCOST
  /PRINT=DISTANCE.
```

```
Squared Euclidean Dissimilarity Coefficient Matrix

Case        1          2          3          4          5          6          7          8

  2       .4922
  3       .3749      .5297
  4      7.0040     8.2298     4.8424
  5      6.1889     7.0897     4.4835      .8700
  6      2.5848     1.6534     3.7263    17.0154    15.2734
  7      4.0720     1.8735     3.1573    12.1251    11.5371     3.1061
  8      3.3568     1.5561     3.6380    14.8000    12.0038     1.3526     2.0742
  9      3.0662     5.4473     4.9962    11.4721     9.5339     7.4577    13.3723     9.6850
 10      3.9181     6.8702     5.8179    11.5391    10.0663     8.9551    15.7993    11.5019
 11       .2474      .3160      .7568     8.4698     6.8353     1.8432     3.6498     1.9953
 12      2.5940     4.1442     4.4322    12.1519     9.1534     5.4981    11.2604     6.4385
 13      1.1281     2.8432     1.7663     5.9995     4.9519     6.0530     9.0610     6.8673
 14      5.6782     5.3399     4.2859     4.2382     1.6427    11.5628     8.6397     7.0724
 15      8.3245    10.1947     6.6075      .7483      .6064    19.5528    16.0117    16.9620
 16     16.4081    19.7255    20.8463    33.3380    28.0650    17.6015    32.1339    20.5466
 17       .5952      .6788     1.4051    10.0509     7.9746     1.6159     4.3782     1.8230
 18      1.9394      .6307     2.1757    11.9216     9.5828     1.2688     1.7169      .3092
 19     13.1887    17.6915    16.7104    23.2048    19.8574    19.0673    30.9530    22.3479
 20      4.4010     7.4360     6.2635    10.8241     9.1372    10.4511    16.4825    12.7426

Case        9         10         11         12         13         14         15         16

 10       .9349
 11      3.4745     4.5082
 12       .6999     1.5600     2.2375
 13      1.6931     1.3437     1.6100     1.6536
 14     10.2578    10.9762     5.1046     7.8646     5.4275
 15     10.2201    10.3631     9.6179    10.9556     5.9694     4.1024
 16      8.6771     6.9127    15.2083     7.1851    12.2231    24.6793    29.7992
 17      3.3828     4.2251      .1147     1.8315     1.7851     5.6395    10.9812    13.1806
 18      7.3607     9.4595     1.0094     4.9491     5.0762     5.9553    13.7962    20.0105
 19      4.6046     3.0565    13.4011     5.3477     7.9175    20.5149    19.3851     2.8209
 20       .3069      .7793     5.1340     1.5271     1.9902    10.8954     9.0403     9.0418

Case       17         18         19

 18      1.0802
 19     12.3170    20.1156
 20      5.1327    10.0114     3.6382
```

The first entry in Figure 22.6b is the distance between Case 1 and Case 2, Budweiser and Schlitz. This can be calculated from the standardized values in Figure 22.6a as

$$D^2=(0.38-0.61)^2+(0.01-0.62)^2+(0.34-0.61)^2+(-0.46-(-0.46))^2 \quad \textbf{Equation 22.6}$$
$$=0.49$$

Since the distance between pairs of cases is symmetric (that is, the distance between Case 3 and Case 4 is the same as the distance between Case 4 and Case 3), only the lower half of the distance matrix is displayed.

22.7 Icicle Plots

Once the distance matrix has been calculated, the actual formation of clusters can commence. Figure 22.7a summarizes a cluster analysis that uses the complete linkage method. This type of figure is sometimes called a vertical icicle plot because it resembles a row of icicles hanging from eaves.

Figure 22.7a Vertical icicle plot for the 20 beers

```
CLUSTER ZCALORIE ZSODIUM ZALCOHOL ZCOST
 /ID=BEER /METHOD=COMPLETE
 /PLOT=VICICLE.
```

```
  Vertical Icicle Plot using Complete Linkage

    (Down) Number of Clusters  (Across) Case Label and number

    O  P  M  C  B  S  M  B  K  H  K  A  H  S  O  H  C  S  L  B
    L  A  I  O  U  C  I  E  I  E  R  U  E  T  L  A  O  C  O  U
    Y  B  C  O  D  H  L  C  R  I  O  G  I  R  D  M  O  H  W  D
    M  S  H  R  W  L  L  K  I  N  N  S  L  O     M  R  L  E  W
    P  T  E  S  E  I  E  S  N  E  E  B  E  H  M  S  S  I  N  E
    I     L     I  T  R        K  N  E  M  S  I        T  B  I
    A  E  O  L  S  Z           E  B  R  A     L        Z  R  S
       X  B  I  E     L        N  O  G  N  B  W           A  E
    G  T     G  R  L  I           U  E  S  O  A           U  R
    O  R  L  H     I  T           R  R     H  U
    L  A  I  T  L  G  E           G     O  E  K
    D     G     I  H                    L  M  E
       L  H     G  T                    D  I  E
    L  I  T     H                          A
    I  G        T                       S  N
    G  H                                T
    H  T                                Y  S
    T                                   L  T
                                        E  Y
                                           L

    1  1  1  1  1  2     1  1           1        1  1
    9  6  3  2  0  0  9  4  5  5  4  7  8  8  6  7  1  2  3  1
 1 +XXXXXXXXXXXXXXXXXXXXXXXXXXXXXXXXXXXXXXXXXXXXXXXXXXXXXXXXXX
 2 +XXXX  XXXXXXXXXXXXXXXXXXXXXXXXXXXXXXXXXXXXXXXXXXXXXXXXXXXX
 3 +XXXX  XXXXXXXXXXXXXXXXXXXXXXXXX  XXXXXXXXXXXXXXXXXXXXXXXXX
 4 +XXXX  XXXXXXXXXXXXX  XXXXXXXXXX  XXXXXXXXXXXXXXXXXXXXXXXXX
 5 +XXXX  XXXXXXXXXXXXX  XXXXXXXXXX  XXXXXXXXXX  XXXXXXXXXXXXX
 6 +XXXX  XXXXXXXXXXXXX  X  XXXXXXX  XXXXXXXXXX  XXXXXXXXXXXXX
 7 +XXXX  XXXXXXXXXXXXX  X  XXXXXXX  X  XXXXXXX  XXXXXXXXXXXXX
 8 +X  X  XXXXXXXXXXXXX  X  XXXXXXX  X  XXXXXXX  XXXXXXXXXXXXX
 9 +X  X  X  XXXXXXXXXX  X  XXXXXXX  X  XXXXXXX  XXXXXXXXXXXXX
10 +X  X  X  X  XXXXXXX  X  XXXXXXX  X  XXXXXXX  XXXXXXXXXXXXX
11 +X  X  X  X  XXXXXXX  X  XXXXXXX  X  XXXXXXX  XXXX  XXXXXXX
12 +X  X  X  X  XXXXXXX  X  XXXXXXX  X  XXXX  X  XXXX  XXXXXXX
13 +X  X  X  X  X  XXXX  X  XXXXXXX  X  XXXX  X  XXXX  XXXXXXX
14 +X  X  X  X  X  XXXX  X  XXXX  X  X  XXXX  X  XXXX  XXXXXXX
15 +X  X  X  X  X  XXXX  X  X  X  X  X  XXXX  X  XXXX  XXXXXXX
16 +X  X  X  X  X  XXXX  X  X  X  X  X  XXXX  X  XXXX  X  XXXX
17 +X  X  X  X  X  XXXX  X  X  X  X  X  XXXX  X  XXXX  X  X  X
18 +X  X  X  X  X  XXXX  X  X  X  X  X  X  X  X  XXXX  X  X  X
19 +X  X  X  X  X  X  X  X  X  X  X  X  X  X  X  XXXX  X  X  X
```

The columns of Figure 22.7a correspond to the objects being clustered. They are identified both by a sequential number ranging from 1 to the number of cases and, when possible, by the labels of the objects. Thus, the first column corresponds to beer number 19, Olympia Gold Light, while the last column corresponds to the first beer in the file, Budweiser. In order to follow the sequence of steps in the cluster analysis, the figure is read from bottom to top.

As previously described, all cases are considered initially as individual clusters. Since there are twenty beers in this example, there are 20 clusters. At the first step the two closest cases are combined into a single cluster, resulting in 19 clusters. The bottom line of Figure 22.7a shows these 19 clusters. Each case is represented by a single X separated by blanks. The two cases that have been merged into a single cluster, Coors and Hamms, do not have blanks separating them. Instead they are represented by consecutive X's. The row labeled **18** in Figure 22.7a corresponds to the solution at the next step, when 18 clusters are present. At this step Miller Lite and Schlitz Light are merged into a single cluster. Thus, at this point there are 18 clusters, 16 consisting of individual beers and 2 consisting of pairs of beers. At each subsequent step an additional cluster is formed by joining either a case to an already existing multicase cluster, two separate cases into a single cluster, or two multicase clusters.

For example, the row labeled 5 in Figure 22.7a corresponds to a solution that has five clusters. Beers 19 and 16, the very light beers, form one cluster; beers 13, 12, 10, 20, and 9 form the next. These beers, Michelob Light, Coors Light, Budweiser Light, Schlitz Light, and Miller Light, are all light beers, but not as light as the two in the first cluster. The third cluster consists of Becks, Kirin, Heineken, and Kronenbourg. These are all imported beers. Although no variable in this example explicitly indicates whether beers are domestic or imported, the cost variable (see Figure 22.6b) causes the imported beers to cluster together since they are quite a it more expensive than the domestic ones. A fourth cluster consists of Augsberger, Heilemans Old Style, Strohs Bohemian Style, and Old Milwaukee. Inspection of Figure 22.7b shows that all of these beers are distinguished by high sodium content. The last cluster consists of five beers, Hamms, Coors, Schlitz, Lowenbrau, and Budweiser. These beers share the distinction of being average. That is, they are neither particularly high nor particularly low on the variables measured. Note from Figure 22.7b that, based on the standard deviations, beers in the same cluster, when compared to all beers, are more homogeneous on the variables measured.

Figure 22.7b   Cluster characteristics

```
CLUSTER ZCALORIE ZSODIUM ZALCOHOL ZCOST
 /ID=BEER
 /SAVE CLUSTER(5)
 /METHOD=COMPLETE(CLUSMEM).
VALUE LABELS CLUSMEM5 1 'AVERAGE' 2 'EXPENSIVE'
 3 'HIGH NA' 4 'LIGHT' 5 'VERY LIGHT'.
TABLES OBSERVATION= COST CALORIES ALCOHOL SODIUM
 /FTOTAL=TOTAL
 /FORMAT=CWIDTH(10,9)
 /TABLE= CLUSMEM5+TOTAL BY CALORIES +COST+ALCOHOL+SODIUM
 /STATISTICS=MEAN STDDEV.
```

	CALORIES PER 12 FLUID OUNCES		COST PER 12 FLUID OUNCES		ALCOHOL BY VOLUME (IN %)		SODIUM PER 12 FLUID OUNCES IN MG	
	Mean	Standard Deviation	Mean	Standard Deviation	Mean	Standard Deviation	Mean	Standard Deviation
CLUSMEM5								
AVERAGE	146	8	.44	.02	4.7	.2	17	2
EXPENSIVE	155	10	.76	.03	5.0	.2	11	6
HIGH NA	153	15	.38	.07	4.9	.4	25	2
LIGHT	109	16	.46	.03	4.1	.2	10	3
VERY LIGHT	70	3	.42	.06	2.6	.4	11	6
TOTAL	132	30	.50	.14	4.4	.8	15	7

Cluster formation continues in Figure 22.7a until all cases are merged into a single cluster, as shown in the first row. Thus, all steps of the cluster analysis are displayed in Figure 22.7a. If we were clustering people instead of beers, the last row would be individual persons, higher up they would perhaps merge into families, these into neighborhoods, and so forth. Often there is not one single, meaningful cluster solution, but many, depending on what is of interest.

22.8
The Agglomeration Schedule

The results of the cluster analysis are summarized in the *agglomeration schedule* in Figure 22.8, which contains the number of cases or clusters being combined at each stage. The first line is Stage 1, the 19-cluster solution. Beers 11 and 17 are combined at this stage, as shown in the columns labeled **Clusters Combined.** The squared Euclidean distance between these two beers is displayed in the column labeled **Coefficient.** Since this is the first step, this coefficient is identical to the distance measure in Figure 22.6b for Cases 11 and 17. The last column indicates at which stage another case or cluster is combined with this one. For example, at the tenth stage, Case 1 is merged with Cases 11 and 17 into a single cluster. The column entitled **Stage Cluster 1st Appears** indicates at which stage a cluster is first formed. For example, the entry of 4 at Stage 5 indicates that Case 1 was first involved in a merge in the previous step (Stage 4). From the line for Stage 4, you can see that, at this point, Case 1 was involved in a merge with Case 3. From the last column of Stage 5 we see that the new cluster (Cases 1, 2, and 3) is next involved in a merge at Stage 10, where the cases combine with Cases 11 and 17.

Figure 22.8 Agglomeration schedule using complete linkage

```
CLUSTER ZCALORIE ZSODIUM ZALCOHOL ZCOST
 /ID=BEER
 /PRINT=SCHEDULE
 /METHOD=COMPLETE.
```

Agglomeration Schedule using Complete Linkage

Stage	Clusters Cluster 1	Combined Cluster 2	Coefficient	Stage Cluster 1st Appears Cluster 1	Cluster 2	Next Stage
1	11	17	.114695	0	0	10
2	9	20	.306903	0	0	8
3	8	18	.309227	0	0	9
4	1	3	.374859	0	0	5
5	1	2	.529696	4	0	10
6	5	15	.606378	0	0	7
7	4	5	.870016	0	6	15
8	9	10	.934909	2	0	11
9	6	8	1.352617	0	3	14
10	1	11	1.405148	5	1	16
11	9	12	1.559987	8	0	12
12	9	13	1.990205	11	0	17
13	16	19	2.820896	0	0	19
14	6	7	3.106108	9	0	16
15	4	14	4.238164	7	0	17
16	1	6	4.378198	10	14	18
17	4	9	12.151937	15	12	18
18	1	4	19.552841	16	17	19
19	1	16	33.338028	18	13	0

The information in Figure 22.8. that is not available in the icicle plot is the value of the distance between the two most dissimilar points of the clusters being combined at each stage (the column labeled **Coefficient**). By examining these values, you can get an idea of how unlike the clusters being combined are. Small coefficients indicate that fairly homogeneous clusters are being merged. Large coefficients indicate that clusters containing quite dissimilar members are being combined. The actual value depends on the clustering method and the distance measure used.

These coefficients can also be used for guidance in deciding how many clusters are needed to represent the data. You usually want to stop agglomeration as soon as the increase between two adjacent steps becomes large. For example, in Figure 22.8 there is a fairly large increase in the value of the distance measure from a four-cluster to a three-cluster solution (Stages 16 and 17).

22.9
The Dendrogram

Another way of visually representing the steps in a hierarchical clustering solution is with a display called a *dendrogram*. The dendrogram shows the clusters being combined and the values of the coefficients at each step. The dendrogram produced by the SPSS CLUSTER procedure does not plot actual distances but rescales them to numbers between 0 and 25. Thus, the ratio of the distances between steps is preserved. The scale displayed at the top of the figure does not correspond to actual distance values.

To understand how a dendrogram is constructed, consider a simple four-beer example. Figure 22.9a contains the icicle plot for clustering Kirin, Becks, Old Milwaukee, and Budweiser. From the icicle plot, you can see that at the first step Budweiser and Old Milwaukee are combined, at the second step Becks and Kirin are merged, and at the last step all four beers are merged into a single cluster.

Figure 22.9a   Vertical icicle plot for the four-beer example

```
SELECT IF (ID EQ 1 OR ID EQ 6 OR ID EQ 14 OR ID EQ 15).
CLUSTER ZCALORIE ZSODIUM ZALCOHOL ZCOST
 /ID=BEER
 /METHOD=COMPLETE
 /PLOT=VICICLE.
```

```
Vertical Icicle Plot using Complete Linkage

  (Down) Number of Clusters   (Across) Case Label and number

        K   B   O   B
        I   E   L   U
        R   C   D   D
        I   K       W
        N   S   M   E
                L   I
                W   S
                A   E
                U   R
                K
                E
                E




          4   3   2   1
     1  +XXXXXXXXXX
     2  +XXXX  XXXX
     3  +X  X  XXXX
```

The distances at which the beers are combined are shown in the agglomeration schedule in Figure 22.9b. From this schedule, we see that the distance between Budweiser and Old Milwaukee is 2.017 when they are combined. Similarly when Becks and Kirin are combined, their distance is 6.323. Since the method of complete linkage is used, the distance coefficient displayed for the last stage is the largest distance between a member of the Budweiser-Milwaukee cluster and a member of the Becks-Kirin cluster. This distance is 16.789.

Figure 22.9b   Agglomeration schedule for the four-beer example

```
SELECT IF (ID EQ 1 OR ID EQ 6 OR ID EQ 14 OR ID EQ 15).
CLUSTER ZCALORIE ZSODIUM ZALCOHOL ZCOST
 /ID=BEER
 /PRINT=SCHEDULE
 /METHOD=COMPLETE.
```

Agglomeration Schedule using Complete Linkage

| | Clusters Combined | | | Stage Cluster 1st Appears | | Next |
Stage	Cluster 1	Cluster 2	Coefficient	Cluster 1	Cluster 2	Stage
1	1	2	2.017018	0	0	3
2	3	4	6.323439	0	0	3
3	1	3	16.789215	1	2	0

The information in Figure 22.9b is displayed in the dendrogram in Figure 22.9c, which is read from left to right. Vertical lines denote joined clusters. The position of the line on the scale indicates the distance at which clusters were joined. Since the distances are rescaled to fall in the range of 1 to 25, the largest distance, 16.8, corresponds to the value of 25. The smallest distance, 2.017, corresponds to the value 1. The second distance (6.32) corresponds to a value of about 8. Note that the ratio of the rescaled distances is, after the first, the same as the ratios of the original distances.

The first two clusters that are joined are Budweiser and Old Milwaukee. They are connected by a line that is one unit from the origin since this is the rescaled distance between these points. When Becks and Kirin are joined, the line that connects them is 8 units from the origin. Similarly, when these two clusters are merged into a single cluster, the line that connects them is 25 units from the origin. Thus, the dendrogram indicates not only which clusters are joined but also the distance at which they are joined.

Figure 22.9c   Dendrogram for the four-beer example

```
SELECT IF (ID EQ 1 OR ID EQ 6 OR ID EQ 14 OR ID EQ 15).
CLUSTER ZCALORIE ZSODIUM ZALCOHOL ZCOST
 /ID=BEER
 /METHOD=COMPLETE
 /PLOT=DENDROGRAM.
```

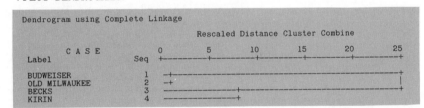

Figure 22.9d contains the dendrogram for the complete 20-beer example. Since many of the distances at the beginning stages are similar in magnitude, you cannot tell the sequence in which some of the early clusters are formed. However, at the last three stages the distances at which clusters are being combined are fairly large. Looking at the dendrogram, it appears that the five-cluster solution (very light beers, light beers, imported beers, high-sodium beers, and "average" beers) may be appropriate since it is easily interpretable and occurs before the distances at which clusters are combined become too large.

Figure 22.9d Dendrogram using complete linkage for the 20 beers

```
CLUSTER ZCALORIE ZSODIUM ZALCOHOL ZCOST
 /ID=BEER
 /METHOD=COMPLETE
 /PLOT=DENDROGRAM.
```

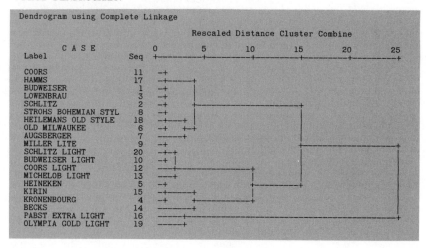

22.10
Some Additional Displays and Modifications

The agglomeration schedule, icicle plot, and dendrogram illustrate the results produced by a hierarchical clustering solution. Several variations of these plots may also be useful. For example, when there are many cases, the initial steps of the cluster analysis may not be of particular interest. You might want to display solutions for only certain numbers of clusters. Or you might want to see the results at every *k*th step. Figure 22.10a contains the icicle plot of results at every fifth step.

Figure 22.10a Icicle plot with results at every fifth step

```
CLUSTER ZCALORIE ZSODIUM ZALCOHOL ZCOST
 /ID=BEER
 /METHOD=COMPLETE
 /PLOT=VICICLE(1,19,5).
```

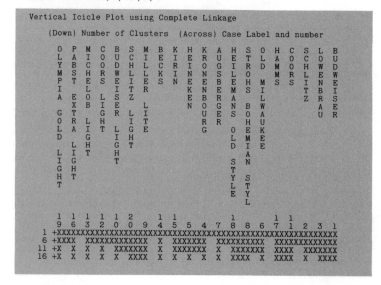

When there are many cases, all of them may not fit across the top of a single page. In this situation it may be useful to turn the icicle plot on its side. This is called a horizontal icicle plot. Figure 22.10b contains the horizontal icicle plot corresponding to Figure 22.7a.

Figure 22.10b Horizontal icicle plot

```
CLUSTER ZCALORIE ZSODIUM ZALCOHOL ZCOST
 /ID=BEER
 /METHOD=COMPLETE
 /PLOT=HICICLE.
```

```
      Horizontal Icicle Plot Using Complete Linkage

                                   Number of Clusters

                                          1111111111
                C A S E            1234567890123456789
           Label            Seq    +++++++++++++++++++

      OLYMPIA GOLD LIGHT     19    XXXXXXXXXXXXXXXXXXX
                                   XXXXXXX
                                   XXXXXX
      PABST EXTRA LIGHT      16    XXXXXXXXXXXXXXXXXXX
                                   X
                                   X
      MICHELOB LIGHT         13    XXXXXXXXXXXXXXXXXXX
                                   XXXXXXXX
                                   XXXXXXXX
      COORS LIGHT            12    XXXXXXXXXXXXXXXXXXX
                                   XXXXXXXXX
                                   XXXXXXXXX
      BUDWEISER LIGHT        10    XXXXXXXXXXXXXXXXXXX
                                   XXXXXXXXXXXX
                                   XXXXXXXXXXXX
      SCHLITZ LIGHT          20    XXXXXXXXXXXXXXXXXXX
                                   XXXXXXXXXXXXXXXX
                                   XXXXXXXXXXXXXXXX
      MILLER LITE             9    XXXXXXXXXXXXXXXXXXX
                                   XXX
                                   XXX
      BECKS                  14    XXXXXXXXXXXXXXXXXXX
                                   XXXXX
                                   XXXXX
      KIRIN                  15    XXXXXXXXXXXXXXXXXXX
                                   XXXXXXXXXXXXX
                                   XXXXXXXXXXXXX
      HEINEKEN                5    XXXXXXXXXXXXXXXXXXX
                                   XXXXXXXXXXXX
                                   XXXXXXXXXXXX
      KRONENBOURG             4    XXXXXXXXXXXXXXXXXXX
                                   XX
                                   XX
      AUGSBERGER              7    XXXXXXXXXXXXXXXXXXX
                                   XXXXXX
                                   XXXXXX
      HEILEMANS OLD STYLE    18    XXXXXXXXXXXXXXXXXXX
                                   XXXXXXXXXXXXXXX
                                   XXXXXXXXXXXXXXX
      STROHS BOHEMIAN STYL    8    XXXXXXXXXXXXXXXXXXX
                                   XXXXXXXXXXX
                                   XXXXXXXXXXX
      OLD MILWAUKEE           6    XXXXXXXXXXXXXXXXXXX
                                   XXXX
                                   XXXX
      HAMMS                  17    XXXXXXXXXXXXXXXXXXX
                                   XXXXXXXXXXXXXXXXX
                                   XXXXXXXXXXXXXXXXX
      COORS                  11    XXXXXXXXXXXXXXXXXXX
                                   XXXXXXXXX
                                   XXXXXXXXX
      SCHLITZ                 2    XXXXXXXXXXXXXXXXXXX
                                   XXXXXXXXXXXXXX
                                   XXXXXXXXXXXXXX
      LOWENBRAU               3    XXXXXXXXXXXXXXXXXXX
                                   XXXXXXXXXXXXXX
                                   XXXXXXXXXXXXXX
      BUDWEISER               1    XXXXXXXXXXXXXXXXXXX
```

Although the composition of clusters at any stage can be discerned from the icicle plots, it is often helpful to display the information in tabular form. Figure 22.10c contains the cluster memberships for the cases at different stages of the solution. From Figure 22.10c, you can easily tell which clusters cases belong to in the two- to five-cluster solutions.

Figure 22.10c   Cluster membership at different stages

```
CLUSTER ZCALORIE ZSODIUM ZALCOHOL ZCOST
  /ID=BEER
  /PRINT=CLUSTER(2,5)
  /METHOD=COMPLETE.
```

Cluster Membership of Cases using Complete Linkage

		Number of Clusters			
Label	Case	5	4	3	2
BUDWEISER	1	1	1	1	1
SCHLITZ	2	1	1	1	1
LOWENBRAU	3	1	1	1	1
KRONENBOURG	4	2	2	2	1
HEINEKEN	5	2	2	2	1
OLD MILWAUKEE	6	3	1	1	1
AUGSBERGER	7	3	1	1	1
STROHS BOHEMIAN STYL	8	3	1	1	1
MILLER LITE	9	4	3	2	1
BUDWEISER LIGHT	10	4	3	2	1
COORS	11	1	1	1	1
COORS LIGHT	12	4	3	2	1
MICHELOB LIGHT	13	4	3	2	1
BECKS	14	2	2	2	1
KIRIN	15	2	2	2	1
PABST EXTRA LIGHT	16	5	4	3	2
HAMMS	17	1	1	1	1
HEILEMANS OLD STYLE	18	3	1	1	1
OLYMPIA GOLD LIGHT	19	5	4	3	2
SCHLITZ LIGHT	20	4	3	2	1

22.11 MORE ON CALCULATING DISTANCES AND SIMILARITIES

There are many methods for estimating the distance or similarity between two cases. But even before these measures are computed, you must decide whether the variables need to be rescaled. When the variables have different scales, such as cents and calories, and they are not standardized, any distance measure will reflect primarily the contributions of variables measured in the large units. For example, the beer data variables were standardized prior to cluster analysis to have a mean of 0 and a standard deviation of 1. Besides standardization to Z scores, variables can be standardized by dividing by just the standard deviation, the range, the mean, or the maximum. See Romesburg (1984) or Anderberg (1973) for further discussion.

Based on the transformed data it is possible to calculate many different types of distance and similarity measures. Different distance and similarity measures weight data characteristics differently. The choice among the measures should be based on which differences or similarities in the data are important for a particular application. For example, if one is clustering animal bones, what may matter is not the actual differences in bone size but relationships among the dimensions, since we know that even animals of the same species differ in size. Bones with the same relationship between length and diameter should be judged as similar, regardless of their absolute magnitudes. See Romesburg (1984) for further discussion.

The most commonly used distance measure, the squared Euclidean distance, has been discussed previously. Sometimes its square root, the Euclidean distance, is also used. A distance measure that is based on the absolute values of differences is the *city-block* or *Manhattan* distance. For two cases it is just the sum of the absolute differences of the values for all variables. Since the differences are not squared, large differences are not weighted as heavily as in the squared Euclidean distances. The *Chebychev* distance defines the distance between two cases as the maximum absolute difference in the values over all variables. Thus, it ignores much of the available information.

When variables are binary, special distance and similarity measures are required. Many are based on the familiar measures of association for contingency tables. See Chapter 24 for further description of the numerous measures computed by the PROXIMITIES procedure.

22.12 METHODS FOR COMBINING CLUSTERS

Many methods can be used to decide which cases or clusters should be combined at each step. In general, clustering methods fall into three groups: linkage methods, error sums of squares or variance methods, and centroid methods. All are based on either a matrix of distances or a matrix of similarities between pairs of cases. The methods differ in how they estimate distances between clusters at successive steps. Since the merging of clusters at each step depends on the distance measure, different distance measures can result in different cluster solutions for the same clustering method. See Milligan (1980) for comparisons of the performance of some of the different clustering methods.

One of the simplest methods for joining clusters is *single linkage,* sometimes called "nearest neighbor." The first two cases combined are those with the smallest distance, or greatest similarity, between them. The distance between the new cluster and individual cases is then computed as the minimum distance between an individual case and a case in the cluster. The distances between cases that have not been joined do not change. At every step the distance between two clusters is taken to be the distance between their two closest points.

Another commonly used method is called *complete linkage,* or the "furthest neighbor" technique. In this method the distance between two clusters is calculated as the distance between their two furthest points.

The *average linkage between groups method,* often called UPGMA (unweighted pair-group method using arithmetic averages), defines the distance between two clusters as the average of the distances between all pairs of cases in which one member of the pair is from each of the clusters. For example, if Cases 1 and 2 form cluster A and Cases 3, 4, and 5 form cluster B, the distance between clusters A and B is taken to be the average of the distances between the following pairs of cases: (1,3) (1,4) (1,5) (2,3) (2,4) (2,5). This differs from the linkage methods in that it uses information about all pairs of distances, not just the nearest or the furthest. For this reason it is usually preferred to the single and complete linkage methods for cluster analysis.

The UPGMA method considers only distances between pairs of cases in different clusters. A variant of it, *the average linkage within groups,* combines clusters so that the average distance between all cases in the resulting cluster is as small as possible. Thus, the distance between two clusters is taken to be the average of the distances between all possible pairs of cases in the resulting cluster.

Another frequently used method for cluster formation is *Ward's method.* For each cluster the means for all variables are calculated. Then for each case the squared Euclidean distance to the cluster means is calculated. These distances are summed for all of the cases. At each step, the two clusters that merge are those that result in the smallest increase in the overall sum of the squared within-cluster distances.

The *centroid method* calculates the distance between two clusters as the distance between their means for all of the variables. One disadvantage of the centroid method is that the distance at which clusters are combined can actually decrease from one step to the next. Since clusters merged at later stages are more dissimilar than those merged at early stages, this is an undesirable property.

In the centroid method, the centroid of a merged cluster is a weighted combination of the centroids of the two individual clusters, where the weights are proportional to the sizes of the clusters. In the *median method,* the two clusters being combined are weighted equally in the computation of the centroid, regardless of the number of cases in each. This allows small groups to have equal effect on the characterization of larger clusters into which they are merged. Squared Euclidean distances should be used with both centroid and median methods.

Some of the above methods, such as single and complete linkage and the average distances between and within clusters, can be used with similarity or distance measures. Other methods require particular types of distance measures. In particular, the median, centroid, and Ward's methods should use squared Euclidean distances. When similarity measures are used, the criteria for combining is reversed. That is, clusters with large similarity-based measures are merged.

22.13 CLUSTERING VARIABLES

In the previous example, the units used for cluster analysis were individual cases (the different brands of beer). Cluster analysis can also be used to find homogeneous groups of variables. For example, consider the 14 community variables described in Chapter 21. We could use cluster analysis to group the 88 counties included in the study and then examine the resulting clusters to establish the characteristics they share. Another approach is to cluster the 14 variables used to describe the communities. In this case, the unit used for analysis is the variable. The distance or similarity measures are computed for all pairs of variables. (Distances can be calculated in the PROXIMITIES procedure; see Chapter 24).

Figure 22.13 contains the results of clustering the community variables using the absolute value of the correlation coefficient as a measure of similarity. The absolute value of the coefficient is used since it is a measure of the strength of the relationship. The sign indicates only the direction. If you want clusters for positively correlated variables only, the sign of the coefficient should be maintained.

The clustering procedure is the same whether variables or cases are clustered. It starts out with as many clusters as there are variables. At each successive step, variables or clusters of variables are merged, as shown in the icicle plot in Figure 22.13.

Consider the four-cluster solution. The HEALTH, COMMEFFC, CHLDNEGL, and UNEMPLOY variables form one cluster; the FARMERS, INDUSTZN, COMMERCL, RETAILNG, FEMEMPLD, and NEWSCIRC variables form the second cluster; MENTALIL is a cluster by itself; and the fourth cluster is MIGRNPOP, DWELGNEW, and POPSTABL.

If you've read Chapter 21, this solution should appear familiar. The groupings of the variables are exactly those established by the factor analysis. The first cluster is the WELFARE factor, the second the URBANISM, and the fourth INFLUX. In both cases the extent of mental illness does not appear to be related to the remainder of the variables.

Figure 22.13 Cluster analysis of the community variables

```
MATRIX DATA VARIABLES=POPSTABL NEWSCIRC FEMEMPLD FARMERS RETAILNG
    COMMERCL INDUSTZN HEALTH CHLDNEGL COMMEFFC DWELGNEW MIGRNPOP
    UNEMPLOY MENTALIL
    /CONTENTS=PROX
    /N=88.
BEGIN DATA.
1.
-.175 1.
-.276 .616 1.
 .369 -.625 -.637 1.
-.127 .624 .736 -.519 1.
-.069 .652 .589 -.306 .727 1.
-.106 .712 .742 -.545 .785 .911 1.
-.149 -.030 .241 -.068 .100 .123 .129 1.
-.039 -.171 -.589 .257 -.557 -.357 -.424 -.407 1.
-.005 .100 .471 -.213 .452 .287 .357 .732 -.660 1.
-.670 .188 .413 -.579 .165 .030 .203 .290 -.138 .311 1.
-.476 -.086 .064 -.198 .007 -.068 -.024 .083 .148 .067 .505 1.
 .137 -.373 -.689 .450 -.650 -.424 -.528 -.348 .733 -.601 -.266 .181
1.0
 .237 .046 -.237 .121 -.190 -.055 -.095 -.279 .247 -.324 -.266 -.307 .217
1.
END DATA.
PROXIMITIES  /MATRIX=IN (*)
 /MEASURE=NONE ABSOLUTE
 /MATRIX=OUT (*).
CLUSTER /MATRIX=IN (*).
```

```
Vertical Icicle Plot using Average Linkage (Between Groups)

  (Down) Number of Clusters   (Across) Case Label and number

      U  C  C  H  F  I  C  R  F  N  M  M  D  P
      N  H  O  E  A  N  O  E  E  E  E  I  W  O
      E  L  M  A  R  D  M  T  M  W  N  G  E  P
      M  D  M  L  M  U  M  A  E  S  T  R  L  S
      P  N  E  T  E  S  E  I  M  C  A  N  G  T
      L  E  F  H  R  T  R  L  P  I  L  P  N  A
      O  G  F     S  Z  C  N  L  R  I  O  E  B
      Y  L  C        N  L  G  D  C  L  P  W  L

      1     1                       1  1  1
      3  9  0  8  4  7  6  5  3  2  4  2  1  1
   1 +XXXXXXXXXXXXXXXXXXXXXXXXXXXXXXXXXXXXXXXXX
   2 +XXXXXXXXXXXXXXXXXXXXXXXXXXXXX  XXXXXXXXX
   3 +XXXXXXXXXXXXXXXXXXXXXXXXXXXX   X  XXXXXXX
   4 +XXXXXXXXXX   XXXXXXXXXXXXXXXX  X  XXXXXXX
   5 +XXXXXXXXXX   XXXXXXXXXXXXXXXX  X  X XXXX
   6 +XXXX  XXXX   XXXXXXXXXXXXXXXX  X  X  XXXX
   7 +XXXX  XXXX  X  XXXXXXXXXXXX    X  X  XXXX
   8 +XXXX  XXXX  X  XXXXXXXXX  X  X  X  XXXX
   9 +XXXX  XXXX  X  XXXXXXXXX  X  X  X  X  X
  10 +XXXX  XXXX  X  XXXXXXX  X  X  X  X  X  X
  11 +XXXX  X  X  X  XXXXXXX  X  X  X  X  X  X
  12 +X  X  X  X  X  XXXXXX  X  X  X  X  X  X
  13 +X  X  X  X  X  XXXX  X  X  X  X  X  X  X
```

This is not a chance occurrence. Although factor analysis has an underlying theoretical model and cluster analysis is much more ad hoc, both identify related groups of variables. However, factor analysis allows variables to be either positively or negatively related to a factor. Cluster analysis can be restricted to search only for positive associations between variables. Thus, if the absolute values of the correlation coefficients are not taken, variables that correlate negatively with a factor do not appear in the same cluster with variables that correlate positively. For example, the FARMERS variable would not appear with the other urbanism variables. Factor analysis and cluster analysis need not always arrive at the same variable groupings, but it is comforting when they do.

22.14
RUNNING
PROCEDURE
CLUSTER

Use the CLUSTER procedure to obtain hierarchical clusters for cases when the number of cases is not too large. (If the number of cases exceeds several hundred, use the QUICK CLUSTER procedure described in Chapter 23.) Variables can also be clustered if the data are in the appropriate format (for example, if you have a correlation matrix or some other measure of distance). CLUSTER provides several measures of dissimilarity and allows you to specify missing-value treatment. A matrix of similarity or dissimilarity coefficients can be entered and used to cluster cases or variables.

Procedure PROXIMITIES, described in Chapter 24, is useful for computing a wide variety of distance and similarity coefficients for either cases or variables. Options for standardizing matrix data are also available. (The CLUSTER procedure does not allow for data standardizations. Examples in this chapter were first standardized with the DESCRIPTIVES procedure; see Chapter 8.) Proximity matrices from procedure PROXIMITIES can be used in the CLUSTER procedure, as well as in other procedures that permit matrix input.

By default, CLUSTER performs cluster analysis using the average linkage between groups and squared Euclidean distances and displays the agglomeration schedule and a vertical icicle plot (see Sections 22.16 through 22.19).

22.15
Specifying the Variables

The first specification on CLUSTER is a list of variables to use in computing similarities or distances between cases, as in

```
CLUSTER ZCALORIE ZSODIUM ZALCOHOL ZCOST.
```

The variable list is the only required specification and must precede any optional subcommands. If you are using matrix data, specified with the MATRIX subcommand (see Section 22.22), the variable list should be omitted.

22.16
METHOD Subcommand

The METHOD subcommand specifies the clustering method. If you do not specify a method, CLUSTER uses the average linkage between groups method (see Section 22.12). You can specify more than one method on a single METHOD subcommand.

BAVERAGE   *Average linkage between groups (UPGMA).* This is the default.
WAVERAGE   *Average linkage within groups.*
SINGLE   *Single linkage or nearest neighbor.*
COMPLETE   *Complete linkage or furthest neighbor.*
CENTROID   *Centroid clustering (UPGMC).* Squared Euclidean distances are commonly used with this method.
MEDIAN   *Median clustering (WPGMC).* Squared Euclidean distances are commonly used with this method.
WARD   *Ward's method.* Squared Euclidean distances are commonly used with this method.

For example, the command

```
CLUSTER ZCALORIE ZSODIUM ZALCOHOL ZCOST
 /METHOD=SINGLE COMPLETE.
```

requests clustering with both the single and complete methods.

22.17
MEASURE Subcommand

Use the MEASURE subcommand to specify the distance measure to use for clustering cases (see Section 22.2 and 22.11). If you omit MEASURE, CLUSTER uses squared Euclidean distances. You can specify only one distance measure.

MEASURE has the following keywords:

SEUCLID *Squared Euclidean distances.* This is the default. SEUCLID is the measure commonly used with the centroid, median, and Ward's methods of clustering. The distance between two cases is the sum of the squared diferences in value for each variable:

$$\text{Distance}(X, Y) = \sum_i (X_i - Y_i)^2$$

EUCLID *Euclidean distances.* The distance between two cases is the square root of the sum of the squared differences in values for each variable:

$$\text{Distance}(X, Y) = \sqrt{\sum_i (X_i - Y_i)^2}$$

COSINE *Cosine of vectors of variables.* This is a pattern similarity measure:

$$\text{Similarity}(X, Y) = \frac{\sum_i (X_i Y_i)}{\sqrt{\sum_i (X_i^2) \sum_i (Y_i^2)}}$$

BLOCK *City-block or Manhattan distances.* The distance between two cases is the sum of the absolute differences in values for each variable:

$$\text{Distance}(X, Y) = \sum_i |X_i - Y_i|$$

CHEBYCHEV *Chebychev distance metric.* The distance between two cases is the maximum absolute difference in values for any variable:

$$\text{Distance}(X, Y) = MAX_i |X_i - Y_i|$$

POWER(p,r) *Distances in an absolute power metric.* The distance between two cases is the rth root of the sum of the absolute differences to the pth power in values on each variable:

$$\text{Distance}(X, Y) = \left(\sum_i |X_i - Y_i|^p\right)^{\frac{1}{r}}$$

Appropriate selection of integer parameters p and r yields Euclidean, squared Euclidean, Minkowski, city-block, minimum, maximum, and many other distance metrics.

DEFAULT

22.18
PRINT Subcommand

CLUSTER automatically displays the clustering method, the similarity or distance measure used for clustering, and the number of cases. Use the PRINT subcommand to obtain additional output.

SCHEDULE *Agglomeration schedule.* Display the order in which and distances at which clusters combine to form new clusters as well as the last cluster level at which a case (or variable) joined the cluster (see Figures 22.8 and 22.9b). The agglomeration schedule is displayed by default if you do not specify PRINT. If you specify PRINT, you must request SCHEDULE explicitly.

CLUSTER(min,max) *Cluster membership. Min* and *max* specify the minimum and maximum numbers of clusters in the cluster solutions. For each case, CLUSTER displays an identifying label and values indicating which cluster the case belongs to in a given cluster solution. Cases are identified by case number plus the value of any string variable specified on the ID subcommand (see Section 22.20).

DISTANCE *Matrix of distances or similarities between items.* The type of matrix produced (similarities or dissimilarities) depends upon the measure selected. With a large number of clustered cases, DISTANCE uses considerable computer processing time.

NONE   *No display output.* Use PRINT=NONE when you want to suppress all display output, such as when you are using SAVE.

For example, the command

```
CLUSTER ZCALORIE ZSODIUM ZALCOHOL ZCOST
 /ID=BEER
 /PRINT=CLUSTER(2,5)
 /METHOD=COMPLETE.
```

produces Figure 22.10c.

22.19
PLOT Subcommand

CLUSTER produces the vertical icicle plot by default. Use the PLOT subcommand to obtain a horizontal icicle plot or a dendrogram. When you specify PLOT, only the requested plots are produced.

VICICLE(min,max,inc)   *Vertical icicle plot.* The optional *min*, *max*, and *inc* specifications indicate the minimum and maximum numbers of cluster solutions to plot and the increment to use between cluster levels. Min, max, and inc must be integers. By default, the increment is 1 and all cluster solutions are plotted. VICICLE is the default if the PLOT subcommand is omitted.

HICICLE(min,max,inc)   *Horizontal icicle plot.* Has the same specifications as VICICLE. (See Figure 22.10b.)

DENDROGRAM   *Dendrogram.* The dendrogram is scaled by joining the distances of the clusters. (See Figures 22.9c and 22.9d.)

NONE   *No display output.* Use PLOT=NONE to suppress all plots.

For example, Figure 22.10a was produced by the following command:

```
CLUSTER ZCALORIE ZSODIUM ZALCOHOL ZCOST
 /ID=BEER
 /METHOD=COMPLETE
 /PLOT=VICICLE(1,19,5).
```

If there is insufficient memory to plot a dendrogram or icicle plot, CLUSTER performs the cluster analysis, skips the plot, and displays an error message. To obtain a plot when this occurs, request more memory or specify an increment for VICICLE or HICICLE.

22.20
ID Subcommand

By default, CLUSTER identifies cases by case number. Name a string variable on the ID subcommand to identify cases with string values. For example, the subcommand

```
 /ID=BEER
```

produces the beer-name labels in Figures 22.7a, 22.9a, 22.9c, 22.9d, 22.10a, 22.10b, and 22.10c.

22.21
MISSING Subcommand

CLUSTER uses listwise deletion as the default missing-value treatment. A case with missing values for any clustering variable is excluded from the analysis. Use the MISSING subcommand to treat user-defined missing values as valid.

INCLUDE   *Include user-missing values.*

LISTWISE   *Delete cases with missing values listwise.* This is the default.

Cases with system-missing values for clustering variables are never included in the analysis.

22.22
MATRIX Subcommand

The CLUSTER procedure can read and write proximity-type matrix materials. The MATRIX subcommand has the following two keywords:

OUT *Write matrix materials.* After OUT, specify in parentheses either a name for the matrix file or an asterisk (*) to replace the active system file with the matrix.

IN *Read matrix materials.* After IN, specify in parentheses either the name of the matrix file to read or an asterisk (*) to read the matrix materials from the active file.

For example, the following commands were used to produce Figure 22.13 from a proximities matrix:

```
PROXIMITIES  /MATRIX=IN (*)
 /MEASURE=NONE ABSOLUTE
 /MATRIX=OUT (*).
 CLUSTER /MATRIX=IN (*).
```

If you specify MATRIX=IN, you can omit the variable list on CLUSTER. By default, all variables in the matrix are included. You can use the variable list to specify a subset of the matrix, but you must use variable names defined on the matrix system file. (See Chapter 24 for a discussion of matrix system files created with the PROXIMITIES procedure and the *SPSS Reference Guide* for a complete discussion of matrix system files.)

You must use a slash to separate the MATRIX subcommand from the command keyword CLUSTER and other subcommands.

22.23
SAVE Subcommand

Use the SAVE subcommand to save cluster memberships at specified cluster levels as new variables on the active system file. You must specify a rootname for each cluster method for which you want to save cluster membership, as in:

```
CLUSTER A B C
 /METHOD=BAVERAGE(CLUSMEM)
 /SAVE=CLUSTERS(3,5).
```

This command saves each case's cluster memberships for the three-, four-, and five-cluster solutions. The new variables derive their names from the rootname CLUSMEM and appear on the active system file in the order CLUSMEM5, CLUSMEM4, and CLUSMEM3. CLUSTER prints the names of variables it adds to the active system file.

Contents

23 Cluster Analysis for Large Files: Procedure QUICK CLUSTER

Chapter 22 discusses the basics of cluster analysis and describes a commonly used method for cluster formation—agglomerative hierarchical clustering. This is but one of many methods available for cluster formation. For a particular problem, selection of a method to use depends not only on the characteristics of the various methods but also on the data set to be analyzed. For example, when the number of cases is large, algorithms that require many computations or storage of all cases in a computer's "memory" may pose difficulties in terms of either time required to perform the computations or available memory.

This chapter describes the QUICK CLUSTER procedure, which can be used to cluster large numbers of cases efficiently without requiring substantial computer resources. Unlike the CLUSTER procedure, which results in a series of solutions corresponding to different numbers of clusters, the QUICK CLUSTER procedure produces only one solution for the number of clusters requested. The number of clusters must be specified by the user.

23.1 THE METHOD

The algorithm used for determining cluster membership in the QUICK CLUSTER procedure is based on nearest centroid sorting (Anderberg, 1973). That is, a case is assigned to the cluster for which the distance between the case and the center of the cluster (centroid) is smallest. The actual mechanics of the procedure depend on the information available. If the cluster centers are known, they can be specified, and case assignment is based on them. Otherwise, cluster centers are estimated from the data.

23.2 Classification When Cluster Centers Are Known

Since QUICK CLUSTER requires a user-specified number of clusters, you may want to use the CLUSTER procedure on a random sample or subset of cases to help determine the number of clusters, before using the QUICK CLUSTER procedure on all cases. The CLUSTER procedure can also be used to determine the initial cluster centers for the QUICK CLUSTER procedure.

Consider the beer data described in Chapter 22. Using the CLUSTER procedure, we identified five interpretable clusters for twenty beers. If there are additional beers that we want to classify into one of these five clusters, we can use the QUICK CLUSTER procedure as a quick and efficient means of doing so (although QUICK CLUSTER is usually most useful if the number of cases is in the range of 200 or more). Each of the new beers is assigned to the cluster to whose center it is closest. For each cluster, the center is just the mean of the four variables for cases in the cluster. These values, standardized, are shown in Figure 23.2a. (The unstandardized values are shown in Chapter 22.)

369

Figure 23.2a Standardized means for the five clusters

```
SELECT IF (NEWOLD EQ 1).
DESCRIPTIVES VARIABLES=CALORIES COST ALCOHOL SODIUM /SAVE.
CLUSTER ZCALORIE ZCOST ZALCOHOL ZSODIUM
 /METHOD=COMPLETE(CLUSMEM) /SAVE=CLUSTERS(5).
VALUE LABELS CLUSMEM5 1 'AVERAGE' 2 'EXPENSIVE' 3 'HIGH NA'
 4 'LIGHT' 5 'VERY LIGHT'.
MEANS TABLES=ZCALORIE ZCOST ZALCOHOL ZSODIUM BY CLUSMEM5 /CELLS=MEAN.
```

- - Description of Subpopulations - -					- - Description of Subpopulations - -			
Summaries of		ZCALORIE			Summaries of		ZALCOHOL	
By levels of		CLUSMEM5			By levels of		CLUSMEM5	
Variable	Value	Label	Mean		Variable	Value	Label	Mean
CLUSMEM5	1	AVERAGE	.4362		CLUSMEM5	1	AVERAGE	.3421
CLUSMEM5	2	EXPENSIVE	.7551		CLUSMEM5	2	EXPENSIVE	.7039
CLUSMEM5	3	HIGH NA	.6890		CLUSMEM5	3	HIGH NA	.6382
CLUSMEM5	4	LIGHT	-.7667		CLUSMEM5	4	LIGHT	-.4474
CLUSMEM5	5	VERY LIGHT	-2.0621		CLUSMEM5	5	VERY LIGHT	-2.4211

- - Description of Subpopulations - -					- - Description of Subpopulations - -			
Summaries of		ZCOST			Summaries of		ZSODIUM	
By levels of		CLUSMEM5			By levels of		CLUSMEM5	
Variable	Value	Label	Mean		Variable	Value	Label	Mean
CLUSMEM5	1	AVERAGE	-.3790		CLUSMEM5	1	AVERAGE	.3418791
CLUSMEM5	2	EXPENSIVE	1.8498		CLUSMEM5	2	EXPENSIVE	-.6381744
CLUSMEM5	3	HIGH NA	-.7928		CLUSMEM5	3	HIGH NA	1.4510870
CLUSMEM5	4	LIGHT	-.2538		CLUSMEM5	4	LIGHT	-.7217448
CLUSMEM5	5	VERY LIGHT	-.5320		CLUSMEM5	5	VERY LIGHT	-.6761610

The cases in the new data set are standardized using the means and standard deviations of the original data set (see Chapter 22). The COMPUTE commands that create the standardized variables and the computed values are shown in Figure 23.2b.

Figure 23.2b Original and standardized values for the 15 new beers

```
COMPUTE ZCALORIE=(CALORIES-132.4)/30.26.
COMPUTE ZCOST=(COST-.4965)/.1438.
COMPUTE ZALCOHOL=(ALCOHOL-4.44)/.76.
COMPUTE ZSODIUM=(SODIUM-14.95)/6.58.
FORMATS ZCALORIE ZCOST ZALCOHOL ZSODIUM (F5.2).
TEMPORARY.
SELECT IF (NEWOLD EQ 0).
LIST VARIABLES=BEER CALORIES SODIUM ALCOHOL COST
 ZCALORIE ZSODIUM ZALCOHOL ZCOST.
```

BEER	CALORIES	SODIUM	ALCOHOL	COST	ZCALORIE	ZSODIUM	ZALCOHOL	ZCOST
MILLER HIGH LIFE	149	17	4.7	.42	.55	.31	.34	-.53
MICHELOB	162	10	5.0	.50	.98	-.75	.74	.02
LABATTS	147	17	5.0	.53	.48	.31	.74	.23
MOLSON	154	17	5.1	.56	.71	.31	.87	.44
HENRY WEINHARD	149	7	4.7	.61	.55	-1.21	.34	.79
ANCHOR STEAM	154	17	4.7	1.20	.71	.31	.34	4.89
SCHMIDTS	147	7	4.7	.30	.48	-1.21	.34	-1.37
PABST BLUE RIBBON	152	8	4.9	.38	.65	-1.06	.61	-.81
OLYMPIA	153	27	4.6	.44	.68	1.83	.21	-.39
DOS EQUIS	145	14	4.5	.70	.42	-.14	.08	1.42
SCOTCH BUY (SAFEWAY)	145	18	4.5	.27	.42	.46	.08	-1.58
BLATZ	144	13	4.6	.30	.38	-.30	.21	-1.37
ROLLING ROCK	144	8	4.7	.36	.38	-1.06	.34	-.95
TUBORG	155	13	5.0	.43	.75	-.30	.74	-.46
ST PAULI GIRL	144	21	4.7	.77	.38	.92	.34	1.90

Number of cases read: 15   Number of cases listed: 15

Next, the Euclidean distance (Chapter 22) to each of the cluster centers is s calculated for each case in the new data set. The cluster centers are simply the means from Figure 23.2a and are specified on the INITIAL subcommand on QUICK CLUSTER (Figure 23.2c). The output displays these centers as **Classification Cluster Centers,** since they will be used to assign cases to clusters.

Figure 23.2c   Classification cluster centers

```
TEMPORARY.
SELECT IF (NEWOLD EQ 0).
QUICK CLUSTER ZCALORIE ZCOST ZALCOHOL ZSODIUM
 /CRITERIA=CLUSTERS(5) NOUPDATE
 /INITIAL=(.436   -.379    .342     .342
            .755  1.85     .704    -.639
            .689  -.793    .638    1.45
           -.767  -.254   -.447    -.722
          -2.06   -.532  -2.42     -.676).
```

Cluster	ZCALORIE	ZCOST	ZALCOHOL	ZSODIUM
1	.4360	-.3790	.3420	.3420
2	.7550	1.8500	.7040	-.6390
3	.6890	-.7930	.6380	1.4500
4	-.7670	-.2540	-.4470	-.7220
5	-2.0600	-.5320	-2.4200	-.6760

Classification Cluster Centers.

The first new beer to be classified is Miller High Life. From Figure 23.2b, its standardized value for calories is 0.55, for cost is -0.53, for alcohol is 0.34, and for sodium is 0.31. Its Euclidean distance to Cluster 1 is

$$\sqrt{(0.55-0.44)^2 + (-0.53-(-0.38))^2 + (0.34-0.34)^2 + (0.31-0.34)^2} = 0.19$$

Equation 23.2a

Distances to the other cluster centers are computed in the same way. The distance to Cluster 2 is 2.6, to Cluster 3 is 1.21, to Cluster 4 is 1.87, and to Cluster 5 is 3.92. Since the distance is smallest to Cluster 1, Miller High Life is assigned to it.

Figure 23.2d contains the cluster numbers to which the new beers are assigned, as well as the Euclidean distance from the case to the center of the cluster to which it is assigned. As shown in Figure 23.2e, ten beers are assigned to Cluster 1, four to Cluster 2, and one to Cluster 3. No beers are assigned to the last two clusters.

Figure 23.2d   Case listing of cluster membership

```
QUICK CLUSTER ZCALORIE ZCOST ZALCOHOL ZSODIUM
 /CRITERIA=CLUSTERS(5) NOUPDATE
 /INITIAL=(.436   -.379    .342     .342
            .755  1.85     .704    -.639
            .689  -.793    .638    1.45
           -.767  -.254   -.447    -.722
          -2.06   -.532  -2.42     -.676)
 /PRINT=ID(BEER) CLUSTER.
```

Case listing of Cluster membership.

BEER	Cluster	Distance
MILLER HIGH LIFE	1	.192
MICHELOB	1	1.345
LABATTS	1	.730
MOLSON	1	1.014
HENRY WEINHARD	2	1.274
ANCHOR STEAM	2	3.208
SCHMIDTS	1	1.839
PABST BLUE RIBBON	1	1.502
OLYMPIA	3	.699
DOS EQUIS	2	.969
SCOTCH BUY (SAFEWAY)	1	1.231
BLATZ	1	1.184
ROLLING ROCK	1	1.511
TUBORG	1	.817
ST PAULI GIRL	2	1.643

Figure 23.2e Number of cases in each cluster

```
Number of Cases in each Cluster.

    Cluster        unweighted cases      weighted cases

       1                  10.0                 10.0
       2                   4.0                  4.0
       3                   1.0                  1.0
       4                    .0                   .0
       5                    .0                   .0

Missing                     0
Total                     15.0                 15.0
```

Once the beers have been assigned to clusters, it is possible to calculate the actual centers of the resulting clusters, which are just the average values of the variables for cases in the cluster. These values, labeled **Final Cluster Centers,** are shown in Figure 23.2f. Since no cases were assigned to the last two clusters, system-missing values are displayed. From this table, we can see that the clusters do not differ much in average calories, since all three have similar standardized values. Cluster 2 has the beers with the highest cost, while Cluster 3 contains the high-sodium beers.

Figure 23.2f Final cluster centers

```
Final Cluster Centers.

    Cluster     ZCALORIE        ZCOST        ZALCOHOL        ZSODIUM

       1          .5783        -.6363          .5000         -.3267
       2          .5155        2.2497          .2763         -.0304
       3          .6808        -.3929          .2105         1.8313
       4            .              .              .              .
       5            .              .              .              .
```

Once clusters have been formed, you can assess how "well-separated" they are by calculating the distances between their centers. Hopefully, the clusters will have centers that are far apart, with cases within a cluster hovering fairly closely to the cluster's center.

Euclidean distances between pairs of final cluster centers are displayed in Figure 23.2g. For example, the distance between Clusters 1 and 2 is

$$\sqrt{(0.58-0.52)^2 + (-0.64-2.25)^2 + (0.50-0.28)^2 + (-0.33-(-0.03))^2} \quad = 2.91$$

Equation 23.2b

Similarly, the distance between Clusters 1 and 3 is 2.19, while the distance between Clusters 2 and 3 is 3.24.

Figure 23.2g Euclidean distances between clusters

```
QUICK CLUSTER ZCALORIE ZCOST ZALCOHOL ZSODIUM
 /CRITERIA=CLUSTERS(5) NOUPDATE
 /INITIAL=(.436   -.379    .342      .342
           .755   1.85     .704     -.639
           .689   -.793    .638     1.45
          -.767   -.254   -.447     -.722
          -2.06   -.532  -2.42      -.676)
 /PRINT=DISTANCE.
```

```
Distances between Final Cluster centers.

    Cluster          1            2            3            4            5

       1          .0000
       2         2.9104        .0000
       3         2.1933       3.2374        .0000
       4            .            .            .          .0000
       5            .            .            .            .          .0000
```

The table of final cluster centers (Figure 23.2f) contains the average values of the variables for each cluster but provides no idea of the variability. One way of assessing the between-cluster to within-cluster variability is to compute a one-way analysis of variance for each of the variables and examine the ratio of the between-cluster to within-cluster mean squares.

Figure 23.2h contains the mean squares for examining differences between the clusters. The between-clusters mean square is labeled **Cluster MS,** and the within-cluster mean square is labeled **Error MS.** Their ratio is in the column labeled **F.** Large ratios and small observed significance levels are associated with variables that differ between the clusters. However, the F tests should only be used for descriptive purposes since the clusters have been chosen to maximize the differences among cases in different clusters. The observed significance levels are not corrected for this and thus cannot be interpreted as tests of the hypothesis that the cluster means are equal.

Figure 23.2h   Cluster mean squares

```
QUICK CLUSTER ZCALORIE ZCOST ZALCOHOL ZSODIUM
 /CRITERIA=CLUSTERS(5) NOUPDATE
 /INITIAL=(.436  -.379   .342    .342
           .755  1.85    .704   -.639
           .689  -.793   .638   1.45
          -.767  -.254  -.447   -.722
          -2.06  -.532  -2.42   -.676)
 /PRINT=ANOVA.
```

Analysis of Variance.						
Variable	Cluster MS	DF	Error MS	DF	F	Prob
ZCALORIE	.0124	2	.0334	12.0	.3712	.698
ZCOST	12.0558	2	1.2003	12.0	10.0438	.003
ZALCOHOL	.0952	2	.0586	12.0	1.6256	.237
ZSODIUM	2.1316	2	.5242	12.0	4.0665	.045

As expected from Figure 23.2f, the calories variable (ZCALORIE) does not differ between the clusters. The F value is small, and the associated significance level is large. Beers in the three clusters also have fairly similar alcohol content (ZALCOHOL). However, they do seem to be different in sodium (ZSODIUM) and cost (ZCOST).

23.3
Classification When Cluster Centers Are Unknown

In the previous example, the cluster centers for classifying cases were already known. The initial cluster solution and the center values were obtained from the CLUSTER solution. In many situations the center values for the clusters are not known in advance. Instead, they too must be estimated from the data. Several different methods for estimating cluster centers are available. Most of them involve examining the data several times.

Good cluster centers separate the cases well. One strategy is to choose cases that have large distances between them and use their values as initial estimates of the cluster centers. The number of cases selected is the number of clusters specified.

The algorithm for this strategy proceeds as follows. The first k cases in the data file, where k is the number of clusters requested, are selected as temporary centers. As subsequent cases are processed, a case replaces a center if its smallest distance to a center is greater than the distance between the two closest centers. The center that is closer to the case is replaced. A case also replaces a center if the smallest distance from the case to a center is larger than the smallest distance between that center and all other centers. Again, it replaces the center closest to it.

To illustrate the basics of the QUICK CLUSTER procedure when centers are estimated from the data, let's consider the beers again, this time using QUICK CLUSTER to cluster all 35 beers into 5 clusters.

23.4
Selecting Initial Cluster Centers

The first step of cluster formation, as previously described, is selection of the first guesses at cluster centers. Although we need not specify anything else about the clusters, we must indicate the number of clusters to be formed. Figure 23.4a contains the values of five centers selected by the program. They are labeled **Initial Cluster Centers.** Each center corresponds to a beer. The first center is Schlitz Light, the second, Kronenbourg, the third, Pabst Extra Light, the next, Anchor Steam, and the last, Heileman's Old Style. These are, in terms of the variables under consideration, well-separated beers. Schlitz Light is a low-calorie beer; Kronenbourg is a low-sodium beer; Pabst Extra Light is a very light beer; Anchor Steam is a very expensive beer; and Heileman's Old Style is a rather average beer, though somewhat higher in sodium than most.

Figure 23.4a   Initial cluster centers for all 35 beers

```
DESCRIPTIVES CALORIES (ZCAL) SODIUM (ZSOD) ALCOHOL (ZALC) COST(ZCST).
QUICK CLUSTER ZCAL ZSOD ZALC ZCST
  /CRITERIA=CLUSTERS(5).
```

Initial Cluster Centers.

Cluster	ZCAL	ZSOD	ZALC	ZCST
1	-1.7496	-1.2461	-.6255	-.1907
2	1.2365	-1.2461	1.0330	1.1973
3	-2.9358	.0558	-3.7765	-.6711
4	.5820	.3813	.2038	3.7064
5	.1730	1.5204	.5354	-.4042

After the initial cluster centers have been selected, all cases are grouped into the cluster with the closest center. Once all cases have been assigned to clusters, average values for the variables are computed from the cases that have been assigned to each cluster and the cases that were the initial cluster centers. These values, shown in Figure 23.4b, are the **Classification Cluster Centers** since they will be used to classify the cases at the next step.

Figure 23.4b   Classification cluster centers

Classification Cluster Centers.

Cluster	ZCAL	ZSOD	ZALC	ZCST
1	-1.5138	-.9695	-.6928	-.2315
2	.8498	-1.0563	.7817	.8577
3	-2.9085	-.1534	-3.6521	-.6237
4	.5820	.3813	.2038	3.7064
5	.3333	.8370	.4196	-.3716

Examination of the classification cluster centers shows that the average profile of the clusters has not changed much from that suggested by the initial centers. The first cluster remains the light beers; the second, low-sodium beers; and so forth. The fourth cluster contains only Anchor Steam, a beer far removed from the others because of its very steep price, almost four standard deviations above the rest.

23.5
A Second Round of Classification

Although at this step all cases have been allocated to clusters based on the initial center values, clustering results can be improved by classifying the cases again using the classification cluster centers. Again, the same rule is used for the formation of clusters. Each case is assigned to the cluster for which its distance to the classification center is smallest. Beer names, cluster numbers, and distances to the cluster centers are shown in Figure 23.5a for the first 10 beers. The count of the number of cases in each cluster is shown in Figure 23.5b.

Figure 23.5a   Case listing of cluster membership

```
QUICK CLUSTER ZCAL ZSOD ZALC ZCST
 /CRITERIA=CLUSTERS(5)
 /PRINT=ID(BEER)  CLUSTER.
```

```
Case listing of Cluster membership.

BEER                        Cluster      Distance

  MILLER HIGH LIFE             5           .513
  BUDWEISER                    5           .827
  SCHLITZ                      5           .217
  LOWENBRAU                    5           .904
  MICHELOB                     2           .942
  LABATTS                      5           .735
  MOLSON                       5           .953
  HENRY WEINHARD               2           .827
  KRONENBOURG                  2           .603
  HEINEKEN                     2           .805
  .
  .
  .
```

Figure 23.5b   Number of cases in each cluster

```
Number of Cases in each Cluster.

  Cluster      unweighted cases      weighted cases

     1              5.0                  5.0
     2              9.0                  9.0
     3              2.0                  2.0
     4              1.0                  1.0
     5             18.0                 18.0

Missing            0
Total             35.0                 35.0
```

Once the cases have been classified a second time, average values of the variables are again computed. These are termed final cluster centers and are shown in Figure 23.5c. The resulting five clusters are quite similar to those obtained with the CLUSTER procedure (Chapter 22) using a subset of the beers. Cluster 1 is the light beers, Cluster 3 is the very light beers, and Cluster 5 is the average beers. Anchor Steam, which was not included in the previous analysis, constitutes a separate cluster.

Figure 23.5c   Final cluster centers

```
Final Cluster Centers.

  Cluster      ZCAL        ZSOD        ZALC        ZCST

     1       -1.2505      -.7253      -.7913      -.2440
     2         .5093      -.9748       .4617       .3491
     3       -2.8540      -.6765     -3.2790      -.4576
     4         .5820       .3813       .2038      3.7064
     5         .3775       .7429       .3420      -.2618
```

Euclidean distances between the final cluster centers are shown in Figure 23.5d. Based on this, you can assess how different the final clusters are. The largest distance is between the very light beers and Anchor Steam; the smallest distance is between the average beers and the light beers. From Figure 23.5e, it appears that for all of the variables, variability within a cluster is less than the variability between the clusters.

Figure 23.5d Euclidean distances between clusters

```
QUICK CLUSTER ZCAL ZSOD ZALC ZCST
 /CRITERIA=CLUSTERS(5)
 /PRINT=DISTANCE.
```

```
Distances between Final Cluster centers.

 Cluster            1           2           3           4           5

    1            .0000
    2           2.2541       .0000
    3           2.9678      5.1034       .0000
    4           4.6020      3.6307      6.5110       .0000
    5           2.4679      1.8318      5.0603      3.9923       .0000
```

Figure 23.5e Cluster mean squares

```
QUICK CLUSTER ZCAL ZSOD ZALC ZCST
 /CRITERIA=CLUSTERS(5)
 /PRINT=ANOVA.
```

```
Analysis of Variance.

 Variable      Cluster MS    DF       Error MS      DF          F      Prob

 ZCAL            7.3370       4         .1551      30.0      47.3136   .000
 ZSOD            5.5445       4         .3941      30.0      14.0701   .000
 ZALC            7.1748       4         .1767      30.0      40.6070   .000
 ZCST            4.1961       4         .5738      30.0       7.3123   .000
```

23.6 RUNNING PROCEDURE QUICK CLUSTER

The QUICK CLUSTER procedure allocates cases to clusters when the number of clusters to be formed is known. It is particularly useful when the number of cases is large, since it requires substantially less computer memory and computation time than does the CLUSTER procedure. The algorithm classifies cases into clusters based on distances to the cluster centers. Cluster centers can either be specified by the user or estimated from the data.

Available output includes estimates of initial, updated, and final cluster centers, distances between all pairs of final cluster centers, cluster membership and distance to the cluster center for all cases, and analysis of variance tables for variables used in the clustering. For each case, cluster membership and distance to the cluster center can be saved as new variables on the active file.

23.7 Variable Specification

The only required specification for QUICK CLUSTER is the list of variables to be used for forming the clusters. The command

```
QUICK CLUSTER ZCALORIE ZCOST ZALCOHOL ZSODIUM.
```

produces a default clustering of cases into two groups based on the values of the four variables. The variable list must precede any optional subcommands.

23.8 CRITERIA Subcommand

Use the CRITERIA subcommand to specify the number of clusters and options for the QUICK CLUSTER algorithm. You can use any of the following keywords with the CRITERIA subcommand:

CLUSTERS(k) *Number of clusters to be formed.* The default is two clusters.

NOINITIAL *No initial cluster center selection.* This keyword specifies that as initial centers, QUICK CLUSTER uses the first k cases without missing values, where k is the number of clusters specified on the CLUSTER keyword. This does not require an extra pass of the data and saves processing time, but it may result in a poor solution.

NOUPDATE *No updating of cluster centers.* This option produces a very quick clustering, but the results are not as good as those from the default procedure. This keyword is required if cluster centers specified with the INITIAL subcommand are to be used for classification.

For example, the command

```
QUICK CLUSTER ZCALORIE ZCOST ZALCOHOL ZSODIUM
 /CRITERIA=CLUSTERS(5).
```

asks for 5 clusters. By default, well-spaced cases are selected as initial centers.

23.9
INITIAL Subcommand

Use the INITIAL subcommand to set the initial cluster centers in your program. You must include a value for each clustering variable for as many clusters as you request. If you specify four clustering variables and five clusters, you must supply 20 values, as in

```
QUICK CLUSTER ZCALORIE ZCOST ZALCOHOL ZSODIUM
 /CRITERIA=CLUSTERS(5) NOUPDATE
 /INITIAL=( .436   -.379    .342     .342
            .755   1.85     .704    -.639
            .689   -.793    .638    1.45
           -.767   -.254   -.447    -.722
          -2.06    -.532  -2.42     -.676).
```

In this example, the first cluster has a value of 0.436 for ZCALORIE, −0.379 for ZCOST, 0.342 for ZALCOHOL, and 0.342 for ZSODIUM.

One way to obtain initial cluster center values is to use the CLUSTER procedure (see Chapter 22) on a random sample or subset of cases before using QUICK CLUSTER on all cases.

23.10
FILE Subcommand

Use the FILE subcommand to obtain initial cluster centers from an SPSS system file. Use the following command to read initial cluster centers from a system file:

```
QUICK CLUSTER A B C D
 /FILE=INIT
 /CRITERIA=CLUSTER(3).
```

In this example, the initial cluster centers are read from file INIT.

23.11
PRINT Subcommand

By default, QUICK CLUSTER displays the initial cluster centers, the centers used for classification, and, when clustering is complete, average values for the variables in each cluster as well as the number of cases in each cluster. To obtain additional output, use the PRINT subcommand with the following keywords:

INITIAL *Initial cluster centers.* The initial cluster centers are displayed by default if you omit the PRINT subcommand or specify PRINT with no subsequent keywords. If you specify any keywords on the PRINT subcommand, you must explicitly specify INITIAL to obtain initial cluster centers.

ID(varname) *Identifying variable for cases.* You can name any variable on your file as the identifier. QUICK CLUSTER uses the values of this variable to identify cases in procedure output (see Figure 23.2d). By default, QUICK CLUSTER identifies cases by case number.

CLUSTER *Cluster membership.* Keyword CLUSTER displays an identifying label for each case, a value indicating the cluster to which each case belongs, and the distance between each case and its classification cluster center (see Figure 23.2d). If you cluster a very large number of cases, this option produces a large volume of output.

DISTANCE   *Distances between final cluster centers.* Use this option to determine how well separated individual pairs of clusters are (see Figure 23.2g). When you request a very large number of clusters, this option can be computationally expensive.

ANOVA   *Univariate* F *tests for each clustering variable.* For each clustering variable, this option displays a univariate F test for the derived clusters (see Figure 23.2h). The F tests are only descriptive. You should *not* interpret the resulting probabilities to test the null hypothesis of no differences among clusters. Cases are systematically assigned to clusters to maximize differences on the clustering variables.

NONE   *Minimum output.* You can use the keyword NONE on the PRINT subcommand for QUICK CLUSTER to display only the classification and final cluster centers and the number of cases in each cluster. NONE also overrides any other specification you use on the PRINT subcommand.

For example, the command

```
QUICK CLUSTER ZCALORIE ZCOST ZALCOHOL ZSODIUM
 /CRITERIA=CLUSTERS(5) NOUPDATE
 /INITIAL=( .436   -.379    .342     .342
            .755   1.85     .704    -.639
            .689   -.793    .638    1.45
           -.767   -.254   -.447    -.722
           -2.06   -.532   -2.42    -.676)
 /PRINT=DISTANCE ANOVA.
```

requests that the distances between pairs of final clusters and an analysis of variance table be included in the display.

23.12
MISSING Subcommand

By default, QUICK CLUSTER eliminates from the analysis cases with system- or user-missing values for any variable on the variable list. Use the MISSING subcommand with one of the following keywords to change the missing-value treatment:

LISTWISE   *Delete cases with missing values on any variable.* This is the default.
PAIRWISE   *Assign cases to clusters based on distances computed from all variables with non-missing values.*
INCLUDE   *Treat user-missing values as non-missing.*

For example, the command

```
QUICK CLUSTER ZCALORIE ZCOST ZALCOHOL ZSODIUM
 /MISSING=INCLUDE.
```

requests that cases with user-missing values be included in the analysis.

23.13
OUTFILE Subcommand

Use the OUTFILE subcommand to save the final cluster centers on an SPSS system file. You can later use these final cluster centers as initial cluster centers for a different sample of cases that use the same variables. You can also cluster the final cluster centers themselves to obtain clusters of clusters. For example, the command

```
QUICK CLUSTER A B C D
 /CRITERIA=CLUSTER(3)
 /OUTFILE=QC1.
```

writes the cluster centers to file QC1.

23.14
SAVE Subcommand

Use the SAVE subcommand to save the cluster membership of cases and to save the distances from the classification cluster centers as new variables on the active system file.

CLUSTER(varname)   *Cluster membership.* The saved variable has integer values indicating the cluster to which each case belongs. The values range from 1 to the number of clusters.

DISTANCE(varname)   *Distance from nearest classification cluster center.*

23.15
Annotated Example

The following SPSS commands created the output in Figures 23.2c, 23.2d, 23.2e, 23.2f, 23.2g, and 23.2h.

```
DATA LIST FIXED /NEWOLD 1 RATING 3 BEER 5-26 (A) ORIGIN 29
 AVAIL 31 PRICE 33-35 COST 37-39 CALORIES 41-43
 SODIUM 45-46 ALCOHOL 48-49 CLASS 51 LIGHT 53.
COMPUTE ZCALORIE=(CALORIES-132.4)/30.26.
COMPUTE ZCOST=(COST-.4965)/.1438.
COMPUTE ZALCOHOL=(ALCOHOL-4.44)/.76.
COMPUTE ZSODIUM=(SODIUM-14.95)/6.58.
BEGIN DATA.
data records
END DATA.
TEMPORARY.
SELECT IF (NEWOLD EQ 0).
QUICK CLUSTER ZCALORIE ZCOST ZALCOHOL ZSODIUM
 /CRITERIA=CLUSTERS(5) NOUPDATE
 /INITIAL=(.436   -.379    .342     .342
           .755   1.85     .704    -.639
           .689   -.793    .638    1.45
          -.767   -.254   -.447    -.722
         -2.06    -.532   -2.42    -.676)
 /PRINT=ID(BEER) CLUSTER DISTANCE ANOVA.
```

- The DATA LIST command defines the variables names and tells SPSS that the data are in fixed format. Each variable name is followed by a column location.

- The four COMPUTE commands create the standardized variables needed for input to the QUICK CLUSTER command. COMPUTE statements, rather than procedure DESCRIPTIVES, are used so that the standardized values are based on the means and standard deviations of the original 20 beers analyzed in Chapter 22.

- The TEMPORARY and SELECT IF commands temporarily select only those beers that were not analyzed in Chapter 22. The variable NEWOLD is coded 0 for the new beers and 1 for the beers previously analyzed.

- The QUICK CLUSTER command names the four standardized variables as the variables to be used for forming clusters.

- The CRITERIA subcommand tells SPSS to form five clusters. Since the values of the initial cluster centers are given on the INITIAL subcommand, the keyword NOUPDATE is required on the CRITERIA subcommand.

- The INITIAL subcommand specifies the initial cluster centers for the QUICK CLUSTER procedure. In this case, the standardized mean values for each of the four variables within each of the five cluster categories, based on the CLUSTER analysis of the original 20 beers, were used.

- The PRINT subcommand asks for all available output, with the values of string variable BEER used to label cases.

Contents

24 Proximity Measures: Procedure PROXIMITIES

Many statistical procedures such as cluster analysis, factor analysis, and multidimensional scaling have as their starting point a matrix of similarities or dissimilarities between pairs of cases or variables. Based on these measures, clusters are formed, factors extracted, and structures and dimensions identified.

There are many different measures that can be used to quantify similarity or dissimilarity. The Pearson correlation coefficient is one of the most frequently used measures of similarity between two variables. Large absolute values of the correlation coefficient indicate that two variables are similar. In general, measures of similarity are constructed so that large values indicate much similarity and small values indicate little similarity.

Unlike similarity measures, which estimate the amount of closeness between two objects, dissimilarity measures estimate the distance or unlikeness of two objects. A large dissimilarity value tells you that two objects are far apart. The larger the measure, the more distant or unlike the two objects are. The squared Euclidean distance, discussed in the CLUSTER chapter, is one of the most commonly used dissimilarity measures when data are interval or ratio.

24.1 SELECTING A MEASURE

In order to decide which similarity or dissimilarity measure to use, you must consider the characteristics of your data. Special measures are available for interval data, frequency counts, and binary data. You must also decide whether you want to standardize the original data in some fashion, and whether you want to standardize the resulting distance measure in some way.

24.2 Standardizing the Data

Suppose you want to look at the distances between pairs of automobiles. For each make of car, you have recorded expected mileage per gallon, engine displacement, curb weight, number of cylinders, and horsepower. These variables are measured on scales that have very different ranges. The number of cylinders probably won't exceed twelve, while the curb weight may well exceed 5000 pounds. If we compute a distance measure that is based on the differences of the values of all of the variables, the variables that have large values will overwhelm the variables with smaller values. For example, a difference of 4 cylinders will be nothing compared to a difference of 100 pounds.

One way to overcome this difficulty is to standardize the variables in some fashion. For example, you can transform each variable to a standardized variable with a mean of 0 and a standard deviation of 1. The contributions of all the variables to the distance measure will then be more comparable. The PROXIMITIES procedure offers several methods for standardization wiich are described in Section 24.9.

24.3
Measures for Interval Data

Chapter 22 gives an example of using and computing the squared Euclidean distance between two cases for cluster analysis. Sometimes its square root, the Euclidean distance, is also used.

A distance measure that is based on the absolute values of differences, instead of their squares, is the *city-block* or *Manhattan distance*. For two cases it is just the sum of the absolute differences of the values for all variables. Since the differences are not squared, large differences are not weighted as heavily as in the squared Euclidean distances.

The *Chebychev distance* defines the distance between two cases as the maximum absolute difference in the values over all variables. Thus it ignores much of the available information.

PROXIMITIES can calculate a variety of other measures, as described in Section 24.12.

24.4
Measures for Frequency Data

When the variables are frequency counts, measures of dissimilarity based on the chi-square statistic can be computed. For example, suppose you want to see how dissimilar authors are in their use of articles. For each author you count the number of times "a," "the" and "an" occur in 600-word passages. For two authors you obtain the following results:

	a	the	an
Author 1	41	23	10
Author 2	32	10	28

You can calculate a dissimilarity measure that is based on the chi-square test of independence. In this example the chi-square value is 14.66, and the chi-square based dissimilarity measure, which is the square root of chi-square, is 3.83.

Since the value of the chi-square statistic depends on the sample size, there is a variant of the chi-square dissimilarity measure that attempts to take sample size into account so that the values of the measure don't depend as much on the actual observed frequencies. The phi-squared measure attempts to normalize the chi-square dissimilarity measure by dividing it by the square root of the sum of the frequencies in the table. In this example the sum of the frequencies is 144, and the value of phi-squared is 0.32 (3.83 divided by the square root of 144).

24.5
Measures for Binary Data

There are numerous similarity coefficients for sets of binary variables. They differ in the importance they attach to the different cells of a 2 × 2 table.

Consider the following two cases and their values for seven binary variables:

	V1	V2	V3	V4	V5	V6	V7
Case 1	0	0	0	0	1	1	1
Case 2	1	1	0	0	1	1	0

We can summarize the results in the following table:

		Case 1	
		Present	Absent
Case 2	Present	2	2
	Absent	1	2

The first cell of the table tells you that for two variables both cases have values of present. Similarly, for two variables both cases have values of absent. For the remaining three variables the cases have different values.

The importance attached to the various cells of the table depends on the nature of the variables. For example, if both cases responded "no" to the question "Have you ever won at least a million dollars in the state lottery?" that doesn't convey much information about similarity. On the other hand a positive answer to the same question may indicate remarkable similarity between the two cases. However, if the question is "Do you own a television set?", matches on the negative may be more informative than matches on the positive. In such situations we may want to weight the positive-positive cell and the negative-negative cell differently.

Similarity measures for binary variables differ in their treatment of the four cells of the table. Some measures exclude the negative-negative cell altogether. Some measures weight matches more than mismatches, and others weight mismatches more than matches. Selection of an appropriate measure must depend on the nature of the variables and the information they convey.

Consider the values of several coefficients for the previous table. The simple matching measure is defined as the number of matches over the total number of variables. In this example we have four matches out of seven variables. The simple matching coefficient is 0.5714. Positive matches and negative matches are treated equally.

The Russell and Rao similarity measure is computed by dividing the number in the positive-positive cell by the total number of entries. For this table its value is 2/7 or 0.28. Note that this measure excludes negative-negative matches from the numerator but not from the denominator.

The Jaccard measure excludes the negative-negative cell from both the numerator and the denominator. For this table the Jaccard measure is 2/5, or 0.4.

The Dice measure excludes negative-negative matches from both the numerator and the denominator and assigns a double weight to the positive-positive cell. For this example the numerator is twice the number of matches, or 4, and the denominator is twice the number of positive positive matches plus the number of nonmatches, or 7. The value of the Dice coefficient is 0.5714.

24.6
Other Types of Binary Coefficients

Binary similarity coefficients that measure how well one variable predicts the other can also be computed. One of these is the symmetric Goodman and Kruskal's lambda, discussed in Chapter 10. Yule's Y and Yule's Q can also be used. Measures based on conditional probabilities are also available. PROXIMITIES can calculate a wide variety of binary coefficients, as described in Section 24.14.

24.7
RUNNING PROCEDURE PROXIMITIES

PROXIMITIES computes measures of similarity, dissimilarity, or distance. PROXIMITIES lets you choose among a great variety of different measures. It computes the measures between pairs of cases or pairs of variables for moderate-sized data sets. You can use output from PROXIMITIES as input matrices for procedure ALSCAL (Chapter 25), CLUSTER (Chapter 22), or FACTOR (Chapter 21). To learn more about proximity matrices and their uses, consult Anderberg (1973) and Romesburg (1984).

24.8
Variable Specification

The only required specification on the PROXIMITIES command is a list of variables to use for computing proximities. The variable list appears immediately after the PROXIMITIES command. If your data are matrix materials specified with the MATRIX=IN subcommand (see Section 24.19), you can omit the variable list. By default, all variables in the matrix are included.

24.9
STANDARDIZE Subcommand

Use the STANDARDIZE subcommand to standardize data values for either cases or variables before computing proximities. You can specify one of two options to control the direction of standardization:

VARIABLE   *Standardize the values for each variable.* This is the default if you use the STANDARDIZE subcommand without any additional specifications.

CASE   *Standardize the values within each case.*

In addition to specifying VARIABLE or CASE, you can also specify one of the following standardization methods:

Z   *Standardize values to Z scores, having 0 mean and unit standard deviation.* PROXIMITIES subtracts the mean from each value for the variable or case being standardized and then divides by the standard deviation of the values. If a standard deviation is 0, PROXIMITIES sets all values for the case or variable to 0. This is the default if you use the STANDARDIZE subcommand without specifying a method.

RANGE   *Standardize values to unit range.* PROXIMITIES divides each value for the variable or case being standardized by the range of the values. If the range is 0, PROXIMITIES leaves all values unchanged.

RESCALE   *Standardize values to a range of 0 to 1.* From each value for the variable or case being standardized, PROXIMITIES subtracts the minimum value and then divides by the range. If a range is 0, PROXIMITIES sets all values for the case or variable to 0.50.

MAX   *Standardize values to a maximum magnitude of 1.* PROXIMITIES divides each value for the variable or case being standardized by the maximum of the values. If the maximum of a set of values is 0, PROXIMITIES uses an alternative process to produce a comparable standardization: it divides by the absolute magnitude of the smallest value and adds 1.

MEAN   *Standardize values to unit mean.* PROXIMITIES divides each value for the variable or case being standardized by the mean of the values. If a mean is 0, PROXIMITIES adds 1 to all values for the case or variable to produce a mean of 1.

SD   *Standardize values to unit standard deviation.* PROXIMITIES divides each value for the variable or case being standardized by the standard deviation of the values. PROXIMITIES does not change the values if their standard deviation is 0.

NONE   *Do not standardize.* Compute proximities using the original values. This is the default if you do not use the STANDARDIZE subcommand.

You can specify both direction and method of standardization on one STANDARDIZE subcommand, as in:

/STANDARDIZE=CASE MEAN

If you use the STANDARDIZE subcommand alone, without specifying a direction or method, variables are standardized to Z-score values by default.

24.10
VIEW Subcommand

Use the VIEW subcommand to indicate whether to compute proximities between cases or between variables.

CASE *Compute proximity values between cases.* This is the default.
VARIABLE *Compute proximity values between variables.*

24.11
MEASURE Subcommand

By default, PROXIMITIES uses the Euclidean distance measure to calculate the distance between two items. Use the MEASURE subcommand to choose the similarity, dissimilarity, or distance measure that PROXIMITIES computes and to specify any transformations for the measure.

PROXIMITIES computes measures for continuous data, frequency count data, or binary data (see Sections 24.12 through 24.14). You can specify only one measure on each PROXIMITIES command.

If you are using an existing proximities matrix, specify the following:

NONE *Do not compute proximity measures.* Use the NONE specification only if you enter an existing proximity matrix using the IN keyword on the MATRIX subcommand. This lets you apply the ABSOLUTE, REVERSE, and/or RESCALE transformations to an existing matrix of proximity values.

Each entry in the proximity matrix that PROXIMITIES computes represents a pair of items. The items can be either cases or variables, as specified on the VIEW subcommand (see Section 24.10). When the items are cases, the computation for each pair of cases involves pairs of values for specified variables. When the items are variables, the computation for each pair of variables involves pairs of values for the variables across all the cases.

24.12
Measures for Continuous Data

To obtain proximities for continuous data, you can use one of eight specifications on the MEASURE subcommand:

EUCLID *Euclidean distance.* This is the default specification for MEASURE. The distance between two items, x and y, is the square root of the sum of the squared differences between the values for the items.

$$EUCLID(x,y) = \sqrt{\Sigma_i(x_i - y_i)^2}$$

SEUCLID *Squared Euclidean distance.* The distance between two items is the sum of the squared differences between the values for the items.

$$SEUCLID(x,y) = \Sigma_i(x_i - y_i)^2$$

CORRELATION *Correlation between vectors of values.* This is a pattern similarity measure.

$$CORRELATION(x,y) = \frac{\Sigma_i(Z_{xi}Z_{yi})}{N-1}$$

where Z_{xi} is the (standardized) Z-score value of x for the ith case or variable, and N is the number of cases or variables.

COSINE   *Cosine of vectors of values.* This is a pattern similarity measure.

$$COSINE(x,y) = \frac{\Sigma_i(x_i y_i)}{\sqrt{(\Sigma_i x_i^2)(\Sigma_i y_i^2)}}$$

CHEBYCHEV   *Chebychev distance metric.* The distance between two items is the maximum absolute difference between the values for the items.

$$CHEBYCHEV(x,y) = max_i|x_i - y_i|$$

BLOCK   *City-block, or Manhattan, distance.* The distance between two items is the sum of the absolute differences between the values for the items.

$$BLOCK(x,y) = \Sigma_i|x_i - y_i|$$

MINKOWSKI(p)   *Distance in an absolute Minkowski power metric.* The distance between two items is the *p*th root of the sum of the absolute differences to the *p*th power between the values for the items. Appropriate selection of the integer parameter *p* yields Euclidean and many other distance metrics.

$$MINKOWSKI(x,y) = (\Sigma_i|x_i - y_i|^p)^{1/p}$$

POWER(p,r)   *Distances in an absolute power metric.* The distance between two items is the *r*th root of the sum of the absolute differences to the *p*th power between the values for the items. Appropriate selection of integer parameters *p* and *r* yields Euclidean, squared Euclidean, Minkowski, city-block, and many other distance metrics.

$$POWER(x,y) = (\Sigma_i|x_i - y_i|^p)^{1/r}$$

24.13
Measures for Frequency Count Data

You can use either of two specifications on the MEASURE subcommand to obtain proximities for frequency count data:

CHISQ   *Chi-square test of equality for two sets of frequencies.* The magnitude of this dissimilarity measure depends on the total frequencies of the two cases or variables whose proximity is computed. Expected values are from the model of independence of cases (or variables) x and y.

$$CHISQ(x,y) = \sqrt{\frac{\Sigma_i(x_i - E(x_i))^2}{E(x_i)} + \frac{\Sigma_i(y_i - E(y_i))^2}{E(y_i)}}$$

PH2   *Phi-squared between sets of frequencies.* This is the CHISQ dissimilarity measure normalized by the square root of the combined frequency. Therefore, its value does not depend on the total frequencies of the two cases or variables whose proximity is computed.

$$PH2(x,y) = \sqrt{\frac{\dfrac{\Sigma_i(x_i - E(x_i))^2}{E(x_i)} + \dfrac{\Sigma_i(y_i - E(y_i))^2}{E(y_i)}}{N}}$$

**24.14
Measures for Binary Data**

Different binary measures emphasize different aspects of the relation between sets of binary values. However, you specify all the measures in the same way. Each has two optional integer-valued parameters, *p* (present) and *np* (not present). If you specify both parameters, PROXIMITIES uses the value of the first as an indicator that a characteristic is present and the value of the second as an indicator that a characteristic is absent. PROXIMITIES skips all other values. For example, the specification

/MEASURE=RR(1,2)

tells PROXIMITIES to compute Russell and Rao coefficients from data in which 1 indicates the presence of a characteristic and 2 indicates the absence of a characteristic. Other values are ignored. If you specify only the first parameter, PROXIMITIES uses that value to indicate presence and all other values to indicate absence. For example, the specification

/MEASURE=SM(2)

tells PROXIMITIES to compute simple matching coefficients from data in which 2 indicates presence and all other values indicate absence. If you specify no parameters, PROXIMITIES assumes that 1 indicates presence and 0 indicates absence.

Using the indicators for presence and absence within each item (case or variable), PROXIMITIES constructs a 2×2 contingency table for each pair of items in turn. It uses this table to compute a proximity measure for the pair.

	Item 2 characteristics	
	Present	Absent
Item 1 characteristics		
Present	a	b
Absent	c	d

PROXIMITIES computes all binary measures from the values of a, b, c, and d. These values are tallies across variables (when the items are cases) or tallies across cases (when the items are variables). For example, if variables V, W, X, Y, Z have values 0, 1, 1, 0, 1 for Case 1 and values 0, 1, 1, 0, 0 for Case 2 (where 1 indicates presence and 0 indicates absence), the contingency table is

	Item 2 characteristics	
	Present	Absent
Item 1 characteristics		
Present	2	1
Absent	0	2

The available binary measures include matching coefficients, conditional probabilities, predictability measures, and others.

Matching Coefficients. Table 24.14 shows a classification scheme for the PROXIMITIES matching coefficients. In this scheme, *matches* are joint presences (value a in the contingency table) or joint absences (value d). *Nonmatches* are equal in number to value b plus value c. Matches and nonmatches may be weighted equally or not. The three coefficients JACCARD, DICE, and SS2 are related monotonically; SM, SS1, and RT also are related monotonically. All the coefficients in Table 24.14 are similarity measures, and all except two (K1 and SS3) range from 0 to 1. K1 and SS3 have a minimum value of 0 and no upper limit.

Table 24.14 Binary matching coefficients in PROXIMITIES

	Joint absences excluded from numerator	Joint absences included in numerator
All matches included in denominator		
Equal weight for matches and nonmatches	RR	SM
Double weight for matches		SS1
Double weight for nonmatches		RT
Joint absences excluded from denominator		
Equal weight for matches and nonmatches	JACCARD	
Double weight for matches	DICE	
Double weight for nonmatches	SS2	
All matches excluded from denominator		
Equal weight for matches and nonmatches	K1	SS3

RR(p,np) — *Russell and Rao similarity measure.* This is the binary dot product.

$$RR(x,y) = \frac{a}{a + b + c + d}$$

SM(p,np) — *Simple matching similarity measure.* This is the ratio of the number of matches to the total number of characteristics.

$$SM(x,y) = \frac{a + d}{a + b + c + d}$$

JACCARD(p,np) — *Jaccard similarity measure.* This is also known as the *similarity ratio.*

$$JACCARD(x,y) = \frac{a}{a + b + c}$$

DICE(p,np) — *Dice (or Czekanowski or Sorenson) similarity measure.*

$$DICE(x,y) = \frac{2a}{2a + b + c}$$

SS1(p,np) *Sokal and Sneath similarity measure 1.*

$$SS1(x,y) = \frac{2(a + d)}{2(a + d) + b + c}$$

RT(p,np) *Rogers and Tanimoto similarity measure.*

$$RT(x,y) = \frac{a + d}{a + d + 2(b + c)}$$

SS2(p,np) *Sokal and Sneath similarity measure 2.*

$$SS2(x,y) = \frac{a}{a + 2(b + c)}$$

K1(p,np) *Kulczynski similarity measure 1.* This measure has a minimum value of 0 and no upper limit. It is undefined when there are no nonmatches ($b=0$ and $c=0$). Therefore, PROXIMITIES assigns an artificial upper limit of 9999.999 to K1 when it is undefined or exceeds this value.

$$K1(x,y) = \frac{a}{b + c}$$

SS3(p,np) *Sokal and Sneath similarity measure 3.* This measure also has a minimum value of 0, has no upper limit, and is undefined when there are no nonmatches ($b=0$ and $c=0$). As with K1, PROXIMITIES assigns an artificial upper limit of 9999.999 to SS3 when it is undefined or exceeds this value.

$$SS3(x,y) = \frac{a + d}{b + c}$$

Conditional Probabilities. The following three binary measures yield values that you can interpret in terms of conditional probability. All three are similarity measures.

K2(p,np) *Kulczynski similarity measure 2.* This yields the average conditional probability that a characteristic is present in one item given that the characteristic is present in the other item. The measure is an average over both items acting as predictors. It has a range of 0 to 1.

$$K2(x,y) = \frac{a/(a + b) + a/(a + c)}{2}$$

SS4(p,np) *Sokal and Sneath similarity measure 4.* This yields the conditional probability that a characteristic of one item is in the same state (presence or absence) as the characteristic of the other item. The measure is an average over both items acting as predictors. It has a range of 0 to 1.

$$SS4(x,y) = \frac{a/(a + b) + a/(a + c) + d/(b + d) + d/(c + d)}{4}$$

HAMANN(p,np) *Hamann similarity measure.* This measure gives the probability that a characteristic has the same state in both items (present in both or absent from both) minus the probability that a characteristic has different states in the two items (present in one and absent from the other). HAMANN has a range of -1 to $+1$ and is monotonically related to SM, SS1, and RT.

$$\text{HAMANN}(x,y) = \frac{(a + d) - (b + c)}{a + b + c + d}$$

Predictability Measures. The following four binary measures assess the association between items as the predictability of one given the other. All four measures yield similarities.

LAMBDA(p,np) *Goodman and Kruskal lambda (similarity).* This coefficient assesses the predictability of the state of a characteristic on one item (presence or absence) given the state on the other item. Specifically, lambda measures the proportional reduction in error using one item to predict the other, when the directions of prediction are of equal importance. Lambda has a range of 0 to 1.

$$\text{Lambda}(x,y) = \frac{\max(a,b) + \max(c,d) + \max(a,c) + \max(b,d) - \max(a + c, b+d) - \max(a +b, c + d)}{2(a + b + c + d)}$$

D(p,np) *Anderberg's D (similarity).* This coefficient assesses the predictability of the state of a characteristic on one item (presence or absence) given the state of the other. D measures the actual reduction in the error probability when one item is used to predict the other. The range of D is 0 to 1.

$$D(x,y) = \frac{\max(a,b) + \max(c,d) + \max(a,c) + \max(b,d) + \max(a + c, b+d) + \max(a +b, c + d)}{2(a + b + c + d)}$$

Y(p,np) *Yule's Y coefficient of colligation (similarity).* This is a function of the cross ratio for a 2×2 table. It has a range of -1 to $+1$.

$$Y(x,y) = \frac{\sqrt{ad} - \sqrt{bc}}{\sqrt{ad} + \sqrt{bc}}$$

Q(p,np) *Yule's Q (similarity).* This is the 2×2 version of Goodman and Kruskal's ordinal measure *gamma*. Like Yule's Y, Q is a function of the cross ratio for a 2×2 table and has a range of -1 to $+1$.

$$Q(x,y) = \frac{ad - bc}{ad + bc}$$

Other Binary Measures. The remaining binary measures available in PROXIMITIES are either binary equivalents of association measures for continuous variables or measures of special properties of the relation between items.

OCHIAI(p,np)   *Ochiai similarity measure.* This is the binary form of the cosine. It has a range of 0 to 1 and is a similarity measure.

$$\text{OCHIAI}(x,y) = \sqrt{\frac{a}{a+b} \cdot \frac{a}{a+c}}$$

SS5(p,np)   *Sokal and Sneath similarity measure 5.* This is a similarity measure. Its range is 0 to 1.

$$\text{SS5}(x,y) = \frac{ad}{\sqrt{(a+b)(a+c)(b+d)(c+d)}}$$

PHI(p,np)   *Fourfold point correlation (similarity).* This is the binary form of the Pearson product-moment correlation coefficient. Phi is a similarity measure, and its range is 0 to 1.

$$\text{PHI}(x,y) = \frac{ad-bc}{\sqrt{(a+b)(a+c)(b+d)(c+d)}}$$

BEUCLID(p,np)   *Binary Euclidean distance.* This is a distance measure. Its minimum value is 0, and it has no upper limit.

$$\text{BEUCLID}(x,y) = \sqrt{b+c}$$

BSEUCLID(p,np)   *Binary squared Euclidean distance.* This is also a distance measure. Its minimum value is 0, and it has no upper limit.

$$\text{BSEUCLID}(x,y) = b + c$$

SIZE(p,np)   *Size difference.* This is a dissimilarity measure with a minimum value of 0 and no upper limit.

$$\text{SIZE}(x,y) = \frac{(b-c)^2}{(a+b+c+d)^2}$$

PATTERN(p,np)   *Pattern difference.* This is also a dissimilarity measure. Its range is 0 to 1.

$$\text{PATTERN}(x,y) = \frac{bc}{(a+b+c+d)^2}$$

BSHAPE(p,np)   *Binary shape difference.* This dissimilarity measure has no upper or lower limit.

$$\text{BSHAPE}(x,y) = \frac{(a+b+c+d)(b+c)-(b-c)^2}{(a+b+c+d)^2}$$

DISPER(p,np)   *Dispersion similarity measure.* This similarity measure has a range of -1 to $+1$.

$$DISPER(x,y) = \frac{ad - bc}{(a + b + c + d)^2}$$

VARIANCE(p,np)   *Variance dissimilarity measure.* This dissimilarity measure has a minimum value of 0 and no upper limit.

$$VARIANCE(x,y) = \frac{b + c}{4(a + b + c + d)}$$

BLWMN(p,np)   *Binary Lance-and-Williams nonmetric dissimilarity measure.* Also known as the Bray-Curtis nonmetric coefficient, this dissimilarity measure has a range of 0 to 1.

$$BLWMN(x,y) = \frac{b + c}{2a + b + c}$$

24.15
Measure Transformations

In addition to selecting a method, you can use the MEASURE subcommand to specify any combination of the following three transformations:

ABSOLUTE   *Take the absolute values of the proximities.* Use ABSOLUTE when the sign indicates the direction of the relations (as with correlation coefficients), but only the magnitude of the relations is of interest.

REVERSE   *Transform similarity values into dissimilarities, or vice versa.* Use this specification to reverse the ordering of the proximities by negating the values.

RESCALE   *Rescale the proximity values to a range of 0 to 1.* RESCALE standardizes the proximities by first subtracting the value of the smallest and then dividing by the range. You would not usually use RESCALE with measures that are already standardized on meaningful scales, as are correlations, cosines, and many binary coefficients.

If you specify more than one transformation, PROXIMITIES does them in the order listed above: first ABSOLUTE, then REVERSE, then RESCALE.

You can specify both a measure and one or more transformations on the same MEASURE subcommand, as in:

```
PROXIMITIES VAR1 VAR2 VAR3
 MEASURE=SEUCLID ABSOLUTE REVERSE.
```

24.16
PRINT Subcommand

PROXIMITIES always displays the name of the measure it computes and the number of cases. In addition, you can use either of the following keywords with the PRINT subcommand to display the proximity matrix.

PROXIMITIES   *Display the matrix of the proximities between items.* This is the default. The matrix may have been read in or computed. When the number of cases or variables is large, this specification produces a large volume of output and uses significant computer time.

NONE   *Do not display the matrix of proximities.*

24.17
ID Subcommand

Use the ID subcommand to specify an identifying string variable for cases. You can name any string variable on your file as the identifier. PROXIMITIES uses the values of this variable to identify cases in output. By default, it identifies cases by case number alone. The form of the subcommand is

```
/ID=varname
```

24.18
MISSING Subcommand

You can use the MISSING subcommand to change or make explicit the treatment of cases with missing values. The available keywords are:

LISTWISE   *Delete cases with missing values listwise.* This is the default.

INCLUDE   *Include cases with user-missing values.* This option deletes listwise only those cases with system-missing values.

24.19
MATRIX Subcommand

PROXIMITIES can both read and write matrix materials. It writes proximity-type matrices that can be used by PROXIMITIES or other procedures. Procedures CLUSTER and ALSCAL can read a proximity matrix directly. Procedure FACTOR can read a correlation matrix written by PROXIMITIES, but you must first use RECODE to change the ROWTYPE_ value PROX to a ROWTYPE_ value CORR (see Section 24.20). Also, if using a proximity matrix in FACTOR, you cannot use the ID subcommand in PROXIMITIES.

Use the MATRIX subcommand to read and write matrix materials. The MATRIX subcommand has the following two keywords:

OUT   *Write matrix materials.* After OUT, specify in parentheses either a name for the matrix system file or an asterisk (*) to replace the active system file with the matrix.

IN   *Read matrix materials.* After IN, specify in parentheses either the name of the matrix system file to read or an asterisk (*) to read matrix material from the active system file.

You can specify both MATRIX=IN and MATRIX=OUT on the same PROXIMITIES command, as in:

```
PROXIMITIES /MATRIX=IN(*)
/MEASURE=NONE ABSOLUTE
/MATRIX=OUT(ABSMTRX).
```

If you specify MATRIX=IN, you can omit the variable list. By default, all variables in the matrix are included. You can use the variable list to specify a subset of the matrix, but you must use variable names defined on the matrix system file. Use a slash to separate the MATRIX subcommand from the command keyword PROXIMITIES and other subcommands.

If VIEW=VARIABLE, the variables on the new matrix system file will have the names and labels of the original variables. If VIEW=CASE (the default), the names of the variables on the new matrix system file will be CASE1, CASE2...CASEn, where n is the number of cases in the file or in the largest split-file group. The new matrix system file will preserve the names and values of any split-file variables in effect.

24.20
Recoding a PROXIMITIES
Matrix for Procedure FACTOR

Before you can use the PROXIMITIES matrix for FACTOR, you must use the RECODE command to recode the ROWTYPE_ values, changing them from PROX to CORR, as in:

```
GET FILE=CRIME.
PROXIMITIES MURDER TO MOTOR
  /MEASURE=CORR
  /MATRIX=OUT(*).
RECODE ROWTYPE_ ('PROX' = 'CORR').
FACTOR MATRIX IN(COR=*).
```

24.21
Annotated Example

This example shows how PROXIMITIES can produce matrix materials for CLUSTER.

```
DATA LIST / CITY 1-17(A) MURDER 18-21 RAPE 23-25 ROBBERY 27-30
   ASSAULT 32-34 BURGLARY 36-39 LARCENY 41-44 MOTOR 46-49.
BEGIN DATA.
San Francisco      17.0 101 1016 542 2618 5149 1290
Dallas             34.8 111  505 647 2997 5443  890
Baltimore          31.0  71 1072 788 2139 4367  856
Los Angeles        27.4  88  714 685 2596 3549 1373
Detroit            35.9 109  907 619 2598 2820 1708
Houston            40.4  91  575 171 3022 3335 1517
New York           24.4  55 1161 622 2506 3106 1262
San Diego          11.6  40  348 256 2406 4730  902
Cleveland          45.6 102  958 514 2412 2364 2251
Washington, D.C.   27.4  75 1055 452 2051 4393  550
Indianapolis       17.9  85  400 310 1664 3683  672
San Antonio        20.6  44  204 224 1990 3588  560
Chicago            28.0  54  473 354 1091 3074 1027
Milwaukee           9.8  44  247 171 1325 3498  655
Philadelphia       21.9  48  503 255 1193 1927  752
END DATA.
PROXIMITIES MURDER TO MOTOR
  /VIEW=VARIABLE
  /MATRIX=OUT(*).
CLUSTER
  /MATRIX=IN(*)
  /PRINT=DISTANCE SCHEDULE.
```

- The PROXIMITIES command specifies the variables MURDER through MOTOR for computing the data matrix.
- The VIEW subcommand indicates that proximities are to be computed between variables, not cases.
- The MATRIX subcommand writes the computed matrix to the active system file for CLUSTER to read. Since the MEASURE subcommand is not specified, the computed matrix will consist of Euclidean distances.
- The CLUSTER command omits the variable list. By default, all variables from the matrix are used in the cluster analysis.
- The MATRIX subcommand indicates that the matrix data are in the active system file.
- The PRINT subcommand requests the cluster agglomeration schedule as well as the computed distances between cases.

Contents

25 Multidimensional Scaling: Procedure ALSCAL

This chapter was written by Forrest W. Young and David F. Harris, University of North Carolina, Psychometric Laboratory.

What characteristics of automobiles do people consider when they are deciding which car to buy: its economy? its sportiness? its reliability? What aspects of political candidates are important when a voter is making a decision? the candidate's party? the candidate's position on defense issues? What interpersonal characteristics come into play when one member of a work group is talking to another member: the status of the two members? their knowledge about the task of the work group? their socioeconomic characteristics?

How do you even go about answering such questions? The variables mentioned in the first paragraph are subjective, as are their units and the values of these units. These variables are presumed to exist in the minds of people, and do not have an independent, objective existence.

There are at least two ways of answering the questions posed above; at least two ways to construct objective scales that can be reasonably thought to correspond to a person's internal "scales." One of these ways is to obtain multivariate data and then use factor analysis (see Chapter 21).

The other way is to obtain dissimilarity data and to then use multidimensional scaling to analyze the data. In this chapter we focus on the multidimensional scaling of dissimilarity data as a way to construct objective scales of subjective attributes.

25.1 DATA, MODELS, AND ANALYSIS OF MULTIDIMENSIONAL SCALING

What is multidimensional scaling? Multidimensional scaling (MDS) is designed to analyze distance-like data called dissimilarity data, i.e., data that indicate the degree of dissimilarity (or similarity) of two things. For example, MDS could be used with data that indicates the apparent (dis)similarity of a pair of political candidates, or a pair of automobiles. MDS analyzes the dissimilarity data in a way which displays the structure of the distance-like data as a geometrical picture. MDS has its origins in psychometrics where it was proposed to help understand people's judgments of the similarity of members of a set of objects. MDS has now become a general data analysis technique used in a wide variety of fields.

What are dissimilarities data? MDS pictures the structure of a set of objects from data that approximate the distances between pairs of the objects. The data, which are called similarities, dissimilarities, distances, or proximities, must reflect the amount of (dis)similarity between pairs of objects. In this chapter we use the term dissimilarity generically to refer to both similarities (where large number refer to great similarity) and dissimilarities (where large numbers refer to great dissimilarity).

Traditionally, dissimilarity data are subjective data obtained by asking people to judge the dissimilarity of pairs of things, where the things are automobiles, political candidates, types of wines, etc. But dissimilarity data can also be objective measures such as the driving time between pairs of cities, or the frequency with which pairs of people in a work group talk to each other. Finally, dissimilarity data can be calculated from multivariate data, as when we use voting records in the United States Senate to calculate the proportion of agreement in the votes cast by pairs of senators. However, the data must always represent the degree of dissimilarity of pairs of objects or events.

There may be one or more matrices of dissimilarity data. For example, if we have observed the frequency with which pairs of people in a business communicate with each other, then we have a single similarity matrix, where the frequency with which a pair of people communicate indicates the similarity of the pair of people. On the other hand, if we have judgments of dissimilarity of pairs of automobiles from many drivers, then we have many dissimilarity matrices, one for each driver.

What is the MDS model? Each object or event is represented by a point in a multidimensional space. The points are arranged in this space so that the distances between pairs of points have the strongest possible relation to the similarities among pairs of objects. That is, two similar objects are represented by two points that are close together, and two dissimilar objects are represented by two points that are far apart. The space is usually a two- or three-dimensional Euclidean space but may have more dimensions. This model is called the Euclidean model. Sometimes, a model that was originally designed to portray individual differences in judgments of dissimilarity is used. This model, which is called the INDSCAL (individual differences scaling) model, uses weights for individuals on the dimensions of the Euclidean space. The model is discussed more below.

What types of MDS analyses are there? MDS is a generic term that includes many different specific types of analyses. The kind of MDS analysis depends on the number of dissimilarity matrices, the measurement level of the dissimilarity data, and the MDS model used to analyze the data.

First of all, we can classify the kinds of MDS analyses according to how many matrices there are and what model is being used in the analysis. This give us four kinds of MDS analyses: classical MDS (one matrix, Euclidean model), replicated MDS (several matrices, Euclidean model), weighted MDS (several matrices, weighted Euclidean model—also called the INDSCAL model), and generalized MDS (several matrices, general Euclidean model). For the INDSCAL and generalized models, you need more than one data matrix.

We can also classify the kinds of MDS according to whether the dissimilarities data are measured on an ordinal scale (called nonmetric MDS) or measured on an interval or ratio scale (metric MDS). The nonmetric/metric distinction can be combined with the classical/replicated/weighted distinction to provide six different types of MDS. We discuss these types in the next sections.

The ALSCAL procedure is capable of many kinds of analyses, not all of which are covered in this chapter. See Young and Lwyckyj (1979) or Young and Hamer (1987) for more information.

25.2
Example: Flying Mileages

The purpose of MDS is to construct a map of the locations of some objects relative to each other from data that specify how different the objects are from each other. The problem is like the problem faced by a surveyor who has surveyed the distances between a set of places and then needs to draw a map showing where those places are relative to each other.

Consider a road map showing cities and the roads between them. On such a map there is usually a small table of driving mileages between major cities on the map. In our example we start with such a table, except that it is a table of flying mileages (rather than driving mileages). With ALSCAL, we can use these data to construct a map showing where the cities are, relative to each other. We use these data because most of us are familiar with the relative locations of the large cities in the United States. We know what structure to expect, and we will be looking to see if ALSCAL can show us that structure.

In Figure 25.2 we present a matrix of dissimilarity data. These data are actually the flying mileages between 10 American cities. The cities are the "objects," and the mileages are the "dissimilarities."

Figure 25.2a Flying mileages between 10 American cities

```
ATLT CHIC DENV HOUS L.A. MIAM N.Y. S.F. SEAT D.C.
   0  587 1212  701 1936  604  748 2319 2182  543    ATLANTA
 587    0  920  940 1745 1188  713 1858 1737  597    CHICAGO
1212  920    0  879  831 1716 1631  949 1021 1494    DENVER
 701  940  879    0 1374  968 1420 1645 1891 1220    HOUSTON
1936 1745  831 1374    0 2339 2451  347  959 2300    LOS ANGELES
 604 1188 1726  968 2339    0 1092 2594 2734  923    MIAMI
 748  713 1631 1420 2451 1092    0 2571 2408  205    NEW YORK
2139 1858  949 1645  347 2594 2571    0  678 2442    SAN FRANCISCO
2182 1737 1021 1891  959 2734 2408  678    0 2329    SEATTLE
 543  597 1494 1220 2300  923  205 2442 2329    0    WASHINGTON D. C.
```

Figure 25.2b shows the map plotted with ALSCAL, based on these data.

Figure 25.2b   ALSCAL plot of intercity flying mileage

```
TITLE 'INTERCITY FLYING MILEAGES'
DATA LIST /ATLANTA 2-5 CHICAGO 7-10 DENVER 12-15 HOUSTON 17-20
 LOSANGEL 22-25 MIAMI 27-30 NEWYORK 32-35 SANFRAN 37-40
 SEATTLE 42-45 WASHDC 47-50 CITYNAME 55-69 (A).
BEGIN DATA.
    0                                                      ATLANTA
  587    0                                                 CHICAGO
 1212  920    0                                            DENVER
  701  940  879    0                                       HOUSTON
 1936 1745  831 1374    0                                  LOS ANGELES
  604 1188 1726  968 2339    0                             MIAMI
  748  713 1631 1420 2451 1092    0                        NEW YORK
 2139 1858  949 1645  347 2594 2571    0                   SAN FRANCISCO
 2182 1737 1021 1891  959 2734 2408  678    0              SEATTLE
  543  597 1494 1220 2300  923  205 2442 2329    0         WASHINGTON D.C.
END DATA.
ALSCAL VARIABLES=ATLANTA TO WASHDC
 /PLOT.
```

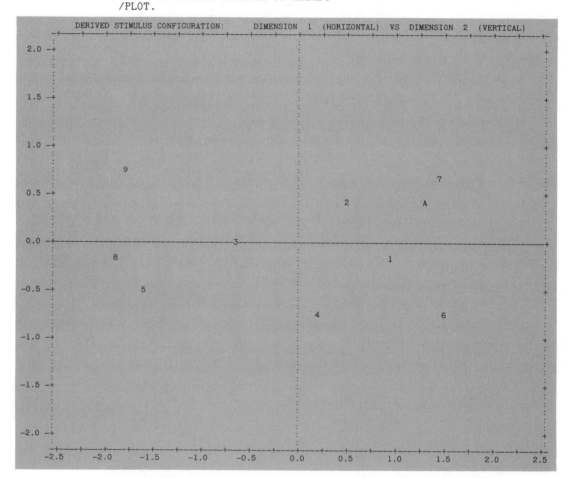

On the basis of the ALSCAL plot we can produce the map of relative locations of the 10 cities in the United States (Figure 25.2c). This map has 10 points, one for each city. Cities that are similar (have short flying mileages) are represented by points that are close together, and cities that are dissimilar (have long mileages) by points that are far apart. Note that the orientation is arbitrary. For this particular analysis ALSCAL has determined the dimensions such that the first one is the longest, the second one the next longest, etc. By coincidence, ALSCAL also places north on top (rather than bottom), and west on the left (instead of right).

Figure 25.2c Map based on ALSCAL plot

25.3
THE NATURE OF DATA ANALYZED BY ALSCAL

ALSCAL analyzes dissimilarity data. The data can either be obtained directly in some empirical situation, or it can be computed from multivariate data. In either case, the basic nature of dissimilarity data is exemplified by the flying mileages: the individual elements of the data matrix indicate the degree of dissimilarity (or similarity) between the pairs represented by the rows and columns of the matrix. In the flying mileage example the dissimilarities are the various flying mileages, and the pairs of objects are pairs of cities.

ALSCAL is very flexible with regard to the kinds of dissimilarity data that can be analyzed. The data can vary in terms of their measurement level, shape, and conditionality. There can be any pattern of missing data. These aspects are discussed briefly in this section. (For a more detailed discussion, see Young & Hamer, 1987.)

ALSCAL can directly analyze multivariate data, but we don't usually recommend that it be used for this purpose. You can use the PROXIMITIES procedure (see Chapter 24) to calculate dissimilarities from multivariate data, which can then be analyzed by ALSCAL.

25.4
The Measurement Level of Data

The data can be analyzed in ways that respect the basic nature of any of the four commonly identified levels of measurement: nominal, ordinal, interval, or ratio. While the nominal level can be specified, examples of nominal dissimilarities data are exceedingly rare and are not discussed here.

The remaining three levels of measurement (ordinal, interval, and ratio) fall into two categories that define two kinds of data and two kinds of analyses. The ordinal level defines data that are qualitative and analyses that are nonmetric. The interval and ratio levels, on the other hand, define data that are quantitative and analyses that are metric. All three measurement levels, and both metric and nonmetric analyses, will be discussed in this chapter.

25.5
The Shape of Data

A less commonly discussed aspect of data is their shape. Data can be square or rectangular. Square data, in turn, can be symmetric or asymmetric. Thus, we have three basic data shapes: symmetric, asymmetric, and rectangular. ALSCAL can analyze all three shapes.

In this chapter we only discuss square data, both symmetric and asymmetric. For both types of data the rows and columns refer to the same set of objects. For example, the rows and columns of square data may refer to political candidates. In another example, the rows and columns could refer to automobiles. In both examples the data indicate the degree of dissimilarity of a pair of the set of objects. Thus, if the rows and columns refer to automobiles, the data indicate the degree of dissimilarity of pairs of automobiles.

The difference between symmetric and asymmetric data is in whether the degree of dissimilarity between, say, a Ford and a Chevrolet is the same as the dissimilarity between a Chevrolet and a Ford, regardless of the order in which the two objects are considered. If the dissimilarity is the same, then the data are symmetric. Otherwise, they are asymmetric. We consider both kinds of data in this chapter.

ALSCAL can analyze rectangular data, the most common example being multivariate data. Rectangular data elements specify the dissimilarity of all objects in one set to all objects in a second set. But for these data there is no information about the dissimilarity of objects in either set, which is often a problem for MDS. Rectangular data should be analyzed directly by ALSCAL with the greatest care, as the results are often not robust.

25.6
The Conditionality of Data

In this chapter we discuss two kinds of data conditionality: matrix conditionality and row conditionality. Most dissimilarity data are matrix conditional. That is, most dissimilarities are such that the numbers within a matrix are on the same measurement scale. Thus, if we have a matrix where the dissimilarity index is the proportion of times that a pair of senators voted differently out of all their votes during a session of the senate, then all of the proportion indexes are on the same scale, and the data are said to be matrix conditional. As a second example, consider judgments of dissimilarity about pairs of wines made by several different experts. Here, the judgments for a given expert are presumed to be on a single scale, but the experts probably each have their own idiosyncratic ways of responding, so the actual meaning of a specific judgment is conditional on which expert made the judgment. Thus, these data are also matrix conditional.

25.7
Missing Data

The ALSCAL procedure can analyze data with any pattern of missing values. Of course, the more values that are missing from the data, the lower the probable reliability of the analysis. You should always try to have data with as few missing values as possible. Certain patterns of missing data are not susceptible to robust analysis, as discussed by Young and Hamer (1987).

25.8
Multivariate Data

As has been discussed by Young and Hamer (1987), multivariate data can be viewed as rectangular (since the number of observations usually does not equal the number of variables) and column conditional (since the variables are usually measured on different scales). The measurement level of multivariate data often varies from variable to variable, some variables being nominal, others ordinal, and still others interval.

While ALSCAL can analyze multivariate data directly, it rarely produces useful results. If the multivariate data are quantitative (i.e., if all the variables are at the interval or ratio levels of measurement), or if all variables are dichotomous, then the PROXIMITIES procedure can be used to calculate dissimilarity data from the multivariate data, using either the EUCLID or BEUCLID specifications on the MEASURE subcommand (see Chapter 24). These dissimilarities can then be analyzed by ALSCAL.

While ALSCAL can be used to analyze a matrix of dissimilarities calculated by PROXIMITIES from a multivariate matrix, there is no real advantage in doing so if you have only one multivariate matrix, since the analysis will be equivalent to a principal components analysis when the defaults of PROXIMITIES and ALSCAL are used, and since the FACTOR procedure (see Chapter 21) can perform the same analysis more efficiently and easily.

The real strength of ALSCAL with multivariate data is when you have multiple multivariate matrices. In this case you can use split-file processing with PROXIMITIES to calculate a separate dissimilarity matrix for each multivariate matrix. These multivariate matrices can then be simultaneously analyzed by ALSCAL. This feature provides you with three-mode factor analysis, a family of analyses that provide one of the few ways in which multiple-matrix multivariate data can be analyzed in any statistical system.

25.9
CLASSICAL MDS

Classical MDS (CMDS) is the simplest kind of MDS. The identifying aspect of CMDS is that there is only one dissimilarity matrix. ALSCAL can analyze many dissimilarity matrices simultaneously, resulting in other kinds of MDS that are not CMDS. They are discussed later in this chapter.

25.10
Example: Flying Mileages Revisited

Consider the flying mileage example from the beginning of the chapter. This example is classical MDS because there is only one dissimilarity matrix, the matrix of flying mileages shown in Figure 25.2a.

The ALSCAL command

```
ALSCAL VARIABLES=ATLANTA TO WASHDC
 /SHAPE=SYMMETRIC
 /LEVEL=RATIO
 /CRITERIA=STRESSMIN(.001)
 /PRINT=HEADER DATA
 /PLOT.
```

specifies that the data are symmetric and are at the ratio level of measurement. The only model that can be used for a single matrix of dissimilarities is the Euclidean model, and we know that two dimensions are appropriate. We do not need to specify this, since a two-dimensional Euclidean model is the default.

Figure 25.10a summarizes all the subcommand values for the ALSCAL analysis, as requested by the HEADER keyword on the PRINT subcommand. Figure 25.10b gives the raw data matrix (identical to the mileage values in 25.2a), as requested by the DATA keyword.

Figure 25.10a   ALSCAL procedure options

```
ALSCAL PROCEDURE OPTIONS


DATA OPTIONS-

NUMBER OF ROWS (OBSERVATIONS/MATRIX).    10
NUMBER OF COLUMNS (VARIABLES) .  .  .    10
NUMBER OF MATRICES  .  .  .  .  .  .  .   1
MEASUREMENT LEVEL .  .  .  .  .  .  .  .  RATIO
DATA MATRIX SHAPE .  .  .  .  .  .  .  .  SYMMETRIC
TYPE  .  .  .  .  .  .  .  .  .  .  .  .  DISSIMILARITY
APPROACH TO TIES  .  .  .  .  .  .  .  .  LEAVE TIED
CONDITIONALITY .  .  .  .  .  .  .  .  .  MATRIX
DATA CUTOFF AT .  .  .  .  .  .  .  .     0.000000




MODEL OPTIONS-

MODEL .  .  .  .  .  .  .  .    .  .  .  .  EUCLID
MAXIMUM DIMENSIONALITY  .  .  .  .  .  .  2
MINIMUM DIMENSIONALITY  .  .  .  .  .  .  2
NEGATIVE WEIGHTS  .  .  .  .  .  .  .  .  NOT PERMITTED




OUTPUT OPTIONS-

JOB OPTION HEADER .  .  .  .  .  .  .  .  PRINTED
DATA MATRICES  .  .  .  .  .  .  .  .     PRINTED
CONFIGURATIONS AND TRANSFORMATIONS  .    PLOTTED
OUTPUT DATASET .  .  .  .  .  .  .  .     NOT CREATED
INITIAL STIMULUS COORDINATES  .  .  .    COMPUTED




ALGORITHMIC OPTIONS-

MAXIMUM ITERATIONS  .  .  .  .  .  .  .   30
CONVERGENCE CRITERION  .  .  .  .  .  .   0.00100
MINIMUM S-STRESS  .  .  .  .  .  .  .  .  0.00100
MISSING DATA ESTIMATED BY  .  .  .  .     ULBOUNDS
```

Figure 25.10b   Matrix of flying mileages

```
                            RAW (UNSCALED) DATA FOR SUBJECT    1

           1         2         3         4         5         6         7         8         9        10
 1     0.000
 2   587.000     0.000
 3  1212.000   920.000     0.000
 4   701.000   940.000   879.000     0.000
 5  1936.000  1745.000   831.000  1374.000     0.000
 6   604.000  1188.000  1726.000   968.000  2339.000     0.000
 7   748.000   713.000  1631.000  1420.000  2451.000  1092.000     0.000
 8  2139.000  1858.000   949.000  1645.000   347.000  2594.000  2571.000     0.000
 9  2182.000  1737.000  1021.000  1891.000   959.000  2734.000  2408.000   678.000     0.000
10   543.000   597.000  1494.000  1220.000  2300.000   923.000   205.000  2442.000  2329.000     0.000
```

The iteration history in Figure 25.10c is produced by default. However, without the MINSTRESS (0.001) specification on the CRITERIA subcommand, ALSCAL would only produce one iteration, since the default minimum value for s-stress for further iterations is 0.005, and the s-stress value for the first iteration is only 0.003. S-stress is a measure of fit ranging from 1 (worst possible fit) to 0 (perfect fit). Next, the procedure displays two more measures of fit, Kruskal's stress measure (0.003) and the squared correlation coefficient (r-squared = 1.000) between the data and the distances. All three measures of fit, which are discussed and defined below, indicate that the two-dimensional Euclidean model describes these flying mileages perfectly.

Figure 25.10c Iteration history

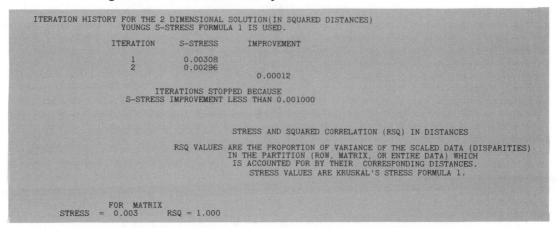

```
ITERATION HISTORY FOR THE 2 DIMENSIONAL SOLUTION(IN SQUARED DISTANCES)
              YOUNGS S-STRESS FORMULA 1 IS USED.

          ITERATION     S-STRESS      IMPROVEMENT

              1          0.00308
              2          0.00296
                                         0.00012

              ITERATIONS STOPPED BECAUSE
       S-STRESS IMPROVEMENT LESS THAN 0.001000


                            STRESS AND SQUARED CORRELATION (RSQ) IN DISTANCES

              RSQ VALUES ARE THE PROPORTION OF VARIANCE OF THE SCALED DATA (DISPARITIES)
                     IN THE PARTITION (ROW, MATRIX, OR ENTIRE DATA) WHICH
                     IS ACCOUNTED FOR BY THEIR  CORRESPONDING DISTANCES.
                       STRESS VALUES ARE KRUSKAL'S STRESS FORMULA 1.



           FOR  MATRIX
     STRESS  =  0.003     RSQ = 1.000
```

The stimulus coordinates in Figure 25.10d are the coordinates used to generate the plot in Figure 25.2b.

Figure 25.10d Stimulus coordinates

```
              CONFIGURATION DERIVED IN 2 DIMENSIONS


                      STIMULUS COORDINATES

                                    DIMENSION
     STIMULUS   STIMULUS  PLOT     1        2
     NUMBER       NAME    SYMBOL

        1        ATLANTA    1     0.9581  -0.1908
        2        CHICAGO    2     0.5088   0.4543
        3        DENVER     3    -0.6443   0.0336
        4        HOUSTON    4     0.2143  -0.7622
        5        LOSANGEL   5    -1.6006  -0.5222
        6        MIAMI      6     1.5119  -0.7707
        7        NEWYORK    7     1.4288   0.6928
        8        SANFRAN    8    -1.8944  -0.1492
        9        SEATTLE    9    -1.7884   0.7654
       10        WASHDC     A     1.3057   0.4488
```

Next, the procedure displays a matrix called **OPTIMALLY SCALED DATA (DISPARITIES) FOR SUBJECT 1**, as shown in Figure 25.10e. For this analysis, in which the data are specified to be at the ratio level of measurement, the values in this matrix of "disparities" are linearly related to the original flying mileages.

Figure 25.10e Optimally scaled data for subject 1

```
                   OPTIMALLY SCALED DATA (DISPARITIES) FOR SUBJECT    1

         1        2        3        4        5        6        7        8        9       10
 1    0.000
 2    0.783    0.000
 3    1.616    1.227    0.000
 4    0.935    1.254    1.172    0.000
 5    2.582    2.327    1.108    1.832    0.000
 6    0.805    1.584    2.302    1.291    3.119    0.000
 7    0.998    0.951    2.175    1.894    3.269    1.456    0.000
 8    2.853    2.478    1.266    2.194    0.463    3.459    3.429    0.000
 9    2.910    2.316    1.362    2.522    1.279    3.646    3.211    0.904    0.000
10    0.724    0.796    1.992    1.627    3.067    1.231    0.273    3.257    3.106    0.000
```

The perfect fit summarized by the three fit indexes is also represented in Figure 25.10f, created by the PLOT subcommand. This plot is a scatterplot of the raw data (horizontally) versus the distances (vertically). The raw data have been standardized, so their units have been changed. The distances are the Euclidean distances between all pairs of points shown in the configuration plot. This plot is an ordinary scatterplot and is interpreted as such. It represents the fit of the distances to the data, which is the fit that is being optimized by the procedure and that is summarized by the fit indexes. In fact, RSQ is simply the squared correlation between the data and the distances. Thus, we look at this scatterplot to see how much scatter there is around the perfect-fit line that runs from the lower left to the upper right. (For similarity data the line runs from the upper left to the lower right). In this analysis we see that there is no scatter and no departure from perfect linear fit.

Figure 25.10f Scatterplot of raw data vs. distances

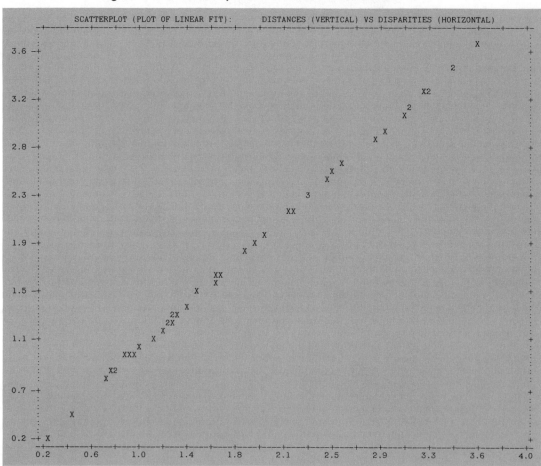

These high-quality results occur since the data have essentially no error, and since we have properly assumed that the data are at the ratio level of measurement. These results also imply that a two-dimensional space is sufficient to explain the flying mileages between cities in the United States. These results, then, assure us that ALSCAL is doing what it is supposed to do since it is recovering structure that we know to be in the data.

25.11
The Euclidean Model

In this section we present the Euclidean model. First we present the algebra of the model, and then the geometry. Then we return to the algebra of the model, this time presented in matrix algebra instead of scalar algebra. Since the details of the matrix algebra are not crucial to the remainder of the chapter, they can be skipped.

25.12
Algebra of the Euclidean Model

Classical MDS employs Euclidean distance to model dissimilarity. That is, the distance d_{ij} between points i and j is defined as

$$d_{ij} = [\Sigma_a^r(x_{ia} - x_{ja})^2]^{1/2} \qquad \text{**Equation 25.12**}$$

where X_{ia} specifies the position (coordinate) of point i on dimension a. The X_{ia} and X_{ja} are the stimulus coordinates in Figure 25.10d, which are used to plot the derived stimulus configuration in Figure 25.2b. The distances d_{ij} are plotted on the vertical axis of the scatterplot in Figure 25.10f, versus the corresponding dissimilarities (after normalization).

Note that there are n points in Figure 25.2b. In this case $n=10$, one for each of the n objects (cities). There are also r dimensions (here, $r=2$). The value of r can be specified on the CRITERIA subcommand. The default is two dimensions. The dissimilarity of objects i and j is denoted as s_{ij}, displayed in Figure 25.10b under the heading **RAW (UNSCALED) DATA FOR SUBJECT 1.** In this case, the "dissimilarities" are the actual flying mileages.

The dimensions of the space can be reflected, translated, permuted, and rotated, and they can all be rescaled by the same scaling factor. They cannot, however, be individually rescaled by different scaling factors.

25.13
Geometry of the Euclidean Model

Geometrically, the Euclidean distance model presented above is a multidimensional generalization of the two-dimensional Pythagorean theorem, as demonstrated in Figure 25.13.

Figure 25.13 Pythagorean theorem

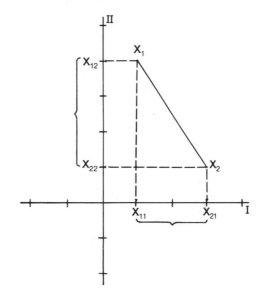

In this figure, the points x_1 and x_2 are shown with dashed lines that project orthogonally onto the two dimensions. The place that these dashed lines project onto the dimensions corresponds to the two coordinates for each point. Thus, the point x_1 has projection x_{11} on dimension 1 and x_{12} on dimension 2, while the point x_2 has projections x_{21} and x_{22} on the two dimensions. By comparing this figure with the previous formula, we see that the formula calculates d_{12} (the length of the hypotenuse of the right triangle) as the square root of the sum of the squared lengths of the two other sides of the triangle, where these squared lengths are $(x_{11}-x_{21})^2$ and $(x_{12}-x_{22})^2$, respectively.

25.14
Matrix Algebra of the Euclidean Model

Using matrix algebra, the Euclidean model can be defined as

$$d_{ij} = [(x_i - x_j)(x_i - x_j)']^{1/2} \qquad \text{Equation 25.14a}$$

where x_i is the ith row of X, consisting of the r coordinates of the ith point on all r dimensions. The dimensions of a Euclidean space can be rotated. This characteristic will be contrasted with other MDS models which are not rotatable.

Normalization. The stimulus coordinates X can be changed in a number of ways that do not change the distances by more than a multiplicative constant (the type of change in scaling of the distances which is permitted by the Euclidean model). Permissible changes in the coordinates include changing the mean of each dimension and multiplying all coordinates by a constant. Since the mean and unit are arbitrary, these are fixed to be the same for all analyses. In particular, the mean of each dimension is made to be 0:

$$\Sigma_i^n x_{ia} = 0.0 \qquad \text{Equation 25.14b}$$

and the dimensions are given an average length equal to the number of points:

$$\Sigma_i^n \Sigma_a^r x_{ia}^2 = nr \qquad \text{Equation 25.14c}$$

Note that nothing is done to rotate the space to any specific orientation. However, the first iteration is begun with the configuration oriented so that the first dimension is the longest, the second the next longest, etc. ("longest" means greatest sum of squared coordinates).

25.15
Details of CMDS

In this section we discuss some important details of CMDS, including the distinction between metric and nonmetric CMDS, the measures of goodness of fit displayed by ALSCAL, and the fundamental CMDS equation.

25.16
Metric CMDS

The seminal MDS work was done by Torgerson (1952) and is now known as metric CMDS. The flying mileage example presented above is an example. It is "metric" because the flying mileages are assumed to be at the ratio level of measurement. It is "classical" because there is exactly one matrix of dissimilarities. For metric classical MDS, ALSCAL fits the squared Euclidean distances D^2 to the dissimilarities S so that they are as much like S as possible, in a least-squares sense. (The matrix D^2 has elements that are the squares of the elements of the matrix D.)

The fitting of the squared Euclidean distances to the dissimilarities is represented by the equation

$$l\{S\} = D^2 + E \qquad\qquad \text{Equation 25.16a}$$

where $l\{S\}$ is read "a linear transformation l of the dissimilarities S." The transformation l takes the matrix S as its argument, and yields as its value the matrix

$$T = l\{S\}. \qquad\qquad \text{Equation 25.16b}$$

If the measurement level is ratio (as in the example), then the linear transformation has a 0 intercept. The intercept can be nonzero when the level is interval. If the data are similarities (as distinct from dissimilarities), the slope of the transformation is negative; if dissimilarities, it is positive. If the data are row conditional the transformations are somewhat more complex, as will be explained below.

Note that the transformations for the interval measurement level are subject to indeterminacies that do not occur at the other measurement levels. If warning messages appear, you should try another measurement level.

Note also that, for technical reasons, similarities are not as robust as dissimilarities for the ALSCAL procedure, so you should convert similarities to dissimilarities before performing multidimensional scaling. This recommendation holds regardless of other analysis details.

In the preceding equation, E is a matrix of errors (residuals). ALSCAL minimizes s-stress, a normalized sums of squares of this matrix, as described below. Thus, the s-stress measure is defined on the squared distances in D^2, whereas the stress and RSQ measures are defined on the (unsquared) distances in D. This point has certain implications for information output by the procedure, as will be discussed in the examples below.

Since the distances D (and the squared distances D^2) are a function of the coordinates X, the goal of CMDS is to calculate the coordinates X so that the sum of squares of E is minimized, subject to suitable normalizations. ALSCAL also calculates the slope (and intercept) of the transformation $l\{S\}$ to minimize E.

25.17
Nonmetric CMDS

The first major breakthrough in multidimensional scaling was due to Shepard (1962) and Kruskal (1964) and is known as nonmetric CMDS. Nonmetric CMDS refers to analyses in which the measurement level is specified to be ordinal by the LEVEL subcommand. For nonmetric CMDS, we define

$$m\{S\} = D^2 + E \qquad\qquad \text{Equation 25.17a}$$

where $m\{S\}$ is "a monotonic transformation m of the dissimilarities S." As with the transformation l, m takes the matrix S as its argument, and yields as its value the matrix

$$T = m\{S\} \qquad\qquad \text{Equation 25.17b}$$

If S is actually dissimilarities, then $m\{S\}$ preserves rank order, whereas if S is actually similarities, then $m\{S\}$ reverses rank order. Thus, for nonmetric CMDS,

ALSCAL solves for the monotonic (order-preserving) transformation $m\{S\}$ and the coordinates X, which together minimize the sum of squares of the errors E (after normalization).

The matrix of transformed dissimilarities $m\{S\}$ (or the matrix $l\{S\}$), appears in ALSCAL ouput under the heading **OPTIMALLY SCALED DATA (DISPARITIES)**, as shown in Figure 25.10e. This terminology refers to the fact that the transformation m (or l) induces a new scaling of the data which is the scaling which optimizes the s-stress index. It also refers to the fact that historically this information was first called "disparities."

The nonmetric minimization problem represents a much more difficult problem to solve than the corresponding metric problem. The nonmetric minimization problem belongs to the general class of problems discussed by Young (1981). These problems require iterative solutions, implying that nonmetric analyses take much more computer time than the metric ones.

25.18 Measures of Fit

As shown in Figure 25.10c, ALSCAL produces an iteration history which lists, for each iteration, the s-stress and improvement of the iteration. Note that the fit formula is based on the squared distances contained in the matrix D^2. This is the s-stress index proposed by Takane et al. (1977). The improvement simply represents the amount of improvement in s-stress from one iteration to the next. S-stress indicates the fit of the squared distances D^2 to the transformed data $m\{S\}$ or $l\{S\}$.

In the presentation above, we denoted the result of either the monotonic and linear transformations of the data by the matrix T, so that $T = m\{S\}$ or $l\{S\}$, depending on measurement level. Then

$$\text{s-stress} = (\ \|E\|\ /\ \|T\|\ )^{1/2} \qquad\qquad \textbf{Equation 25.18a}$$

where the notation $\|E\|$ indicates the sum of all squared elements of the error (residual) matrix E, and $\|T\|$ indicates the sum of all squared elements of the matrix of transformed data T. Note that

$$\|E\| = \|T\text{-}D^2\| \qquad\qquad \textbf{Equation 25.18b}$$

which means that s-stress is the square root of the ratio of the error sums of squares to the total sums of squares, where the error sums of squares is calculated between the squared distances and the transformed data, and the total sums of squares is calculated on the transformed data. That is, s-stress is the square root of the proportion of the total sums of squares of the transformed data which is error, error being indicated by lack of fit of the squared distances to the transformed data.

Except for the s-stress index, all results (including the two additional measures of fit) are reported in terms of the distances D, not squared distances D^2. Two additional indexes of fit are stress and RSQ. The stress index is Kruskal's (1964) stress formula. It is defined in exactly the same fashion as s-stress, except that distances are used instead of squared distances. Note that ALSCAL optimizes s-stress, not stress. This has certain implications about information output by the procedure, which will be discussed in the examples below.

RSQ is the squared simple correlation between corresponding elements of T and D. It can be interpreted as the proportion of variance of the transformed data T that is accounted for by the distances D of the MDS model.

25.19
The Fundamental CMDS Equation

We can now summarize, in a single equation, the CMDS data analysis problem being solved by the ALSCAL procedure. The fundamental equation is:

$$S \overset{t}{=} T = D^2 + E \qquad \text{Equation 25.19}$$

which reads S (the original dissimilarity data) are equal by transformation (the symbol $=^t$ represents the error-free one-to-one transformation) to T (the transformed dissimilarity data), which in turn are equal to the model's squared Euclidean distances D^2 plus error E. ALSCAL solves for D^2 and for $\overset{t}{=}$ so that the sum of squared elements of E is minimized.

We can think of the transformed data T as an interface between the measurement characteristics of S (which may have a variety of measurement levels, shapes, and conditionalities, and which may have missing values) and those of D^2 (which is always at the ratio level of measurement, is always symmetric and unconditional, and never has missing values). T is in fact identical to S when looked at through the filters imposed by S's various measurement characteristics. That is, T and S have identical ordinal characteristics, if the measurement level of S is ordinal. Similarly, T is identical to $D^2 + E$, when viewed through their measurement characteristic's filters.

25.20
Example: Ranked Flying Mileages

As an example of nonmetric CMDS, we now return to the flying mileages, but we use their ranks instead of the actual mileages. We still hope that ALSCAL can construct a reasonable map of the United States, even though we have degraded the information from mileages to ranks, and even though ALSCAL uses ordinal instead of ratio information.

In Figure 25.20a we show the new matrix of dissimilarity data concerning intercity flying mileages. These data differ from the first set of data in that they have been converted into their ranking numbers—i.e., an element in this new data matrix specifies the rank position of the corresponding mileage element in the first data matrix. Note that there are 45 elements, and that the ranks vary from 1 through 45. Thus, the flying mileage between New York and Washington, D.C. is the shortest (rank of 1), while the flying mileage between Miami and Seattle is the longest (45). Since these data are at the ordinal level of measurement, they are suitable for nonmetric CMDS.

Figure 25.20a   Ranked distances between cities

```
 ATLT CHIC DENV HOUS L.A. MIAM N.Y. S.F. SEAT D.C.
                                                      ATLANTA
   4                                                  CHICAGO
  22   13                                             DENVER
   8   15   12                                        HOUSTON
  34   31   11   24                                   LOS ANGELES
   6   21   29   18   39                              MIAMI
  10    9   27   25   42   40                         NEW YORK
  35   32   16   28    2   44   43                    SAN FRANCISCO
  36   30   19   33   17   45   40    7               SEATTLE
   3    5   26   23   37   14    1   41   38          WASHINGTON D. C.
```

A nonmetric CMDS of these data produces the plot in Figure 25.20b, which is virtually indistinguishable from the plot in Figure 25.2b.

Figure 25.20b Plot of nonmetric (ranked) distances

```
ALSCAL VARIABLES=ATLANTA TO WASHDC
 /LEVEL=ORDINAL
 /PLOT.
```

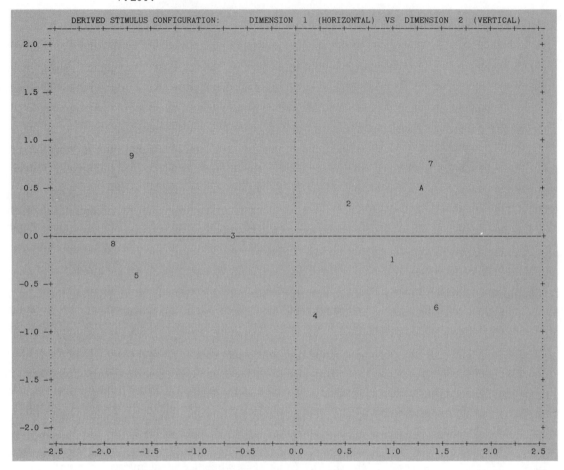

The remaining output for this analysis is shown in Figures 25.20c through 25.20h. Since the PRINT subcommand was not used, the header and matrix of data are not displayed. ALSCAL displays a warning message, telling us that the number of parameters being estimated (which for these data is 20: $n = 10 \times r = 2$) is dangerously large compared to the number of elements in the data matrix (which is $n(n\text{-}1)/2 = 45$). This warning message did not appear for the previous analysis because we had assumed the data were quantitative. In general, we should be cautious when this message appears.

Next, the procedure displays the iteration history for the two-dimensional solution, shown in Figure 25.20c. Note that the s-stress index starts at 0.03346, and after eight iterations reduces to 0.00584, where it stops due to the default minimum improvement criterion of 0.001 being reached. This index of fit is not as good as in the metric CMDS of the flying mileages, reflecting the fact that the precision of the data has been reduced because ranks are used instead of actual mileages.

Figure 25.20c   Iteration history

```
ITERATION HISTORY FOR THE 2 DIMENSIONAL SOLUTION(IN SQUARED DISTANCES)
              YOUNGS S-STRESS FORMULA 1 IS USED.

              ITERATION      S-STRESS        IMPROVEMENT

                  1           0.03346
                  2           0.02259
                                            0.01086
                  3           0.01656
                                            0.00604
                  4           0.01271
                                            0.00385
                  5           0.01009
                                            0.00261
                  6           0.00821
                                            0.00189
                  7           0.00684
                                            0.00137
                  8           0.00584
                                            0.00100

                   ITERATIONS STOPPED BECAUSE
           S-STRESS IMPROVEMENT LESS THAN 0.001000
```

Next, the procedure gives the two additional measures of fit, stress (0.008) and RSQ (1.000), as shown in Figure 25.20d. The stress measure indicates worse fit than in the metric analysis, as would RSQ if more decimal places were displayed. (The RSQ value has been rounded *up* to 1.) Even though the fit has become somewhat worse, the overall conclusion is that the squared distances D^2 of this two-dimensional Euclidean model describe the monotonic transformation of the data $T=m\{S\}$ perfectly.

Figure 25.20d   Measures of fit

```
                    STRESS AND SQUARED CORRELATION (RSQ) IN DISTANCES

         RSQ VALUES ARE THE PROPORTION OF VARIANCE OF THE SCALED DATA (DISPARITIES)
                    IN THE PARTITION (ROW, MATRIX, OR ENTIRE DATA) WHICH
                    IS ACCOUNTED FOR BY THEIR  CORRESPONDING DISTANCES.

                    STRESS VALUES ARE KRUSKAL'S STRESS FORMULA 1.


        FOR  MATRIX
STRESS  =  0.008      RSQ = 1.000
```

Figure 25.20e shows the stimulus coordinates, which are very similar to the coordinates from the metric analysis in Figure 25.10d.

Figure 25.20e   Stimulus coordinates

```
          CONFIGURATION DERIVED IN 2 DIMENSIONS


                 STIMULUS COORDINATES

                                     DIMENSION
     STIMULUS   STIMULUS  PLOT      1          2
     NUMBER       NAME    SYMBOL

        1        ATLANTA    1     1.0194    -0.2397
        2        CHICAGO    2     0.5556     0.3621
        3        DENVER     3    -0.6609    -0.0345
        4        HOUSTON    4     0.1816    -0.8584
        5        LOSANGEL   5    -1.6307    -0.4110
        6        MIAMI      6     1.4378    -0.7781
        7        NEWYORK    7     1.4227     0.7107
        8        SANFRAN    8    -1.9047    -0.0734
        9        SEATTLE    9    -1.7195     0.8553
       10        WASHDC     A     1.2986     0.4668
```

The PLOT subcommand produces four plots for this nonmetric analysis, whereas it produced only two plots for the metric analysis. For both analyses the first two plots are the plot of the derived configuration (Figure 25.20b) and the scatterplot of linear fit.

The scatterplot of linear fit, shown in Figure 25.20f, plots the monotonically transformed data (disparities) $T=m\{S\}$ horizontally versus the distances D vertically. This plot displays the departures from linearity that are measured by the stress and RSQ indexes. We see that there is very little scatter, although what scatter there is appears for the small distances and disparities. For this nearly perfectly fitting analysis there are some departures from perfect fit for the small transformed data but very few for the large transformed data. This is a common result and is an artifact of the fit index s-stress, which tends to overfit large data values and underfit small ones due to the fact that the *squared* distances are being fit to the data.

Figure 25.20f Scatterplot of linear fit

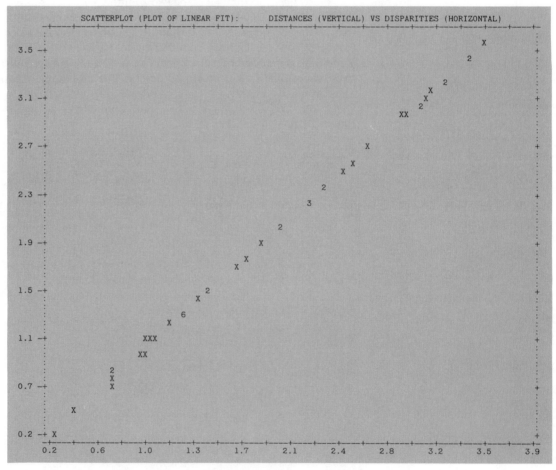

Figure 25.20g is the plot of nonlinear fit. It plots the raw data S horizontally versus the distances D vertically. This plot displays the same departures from fit as in the previous plot, but displays them relative to the raw data instead of the transformed data. Here we see that large ranks are better fit than small ranks.

Figure 25.20g   Plot of nonlinear fit

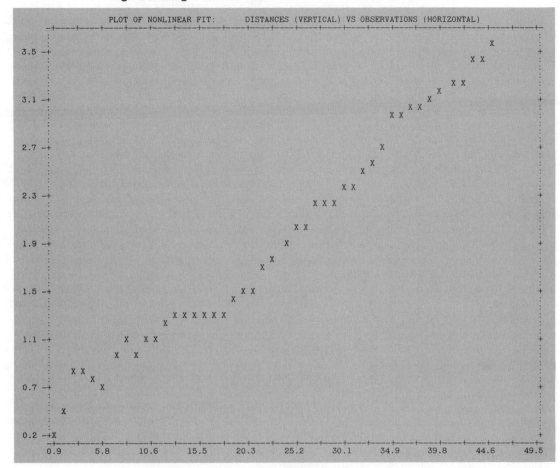

Figure 25.20h is the plot of transformation. It plots the raw data S horizontally versus the monotonically transformed data $T=m\{S\}$ vertically. The transformed data are called the "disparities" by ALSCAL. This plot displays the transformation that rescores the ranked flying mileages so that they are as much like the distances, given that the new scores must be in the same order as the original ranks. Since this is a monotone transformation, the plotted values must never go down as we move from left to right (unless the data are similarities, in which case the transformation line moves monotonically from upper left to lower right). The transformation plot can be placed on top of the nonlinear fit plot and can be interpreted as the monotonic regression line that minimizes error, where error is measured vertically in both plots.

Figure 25.20h Plot of transformation

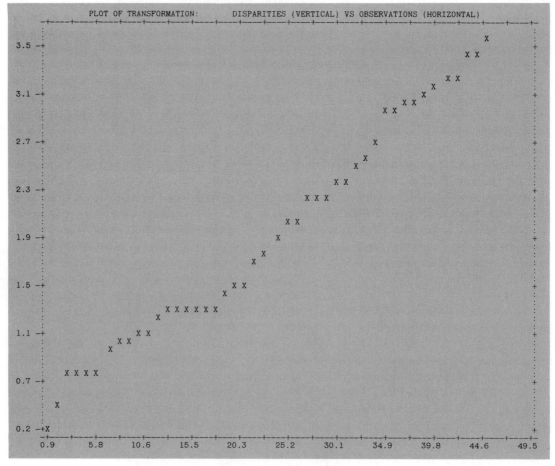

To interpret the transformation plot, we look at its overall shape and smoothness. This particular transformation is quite linear and smooth. The linearity leads us to conclude that the nonmetric analysis of the ranks is essentially the same as the metric analysis of the raw data. This conclusion would be stronger if the nonmetric analysis were of the actual flying mileages. Then, a linear transformation would yield the same results as the metric analysis. The smoothness suggests that we have a reasonably continuous, nondegenerate transformation. In particular, we should be suspicious of transformations that consist of a series of a few horizontal steps. These "step functions" suggest a discontinuous, possibly degenerate transformation.

Our overall conclusion, then, is that the results of the nonmetric analysis of the ranked flying mileages are very concordant with the results of the metric analysis of the flying mileages themselves. Since the transformation is quite linear in the nonmetric analysis, this tells us that the metric analysis, which is more parsimonious, is to be preferred. We can conclude from the two analyses that it is reasonable to assume that the flying mileages are in fact measured at the ratio level of measurement. We can also conclude from the metric analysis that the mileages are nearly error free and are basically two-dimensional.

25.21
REPEATED CMDS

All of the remaining types of MDS that we discuss differ from CMDS in that they are appropriate to data that consist of more than one matrix of dissimilarities. The major ways of analyzing such data are known as replicated MDS and weighted MDS.

In this brief section we mention that one way of analyzing multiple matrices of dissimilarity data is to repeatedly apply classical MDS, once to each matrix. This approach implies that you believe that the many matrices of data have no shared structure. The configurations of points underlying each dissimilarity matrix are presumed to be totally unrelated to each other in any fashion. If the several matrices of data are obtained from several individual judges, then this is an individual differences model that permits the greatest freedom in modeling individual differences. There are, in fact, no constraints. However, this individual differences model is the least parsimonious model, there being an entire configuration of points for each individual. If there are n points (cities, in the previous examples) with coordinates on r dimensions, then there are $n \times r$ parameters per individual. If there are m individuals, then there are $m \times n \times r$ parameters. Not only is this very nonparsimonious, but the results are difficult to interpret, since you are faced with the task of having to compare m separate analyses.

25.22
REPLICATED MDS

Historically, the next major development in the multidimensional scaling literature was replicated MDS (McGee, 1968). Replicated MDS (RMDS) was the first proposal that extended MDS to permit the analysis of more than one matrix of dissimilarities, a particularly important development since researchers typically have more than one dissimilarity matrix. This is not the sole defining characteristic of RMDS, however, as the weighted MDS and generalized MDS analyses discussed in later portions of this chapter also use several matrices of dissimilarities.

The defining characteristic of RMDS is that it applies the Euclidean distance model to several dissimilarity matrices simultaneously. The basic assumption is that the stimulus configuration X applies with equal validity to every matrix of data. Thus, the implication is that all the data matrices are, except for error, the same: they are replicates of each other, there being no systematic differences other than, perhaps, systematic response bias differences. This is the most parsimonious, and the most constrained, model of individual differences in MDS. Note that the number of parameters is the same as in CMDS: There are a total of $n \times r$ parameters for the n points on r dimensions. Another distance model forms the foundation of weighted MDS. This model relaxes the assumption that all data matrices are replicates of each other. The model is less parsimonious and less constrained than RMDS.

For RMDS, the matrix of squared distances D^2 is still defined by the same Euclidean distance formula that is involved in CMDS. The difference is that the data consist of several dissimilarity matrices S_k, $k=1, \ldots, m$, there being m data matrices in total. The analysis is such that the matrix of squared distances D^2 is calculated so that it is simultaneously like all of the several dissimilarity matrices S_k.

25.23
Details of RMDS

In this section we discuss some details of RMDS, including the metric and nonmetric varieties, individual differences in response bias in RMDS, measures of fit in RMDS, and the fundamental RMDS equation.

25.24
Metric RMDS

For metric RMDS, the analysis is based on fitting the equation

$$l_k\{S_k\} = D^2 + E_k \qquad\qquad \text{Equation 25.24}$$

where $l_k\{S_k\}$ is the linear transformation of the kth dissimilarity matrix S_k that best fits the squared Euclidean distances D^2. The data may be similarities or dissimilarities and may be at the ratio or interval levels, just as in metric CMDS. The analysis minimizes the sum of the squared elements, where the sum is taken over all elements in all matrices E_k, subject to normalization of X. The details of the fit index and normalization are discussed later in this chapter.

25.25
Nonmetric RMDS

For nonmetric RMDS, ALSCAL minimizes the several E_k, just as in metric RMDS, except that the equation becomes

$$m_k\{S_k\} = D^2 + E_k \qquad\qquad \text{Equation 25.25}$$

where $m_k\{S_k\}$ is the monotonic transformation of the dissimilarity matrix S_k that is least-squares fit to the squared distances in D^2. The data and their monotonic transformation are the same as for nonmetric CMDS, except that there are k matrices instead of just one.

25.26
Individual Response Bias Differences

It is important to notice that for RMDS each linear or monotonic transformation l_k or m_k is subscripted, letting each data matrix S_k have a unique linear or monotonic relation to the squared Euclidean distances contained in D^2. Since k ranges up to m, there are m separate linear or monotonic transformations, one for each of the m dissimilarity matrices S_k. This implies that RMDS treats all the matrices of the data as being related to each other (through D) by a systematic linear or monotonic transformation (in addition to the random error contained in E_k).

In psychological terms, RMDS accounts for differences in the ways subjects use the response scale (i.e., differences in their response bias). Consider, for example, a response scale consisting of the numbers 1 through 9. Even though each subject has the same scale to respond on, they won't necessarily use the scale the same way. It could be that one subject uses only categories 1, 5, and 9, while another uses only the even numbers, and a third uses only the middle three categories of 4, 5, and 6. These differences in response style (bias) are taken into account by the separate transformations for each subject.

25.27
Measures of Fit

As discussed above for CMDS, ALSCAL produces an iteration history that lists, for each iteration, the s-stress and improvement of the iteration. S-stress uses a formula based on the squared distances contained in the matrix D^2. To define the formula, we begin by denoting the matrix of transformed data by the symbol T_k, where

$$T_k = m_k\{S_k\} \text{ or } L_k\{S_k\}, \text{ depending on measurement level.} \qquad \text{Equation 25.27a}$$

Then

$$\text{s-stress} = [1/m\Sigma_k^m(\|E_k\|/\|T_k\|)]^{1/2}$$ **Equation 25.27b**

where the notation $\|E_k\|$ indicates the sum of all squared elements of the error (residual) matrix E_k, and $\|T_k\|$ indicates the sum of all squared elements of the matrix of transformed data T_k. Note that

$$\|E_k\| = \|T_k - D^2\|$$ **Equation 25.27c**

which means that for RMDS, s-stress is the square root of the mean of the ratio of the error sums of squares for a matrix to the total sums of squares for that matrix, where the error sums of squares is calculated between the squared distances and the transformed data for one matrix, and the total sums of squares is calculated on the transformed data for one matrix. That is, s-stress is the square root of the mean, averaged over the several matrices of data, of the proportion of the total sums of squares for one matrix of transformed data which is error, error being indicated by lack of fit of the squared distances to the transformed data.

In addition, stress and RSQ (but not s-stress) are calculated and displayed for each matrix of data. These are exactly the same formulas as for CMDS, calculated separately for each matrix. Then, the average stress and RSQ (again, not s-stress) are calculated and displayed (labeled as **Overall Stress and RSQ** in the output). (The average stress is the square root of the mean of the squared stress values, while the average RSQ is the mean of the RSQ values.) The stress indexes for each matrix are Kruskal's stress and can be interpreted as such. The RSQ for a matrix indicates the proportion of variance of the disparities in the matrix which is accounted for by the squared distances. The overall RSQ is an average squared correlation, and it indicates the average proportion of variance accounted for in all of the transformed data.

For row conditional data the stress and RSQ (but not s-stress) values are displayed for each row of each matrix, as are the overall indexes for each matrix. The interpretation of these values corresponds to their interpretation for matrix conditional data.

Note: The final s-stress in the iteration list and the overall stress value do not correspond because the former is defined on squared distances and the latter on distances.

25.28
The Fundamental RMDS Equation

We can now summarize, in a single equation, the RMDS data analysis problem being solved by the ALSCAL procedure. The fundamental equation is:

$$S_k \overset{t}{=} T_k = D^2 + E$$ **Equation 25.28**

This equation parallels the fundamental CMDS equation, and is to be understood in a similar fashion.

25.29
Example: Perceived Body-Part Structure

Jacobowitz (see Young, 1974) used RMDS to study the way language develops as children grow to adulthood. In his experiment he asked children and adults to judge the dissimilarity of all pairs of 15 parts of the human body. The judges were five-, seven-, and nine-year-olds, and adults. There were 15 judges at each age. Here we report two separate RMDS analyses, one for the seven-year-olds and the other for the adults. These data, and the RMDS of them, are discussed extensively by Young (1974).

Each of 15 subjects at each of the four age groups was asked to do the following task. The experimenter wrote the 15 body-part terms on a slip of paper, 15 slips in all. The experimenter then selected one of the body-part terms and called it the "standard." He then asked the subject to select the term from the remaining 14 which seemed most similar to the standard. The experimenter then removed this slip, and asked the subject to select the most similar term from the remaining 13. This continued until all 14 "comparison" terms were rank ordered by their similarity to the standard. This task was then repeated 15 times per subject, one time with each term as standard.

Figure 25.29a shows the data for one subject. The value 1 indicates the comparison term that was picked first (most similar), the value 2 is the term picked second, and so forth.

Figure 25.29a   Body-part data for one subject

```
 0  1  2  3  4  9  7 10  6  5  8 12 11 13 14
 2  0  1  3  4  8  6 10 12  5 11  7  9 13 14
 2  1  0  3  4  6  8 12  7 10  5  9 11 13 14
 3  1  2  0  4  5  6  7 10  8  9 12 11 13 14
 3  2  4  1  0  5  9 10  7  8  6 11 12 13 14
 3  2  6  1  8  0  7 10 12  9 14  4 11  5 13
13 11 12 10 14  4  0  1  2  9  3  5  7  6  8
11 12 13 10 14  5  1  0  2  9  3  6  4  7  8
13  8 10 11 14  9  3  5  0  1  2 12  7  4  6
12 11  7 13 14 10  6  4  1  0  2  8  9  3  5
10 11  6  8  7  5  9 14  1  2  0 12 13  4  3
13  9 12 10 14  4  5 11  6  7  8  0  1  2  3
13 12 11 10 14  9  6  2  5  8  7  1  0  3  4
13 11 14 10 12  6  7  9  4  8  5  2  3  0  1
13 12 14 10 11  5  8  9  6  7  3  2  4  1  0
```

Note that each row of the data contains the numbers 1 through 14, plus a 0. The numbers 1 through 14 indicate the judged similarity order, and the 0 indicates that a term was not compared to itself (i.e., zero dissimilarity). The first 15 rows of the data are for the first subject, the second 15 rows for the second, etc. Thus, there are 225 rows of data, 15 sets (for 15 subjects) of 15 rows each (for 15 terms).

Also note that each data matrix is asymmetric, and that the data are row conditional, as the values in a row are only ranked relative to other values in the same row, not in other rows.

The RMDS results for adults and seven-year-olds are shown in Figures 25.29b and 25.29c results. Both figures are based on a plots generated by the ALSCAL procedure. The ALSCAL plot for the adult data is shown in Figure 25.29g.

Figure 25.29b   Three-dimensional body-part RMDS for adults

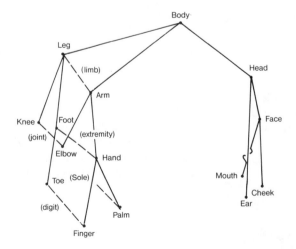

Figure 25.29c   Three-dimensional body-part RMDS for seven-year-olds

The lines were drawn to interpret the psycholinguistic structure that people have for body-part words. Jacobowitz theorized that the structure would be hierarchical. We can see that it is. (Note that there is nothing in the RMDS that forces the structure to be hierarchical. This structure is imposed on the solution by the data themselves, not by the analysis.) This hierarchical structure corresponds, psycholinguistically, to the phrase "has a." We say that a body "has a" head, which in turn "has a" face, which "has a" mouth.

Jacobowitz further theorized that the structure would become more complex as the children become adults. This theory is also supported, since the adults' hierarchy also involves a classification of corresponding arm and leg terms. In Figure 25.29b we have not only drawn the hierarchy, but we have also shown corresponding arm and leg terms linked by the dashed lines. In addition, the implied classification terms are shown in parentheses, and the word sole, which was not a stimulus, is shown in the position that we would predict it to be in if the study were repeated with sole as a 16th stimulus.

The structure for adults shown in Figure 25.29b is based on a three-dimensional RMDS specified by the following ALSCAL command:

```
ALSCAL VARIABLES=CHEEK FACE MOUTH HEAD EAR BODY ARM ELBOW HAND
 PALM FINGER LEG KNEE FOOT TOE
 /LEVEL=ORDINAL
 /SHAPE=ASYMMETRIC
 /CONDITION=ROW
 /CRITERIA=DIMENS(1,3)
 /PLOT.
```

There are 15 matrices of dissimilarity judgments. The judgments are ordinal, asymmetric, and are specified as row conditional (conditionality and asymmetry are explained below). Since the model subcommand is not used, the default Euclidean model is in effect. When the Euclidean model is used with multiple matrices of dissimilarities, the result is RMDS. The CRITERIA=DIMENS(1,3) subcommand tells ALSCAL to do three RMDS analyses, the first with three dimensions, the second with two, and the last with one. The PLOT subcommand causes plots of results to be displayed.

Figure 25.29d shows the iteration history for the three-dimensional solution. The s-stress index starts at 0.24780 and improves only slightly to 0.23621 after six iterations. Iterations stop because the rate of improvement is slow. For this size data, the fit is rather good, but not excellent.

It is not, unfortunately, possible to say exactly what a "good" or "bad" s-stress value is. We do know, however, that the value is a function of many things in addition to the amount of error in the data. For example, s-stress gets larger when the number of stimuli or matrices goes up.

Figure 25.29d   Iteration history for the three-dimensional solution

```
ITERATION HISTORY FOR THE 3 DIMENSIONAL SOLUTION(IN SQUARED DISTANCES)
              YOUNGS S-STRESS FORMULA 1 IS USED.

          ITERATION      S-STRESS         IMPROVEMENT

              1          0.24780
              2          0.24217
                                            0.00563
              3          0.23955
                                            0.00262
              4          0.23798
                                            0.00157
              5          0.23694
                                            0.00104
              6          0.23621
                                            0.00073

              ITERATIONS STOPPED BECAUSE
         S-STRESS IMPROVEMENT LESS THAN 0.001000
```

The next information displayed by ALSCAL is a large number of fit indexes (Figure 25.29e). The stress and RSQ indexes are displayed for every row of every matrix (there are $15 \times 15 = 225$ of these). In addition, an averaged stress and RSQ index is calculated for each matrix (subject). Then, an average RSQ (but not stress) index is displayed for each stimulus (body-part term). Finally, the RSQ and stress indexes are averaged over all data.

Figure 25.29e   Fit indexes

```
              STRESS AND SQUARED CORRELATION (RSQ) IN DISTANCES

      RSQ VALUES ARE THE PROPORTION OF VARIANCE OF THE SCALED DATA (DISPARITIES)
               IN THE PARTITION (ROW, MATRIX, OR ENTIRE DATA) WHICH
                IS ACCOUNTED FOR BY THEIR  CORRESPONDING DISTANCES.

               STRESS VALUES ARE KRUSKAL'S STRESS FORMULA 1.
```

MATRIX 1

STIMULUS	STRESS	RSQ	STIMULUS	STRESS	RSQ	STIMULUS	STRESS	RSQ	STIMULUS	STRESS	RSQ
1	0.073	0.973	2	0.061	0.982	3	0.089	0.965	4	0.043	0.988
5	0.113	0.938	6	0.112	0.876	7	0.077	0.958	8	0.119	0.929
9	0.091	0.954	10	0.117	0.907	11	0.211	0.730	12	0.114	0.917
13	0.091	0.958	14	0.157	0.883	15	0.141	0.887			

```
AVERAGED (RMS) OVER STIMULI
STRESS  =  0.114      RSQ = 0.923
```

MATRIX 2

STIMULUS	STRESS	RSQ	STIMULUS	STRESS	RSQ	STIMULUS	STRESS	RSQ	STIMULUS	STRESS	RSQ
1	0.220	0.764	2	0.360	0.402	3	0.035	0.994	4	0.316	0.389
5	0.157	0.879	6	0.122	0.853	7	0.241	0.614	8	0.211	0.781
9	0.270	0.602	10	0.266	0.527	11	0.032	0.993	12	0.207	0.726
13	0.179	0.836	14	0.167	0.867	15	0.159	0.854			

```
AVERAGED (RMS) OVER STIMULI
STRESS  =  0.215      RSQ = 0.739
```

MATRIX 3

STIMULUS	STRESS	RSQ	STIMULUS	STRESS	RSQ	STIMULUS	STRESS	RSQ	STIMULUS	STRESS	RSQ
1	0.043	0.991	2	0.032	0.995	3	0.088	0.965	4	0.020	0.997
5	0.114	0.937	6	0.058	0.966	7	0.103	0.926	8	0.198	0.805
9	0.153	0.872	10	0.036	0.991	11	0.149	0.859	12	0.071	0.968
13	0.172	0.849	14	0.209	0.794	15	0.137	0.893			

```
AVERAGED (RMS) OVER STIMULI
STRESS  =  0.121      RSQ = 0.921
```

It is useful to look over all of the fit measures to see if there are any that are particularly poor. Figure 25.29e shows the output for the first three subjects. For these data, there are no great anomalies, although we do note, for example, that subject 2 does not fit as well as subjects 1 and 3.

Figure 25.29f shows the stimulus coordinates used to produce the plot of dimensions 1 and 2 in Figure 25.29g, which was generated by the PLOT subcommand. Figure 25.29b is based on this ALSCAL plot.

Figure 25.29f RMDS stimulus coordinates for adults

```
              CONFIGURATION DERIVED IN 3 DIMENSIONS


                        STIMULUS COORDINATES

                                   DIMENSION
         STIMULUS   STIMULUS  PLOT    1        2        3
         NUMBER       NAME   SYMBOL

            1        CHEEK      1    1.6769  -0.7933   0.2862
            2        FACE       2    1.7494  -0.0672   0.5335
            3        MOUTH      3    1.4937  -0.5243   0.8406
            4        HEAD       4    1.6150   0.8473   0.5264
            5        EAR        5    1.3942  -0.7597   1.0267
            6        BODY       6    0.6731   1.9305  -0.4411
            7        ARM        7   -0.4713   0.7897  -1.1979
            8        ELBOW      8   -1.1175   0.0675  -0.9528
            9        HAND       9   -0.5062  -0.4646  -1.2404
           10        PALM       A   -0.0416  -0.9172  -1.5049
           11        FINGER     B   -0.8654  -1.1912  -0.3707
           12        LEG        C   -1.1393   1.1425   0.6027
           13        KNEE       D   -1.5242   0.4754   0.7471
           14        FOOT       E   -1.4223  -0.0403   0.2530
           15        TOE        F   -1.5145  -0.4950   0.8915
```

Figure 25.29g Plot of RMDS stimulus coordinates for adults

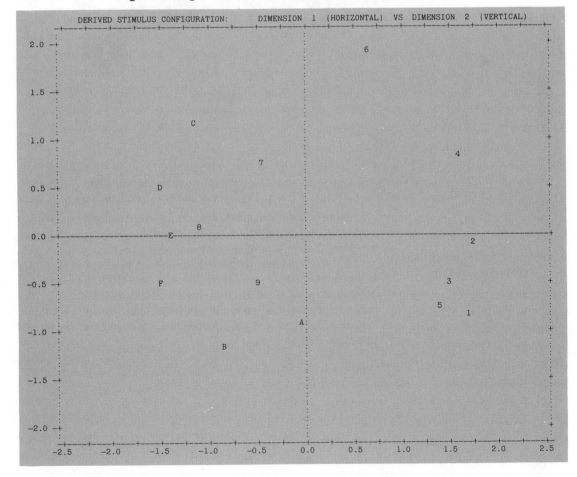

After the configuration plots, the PLOT subcommand creates the scatterplot in Figure 25.29h. This plot is interpreted just like any other scatterplot, including the scatterplots discussed above for the analyses of the flying mileages and their ranks. The scatter is between the transformed data (horizontal, and called "disparities") and the distances between the points in the configuration (vertical). If the scatter is tight, the fit is good; if it is loose, it is bad. The overall RSQ value (0.846) is calculated from this scatterplot and is rather good.

Figure 25.29h   Scatterplot of RMDS results for adults

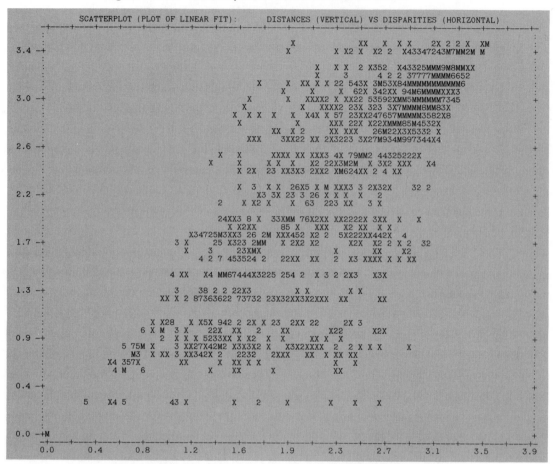

Note that the plot symbols are interpreted as follows: an **X** means that one pair of distances and transformed data is plotted in that spot; a **2** means that two pairs are plotted there; a **3** means that three pairs are plotted there. This continues up to an **M**, which means that more than nine are plotted in that one place. Thus, these symbols indicate the density of the scatter, and should be taken into consideration. While the initial impression of this particular scatterplot is fairly poor, the density indicated by the plotting symbols reveals that the scatter is much more dense along the diagonal than away from it. Thus, the scatter is not as poor as it initially appears.

ALSCAL then goes on to produce the same type of output for the two-dimensional solution and then the one-dimensional solution.

A notable feature of the three separate analyses is that the two-dimensional solution fits somewhat less well, but not a lot less well (s-stress = 0.27912) than the three-dimensional solution, whereas the one-dimensional solution fits quite a lot less well than the two- and three-dimensional solutions (s-stress=0.35197). This suggests that the two-dimensional solution may be the best of these, since it is more parsimonious than the three-dimensional but fits nearly as well, and it fits quite a lot better then the one-dimensional solution.

Another notable feature of the three analyses is that the one-dimensional solution is clearly degenerate. The one-dimensional plot of the derived configuration in Figure 25.29i shows that the points are clustering together into two distinctive clusters: on the right we have all the head terms, with body slightly to their left, whereas all the arm and leg terms are on the far left. The cluster structure shows that the solution is degenerating into a simple geometric pattern, in this case consisting of all points in two places. Also, by looking at the scatterplot in Figure 25.29j, we see a strange pattern that should be taken as another warning: there is a large horizontal gap in the scatter. This gap indicates that there are no medium-sized distances; rather, all distances are either large or small. This is another way of seeing the cluster-like nature of this solution.

Figure 25.29i   Plot of one-dimensional solution

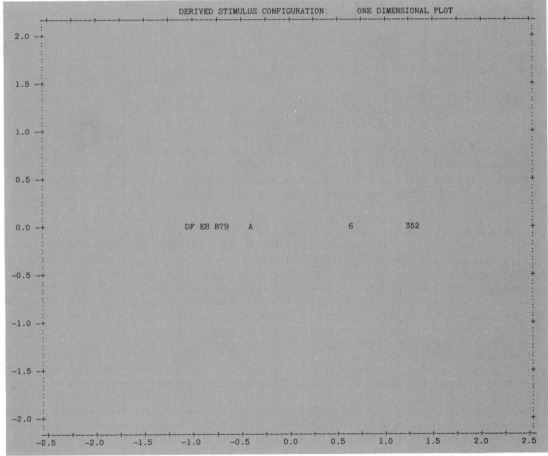

Figure 25.29j   Scatterplot of one-dimensional solution

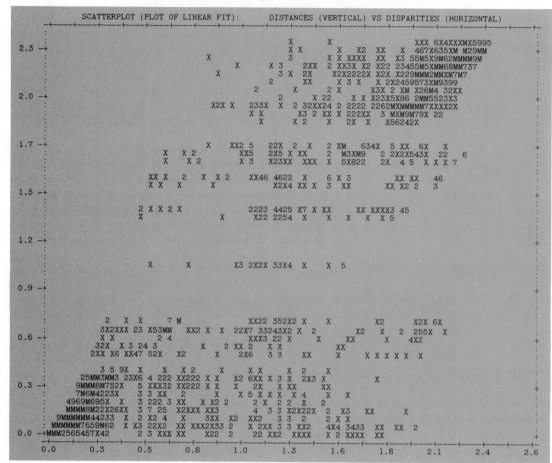

What we conclude from all these clues is that the one-dimensional analysis is actually telling us about the gross (as opposed to fine) structure of the data. The arm and leg terms are seen as being more similar to themselves than they are to the head terms or to the body terms. But the analysis appears to have degenerated into an oversimplified structure, suggesting in this case that we may have too few dimensions.

Figure 25.29k   Plot of two-dimensional solution

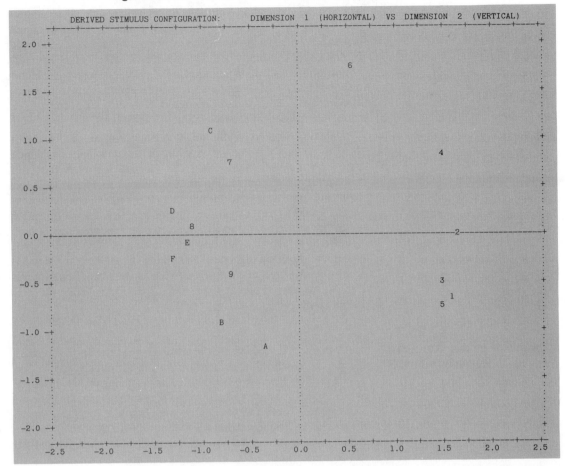

There are some clues that the two-dimensional solution may be partially degenerate. The two-dimensional plot of the derived configuration in Figure 25.29k looks quite circular, another kind of simple geometric pattern that should be interpreted cautiously and that may indicate that the analysis has degenerated into an oversimplified structure. We can see the hierarchical structure in this plot, so the analysis is, perhaps, only partially degenerate. However, caution is appropriate—this space may also be too low in dimensionality.

The conclusion from these three analyses is that the three-dimensional solution is the best. It fits reasonably well and shows no signs of degeneracy, whereas the two-dimensional and one-dimensional solutions seem somewhat questionable.

25.30
WEIGHTED MDS

The second major breakthrough in multidimensional scaling was due to Carroll and Chang (1970). This development, which is called weighted MDS (WMDS), generalized the Euclidean distance model so that the several dissimilarity matrices S_k could be assumed to differ from each other in systematically nonlinear or nonmonotonic ways. Whereas RMDS only accounts for individual differences in response bias, WMDS can also account for individual differences in the perceptual or cognitive processes that generate the responses. For this reason, WMDS is often called individual differences scaling (INDSCAL).

WMDS is based on the weighted Euclidean model. In this model we still have the stimulus space X that we have had in the (unweighted) Euclidean model, but we also have a new weight space W. We can think of the stimulus space X as representing the information that is shared in common across the individuals about the structure of the stimuli, just as in RMDS. In addition, we can think of the weight space W as representing the information that is unique to each individual about the structure of the stimuli, a notion that we did not have in RMDS.

We now turn to a detailed presentation of WMDS. We discuss the geometry, algebra, and matrix algebra of this model in the next three sections. In the fourth section we discuss a number of WMDS details. Then we present an example. Finally, we discuss two statistics developed for WMDS, the weirdness index, and flattened weights.

25.31
Geometry of the Weighted
Euclidean Model

The weighted Euclidean model assumes that the individuals vary in the importance they attach to the dimensions of the stimulus space X. While one individual may perceive one of the dimensions as being more important than another, another individual may have just the opposite perception. The notion of salience is incorporated into the model by weights w_{ka} for each individual k on each dimension a. These weights vary from 0.0 to 1.0. If the weight is large (near 1.0), then the dimension is relatively important; if it is small (near 0), the dimension is not so important.

Geometrically, the weighted Euclidean model represents individual differences in a special space called the weight space. In this space individuals are represented by vectors emanating from the origin of the space. The direction of the vector from the origin represents the relative weighting of each dimension. The length of the vector represents the overall salience of the dimension to the individual.

A schematic diagram of the geometry of the weighted Euclidean model is presented in Figure 25.31a. At the top are two hypothetical data matrices concerning four stimuli (potato, spinach, lettuce and tuna). These matrices are labeled S_2 and S_5, indicating that they are matrices number 2 and 5 of (we assume for this example) five such matrices. (Note that ALSCAL would not actually analyze data matrices that have only four rows and columns, since they are too small to support meaningful results.)

In the middle of Figure 25.31a are two spaces, each two-dimensional. The left-hand space is the hypothetical group stimulus space X. In it are four points labeled x_1 through x_4. These points correspond to the four stimuli. The right-hand space is a hypothetical weight space W with five vectors labeled w_1 through w_5. These vectors correspond to the five data matrices. Note that the dimensionality of X is always the same as that of W in WMDS.

Figure 25.31a   Geometry of the weighted Euclidean model

DATA MATRICES

S_2

	POTATO	SPINACH	LETTUCE	TUNA
POTATO		4	2	3
SPINACH	4		1	6
LETTUCE	2	1		5
TUNA	3	6	5	

S_5

	POTATO	SPINACH	LETTUCE	TUNA
POTATO		1	3	6
SPINACH	1		2	5
LETTUCE	3	2		4
TUNA	6	5	4	

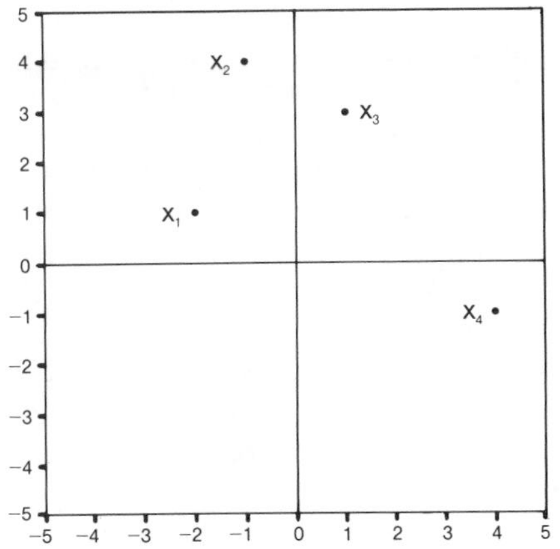

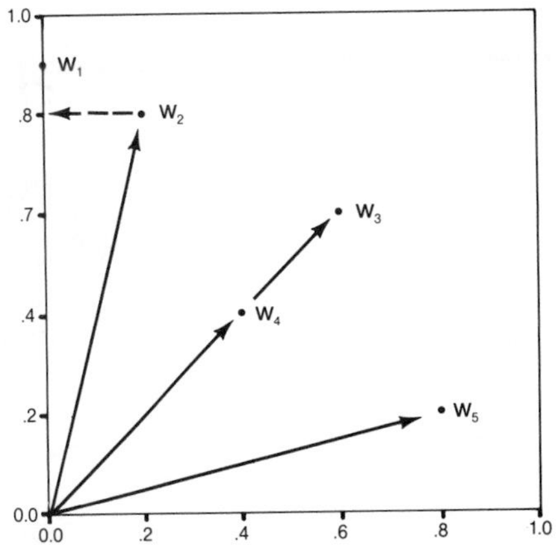

GROUP COORDINATES X		
	I	II
X_1	−2	1
X_2	−1	4
X_3	1	3
X_4	4	−1

MATRIX WEIGHTS W			
	I	II	LENGTH
W_1	0	.9	.90
W_2	.2	.8	.82
W_3	.6	.6	.85
W_4	.4	.4	.56
W_5	.8	.2	.82

GROUP DISTANCES D				
	POTATO	SPINACH	LETTUCE	TUNA
POTATO		3.16	3.61	6.32
SPINACH	3.16		2.24	7.07
LETTUCE	3.61	2.24		5.00
TUNA	6.32	7.07	5.00	

At the bottom of Figure 25.31a we present numerical information that corresponds to the diagrams in the middle of the figure: on the left is the group stimulus coordinates matrix X and in the middle the weights matrix W. The two columns of the matrix X correspond to the two dimensions of the stimulus space. The rows of this matrix specify the positions of each point on each dimension of the stimulus space. The first two columns of the weight matrix W correspond to the two dimensions of the weight space. The values in these columns for each row specify the location of the tips of the weight vectors in the weight space. The third column contains the length of each weight vector in the weight space, which is the square root of the sum of the squares of the other values in the row of the weight matrix. At the bottom-right of the figure is the matrix D of Euclidean distances between the points in the group stimulus space X.

The stimulus space X is the same as that in RMDS and CMDS. For this reason, we use the same notation as that previously used. We call the space the group stimulus space, for the same reasons we called it that for RMDS. The group Euclidean distances D are also the same as the Euclidean distances in the (unweighted) Euclidean model, except that they are for the group stimulus space, and so are called group distances. The group space and its distances present information about how the entire group of individuals (or whatever group of things generated the several data matrices) structures the stimuli, and carries the same interpretation as that for RMDS, with one major (and one minor) exception to be discussed next. Note, however, that this group information does not represent the structure for any individual, as each individual's structure is modified from the group structure by the individual's weights w_k. Rather, the group space represents the information that is shared in common by all the individuals about the structure of the stimuli.

The stimulus space X has the same characteristics for WMDS as it does for CMDS and RMDS, except for two differences. One very important difference is that for WMDS the stimulus space is not rotatable, as will be proven in the matrix algebra section below. The other difference, which is less important but occasionally confusing, is that the dimensions can be stretched or shrunk by separate scaling factors, whereas the Euclidean model requires that the same scaling factor be used for all dimensions. The two models are the same in that for both models the dimensions can be reflected, permuted, and translated.

The fact that the stimulus space is not rotatable is very important because it implies that the dimensions themselves should be meaningful. We should, if the model describes the data accurately, be able to directly interpret the dimensions of the space, not having to worry about rotations of the dimensions into another orientation for interpretation. It should be kept in mind, however, that the stability of the dimensions depends on two things: the goodness of fit of the analysis and the variation in the weights. First, if there is no variation in the orientation of the weight vectors, then the dimensions can be rotated. Also, if there is little variation in the weight vectors' orientations, the orientation of the dimensions is not as tightly determined as when there is great variation. Secondly, if the model fits the data perfectly, then the dimensions are completely stable (unless there is no variation in the weights). However, the degree of stability decreases as the fit decreases. Thus, for a poorly fitting analysis the orientation of the dimensions is not as well determined as for an analysis that fits very well.

We now turn to the weights W. Each individual (each matrix of data) is represented by a weight vector, the vectors being labeled $\mathbf{w}_1$ through $\mathbf{w}_5$ for the five individual matrices. Notice that the weight space only has vectors in the positive quadrant. Generally, only positive weights are interpretable. Thus, by default ALSCAL restricts weights to be nonnegative. Notice also that no weights are greater than 1.00. This is because they have been normalized so that their length equals the proportion of variance accounted for in the individual's data by the model (the RSQ value discussed earlier).

In the weighted Euclidean model, individual differences in perception or cognition are represented by differences in the orientation and length of the vectors w_k in the weight space W. Of these two aspects of a vector, variation in orientation of the vectors is most important as it reflects differences in the importance of the dimensions to the individuals. Two vectors that point in the same exact direction imply that the two individuals have the same relative weighting of the dimensions, regardless of the length of the vectors. The different lengths simply indicate that one person's data is better described by the analysis than the other's, the longer vector (and larger weights) being for the person whose data are better fit.

The nature of the individual differences can be seen most readily by comparing the personal stimulus spaces for the several individuals. The personal stimulus space for an individual is what results after applying the (square root of the) weights for an individual to the group space. The weights shrink the dimensions of the group space, with important dimensions being shrunk less than unimportant dimensions (since weights near 1.00 represent important dimensions, and will shrink a dimension relatively little). Thus, in the personal space important dimensions are longer than unimportant dimensions. The algebra for this will be shown in the next section.

The idea of an individual's personal space is illustrated in Figure 25.31b for three individuals. Information across the top is for individual 2, across the middle is for individual 5, and across the bottom is for individual 4.

Figure 25.31b   Personal space structures

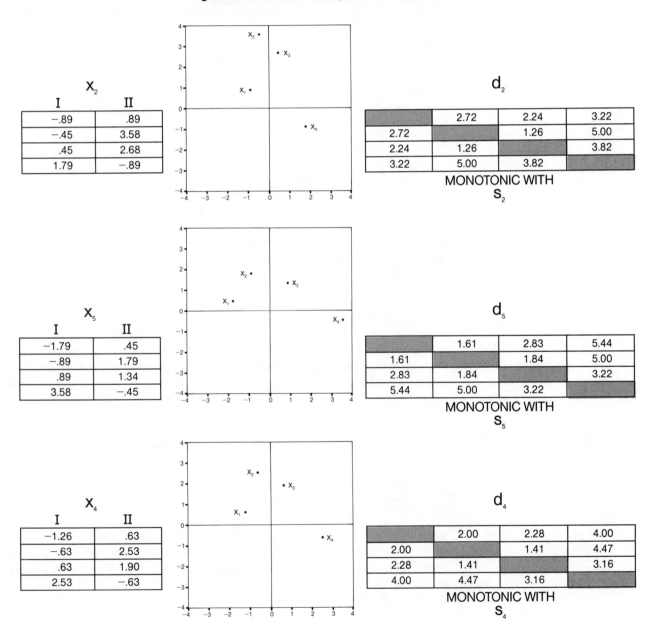

Consider the information across the top of the figure. This information concerns individual 2. On the top-left is this individual's matrix of personal coordinates, labeled $\mathbf{X_2}$. (Note that X_2 is a matrix of coordinates for all the stimuli in the personal space for individual 2, whereas x_2 is a row of coordinates for stimulus 2 in the group stimulus space.) At the top middle is the personal space X_2 for this individual (the coordinates are in the matrix at the top left). At the top right is the individual's matrix of personal distances, labeled $\mathbf{D_2}$, which are unweighted Euclidean distances between the points in the personal space X_2, and weighted Euclidean distances between the points in the group space X as weighted by the square root of the weights w_2 for this individual.

It is informative to compare the personal space structures for each of these three individuals with their weights. Individual 2 has weights of 0.2 and 0.8, as can be seen at the bottom middle of Figure 25.31a. Thus, this individual finds dimension 2 four times as important as dimension 1. This is reflected in the top-middle of Figure 25.31b by the fact that dimension 2 is relatively longer than dimension 1. For this person the personal space is mostly the vertical dimension.

Individual 5 has weights with the pattern that is opposite from individual 2's, being 0.8 and 0.2. These weights indicate that individual 5 finds dimension 2 to be one-fourth as important as dimension 1. We see, in the middle of Figure 25.31b, that person 5's personal space is much longer along dimension 1 than dimension 2 (the space is mostly horizontal).

Individual 4, on the other hand, finds the two dimensions to be equally important, having weights of 0.4 and 0.4 on both dimensions. Thus, this person's own stimulus structure is the same as the group's, except that it has shrunk due to the relatively small weights.

The last point we want to make about the geometry of WMDS is that one individual's personal distances are not related to another individual's personal distances by any type of simple one-to-one function. In particular, they are not linearly related, nor are they even monotonically related. As can be seen in Figure 25.31b, person 2's distances D_2 are not monotonic with person 5's or 4's distances. This implies that it is possible to use the weighted Euclidean model to perfectly describe data in several dissimilarity data matrices even though the data are not even monotonically related to each other! In fact, the top two distance matrices in Figure 25.31b (D_2 and D_5) are monotonically related to the two data matrices S_2 and S_5 in Figure 25.31a, even though the data matrices are not monotonically related to each other. Thus, the structure in X and W perfectly describes the data from these two people, even though their data are not simply related to each other. This is an important distinction from RMDS, where the model assumes that all data matrices are monotonically (or linearly) related to each other, except for error.

25.32
Algebra of the Weighted Euclidean Model

WMDS is based on the following definition of weighted Euclidean distance

$$d_{ijk} = \left[\sum_a^r w_{ka} \left(x_{ia} - x_{ja} \right)^2 \right]^{\frac{1}{2}}$$

Equation 25.32

where $0 \leq w_{ka} \leq 1$, $r \geq 2$, and d_{ijk} is the distance between stimuli i and j as perceived by subject k. We discuss the algebraic characteristics of the weighted distance model in the next several sections, first presenting several concepts in scalar algebra, then several more concepts in matrix algebra.

25.33
Group Stimulus Space

The x_{ia} are the same stimulus coordinates as those in the CMDS and RMDS situations, with the new restriction that one-dimensional solutions are not permitted. Taken together, the x_{ia} form the $n \times r$ stimulus coordinates matrix X. A row of this matrix is denoted x_i and contains all r of the coordinates for stimulus i. As in the RMDS case, the stimulus space X represents the structure of the stimuli as perceived by the entire group of individuals. Thus, it is called the group stimulus space.

As was mentioned above, the WMDS group stimulus space has the same characteristics as the RMDS group stimulus space, except that it is not rotatable, and the dimensions can be arbitrarily rescaled by separate constant factors. We discuss the rotation issue in the matrix algebra section that follows. Here we discuss the rescaling issue.

In WMDS we can rescale each dimension a by a unique constant c_a if we rescale the dimensions of the weight space by corresponding constants c_a^{-2}. This can be shown by noting that

$$d_{ijk} = [\Sigma_a^r w_{ka} c_a^{-2} (c_a x_{ia} - c_a x_{ja})^2]^{1/2} \qquad \text{Equation 25.33a}$$

$$d_{ijk} = [\Sigma_a^r w_{ka} c_a^{-2} c_a^2 (x_{ia} - x_{ja})^2]^{1/2}$$

$$d_{ijk} = [\Sigma_a^r w_{ka} (x_{ia} - x_{ja})^2]^{1/2}$$

which is the basic WMDS equation. This implies that there is an arbitrary normalization of the dimensions that must be defined. This normalization and its implications are discussed below. Note that this arbitrary aspect does not exist in the Euclidean model, since there are no weights that can be rescaled in a way that compensates for rescalings of the stimulus space.

The w_{ka} in the equation above represent the weights that individual k associates with the dimensions a of the stimulus space. As noted above, the weights are collected together into an $m \times r$ matrix W, which has one row for each of the m individuals (data matrices) and one column for each of the r dimensions.

For WMDS, the configuration derived by ALSCAL is normalized as follows. For all models the coordinates are centered

$$\Sigma_i^n x_{ia} = 0.0 \qquad \text{Equation 25.33b}$$

and the length of the stimulus space dimensions are each set equal to the number of points:

$$\Sigma_i^n x_{ia}^2 = n \qquad \text{Equation 25.33c}$$

The weights are normalized so that

$$\Sigma_a^r w_{ka}^2 = r_k^2 \qquad \text{Equation 25.33d}$$

where r_k^2 is RSQ, the squared correlation between subject k's squared weighted Euclidean distances D_k^2 and the same subject's dissimilarity data S_k. This normalization has the characteristic that the sum of an individual's squared weights reflects the proportion of the total variance of the individual's transformed data S_k that is accounted for by the model.

Note that there is a subtle difference in normalization of the stimulus space in the weighted and unweighted models. In the weighted model the dimensions of the stimulus space X are each separately normalized to be of equal length n, whereas in the unweighted model the dimensions are jointly normalized to have an average length of n. Thus, in CMDS and RMDS, you interpret the relative length of the stimulus space dimensions as indicating their relative importance, whereas in WMDS you cannot interpret the relative importance of stimulus space dimensions because they are arbitrarily normalized to be equal. The relative importance of WMDS dimensions is found in the average weights on a dimension, rather than in the spread of the stimulus coordinates. This will be seen in the example below.

25.34
Personal Spaces

One essential difference between the weighted and unweighted Euclidean models is that in WMDS the coordinates x_{ia} of the group stimulus space X can be weighted by the square root of an individual's weights w_{ka} to obtain the individual's personal stimulus space. The coordinates x_{ika} of stimuli in an individual's personal stimulus space X_k are derived from the group space X and the weights W by the equation

$$x_{ika} = x_{ia}(w_{ka})^{1/2}$$

Equation 25.34a

It can be shown that the distances d_{ijk} for an individual can be reexpressed in terms of the coordinates x_{ika} as the simple Euclidean distances in the personal stimulus space:

$$d_{ijk} = [\Sigma_a^r(x_{ika} - x_{jka})^2]^{1/2}$$

Equation 25.34b

25.35
Matrix Algebra of the Weighted Euclidean Model

To state the weighted Euclidean model in matrix algebra we must first define a new set of weight matrices W_k. There are m of these weight matrices W_k, one for each of the m individuals. Each W_k is an $r \times r$ diagonal matrix, with the weights for individual k on the diagonal.

Note that the new diagonal weight matrices W_k are not the same as the previously defined rectangular weight matrix W. However, the new diagonal matrices contain the same information as the earlier rectangular matrix: The rows w_k of the earlier W have become the diagonals of the new W_k (note that lowercase w_k is a row of W, whereas uppercase W_k is a diagonal matrix). Furthermore, the diagonal elements w_{kaa} of matrix W_k correspond to the elements w_{ka} of the kth row of the earlier matrix W.

Now that we have introduced the new notation W_k, we can state the weighted Euclidean model in matrix algebra terminology. The model is:

$$d_{ijk} = [x_i - x_j)W_k(x_i - x_j)']^{1/2}$$

Equation 25.35

25.36
Personal Spaces

We mentioned above that an essential aspect of the weighted model is the notion of an individual's personal stimulus space. The personal space for individual k is represented by the matrix X_k, which is defined as

$$X_k = XW_k^{1/2}$$

Equation 25.36a

giving an alternative expression for weighted Euclidean model as

$$d_{ijk} = [(x_{ik} - x_{jk})(x_{ik} - x_{jk})']^{1/2}$$

Equation 25.36b

where x_{ik} is the ith row of X_k. We see then that this is the same as the formula for Euclidean distance in individual k's personal space.

25.37
Rotation

It is very important to note that the dimensions of the WMDS joint space cannot be orthogonally rotated without violating the basic definition of the model (unlike the CMDS and RMDS dimensions, which can be rotated). This can be seen by defining the rotated stimulus space

$$X^* = XT \hspace{4cm} \textbf{Equation 25.37a}$$

where T is an $r \times r$ orthogonal rotation matrix such that $TT' = T'T = I$. Then it follows that the distances between points in the rotated space are:

$$d_{ijk} = [(x^*_{ik} - x^*_{jk})W_k(x^*_{ik} - x^*_{jk})']^{1/2} \hspace{2cm} \textbf{Equation 25.37b}$$

$$d_{ijk} = [(x_{ik} - x_{jk})TW_kT'(x_{ik} - x_{jk})']^{1/2}$$

$$d_{ijk} = [(x_{ik} - x_{jk})W^*_k(x_{ik} - x_{jk})']^{1/2}$$

While it appears that the distances defined by the last equation satisfy the definition of the weighted Euclidean model, the matrix W^*_k in the last equation is not diagonal, thus violating the definition of the model. Therefore, orthogonal rotation is not allowed.

25.38
Details of WMDS

In this section we discuss the distinction between metric and nonmetric WMDS, the measures of fit in WMDS, and the fundamental WMDS equation.

25.39
Metric and Nonmetric WMDS

WMDS is appropriate for the same type of data as RMDS. However, RMDS generates a single distance matrix D, while WMDS generates m unique distance matrices D_k, one for each data matrix S_k. Just as in RMDS, the data can be symmetric or asymmetric, matrix or row conditional, have missing values, and be at the ordinal, interval, or ratio levels of measurement. Thus, we can have metric or nonmetric WMDS, depending on the measurement level.

The distances D_k are calculated so that they are all as much like their corresponding data matrices S_k as possible. For metric WMDS (when the data are quantitative), the least-squares problem is:

$$l_k\{S_k\} = D^2_k + E_k \hspace{4cm} \textbf{Equation 25.39a}$$

and for nonmetric WMDS (qualitative data), the least-squares problem is

$$m_k\{S_k\} = D^2_k + E_k \hspace{4cm} \textbf{Equation 25.39b}$$

Thus, for WMDS, ALSCAL solves for the $n \times r$ matrix of coordinates X, for the m diagonal $r \times r$ matrices W_k, and also for the m transformations m_k or l_k. It does this so that the sum of squared elements in all error matrices E_k is minimal when summed over all matrices and when subject to normalization constraints on X and W_k. ALSCAL was the first algorithm to incorporate both nonmetric and metric WMDS, as well as the other types of MDS discussed above, and is considered to be the third breakthrough in multidimensional scaling (Takane et al., 1977).

25.40
Measures of Fit

The measures of fit (s-stress, stress, and RSQ) are all defined in the same way as for RMDS, except that the weighted Euclidean distances D_k are used in the measures instead of the unweighted distances.

<table>
<tr><td>

25.41
The Fundamental WMDS
Equation

</td><td>

We can now summarize, in a single equation, the WMDS data analysis problem being solved by the ALSCAL procedure. The fundamental equation is:

$$S_k \overset{t}{=} T_k = D_k^2 + E_k$$

Equation 25.41

This equation parallels the fundamental CMDS and RMDS equations and is to be understood in a similar fashion.

</td></tr>
<tr><td>

25.42
Example: Perceived
Body-Part Structure

</td><td>

We return to the Jacobowitz (Young, 1974) data concerning the way children and adults understand the relationship between various parts of the body. The data are the same as those discussed for RMDS (see Figure 25.29a).

The WMDS results are shown in Figures 25.42a and 25.42b These are the results of applying the WMDS model to the data of both the children and adults simultaneously. Figure 25.42a displays a three-dimensional stimulus space X (with the origin, which is not shown, at the center), and Figure 25.42b shows the positive portion of the three-dimensional weight space W (the origin is where the sides all intersect).

</td></tr>
</table>

Figure 25.42a   Three-dimensional stimulus space

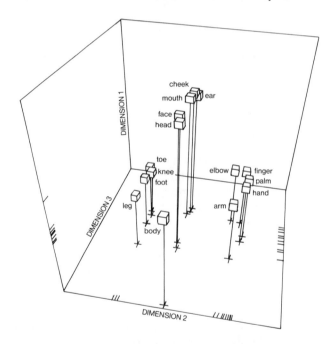

We can see in Figure 25.42a that the stimulus space displays the overall hierarchical structure that was hypothesized by Jacobowitz to exist in this data. We can also see in Figure 25.42b that the weights for adults and children occupy different portions of the space, implying that adults and children have different perceptions/cognitions concerning the body parts.

The weight space shows that the adults generally have a relatively small weight on dimension 2 (they are all on the left side of the space), whereas the children generally have a relatively small weight on dimension 3 (they are at the back of the space). This gives us a way to look at individual differences between adults and children. We can construct a hypothetical adult who has no weight on dimension 2 and a hypothetical child who has no weight on dimension 3 and investigate what structures such people would have.

Figure 25.42b   Positive portion of the three-dimensional weight space

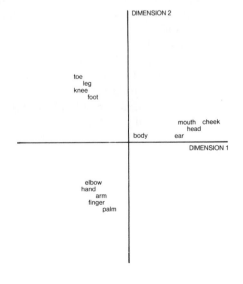

A hypothetical child who has no weight on dimension 3 is one who collapses the three-dimensional space into a two-dimension space consisting only of dimensions 1 and 2. Such a space is presented in Figure 25.42c. We see that this space presents a very simple version of the hierarchical structure, showing only that this hypothetical child differentiates "body" from the other body parts, which in turn are clustered according to whether they are arm parts, leg parts, or head parts. This is a structure for a very young child (in fact, it is rather like the structure derived from the data of the youngest age group, data we do not analyze in this chapter).

Figure 25.42c   Hypothetical child: no weight for dimension 3

A hypothetical adult who has no weight on dimension 2 is one who collapses the three-dimensional space into a two-dimensional space consisting only of dimensions 1 and 3. This space is presented in Figure 25.42d. We see that this space displays both the hierarchy and the classification. Thus, this space represents the structure of a hypothetical individual who has the most developed understanding of the relationships among bodyparts.

Figure 25.42d   Hypothetical adult: no weight for dimension 2

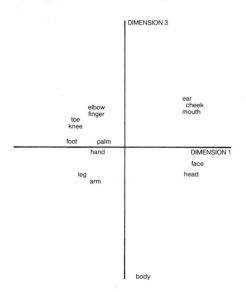

The results shown in Figures 25.42a through 25.42d are based on a three-dimensional WMDS created by the following ALSCAL command:

```
ALSCAL VARIABLES = CHEEK TO TOE
 /LEVEL=ORDINAL
 /SHAPE=ASYMMETRIC
 /CONDITION=ROW
 /CRITERIA=DIMENS(3)
 /MODEL=INDSCAL
 /PLOT.
```

The data are the same as those shown for the RMDS analysis. The ALSCAL command differs in two ways from the command used in the RMDS: First, we have specified CRITERIA=DIMENS(3) because the RMDS analyses suggested that a three-dimensional solution is appropriate. Second, we have used the MODEL=INDSCAL subcommand to obtain the weighted Euclidean model used in WMDS.

Figure 25.42e shows the iteration history for the three-dimensional solution. The initial iteration has an s-stress value of 0.29930. After seven iterations the value has improved modestly to 0.26777. At this point iterations stop because the s-stress improvement is less than 0.00100. As with the RMDS analysis, for this amount of data the fit is good, but not excellent.

Figure 25.42e   Iteration history for the three-dimensional solution

```
ITERATION HISTORY FOR THE 3 DIMENSIONAL SOLUTION(IN SQUARED DISTANCES)
              YOUNGS S-STRESS FORMULA 1 IS USED.

          ITERATION      S-STRESS      IMPROVEMENT

              0          0.29930
              1          0.29704
              2          0.28083
                                          0.01620
              3          0.27487
                                          0.00597
              4          0.27188
                                          0.00298
              5          0.27003
                                          0.00185
              6          0.26874
                                          0.00129
              7          0.26777
                                          0.00098

                  ITERATIONS STOPPED BECAUSE
          S-STRESS IMPROVEMENT LESS THAN 0.001000
```

ALSCAL then generates 450 stress and RSQ indexes (not shown), one for each of the 15 rows of the 30 matrices of data. In addition, there are 30 stress and RSQ indexes for each matrix of data. Then, the RSQ (but not the stress) is calculated for each stimulus, averaged over matrices (this only appears for asymmetric, row conditional data). Finally, the RSQ and stress indexes averaged over all of the data are calculated. This last stress measure is 0.142, which does not equal the s-stress of 0.26777 because these formulas are defined differently, as has been discussed above.

The RSQ values for each matrix (not shown) vary between 0.400 and 0.967, indicating that there are no judges who are being fit very poorly, which in turn indicates that none of the judges are giving purely random judgments. There is some suggestion that the adults fit better than the children, as the adult RSQ's are higher (ranging from 0.606 to 0.967) than the children's (0.400 to 0.933).

The RSQ values for each stimulus vary between 0.698 and 0.810, except for the term "body" which fits noticeably better at 0.864. There seems to be a bit less error, or a bit more agreement, in the placement of "body" in the overall structure. There are no extremely low RSQ's for any given row of any given matrix (suggesting that none of the judged rank-orders are reversed, a not uncommon problem).

Figure 25.42f shows the stimulus coordinates (X), and Figure 25.42g shows the subject weights (W). Displayed with the subject weights is the weirdness index, whose interpretation is briefly noted on the output and is explained extensively in the next section. It is useful to look over the values of the weirdness index for values near 1.0, as these values indicate the associated subject's weights w_k are unusual. We see that some of the weirdness values for the children (first 15 values) range up to 0.47, whereas these values range up to 0.78 for adults, since there are five adults with values higher than the children's values. This suggests that there are more adults than children who have at least one very low weight, indicating that more of the adults tend to have nearly two-dimensional solutions.

Figure 25.42f Stimulus coordinates

```
                    STIMULUS COORDINATES

                                  DIMENSION
  STIMULUS   STIMULUS   PLOT      1         2         3
  NUMBER     NAME       SYMBOL

      1      CHEEK       1      -1.3626   -0.4343   -0.8803
      2      FACE        2      -1.3834   -0.5137    0.4789
      3      MOUTH       3      -1.2947   -0.5572   -0.8309
      4      HEAD        4      -1.3270   -0.4395    0.7631
      5      EAR         5      -1.2865   -0.4261   -1.0799
      6      BODY        6      -0.1830   -0.1310    2.8436
      7      ARM         7       0.5063    1.2065    0.9689
      8      ELBOW       8       0.6162    1.1558   -0.6874
      9      HAND        9       0.4572    1.4547    0.0225
     10      PALM        A       0.3129    1.5981   -0.3816
     11      FINGER      B       0.5302    1.3534   -0.7871
     12      LEG         C       1.0275   -1.0707    0.7943
     13      KNEE        D       1.1487   -1.0832   -0.3346
     14      FOOT        E       1.1124   -1.0603   -0.1659
     15      TOE         F       1.1257   -1.0525   -0.7235
```

Figure 25.42g Subject weights and weirdness index

```
SUBJECT WEIGHTS MEASURE THE IMPORTANCE OF EACH DIMENSION TO EACH SUBJECT.
SQUARED WEIGHTS SUM TO RSQ.

A SUBJECT WITH WEIGHTS PROPORTIONAL TO THE AVERAGE WEIGHTS HAS A WEIRDNESS OF
ZERO, THE MINIMUM VALUE.
A SUBJECT WITH ONE LARGE WEIGHT AND MANY LOW WEIGHTS HAS A WEIRDNESS NEAR ONE.
A SUBJECT WITH EXACTLY ONE POSITIVE WEIGHT HAS A WEIRDNESS OF ONE,
THE MAXIMUM VALUE FOR NONNEGATIVE WEIGHTS.


                      SUBJECT WEIGHTS

                                  DIMENSION
  SUBJECT   PLOT    WEIRD-        1         2         3
  NUMBER    SYMBOL  NESS

      1       1     0.2724      0.7015    0.5753    0.2107
      2       2     0.2309      0.4319    0.4569    0.2207
      3       3     0.1695      0.4460    0.4177    0.3114
      4       4     0.3344      0.6440    0.6723    0.2208
      5       5     0.2284      0.4976    0.5516    0.2904
      6       6     0.1491      0.7490    0.5128    0.2653
      7       7     0.2022      0.3947    0.4223    0.2567
      8       8     0.1994      0.4487    0.4525    0.2367
      9       9     0.3249      0.6779    0.6681    0.2195
     10       A     0.1816      0.4326    0.4388    0.2793
     11       B     0.3661      0.6361    0.6961    0.2101
     12       C     0.1332      0.5225    0.3696    0.3340
     13       D     0.4707      0.8590    0.3695    0.1020
     14       E     0.1506      0.5040    0.4609    0.3294
     15       F     0.3860      0.5750    0.5914    0.1593
     16       G     0.2665      0.8192    0.4246    0.1998
     17       H     0.7846      0.3841    0.0929    0.8280
     18       I     0.1970      0.7663    0.4878    0.2322
     19       J     0.4367      0.4312    0.3531    0.5434
     20       K     0.2454      0.7662    0.3992    0.1986
     21       L     0.4255      0.7677    0.4150    0.1051
     22       M     0.4721      0.9039    0.1455    0.2858
     23       N     0.4154      0.8489    0.4734    0.1217
     24       O     0.4119      0.9019    0.1954    0.2760
     25       P     0.7133      0.9109    0.3039    0.0000
     26       Q     0.0430      0.7531    0.5277    0.3491
     27       R     0.6491      0.2884    0.2988    0.7114
     28       S     0.2312      0.7803    0.3308    0.4263
     29       T     0.5123      0.6727    0.2157    0.6320
     30       U     0.4581      0.7020    0.2432    0.5960

OVERALL IMPORTANCE
OF EACH DIMENSION:              0.4420    0.1972    0.1268
```

Figures 25.42h, 25.42i, and 25.42j show the plots of the stimulus coordinates used to create the three-dimensional display in Figure 25.42a.

Figure 25.42h Plot of stimulus coordinates, dimension 1 vs. dimension 2

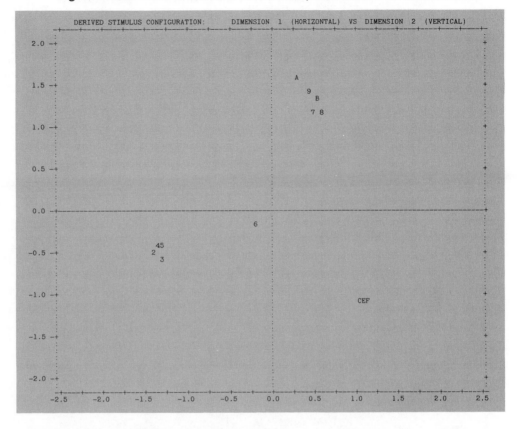

Figure 25.42i Plot of stimulus coordinates, dimension 1 vs. dimension 3

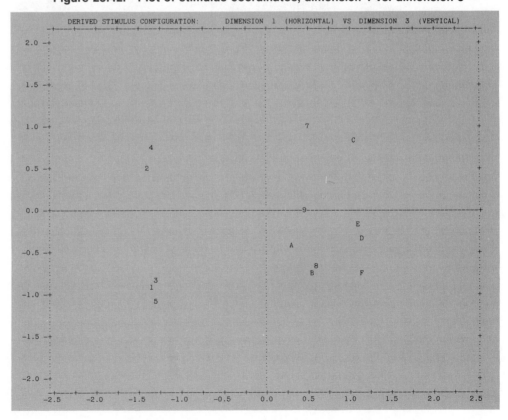

Figure 25.42j   Plot of stimulus coordinates, dimension 2 vs. dimension 3

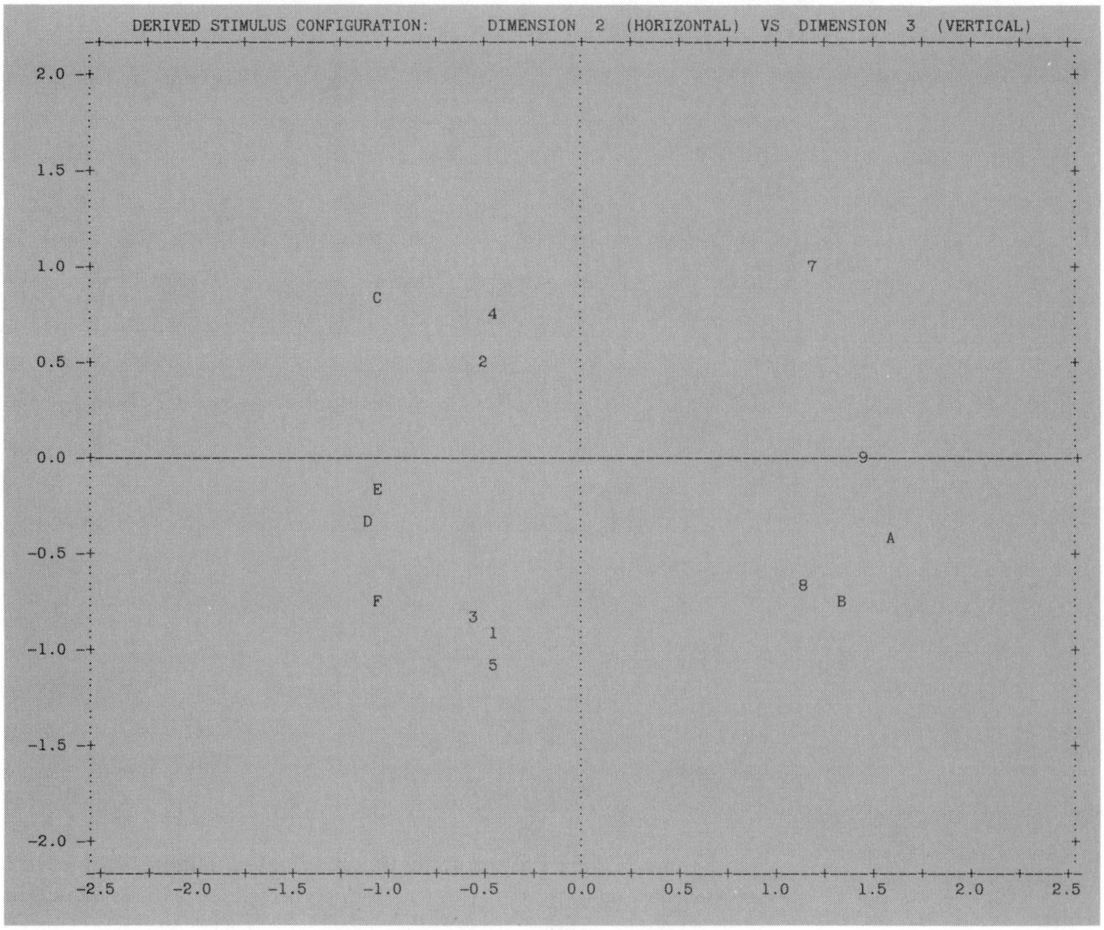

Figures 25.42k, 25.42l, and 25.42m show the plots of derived subject weights. The correct interpretation of the three plots shown here is that the points plotted for each individual represent the ends of vectors drawn from the origin of the space. We interpret both the direction and the length of each vector. If two vectors are in the same direction, they represent subjects who have equivalent weighting schemes (the ratios of one subject's weights on the various dimensions are the same as the ratios of the other subject's weights) and, therefore, the same stimulus structure in their personal stimulus spaces. This is true, even if the vectors are of different lengths, since the length simply indicates goodness of fit (the squared length of a vector—i.e., the sum of the squared weights—equals RSQ).

Figure 25.42k   Plot of derived subject weights, dimension 1 vs. dimension 2

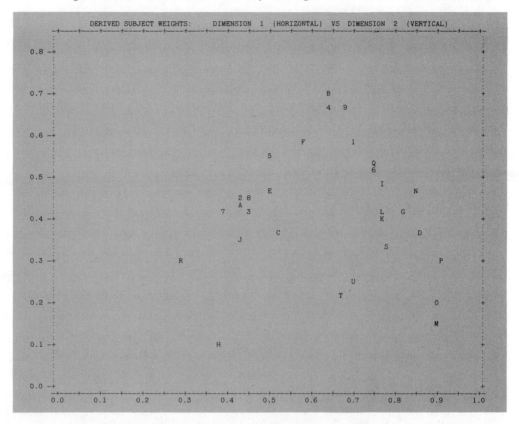

Figure 25.42l   Plot of derived subject weights, dimension 1 vs. dimension 3

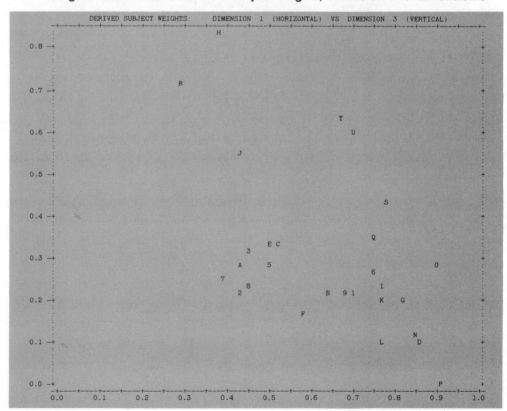

Figure 25.42m   Plot of derived subject weights, dimension 2 vs. dimension 3

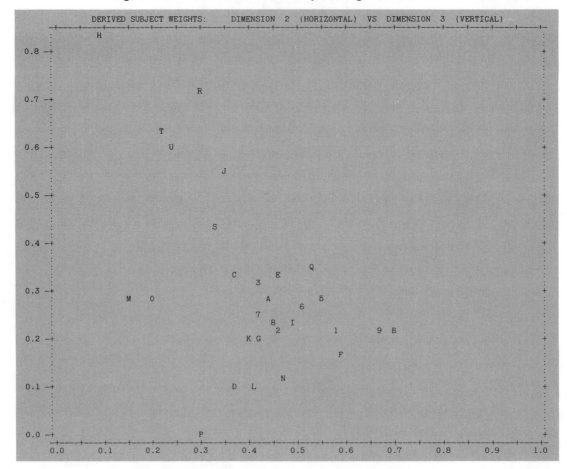

With this in mind, let's look at the three weight space plots. In Figure 25.42k, we note that if we draw a line from the origin through the subject whose plot symbol is **C** (in the middle of the plot), then all the subjects below that line are adults (with one exception), and all the subjects above the line are children (with two exceptions). Thus, essentially all adults weight dimension 1 (horizontal) more heavily relative to dimension 2 (vertical) than is the case for children. More simply stated, adults find dimension 1 more salient than do children.

In Figure 25.42l, which is of dimensions 1 and 3, we can draw a similar line from the origin to just below the subject whose plot symbol is **U**. The five subjects above this line are adults. Thus, some of the adults, but none of the children, find dimension 1 more important than dimension 3. Furthermore, the adults who are below this line are all further from the origin than the children, suggesting that children find neither dimension 1 or 3 as salient as do adults.

Finally, looking at the Figure 25.42m, which displays dimensions 2 and 3, we conclude that some adults find dimension 3 more salient than 2, whereas all children find dimension 2 more salient than 3. Putting all of these observations together, we come to the interpretation presented in the results section above.

Figure 25.42n shows the scatterplot of linear fit, which presents the plot of all of the $15 \times 14 = 210$ transformed dissimilarities for each of the 30 matrices T_k (6300 elements in total) versus their corresponding elements in the matrices D. We see that this plot shows fairly little scatter, particularly when one considers all the M's along the diagonal of the plot. However, there is a definite suggestion of greater scatter for the small distances than for the large distances, an artifact explained above.

Figure 25.42n Scatterplot of linear fit

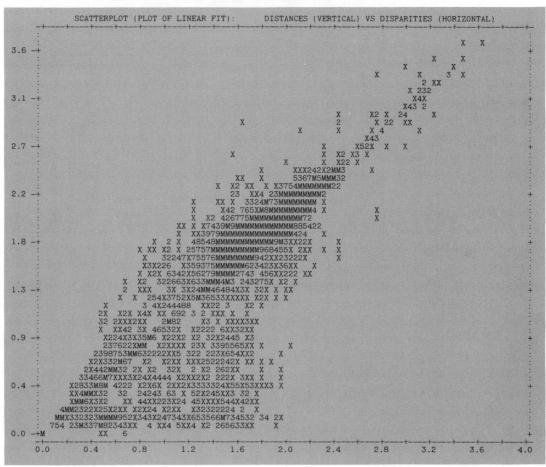

Finally, the matrix and plot of flattened subject weights appear in Figures 25.42o and 25.42p. The meaning of the flattened weights, and their interpretation, is given below.

Figure 25.42o   Flattened subject weights

```
                        FLATTENED SUBJECT WEIGHTS

                                    VARIABLE
        SUBJECT      PLOT       1           2
        NUMBER      SYMBOL
           1           1       0.0357      0.7616
           2           2      -0.6606      1.0043
           3           3      -0.7430      0.4589
           4           4      -0.4095      1.2518
           5           5      -0.8112      1.0037
           6           6       0.1958      0.2681
           7           7      -0.8438      0.8252
           8           8      -0.6181      0.8672
           9           9      -0.2903      1.1490
          10           A      -0.7731      0.7091
          11           B      -0.4645      1.3867
          12           C      -0.3486     -0.0646
          13           D       1.5082     -0.2946
          14           E      -0.6593      0.4649
          15           F      -0.2843      1.3361
          16           G       0.8468     -0.1350
          17           H      -1.4639     -2.2940
          18           I       0.4081      0.1945
          19           J      -1.2060     -0.4081
          20           K       0.7983     -0.1494
          21           L       1.0896      0.1367
          22           M       1.7733     -1.9283
          23           N       1.0198      0.1909
          24           O       1.6020     -1.6055
          25           P       2.3896     -0.5610
          26           Q      -0.0448      0.1518
          27           R      -2.0746     -0.7556
          28           S       0.3398     -0.8998
          29           T      -0.2109     -1.6093
          30           U      -0.1004     -1.4551
```

Figure 25.42p   Plot of flattened subject weights

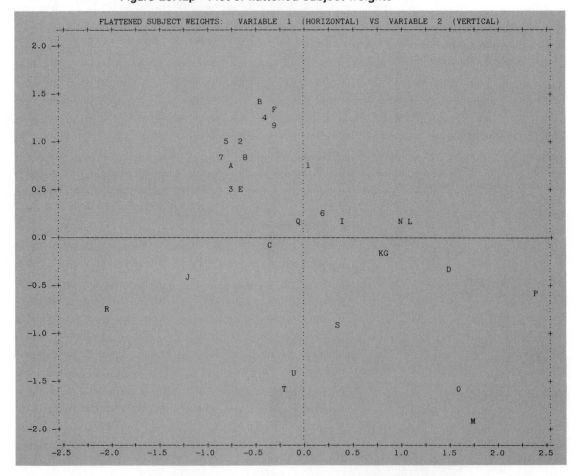

25.43
The Weirdness Index

It has been pointed out by Takane et al. (1977) and especially by MacCallum (1977) that the weights used to represent individual differences in the INDSCAL model are commonly misinterpreted. The correct interpretation of the weights is that they represent the end of a vector directed from the origin of the weight space. Thus, the angle of each subject's vector, relative to the dimensions of the space (and relative to other subjects' vectors) is interpretable. The common mistake is to treat the weights as a point and interpret the distances between points, when instead the weights should be treated as a vector and the angles between vectors be interpreted.

Thus, the common misinterpretation is that subject weight points that are "near each other" in the subject weight space are "similar." However, the correct interpretation is that subject weight vectors which are oriented in "roughly the same direction" are "similar."

The weirdness index is designed to help interpret subject weights. The index, as described below, indicates how unusual or weird each subject's weights are relative to the weights of the typical subject being analyzed. The index varies from 0.00 to 1.00. A subject with a weirdness of 0.00 has weights that are proportional to the average subject's weights (to the mean weights). Such a subject is a totally typical subject. As the weight ratios become more and more extreme, the weirdness index approaches 1.00. Finally, when a subject has only one positive weight, and all the remaining weights are 0, the weirdness index is 1.00. Such a subject is very weird, only using one of the dimensions of the analysis.

Consider the hypothetical subject weight space presented in Figure 25.43a. In this figure we present the weight vector for just one subject. It is shown as a vector directed from the origin of the weight space. The endpoint of the vector, when projected onto dimensions 1 and 2, has Cartesian coordinates w_{k1} and w_{k2}, respectively. In the usual interpretation of individual differences, the subject is said to have weight w_{k1} on dimension 1 and weight w_{k2} on dimension 2, the weights representing the degree of importance (salience or relevance) of the dimensions to the subject.

Figure 25.43a Hypothetical subject weight space

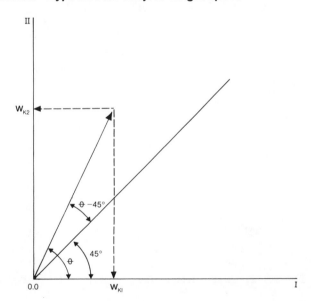

The Cartesian coordinates can be converted into polar coordinates without loss of information. The polar coordinates of vector w_k are the length of the vector and its angle relative to dimension 1. We can represent the length as r_k (not labeled in Figure 25.43a) and the angle as Θ_k (labeled as Θ in the figure). The length r_k is set equal to the square root of the RSQ value displayed by ALSCAL for each subject. Thus, the usual representation of individual differences, namely w_{k1} and w_{k2}, can be changed to the wholly equivalent representation r_k and Θ_k. When there are more than two dimensions, we still have r_k but several Θ_{ka}, one for each dimension a except the last.

The reference axis for the angle Θ is of course, arbitrary. We could have chosen dimension 2 instead of dimension 1. In fact, we could have chosen any other direction through the subject space. The 45° line through Figure 25.43a, for example, could serve as the reference for a new angle $\Theta - 45°$, and we could express the location of the subject's vector by its length and the angle between it and the 45° line.

Consider the 45° line. It has the simple interpretation that it represents equal weighting of both dimensions. Furthermore, as a subject's weight vector departs from this line the subject has a more and more extreme pattern of weights. In the extreme, if the subject's vector lies along one of the dimensions, the subject is using that dimension to the complete exclusion of the other dimension.

This interpretation of the 45° line is, however, entirely dependent on a particular way of arbitrarily normalizing the subject weights. As is shown in the left portion of Figure 25.43b, in ALSCAL the subject weights are normalized so that on the average dimension 1 gets the heaviest weighting, dimension 2 the next heaviest, etc. As was discussed above, this normalization is arbitrary. If instead we were to normalize so that the 45° line represented the typical subject's weights (instead of equal weights), then the line would correspond to the average subject. This modification, which is shown in the right portion of Figure 25.43b, is done by simply defining a new set of weights:

$$w'_{ka} = w_{ka}/\Sigma_k^n w_{ka} \hspace{4cm} \textbf{Equation 25.43a}$$

When there are more than two dimensions, this normalization orients the typical subject's weight vector along the line that is at a 45° angle to all dimensions.

Figure 25.43b Normalized subject weights

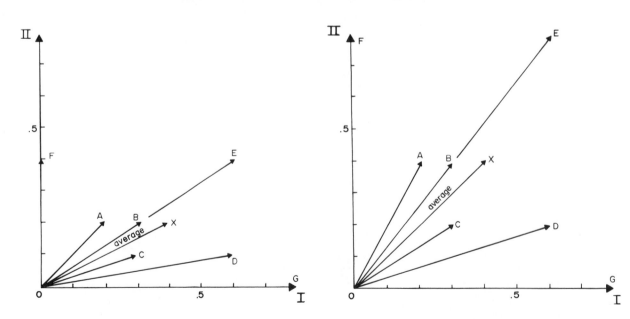

If we make this modification in the normalization of the weights, then departures from the 45° line have a very nice interpretation. First, a subject whose vector is on the 45° line is one who weights the dimensions just as the typical subject does. Second, as a subject's vector departs farther and farther from the line, the subject becomes less and less like the typical subject.

While this normalization has desirable aspects, it is used only in the definition of the weirdness index. In particular, ALSCAL does not normalize the weights in this fashion because it seems to be more desirable to continue with the normalization conventions adopted in other MDS programs. However, this normalization is involved in calculating the weirdness index.

The final steps in defining a convenient index of a subject's "weirdness" (i.e., how far the subject's weight vector is from the average subject's vector) are first to determine the angle between the subject's normalized weight vector and the 45° line, and second to define a function of this angle that varies from 0.00 to 1.00. We do this by defining standardized vectors v_k which are unit-length and colinear with the weight vectors w_k:

$$v_{ka} = w'_{ka}/[\Sigma_a^r(w'_{ka})^2]^{1/2} \qquad\qquad \textbf{Equation 25.43b}$$

The angle between a subject's weight vector and the 45° line can now be defined, in radians, as:

$$\text{Cos}^{-1}[r^{-1/2}(\Sigma_a^r v_{ka})] \qquad\qquad \textbf{Equation 25.43c}$$

This angle varies from a minimum that occurs when the subject's vector coincides with the 45° line (i.e., when the subject's weights are proportional to the average weights) to a maximum value that occurs when the subject's vector coincides with one of the edges of the subject weight space (i.e., when the subject has only one positive weight). A little investigation shows that the maximum angle, in radians, is $\text{Cos}^{-1}(r^{-1/2})$. Thus, if we divide by this maximum value we obtain an index that varies from 0.00 to 1.00. Finally, we divide the previous formula by this maximum value to obtain the complete formula for the weirdness index:

$$\text{Cos}^{-1}[r^{-1/2}(\Sigma_a^r v_{ka})] / \text{Cos}^{-1}(r^{-1/2}) \qquad\qquad \textbf{Equation 25.43d}$$

25.44
Flattened Weights

As was pointed out above, the subject weights in WMDS are often misinterpreted. The common mistake is to interpret the distance between subject points instead of interpreting the angle between subject vectors. In addition, standard statistical procedures are inappropriate for interpreting these weights because the weights present angular information, not linear information.

Because of these characteristics of the weights, ALSCAL calculates and displays information called flattened weights. The weight vectors, when flattened, become weight points. The angles between the vectors, when flattened, become distances between the points. Thus, the flattened-weight variables are ordinary linear variables that can be used in ordinary statistical procedures. However, because of lack of independence between the weights, hypothesis testing is inappropriate. The statistical procedure should be used in a descriptive fashion only.

In ALSCAL, flattened weights are calculated by normalizing each subject's weights so that their sum is 1.00, as is illustrated by the two matrices on the bottom left of Figure 25.44. This defines a set of r normalized weight vectors. The rth one is dropped (because it is a linear combination of the others) and the remaining are centered and normalized, as illustrated by the bottom right matrix in the figure. This is the complete definition of the flattening transformation used in ALSCAL. The rank of the flattened weights matrix is $r-1$. Thus any one of its variables is a linear combination of the remaining variables. Therefore, one of the variables can be dropped.

Figure 25.44   Flattened transformation

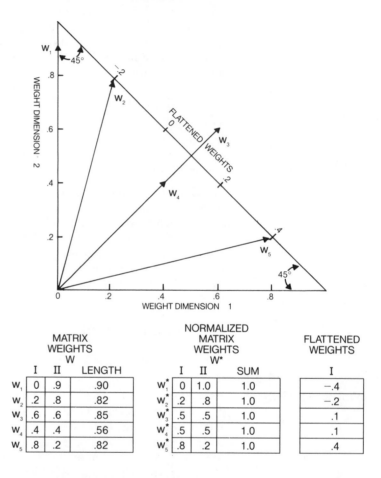

		MATRIX WEIGHTS W					NORMALIZED MATRIX WEIGHTS W*			FLATTENED WEIGHTS	
	I	II	LENGTH			I	II	SUM		I	
w_1	0	.9	.90		w_1^*	0	1.0	1.0		−.4	
w_2	.2	.8	.82		w_2^*	.2	.8	1.0		−.2	
w_3	.6	.6	.85		w_3^*	.5	.5	1.0		.1	
w_4	.4	.4	.56		w_4^*	.5	.5	1.0		.1	
w_5	.8	.2	.82		w_5^*	.8	.2	1.0		.4	

The geometry underlying the idea of flattened weights, as implemented in ALSCAL, is also illustrated in Figure 25.44. The flattening transformation directly projects the weight vectors (labeled $\mathbf{w_1}$ through $\mathbf{w_5}$ in the figure) onto a space having one less dimension than the weight space, and which is at a 45° angle to all dimensions. In the figure, the weight space (whose dimensions are the horizontal and vertical sides of the triangle) is two-dimensional, whereas the flattened weight space (which is the hypotenuse of the triangle) is one-dimensional. Note the weight vector w_3 extends beyond the hypotenuse before flattening, so its projection onto the flattened space is shorter than the original vector. However, the weight vectors

w_1 and w_2 are lengthened in their projection onto the flattened space. Finally, we look at the points in the flattened space defined by the projections from the original weight space.

Notice that this flattening transformation does not map the angles in the weight space onto distances in the flattened space in a one-to-one fashion. (In fact, there is no one-to-one flattening transformation.) An angle that is at the edge of the weight space is represented by a distance which is larger than the distance for an equal angle in the middle of the weight space. That is, subjects who are peripheral in the weight space appear to be even more peripheral in the flattened space.

25.45
RUNNING
PROCEDURE ALSCAL

ALSCAL reads one or more proximity matrices from an active system file. You can use the CLUSTER or PROXIMITIES procedures (see Chapters 22 and 24) to produce these matrices. For the stimuli represented in the matrix or matrices, ALSCAL uses one of five different models to derive stimulus coordinates and/or weights in a multidimensional space. You can specify many forms of multidimensional scaling and unfolding models. You can also display a variety of plots, including those for stimulus coordinates, weights, and transformations.

The only required subcommand for ALSCAL is the VARIABLES subcommand. All other subcommands are optional.

25.46
VARIABLES Subcommand

The VARIABLES subcommand is required. It identifies the variables for the columns of the proximity matrix or matrices that ALSCAL reads from the active system file. You can use the TO keyword to imply consecutive variables on the active system file. You can use a DATA LIST command to enter proximity matrices directly, or you can use the PROXIMITIES procedure to compute them. All the matrix variables must be numeric, and each matrix must have at least four rows and four columns. You can use the SHAPE subcommand to specify the form of the matrix (see Section 25.48).

25.47
INPUT Subcommand

The INPUT subcommand is used when ALSCAL reads inline rectangular data matrices and specifies how many rows are in each matrix. Each case in the active system file represents a single row in the data matrix. (The VARIABLES subcommand specifies the columns.) If you do not use the INPUT subcommand to read rectangular data, ALSCAL assumes that each case in your file represents one row of a single input matrix.

If you have split-file data (see Chapter 2), the number of rows in the input matrix is the number of cases in each split-file group. All split-file groups must have the same number of rows. At least four rows are required.

If your file contains multiple rectangular input matrices, you must specify the number of rows in each, as in

```
ALSCAL VARIABLES = varlist
 /INPUT = ROWS(8)
 /SHAPE=RECTANGULAR
 /CONDITION=ROW
 /LEVEL=ORDINAL.
```

which indicates that there are eight rows per matrix, with each case representing one row. The number of rows per matrix must divide evenly into the total number of observations in the data set.

25.48
SHAPE Subcommand

The SHAPE subcommand specifies the form of the input data matrix or matrices you are scaling. The form may be symmetric, asymmetric, or rectangular.

SYMMETRIC   *Symmetric data matrix or matrices.* This is the default. A matrix is symmetric when the corresponding values in the upper and lower triangles are equal. For example, in a study of automobiles, the similarity of a Ford to a Plymouth might be considered the same as the similarity of a Plymouth to a Ford. ALSCAL only looks at the values below the diagonal, so values on and above the diagonal can be left missing.

ASYMMETRIC   *Asymmetric data matrix or matrices.* The corresponding values in the upper and lower triangles are not all equal. The diagonal is ignored.

RECTANGULAR   *Rectangular data matrix or matrices.* The rows and columns represent different sets of items.

ALSCAL calculates the number of input matrices by dividing the total number of observations in the data set by the number of observations in each matrix. All matrices must contain the same number of observations. This number depends on the SHAPE subcommand and the INPUT subcommand (if used). For example, if you specify SHAPE=SYMMETRIC or SHAPE=ASYMMETRIC, ALSCAL expects square matrix data, and it sets the number of observations in each matrix equal to the number of variables (stimuli being analyzed). If you specify SHAPE= RECTANGULAR, ALSCAL sets the number of column stimuli equal to the number of variables in the analysis. The number of row stimuli is set equal to the number of rows specified in the INPUT subcommand. If no INPUT subcommand is specified, ALSCAL uses the number of cases in the input file or, with split files, the number of cases in the first split-file group. (All groups must contain the same number of cases.)

25.49
LEVEL Subcommand

The LEVEL subcommand identifies the level of measurement for the values in the data matrix or matrices: ordinal, interval, ratio, or nominal. Optionally, you can specify the degree of a polynomial transformation for interval or ratio measurement.

ORDINAL(UNTIE|SIMILAR)   *Ordinal-level data.* This is the default. It treats the data as ordinal, using Kruskal's (1964) least-squares monotonic transformation. The analysis is nonmetric. By default, ties in the data remain tied throughout the analysis and ALSCAL treats the data as dissimilarities. Optionally, you can specify either UNTIE or SIMILAR in parentheses. The UNTIE option allows ties to be untied. The SIMILAR option instructs ALSCAL to treat the data as similarities.

INTERVAL(d)   *Interval-level data.* This specification produces a metric analysis of the data using classical regression techniques. Optionally, you can specify an integer from 1 to 4 in parentheses for the degree of polynomial transformation. The default value is 1.

RATIO(d)   *Ratio-level data.* Like INTERVAL, this specification produces a metric analysis. Optionally, you can specify an integer from 1 to 4 in parentheses for the degree of polynomial transformation. The default value is 1.

NOMINAL	*Nominal-level data.* ALSCAL treats the data as nominal by using Takane et al.'s (1977) least-squares categorical transformation. You can use this specification for a nonmetric analysis of nominal data. This option can be used in only a few situations: when there are few observed categories, when there are many observations in each category, or when the order of the categories is not known.

25.50
CONDITION Subcommand

Conditionality refers to ways in which the numbers in a data set are not comparable. For example, the subjects in a study may all use a 7-point rating scale, but the meaning of the rating-scale responses may differ from subject to subject. Different subjects may use the scale in different ways. You may correctly interpret a response of 3 from one subject as less than a 5 from that same subject, but you may not be justified in interpreting the 3 from the first subject as less than a 5 from another subject. In this case, the meaning of the numbers would be *conditional* on the subject.

The CONDITION subcommand lets you identify the conditionality of the data matrix or matrices you are scaling. In the previous example, you would use CONDITION=MATRIX when the data for different subjects are in different matrices.

MATRIX	*The meaning of the numbers is conditional on the subject.* This specification is the default.
ROW	*The meaning of the numbers is conditional on the row.* You can make meaningful comparisons only among numbers within rows of each matrix. This specification is appropriate only for asymmetric or rectangular data and may not be used when MODEL= ASCAL or MODEL=AINDS.
UNCONDITIONAL	*The meaning of the numbers is not conditional.* You can make meaningful comparisons among all values in the input matrix or matrices.

25.51
FILE Subcommand

To perform an analysis, ALSCAL requires proximity data (see Sections 25.46 through 25.50). With the FILE subcommand, ALSCAL can read a file containing additional data: an initial or fixed configuration for the coordinates of the stimuli and/or weights for the matrices being scaled. You can create this file with an ALSCAL OUTFILE subcommand or with an SPSS input program. The FILE subcommand is *not* used to read matrix system files written by PROXIMITIES or CLUSTER. Use the MATRIX subcommand for those files (Section 25.58).

To use the FILE subcommand, you must specify a filename. You can follow this with optional specifications for the matrices and the types of values in the matrices to be read.

The variables in the configuration/weights file that correspond to successive ALSCAL dimensions must have the names DIM1, DIM2 . . . DIM*r*, where *r* is the maximum number of ALSCAL dimensions. The file must also contain the short string variable TYPE_ to identify the types of values in all the rows. Specify stimulus coordinate values as CONFIG; row stimulus coordinates as ROWCONF; column stimulus coordinates as COLCONF; and subject and stimulus weights, respectively, as SUBJWGHT and STIMWGHT. ALSCAL accepts CONFIG and ROWCONF interchangeably. You can spell out CONFIG, ROWCONF, COL-CONF, SUBJWGHT, and STIMWGHT in full or use just the first three letters of each.

The sets of coordinates or weights in the file must appear in the order CON, ROW, COL, SUB, STI. ALSCAL skips unneeded types as long as they appear in the file in their proper order. Generalized weights (GEM) and flattened subject weights (FLA) may not be initialized or fixed and will always be skipped. (These can be generated by ALSCAL but not entered into the procedure.)

You can enter initial values (option INITIAL) or fixed values (option FIXED) as in an external unfolding model. INITIAL is the default. The FIXED option lets you define an external or hypothesized structure for stimulus coordinates, subject weights, and/or stimulus weights. This option forces ALSCAL to use the defined structure without modification to calculate the best values for all unfixed portions of the structure. In the following example, ALSCAL reads stimulus coordinates as fixed values and stimulus weights as purely initial values.

```
ALSCAL VARIABLES = varlist
 /SHAPE = ASYMMETRIC
 /LEVEL = ORDINAL
 /MODEL = ASCAL
 /FILE  = FIRST
          CONFIG(FIXED)
          STIMWGHT(INITIAL).
```

In the case of split files, ALSCAL reads initial or fixed configurations for each split-file group. If there is only one initial configuration in the file, ALSCAL rereads these initial or fixed values for successive split-file groups.

If you do not include the input matrix specifications for the configuration/ weights file, ALSCAL will read sequentially the TYPE_ values appropriate to the model you specify. For instance, if MODEL=ASCAL and SHAPE= ASYMMETRIC, ALSCAL will automatically check TYPE_ to find rows containing the value CON for stimulus coordinates and the value STI for stimulus weights (see Table 25.51). ALSCAL ignores user-missing values in all variables. The system-missing value is an error in the TYPE_ variable and is converted to 0 in the other variables.

The following list summarizes and further explains the optional specifications on the FILE subcommand. Table 25.51 shows the default matrices ALSCAL reads if you use the FILE subcommand without optional specifications.

CONFIG(type)   *Read stimulus configuration.* The configuration/weights file contains initial stimulus coordinates. Input of this sort is appropriate when SHAPE=SYMMETRIC or SHAPE=ASYMMETRIC or when the number of variables in a matrix equals the number of variables in the ALSCAL command. The value of TYPE_ must be either CON or ROW for all the stimulus coordinates of the configuration.

ROWCONF(type)   *Read row stimulus configuration.* The configuration/weights file contains initial row stimulus coordinates. This specification is necessary if SHAPE=RECTANGULAR. The number of observations equals the number of rows you specify on the INPUT subcommand or, if you do not include INPUT, the number of cases in the proximity file. The command

```
ALSCAL VARIABLES = varlist
 /SHAPE = RECTANGULAR
 /INPUT = ROWS
 /CONDITION = ROW
 /FILE = OUTSET
          ROWCONF.
```

specifies that the file OUTSET contains row stimulus configurations; that the proximity file is rectangular in shape; that each case in the proximity file represents a single row in the data matrix; and that only within-row values in the matrix may be meaningfully compared. The value of TYPE_ must be either ROW or CON for the set of coordinates for each row.

COLCONF(type)   *Read column stimulus configuration.* The configuration/weights file contains initial column stimulus coordinates. This type of file is appropriate only if SHAPE=RECTANGULAR and if the number of observations in the matrix equals the number of variables in the ALSCAL command. The value of TYPE_ must be COL for the set of coordinates for each column.

SUBJWGHT(type)   *Read subject (matrix) weights.* The configuration/weights file contains subject weights. The number of observations in a subject-weights matrix must equal the number of matrices in the proximity file. Subject weights can be used only if MODEL=INDSCAL, MODEL=AINDS, or MODEL=GEMSCAL. The value of TYPE_ for each set of weights must be SUB.

STIMWGHT(type)   *Read stimulus weights.* The configuration/weights file contains stimulus weights. You can use this option only if the number of observations in the configuration/weights file equals the number of matrices in the proximity file. This kind of input can be used only if MODEL=AINDS or MODEL=ASCAL. The value of TYPE_ for each set of weights must be STI.

The (type) specification is optional. You can specify either (FIXED) or (INITIAL). The default is (INITIAL).

Table 25.51   Default input values for the FILE subcommand

Shape	Model	Default
SYMMETRIC	EUCLID	CONFIG (or ROWCONF)
	INDSCAL	CONFIG (or ROWCONF)
		SUBJWGHT
	GEMSCAL	CONFIG (or ROWCONF)
		SUBJWGHT
ASYMMETRIC	EUCLID	CONFIG (or ROWCONF)
	INDSCAL	CONFIG (or ROWCONF)
	GEMSCAL	CONFIG (or ROWCONF)
		SUBJWGHT
	ASCAL	CONFIG (or ROWCONF)
		STIMWGHT
	AINDS	CONFIG (or ROWCONF)
		SUBJWGHT
		STIMWGHT
RECTANGULAR	EUCLID	ROWCONF (or CONFIG)
		COLCONF
	INDSCAL	ROWCONF (or CONFIG)
		COLCONF
		SUBJWGHT
	GEMSCAL	ROWCONF (or CONFIG)
		COLCONF
		SUBJWGHT

25.52
MODEL Subcommand

The MODEL subcommand defines the scaling model for the analysis. You can specify any of five scaling and unfolding model types:

EUCLID   *Euclidean distance model.* This model is the default. It can be used with any type of proximity matrix.

INDSCAL   *Individual differences (weighted) Euclidean distance model.* ALSCAL will scale the data using the weighted individual differences Euclidean distance model, as proposed by Carroll and Chang (1970). You can specify this type of analysis only if you are analyzing more than one data matrix and if you specify more than one dimension on the CRITERIA subcommand (see Section 25.53).

ASCAL   *Asymmetric Euclidean distance model.* You can use this model (Young, 1975b) only if SHAPE=ASYMMETRIC and if the number of dimensions requested on the CRITERIA subcommand is greater than one.

AINDS   *Asymmetric individual differences Euclidean distance model.* This option combines Young's (1975a) asymmetric Euclidean model with the individual differences model as proposed by Carroll and Chang (1970). You can specify MODEL=AINDS only when SHAPE=ASYMMETRIC, when you are analyzing more than one data matrix, and when the number of dimensions on the CRITERIA subcommand is greater than one.

GEMSCAL   *Generalized Euclidean metric individual differences model.* You can control the number of directions for this model with the DIRECTIONS option on the CRITERIA subcommand. By default, the number of directions is set equal to the number of dimensions in the solution. The number of directions you specify can be equal to but not exceed the group space dimensionality. In the following example, the number of directions in the GEMSCAL model is set to 4:

```
ALSCAL VARIABLES = varlist
 /SHAPE = ASYMMETRIC
 /CONDITION = ROW
 /MODEL = GEMSCAL
 /CRITERIA = DIM(4) DIRECTIONS(4).
```

25.53
CRITERIA Subcommand

The CRITERIA subcommand lets you specify aspects of your scaling model and set convergence criteria for the scaling solution. ALSCAL is an iterative algorithm designed to minimize the goodness-of-fit criterion called s-stress. ALSCAL iterates until the amount of improvement in s-stress is less than the CONVERGE value, until the number of completed iterations reaches a maximum, or until the value of s-stress reaches a minimum.

CONVERGE(c)   *Set CONVERGE to c.* This refers to the criterion for improvement in s-stress from one iteration to the next. By default, CONVERGE=0.001. To increase the precision of your solution, you can replace this value with a smaller number. To obtain a less precise solution (perhaps to reduce computer time), specify a larger value, for instance 0.05. Negative values of CONVERGE are not allowed. If CONVERGE=0, the algorithm will iterate 30 times unless you specify a different value with the ITER option.

ITER(ni)   *Set the maximum number of iterations to ni.* The default value is 30. The ITER option lets you set the value higher or lower. A higher value may give you a more precise solution, but it may add substantially to your computer time and costs.

STRESSMIN(s)   *Set the minimum stress value to s.* By default, ALSCAL automatically stops iterating when the value of s-stress reaches 0.005 or less. If you want the iterations to continue beyond this point, you can specify a value smaller than 0.005. A larger value will cause ALSCAL to terminate sooner than usual. You can specify a value for STRESSMIN from 0 to 1.

NEGATIVE   *Allow negative weights in the individual differences models.* By default, ALSCAL does not permit weights to take on negative values. To allow negative weights, specify CRITERIA= NEGATIVE. Weighted models include INDSCAL, ASCAL, and AINDS, but not GEMSCAL. The NEGATIVE option will be ignored if MODEL=EUCLID.

CUTOFF(c)   *Set the cutoff value for treating distances as missing to c.* By default, ALSCAL treats all negative similarities (or dissimilarities) as missing, and 0 and positive similarities as nonmissing (CUTOFF=0). Changing the CUTOFF value causes ALSCAL to treat similarities greater than or equal to that value as nonmissing. User- and system-missing values are considered missing regardless of the CUTOFF specification.

NOULB
Do not estimate upper and lower bounds on missing values. By default, ALSCAL estimates the upper and lower bounds on missing values in order to compute the initial configuration. Specify CRITERIA=NOULB if you do not want upper and lower bounds to be estimated. This specification has no effect during the iterative process, when missing values are ignored.

DIMENS(min,max)
Set the minimum and maximum numbers of dimensions in the scaling solution. By default, ALSCAL calculates a scaling solution with two dimensions. If you want to allow your solution to have other than two dimensions, specify the minimum number and the maximum number of dimensions in parentheses to the right of DIMENS. The minimum and maximum numbers can be any integer values between 2 and 6. You can also specify a single value inside the parentheses to represent both the minimum and the maximum number of dimensions. Thus, DIMENS(3) is equivalent to DIMENS(3,3). The minimum number of dimensions can be set to 1 only if MODEL=EUCLID.

DIRECTIONS(r)
Set the number of principal directions in the generalized Euclidean model to r. This option has no effect for models other than MODEL=GEMSCAL. The number of principal directions can be any positive integer between 1 and the number of dimensions specified on the DIMENS option. By default, ALSCAL will set the number of directions equal to the number of dimensions.

TIESTORE(n)
Set the amount of storage needed for ties to n. This option estimates the amount of storage needed to deal with ties in ordinal data. By default, the amount of storage is set to 1000 or the number of cells in a matrix, whichever is smaller. Should this be insufficient, ALSCAL terminates with a message that more space is needed.

CONSTRAIN
Constrain multidimensional unfolding solution. Use the CONSTRAIN option if you want the initial constraints to remain constant throughout the analysis.

25.54
Specification of Analyses

Table 25.54a summarizes the types of analyses that can be performed for the major forms of proximity matrices you can use with ALSCAL. Tables 25.54b and 25.54c list the specifications necessary to produce these analyses using SPSS ALSCAL, depending on whether you want a nonmetric or metric type of analysis. You can, of course, include additional specifications to control the precision of your analysis with the CRITERIA subcommand.

Table 25.54a   Models for types of matrix input

Matrix mode	Matrix form	Model class	Single matrix	Replications of single matrix	Two or more individual matrices
Object by object	Symmetric	Multi-dimensional scaling	CMDS Classical multidimensional scaling	RMDS Replicated multidimensional scaling	WMDS(INDSCAL) Weighted multidimensional scaling
	Asymmetric single process	Multi-dimensional scaling	CMDS(row conditional) Classical row conditional multidimensional scaling	RMDS(row conditional) Replicated row conditional multidimensional scaling	WMDS(row conditional) Weighted row conditional multidimensional scaling
	Asymmetric multiple process	Internal asymmetric multi-dimensional scaling	CAMDS Classical asymmetric multidimensional scaling	RAMDS Replicated asymmetric multidimensional scaling	WAMDS Weighted asymmetric multidimensional scaling
		External asymmetric multi-dimensional scaling	CAMDS(external) Classical external asymmetric multidimensional scaling	RAMDS(external) Replicated external asymmetric multidimensional scaling	WAMDS(external) Weighted external asymmetric multidimensional scaling
Object by attribute	Rectangular	Internal unfolding	CMDU Classical internal multidimensional unfolding	RMDU Replicated internal multidimensional unfolding	WMDU Weighted internal multidimensional unfolding
		External unfolding	CMDU(external) Classical external multidimensional unfolding	RMDU(external) Replicated external multidimensional unfolding	WMDU(external) Weighted external multidimensional unfolding

Table 25.54b   ALSCAL specifications for nonmetric models

Matrix mode	Matrix form	Model class	Single matrix	Replications of single matrix	Two or more individual matrices
Object by object	Symmetric	Multi-dimensional scaling	`ALSCAL VAR= varlist.`	`ALSCAL VAR= varlist.`	`ALSCAL VAR= varlist /MODEL=INDSCAL.`
	Asymmetric single process	Multi-dimensional scaling	`ALSCAL VAR= varlist /SHAPE=ASYMMETRIC /CONDITION=ROW.`	`ALSCAL VAR= varlist /SHAPE=ASYMMETRIC /CONDITION=ROW.`	`ALSCAL VAR= varlist /SHAPE=ASYMMETRIC /CONDITION=ROW /MODEL=INDSCAL.`
	Asymmetric multiple process	Internal asymmetric multi-dimensional scaling	`ALSCAL VAR= varlist /SHAPE=ASYMMETRIC /MODEL=ASCAL.`	`ALSCAL VAR= varlist /SHAPE=ASYMMETRIC /MODEL=ASCAL.`	`ALSCAL VAR= varlist /SHAPE=ASYMMETRIC /MODEL=AINDS.`
		External asymmetric multi-dimensional scaling	`ALSCAL VAR= varlist /SHAPE=ASYMMETRIC /MODEL=ASCAL /FILE=file COLCONF(FIX).`	`ALSCAL VAR= varlist /SHAPE=ASYMMETRIC /MODEL=ASCAL /FILE=file COLCONF(FIX).`	`ALSCAL VAR= varlist /SHAPE=ASYMMETRIC /MODEL=AINDS /FILE=file COLCONF(FIX).`
Object by attribute	Rectangular	Internal unfolding	`ALSCAL VAR= varlist /SHAPE=REC /INP=ROWS /CONDITION=ROW.`	`ALSCAL VAR= varlist /SHAPE=REC /INP=ROWS /CONDITION(ROW).`	`ALSCAL VAR= varlist /SHAPE=REC /INP=ROWS /CONDITION=ROW /MODEL=INDSCAL.`
		External unfolding	`ALSCAL VAR= varlist /SHAPE=REC /INP=ROWS /CONDITION=ROW /FILE=file ROWCONF(FIX).`	`ALSCAL VAR= varlist /SHAPE=REC /INP=ROWS /CONDITION=ROW /FILE=file ROWCONF(FIX).`	`ALSCAL VAR= varlist /SHAPE=REC /INP=ROWS /CONDITION=ROW /FILE=file ROWCONF(FIX) /MODEL=INDSCAL.`

Table 25.54c ALSCAL specifications for metric models

Matrix mode	Matrix form	Model class	Single matrix	Replications of single matrix	Two or more individual matrices

Object by object	Symmetric	Multi-dimensional scaling	`ALSCAL VAR= varlist`
			`/LEVEL=INT.`
				`ALSCAL VAR= varlist`
				`/LEVEL=INT.`
					`ALSCAL VAR= varlist`
					`/LEVEL=INT`
					`/MODEL=INDSCAL.`

	Asymmetric single process	Multi-dimensional scaling	`ALSCAL VAR= varlist`
			`/SHAPE=ASYMMETRIC`
			`/CONDITION=ROW`
			`/LEVEL=INT.`
				`ALSCAL VAR= varlist`
				`/SHAPE=ASYMMETRIC`
				`/CONDITION=ROW`
				`/LEVEL=INT.`
					`ALSCAL VAR= varlist`
					`/SHAPE=ASYMMETRIC`
					`/CONDITION=ROW`
					`/LEVEL=INT`
					`/MODEL=INDSCAL.`

	Asymmetric multiple process	Internal asymmetric multi-dimensional scaling	`ALSCAL VAR= varlist`
			`/SHAPE=ASYMMETRIC`
			`/LEVEL=INT`
			`/MODEL=ASCAL.`
				`ALSCAL VAR= varlist`
				`/SHAPE=ASYMMETRIC`
				`/LEVEL=INT`
				`/MODEL=ASCAL.`
					`ALSCAL VAR= varlist`
					`/SHAPE=ASYMMETRIC`
					`/LEVEL=INT`
					`/MODEL=AINDS.`

		External asymmetric multi-dimensional scaling	`ALSCAL VAR= varlist`
			`/SHAPE=ASYMMETRIC`
			`/LEVEL=INT`
			`/MODEL=ASCAL`
			`/FILE=file COLCONF(FIX).`
				`ALSCAL VAR= varlist`
				`/SHAPE=ASYMMETRIC`
				`/LEVEL=INT`
				`/MODEL=ASCAL`
				`/FILE=file COLCONF(FIX).`
					`ALSCAL VAR= varlist`
					`/SHAPE=ASYMMETRIC`
					`/LEVEL=INT`
					`/MODEL=AINDS`
					`/FILE=file COLCONF(FIX).`

Object by attribute	Rectangular	Internal unfolding	`ALSCAL VAR= varlist`
			`/SHAPE=REC`
			`/INP=ROWS`
			`/CONDITION=ROW`
			`/LEVEL=INT.`
				`ALSCAL VAR= varlist`
				`/SHAPE=REC`
				`/INP=ROWS`
				`/CONDITION=ROW`
				`/LEVEL=INT.`
					`ALSCAL VAR= varlist`
					`/SHAPE=REC`
					`/INP=ROWS`
					`/CONDITION=ROW`
					`/LEVEL=INT`
					`/MODEL=INDSCAL.`

		External unfolding	`ALSCAL VAR= varlist`
			`/SHAPE=REC`
			`/INP=ROWS`
			`/CONDITION=ROW`
			`/LEVEL=INT`
			`/FILE=file ROWCONF(FIX).`
				`ALSCAL VAR= varlist`
				`/SHAPE=REC`
				`/INP=ROWS`
				`/CONDITION=ROW`
				`/LEVEL=INT`
				`/FILE=file ROWCONF(FIX).`
					`ALSCAL VAR= varlist`
					`/SHAPE=REC`
					`/INP=ROWS`
					`/CONDITION=ROW`
					`/LEVEL=INT`
					`/FILE=file ROWCONF(FIX)`
					`/MODEL=INDSCAL.`

25.55 PRINT Subcommand

You can use the PRINT subcommand to specify additional output not available by default.

DATA *Display input data.* The output includes both the raw data and the scaled data for each subject according to the structure you specified on the SHAPE subcommand.

INTERMED *Display intermediate steps in the scaling process.* Intermediate steps leading up to the final scaling solution are not usually of interest. Some of the items the INTERMED option displays are the raw data, the missing-value pattern, the data with missing-value estimates, the normalized data and means, the squared data with additive constant estimated, and the scalar product for each subject. Since this option can produce a great deal of output, you should use it with caution.

HEADER *Display a header page.* This specification displays a listing of the data, model, output, and algorithmic options in effect for the analysis.

25.56 PLOT Subcommand

The PLOT subcommand plots the multidimensional scaling results.

DEFAULT *Produce default plots.* These are plots of the stimulus coordinates, the matrix weights (if MODEL=INDSCAL, MODEL=AINDS, or MODEL=GEMSCAL), and the stimulus weights (if MODEL=AINDS or MODEL=ASCAL). The default also includes a scatterplot of the linear fit between the data and the model and, for certain types of data, scatterplots of the nonlinear fit and of the data transformation. ALSCAL produces $d*(d-1)/2$ pages of plots for the stimulus space, and, when appropriate, for each of the weight spaces, where d is the number of dimensions in the solution.

ALL   *Plot the stimulus space for each matrix.* You can specify PLOT=ALL to obtain a separate plot of each subject's data transformation (if CONDITION=MATRIX or the data are nominal or ordinal) or a plot for each row (if CONDITION=ROW), and, for weighted models, a separate plot of each subject's weight space. This option can produce thousands of pages of output, especially if CONDITION=ROW.

25.57
OUTFILE Subcommand

The OUTFILE subcommand saves coordinate and weight matrices to the SPSS system file specified immediately after the keyword OUTFILE. This file has a format that the FILE subcommand can use to read initial values. The SPSS system file has an alphanumeric (short string) variable named TYPE_ that identifies the kind of values in each row, a numeric variable DIMENS that specifies the number of dimensions, a numeric variable MATNUM that indicates the subject (matrix) to which each set of coordinates corresponds, and variables DIM1, DIM2...DIMr that correspond to the r ALSCAL dimensions in the model. The values of any split-file variables are also included in this file.

The following list indicates the seven different kinds of ALSCAL file output. Only the first three characters of each identifier are written to variable TYPE_ on the SPSS system file. For example, CONFIG becomes CON.

CONFIG   *Stimulus configuration coordinates for SHAPE=SYMMETRIC or SHAPE=ASYMMETRIC.*

ROWCONF   *Row stimulus configuration coordinates for SHAPE=RECTANGULAR.*

COLCONF   *Column stimulus configuration coordinates for SHAPE =RECTANGULAR.*

SUBJWGHT   *Subject (matrix) weights for MODEL=INDSCAL, MODEL=AINDS, or MODEL=GEMSCAL.*

FLATWGHT   *Flattened subject (matrix) weights for MODEL=INDSCAL, MODEL =AINDS, or MODEL=GEMSCAL.*

GEMWGHT   *Generalized weights for MODEL=GEMSCAL.*

STIMWGHT   *Stimulus weights for MODEL=ASCAL or MODEL=AINDS.*

Table 25.57 shows the types of values that the OUTFILE subcommand automatically writes according to shape and model. For example, if you specify the OUTFILE subcommand with SHAPE=ASYMMETRIC and MODEL= INDSCAL, ALSCAL writes stimulus coordinates, subject weights, and flattened weights to your SPSS system file.

25.58
MATRIX Subcommand

Generally, data read by ALSCAL are already in matrix form. This matrix can be created in either PROXIMITIES or CLUSTER. You do not need to use the MATRIX subcommand to read this file. Simply use the VARIABLES subcommand to indicate the variables (or columns) to be used.

If you use the MATRIX subcommand, the order of rows and columns is unimportant. The MATRIX subcommand has one keyword, IN, which you use to specify the matrix file in parentheses.

(file)   *Read the matrix materials from a matrix system file.*

(*)   *Read the matrix materials from the active system file.* The active system file must be an appropriate matrix system file.

MATRIX=IN cannot be used in place of GET or DATA LIST to create an active system file.

In the following example, ALSCAL reads a distance matrix written to the active system file by PROXIMITIES:

```
GET FILE=CRIME
PROXIMITIES MURDER TO MOTOR
  /ID=CITY
  /MATRIX=OUT(*).
ALSCAL VARIABLES=CASE1 TO CASE8
  /MATRIX=IN(*).
```

Table 25.57   Types of configurations and/or weights in output files

Shape	Model	TYPE_
SYMMETRIC	EUCLID	CON
	INDSCAL	CON
		SUB
		FLA
	GEMSCAL	CON
		SUB
		FLA
		GEM
ASYMMETRIC	EUCLID	CON
	INDSCAL	CON
		SUB
		FLA
	GEMSCAL	CON
		SUB
		FLA
		GEM
	ASCAL	CON
		STI
	AINDS	CON
		SUB
		FLA
		STI
RECTANGULAR	EUCLID	ROW
		COL
	INDSCAL	ROW
		COL
		SUB
		FLA
	GEMSCAL	ROW
		COL
		SUB
		FLA
		GEM

Contents_____

26 Reliability Analysis: Procedure RELIABILITY

From the moment we're born, the world begins to "score" us. One minute after birth, we're rated on the 10-point Apgar scale, followed closely by the five-minute Apgar scale, and then on to countless other scales that will track our intelligence, credit-worthiness, likelihood of hijacking a plane, and so forth. A dubious mark of maturity is when we find ourselves administering these scales.

26.1 CONSTRUCTING A SCALE

When we want to measure characteristics such as driving ability, mastery of course materials, or the ability to function independently, we must construct some type of measurement device. Usually we develop a scale or test that is composed of a variety of related items. The responses to each of the items can be graded and summed, resulting in a score for each case. A question that frequently arises is, How good is our scale? In order to answer this question, consider some of the characteristics of a scale or test.

When we construct a test to measure how well college students have learned the material in an introductory psychology course, the questions actually included in the test are a small sample from all of the items that may have been selected. Though we have selected a limited number of items for inclusion in a test, we want to draw conclusions about the students' mastery of the entire course contents. In fact, we'd like to think that even if we changed the actual items on the test, there would be a strong relationship between students' scores on the test actually given and the scores they would have received on other tests we could have given. A good test is one that yields stable results. That is, it's *reliable.*

26.2 Reliability and Validity

Everyone knows the endearing qualities of a reliable car. It goes anytime, anywhere, for anybody. It behaves the same way under a wide variety of circumstances. Its performance is repeatable. A reliable measuring instrument behaves similarly: the test yields similar results when different people administer it and when alternative forms are used. When conditions for making the measurement change, the results of the test should not.

A test must be reliable to be useful. But it's not enough for a test to be reliable; it must also be *valid.* That is, the instrument must measure what it is intended to measure. A test that requires students to do mirror drawing and memorize nonsense syllables may be quite reliable, but it is a poor indicator of mastery of the concepts of psychology. The test has poor validity.

There are many different ways to assess both reliability and validity. In this chapter, we will be concerned only with measures of reliability.

26.3
Describing Test Results

Before embarking on a discussion of measures of reliability, let's take a look at some of the descriptive statistics that are useful for characterizing a scale. We will be analyzing a scale of the physical activities of daily living in the elderly.[1] The goal of the scale is to assess an elderly person's competence in the physical activities of daily living. Three hundred and ninety-five people were rated on the eight items shown in Figure 26.3a. For each item, a score of 1 was assigned if the patient was unable to perform the activity, 2 if the patient was able to perform the activity with assistance, and 3 if the patient required no assistance to perform the activity.

Figure 26.3a Physical activity items

```
RELIABILITY VARIABLES=ITEM1 TO ITEM8.
```

```
1.      ITEM1        Can eat
2.      ITEM2        Can dress and undress
3.      ITEM3        Can take care of own appearance
4.      ITEM4        Can walk
5.      ITEM5        Can get in and out of bed
6.      ITEM6        Can take a bath or shower
7.      ITEM7        Can get to bathroom on time
8.      ITEM8        Has been able to do tasks for 6 months
```

When we summarize a scale, we want to look at the characteristics of the individual items, the characteristics of the overall scale, and the relationship between the individual items and the entire scale. Figure 26.3b contains descriptive statistics for the individual items.

Figure 26.3b Univariate descriptive statistics

```
RELIABILITY VARIABLES=ITEM1 TO ITEM8
 /STATISTICS=DESCRIPTIVES.
```

		MEAN	STD DEV	CASES
1.	ITEM1	2.9266	.3593	395.0
2.	ITEM2	2.8962	.4116	395.0
3.	ITEM3	2.9165	.3845	395.0
4.	ITEM4	2.8684	.4367	395.0
5.	ITEM5	2.9114	.3964	395.0
6.	ITEM6	2.8506	.4731	395.0
7.	ITEM7	2.7873	.5190	395.0
8.	ITEM8	1.6582	.4749	395.0

You see that the average scores for the items range from 2.93 for item 1 to 1.66 for item 8. Item 7 has the largest standard deviation, 0.5190.

Figure 26.3c Inter-item correlation coefficients

```
RELIABILITY VARIABLES=ITEM1 TO ITEM8
 /STATISTICS=CORRELATIONS.
```

CORRELATION MATRIX

	ITEM1	ITEM2	ITEM3	ITEM4	ITEM5
ITEM1	1.0000				
ITEM2	.7893	1.0000			
ITEM3	.8557	.8913	1.0000		
ITEM4	.7146	.7992	.7505	1.0000	
ITEM5	.8274	.8770	.8173	.8415	1.0000
ITEM6	.6968	.8326	.7684	.8504	.7684
ITEM7	.5557	.5736	.5340	.5144	.5497
ITEM8	.0459	.1427	.0795	.2108	.0949

	ITEM6	ITEM7	ITEM8
ITEM6	1.0000		
ITEM7	.5318	1.0000	
ITEM8	.2580	.1883	1.0000

[1] Thanks to Dr. Michael Counte of Rush-Presbyterian-St. Lukes Medical Center, Chicago, Principal Investigator of the National Institute of Aging Panel Study of Elderly Health Beliefs and Behavior, for making these data available.

The correlation coefficients between the items are shown in Figure 26.3c. The only item that appears to have a small correlation with the other items is item 8. Its highest correlation is 0.26, with item 6.

Additional statistics for the scale as a whole are shown in Figure 26.3d and 26.3e.

Figure 26.3d Scale statistics

```
RELIABILITY VARIABLES=ITEM1 TO ITEM8
 /STATISTICS=SCALE.
```

STATISTICS FOR SCALE	MEAN	VARIANCE	STD DEV	# OF VARIABLES
	21.8152	7.3896	2.7184	8

Figure 26.3e Summary statistics for items

```
RELIABILITY VARIABLES=ITEM1 TO ITEM8
 /SUMMARY=MEANS VARIANCES CORRELATIONS.
```

	MEAN	MINIMUM	MAXIMUM	RANGE	MAX/MIN	VARIANCE
ITEM MEANS	2.7269	1.6582	2.9266	1.2684	1.7649	.1885
ITEM VARIANCES	.1891	.1291	.2694	.1403	2.0864	.0022
INTER-ITEM CORRELATIONS	.5843	.0459	.8913	.8454	19.4033	.0790

The average score for the scale is 21.82, and the standard deviation is 2.7 (Figure 26.3d). The average score on an item (Figure 26.3e) is 2.73, with a range of 1.27. Similarly, the average of the item variances is 0.19, with a minimum of 0.13 and a maximum of 0.27. The correlations between items range from 0.046 to 0.891. The ratio between the largest and smallest correlation is 0.891/0.046, or 19.4. The average correlation is 0.584.

26.4
Relationship Between the Scale and the Items

Now let's take a look at the relationship between the individual items and the composite score.

Figure 26.4 Item-total summary statistics

```
RELIABILITY VARIABLES=ITEM1 TO ITEM8
 /SUMMARY=TOTAL.
```

ITEM-TOTAL STATISTICS	SCALE MEAN IF ITEM DELETED	SCALE VARIANCE IF ITEM DELETED	CORRECTED ITEM-TOTAL CORRELATION	SQUARED MULTIPLE CORRELATION	ALPHA IF ITEM DELETED
ITEM1	18.8886	5.8708	.7981	.7966	.8917
ITEM2	18.9190	5.5061	.8874	.8882	.8820
ITEM3	18.8987	5.7004	.8396	.8603	.8873
ITEM4	18.9468	5.4718	.8453	.8137	.8848
ITEM5	18.9038	5.6202	.8580	.8620	.8852
ITEM6	18.9646	5.3084	.8520	.8029	.8833
ITEM7	19.0278	5.6414	.5998	.3777	.9095
ITEM8	20.1570	6.7316	.1755	.1331	.9435

For each item, the first column of Figure 26.4 shows what the average score for the scale would be if the item were excluded from the scale. For example, we know from Figure 26.3d that the average score for the scale is 21.82. If item 1 were eliminated from the scale, the average score would be 18.89. This is computed by simply subtracting the average score for the item from the scale mean. In this case it's 21.82 − 2.93 = 18.89. The next column is the scale variance if the item were eliminated. The column labeled **CORRECTED ITEM-TOTAL CORRELATION** is the Pearson correlation coefficient between the score on the individual item and the sum of the scores on the remaining items. For example, the correlation between the score on item 8 and the sum of the scores of items 1 through 7 is only 0.176. This indicates that there is not much of a relationship between the eighth item and the other items. On the other hand, item 2 has a very high correlation, 0.887, with the other items.

Another way to look at the relationship between an individual item and the rest of the scale is to try to predict a person's score on the item based on the scores obtained on the other items. We can do this by calculating a multiple regression equation with the item of interest as the dependent variable and all of the other items as independent variables. The multiple R^2 from this regression equation is displayed for each of the items in the column labeled **SQUARED MULTIPLE CORRELATION**. We can see that almost 80% of the observed variability in the responses to item 1 can be explained by the other items. As expected, item 8 is poorly predicted from the other items. Its multiple R^2 is only 0.13.

26.5
THE RELIABILITY COEFFICIENT

By looking at the statistics shown above, we've learned quite a bit about our scale and the individual items of which it is composed. However, we still haven't come up with an index of how reliable the scale is. There are several different ways to measure reliability:

- You can compute an estimate of reliability based on the observed correlations or covariances of the items with each other.
- You can correlate the results from two alternate forms of the same test or split the same test into two parts and look at the correlation between the two parts.

(See Lord & Novick, 1968, and Nunnally, 1978.)

One of the most commonly used reliability coefficients is *Cronbach's alpha.* Alpha (or α) is based on the "internal consistency" of a test. That is, it is based on the average correlation of items within a test, if the items are standardized to a standard deviation of 1; or on the average covariance among items on a scale, if the items are not standardized. We assume that the items on a scale are positively correlated with each other because they are measuring, to a certain extent, a common entity. If items are not positively correlated with each other, we have no reason to believe that they are correlated with other possible items we may have selected. In this case, we do not expect to see a positive relationship between this test and other similar tests.

26.6
Interpreting Cronbach's Alpha

Cronbach's α has several interpretations. It can be viewed as the correlation between this test or scale and all other possible tests or scales containing the same number of items, which could be constructed from a hypothetical universe of items that measure the characteristic of interest. In the physical activities scale, for example, the eight questions actually selected for inclusion can be viewed as a sample from a universe of many possible items. The patients could have been asked whether they can walk up a flight of stairs, or get up from a chair, or cook a meal, or whether they can perform a myriad of other activities related to daily living. Cronbach's α tells us how much correlation we expect between our scale and all other possible eight-item scales measuring the same thing.

Another interpretation of Cronbach's α is the squared correlation between the score a person obtains on a particular scale (the observed score) and the score he would have obtained if questioned on *all* of the possible items in the universe (the true score).

Since α can be interpreted as a correlation coefficient, it ranges in value from 0 to 1. (Negative α values can occur when items are not positively correlated among themselves and the reliability model is violated.)

Figure 26.6 Cronbach's alpha

```
RELIABILITY VARIABLES=ITEM1 TO ITEM8
  /SCALE(ALPHA)=ALL  /MODEL=ALPHA
  /SCALE(SPLIT)=ALL  /MODEL=SPLIT
  /SCALE(ML)=ALL  /MODEL=PARALLEL.
```

```
RELIABILITY COEFFICIENTS      8 ITEMS

ALPHA =    .9089              STANDARDIZED ITEM ALPHA =    .9183
```

Cronbach's α for the physical activity scale is shown in Figure 26.6. Note that the value, 0.91, is large, indicating that our scale is quite reliable. The other entry in Figure 26.6, labeled **STANDARDIZED ITEM ALPHA,** is the α value that would be obtained if all of the items were standardized to have a variance of 1. Since the items in our scale have fairly comparable variances, there is little difference between the two α's. If items on the scale have widely differing variances the two α's may differ substantially.

Cronbach's α can be computed using the following formula:

$$\alpha = \frac{k\,\overline{cov}/\overline{var}}{1 + (k\text{-}1)\,\overline{cov}/\overline{var}}$$

Equation 26.6a

where k is the number of items in the scale, $\overline{cov}$ is the average covariance between items, and $\overline{var}$ is the average variance of the items. If the items are standardized to have the same variance, the formula can be simplified to

$$\alpha = \frac{k\overline{r}}{1 + (k\text{-}1)\overline{r}}$$

Equation 26.6b

where $\overline{r}$ is the average correlation between items.

Looking at Equation 26.6b, we can see that Cronbach's α depends on both the length of the test (k in the formula) and the correlation of the items on the test. For example, if the average correlation between items is 0.2 on a 10-item scale, α is 0.71. If the number of items is increased to 25, α is 0.86. You can have large reliability coefficients even when the average inter-item correlation is small, if the number of items on the scale is large enough.

26.7
Alpha If Item Deleted

When we are examining individual items, as in Figure 26.4, you may want to know how each of the items affects the reliability of the scale. This can be accomplished by calculating Cronbach's α when each of the items is removed from the scale. These α's are shown in the last column of Figure 26.4. You can see that eliminating item 8 from the physical activity scale causes α to increase from 0.9089 (as in Figure 26.6) to 0.9435 (Figure 26.4). From the correlation matrix in Figure 26.3c we saw that item 8 is not strongly related to the other items, so we would expect that eliminating it from the scale would increase the overall reliability of the scale. Elimination of any of the other items from the scale causes little change in α.

26.8
THE SPLIT-HALF RELIABILITY MODEL

Cronbach's α is based on correlations of items on a single scale. It's a measure based on the internal consistency of the items. Other measures of reliability are based on splitting the scale into two parts and looking at the correlation between the two parts. Such measures are called *split-half* coefficients. One of the disadvantages of this method is that the results depend on the allocation of items to halves. The coefficient you get depends on how you split your scale. Sometimes split-half methods are applied to situations in which two tests are administered, or the same test is administered twice.

Figure 26.8a Split-half statistics

```
RELIABILITY VARIABLES=ITEM1 TO ITEM8
 /STATISTICS=DESCRIPTIVES CORRELATIONS SCALE
 /SUMMARY=MEANS VARIANCES CORRELATIONS
 /SCALE(SPLIT)=ALL /MODEL=SPLIT.
```

	# OF CASES =	395.0					
				# OF			
STATISTICS FOR	MEAN	VARIANCE	STD DEV	VARIABLES			
PART 1	11.6076	2.1527	1.4672	4			
PART 2	10.2076	1.8959	1.3769	4			
SCALE	21.8152	7.3896	2.7184	8			
ITEM MEANS	MEAN	MINIMUM	MAXIMUM	RANGE	MAX/MIN	VARIANCE	
PART 1	2.9019	2.8684	2.9266	.0582	1.0203	.0007	
PART 2	2.5519	1.6582	2.9114	1.2532	1.7557	.3575	
SCALE	2.7269	1.6582	2.9266	1.2684	1.7649	.1885	
ITEM VARIANCES	MEAN	MINIMUM	MAXIMUM	RANGE	MAX/MIN	VARIANCE	
PART 1	.1593	.1291	.1907	.0616	1.4774	.0007	
PART 2	.2190	.1571	.2694	.1123	1.7147	.0021	
SCALE	.1891	.1291	.2694	.1403	2.0864	.0022	
INTER-ITEM							
CORRELATIONS	MEAN	MINIMUM	MAXIMUM	RANGE	MAX/MIN	VARIANCE	
PART 1	.8001	.7146	.8913	.1768	1.2474	.0039	
PART 2	.3985	.0949	.7684	.6735	8.0973	.0606	
SCALE	.5843	.0459	.8913	.8454	19.4033	.0790	

Figure 26.8a contains summary statistics that would be obtained if we split the physical ability scale into two equal parts. The first four items are part 1, while the second four items are part 2. Note that separate descriptive statistics are given for each of the parts, as well as for the entire scale. Reliability statistics for the split model are shown in Figure 26.8b.

Figure 26.8b Split-half reliability

```
RELIABILITY VARIABLES=ITEM1 TO ITEM8
 /SCALE(ALPHA)=ALL /MODEL=ALPHA
 /SCALE(SPLIT)=ALL /MODEL=SPLIT
 /SCALE(ML)=ALL /MODEL=PARALLEL.
```

RELIABILITY COEFFICIENTS	8 ITEMS		
CORRELATION BETWEEN FORMS =	.8269	EQUAL LENGTH SPEARMAN-BROWN =	.9052
GUTTMAN SPLIT-HALF =	.9042	UNEQUAL-LENGTH SPEARMAN-BROWN =	.9052
ALPHA FOR PART 1 =	.9387	ALPHA FOR PART 2 =	.7174
4 ITEMS IN PART 1		4 ITEMS IN PART 2	

The correlation between the two halves, labeled on the output as **CORRELATION BETWEEN FORMS**, is 0.8269. This is an estimate of the reliability of the test if it has four items. The equal length Spearman-Brown coefficient, which has a value of 0.9052 in this case, tells us what the reliability of the eight-item test would be if it was made up of two equal parts that have a four-item reliability of 0.8269. (Remember, the reliability of a test increases as the number of items on the test increase, provided that the average correlation between items does not change.) If the number of items on each of the two parts is not equal, the unequal length

Spearman-Brown coefficient can be used to estimate what the reliability of the overall test would be. In this case, since the two parts are of equal length, the two Spearman-Brown coefficients are equal. The Guttman split-half coefficient is another estimate of the reliability of the overall test. It does not assume that the two parts are equally reliable or have the same variance. Separate values of Cronbach's α are also shown for each of the two parts of the test.

26.9
OTHER RELIABILITY MODELS

In the previous models we've considered, we didn't make any assumptions about item means or variances. If we have information about item means and variances, we can incorporate this additional information in the estimation of reliability coefficients. Two commonly used models are the *strictly parallel* model and the *parallel* model. In the strictly parallel model, all items are assumed to have the same means, the same variances for the true (unobservable) scores, and the same error variances over replications. When the assumption of equal means is relaxed, we have what's known as a parallel model.

Additional statistics can be obtained from a strictly parallel or parallel model. Figure 26.9a contains a test of the goodness-of-fit for the parallel model applied to the physical activity data. (This model is not appropriate for these data. We'll use it, however, to illustrate the output for this type of model.)

Figure 26.9a   Goodness-of-fit for parallel model

```
RELIABILITY VARIABLES=ITEM1 TO ITEM8
 /SCALE(ALPHA)=ALL /MODEL=ALPHA
 /SCALE(SPLIT)=ALL /MODEL=SPLIT
 /SCALE(ML)=ALL  /MODEL=PARALLEL.
```

```
TEST FOR GOODNESS OF FIT OF MODEL            PARALLEL

 CHI SQUARE =      1660.1597      DEGREES OF FREEDOM =        34
 LOG OF DETERMINANT OF UNCONSTRAINED MATRIX =     -21.648663
 LOG OF DETERMINANT OF CONSTRAINED MATRIX   =     -17.403278
 PROBABILITY =   .0000
```

As you can see, the chi-square value is very large and we must reject the hypothesis that the parallel model fits. If the parallel model were appropriate we could consider the results, which are shown in Figure 26.9b.

Figure 26.9b   Maximum-likelihood reliability estimate

```
   PARAMETER ESTIMATES

 ESTIMATED COMMON VARIANCE =        0.1891
            ERROR VARIANCE =        0.0842
             TRUE VARIANCE =        0.1049
 ESTIMATED COMMON INTERITEM CORRELATION =     0.5549

 ESTIMATED RELIABILITY OF SCALE   =   .9089
 UNBIASED ESTIMATE OF RELIABILITY =   .9093
```

The first entry is an estimate of the common variance for an item. It is the sum of the true variance and the error variance, which are displayed below it. An estimate of the common inter-item correlation, based on the model, is also shown. Figure 26.9b also shows two reliability coefficients. The first is a maximum-likelihood estimate of the reliability coefficient, while the second is the maximum-likelihood estimate corrected for bias. If either the parallel or the strictly parallel model fits the data, then the best linear combination of the items is simply their sum.

26.10
RUNNING
PROCEDURE
RELIABILITY

Use RELIABILITY to analyze *additive* scales: scales formed by simply adding a number of component variables, or items. RELIABILITY can efficiently analyze different groups of items to help you choose the best scale. RELIABILITY does not create the scale for you. After choosing the items that you want, on the basis of the reliability analysis, use the COMPUTE command to form the scale as the sum of the items.

26.11
VARIABLES Subcommand

The VARIABLES subcommand specifies a group of variables for subsequent analysis. It must be the first subcommand. You can enter more than one VARIABLES subcommand; each one specifies variables for the following SCALE subcommands, up to the next VARIABLES subcommand (if any). You can specify VARIABLES=ALL to use all variables in the active system file as scale components.

For example, the command

```
RELIABILITY VARIABLES=ITEM1 TO ITEM8.
```

specifies all variables from ITEM1 through ITEM8 on the active system file.

26.12
SCALE Subcommand

By default, RELIABILITY includes all variables named on the the VARIABLES subcommand in building the model. Use the SCALE subcommand to choose a subset of variables for analysis. Specifications on SCALE consist of a scale name of up to eight characters (enclosed in parentheses) and a list of the variables making up the scale. Specify ALL to use all the variables on the VARIABLES subcommand.

You can use more than one SCALE subcommand to analyze the items on the preceding VARIABLES subcommand. For example, the command

```
RELIABILITY VARIABLES=ITEM1 TO ITEM8
 /SCALE(ALL)=ALL
 /SCALE(ALLBUT8)=ITEM1 TO ITEM7
 /SCALE(FIRST4)=ITEM1 TO ITEM4.
```

specifies three different scales and names them ALL, ALLBUT8, and FIRST4. The keyword TO on the SCALE subcommand refers to the order that variables are listed on the preceding VARIABLES subcommand, not their order in the active system file.

26.13
MODEL Subcommand

The default model for reliability analysis is ALPHA, which calculates Cronbach's α coefficient for each SCALE subcommand. To use a different model, specify the MODEL subcommand after the SCALE to which the model applies. Available models are:

ALPHA   *Cronbach's α.* This is the default.

SPLIT (n)   *Split-half coefficients.* A split-half reliability analysis is performed, based on the order in which you named the items on the preceding SCALE subcommand. The first half of the items (rounding up if the number of items is odd) form the first part, and the remaining items form the second part.
After the keyword SPLIT, you can specify in parentheses the number of items to be placed in the *second* part. Thus /MODEL= SPLIT(5) indicates that the last five items on the SCALE subcommand should form the second part, and the items that precede them should form the first part.

GUTTMAN   *Guttman's lower bounds for true reliability.*

PARALLEL   *Maximum-likelihood reliability estimate under parallel assumptions.* This model assumes that the items all have equal variance.

STRICTPARALLEL   *Maximum-likelihood reliability estimate under strictly parallel assumptions.* This model assumes that the items have the same variance and mean.

You can only specify one MODEL subcommand after each SCALE subcommand. To use more than one model on the same scale, specify several SCALE subcommands, each followed by MODEL. For example:

```
RELIABILITY VARIABLES=ITEM1 TO ITEM8
 /SCALE(ALPHA)=ALL  /MODEL=ALPHA
 /SCALE(SPLIT)=ALL  /MODEL=SPLIT
 /SCALE(ML)=ALL  /MODEL=PARALLEL.
```

26.14
Obtaining Statistics

Use the SUMMARY and STATISTICS subcommands to obtain additional statistics from RELIABILITY. Use these subcommands only once for each RELIABILITY procedure; they apply to all the SCALE subcommands in the procedure.

26.15
SUMMARY Subcommand

SUMMARY provides comparisons of various statistics over all items in a scale, as well as comparisons of each item to the others taken as a group. Available keywords are:

MEANS   *Summary statistics for item means.* The average item mean, the largest, smallest, range, and variance of item means, and the ratio of the largest to the smallest item mean.

VARIANCES   *Summary statistics for item variances.* Same statistics as those displayed for MEANS.

COVARIANCES   *Summary statistics for inter-item covariances.* Same statistics as those displayed for MEANS.

CORRELATIONS   *Summary statistics for inter-item correlations.* Same statistics as those displayed for MEANS.

TOTAL   *Summary statistics comparing each item to the scale composed of the other items.* TOTAL compares scale mean and variance if the item were deleted; correlation between the item and the scale if it were deleted; squared multiple correlation with the other items; and Cronbach's α if the item were deleted.

ALL   *All available summary statistics.*

For example, Figures 26.3e and 26.4 were obtained by specifying:

```
RELIABILITY VARIABLES=ITEM1 TO ITEM8
 /SUMMARY=MEANS VARIANCES CORRELATIONS TOTAL.
```

26.16
STATISTICS Subcommand

The STATISTICS command computes a variety of descriptive and diagnostic statistics. The available keywords are:

DESCRIPTIVES   *Item means and standard deviations.*

COVARIANCES   *Inter-item variance-covariance matrix.*

CORRELATIONS   *Inter-item correlation matrix.*

SCALE   *Scale mean and variance.*

ANOVA   *Repeated-measures analysis of variance table.*

TUKEY   *Tukey's estimate of the power to which the scale must be raised to achieve additivity.* This tests the assumption that there is no multiplicative interaction among the items.

HOTELLING   *Hotelling's T^2.* This tests the hypothesis that item means are equal.

FRIEDMAN	*Friedman's chi-square and Kendall's coefficient of concordance.* You can request this in addition to ANOVA if your items have the form of ranks. The chi-square test replaces the usual *F* test in the ANOVA table.
COCHRAN	*Cochran's* Q. You can request this in addition to ANOVA if your items are all dichotomies. The *Q* statistic replaces the usual *F* test in the ANOVA table.
ALL	*All available statistics.*

For example, Figures 26.3b, 26.3c, and 26.3d were obtained by specifying:

```
RELIABILITY VARIABLES=ITEM1 TO ITEM8
 /STATISTICS=DESCRIPTIVES CORRELATIONS SCALE.
```

26.17
Annotated Example

The following commands produce all the figures in this chapter:

```
DATA LIST FREE/ ID ITEM1 TO ITEM8.
BEGIN DATA.
3433 3 3 3 3 3 3 2 2
1418 3 3 3 3 3 3 3 2
2180 3 2 3 2 3 2 3 1
...
END DATA.
VARIABLE LABELS ITEM1 'Can eat'
 ITEM2 'Can dress and undress'
 ITEM3 'Can take care of own appearance'
 ITEM4 'Can walk'
 ITEM5 'Can get in and out of bed'
 ITEM6 'Can take a bath or shower'
 ITEM7 'Can get to bathroom on time'
 ITEM8 'Has been able to do tasks for 6 months'.
VALUE LABELS ITEM1 TO ITEM8 1 'Unable to perform'
 2 'Needs assistance'       3 'Needs no assistance'.
RELIABILITY VARIABLES=ITEM1 TO ITEM8
 /STATISTICS=DESCRIPTIVES CORRELATIONS SCALE
 /SUMMARY=MEANS VARIANCES CORRELATIONS TOTAL
 /SCALE(ALPHA)=ALL /MODEL=ALPHA
 /SCALE(SPLIT)=ALL /MODEL=SPLIT
 /SCALE(ML)=ALL /MODEL=PARALLEL.
```

- The DATA LIST command indicates that the variables ID and ITEM1 to ITEM8 are to be read in freefield format.

- The VARIABLE LABELS and VALUE LABELS commands provide descriptive labels.

- The RELIABILITY command names all eight items on the VARIABLES subcommand.

- The STATISTICS subcommand requests descriptive statistics (Figure 26.3b), the correlation matrix (Figure 26.3c), and scale statistics (Figure 26.3d).

- The SUMMARY subcommand requests summary tables of means, variances, and correlations (Figure 26.3e), as well as item-total summary statistics (Figure 26.4).

- A series of SCALE subcommands follow. Each provides a scale name (in parentheses) and specifies that all eight variables should be included in the scale. Scale names are arbitrary (although limited to 8 letters or numbers); these were chosen to indicate the model used for each scale.

- Each SCALE subcommand is followed by a MODEL subcommand that specifies the model for that scale.

Contents_____

27 Reporting Results: Procedure Report

Case listings and descriptive statistics are basic tools for studying and presenting data. You can obtain case listings with LIST, frequency counts and descriptive statistics with FREQUENCIES and DESCRIPTIVES, and subpopulation statistics with MEANS. Each of these procedures uses a format designed to make the information clear; but if that format isn't what you need for presentation, there is little you can do to change it. REPORT gives you the control you need over data presentation.

REPORT is a formatting tool. It allows you to present case listings and summary statistics (including frequencies) in report format. Your report can be one page long, or it can be hundreds of pages long. With REPORT's subcommands and keywords you can specify the variables you want to summarize or list and organize them into subgroups. You can calculate summary statistics on the report variables and also calculate cross-variable statistics that are not available in other procedures, such as the ratio of two means.

27.1
BASIC REPORT CONCEPTS

This section introduces you to the two basic elements of a report: its contents, and the organization of those contents. To illustrate these concepts (and others in this chapter), we'll use information from a retail company's personnel file. The file contains data such as employees' names, salaries, employment grades, length of time in grade, overall length of employment, store branch and department, shift, and so forth.

27.2
Report Contents: Summaries and Listings

Reports contain summary statistics calculated for groups of cases, listings of individual cases, or a combination of both statistics and listings.

27.3
Summary Reports

Summary reports display summary statistics but do not display case listings. The summary information consists of the statistic or statistics you request for the report variables. Each statistic is displayed in a separate row on the report, referred to as a *summary line*. The cells within the summary line display the statistical values. Figure 27.3 shows a summary report presenting means as the summary statistics.

Figure 27.3   Summary personnel report

```
SET WIDTH=80.
SORT CASES BY DIVISION.
REPORT FORMAT=AUTOMATIC
 /VARIABLES=AGE TENURE JTENURE SALARY
 /BREAK=DIVISION
 /SUMMARY=MEAN.
```

Personnel Data					PAGE	1
Division	Age	Tenure in Company	Tenure in Grade	Salary—Annual		
Carpeting						
Mean	30.75	4.04	3.31	$11,754		
Appliances						
Mean	31.11	3.81	3.54	$12,508		
Furniture						
Mean	36.87	4.79	4.08	$13,255		
Hardware						
Mean	36.20	4.60	4.57	$17,580		

27.4
Listing Reports

Listing reports list individual cases. The case listings display the values and/or labels recorded for each of the report variables. In addition to case listings, a listing report can display summary statistics. Figure 27.4a presents a report that contains case listings, and 27.4b shows one that contains both listings and summaries.

Figure 27.4a   Personnel report with case listings

```
SORT CASES BY DIVISION.
REPORT FORMAT=AUTOMATIC LIST
 /VARIABLES=AGE TENURE JTENURE SALARY
 /BREAK=DIVISION.
```

Personnel Data					PAGE	1
Division	Age	Tenure in Company	Tenure in Grade	Salary—Annual		
Carpeting	27.00	3.67	2.17	$9,200		
	22.00	3.92	3.08	$10,900		
	23.00	3.92	3.08	$10,900		
	24.00	4.00	3.25	$10,000		
	30.00	4.08	3.08	$10,000		
	27.00	4.33	3.17	$10,000		
	33.00	2.67	2.67	$9,335		
	33.00	3.75	3.25	$10,000		
	44.00	4.83	4.33	$15,690		
	36.00	3.83	3.25	$10,000		
	35.00	3.50	3.00	$15,520		
	35.00	6.00	5.33	$19,500		
Appliances	21.00	2.67	2.67	$8,700		
	26.00	2.92	2.08	$8,000		
	32.00	2.92	2.92	$8,900		
	33.00	3.42	2.92	$8,900		
	34.00	5.08	4.50	$15,300		
	24.00	3.17	3.17	$8,975		
	42.00	6.50	6.50	$18,000		
	30.00	2.67	2.67	$7,500		
	38.00	5.00	4.42	$28,300		

Figure 27.4b   Personnel report with case listings and summaries

```
SORT CASES BY DIVISION.
REPORT FORMAT=AUTOMATIC LIST
 /VARIABLES=AGE TENURE JTENURE SALARY
 /BREAK=DIVISION
 /SUMMARY=MEAN.
```

| Personnel Data | | | | PAGE 1 |
Division	Age	Tenure in Company	Tenure in Grade	Salary—Annual
Carpeting	27.00	3.67	2.17	$9,200
	22.00	3.92	3.08	$10,900
	23.00	3.92	3.08	$10,900
	24.00	4.00	3.25	$10,000
	30.00	4.08	3.08	$10,000
	27.00	4.33	3.17	$10,000
	33.00	2.67	2.67	$9,335
	33.00	3.75	3.25	$10,000
	44.00	4.83	4.33	$15,690
	36.00	3.83	3.25	$10,000
	35.00	3.50	3.00	$15,520
	35.00	6.00	5.33	$19,500
Mean	30.75	4.04	3.31	$11,754
Appliances	21.00	2.67	2.67	$8,700
	26.00	2.92	2.08	$8,000
	32.00	2.92	2.92	$8,900
	33.00	3.42	2.92	$8,900
	34.00	5.08	4.50	$15,300
	24.00	3.17	3.17	$8,975
	42.00	6.50	6.50	$18,000
	30.00	2.67	2.67	$7,500
	38.00	5.00	4.42	$28,300
Mean	31.11	3.81	3.54	$12,508

27.5
Report Organization

A report is organized into columns and rows. Each column is defined by a variable. The columns on the left are the *break variables*—those whose values divide the report into subgroups. In Figures 27.3, 27.4a, and 27.4b, DIVISION is the break variable. The other columns, on the right, are the *report variables*—those whose values are listed or summarized. The order of the columns is the order in which you specify the variables.

The rows consist of case listings or summary statistics. The order of the rows is the order of the cases in the file. (See Section 27.15 for more information about the order of cases.)

27.6
BUILDING THE
REPORT

Four basic subcommands determine the appearance of reports:

FORMAT   Determines the report's general layout and whether cases are listed.

VARIABLES   Specifies the *report variables* that are listed and/or summarized in columns in the report.

BREAK   Specifies the *break variable(s)* that break the report rows into subgroups. Break variables are always displayed as the leftmost columns on the report.

SUMMARY   Names a statistic or set of statistics to calculate.

REPORT has other subcommands, but the four above are the ones you'll use most often. They are described in more detail below.

27.7
Required Subcommands

For summary reports, there are three required subcommands: VARIABLES, BREAK, and SUMMARY, as in:

```
REPORT VARIABLES=AGE TENURE SALARY
 /BREAK=DIVISION
 /SUMMARY=MEAN.
```

All other subcommands are optional for summary reports.
    For listing reports, there are two required subcommands: FORMAT and VARIABLES, as in:

```
REPORT FORMAT=LIST
 /VARIABLES=LNAME AGE TENURE SALARY.
```

All other subcommands are optional for listing reports.

27.8
Subcommand Order

Each of the four basic subcommands, when used, must follow this order: FORMAT, followed by VARIABLES, BREAK, and SUMMARY. You can specify multiple BREAK and SUMMARY subcommands.

27.9
Choosing Formats and
Obtaining Listings

Use the FORMAT subcommand to choose reports containing listings, summaries, or both. Summary reports are produced by default. To produce a listing report, use the keyword LIST, as in:

```
REPORT FORMAT=LIST
```

The keyword LIST applies to all variables named on the VARIABLES subcommand.
    A wide variety of formatting options are available with REPORT. To facilitate report design, you can specify

```
 /FORMAT=AUTOMATIC
```

which automatically implements the basic format features you are most likely to use. All the output examples in this chapter use this format. See Section 27.37 for a comparison of the AUTOMATIC and default (MANUAL) settings.

27.10
Specifying Report
Variables

The required VARIABLES subcommand determines the variables that appear in the report columns and the order in which they appear. The minimum VARIABLES specification is a list of variables, as in

```
 /VARIABLES=LNAME AGE TENURE JTENURE
```

which instructs REPORT to list or summarize data for the variables LNAME, AGE, TENURE, and JTENURE. The order in which you specify the variables on the VARIABLES subcommand determines the order in which they appear in the report.

27.11
Defining Break Groups

The BREAK subcommand specifies the variable whose values break the report rows into subgroups. For example, the REPORT subcommand

```
 /BREAK=DIVISION
```

specifies a subgroup for each value of DIVISION.

The BREAK subcommand is required on all summary reports but is optional on listing reports. If you do not want to break a listing report into subgroups, omit the BREAK subcommand.

The REPORT command does not organize data itself, so you must first use the SORT command to organize cases into the break groups you intend to specify on the BREAK subcommand (see Section 27.15).

27.12
Requesting Summary Statistics

To request statistics for subgroups of cases on a summary or listing report, specify the statistic on a SUMMARY subcommand immediately after a BREAK subcommand. You cannot use a SUMMARY subcommand without a corresponding BREAK subcommand, and the BREAK subcommand must precede its associated SUMMARY subcommands.

For example, the commands

```
SORT CASES BY DIVISION.
REPORT FORMAT=AUTOMATIC
 /VARIABLES=AGE TENURE JTENURE SALARY
 /BREAK=DIVISION
 /SUMMARY=MEAN.
```

request the mean values for AGE, TENURE, JTENURE, and SALARY within each category of the variable DIVISION, as shown in Figure 27.3.

For a complete list of the summaries available in REPORT, see Sections 27.42 through 27.45.

27.13
Adding Statistics

To add more summaries, you simply add more SUMMARY subcommands. For example, the following commands

```
SORT CASES BY DIVISION.
REPORT FORMAT=AUTOMATIC
 /VARIABLES=AGE TENURE JTENURE SALARY
 /BREAK=DIVISION
 /SUMMARY=MEAN
 /SUMMARY=MIN
 /SUMMARY=MAX.
```

request the minimum and maximum values in addition to the means for variables AGE, TENURE, JTENURE, and SALARY. Each summary appears on its own line on the report.

27.14
Adding Break Levels

You might want to subdivide data into multiple break levels, adding break columns on the left of the report. To do this, specify multiple BREAK subcommands. Successive BREAK subcommands group the data within categories of variables specified on preceding BREAK subcommands.

Before specifying a report with multiple break levels, use SORT CASES to sort the break variables into the order you intend to use them (see Section 27.15). Then specify successive BREAK subcommands, as in:

```
SORT CASES BY DIVISION STORE.
REPORT FORMAT=AUTOMATIC
 /VARIABLES=AGE TENURE SALARY
 /BREAK=DIVISION
 /SUMMARY=MEAN
 /SUMMARY=VALIDN
 /BREAK=STORE
 /SUMMARY=MEAN.
```

Figure 27.14 shows a portion of the report. The DIVISION and STORE columns are defined by the break variables. Only the means are shown for each level of store branch within division. Both means and the number of valid cases are shown for each division.

Figure 27.14   Personnel report with multiple breaks

```
Personnel Data                                                        PAGE    1

                              Tenure
                  Branch         in
Division          Store      Age  Company  Salary—Annual
                  ─────      ───  ───────  ─────────────

Carpeting         Suburban

                  Mean       26.75   4.37     $12,625

                  Downtown

                  Mean       32.75   3.87     $11,318
Mean                         30.75   4.04     $11,754
N                               12     12           12
```

When you specify a SUMMARY subcommand, REPORT calculates the statistic you request only for the specified break level. If you want the same statistic for multiple break levels, you must request it at each desired level (see Section 27.45 for a shortcut). If you don't want any summary statistics at a given break level, omit the SUMMARY subcommand at that level.

27.15
Preparing Data for
REPORT

REPORT does not organize the data itself as it reads the cases and computes the summaries. Instead, it simply reads cases in the order they reside in the file, listing them (if you request a listing) while keeping track of information you request for summaries.

For example, when REPORT calculates a statistic, it calculates it for the subgroup defined by the first value of the break variable. When the value of the break variable changes in the data, REPORT calculates and displays the statistics you requested. It then displays the next value of the break variable and resumes reading cases until the value of the break variable changes again. It displays the requested summary statistics every time it reads a change in the value for the break variable.

Therefore, before you run REPORT, the data must be organized in the file in such a way that all cases with the same value for the break variable reside together. It doesn't matter if the values are in ascending, descending, or some other order—only that all the cases in the same group are together.

To organize data in the file, use the SORT CASES command immediately before the REPORT command. For example, the command

SORT CASES BY DIVISION.

organizes the data in Figure 27.3 by the subgroups Carpeting, Appliances, Furniture, and Hardware. If you wanted to further subdivide these divisions according to the subgroupings of other variables, you would name additional variables on the SORT CASES command. For example, the command

SORT CASES BY DIVISION STORE.

groups the data into the divisions of Carpeting, Appliances, Furniture, and Hardware and then organizes the data within each of the divisions according to the subgroups of the variable STORE, which are Suburban and Downtown. For more information on SORT CASES, see Chapter 4.

27.16
Trial Runs

Because REPORT is so flexible and its output can have so many components, you may want to experiment with the report layout before you run the final report. If you have a large data file, you can experiment with a subset of the data until you obtain your intended format.

To process a subset of the data, use one of the following techniques:

- Use the N OF CASES command to limit the number of cases read. The system does not attempt to read more cases than the number specified on the N OF CASES command. For example, if the file contains 10,000 cases and you specify 10 on the N OF CASES command, REPORT reads only the first 10 cases.
- If the REPORT contains break variables, and the labeling and spacing of breaks are important considerations, you can obtain a subset of the entire file containing cases from several breaks by using the SAMPLE command.

See Chapter 3 for more information about N OF CASES and SAMPLE.

27.17
REFINING THE REPORT

In addition to specifying the basic report structure as described above, REPORT gives you the ability to refine various report components. These include the following:

- Titles and footnotes.
- Margins and alignment.
- Column contents and labeling.
- Horizontal spacing.
- Summary statistics.
- String variables.

27.18
Adding Titles and Footnotes

The optional TITLE and FOOTNOTE subcommands in REPORT enable you to place titles and footnotes on the left, in the center, and on the right of each page of a report. Enclose each line of the title or footnote in apostrophes, separating lines by a comma or a space. To include an apostrophe in a title, either enclose the string in quotation marks or use double apostrophes not separated by a space. For example,

```
SORT CASES BY DIVISION.
REPORT FORMAT=AUTOMATIC LIST
 /VARIABLES=LNAME AGE TENURE SALARY
 /BREAK=DIVISION
 /SUMMARY=MEAN
 /TITLE= 'Personnel Report' "Employees' Profile".
```

specifies a two-line title. *Personnel Report* is displayed on the first title line, and *Employees' Profile* is displayed beneath it on the second title line. The quotation marks enclosing the second title line assure the apostrophe will be displayed in the title.

If you don't specify a title, SPSS uses its system title as a default when the report width is greater than or equal to the system title's width plus 12. To specify a blank title line, type a space between apostrophes. There is no default footnote.

To specify the left, right, or center positions for either titles or footnotes, use the following keywords:

```
/TITLE=
LEFT    'title'      Left-justified title
RIGHT   'title'      Right-justified title
CENTER 'title'       Centered title

/FOOTNOTE=
LEFT    'title'      Left-justified note
RIGHT   'title'      Right-justified note
CENTER 'title'       Centered note
```

Using TITLE or FOOTNOTE with no reference to a position is equivalent to specifying the center position. However, if you specify a left or right position on the same subcommand, you must use the keyword CENTER to specify the center position. To specify multiple title and footnote lines in any given position, specify each line in apostrophes. Do not repeat the positional keywords. For example,

```
/TITLE=LEFT  'Personnel Report' 'As of January 1, 1987'
RIGHT 'ACME Products' '2201 LaSalle Park'
'Chicago, Illinois 60611'.
```

produces a two-line left title and a three-line right title. Notice that LEFT, RIGHT, and CENTER are not separated by slashes.

Titles and footnotes are displayed on each page of a multiple-page report. The LEFT, RIGHT, and CENTER alignments are relative to the report's margins. If you specify a title or footnote that is wider than the report width, REPORT generates an error message. To specify report margins, use the FORMAT subcommand and the MARGINS keyword (see Section 27.37). Otherwise, REPORT uses the system default page width to determine placement of titles and footnotes.

You can specify titles and footnotes anywhere after the FORMAT subcommand (except between BREAK and SUMMARY) as long as all title subcommands precede all footnote subcommands. There is no fixed limit to the number of title or footnote lines you can define on a report.

For a complete list of keywords available with TITLE and FOOTNOTE, see Section 27.46.

27.19
Column Contents and Labeling

Sections 27.20 through 27.25 discuss options for controlling the contents, layout, and labeling of columns.

27.20
Column Headings

Each column in a report has a heading. By default, REPORT uses the variable label for the heading. If there is no label, REPORT uses the variable name.

REPORT wraps default column headings within their column widths, using as many lines as necessary and attempting to split lines meaningfully at spaces. With FORMAT=AUTOMATIC, REPORT centers each column heading within the width of its column. However, when value labels or string values exceed the width of the longest word in the heading, REPORT left-justifies the heading.

To specify a column heading, enclose the heading in apostrophes or quotation marks following the variable name on either the VARIABLES or BREAK subcommand. To display a heading on multiple lines, enclose each line within its own set of apostrophes or quotation marks. To include an apostrophe in the heading, use quotation marks around the heading. For example,

```
SORT CASES BY DIVISION.
REPORT FORMAT=AUTOMATIC LIST
 /VARIABLES=LNAME 'Employee'
 AGE "Employee's Age" TENURE JTENURE
 /BREAK=DIVISION 'Company' 'Division'
 /SUMMARY=MEAN.
```

produces the report in Figure 27.20 (only the first few lines of the report are shown). Each heading is centered, except for Company Division and Employee. The column headings for DIVISION and LNAME are left-justified because REPORT left-justifies column headings if a value label or string value is wider than the longest word in the column heading.

Figure 27.20   Column headings

```
Personnel Data                                                      PAGE    1

                                                 Tenure      Tenure
                                                   in          in
Company                                          Company     Grade
Division        Employee        Employee's Age
--------        --------                         --------    --------

Carpeting       Ford                27.00          3.67        2.17
                Cochran             22.00          3.92        3.08
                Hoawinski           23.00          3.92        3.08
                Gates               24.00          4.00        3.25
                Mulvihill           30.00          4.08        3.08
                Lavelle             27.00          4.33        3.17
                Mahr                33.00          2.67        2.67
```

27.21
Column Widths and Spacing

When you don't specify a column width for a variable, REPORT determines a default width, using the *largest* of the following for each variable:

- The widest print format in the column, whether it is a variable print format or a summary print format.
- The width of any temporary variable you define with REPORT's STRING subcommand.
- If you assign a column heading, the length of the longest line in that heading. For example, VARS = TENURE 'Tenure in Company' 'Measured' 'in Months' specifies 'Tenure in Company' as the longest line in a three-line heading.
- When no column heading is specified, the length of the longest word in the variable label, or the length of the variable name. (If FORMAT=MANUAL, variable labels are not evaluated.)
- If you specify (LABEL), the length of the variable's longest value label. (With FORMAT=AUTOMATIC, (LABEL) is the default for break variables.) REPORT reads value labels from the dictionary, so it's possible for you to exclude a value from your report, yet still have that value's label determine the width of a column. If FORMAT=MANUAL, REPORT uses the length of the variable's longest value label, up to 20 characters; 20 is the largest value it uses for this criterion with MANUAL format.

To override the default, specify a column width in parentheses following the variable name on the VARIABLES or BREAK subcommand, as in:

```
REPORT FORMAT=AUTOMATIC
 /VARIABLES=LNAME (10) AGE
 /BREAK=DIVISION (5)
 /SUMMARY=MEAN.
```

27.22
Intercolumn Spacing and
Automatic Fit

REPORT leaves from one to four spaces between columns. With AUTOMATIC format, if the report is too wide for the report margins, REPORT will attempt to make the report fit by incrementally reducing intercolumn spacing, until it reaches a minimum intercolumn space of 1.

27.23
Labels versus Values

Frequently when you run a listing report you want to see value labels for the report variables rather than the values themselves. For example, if you want to run a personnel report that includes an employee's sex, you might prefer to see the labels Female and Male rather than the values 1 and 2 on the report. By specifying the keyword (LABEL) after the variable name on the VARIABLES subcommand, you instruct REPORT to display labels rather than values for that variable.

For example, the following commands produce a listing report that shows the sex, age, job grade, and work shift for each employee:

```
SORT CASES BY LNAME.
REPORT FORMAT=AUTOMATIC LIST
 /VARIABLES=LNAME SEX(LABEL) AGE JOBGRADE(LABEL) SHIFT(LABEL).
```

The keyword (LABEL) generates a descriptive report, as you can see in Figure 27.23 (only part of the report is shown).

Figure 27.23   Personnel report with keyword (LABEL)

```
Personnel Data                                                    PAGE     1

Last Name          Sex           Age      Job Grade             Shift
---------          ---           ---      ---------             -----

Baker              Male         42.00     Sales Staff           Weekend
Blount             Male         41.00     Sales Staff           Weekend
Carlyle            Female       40.00     Sales Staff           Weekend
Cochran            Female       22.00     Sales Staff           First
Cochran            Male         39.00     Sales Staff           Second
Dan                Male         36.00     Sales Staff           Weekend
Farkas             Male         37.00     Sales Staff           First
Ford               Female       27.00     Support Staff         First
Ford               Female       36.00     Sales Staff           Weekend
Gates              Female       24.00     Sales Staff           Second
Golden             Female       42.00     Sales Staff           First
Gonzales           Female       42.00     Support Staff         First
Hoawinski          Female       23.00     Sales Staff           First
Jacobesen          Male         44.00     Supervisory Staff     Second
Johnson            Female       42.00     Sales Staff           Second
```

If the variable list contains a set of inclusive variables implied by the keyword TO, (LABEL) applies to the entire set of variables in the list. For example, in

```
/VARIABLES=V1 TO V5 (LABEL)
```

(LABEL) applies to all variables implied by V1 TO V5. However, (LABEL) cannot be implied for a set of variables named individually. For example, in

```
/VARIABLES=V1 V2 V3 V4 V5 (LABEL)
```

(LABEL) applies only to V5.

27.24
Stacking Report Variables

When FORMAT=LIST, REPORT permits you to stack report variables together in a single column by linking them with plus (+) signs on the VARIABLES subcommand. For example,

```
TITLE Personnel Data.
SORT CASES BY DIVISION LNAME.
REPORT FORMAT=AUTOMATIC LIST
 /VARIABLES=LNAME
  TENURE + STORE(LABEL) 'Tenure' 'and' 'Location'
  AGE SALARY
 /BREAK=DIVISION
 /SUMMARY=MEAN.
```

stacks the variables TENURE and STORE in a single column, as shown in Figure 27.24 (only one division is shown). LNAME, AGE, and SALARY are unaffected. The stacked variables each start a new line on the report and are listed in the order they are specified on the VARIABLES subcommand. REPORT will not split the values for a single case across page breaks in the report.

Figure 27.24   Report with stacked report variables

```
Personnel Data                                                    PAGE    1

                              Tenure
                               and
   Division    Last Name     Location     Age     Salary—Annual
   _____    _____     _____     ___     _____

   Carpeting   Cochran          3.92      22.00      $10,900
                                Suburban
               Dan              3.83      36.00      $10,000
                                Downtown
               Ford             3.67      27.00       $9,200
                                Suburban
               Gates            4.00      24.00      $10,000
                                Downtown
               Hoawinski        3.92      23.00      $10,900
                                Suburban
               Jones            4.83      44.00      $15,690
                                Downtown
               Katz             3.75      33.00      $10,000
                                Downtown
               Lavelle          4.33      27.00      $10,000
                                Downtown
               Mahr             2.67      33.00       $9,335
                                Downtown
               McAndrews        3.50      35.00      $15,520
                                Downtown
               Mulvihill        4.08      30.00      $10,000
                                Downtown
               Tygielski        6.00      35.00      $19,500
                                Suburban

   Mean                         4.04      30.75      $11,754
```

REPORT reads values from all the stacked variables when it determines column widths. However, REPORT uses the default heading from the first variable on the stacked list (if you don't specify a heading), and it uses only values from the first variable on the stacked list to calculate summaries.

27.25
Creating Empty Columns

You can add space between columns by creating a dummy variable on the VARIABLES subcommand. Since a dummy variable has no values, its column will be blank. To insert this blank column between other variables' columns, specify the variable name followed by the keyword (DUMMY) between the names of the variables whose columns are to be separated by the blank column. For example,

```
/VARIABLES=AGE TENURE XX(DUMMY) (7) ' ' SALARY
```

places a blank column 7 spaces wide between the columns for TENURE and SALARY. The blank title specified between apostrophes overrides the default column heading.

The space created by dummy variables is also useful for holding the results of composite functions (see Section 27.32).

27.26
Horizontal Spacing

The keyword LIST on FORMAT has an optional argument, (n), that controls the spacing of cases in listing reports. By default, there are no blank lines between cases. An integer value in parentheses specifies a blank line after every *n* cases. For example, LIST(1) produces a double-spaced listing and LIST(3) lists cases in sets of three. The spacing option makes it easier to read reports with many cases.

The following commands generate the report shown in Figure 27.26 (only part of the report is shown):

```
SORT CASES BY LNAME.
REPORT FORMAT=AUTOMATIC LIST(3)
 /VARIABLES=LNAME AGE TENURE JTENURE.
```

To insert a blank line between several variables that are stacked in one column (see Section 27.24), specify either (DUMMY) after a nonexistent variable name or a blank space between two plus signs.

Figure 27.26   Personnel report with optional spacing

```
Personnel Data                                                    PAGE    1

                                 Tenure      Tenure
                                   in          in
Last Name              Age      Company      Grade
-----------            ----     -------      ------

Baker                 42.00       5.25        3.75
Blount                41.00       5.25        3.75
Carlyle               40.00       6.00        6.00

Cochran               22.00       3.92        3.08
Cochran               39.00       5.50        5.50
Dan                   36.00       3.83        3.25

Farkas                37.00       4.42        3.67
Ford                  27.00       3.67        2.17
Ford                  36.00       4.50        3.67
```

Other keywords in REPORT allow you to control spacing between titles and column headings, between headings and listings, between individual rows within the body of the report, and between the body of the report and footnotes. See Sections 27.37 through 27.47 for a complete list of subcommands and all available keywords.

27.27
Summary Statistics

REPORT gives you precise control over the types of summaries to be displayed and their appearance on the report. Sections 27.28 through 27.32 describe summary specifications.

27.28
Selecting Variables for Statistics

A statistic specified on the SUMMARY subcommand is calculated for all the variables named on the VARIABLES subcommand. If you want the statistic to be calculated only for selected report variables, name the desired variables in parentheses on the SUMMARY subcommand, as in

```
SORT CASES BY DIVISION.
REPORT FORMAT=AUTOMATIC LIST
 /VARIABLES=LNAME AGE TENURE JTENURE SALARY
 /BREAK=DIVISION
 /SUMMARY=MEAN(JTENURE, SALARY).
```

You cannot use the TO keyword on SUMMARY to imply a set of variables.

27.29
Summaries Across Break Groups (Report Totals)

The keyword (TOTAL) on the BREAK subcommand calculates summary statistics for all the cases in the report. These totals are displayed at the end of the report. You can specify (TOTAL) for both listing and summary reports.

To generate a report that has break-level summaries plus total summaries, specify (TOTAL) on the BREAK subcommand that precedes the summary whose totals you want. This must be the first BREAK subcommand specified, as in:

```
SORT CASES BY STORE DIVISION.
REPORT FORMAT=AUTOMATIC
 /VARIABLES=AGE TENURE JTENURE SALARY
 /BREAK=STORE(TOTAL)
 /SUMMARY=VALIDN (AGE)
 /BREAK=DIVISION
 /SUMMARY=MEAN.
```

The first set of BREAK and SUMMARY subcommands calculates the number of employees who work at each branch store and the total number of employees who work for the company by counting those that have valid values for AGE. Figure 27.29a shows the report.

Figure 27.29a Summary report with totals

```
Personnel Data                                                    PAGE    1

                                   Tenure     Tenure
                                     in         in
Branch
Store       Division        Age    Company    Grade     Salary—Annual
──────      ────────        ───    ───────    ─────     ─────────────

Suburban    Carpeting
            Mean           26.75     4.37       3.42       $12,625

            Appliances
            Mean           30.20     4.05       3.77       $14,395

            Furniture
            Mean           35.29     4.71       4.32       $12,975

            Hardware
            Mean           32.00     4.33       4.33       $22,500
N                           17

Downtown    Carpeting
            Mean           32.75     3.87       3.25       $11,318

            Appliances
            Mean           32.25     3.52       3.25       $10,150

            Furniture
            Mean           38.25     4.86       3.86       $13,500

            Hardware
            Mean           37.25     4.67       4.62       $16,350
N                           24

TOTAL
N                           41
```

When the statistics you want REPORT to calculate for the totals differ from those you want it to calculate at the various break levels, specify (TOTAL) on a BREAK subcommand and do not name a variable; then use as many SUMMARY subcommands as you need to specify the summary totals you want REPORT to calculate. Name your break variables on subsequent BREAK subcommands. For example, when you specify

```
SORT CASES BY DIVISION.
REPORT FORMAT=AUTOMATIC
 /VARIABLES=AGE TENURE JTENURE SALARY
 /BREAK=(TOTAL)
 /SUMMARY=VALIDN (AGE)
 /BREAK=DIVISION
 /SUMMARY=MEAN.
```

REPORT calculates the total number of employees in the company but does not calculate the number of employees within each division. It calculates a mean for each division but does not calculate a mean for the entire company (see Figure 27.29b).

Figure 27.29b   Totals that differ from break level summaries

```
Personnel Data                                                       PAGE    1

                        Tenure    Tenure
                          in        in
Division        Age     Company    Grade    Salary--Annual
----------      ----    -------   -------   --------------

Carpeting

Mean           30.75     4.04      3.31        $11,754

Appliances

Mean           31.11     3.81      3.54        $12,508

Furniture

Mean           36.87     4.79      4.08        $13,255

Hardware

Mean           36.20     4.60      4.57        $17,580


N                41
```

You can also specify (TOTAL) on a BREAK subcommand that does not name a variable to obtain totals for a listing report that does not contain break levels. Use as many SUMMARY subcommands as you need to specify the totals you want REPORT to calculate, as in:

```
SORT CASES BY LNAME.
REPORT FORMAT=AUTOMATIC LIST
 /VARIABLES=LNAME AGE TENURE JTENURE SALARY
 /BREAK=(TOTAL)
 /SUMMARY=MEAN
 /SUMMARY=VALIDN (JTENURE).
```

Each statistic specified on a SUMMARY subcommand is calculated for all the cases in the report. Though the file is sorted by LNAME to alphabetize the listing, SORT CASES is optional since the report has no break variables.

Figure 27.29c shows the last lines of the report. The mean values are those for the entire 41 employees. The summary titles Mean and N begin in the leftmost column and are left-justified.

Figure 27.29c   Listing report with totals

```
Personnel Data                                                       PAGE    1

                        Tenure    Tenure
                          in        in
Last Name       Age     Company    Grade    Salary--Annual
----------      ----    -------   -------   --------------


    .
    .
Sedowski       30.00     2.67      2.67         $7,500
Shavilje       32.00     2.92      2.92         $8,900
Snolik         34.00     5.08      4.50        $15,300
Syms           32.00     4.33      4.33        $22,500
Totman         41.00     4.50      3.50        $13,300
Tygielski      35.00     6.00      5.33        $19,500
Wajda          26.00     3.17      3.17         $8,975
Washington     32.00     4.42      3.67        $14,400
White          25.00     3.92      3.33        $11,000
Wilson         36.00     4.42      3.75        $14,000

Mean
               33.73     4.34      3.79        $13,179

N
                41
```

27.30
Summary Titles

By default, REPORT uses its own summary titles (see Section 27.42) to identify each statistic you request on the SUMMARY subcommand. It displays the summary title in the column corresponding to the break being summarized, aligning the titles with the labels or values in the column. The title is displayed in mixed case or upper case, depending upon your system's default specifications.

You can change the default summary title by enclosing a one-line title in apostrophes or quotation marks, as in

```
/SUMMARY=STDDEV 'Standard Deviation'
```

Use leading blanks to indent summary titles within the break column.

If you specify a summary title wider than its break column, the title extends into the break column to its right. If the width of the available break columns is insufficient to display the full summary title, the title is truncated.

Although summary titles can only be one line long, when you use multiple SUMMARY subcommands you can continue a summary title from one summary line to another. For example,

```
/SUMMARY=SUM 'Sums and Averages'
/SUMMARY=MEAN 'Based on 1986 5% Sample'
```

produces a two-line summary with a title continuing from the first to the second line. You can also specify a blank title for any summary line.

27.31
Print Formats for Summary Statistics

Every summary function has a default display format. You can override these defaults by specifying your own format (COMMA, DOLLAR, or PLAIN to override COMMA or DOLLAR when they are the default) and/or an alternative number of decimal places. Specify the format and number of decimals, each enclosed in separate parentheses, following the variable name, as in:

```
/SUMMARY=MEAN(SALARY(COMMA)(2))
```

You must specify a variable name before the format and decimal specifications. In this example, the SUMMARY subcommand displays the mean of SALARY without a dollar sign and with two decimal digits.

If the column is not wide enough to display the specified decimal digits for a given function, REPORT displays fewer decimal places. REPORT uses scientific notation or displays asterisks if the column is not wide enough to display the integer portion of the number.

27.32
Composite Functions

A composite function operates on simple aggregate statistics and their arguments to produce a single result. For example, say you want to run a listing report that shows the average age, tenure, and salary of employees, and also reflects what the average salary will be when next year's 7% across-the-board salary increase takes effect. The following commands produce such a report:

```
SORT CASES BY DIVISION LNAME
REPORT FORMAT=AUTOMATIC LIST
  /VARIABLES=LNAME AGE TENURE SALARY
  /BREAK=DIVISION
  /SUMMARY=MEAN
  /SUMMARY=MULTIPLY(MEAN(SALARY)1.07) '7% Raise'.
```

Note that the summary title is specified after the final parentheses enclosing the arguments, not between the function name (MULTIPLY) and its arguments.

Figure 27.32 shows one division from the report. Note that the composite function computes only one result.

Figure 27.32   Report with composite function

```
Personnel Data                                                         PAGE    1

                                     Tenure
                                       in
Division        Last Name      Age   Company    Salary——Annual
—————————       —————————      ———   ———————    —————————————

Carpeting       Cochran       22.00    3.92       $10,900
                Dan           36.00    3.83       $10,000
                Ford          27.00    3.67        $9,200
                Gates         24.00    4.00       $10,000
                Hoawinski     23.00    3.92       $10,900
                Jones         44.00    4.83       $15,690
                Katz          33.00    3.75       $10,000
                Lavelle       27.00    4.33       $10,000
                Mahr          33.00    2.67        $9,335
                McAndrews     35.00    3.50       $15,520
                Mulvihill     30.00    4.08       $10,000
                Tygielski     35.00    6.00       $19,500

Mean                          30.75    4.04       $11,754
7% Raise                                          $12,577
```

By default, REPORT displays the result of the composite function calculation in the column defined by the first variable in the function that is also named on the VARIABLES subcommand. To move the result to another variable's column, specify that variable's name in parentheses after you completely define the composite function's argument. For example,

`/SUMMARY=MULTIPLY(MEAN(SALARY)1.07)` **(LNAME)**

places the result in the column defined by LNAME. Without (LNAME), this summary would appear in the column for SALARY. Unlike simple functions, the composite function result can be placed in any report column, including those defined by dummy variables or string variables.

It is often advisable to specify the format and number of decimal digits you want to display. Specify print formats for composites within parentheses following the name of the variable in whose column the result is to be displayed. For example, the specification

`/MULTIPLY(MEAN(SALARY)1.07)` **(SALARY(DOLLAR))** `'7% Raise'`

specifies that the increased average salary in Figure 27.32 be displayed in dollar format in the SALARY column.

You can use any numeric SPSS variables, not just REPORT variables, as arguments to composite functions. You do not have to name a variable on the VARIABLES subcommand to use it in a composite function. You cannot use a composite function as an argument to a composite function. You can only use simple functions, variables, and constants.

Composite functions in REPORT give you the ability to choose the column in which a summary statistic will appear and also to generate summaries for variables that don't have their own columns in the report.

For a complete list of the composite functions available in REPORT, see Section 27.44.

27.33
Using Strings

The STRING subcommand enables you to link together SPSS variables and user-specified string values (constants) to create new temporary variables you can use in REPORT. You can link together both alphanumeric and numeric variables and also intermix them.

For example, the subcommand

```
/STRING=PHONE (AREA '/' EXCH '-' NUM)
```

creates a string variable named PHONE, which comprises three variables and two user-specified string values.

- The STRING subcommand must precede the VARIABLES subcommand.
- New STRING variables are temporary and available to the REPORT procedure only. The name you assign them must be unique and must follow SPSS variable-naming conventions.
- You cannot use the keyword TO to imply a list of variables on the STRING subcommand.

You can use STRING variables on both the VARIABLES and BREAK subcommands, specifying column headings for them as you do for any other variables.

27.34
A STRING Application

One use of the STRING subcommand is to separate report columns with a column of special characters, such as asterisks or vertical bars. For example,

```
REPORT FORMAT=AUTOMATIC LIST
  /STRING=FILL1('|') FILL2('|')
  /VARIABLES=LNAME FILL1(1) ' ' TENURE  FILL2(1) ' ' SALARY.
```

defines two string variables, both with a value of '|' for each case. Naming the string variables between other variables on the VARIABLES subcommand produces a vertical column of bars between each column of the report. The (1) after each string variable on VARIABLES specifies a column width of 1; the space between apostrophes specifies a blank column heading. Figure 27.34 shows the first few lines of the report.

Figure 27.34 Column of special characters

```
Personnel Data                                                PAGE    1

                     Tenure
                       in
Last Name            Company        Salary--Annual
--------------       -------        --------------

Ford                  3.67    |        $9,200
Cochran               3.92    |       $10,900
Hoawinski             3.92    |       $10,900
Gates                 4.00    |       $10,000
Mulvihill             4.08    |       $10,000
Lavelle               4.33    |       $10,000
Mahr                  2.67    |        $9,335
Katz                  3.75    |       $10,000
Jones                 4.83    |       $15,690
  .
  .
  .
```

27.35
SUMMARY

REPORT has a full range of keywords that allow you to control the format and layout of a report. Table 27.35 will help you determine the subcommands and keywords to use to achieve the results you want. You can then consult Sections 27.37 through 27.47 for a complete list of subcommands and keywords.

Table 27.35 Summary of REPORT keywords

Function	Subcommand	Keyword
Adjusting margins	FORMAT	MARGINS(l,r)
Aligning report	FORMAT	ALIGN(LEFT|CENTER|RIGHT)
Aligning report contents	VARIABLES, BREAK	(OFFSET(n|CENTER))
Column contents	FORMAT	LIST NOLIST MISSING ' '
	VARIABLES, BREAK	(VALUE|LABEL)
	BREAK	NAME|NONAME
Moving summary titles	SUMMARY	( ) col number
Page lengths	FORMAT BREAK	LENGTH(*|n) (PAGE(RESET))
Page numbers	FORMAT	PAGE1(n)
Shifting column headings	FORMAT	CHALIGN(TOP|BOTTOM) TSPACE(n)
	VARIABLES, STRING, BREAK	' ' literal
	VARIABLES, BREAK	(CENTER, LEFT, RIGHT)
Spacing between columns	FORMAT VARIABLES	COLSPACE (4 n) (DUMMY)
Spacing between rows	FORMAT	TSPACE(n) CHDSPACE(n) LIST(n) BRKSPACE(n) SUMSPACE(n) FTSPACE(n)
	VARIABLES BREAK, SUMMARY	(DUMMY) (SKIP(n))
Column widths	VARIABLES, STRING, BREAK	(n) following varname
Totals on listing reports	BREAK	(TOTAL)
Underscores between listings and summaries	BREAK	UNDERSCORE
Underscores below column headings	FORMAT	UNDERSCORE(ON|OFF)

27.36
Running Procedure
REPORT

Sections 27.37 through 27.47 provide a complete description of all subcommands and keywords available with REPORT.

27.37
FORMAT Subcommand

Use the FORMAT subcommand to choose reports containing listings, summaries, or both. FORMAT also controls the overall width and length of the report and vertical spacing.

Keyword specifications and their arguments can be named in any order. The following can be specified on FORMAT:

AUTOMATIC
MANUAL
The default settings. AUTOMATIC facilitates report design by doing the following: displays labels for break variables; centers all data; centers column headings but left-justifies column headings if value labels or string values exceed the width of the longest word in the heading; bottom aligns and underscores column headings; extends column widths to accommodate the longest word in a variable label or the variable's longest value label; shrinks a report that is too wide for its margins. MANUAL does the following: displays values for break variables; right-justifies numeric values and their column headings; left-justifies value labels and string values and their column headings; top aligns and does not underscore column headings; extends column widths to accommodate the variable's longest value label (but not the longest word in the variable label), up to a width of 20; generates an error message when a report is too wide for its margins. MANUAL is the default.

LIST[(n)]
NOLIST
Listing of individual cases. List the values of all variables named on the VARIABLES subcommand for each case. The optional *n* indicates that a blank line be inserted after every *n* cases; the default is not to insert blank lines. Values for cases are listed using the default formats for the variables. The default is the alternative NOLIST, which requests that no case listing be produced.

PAGE(n)
Number for the first page of the report. The default is 1.

LENGTH(t,b)
Top and bottom lines of the report. The value for the bottom line cannot be greater than the system page length. The system page length is controlled by SET. By default, the top of the report begins at line 1 and the bottom of the report is the last line of the system page length. You can use an asterisk to indicate a default value.

MARGINS(l,r)
The columns for the left and right margins. By default, the left margin is print column 1 and the right margin is the rightmost print column of the system page width, which is controlled by the SET command. The right column cannot be beyond the width specified on SET. You can use an asterisk to indicate a default value.

ALIGN
The report's placement relative to its margins. The specification is either (LEFT), (CENTER), or (RIGHT). (LEFT) left-justifies the report. (CENTER) centers the report between its margins. (RIGHT) right-justifies the report. The default is (LEFT).

COLSPACE(n)
Number of spaces between each column. The default is the lesser of either 4 or the result obtained by first subtracting the combined column widths of the break and report variables from the REPORT margins and then dividing the difference by the number of columns minus 1. When AUTOMATIC is in effect, REPORT overrides the specified column spacing if necessary to fit the report between its margins.

CHALIGN
Alignment of column headings. The specification is either (TOP) or (BOTTOM). (TOP) aligns all column headings with the first, or top, line of multi-line headings. (BOTTOM) aligns headings with the last, or bottom, line of multi-line headings. The default when AUTOMATIC is in effect is (BOTTOM); when MANUAL is in effect, it is (TOP).

UNDERSCORE   *Heading underscores.* The specification is either (ON) or (OFF). (ON) underscores the bottom line of each column heading for the full width of the column. (OFF) does not underscore column headings. The default when AUTOMATIC is in effect is (ON); when MANUAL is in effect, it is (OFF).

TSPACE(n)   *Number of blank lines between the report title and the column heads.* The default is 1.

CHDSPACE(n)   *Number of blank lines beneath the longest column head.* The default is 1.

BRKSPACE(n)   *Number of blank lines between the break head and the next line.* The next line is a case if LIST is in effect or the first summary line if NOLIST is in effect. BRKSPACE(−1) places the first summary statistic or the first case listing on the same line as the break value. When a summary line is placed on the same line as the break value, the summary title is suppressed. When AUTOMATIC is in effect, the default is -1; when MANUAL is in effect, it is 1.

SUMSPACE(n)   *The number of blank lines between the last summary line at the lower break and the first summary line at the higher break when they break simultaneously.* SUMSPACE also controls spacing between the last case listed and the first summary line if LIST is in effect. The default is 1.

FTSPACE(n)   *The minimum number of blank lines between the last listing on the page and the footnote.* The default is 1.

MISSING 's'   *Missing-value symbol.* The symbol can be only one character and is used to represent both system- and user-missing values. The default is a period (.).

27.38
OUTFILE Subcommand

By default, REPORT directs its output to the same output file as the rest of the output in your job. You can use the OUTFILE subcommand to send a report to a separate listing file. You must specify the OUTFILE subcommand after the FORMAT subcommand and before any BREAK subcommands. For example, the commands

```
SORT CASES BY DIVISION.
REPORT FORMAT=AUTOMATIC
 /OUTFILE=RPTLST
 /VARIABLES=AGE TENURE SALARY
 /BREAK=DIVISION
 /SUMMARY=MEAN.
```

send the report to a file named RPTLIST. This separate listing file receives only the report, without command printback or system messages. To append other reports to the same listing file, name the same file on the OUTFILE subcommand of subsequent REPORT procedures.

27.39
VARIABLES Subcommand

The required VARIABLES subcommand names the variables to be listed and summarized in the report. Optionally, you can use VARIABLES to control column titles, column widths, and the contents of report columns. The minimum VARIABLES specification is a list of variables. These are the report variables. The number of variables that can be named is limited by the system page width.

    The following keywords can be specified with the VARIABLES subcommand:

(VALUE)   *Contents of the report column assigned to the variable.* (VALUE)
(LABEL)   specifies that values of the variable be displayed in the column. This is the default. The alternative keyword (LABEL) displays value labels if

value labels are defined, and values otherwise. (VALUE) and (LABEL) have no effect unless LIST has been specified on the FORMAT subcommand.

When AUTOMATIC is in effect, value labels or string values are centered in the column based on the length of the longest value label or string variable format specification (if a string variable has a format of (A12), all values for the variable are assumed to be 12 characters long); numeric values are centered based on the width of the widest value or summary format. When MANUAL is in effect, value labels or string values are left-justified in the column; numeric values are right-justified.

(DUMMY) *Dummy variable.* (DUMMY) defines a report column for a variable that does not exist in the active system file. Such dummy variables are used to control spacing or to reserve space for statistics computed upon other variables. Do not name an existing variable as a dummy variable.

'column title' *Title used for the report column assigned to the variable.* Specify multiple-line titles by enclosing each line in a set of apostrophes or quotes. Separate the specifications for title lines with at least one blank.

If no column title is specified, the default column title is the variable label or the variable name if no variable label has been specified.

Default column titles wrap for as many lines as are required to display the entire label. If AUTOMATIC is in effect, user-specified column titles appear exactly as specified, even if the column width must be extended. If MANUAL is in effect, user-specified titles wrap to fit within the column width.

(LEFT) *Alignment of the column heading.* If AUTOMATIC is in effect, column
(CENTER) headings are centered within their columns by default; if value labels or
(RIGHT) string values exceed the width of the longest word in the heading, the heading is left-justified. If MANUAL is in effect, column headings are by default left-justified for value labels or string values and right-justified for numeric values.

(width) *Width for the report column.* If no width is specified for a variable, REPORT determines a default width using the criteria described in Section 27.21. If you specify a width that is not wide enough to display numeric values, REPORT first rounds decimal digits, then converts to scientific notation if possible, and then displays asterisks. Value labels or string values that exceed the width are truncated.

(OFFSET) *Position of the report column contents.* The specification is either (n) or (CENTER). (OFFSET(n)) indicates the number of spaces to offset. Contents are offset from the left for value labels or string values, and from the right for numeric values. (OFFSET(CENTER)) centers contents within the center of the column. If AUTOMATIC is in effect, the default is CENTER. (However, entering a number on OFFSET offsets the contents from the justified position, not from the center.) If MANUAL is in effect, the default is 0.

27.40
STRING Subcommand

The optional STRING subcommand concatenates variables and user-specified strings into temporary string variables that exist only within REPORT. The minimum specification is a name for the string variable followed by a variable name or a user-specified string enclosed in parentheses. The name assigned to the string variable must be unique. Any combination of string variables, numeric variables, and user-specified strings can be used enclosed in parentheses to define the string.

The following keywords can be specified with the STRING subcommand:

(width) *Column width of the preceding variable.* The default width is the dictionary width of the variable. If the width specified is less than required by the value, asterisks are displayed for numeric values, and string values are truncated on the right. If the width exceeds the width of a value, values of numeric variables are padded with zeros on the left and values of string variables are padded with blanks on the right.

The maximum width for numeric variables within the string definition is 16. The maximum width for a string variable is the system page width.

(BLANK) *Left-pad values of the preceding numeric variable with blanks.* If the specification is omitted, the default is to left-pad values of numeric variables with zeros. If a numeric variable has a DOLLAR or COMMA format, it is automatically left-padded with blanks.

'literal' *A user-specified string.* Any combination of characters can be specified, enclosed in apostrophes or quotes.

27.41
BREAK Subcommand

The BREAK subcommand specifies the variables that define the subgroups for the report. BREAK also allows you to control the titles, width, and contents of break columns and to begin a new page for each level of the break variable. The BREAK subcommand must precede the SUMMARY subcommand that defines the summary line for the break.

Multiple BREAK subcommands can be used, and more than one variable can be named on a single BREAK subcommand. If more than one variable is specified on a BREAK subcommand, a single break column is used. Multiple BREAK subcommands or multiple variables on a BREAK subcommand specify subgroups within categories of variables named on preceding BREAK subcommands or preceding variables named on the same BREAK subcommand.

The following keywords are available with the BREAK subcommand:

(VALUE)
(LABEL) *Contents of the break column.* (VALUE) specifies that values of the break variables be displayed in the column. The alternative keyword (LABEL) displays value labels if value labels have been defined, and values otherwise. The value is displayed only once for each break change and is not repeated at the top of the page in a multiple-page break group. When AUTOMATIC is in effect, the default is (LABEL); when MANUAL is in effect, it is (VALUE).

When AUTOMATIC is in effect, value labels and string values are centered in the column based on the length of the longest string or label; numeric values are centered based on the width of the widest value or summary format. When MANUAL is in effect, value labels and string values are left-justified in the column; numeric values are right-justified.

'column head' *Title used for the break column.* Specify multiple-line titles by enclosing each line in a set of apostrophes or quotes. Separate the specifications for title lines with at least one blank.

The default title is the variable label of the break variable or the variable name if no label has been defined. If the break column is defined by more than one variable, the label or name of the first variable is used.

Default column titles wrap for as many lines as are required to display the entire label. User-specified column titles appear exactly as specified, even if the column width must be extended.

(LEFT)
(CENTER)
(RIGHT) *Alignment of the column heading.* When AUTOMATIC is in effect, column headings are by default centered within their columns. However, if value labels or string values exceed the width of the longest word in the heading, the heading is left-justified. When MANUAL is in effect, column headings are by default left-justified

for value labels or string values, and right-justified for numeric values.

(width)	*Column width for the break column.* If no width is specified for a variable, REPORT determines a default width using the criteria described in Section 27.21. If you specify a width that is not wide enough to display numeric values, REPORT first rounds decimal digits, then converts to scientific notation if possible, and then displays asterisks. Value labels or string values that exceed the width are truncated.
(OFFSET)	*Position of the break column contents.* The specification is either (n) or (CENTER). (OFFSET(n)) indicates the number of spaces to offset. Contents are offset from the left for value labels or string values, and from the right for numeric values. (OFFSET(CENTER)) centers contents within the center of the column. If AUTOMATIC is in effect, the default is CENTER. (However, entering a number on OFFSET offsets the contents from the justified position, not from the center.) If MANUAL is in effect, the default is 0.
(UNDERSCORE)	*Heading underscores.* The specification is either (ON) or (OFF). (UNDERSCORE(ON)) underscores the bottom line of each column heading for the full width of the column. (UNDERSCORE(OFF)) does not underscore column headings. The default when AUTOMATIC is in effect is (ON); when MANUAL is in effect, it is (OFF).
(TOTAL) **(NOTOTAL)**	*(TOTAL) calculates summary statistics specified on the next SUMMARY subcommand for all the cases on the report.* (NOTOTAL) is the default and displays summary statistics only for each break. (TOTAL) should be specified only on the first BREAK subcommand.
(SKIP) **(PAGE)**	*Vertical spacing between the last summary line for a break and the next break.* The specification is either (n) or (PAGE). If (SKIP(n)) is specified, each break begins following n blank lines. The default is 1. If (PAGE) is specified, each break begins on a new page. If (RESET) is specified on (PAGE), the page counter resets to the PAGE1 setting on the FORMAT subcommand every time the break value changes for the specified variable. (PAGE(RESET)) is not allowed on listing reports with no break levels.
(NAME) **(NONAME)**	*Display the name of the break variable alongside each value or value label of the break variable.* (NAME) requires 10 spaces (the maximum eight-character length of SPSS variable names plus two parentheses) in addition to the space needed to display break values or value labels. (NAME) is ignored if the break-column width is insufficient. The default is (NONAME), which does not display the break variable name next to the variable label or value.

27.42
SUMMARY Subcommand

The SUMMARY subcommand calculates a wide range of aggregate and composite statistics. A SUMMARY subcommand must be specified unless LIST is specified on the FORMAT subcommand, and a BREAK subcommand must precede the SUMMARY subcommand(s). Multiple SUMMARY subcommands can be specified after a BREAK subcommand.

Each SUMMARY subcommand following a BREAK subcommand specifies a new summary line. SUMMARY subcommands apply only to the preceding BREAK subcommand. If there is no SUMMARY subcommand after a BREAK subcommand, no statistics are displayed for that break level.

27.43
Aggregate Functions

Use the aggregate functions to request descriptive statistics on report variables. If no variable names are given as arguments to an aggregate function, the statistic is calculated for all variables named on the VARIABLES subcommand, that is, for all report variables. To request an aggregate function for a subset of the report variables, specify the list of report variables in parentheses after the function keyword. All variables specified on an aggregate function must have been named on the VARIABLES subcommand.

To use several aggregate functions on the same report variable, specify multiple SUMMARY subcommands. The results are displayed on different summary lines.

The following aggregate functions are available with the SUMMARY subcommand:

VALIDN	*Valid number of cases.* This is the only function that operates on string variables.
SUM	*Sum of values.*
MIN	*Minimum value encountered.*
MAX	*Maximum value encountered.*
MEAN	*Mean.*
STDDEV	*Standard deviation.* Aliases are SD and STDEV.
VARIANCE	*Variance.*
KURTOSIS	*Kurtosis.*
SKEWNESS	*Skewness.*
MEDIAN(min,max)	*Median value for values within the range.* The median is based on integer values. Noninteger values are truncated before the median is calculated.
MODE(min,max)	*Modal value for values within the range.* MODE sets up integer-valued bins for counting all values in the specified range. Noninteger values are truncated when the mode is calculated.
PCGT(n)	*Percentage of cases with values greater than specified value.*
PCLT(n)	*Percentage of cases with values less than specified value.*
PCIN(min,max)	*Percentage of cases within the inclusive value range specified.*
FREQUENCY(min,max)	*Frequency counts for values within the inclusive range.* FREQUENCY sets up integer-valued bins for counting all values in the specified range. Noninteger values are truncated when the frequency is computed. FREQUENCY cannot be mixed with other aggregate statistics on a summary line.
PERCENT(min,max)	*Percentages for values within the inclusive range.* PERCENT sets up integer-valued bins for counting all values in the specified range. Noninteger values are truncated when the frequency is computed. PERCENT cannot be mixed with other aggregate statistics on a summary line.

27.44
Composite Functions

Use composite functions to obtain statistics based on aggregated statistics, to place a summary statistic in a column other than that of the report variable on which it was calculated, or to manipulate variables not named on the VARIABLES subcommand. Composite functions can be computed using constants and any variable in the active system file.

The following aggregate functions can also be used as arguments to composite functions: VALIDN, SUM, MIN, MAX, MEAN, STDEV, VARIANCE, KURTOSIS, and SKEWNESS. When used within composite functions, aggregate functions can have only one variable as an argument.

Although the syntax for composite functions is similar to the syntax for aggregate functions, the specifications are used in different ways. The general format for specifying a composite function is

composite(agg) ['title'] [(col #)] [(varname[(format)] [(d)])]

where *composite* is the composite function and *agg* is the aggregate statistic used as its argument. The optional specifications in brackets are:

'title'	*Specified summary title.*
(col #)	*Number of the break column to which you want to move the summary title.*
(varname)	*Name of the report variable whose column will display the result of the composite function calculation.*
(format)	*Format for the display.* Valid formats are PLAIN, DOLLAR, and COMMA. PLAIN is the default.
(d)	*Number of decimal places displayed for the result of the composite function calculation.*

The following composite functions are available with the SUMMARY subcommand:

DIVIDE(agg() agg() [factor])	*Divide the first argument by the second and multiply by the optional factor.*
MULTIPLY(agg() ... agg())	*Multiply the arguments.*
PCT(agg() agg())	*Percentage of the first argument over the second.*
SUBTRACT(agg()agg())	*Subtract the second argument from the first argument.*
ADD(agg() ... agg())	*Add the arguments.*
GREAT(agg() ... agg())	*Give the maximum of the arguments.*
LEAST(agg() ... agg())	*Give the minimum of the arguments.*
AVERAGE(agg() ... agg())	*Give the average of the arguments.*

27.45
Other SUMMARY Keywords

Spacing between multiple summary lines for a single break and references to previously defined summary lines are controlled by the following keywords:

SKIP(n)	*Blank lines before the summary line.* SKIP is not enclosed in parentheses. The default is 0. SKIP on the first SUMMARY subcommand for a BREAK skips the specified lines after skipping the number of lines specified for BRKSPACE on FORMAT.
PREVIOUS(n)	*Use the SUMMARY subcommands for the nth BREAK.* If no specification is given in parentheses, PREVIOUS points to the set of SUMMARY subcommands for the previous BREAK. If an integer specification is given, the SUMMARY subcommands from the *n*th BREAK are used.

No other specification can be used on SUMMARY with PREVIOUS. For a multiple-break report for which you want the same sets of summaries, specify SUMMARY subcommands for the higher BREAK subcommand and keyword PREVIOUS for lower breaks.

27.46
TITLE and FOOTNOTE Subcommands

Use the TITLE and FOOTNOTE subcommands for optional titles and footnotes for reports. They can be placed anywhere after the FORMAT subcommand except among the BREAK and SUMMARY subcommands. TITLE subcommands should be specified before any FOOTNOTE subcommands.

A title or footnote is specified by providing a string in apostrophes or quotes. If the title or footnote is more than one line, enclose each line in apostrophes or quotes and separate the specifications for each line by at least one blank.

The following keywords are available with the TITLE and FOOTNOTE subcommands. These keywords are specified before the string that defines the title or footnote.

CENTER *Centered title or footnote.* This is the default.
LEFT *Left-justified title or footnote.*
RIGHT *Right-justified title or footnote.*

All three keywords can appear on one TITLE or FOOTNOTE subcommand, but each can be specified only once.

The LEFT, RIGHT, and CENTER alignments are relative to the report's margins, defined by the MARGINS keyword on the FORMAT subcommand. The default report margins are the system default page margins.

Three special arguments can be specified within the title or footnote string:

)PAGE *Display the page number right-justified in a five-character field.*
)DATE *Display the current date in the form* dd/mmm/yy *right-justified in a nine-character field.*
)var *Display this variable's value label in this relative position.* If you specify a variable that has no value label, the value itself will be displayed, formatted according to its print format. You cannot specify a scratch or system variable, nor can you specify a variable you create with the STRING subcommand. In addition, you cannot use variables named DATE or PAGE in the *)var* argument because they will only display the current date or a page number. If you want to use a variable named DATE or PAGE, change the variable's name with the RENAME VARIABLES command before you use it in the *)var* argument.

Each variable you specify with *)var* must be one you've defined in the active system file, but it does not have to be included on the VARIABLES subcommand.

One label or value from each variable specified in a)variable argument is displayed on every page of the report. The label REPORT displays varies from page to page and is chosen from cases determined as follows:

- If a new page starts with a case listing, REPORT takes the labeled value from the first case listed.
- If a new page starts with a BREAK line, REPORT takes the labeled value from the first case of the new break group.
- If a new page starts with a summary line, REPORT takes the labeled value from the last case of the break group being summarized.

27.47
MISSING Subcommand

Use the optional MISSING subcommand to control the handling of cases with missing values on the VARIABLES and SUMMARY subcommands. By default, cases with missing values are included in case listings but are excluded from the calculation of functions on a function-by-function basis.

The following keywords are available for the MISSING subcommand:

VAR *Missing values are treated separately for each variable.* Missing values are displayed in case listings but are not included in summary statistics. This is the default.
NONE *User-missing values are treated as valid values.* This keyword applies to all variables named on the VARIABLES subcommand.
LIST[([varlist][n])] *Any case with the specified number of missing values among the specified list of variables is eliminated.* If no *n* is specified, the default is 1. If no variables are specified, all variables named on the VARIABLES subcommand are assumed.

27.48
Annotated Example

This example produces a report that summarizes information from a retail company's personnel file. It reports summary statistics for employees in each division of the company within each store. The commands are:

```
GET FILE=CHIGLIVE.
SET CASE=UPLOW.
PRINT FORMATS SALARY(DOLLAR7.0).
SORT CASES BY STORE DIVISION.
REPORT FORMAT=AUTOMATIC MARGINS(1,72) LENGTH(1,24) BRKSPACE(-1)
 /VARIABLES=AGE TENURE JTENURE SPACE(DUMMY)' '(4) SALARY
 /TITLE='Chicago Home Furnishing'
 /FOOTNOTE=LEFT 'Tenure measured in months'
 /BREAK=STORE
 /SUMMARY=MEAN 'Average:'
 /SUMMARY=VALIDN '  Count:'(AGE)
 /BREAK=DIVISION 'Product' 'Division' (SKIP(0))
 /SUMMARY=MEAN.
```

- The GET command retrieves the system file containing information on the employees in the company.

- The SET command ensures that any variable or value labels that were defined in upper and lower case are displayed in upper and lower case in the output.

- The PRINT FORMATS command ensures that summaries for variable SALARY are displayed using dollar format.

- The SORT CASES command sorts the file into the order required for REPORT.

- The FORMAT subcommand produces a summary report by default. The AUTOMATIC keyword implements REPORT's automatic format settings. The MARGINS keyword sets the left margin at column 1 and right margin at column 72. The LENGTH keyword sets the top of the report on the first line of each page and the bottom of the report on line 24. The BRKSPACE keyword places the summary for each break of DIVISION on the same line as each label of DIVISION.

- The VARIABLES subcommand defines five columns in the body of the report. The keyword (DUMMY) creates the dummy variable SPACE for spacing purposes.

- The TITLE subcommand defines a one-line centered title.

- The FOOTNOTE subcommand defines a one-line left-justified footnote.

- The first BREAK subcommand defines the major break in this two-break report. Variable STORE breaks the file into two categories: the downtown store and the suburban store. Value labels for STORE are displayed in the break column.

- The first two SUMMARY subcommands display two lines of summary statistics for each store. The first SUMMARY subcommand computes means for AGE, TENURE, JTENURE, and SALARY. The second SUMMARY subcommand computes the number of employees in each store. Summary titles are assigned to each summary function.

- The second BREAK subcommand breaks the file into divisions within each store. The SKIP specification suppresses blank lines between the summary for each division. A column heading is defined for DIVISION.

- The last SUMMARY subcommand computes means for AGE, TENURE, JTENURE, and SALARY for each division.

Figure 27.48 Summary report

```
                          Chicago Home Furnishing

                                      Tenure    Tenure
                 Product               in        in
 Branch          Product              in        in
 Store           Division     Age    Company    Grade      Salary—Annual
 ────────        ────────    ─────   ───────   ───────     ─────────────

 Suburban        Carpeting   26.75    4.37      3.42           $12,625
                 Appliances  30.20    4.05      3.77           $14,395
                 Furniture   35.29    4.71      4.32           $12,975
                 Hardware    32.00    4.33      4.33           $22,500

 Average:                    31.59    4.42      3.95           $13,871
   Count:                      17

 Downtown        Carpeting   32.75    3.87      3.25           $11,318
                 Appliances  32.25    3.52      3.25           $10,150
                 Furniture   38.25    4.86      3.86           $13,500
                 Hardware    37.25    4.67      4.62           $16,350

 Average:                    35.25    4.28      3.68           $12,689
   Count:                      24

 Tenure measured in months
```

Bibliography

Anderberg, M. R. 1973. *Cluster analysis for applications.* New York: Academic Press.

Anderson, R., and S. Nida. 1978. Effect of physical attractiveness on opposite and same-sex evaluations. *Journal of Personality,* 46:3, 401–413.

Beard, C. M., V. Fuster, and L. R. Elveback. 1982. Daily and seasonal variation in sudden cardiac death, Rochester, Minnesota, 1950–1975. *Mayo Clinic Proceedings,* 57, 704–706.

Belsley, D. A., E. Kuh, and R. E. Welsch. 1980. *Regression diagnostics: Identifying influential data and sources of collinearity.* New York: John Wiley and Sons.

Benedetti, J. K., and M. B. Brown. 1978. Strategies for the selection of log-linear models. *Biometrics,* 34, 680–686.

Berk, K. N. 1978. Comparing subset regression procedures. *Technometrics,* 20, 1–6.

Bishop, Y. M. M., S. E. Feinberg, and P. W. Holland. 1975. *Discrete multivariate analysis: Theory and practice.* Cambridge, Mass: MIT Press.

———. 1977. Tolerance and condition in regression computation. *Journal of the American Statistical Association,* 72, 863–866.

Black and Sherba. 1983. Contracting to problem solve to lose weight. *Behavior Therapy,* 14, 105–109.

Blalock, H. M. 1979. *Social statistics.* New York: McGraw-Hill.

Blom, G. 1958. *Statistical estimates and transformed beta variables.* New York: John Wiley and Sons.

Bock, R. D. 1975. *Multivariate statistical methods in behavioral research.* New York: McGraw-Hill.

Borgatta, E. F., and G. W. Bohrnstedt. 1980. Level of measurement once over again. *Sociological methods and research,* 9:2, 147–160.

Carroll, J.D., and J.J. Chang. 1970. Analysis of individual differences in multidimensional scaling via and N-way generalization of "Eckart-Young" decomposition. *Psychometrika,* 35, 238–319.

Cattell, R. B. 1966. The meaning and strategic use of factor analysis. In *Handbook of Multivariate Experimental Psychology,* ed. R. B. Cattell. Chicago: Rand McNally.

Cedercreutz, C. 1978. Hypnotic treatment of 100 cases of migraine. In F. H. Frankel and H. S. Zamansky, eds. *Hypnosis at its bicentennial.* New York: Plenum.

Chambers, J. M., W. S. Cleveland, B. Kleiner, and P. A. Tukey. 1983. *Graphical methods for data analysis.* Belmont, Ca.: Wadsworth International Group; Boston: Duxbury Press.

Churchill, G. A., Jr. 1979. *Marketing research: Methodological foundations.* Hinsdale, IL: Dryden Press.

Cohen, J. 1960. A coefficient of agreement for nominal scales. *Educational and Psychological Measurement.* 20, 37–46.

Conover, W. J. 1974. Some reasons for not using the Yates continuity correction on 2 × 2 contingency tables. *Journal of the American Statistical Association,* 69, 374–376.

———. 1980. *Practical nonparametric statistics,* 2nd edition. New York: Wiley.

Consumer Reports. 1983. Beer. *Consumer Reports* July, 342–348.

Cook, R. D. 1977. Detection of influential observations in linear regression. *Technometrics,* 19, 15–18.

Daniel, C., and F. Wood. 1980. *Fitting Equations to Data,* revised edition. New York: John Wiley & Sons.

Daugirdas, J. T. 1981. Unpublished data.

Davis, J. A. 1982. *General social surveys, 1972–1982: Cumulative codebook.* Chicago: National Opinion Research Center.

Davis, H., and E. Ragsdale. 1983. Unpublished working paper. Chicago: University of Chicago, Graduate School of Business.

Dillon, W. R., and M. Goldstein. 1984. *Multivariate analysis: Methods and applications.* New York: John Wiley & Sons.

Dineen, L. C., and B. C. Blakesley. 1973. Algorithm AS 62: A generator for the sampling distribution of the Mann-Whitney U statistic. *Applied Statistics,* 22, 269–273.

Draper, N. R., and H. Smith. 1981. *Applied regression analysis.* New York: John Wiley and Sons.

Duncan, O.D. 1966. Path analysis: Sociological examples. *American Journal of Sociology,* 72, 1–16.

Everitt, B. S. 1977. *The analysis of contingency tables.* London: Chapman and Hall.

——. 1980. *Cluster analysis.* 2nd ed. London: Heineman Educational Books Ltd.

Fienberg, S. E. 1977. *The analysis of cross-classified categorical data.* Cambridge: MIT Press.

Finn, J. D. 1974. *A general model for multivariate analysis.* New York: Holt, Rinehart, and Winston.

Fox, J. 1984. *Linear statistical models and related methods.* New York: John Wiley & Sons.

Frane, J. W. 1976. Some simple procedures for handling missing data in multivariate analysis. *Psychometrika,* 41, 409–415.

——. 1977. A note on checking tolerance in matrix inversion and regression. *Technometrics,* 19, 513–514.

Goodman, L. A., and W. H. Kruskal. 1954. Measures of association for cross-classification. *Journal of the American Statistical Association,* 49, 732–764.

Greeley, A. M., W. C. McCready and G. Theisen. 1980. *Ethnic drinking subcultures.* New York: Praeger Publishers.

Haberman, S. J. 1978. *Analysis of qualitative data,* Vol. 1. New York: Academic Press.

Hansson, R. O., and K. M. Slade. 1977. Altruism toward a deviant in city and small town. *Journal of Applied Social Psychology,* 7:3, 272–279.

Harman, H. H. 1967. *Modern factor analysis.* 2nd ed. Chicago: University of Chicago Press.

Hoaglin, D. C., and R.E. Welsch. 1978. The hat matrix in regression and ANOVA. *American Statistician,* 32, 17–22.

Hoaglin, D. C., F. Mosteller, and J. W. Tukey. 1983. *Understanding robust and exploratory data analysis.* New York: Wiley and Sons.

Hocking, R. R. 1976. The analysis and selection of variables in linear regression. *Biometrics,* 32, 1–49.

Hogg, R. V. 1979. An introduction to robust estimation. *Robustness in Statistics,* 1–18.

Jonassen, C. T., and S. H. Peres. 1960. *Interrelationships of dimensions of community systems.* Columbus: Ohio State University Press.

Judge, G. G., W. E. Griffiths, R. C. Hill, H. Lutkepohl, and T. C. Lee. 1985. *The theory and practice of econometrics,* 2nd edition. New York: John Wiley and Sons.

Kaiser, H. F. 1974. An index of factorial simplicity. *Psychometrika,* 39, 31–36.

Kim, J. O., and C. W. Mueller. 1978. *Introduction to factor analysis.* Beverly Hills: Sage Press.

King, M. M., et al. 1979. Incidence and growth of mammary tumors induced by 7,12-dimethylbenz(a) anthracene as related to the dietary content of fat and antioxident. *Journal of the National Cancer Institute,* 63:3, 657–663.

Kleinbaum, D. G., L. L. Kupper, and H. Morgenstern. 1982. *Epidemiological research: Principles and quantitative methods.* Belmont, California: Wadsworth, Inc.

Kleinbaum, D. G., and L. L. Kupper. 1978. *Applied regression analysis and other multivariable methods.* North Scituate, Massachusetts: Duxbury Press.

Kruskal, J. B. 1964. Nonmetric multidimensional scaling. *Psychometrika* 29, 1–27,115–129.

Kruskal, J. B., and M. Wish. 1978. *Multidimensional scaling.* Beverly Hills: Sage Publications, Inc.

Lachenbruch, P. A. 1975. *Discriminant analysis.* New York: Hafner Press.

Lee, E. T. 1980. *Statistical methods for survival data analysis.* Belmont, CA: Lifetime Learning Publications.

Lehmann, E. L. 1975. *Nonparametrics: Statistical methods based on ranks.* San Francisco: Holden-Day.

Loether, H. J., and D. G. McTavish. 1976. *Descriptive and inferential statistics: An introduction.* Boston: Allyn and Bacon.

Lord, F. M. and M. R. Novick. 1968. *Statistical theories of mental test scores.* Reading, MA: Addison-Wesley.

MacCallum, R.C. 1977. Effects of conditionality on INDSCAL and ALSCAL weights. *Psychometrika,* 42, 297–305.

Mantel, N. 1974. Comment and a suggestion on the Yates continuity correction. *Journal of the American Statistical Association,* 69, 378–380.

McGee, V.C. 1968. Multidimensional scaling of *n* sets of similarity measures: A nonmetric individual differences approach. *Multivariate Behavioral Research,* 3, 233–248.

Meyer, L. S., and M. S. Younger. 1976. Estimation of standardized coefficients. *Journal of the American Statistical Association,* 71, 154–157.

Milligan, G. W. 1980. An examination of the effect of six types of error perturbation on fifteen clustering algorithms. *Psychometrika,* 45, 325–342.

Milligan, G. W., and P.D. Isaac. 1980. The validation of four ultrametric clustering algorithms. *Pattern Recognition,* 12, 41–50.

Morrison, D. F. 1967. *Multivariate statistical methods.* New York: McGraw-Hill.

Neter, J., W. Wasserman, and R. Kutner. 1985. *Applied linear statistical models.* 2nd ed. Homewood, Illinois: Richard D. Irwin Inc.

Norusis, M. J. 1985. *SPSS-X advanced statistics guide.* Chicago: SPSS Inc.

Nunnally, J. 1978. *Psychometric theory.* 2nd ed. New York: McGraw-Hill.

Olson, C. L. 1976. On choosing a test statistic in multivariate analysis of variance. *Psychological Bulletin,* 83, 579–586.

Overall, J. E., and C. Klett. 1972. *Applied multivariate analysis.* New York: McGraw-Hill.

Paul, O., et al. 1963. A longitudinal study of coronary heart disease. *Circulation,* 28, 20–31.

Rabkin, S. W., F. A. Mathewson, and R. B. Tate. 1980. Chronobiology of cardiac sudden death in men. *Journal of the American Medical Association,* 244:12, 1357–1358.

Roberts, H. V. 1979. *An analysis of employee compensation.* Report 7946, Center for Mathematical Studies in Business and Economics, University of Chicago: October.

——. 1980. Statistical bases in the measurement of employment discrimination. In E. Robert Livernash, ed., *Comparable worth: issues and alternatives.* Washington, D.C.: Equal Employment Advisory Council, 173–195.

Romesburg, H. C. 1984. *Cluster analysis for researchers.* Belmont, California: Lifetime Learning Publications.

Schiffman, S. S., M. L. Reynolds, and F. W. Young. 1981. *Introduction to multidimensional scaling.* New York: Academic Press.

Shepard, R. N. 1962. The analysis of proximities: Multidimensional scaling with an unknown distance function. I and II. *Psychometrika* 27, 125–140.

Siegel, S. 1956. *Nonparametric statistics for the behavioral sciences.* New York: McGraw-Hill.

Sigall, H., and N. Ostrove. 1975. Beautiful but dangerous: effects of offender attractiveness and nature of the crime on juridic judgment. *Journal of Personality and Social Psychology,* 31, 410–414.

Smirnov, N. V. 1948. Table for estimating the goodness of fit of empirical distributions. *Annals of Mathematical Statistics,* 19, 279–281.

Sneath, P. H. A., and R. R. Sokal. 1973. *Numerical taxonomy.* San Francisco: W.H. Freeman and Co.

Snedecor, G. W., and W. G. Cochran. 1967. *Statistical methods.* Ames, Iowa: Iowa State University Press.

Somers, R. H. 1962. A new symmetric measure of association for ordinal variables. *American Sociological Review,* 27, 799–811.

Speed, M. F. 1976. Response curves in the one way classification with unequal numbers of observations per cell. *Proceedings of the Statistical Computing Section,* American Statistical Association.

SPSS Inc. 1985. *SPSS statistical algorithms.* Chicago: SPSS Inc.

SPSS Inc. 1988. *SPSS-X user's guide,* 3rd edition. Chicago: SPSS Inc.

Stevens, S. S. 1946. On the theory of scales of measurement. *Science,* 103, 677–680.

Stoetzel, J. 1960. A factor analysis of liquor preference of French consumers. *Journal of Advertising Research,* 1:1, 7–11.

Takane, Y., F. W. Young, and J. de Leeuw. 1977. Nonmetric individual differences multidimensional scaling: An alternating least squares method with optimal scaling features. *Psychometrika,* 42, 7–67.

Tatsuoka, M. M. 1971. *Multivariate analysis.* New York: John Wiley and Sons.

Theil, H. 1967. *Economics and information theory.* Chicago: Rand McNally.

Torgerson, W. S. 1952. Multidimensional scaling: I. Theory and method. *Psychometrika* 17, 401–419.

Tucker, L. R. 1971. Relations of factor score estimates to their use. *Psychometrika,* 36, 427–436.

Tucker, R. F., R. F. Koopman, and R. L. Linn. 1969. Evaluation of factor analytic research procedures by means of simulated correlation matrices. *Psychometrika,* 34, 421–459.

Tukey, J. W. 1962. The future of data analysis. *Annals of Mathematical Statistics,* 33, 22.

Velleman, P. F., and R. E. Welsch. 1981. Efficient computing of regression diagnostics. *American Statistician,* 35, 234–242.

Winer, B. J. 1971. *Statistical principles in experimental design.* New York: McGraw-Hill.

Wright, S. 1960. Path coefficients and path regressions: alternative or complementary concepts? *Biometrics.* 16, 189–202.

Wynder, E. L. 1976. Nutrition and cancer. *Federal Proceedings,* 35, 1309–1315.

Wyner, G. A. 1980. Response errors in self-reported number of arrests *Sociological Methods and Research,* 9:2, 161–177.

Young, F.W. 1974. Scaling replicated conditional rank order data. In D. Heise, ed. *Sociological methodology.* American Sociological Association, 129–170.

Young, F.W., and R.M. Hamer. 1979. *Multi-dimensional scaling: history, theory & applications.* Hillsdale, NJ: Erlbaum

Young, F.W., and R. Lewyckyj. 1979. *ALSCAL–4 user's guide.* Carrboro, NC: Data Analysis and Theory Associate.

Index